Engineered Wood Products

A Guide for Specifiers, Designers and Users

Edited by
Stephen Smulski, Ph. D.

ISBN 0-9656736-0-X

Contents

Acknowledgements

The editor and the PFS Research Foundation, Inc. wish to acknowledge the contributions of the individuals and organizations who helped make this book possible. First and foremost, we extend our deepest appreciation to the authors for the considerable time and effort they expended at our request in writing the chapters herein, and for their willingness to share their knowledge, experience and expertise in engineered wood products with others. Our sincere gratitude also goes to Ed Starostovic and Larry Beineke, PFS/TECO Corporations; Paul Fisette, University of Massachusetts; Robert Hoffman, Muncy Homes Inc.; Alan Marra, Professor Emeritus, University of Massachusetts; Erwin Schaffer, Schaffer Forensic Engineering; Stan Suddarth, Professor Emeritus, Purdue University; and Steven Winter, Steven Winter Associates, Inc.; for taking on the task of reviewing the draft manuscript and for providing the insightful comments and criticisms which improved it. We are grateful to Thomas Brassell, American Institute of Timber Construction; R. Larry Foley and David Soderquist, Willamette Industries, Inc. and Charles Goehring, Truss Plate Institute, for reviewing individual chapters, and to Jim Rothman, PFS/TECO Corporations and James Bihr, James Bihr & Associates for their ad hoc comments. Finally, we thank the Wood I-Joist Manufacturers Association for allowing us to reprint *Technical Bulletin No. 1 Design Guidelines*.

Stephen Smulski, Ph. D., editor
PFS Research Foundation, Inc.

About PFS/TECO Corporations

PFS Corporation was chartered in 1959 as Plywood Fabricator Service, a nonprofit quality control agency affiliated with the Douglas Fir Plywood Association (now APA-The Engineered Wood Association) that served the plywood industry. As factory production of structural components and entire buildings became widespread, PFS expanded its scope to include plan review and inspection services for the housing industry. It changed its name to Product Fabrication Service, and in 1972, moved its headquarters from Tacoma, Washington to its current location in Madison, Wisconsin. Formed in 1978, the present PFS Corporation is a regular tax-paying corporation owned principally by Ed Starostovic and is an internationally-recognized quality assurance/inspection/testing agency for engineered wood products, structural and non-structural wood-based panels, structural adhesives, prefabricated components and building systems, fire resistance rated assemblies, and solid fuel burning appliances. Today, PFS Corporation provides certification services to most of the manufacturers of engineered wood products in North America.

The Timber Engineering Company (TECO) was established in 1933 as a subsidiary of the National Lumber Manufacturers Association (now the American Forest & Paper Association or AF&PA). After establishing a laboratory in Washington, D. C. in 1944, TECO became one of the pre-eminent wood research and testing organizations. In addition to its testing and certification services, TECO developed and commercialized numerous metal connectors and framing anchors for wood still known as "TECO fasteners." TECO moved to Corvallis, Oregon in 1958, relocating to its present site in Eugene, Oregon, in 1967. TECO became a private tax-paying corporation in 1969 when it split from AF&PA. In the mid-1980s, the panel certification portion of TECO was created separately as Timberco, Inc. d/b/a TECO. In 1992 TECO's testing and certification operation was bought by Ed Starostovic. Today, as part of PFS/TECO Corporations, TECO is an internationally-recognized certification/compliance/inspection/testing agency for structural and non-structural wood-based panels, engineered wood products and wood components and assemblies.

In 1994, PFS/TECO Corporations president Ed Starostovic formed the nonprofit PFS Research Foundation, Inc. to foster the development and advancement of state-of-the-art quality control methodologies in the engineered wood products industry, and to facilitate technology transfer. *Engineered Wood Products A Guide for Specifiers, Designers and Users* is the first step towards achieving that goal.

Preface

This book is the first of its kind. It is the first publication that brings together between two covers a comprehensive chapter dedicated to each of today's structural engineered wood products, as well as complementary chapters on use considerations, quality assurance, and building code acceptance.

While hundreds of articles on engineered wood products have been published, they are sprinkled across dozens of scientific journals and texts. The search for information starts efficiently enough with a scan of a subject/title/author index or an electronic data base, but ends up as a time-consuming quest for a multiplicity of periodicals and books. Often, the articles are written in the ponderous prose of academia or in engineering jargon understandable to but a knowing few. Packed with scientific minutiae, these sources rarely include practical information about specifying, designing with and building with engineered wood products. Articles in trade magazines are easily understood and more likely to contain information useful to the practitioner. But unless available in the workplace, subscription-only publications can be difficult to track down.

It is primarily for these reasons that this book was written. Intended to present useful and practical information about engineered wood products to architects, designers, contractors, building officials, and others who specify these products, or design, build and inspect structures made with them, it is a comprehensive technical book written in plain language. In Chapters 1 through 6, the history, manufacture, uses, and use considerations for each of today's structural engineered wood products—glued-laminated timber, plywood, metal plate connected wood trusses, wood I-joists, oriented strand board and waferboard, and structural composite lumber—is described. Considerations critical to achieving fire resistance in structures built with these products are outlined in Chapter 7; in-service environmental factors that can influence their long term performance and durability are explained in Chapter 8. The third-party quality control and inspection requirements that ensure that engineered wood products will perform as expected are detailed in Chapter 9. In Chapter 10, the process by which the manufacturers of engineered wood products gain model building code acceptance of their products is reviewed, as are the relevant product standards cited in the codes. Finally, in Chapter 11, an overview of a newly-introduced alternative building design methodology applicable to all structural wood products—load and resistance factor design—is discussed. A list of references is provided at the end of each chapter so that the interested reader can dig deeper.

Like the first edition of all books, this one likely contains some errors and omissions. Readers are invited and encouraged to bring them to my attention.

Stephen Smulski, Ph. D., editor
Shutesbury, Massachusetts
January 1997

Introduction

Stephen Smulski, Ph. D.

Wood Science Specialists Inc.
Shutesbury, Massachusetts

Recently, I read two books by historian Ralph Andrews. *This Was Logging* and *This Was Sawmilling* chronicle a century of lumbering in the old-growth forests of the Pacific Northwest (1, 2). The photographs of skyscraping trees and mountains of massive logs, and the billions of board feet of lumber sawn from them, are truly amazing.

It's no accident that Andrews titled his anthologies in the past tense. Gone forever are the days when sawmills spewed forth an uninterrupted stream of high-grade timber and wide dimension lumber. Since, and as a result of, the "glory days of logging" described by Andrews, the forest resource has changed irrevocably, and so too have the wood products made from it.

A non-renewable resource in truth, the old-growth forests from which trees have been harvested since the first settlers arrived in North America nearly 400 years ago are almost gone. Most of what is left is wisely set aside in national parks, wilderness areas and in other holdings which prohibit harvesting. Today, America's truly renewable forest resource consists of second- and third-growth trees managed under sustainable forestry practices for harvest on 30- to 80-year rotations. This means that the trees are smaller in diameter when felled, and the timbers and lumber sawn from them contain more natural characteristics such as knots and juvenile wood that affect strength and in-service performance. While the smaller sizes of sawn timbers (up to 10x10) and dimension lumber (up to 2x10) will always be plentiful, the future availability of larger members, especially in the higher structural grades, is arguably uncertain.

At the same time, the Nation's demand for wood products continues to rise. Not surprisingly, the United States is both the world's largest producer and consumer of wood products. Annual per capita consumption is about 230 board feet of lumber, 110 square feet of panels (3/8-inch basis) and 750 pounds of paper, or the equivalent of a 100-foot tall tree 18 inches in diameter for each of America's 265 million citizens. Much of the lumber and panels goes into the 1 million or so new single-family homes built every year in the United States, each of which uses on average 16,900 board feet of lumber and 10,000 square feet of panels (3).

For these reasons, engineered wood products—glued-laminated timber, plywood, metal plate connected wood trusses, wood I-joists, oriented strand board (OSB) and waferboard, laminated veneer lumber (LVL), parallel strand lumber (PSL) and laminated strand lumber (LSL)—represent the future of the structural wood products industry in North America. The advantages that engineered wood products hold over the sawn timbers and lumber they replace sound almost too good to be true.

The fact is, they are true. All of these products can be made from trees no larger than 12 inches in diameter or from lumber no wider than a 2x4. Some, such as OSB and LSL, are made from underutilized species and "weed" trees like aspen that formerly had no commercial value. The introduction of performance-based standards for engineered wood products has further broadened the array of non-traditional species and species mixtures now being used. With the kerfless cutting of logs into veneer and strands, the wood of each harvested tree is used more completely.

ix

Ultrasonic grading of veneer allows for the optimum placement of wood according to stiffness and strength in LVL and PSL, while machine stress rating of dimension lumber permits the strategic positioning of lumber in metal plate connected wood trusses and glued-laminated timbers. And where a conventionally framed roof might require 2x8 rafters 16 inches on center, for instance, metal plate connected wood trusses for the same roof might be made entirely of 2x4s spaced 24 inches on center and use 15 to 25 percent less wood.

Because knots and other natural strength-reducing characteristics are restricted to a single strand, veneer, or lamination, they are smaller and dispersed harmlessly throughout the product's volume. As a result, the range of stiffness and strength among individual pieces of engineered wood products is considerably narrower than that of sawn timber and lumber. So, allowable design values are higher, as is the predictability of in-service performance. Capable of bridging long spans, these products eliminate the need for interior bearing walls and obstructing columns, and open unlimited possibilities for floor plans.

With the exception of metal plate connected wood trusses, engineered wood products are manufactured from wood at a moisture content well below the 16 to 19 percent typical of sawn framing lumber. As a consequence, they shrink, check, and warp much less than sawn lumber after being installed. In addition, fastener pops, floor squeaks, drywall cracks, and other shrinkage-related problems in buildings are few and far between.

As always happens, new technological solutions (wood I-joists, OSB, LVL, PSL and LSL are only about 30 years old) are accompanied by new considerations. For instance, except for span-rated plywood and OSB, engineered wood products are proprietary and not necessarily interchangeable. This means that LVL made by one manufacturer cannot be substituted for that made by another simply because both have the same dimensions. Likewise, the proper way to make the angled connections between wood I-joists and ridge beams or wall plates in sloped roofs may not be apparent to the carpenter accustomed to building with dimension lumber. On the other hand, the same methods for achieving fire resistance in structures framed with sawn timbers and lumber apply without modification to those built with engineered wood products.

Because of their advantages, use of engineered wood products continues to expand. According to a recent survey, from 1990 to 1992, use of LVL in North America grew by 8 percent, PSL by 44 percent, wood I-joists by 47 percent, and parallel-chord trusses by 10 percent (4). During the same two-year period, housing starts in the United States inched upward only 1 percent, while in Canada, they fell 10 percent. The study also noted that the greatest hindrance to increased use of engineered wood products was the lack of knowledge by architects, designers, engineers and builders alike concerning the details of their use.

I hope that this book accomplishes what Ralph Andrews' loggers set out to do in the dark, wet forests of the Pacific Northwest: "Let sunlight into the swamp."

Chapter 1

Glued-Laminated Timber

Russell C. Moody and Roland Hernandez

USDA Forest Service, Forest Products Laboratory[1]
Madison, Wisconsin

Structural glued-laminated timber is one of the oldest engineered wood products. It is defined in *ASTM D3737 Standard Method for Establishing Stresses for Structural Glued-Laminated Timber (Glulam)* as "a material glued up from suitably selected and prepared pieces of wood either in a straight or curved form with the grain of all pieces essentially parallel to the longitudinal axis of the member" (1). A stress-rated structural product, glued-laminated timber consists of two or more layers of lumber called laminations, that are nominally 1 or 2 inches thick. The maximum lamination thickness permitted in the United States under *ANSI/AITC A190.1 American National Standard for wood products – Structural Glued-laminated Timber* is 2 inches (2). *ANSI/AITC A190.1* requires that glued-laminated timber be fabricated in an approved (i.e., third-party inspected) manufacturing plant. By joining lumber end to end, edge to edge, and face to face, the size of a glued-laminated timber is limited only by the capabilities of the manufacturing plant and the height and width restrictions imposed by the transportation method.

Species and species combinations commonly used for glued-laminated timber in the United States include Douglas fir-larch, southern pine, hem-fir, and spruce-pine-fir (SPF). Nearly any species or species combination can be used provided its mechanical and physical properties are suitable and their lumber can be glued to meet the requirements of *ANSI/AITC A190.1*. Industry standards currently cover the use of many softwoods (3, 4) and hardwoods (5), and procedures are in place for including other species if and when there is the need (1).

Advantages of Glued-Laminated Timber

Compared with sawn timber as well as other structured materials, glued-laminated timber offers a number of advantages.

Figure 1. Straight members have been manufactured in lengths of up to 140 ft.

Size

Glued-laminated timber permits the creation of structural members that are much larger than the trees from which the component lumber is sawn. Whereas the forest products industry in the United States once had ready access to large-diameter, old-growth trees that yielded large sawn timbers, the present trend is to harvest smaller trees on much shorter rotations. As a result, nearly all modern sawmills are built to process relatively small logs. However, by combining small pieces of lumber in the form of glued-laminated timber, large structural members can be created. Straight members up to 100 feet long are not uncommon, with some spanning up to 140 feet (Fig. 1). Members deeper than 7 feet and wider than 20 inches have been produced. Thus, the glued-laminated timber process offers large timbers from small trees.

Figure 2. The double curvature of these members is easily obtained by bending laminations during lay-up.

Architectural Freedom

The long, clear spans afforded by glued-laminated timber allow for open floor plans unconstrained by columns. Because of their natural beauty, glued-laminated timbers are most often left exposed as a decorative element in residences, churches, shopping centers, and other public-use structures. By bending the lumber during the manufacturing process, a variety of architectural effects, including arches and compound curves, can be created that are difficult or even impossible to achieve with other structural materials (Fig. 2).

Kiln-Dried Lumber

The lumber used in fabricating glued-laminated timber must be kiln dried prior to assembly; therefore, the effect of checks, splits, warpage, and other defects, which normally develop as sawn timbers dry in service, on the strength and appearance of laminated members is minimized. In addition, structures built with glued-laminated timber can be designed on the basis of seasoned wood, which permits the use of higher allowable design values than can be assigned to unseasoned timber. Thus, there is both an appearance advantage—minimal checking—and a structural advantage—higher allowable design values—when using glued-laminated timber compared with sawn timber.

Variable Cross Section

Structural members may be designed with a variable cross section along their length, as determined by the strength and stiffness requirements of the application. For example, the central section of a glued-laminated timber can be made deeper to account for the increased stress that occurs in this region (Fig. 3). Arches often have a variable cross section for the same reason.

Figure 3. Strength where strength is needed; the central portion of this member has been made deeper to accommodate the increased stress that occurs in this region.

Efficient Use of Lumber Grades

A major advantage of glued-laminated timber is that the laminating process allows for the strategic placement of different grades of lumber within a member. Typically, the best grades of lumber are placed in the highly stressed laminations near the top and bottom of the member, while the lower grades of lumber may make up the inner half or more of the member. This means that a large quantity of lower grade lumber can be used for these less highly stressed laminations. Species can also be varied within a member to match the structural requirements of the laminations.

Environmentally Friendly

Much has been discussed and written regarding the relative effects on the environment of using wood, concrete, steel, and other structural materials. Several analyses have shown that wood's renewability, relatively low energy consumption during manufacture, carbon storage capability, and recyclability offers potential long-term environmental advantages compared with other structural materials (6, 7, 8, 9). Although aesthetic and economic considerations are usually the major factors influencing material selection, the environmental advantages of using wood may have an increasingly important effect on material selection.

The advantages of glued-laminated timber are tempered by certain factors not encountered in the production of sawn timber. In those instances where sawn timbers are available in the required size, the extra processing in making glued-laminated timber may increase its cost to more than that of the sawn timbers. The manufacture of glued-laminated timber requires specialized equipment, adhesives, plant facilities, and manufacturing skills that are not needed to produce sawn timbers. In addition, because of the large sizes in which both straight and curved glued-laminated timbers are available, shipping, handling, and storage must be considered early in the building design process.

History

Glued-laminated timber, as it is known today, was first used in 1893 to construct an auditorium in Basel, Switzerland. Patented as the "Hetzer System," it used adhesives that by today's standards are not waterproof. As a consequence, its applications were limited to dry-use conditions.

One of the first examples of glued-laminated timber arches designed and built using engineering principles is a building erected in 1934 at the Forest Products Laboratory, in Madison, Wisconsin (Fig. 4). Arches for this building, and for many of the nation's early buildings framed with glued-laminated timber, were produced by a company in Peshtigo, Wisconsin, which was founded by a German immigrant who transferred the technology to the United States. Several more companies were established in the late 1930s, and using the same technology, fabricated glued-laminated timbers for gymnasiums, churches, halls, factories, and barns.

During World War II, the need for large structural members to construct military buildings, such as warehouses and aircraft hangers, sparked additional interest in glued-laminated

Figure 4. Erected at the Forest Products Laboratory in Madison, Wisconsin, in 1934, this building is one of the first constructed with glued-laminated timber arches designed and built using engineering principles.

timber. The development of waterproof synthetic resin adhesives permitted the use of glued-laminated timber in bridges and other exterior applications where members required preservative treatment. By the early 1950s, there were at least a dozen manufacturers of glued-laminated timber in the United States. In 1952, these manufacturers joined to form the American Institute of Timber Construction (AITC). This association sponsored the first national manufacturing standard in 1963, *CS 253-63 Structural Glued-laminated Timber* (10). AITC has continued to sponsor revisions to the standard. The first was *PS 56-73* in 1973 that also became an ANSI standard, *A190.1-1973*. *ANSI A190.1* was revised in 1982 and 1992. The latest version is known as *ANSI/AITC A190.1-1992* (2).

At present, about 30 manufacturers across the United States and Canada are qualified to produce glued-laminated timber according to the requirements of *ANSI/AITC A190.1*. Total annual production is approximately 300 million board feet. Through the 1980s, nearly all glued-laminated timber production was used domestically. An export market was developed during the 1990s, and a substantial quantity of material is now shipped to Pacific Rim countries, with most going to Japan.

Manufacture of Glued-Laminated Timber

The manufacture of glued-laminated timber must follow recognized national standards to justify the specified engineering design values assigned to it. Properly manufactured glued-laminated timber demonstrates a balance in structural performance between the quality of the wood and that of the adhesive bonds.

ANSI/AITC A190.1 has a two-step approach to all phases of the manufacturing process. The first is a qualification step in which all equipment and personnel critical to the production of a quality product are thoroughly examined by a third-party agency. Upon successful qualification, daily quality assurance procedures and criteria are established that are targeted to keep each of the critical phases of the manufacturing process under control. Typically, one employee is assigned responsibility for supervising the daily testing and inspection. The third-party agency makes unannounced visits to the plant to review the manufacturing process, inspect the finished product, and examine the daily records of the in-plant quality assurance testing.

Several third-party agencies provide the qualification services and inspection supervision required by *ANSI/AITC A190.1* including the American Institute of Timber Construction, Englewood, Colorado; American Wood Systems, Tacoma, Washington; PFS/TECO Corporations, Madison, Wisconsin; and Timber Products Inspection, Conyers, Georgia. A current listing of manufacturers who are qualified according to the standard is available from these agencies.

The glued-laminated timber manufacturing process consists of four phases:

1. drying and grading the lumber

2. end jointing the lumber into longer laminations

3. face gluing the laminations

4. finishing and fabrication

A fifth phase—preservative treatment—is necessary in those applications where glued-laminated timber will be used in high moisture content environments or outdoors. A final important step is protection of the glued-laminated timber against moisture absorption and surface marring during transit, storage, and handling.

Lumber Drying and Grading

To minimize dimensional change following manufacture, as well as to take advantage of the higher allowable design values assigned to lumber compared with large sawn timbers, it is critical that the lumber be properly dried. This generally means kiln drying. For most applications, the maximum moisture content of laminations permitted under *ANSI/AITC A190.1* is 16 percent, which results in a member with an average moisture content of about 12 percent. In addition, the maximum range in moisture content permitted among laminations is limited to 5 percentage points to minimize differential changes in their dimensions following face gluing. Some plants use lumber at or slightly below 12 percent moisture content for two reasons. One is that the material is more easily end jointed at 12 percent moisture content than at higher values when the adhesive is cured by radio-frequency methods. The second reason is that lumber manufactured at 12 percent moisture content is closer to the average equilibrium moisture content that exists for most interior applications in the United States. Exceptions include some drier areas in the southwest that have lower equilibrium moisture content values and some exterior applications that may have higher values. Matching the moisture content of the glued-laminated timber at the time of manufacture to that which it will attain in service minimizes the shrinkage and swelling, which causes checks and splits.

The average moisture content of the lumber entering the manufacturing process can be determined by sampling from the lumber supply using a hand-held moisture meter. Alternatively, many manufacturers use a continuous in-line meter that checks the moisture content of each piece of lumber as it enters the process. Those pieces with a moisture content greater than a given threshold value are removed and re-dried.

Grading standards published by the regional lumber grading associations describe the natural characteristics and machining imperfections permitted in the various grades of lumber (11, 12). Manufacturing standards for glued-laminated timber like *AITC 117-Manufacturing Standard Specification for Structural Glued-laminated Timber of Softwood Species* describe the combination of lumber grades that must be used to achieve specific design values (4). Two types of lumber grading are used for laminating: visual grading and E-rating.

The rules for visually graded lumber are based entirely on those characteristics that are readily apparent. Lumber grade descriptions list the limiting characteristics for knot size, slope of grain, wane, and other strength-reducing characteristics that naturally occur in lumber. Under the Western Wood Product Association's *Western Lumber Grading Rules* (12), for example, knot size in visually graded western species is limited to:

Laminating grade	Maximum knot size
L1	1/4 of width
L2	1/3 of width
L3	1/2 of width

With E-rated or mechanically graded lumber, the stiffness of each piece is first measured directly with one of several nondestructive methods. Those pieces that qualify for a specific grade are then visually inspected to ensure that they meet the requirement for maximum allowable edge-knot size. The various grades of E-rated lumber are expressed in terms of their modulus of elasticity (E) and limiting edge-knot size. A piece graded 2.0E-1/6, for instance, has a modulus of elasticity of 2.0 million psi and an edge knot no larger than 1/6 of its width.

Manufacturers generally purchase graded lumber and verify the grades through visual inspection and, if E-rated, by testing. To qualify for some of the higher design stresses for glued-laminated timber, manufacturers must conduct additional grading in-plant to identify lumber to be used in the outer tension zone of certain members. High quality lumber with high tensile strength is required for the outer 5 percent of the tension side of a glued-laminated beam. Special grading criteria for "tension laminations" are given in *AITC 117-Manufacturing*. Alternatively, a fabricator can purchase special lumber that is manufactured under a quality assurance system to provide the required tensile strength. Another option employed by at least one manufacturer is to use high tensile strength laminated veneer lumber (LVL) for tension laminations.

Recently, some manufacturers have started using fiber-reinforced plastics on the tension side of glued-laminated timbers to enhance bending strength. Fiber-reinforced members are reportedly up to three times stronger than all-wood members. Because of its exceptional tensile strength, the fiber reinforcement can displace up to 30 percent of the wood required for an all-wood member. The result is a member smaller in cross section and lighter in weight that can span longer distances.

End Jointing

To manufacture glued-laminated timber in lengths beyond those commonly available for sawn lumber, laminations must be made by end jointing lumber. The most common end joint is a structural finger joint about 1.1 inches long (Fig. 5). Other end-joint configurations are also acceptable, provided they meet specific strength and durability requirements. One advantage of finger joints compared with other types of end joints—scarf joints, for example—is that only a short length of the starting lumber is "lost" during manufacture. Finger joints are also easily and quickly made with continuous production equipment. Well-made finger joints are critical to ensure the adequate performance of glued-laminated timber in service. Careful control of the end jointing process at each stage—lumber quality, cutting the joint, application of adhesive, mating lumber, application of end pressure, and curing the adhesive—is necessary to produce consistent, high strength joints.

Prior to manufacture, the ends of the lumber are inspected to ensure that there are no knots or other features present that would impair joint strength. Finger joints are then machined on both ends of the lumber with special cutter heads. A structural adhesive is applied, and the joints in successive pieces of lumber are mated. The adhesive is then cured with the joint under end pressure. Most manufacturers use a continuous radio-frequency curing system that rapidly heats and partially sets the adhesive in a matter of seconds. Finger joints achieve most of their strength at this time; residual heat permits the adhesive to completely cure and reach full strength in a few hours.

Structural finger joints have the potential to attain 75 percent or more of the tensile strength of clear wood for many species of lumber. Because most grades of lumber used in fabricating glued-laminated timber permit knots and other natural characteristics that reduce the strength of the lumber by at least 25 percent below that of clear wood, finger joints are adequate for most applications.

Figure 5. Structural finger joints used in glued-laminated timber typically attain at least 75 percent of the tensile strength of clear wood.

ANSI/AITC A190.1 requires that a manufacturer qualify its production end joint to meet the required strength level of the highest strength grade of glued-laminated timber it is going to produce. This necessitates that the results of tensile tests of end-jointed lumber meet certain strength criteria, and that adhesive durability test results do the same. When these criteria are met, daily quality control testing in tension of full-sized end joints is performed to ensure that the required strength level is being maintained. Adhesive durability tests in which end joints are subjected to repeated cycles of wetting and drying to verify their resistance to delamination are also required.

A continuing challenge in the glued-laminated timber production process is to detect and eliminate the occasional low strength end joint. Visual inspection and other nondestructive techniques have been shown not to be fully effective in detecting low strength joints. An approach used by many manufacturers to ensure the quality of critical end joints is the use of proof loading. With this method, a specified bending or tension load is applied to critical laminations that will be placed on the tension side of members to verify end joint strength. By applying loads that are related to the strength needed, low strength joints can be identified. The qualification procedures for proof loading equipment must prove that the loads applied do not damage the laminations that are accepted.

Face Gluing

The assembly of laminations into full depth members is another critical stage in the glued-laminated timber manufacturing process. The proper adhesives and procedures that develop the required interlayer shear strength are determined during the plant's qualification phase. The plant has considerable flexibility in the types of adhesives and procedures that it may use, provided they meet specific shear strength and durability requirements for the species. To obtain clean, parallel, and gluable surfaces, the best procedure is to plane the two wide faces of the laminations just prior to the gluing process. This ensures that the final assembly will be rectangular and the pressure will be applied evenly. Adhesives that have been pre-qualified are then spread, normally with a glue extruder. Phenol resorcinol is the most commonly used adhesive for face gluing, but other adhesives that have been adequately evaluated and proven to meet performance and durability requirements may also be used.

Laminations are then assembled into the specified lay-up pattern. Straight beams may or may not have a camber built in. Laminations wider than about 11 inches (a 2 by 12) are made by placing narrower pieces side-by-side during face gluing, such that the edge joints in adjacent laminations are offset. Laminations for curved members and arches are glued and cured in curved forms that define their shape. The degree of curvature in a glued-laminated timber is controlled by the thickness of its laminations. In general, the radius of curvature is limited to between 100 and 125 times the thickness of the lamination. As such, only low curvature is possible in members made with nominal 2-inch-thick lumber. Those needing moderate curvature are generally manufactured with nominal 1-inch lumber, whereas laminations 1/2 inch or thinner may be required for members with sharp curves.

After the adhesive is given sufficient time to begin to penetrate into the wood, pressure is applied. The most common method of exerting pressure is with clamping beds in which a mechanical or hydraulic system brings the laminations into intimate contact (Fig. 6). With this batch-type process, the adhesive is allowed to cure at room temperature for 6 to 24 hours before pressure is released. Some of the newer clamping systems combine continuous hydraulic presses and radio-frequency curing to reduce the face gluing process from hours to minutes. Upon completion of the process, the adhesive usually has most of its ultimate strength. Curing continues for the next few days, but at a much slower rate.

The face gluing process is monitored at the lumber planing, adhesive mixing and application, and clamping stages. Adhesive bond quality is evaluated by conducting shear tests on small samples taken from end trim cut off the finished glued-laminated timber. The target shear strength is prescribed in *ANSI/AITC A190.1* and equals about 90 percent of the average shear strength of the wood species from which the member is made. Thus, these adhesive bonds are expected to develop nearly the full strength of the wood soon after manufacture.

M 138 309

Figure 6. After being placed in the clamping bed, the laminations of these arches are forced together with an air-driven screw clamp.

Finishing and Fabrication

After the glued-laminated timber is removed from the clamping system, the wide faces (sides) are planed or sanded to remove beads of adhesive that have squeezed out between laminations and smooth any slight irregularities between the edges of laminations. This results in the finished glued-laminated timber being slightly less in width than the dimension lumber from which it was made. The narrow faces (top and bottom) of the member may be lightly planed or sanded, depending on appearance requirements. Edges (corners) are often eased (rounded) as well.

The specified appearance of the member dictates the additional finishing required at this stage of manufacture, but this does not affect the strength or stiffness of the members. Three appearance classes are included in the industry standard: Industrial, Architectural, and Premium (13). Industrial class is used when appearance is not a primary concern, such as factories and warehouses. To some, this is the most natural look for a glued-laminated timber. Architectural class is suitable for most applications where appearance is an important requirement. Premium is the highest appearance class. The primary difference between the classes is the amount of knot holes and occasional planer skips that are permitted. The higher classes require additional attention to filling knot holes and other voids; higher class finishes also increase the cost.

The glued-laminated timber industry is considering the addition of a fourth appearance class called "Framing". Whereas the three previously mentioned classes normally result in a member width less than the lumber width, the proposed "Framing" class would be finished to the same width as the lumber to be compatible with the common widths of framing lumber. This would result in an appearance called "hit and miss" planing and would be intended for uses in which the member is to be covered or the appearance is of minimal importance. In addition, some manufacturers offer members with resawn surfaces that mimic rough-sawn timbers.

The next step in the glued-laminated timber manufacturing process is fabrication. Here final cuts are made, holes drilled, connectors added, and, if specified, a sealer or finish is applied. Depending on the member's intended use, some prefabrication of parts may be done at this point. Trusses may be partially or fully assembled. Moment splices may be fully constructed, then disconnected for transport. Application of end sealers, surface sealers and primer coats, and wrapping glued-laminated timber with a water-resistant covering all help to minimize changes in moisture content between manufacture and installation.

Preservative Treatment

In service environments where the moisture content of a glued-laminated timber will approach or exceed 20 percent, such as in most exterior and some interior uses, the finished member or its lumber laminations should be treated with a preservative as per *AITC 109 Standard for Preservative Treatment of Structural Glued-laminated Timber* (14). Three types of preservatives are used: creosote solutions, oilborne treatments, and waterborne treatments. All these preservative treatments result in a lumber surface that is difficult to bond. Creosote and oilborne preservatives are usually applied to the finished glued-laminated timber after all cutting and boring of holes by the fabricator are completed. The waterborne process can lead to excessive checking if applied to large members and is best applied to the lumber prior to laminating. Recommended retention levels for each preservative type are given in *AITC 109*, along with the appropriate quality assurance procedures.

Creosote treatment is best for glued-laminated timber slated for use in the most severe exposures. It provides excellent protection against decay, insects, and marine borers in uses such as bridges, wharves, and marine structures. Creosote-treated wood has a dark, oily surface that is difficult to alter. This, coupled with a distinct odor, restricts its use to nonresidential structures and where there is no direct contact with humans. One advantage of creosote is that the water repellency it imparts to treated members renders them much less susceptible to the rapid changes in moisture content which can cause checks and splits.

Glued-laminated timber can be treated with oilborne pentachlorophenol dissolved in oil (Type A), light hydrocarbons (Type C), or other solvents listed in *P9 Standards for Solvents and Formulations for Organic Preservative Systems* published by the American Wood-Preserver's Association (AWPA) (15). Type A treatment results in an oily surface; members treated with it cannot be painted. When a paintable surface is needed, Type C treatments should be specified. Penta, as it is called, also imparts water repellency and offers protection against decay and insects, but not marine borers. Glued-laminated timber bridge members in freshwater and utility structures are often penta treated. Other oilborne preservatives used for glued-laminated timbers include copper naphthenate and copper-8-quinolinolate, the only wood preservative approved for use in wood products that may come in contact with food stuffs.

Waterborne treatments can be applied to the lumber prior to the laminating process but are not recommended for use in treating finished glued-laminated timber (16) because of the checks, splits, and warpage that can occur when the members are re-dried after treatment. Preservatives for waterborne treatment conform to AWPA's *P5 Standards for Waterborne Preservatives* and are based on water-soluble chemicals that become fixed in the wood (17). The protection against decay and insects afforded by these waterborne treatments depends on the depth that the chemicals penetrate into the lumber. Some species are easily penetrated with preservatives—southern pine, for example—and others like Douglas-fir and western hemlock are not. As a consequence, different chemical formulations and treatment processes are used for different species. The challenge in the use of waterborne treatments is to obtain the required strength and durability in the gluelines because the surfaces are more difficult to bond. Manufacturers who are qualified to glue waterborne-treated lumber use special manufacturing procedures.

A major advantage of waterborne treatments is that they result in a surface that is easily finished. From an appearance standpoint, the main effect is that different formulations can produce a green, gray, or brown tint. Care must be used in selecting connection hardware to ensure that it will resist the potentially corrosive interactions with the chemical treatment. Also, glued-laminated timber treated with waterborne preservatives is much more susceptible to changes in moisture content and results in a greater tendency for checking, splitting, and dimensional instability than members protected with either creosote or oilborne treatments.

Fire

Like all wood products, glued-laminated timber is combustible. But because of their large cross-sectional areas and the slow rate at which their surfaces char, glued-laminated timbers exposed to fire will safely carry loads substantially longer than unprotected steel, which begins to soften and lose its strength at about 500°F. When needed, members with a 1-hour fire rating can be made by adding an extra "tension lamination." The fire and flame spread resistance of glued-laminated timber can also be enhanced with the application of fire-resistant surface coatings or pressure impregnation with fire retardants.

Applications for Glued-Laminated Timber

Although the major use of glued-laminated timber is in the roof systems of commercial buildings, it is being used increasingly in residential roof and floor systems and in a multitude of special industrial uses. Wood, in general, has distinct advantages for roof systems because of its favorable strength-to-weight ratio. Glued-laminated timber offers the additional advantage of virtually unlimited flexibility in shape and size.

Commercial and Residential Buildings

Rectangular Beams—Glued-laminated timber beams are popular as the main load-carrying members in flat and low-slope roof systems for single-story warehouses, shopping centers, and factories. The volume of wood required to carry the roof design loads is decreased by using main beams cantilevered over interior supports, with smaller beams spanning between them (Fig. 7). Main members are often spaced 20 to 30 feet apart, with purlins of smaller glued-laminated timber, sawn timbers, wood I-joists, or metal plate connected wood trusses spanning between them. Depending on the snow and other live loads, either 2x4s or 2x6s on edge span from purlin to purlin, which are 8 feet on-center. Structural sheathing is attached directly to the 2-foot on-center 2x4 or 2x6 sub-purlins. Exterior walls are often cast concrete or concrete block. Interior supports may be glued-laminated timber or steel columns. With the main beams erected with a fork lift and the purlin assemblies prefabricated on the ground, large roofs can be constructed in a relatively short time.

Pitched and Curved Beams—Roof systems made with pitched and tapered curved glued-laminated timber beams provide both a pitched roof and an interior space with extra ceiling height, without increasing the height of the supporting wall. Applications for these members include office, retail, institutional, and other buildings that call for long, clear spans and high ceilings.

Figure 7. Cantilevered systems are popular in commercial buildings with low-slope and flat roofs.

Trusses—Many kinds of trusses are fabricated with glued-laminated timber. The most common are bowstring, parallel chord, and pitched chord configurations. Glued-laminated timber is particularly suited to bowstring trusses because the top chord can be manufactured to the desired curvature. Connections between chords and webs are most often made with steel plates and through-bolts. Depending on the size and shape of the truss, some pre-assembly of members can often be done off-site.

Headers and Beams for Residential Construction—Many building material suppliers carry stock glued-laminated timbers in standard sizes for use as headers and beams in house construction. Applications include structural ridge beams, exposed roof rafters, floor girders, and headers for large openings, such as picture windows and patio and garage doors. Stock members for residential applications are available in various depths and in 3-1/2 or 5-1/2 inch widths to match walls constructed with 2x4 and 2x6 studs. Other residential uses include stair treads and stringers and fireplace mantels.

Multistory Heavy Timber—Office and retail buildings up to five stories high have been built using glued-laminated timber as the main load-carrying members, most often in the exposed post-and-beam style.

Arches—Glued-laminated timber arches provide for both the efficient transfer of roof loads directly to the foundation and dramatic architectural effects. Their numerous shapes allow architects to create unique structures with sweeping lines. Glued-laminated timber arches have been used widely in bridges, religious structures, concert halls, swimming pool enclosures, skating rinks, and other sports venues (Fig. 8).

Figure 8. Kraft paper covering these glued-laminated timber arches protects their surfaces during transport and erection.

Domes—The high strength-to-weight ratio of glued-laminated timber makes it advantageous for use in long-span domes for sports arenas, auditoriums, and other assembly-use buildings. These large, support-free circular structures use members arranged in radial rib, VARAX™, or Triax® patterns. Radial rib designs consist of circular arches that radiate outward from the crown (top) of the dome to its base. Both VARAX™ and Triax® domes use glued-laminated timbers arranged in triangular patterns. An example of a VARAX™ structure is the 530-foot-diameter Tacoma Dome in Tacoma, Washington (Fig. 9).

Figure 9. Triangulated members form the roof of the 530-foot clear span Tacoma Dome.

Figure 10. Preservative-treated laminations are used for the end of this glued-laminated post that will be in or near the ground.

Construction Posts—Post-frame buildings are widely used for farm structures and light commercial buildings. Glued-laminated timbers are sometimes used for the posts or wall columns. This provides for the option of making only that part of the post that is embedded in the ground (soil-floor buildings) or near the groundline (slab-on-grade buildings) with preservative-treated lumber, while using untreated lumber for the remainder (Fig. 10).

Figure 11. Timber bridge constructed of glued-laminated timber stringers and a transverse glued-laminated timber deck.

Bridges

The main use of glued-laminated timber in bridges is for parts of the superstructure, such as girders and decking (18). One popular type of bridge consists of glued-laminated timber stringers, spanning between supports and glued-laminated timber decking placed transverse to them (Fig. 11). For spans up to 25 to 30 feet, a longitudinal glued-laminated timber deck that requires no stringers is often used (Fig. 12). Special architectural effects can be achieved by supporting the main span with glued-laminated timber arches (Fig. 13).

Figure 12. The longitudinal glued-laminated timber deck of this timber bridge does not require stringers.

Figure 13. Graceful glued-laminated timber arches support this bridge.

Figure 14. The unique shape requirements of this utility structure were met with glued-laminated timber (courtesy of Hughes Brothers, Seward, Nebraska).

Utility Structures

Glued-laminated timber is used in power transmission towers, light standards, and other utility applications to meet special size and shape requirements that cannot be obtained using conventional wood poles (Fig. 14). Glued-laminated timber cross arms and davit arms are used to support wires on wood poles (Fig. 15).

Architectural sculptures are another example of using glued-laminated timber when special sizes and shapes are required (Fig. 16).

1 - 21

Figure 15.
Glued-laminated
timber davit arms
on a conventional
wood pole
(courtesy of
Hughes Brothers,
Seward,
Nebraska).

M 138 316

Figure 16. Sculpture illustrates the dramatic architectural effects possible with glued-laminated timber.

Types and Properties of Glued-laminated Timber

Because the laminating process disperses strength-reducing characteristics like knots and slope of grain throughout the volume of a member, glued-laminated timbers have higher allowable design values than sawn timbers. The improved properties are due, in part, to a re-distribution of stresses around low strength regions within the laminations because of the layered construction of glued-laminated timbers. Also, glued-laminated timbers are specially designed to resist stresses based on their intended use as bending, axial, curved, or tapered members by strategically placing higher grade laminations where strength is needed. The configuration or location of various grades of lumber within the cross section of a glued-laminated timber is referred to as a glued-laminated timber combination.

Types

Bending Members—Glued-laminated timbers intended to carry flexural loads are designed using bending combinations. Referred to as horizontally laminated members, these members are based on combinations that provide the most efficient and economical cross section for resisting the bending stress caused by loads applied perpendicular to the wide faces of the laminations. Typically, lower grades of laminating lumber are used for the center portion of the combination, or core, where bending stress is low, and higher grades are placed on the outside faces where bending stress is relatively high (Fig. 17).

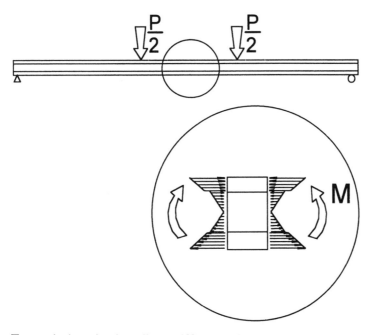

Figure 17. Stresses that develop in a glued-laminated timber bending member when loaded. Discontinuity in stress is due to the difference in the stiffness and strength of the different grades of lumber used for the faces and core.

To optimize the bending stiffness of this type of glued-laminated timber, equal amounts of high quality laminations may be included on both of the outside faces to produce a "balanced" combination. When the goal is to optimize bending strength, the combination can be "unbalanced" with additional high quality laminations placed on the tension side of the member. The high quality lumber used for the outer 5 percent on the tension side of both balanced and unbalanced bending combination members has stringent requirements for knot size, slope of grain, and the extent of grain deviation.

Unbalanced combinations are suitable for most uses where simple beams are required. When the glued-laminated timber is continuous over supports, however, the combination may need to be designed as a balanced member because both the top and bottom of the beam may be subject to high tensile stresses. In this case, the tension lamination requirements apply equally to both the top and bottom laminations.

Axial Members and Those Loaded Parallel to the Wide Face—Axial combinations were developed to optimize the cross section of glued-laminated timbers designed to resist the axial tension and compression. They are also used for so-called vertically laminated members—glued-laminated timber in which flexural loads are applied parallel to the wide faces of the laminations (Fig. 18). Unlike bending combinations, the same grade of lamination is generally used throughout the cross section of the member. Axial combinations may also be loaded perpendicular to the wide face of the laminations, but use of a uniform lumber grade often results in a less efficient and economical member than with a bending combination. As with bending combinations, different knot and slope-of-grain requirements apply, based on the intended use of the axial combination as a tension or bending member.

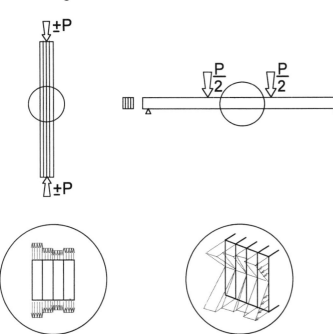

Figure 18. Stresses that develop in glued-laminated timber axial combination members when loaded.

Curved Members—The same combinations that are used for straight, horizontally laminated bending members are also used for curved members. However, an important consideration with these members is the development of radial stresses in the curved portion (Fig. 19) (commonly referred to as radial tension). Loads that tend to flatten or decrease the curvature of a curved member induce radial tension stresses perpendicular to the wide faces of the laminations. As the radius of curvature of the glued-laminated timber decreases, the radial stresses in the curved portion increase. Because of the relatively low strength of lumber in tension perpendicular-to-grain compared with tension parallel-to-grain, these radial stresses can become a critical factor in designing curved glued-laminated timber combinations. When loads are applied that tend to increase the radius of curvature (close up the curved member), radial compression occurs. This does not usually control the design.

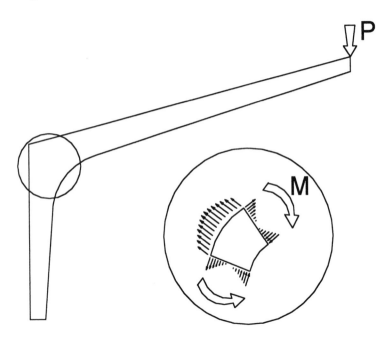

Figure 19. Both bending stresses and radial stresses develop in a curved glued-laminated timber when loaded.

Curved members are commonly manufactured with either nominal 1-inch- (actual 0.75-inch-) or 2-inch- (actual 1.5-inch-) thick lumber. It is recommended that the ratio of lamination thickness, t, to the radius of curvature, R, not exceed 1/100 for hardwoods and southern pine and 1/125 for other softwoods (1). Thus, the curvature that is obtainable with nominal 1-inch lumber will be sharper than that for 2-inch lumber and sharper for hardwoods and southern pine than for other softwoods.

Tapered Members—Straight or curved beams of glued-laminated timber can be tapered to achieve architectural effects, provide pitched roofs, facilitate drainage, and lower wall height requirements at the end supports. The taper is created by sawing across one or more laminations at the desired slope. The cut should be made only on the compression side (top) of a glued-laminated timber, because interrupting the continuity of the tension-side laminations would decrease strength. Common forms of tapered combinations include single tapered (a continuous slope from end to end), double tapered (two slopes that form a peak), tapered both ends (slope at each end of a flat middle), and tapered one end (slope at only one end) (Fig. 20).

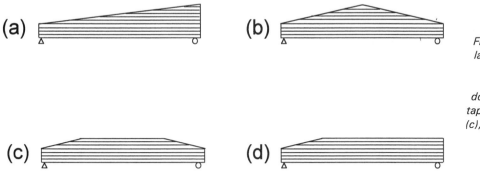

Figure 20. Glued-laminated timbers may be single tapered (a), double tapered (b), tapered at both ends (c), or tapered at one end (d).

Mechanical Properties

Although a glued-laminated timber is a composite of different pieces of lumber of varying grade, strength, and stiffness that are bonded together, its mechanical properties can be estimated with good results using simplified analysis methods. Industry-accepted methods for establishing and/or estimating the mechanical properties of glued-laminated timber are given in *ASTM D3737* (1).

Modulus of Elasticity—The modulus of elasticity (MOE) of a glued-laminated timber is directly related to the MOE of its individual laminations. The MOE of a lamination can be determined with a number of different methods, each of which is usually related to the results of a static test in which the lamination is tested at a span-to-depth ratio of 100:1 under center-point loading. Under these conditions, the MOE of the lamination calculated from load-deflection data is essentially unaffected by shear deformation and approaches the true MOE. The MOE of a horizontally laminated member made with a bending combination is taken as 95 percent of the MOE value determined in a transformed section analysis. For a vertically laminated member, the MOE is taken as 95 percent of the average MOE for all the individual laminations. The 5 percent reduction is applied to these types of members to offset the shear deflection that actually occurs in bending members within the normal range of sizes where the length of the member is 15 to 20 times its depth.

The MOE for glued-laminated timbers subject to axial loads is estimated using the weighted average of the MOE values of the individual laminations. Although no reduction for shear deformation is necessary, values published in industry standards applicable to axial loading include a 5-percent reduction. This avoids having two different allowable values of MOE for the same member.

Strength—The strength properties of glued-laminated timber are determined with the use of stress index values and stress modification factors (1). Stress index values are based on the strength properties of clear, straight-grained wood. These values are determined by adjusting fifth-percentile strength values of clear wood by factors that account for safety and moisture content. Properties of clear, straight-grained wood are published in *ASTM D2555 Standard Test Methods for Establishing Clear Wood Strength Values* (19). Because lumber is not clear and straight grained, stress modification factors are applied to the calculated stress indices. The magnitude of the modification factors is based on the strength-reducing characteristics such as knots, slope of grain, checks, splits, and wane that are allowed in the particular grade of lumber being used. The larger or more severe the characteristic, the smaller the stress modification factor.

The primary characteristics involved in determining the stress modification factors for the bending strength of a glued-laminated timber are knots and slope of grain. If the member is horizontally laminated (load applied perpendicular to the wide faces of the laminations), knots present in the outer laminations are more critical than knots in the core laminations. For this reason, the location of knots within a beam, and their effect on strength, is accounted for in an analysis technique called the I_K/I_G method (20). In this method, I_K refers to the moment of inertia of all knots within 6 inches of the critical cross section, and I_G is the gross moment of inertia of the cross section. The ratio I_K/I_G is related to the stress modification factor for bending (SMF_b):

$$SMF_b = \left(1 + 3\frac{I_K}{I_G}\right)\left(1 - \frac{I_K}{I_G}\right)^3\left(1 - \frac{1}{2}\left(\frac{I_K}{I_G}\right)\right)$$

For vertically laminated members (load applied parallel to the wide faces of the laminations) subject to bending loads, as well as both tension and compression members, the stress modification factors are also determined based on knot properties of the lumber.

In each case (horizontally laminated bending, vertically laminated bending, compression and tension), the stress modification factors determined for knots are then compared with the stress modification factors for slope of grain. The controlling values—the smaller of SMF with respect to knots or SMF for slope of grain—are used for each of the strength properties.

When estimating horizontal shear values for glued-laminated timber, stress modification factors are assumed to be equal to 1.0, if strength-reducing defects such as checks, splits, and wane are limited in horizontally laminated members. The situation is different for vertically laminated members. If defects exist in any one lamination, then the stress modification factor for each lamination with defects is reduced by half, and the stress modification factor for the entire member is equal to [N - (n/2)]/N. Here N is the total number of laminations in the glued-laminated timber, and n is the total number of laminations with defects.

Stress modification factors are also equal to 1.0 when determining allowable strength values in both compression perpendicular-to-grain and in radial tension. These properties, along with horizontal shear for defect-free laminations, are assumed to be equal to the values for clear wood, because they are not affected by slope of grain or the effects of the laminated construction of the member.

Allowable Design Values

When the stress modification factors, whether governed by knots or slope of grain, are determined for each property, they are multiplied by the calculated stress indices. The products of this multiplication are estimates of the allowable stress for glued-laminated timber, not estimates of its actual strength. This is because the clear wood properties on which the stress indices are based were adjusted downward to include a factor of safety and account for duration of load effects. These allowable property values correspond to the tabulated design values for the combinations listed in *AITC 117-Design* (3). In assigning these allowable properties, it is assumed that the end jointing of the lumber and the face gluing of the laminations meet the calculated levels required by *ANSI/AITC A190.1* (2). If tests show that the performance of the end joints does not meet the target level of glued-laminated timber performance, then the allowable properties of the member must be adjusted to reflect the actual end-joint performance.

Physical Properties

With few exceptions, the physical properties of a glued-laminated timber are identical to those of the wood from which it is made. Examples include appearance, working qualities, weathering, decay resistance, chemical resistance, and coefficient of friction. Thermal and electrical properties are point-to-point characteristics that depend on whether the behavior is being analyzed along the length of a lamination or across several laminations. Density and moisture content are volume-based properties that also vary from point-to-point, depending on whether they are being determined for a localized portion of a lamination or an entire cross section.

A critical physical property for glued-laminated timber is the shrinkage and swelling that accompanies changes in moisture content. Residual stresses can be locked into wood adjacent to the gluelines during manufacture when laminations of varying moisture content are bonded together. In addition, because different laminations will shrink and swell by various amounts as their moisture content changes as a result of small variations in density, growth ring orientation, and grain angle, stresses can also develop in service. In severe cases, the residual stresses and in-service movement may be large enough to cause checking near the gluelines. Although almost always an aesthetic problem only, surface checking can be minimized by specifying that the glued-laminated timber be manufactured from lumber at a moisture content close to the equilibrium moisture content of the intended service environment. As previously noted, the maximum moisture content permitted in *ANSI/AITC A190.1* is 16 percent, resulting in an average moisture content near 12 percent, which is appropriate for most covered exterior or interior applications in the United

States. In instances where the equilibrium moisture content is known to be significantly less, a lower moisture content at time of manufacture should be specified.

A rule of thumb that can be used to estimate the extent of dimensional changes is that cross-section dimensions will change 1 percent for each 4 to 5 percentage point change in moisture content. Thus, if the equilibrium moisture content is about 8 percent, a 24-inch-deep member might be expected to shrink about 1/4 inch in depth as it dries from 12 to 7 or 8 percent.

Designing With Glued-Laminated Timber

The design procedures and considerations described here apply only to glued-laminated timber combinations that conform to *AITC 117 Standard Specification for Structural Glued-laminated Timber of Softwood Species* (3, 4), *AITC 119 Standard Specification for Hardwood Glued-laminated Timber* (5), and are manufactured in accordance with *ANSI/AITC A190.1. AITC 117* consists of *Manufacturing* (4), which provides details for the many combinations of glued-laminated timber made from visually graded and E-rated softwood lumber and *Design* (3), which furnishes design values for the strength and stiffness of glued-laminated timber. *AITC 119* supplies similar information for members made from hardwoods. These standards are based on laterally braced, straight members with an average moisture content of 12 percent. For bending members, the design values are based on an assumed reference member size of 12 inches deep, 5.125 inches wide, and 21 feet long. Detailed design information is given in the *Timber Construction Manual* (21).

Tabular Design Values

Allowable design values given in *AITC 117-Design* and *AITC 119* include bending (F_b), tension parallel-to-grain (F_t), shear parallel-to-grain (F_v), compression perpendicular-to-grain (F_{cperp}), compression parallel-to-grain (F_c), modulus of elasticity (E), and radial tension perpendicular-to-grain (F_{rt}).

Because glued-laminated timber may have different properties when loaded perpendicular (horizontally laminated) or parallel (vertically laminated) to the wide faces of its laminations, a common naming pattern is used to specify the design values that correspond to each orientation. Design values for horizontally laminated members are denoted with the subscript "x", and those for vertically laminated members use "y". For example, F_{bx} refers to the allowable design bending stress for a horizontally laminated bending member, and E_y denotes the allowable design modulus of elasticity for a vertically laminated member.

End-Use Adjustment Factors

When glued-laminated timber is exposed to end-use or service conditions other than the reference condition described in the table, the published allowable design values require adjustment.

Volume—The volume factor, C_V, accounts for the known reduction in strength that occurs when the length, width, and depth of glued-laminated timber increase beyond the reference size of 12 inches deep, 5.125 inches wide, and 21 feet long. The decrease is due to the greater probability of the occurrence of critical strength-reducing characteristics, such as knots and slope of grain, in larger volume beams. The volume factor adjustment is given in *AITC Technical Note No. 21, Use of a Volume Effect Factor in the Design of Glued-laminated Timber Beams* (22) as

$$C_V = \left(\frac{12}{d}\right)^{0.10} \left(\frac{5.125}{w}\right)^{0.10} \left(\frac{21}{L}\right)^{0.10}$$

for Douglas-fir and other species, where d is depth (inches); w is width (inches); and L is length (feet). The one exception is southern pine, where:

$$C_V = \left(\frac{12}{d}\right)^{0.05} \left(\frac{5.125}{w}\right)^{0.05} \left(\frac{21}{L}\right)^{0.05}$$

Moisture Content—A moisture content factor, C_M, is used to account for the reduction in stiffness and strength that occurs when moisture content increases. In *AITC 117-Design*, C_M is given as 1.0 when the equilibrium moisture content of glued-laminated timber in service will be 16 percent or less. Under exterior or other conditions that will result in a moisture content greater than 16 percent—a swimming pool enclosure, for example, or when members are in ground contact, the following values apply:

	F_b	F_t	F_v	F_{cperp}	F_c	E
C_M	0.8	0.8	0.875	0.53	0.73	0.833

Loading—An adjustment that accounts for how a member is actually loaded is also necessary, because the volume factor adjustments are derived assuming a uniform load. The loading factor, K_L, recommended in *AITC Technical Note No. 21* and the *National Design Specification for Wood Construction (NDS)* (23) is 1.00 for uniform loading on a simple span, 1.08 for center-point loading on a simple span, and 0.92 for constant stress over the full length of the member. K_L for other loading conditions can be estimated using the proportion of the length of the member subjected to 80 percent or more of the maximum stress, l_o (24):

$$K_L = \left(\frac{0.45}{l_o}\right)^{0.1}$$

Tension Lamination—Special tension lamination provisions must be followed by fabricators in order for the glued-laminated timber beam to achieve the specified design bending strength. Allowable properties tabulated in *AITC 117* and *AITC 119* are applicable to members with these special tension laminations. If the glued-laminated timber combination does not include a special tension lamination, a strength reduction factor must be applied. According to *ASTM D3737*, the appropriate tension lamination factor, C_{TL}, is 1.00 for members with special tension laminations as per *AITC 117* and *AITC 119*, 0.85 for members without tension laminations whose depth is less than or equal to 15 inches and 0.75 for members without tension laminations greater than 15 inches deep.

Curvature—A curvature factor, C_c, is applied to account for the residual stresses in the curved portion of a curved glued-laminated timber created during manufacture. The factor does not apply to the design values for the straight portion of the member, regardless of the curvature elsewhere. The curvature factor is given in the *NDS* as

$$C_c = 1 - 2000 \left(\frac{t}{R} \right)^2$$

where t, R, and limits on the ratio t/R are as described previously.

Flat Use—The *NDS* recommends that a flat use factor, C_{fu}, be applied to bending design values when members are loaded parallel to the wide faces of their laminations and are less than 12 inches deep (23):

Member dimension parallel to wide faces of laminations (inches)	C_{fu}
10-3/4 or 10-1/2	1.01
8-3/4 or 8-1/2	1.04
6-3/4	1.07
5-1/8 or 5	1.10
3-1/8 or 3	1.16
2-1/2	1.19

Lateral Stability—Bending and compression members may exhibit lateral buckling if they are not properly restrained at intervals along their length. The lateral stability factor, C_L, accounts for the amount of lateral support applied to a glued-laminated timber and is a function of the member's cross-sectional dimensions and its effective length. Members that are fully supported have no adjustment applied to them ($C_L = 1.0$). Lateral stability factors and methods for calculating member effective length for glued-laminated timber are specified in the *NDS* and the *Timber Construction Manual.*

Specifying Glued-Laminated Timber

A specification for glued-laminated timber typically includes wood species; appearance grade; actual dimensions; and finishing and wrapping requirements. For members used in commercial construction, allowable design values are specified, as well as camber, location of connector holes, connection hardware and when appropriate, preservative and fire retardant treatment. Specifying and selecting members for use as beams and headers in house construction is fairly simple. Many retail building materials suppliers carry stock glued-laminated timbers in the sizes (except for length, of course), stiffnesses and strengths needed to carry typical residential loads. Regardless of the application, most manufacturers of glued-laminated timber have engineers in-house who will assist architects, designers and contractors in developing specifications and selecting members for specific applications.

Building With Glued-Laminated Timber

Protection During Transport

To maintain glued-laminated timber at the moisture content of about 12 percent at which it is made, members must be protected from direct wetting from the time they leave the factory until they are under cover in the structure. Types of protection include end sealers, surface sealers, primer coats, and wrappings. The type of protection selected depends on the end use of the member and final finishing requirements. Protection options are detailed in *AITC 111 Recommended Practice for Protection of Structural Glued-Laminated Timber During Transit, Storage, and Erection* (25).

End sealers retard the movement of moisture in and out of members and minimize end checking. If the end-use conditions are such that end checking will be a major consideration, then a sealer should be applied to the fresh-cut ends of members after trimming. In cases where the ends of the members will be exposed in use, a colorless sealer should be used.

Surface sealers on glued-laminated timber increase resistance to soiling, control grain raising, minimize checking, and serve as a moisture retardant. There are two types of surface sealers: translucent penetrating, and primer and nonpenetrating. Translucent penetrating sealers have a low solids content, which results in limited protection. This type of sealer is applied when stains will be used as the final finish. Primer and nonpenetrating sealer coats have higher solids content and provide more protection. Since they obscure the surface of the member, primer and nonpenetrating sealers should not be used when a natural finish or stain is to be applied.

Wrapping glued-laminated timber with a water-resistant covering for shipment provides additional protection from moisture and surface damage. Members can be wrapped individually, wrapped as a solid-piled bundle, or load-wrapped. With the first two techniques, all surfaces of the member or bundle are protected with the wrapping, whereas only the top, sides, and ends of a load-wrapped bundle are covered. Individual wrapping is recommended when appearance is of prime importance and the additional protection is desired throughout all stages of erection. Bundle and load wrapping limits the protection of the members up until the time that they are individually handled.

Unloading and Handling

When unloading and handling glued-laminated timber, care should be taken to prevent damage to surfaces and overstressing of the member. The typically smaller members used in residential construction can often be lifted in place by hand, and the larger members used in commercial projects are hoisted by forklift or crane. To avoid marring surfaces when lifting members by crane, webbed belt slings should be used. Cable slings or chokers should not be used unless blocking is placed between the cable and the sides and corners of the member. To prevent overstressing of members during handling, spreader bars of suitable length should be used when hoisting long members. Whenever possible, members should be lifted on edge.

On-Site Storage

To avoid warpage and prevent overstressing, glued-laminated timber should be stored at the job site on a level area on blocking, spaced to provide uniform and adequate support. If covered storage is not available, the members should be blocked well off the ground at a well-drained location. Stored members should be separated with stickers arranged vertically over the supports so that air circulates around all four sides of each member. If a paved surface is unavailable, the ground under the members should be covered with polyethylene to prevent members from absorbing soil moisture. Lengthy glued-laminated timber should be stored on edge on blocking.

Installation

The typically straight, glued-laminated timber beams and headers used in residential construction rarely require pre-assembly and are simply placed onto their supports one at a time. However, sometimes pre-assembly of complicated glued-laminated timber components is done prior to erection. For examples, trusses are usually shipped partially or completely disassembled; then assembled on the ground at the site and lifted into place. Arches, which are generally shipped in halves, may be assembled on the ground or connected after the two halves have been erected. When components are assembled on the ground, they should be supported on level blocking to permit connections to be fitted properly and tightened securely without damage.

Before erection, the assembly should be checked to ensure that all prescribed dimensions are correct. Erection should be planned and executed in such a way that the close fit and neat appearance of joints and the structure as a whole will not be impaired. Anchor bolts in foundations, floor slabs, and on top of walls should be checked prior to erection to ensure that they are structurally sound, accessible, and free of obstructions. The weight and balance point of members—especially curved members and arches—should be determined before lifting begins.

Because glued-laminated timbers are typically highly stressed and used in nonrepetitive framing applications, field modifications, such as drilling, notching, and tapering, should not be done without first seeking the advice of the fabricator or a professional engineer.

Construction Details
A common problem associated with glued-laminated timber design is incorrectly accounting for the behavior of the members in a changing environment and exposure to exterior conditions. Recommendations on glued-laminated timber construction details, such as the types, tolerances, and installation of connections, are given in *AITC 104 Typical Construction Details* (26). As mentioned previously, glued-laminated timber can be expected to expand or contract approximately 1 percent for every 4 to 5 percentage point change in moisture content. This degree of dimensional change could cause splitting in the member as a result of the high stresses caused at the connections. Drawings of correctly and incorrectly designed connections are provided in *AITC 104*, which addresses member splitting caused by moisture change. To prevent decay in the wood, connection details are also included that avoid direct contact between the wood and the surrounding material, as well as provide proper drainage in case of moisture entrapment. Although these details are almost always worked out during the building design phase, on-site inspections should be made to ensure that they are being followed during construction.

Bracing
Glued-laminated timbers need to be adequately braced both during construction and after installation. Erection bracing is temporary bracing installed during construction to hold members safely and securely in position until permanent bracing is in place. Permanent bracing is designed such that it becomes an integral part of the completed structure. Bracing may include sway bracing, guy ropes, steel tie rods with turnbuckles, struts, shoes, and similar items. As erection progresses, bracing is securely fastened in place to temporarily carry all dead loads, erection stresses, and wind, snow, and other weather-related conditions.

Final Alignment and Seasoning
Although the smaller glued-laminated timbers used in residential construction are often fastened with nails and spikes, the large members found in commercial construction are most usually secured with through-bolts inserted into heavy gauge steel straps, plates, and framing anchors. Bolts are only partially tightened during erection; final tightening is not done until the entire structure has been properly aligned. Temporary erection bracing should be removed only after roof and floor diaphragms and permanent bracing are installed, the structure has been properly aligned, and connections and fastenings have been fully tightened. Heat should not be turned on as soon as the structure is enclosed; otherwise,

excessive checking may occur as a result of a rapid lowering of the relative humidity within the building. A gradual seasoning period at moderate temperatures should be provided.

Maintenance

The glued-laminated timber in properly designed and built structures should require a minimum of maintenance. Problems that develop are usually related to elevated moisture levels in localized areas of untreated members. For buildings, changing use or building modifications, particularly additions, can introduce sources of moisture. It is imperative that the moisture content of all parts of untreated members be kept below 19 percent. This can be easily accomplished by proper design that does not permit exposure of untreated wood on the exterior, proper operation of mechanical systems that limits condensation, and proper maintenance of the building envelope that does not permit entrance of free water through the roof, walls, or floor systems.

References

1. American Society for Testing and Materials. 1992. ASTM D3737 Standard Method for Establishing Stresses for Structural Glued-laminated Timber (Glulam). ASTM. West Conshohocken, Pennsylvania.

2. American Institute of Timber Construction. 1992. ANSI/AITC A190.1 American National Standard for wood products—Structural Glued-laminated Timber. AITC. Englewood, Colorado.

3. American Institute of Timber Construction. 1993a. AITC 117-Design Standard Specification for Structural Glued-laminated Timber of Softwood Species. AITC. Englewood, Colorado.

4. American Institute of Timber Construction. 1993b. AITC 117-Manufacturing Standard Specification for Structural Glued-Laminated Timber of Softwood Species. AITC. Englewood, Colorado.

5. American Institute of Timber Construction. 1995. AITC 119 Standard Specification for Hardwood Glued-Laminated Timber. AITC. Englewood, Colorado.

6. Bowyer, J. 1995. Wood and other raw materials for the 21st century. Forest Products Journal. 45(2): 17-24.

7. Forintek Canada Corporation and W.B. Trusty & Associates. 1991. Building Materials in the Context of Sustainable Developments. Forintek Canada Corporation. Vancouver, British Columbia, Canada.

8. Jahn, E. and S. Preston. 1976. Timber: More Efficient Utilization. Science. 191(4227): 757-761.

9. Koch, P. 1992. Wood versus non-wood materials in U.S. residential construction: some energy-related global implications. Forest Products Journal. 42(5): 31-42.

10. United States Department of Commerce. 1963. U.S. Commercial Standard CS 253-63 Structural Glued-laminated Timber. USDC. Washington, D. C.

11. Southern Pine Inspection Bureau. 1994. Standard Grading Rules for Southern Pine Lumber. SPIB. Pensacola, Florida.

12. Western Wood Products Association. 1991. Western Lumber Grading Rules. WWPA. Portland, Oregon.

13. American Institute of Timber Construction. 1984b. AITC 110 Standard Appearance Grades for Structural Glued-laminated Timber. AITC. Englewood, Colorado.

14. American Institute of Timber Construction. 1990. AITC 109 Standard for Preservative Treatment of Structural Glued-laminated Timber. AITC. Englewood, Colorado.

15. American Wood-Preservers' Association. 1995. P9 Standards for Solvents and Formulations for Organic Preservative Systems. AWPA. Woodstock, Maryland.

16. American Wood-Preservers' Association. 1995. C28 Standard for Preservative Treatment of Structural Glued-laminated Members and Laminations Before Gluing of Southern Pine, Coastal Douglas Fir, Hem Fir and Western Hemlock by Pressure Process. AWPA. Woodstock, Maryland.

17. American Wood-Preservers' Association. 1995. P5 Standards for Waterborne Preservatives. AWPA. Woodstock, Maryland.

18. Ritter, M. 1992. Timber Bridges Design, Construction, Inspection, and Maintenance. EM-7700-8. United States Department of Agriculture. Washington, D. C.

19. American Society for Testing and Material. 1988. ASTM D2555 Standard Test Methods for Establishing Clear Wood Strength Values. ASTM. West Conshohocken, Pennsylvania.

20. Freas, A. and M. Selbo. 1954. Fabrication and Design of Glued-laminated Wood Structural Members. Technical Bulletin No. 1069. U.S. Department of Agriculture.

21. American Institute of Timber Construction. 1994. Timber Construction Manual. AITC. Englewood, Colorado.

22. American Institute of Timber Construction. 1991a. AITC Technical Note No. 21 Use of a Volume Effect Factor in the Design of Glued-laminated Timber Beams. AITC. Englewood, Colorado.

23. American Forest & Paper Association. 1991. National Design Specification for Wood Construction. AF&PA. Washington, D. C.

24. Moody, R., C. Dedolph, Jr. and P. Plantinga. 1988. Analysis of size effect for glued-laminated timber beams. Pages 892-898 *in* Proceedings of the International Conference on Timber Engineering Volume I. Forest Products Research Society. Madison, Wisconsin.

25. American Institute of Timber Construction. 1979. AITC 111 Recommended Practice for Protection of Structural Glued-laminated Timber During Transit, Storage and Erection. AITC. Englewood, Colorado.

26. American Institute of Timber Construction. 1984a. AITC 104 Typical Construction Details. AITC. Englewood, Colorado.

Chapter 2

Plywood

Michael McKay

TECO Corporation
Eugene, Oregon

Thin sheets of wood called veneer, cross-laminated and glued, have been used in decorative objects and furniture since the Pharaohs ruled Egypt 3,500 years ago. But plywood, as we now think of it, did not make its debut until early this century when the Portland Manufacturing Company of St. Johns, Oregon, displayed its panels at the 1905 Lewis and Clark Centennial Exposition in Portland, Oregon.

Almost immediately, the panels found use in doors, furniture, trunks, crates and other applications where their large size and dimensional stability were advantageous. In 1933 the Douglas Fir Plywood Association was formed to promote and expand the uses of plywood. Headquartered in Tacoma, Washington, the organization has since twice changed its name, first to the American Plywood Association in 1964, and more recently, to APA-The Engineered Wood Association. Along with TECO of Madison, Wisconsin, and Pittsburgh Testing Laboratories of Eugene, Oregon, APA-The Engineered Wood Association conducts quality assurance inspections and certifies plywood's conformance with applicable product standards for softwood plywood mills nationwide.

Though plywood is today used extensively for sheathing in residential and commercial construction, some builders were reluctant to use the early panels because the blood and soybean protein-based glues used were not waterproof, and some panels delaminated when they got wet. The advent of waterproof synthetic adhesives in 1934 virtually eliminated the problem and eased builders' concerns. Plywood use grew explosively during World War II, when it was used extensively for boats, aircraft, footlockers, crating and buildings. Demand continued to rise during the housing boom of the 1950s, when it saw widespread use as sheathing, doors and cabinets. Today, structural use plywood panels are used extensively in residential and commercial construction.

Originally centered in the Pacific Northwest where it made use of principally large-diameter, old-growth Douglas-fir, the plywood industry expanded into the southeastern United States in the 1970s once the technological problems of achieving consistently good adhesive bonds with southern pine veneers were overcome. Today, over 20 billion square feet of plywood based on a 3/8 inch panel thickness is produced annually in the United States, with about half of it made from southern pine trees 16 inches or less in diameter. While the majority of softwood plywood is used for roof, wall and floor sheathing in residential and commercial construction, plywood also finds use as siding, paneling, shipping containers, boxcar and truck floors, concrete forms, highway signs, stressed-skin panels, wood I-joist webs, and in numerous other construction and industrial applications.

Plywood Terminology

Plywood terminology is unique and confusing. Because of their specialized meaning, important terms used in describing plywood are defined here for convenience:

A *ply* is a single veneer lamina in a bonded plywood panel.

A *layer* is a single veneer ply or two or more plies laminated together such that the grain direction of each is parallel. The latter is referred to as a parallel-laminated layer.

The *face* of a plywood panel is the side of the panel that is of higher quality veneer on any panel whose outer plies (face and back) are of different grades. Where the grading rules make no distinction between the outer plies, either side is the face.

The *back* of a plywood panel is the side of the panel that is of lower quality veneer on any panel whose outer plies (face and back) are of different grades.

Inner plies are the plies other than the face and back plies in a plywood panel. Centers, cores and crossbands are inner plies.

A *center* is any inner layer whose grain direction runs parallel to that of the outer plies. Some centers consist of parallel-laminated plies.

A *core* or *crossband* is an inner layer whose grain direction runs perpendicular to that of the outer plies. Some cores or crossbands consist of parallel-laminated plies.

Width refers to the distance across the grain of the face and back plies.

Length refers to the distance along the grain of the face and back plies.

Group is a term used to classify the wood species permitted for use in softwood plywood. Each species is assigned to one of five groups, depending on its stiffness and strength.

A *grade name* is a term used to identify plywood panels having special characteristics, requirements or uses, such as Marine, Decorative and Underlayment.

Delamination is a visible separation at the interface between plies that have been spread with adhesive and were in firm contact during pressing. Wood characteristics such as checks, splits and broken grain are not delamination.

Touch-sanded describes a panel that has been lightly sanded to achieve a specific thickness.

As defined in *Voluntary Product Standard PS 1-95 Construction and Industrial Plywood*, "Plywood is a flat panel built up of sheets of veneer called plies, united under pressure by a bonding agent to create a panel with an adhesive bond between plies as strong as or stronger than the wood." (1). Plywood is always constructed with an odd number of layers with the grain direction of adjacent layers perpendicular to one another. Since layers can consist of a single ply or of two or more plies laminated such that their grain is parallel, a panel can contain an odd or even number of plies, but always an odd number of layers (Fig. 1). To distinguish the number of plies (individual sheets of veneer in a panel) from the number of layers (the number of times the grain orientation changes), panels are sometimes described as, for example, 3-ply, 3-layer or 4-ply, 3-layer. The outer layers (face and back) and all odd-numbered layers (centers) generally have their grain direction oriented parallel to the length or long dimension of the panel. The grain of even-numbered layers (cores) is perpendicular to the panel's length. The balanced construction achieved by using an odd number of layers with alternating grain direction minimizes dimensional change and warping, and reduces splitting when fasteners are placed close to a panel's edge.

The Manufacture of Plywood

The manufacture of plywood actually begins in the forest. After trees are felled and bucked to length, the logs are graded and sorted to make the most appropriate and efficient use of the wood fiber they contain. Until 15 or so years ago, logs graded as "peelers" were sent to veneer mills or plywood plants; "sawlogs" were shipped to lumber mills. Because of the dwindling availability of the clear, large-diameter peeler logs on which the plywood industry was founded, this has changed. Today, the higher grades of peeler logs are sent to sawmills and, with few exceptions, plywood is made from No. 3 peeler logs or low-grade sawlogs. This came about because of the increasing demand for clearer sawn lumber, and has been made possible by innovations in veneer and plywood manufacturing and testing practices that ensure that the panels are suitable for their intended use.

Logs delivered to a veneer mill are sorted by grade and species, then debarked and crosscut into peeler blocks. Blocks usually are either 4 or 8 feet long, although 6-, 9- and 10-foot lengths are also cut to produce veneer for specialty panels and for panels destined for export. Cores—veneers whose grain is perpendicular to the panel's length—are peeled from the 4-foot-long blocks, while the other lengths may be used for the face, back or center veneers whose grain is parallel to the panel's length.

Peeler blocks are sometimes heated or conditioned by steaming them or immersing them in hot water prior to peeling. This makes the blocks easier to peel, reduces veneer breakage, and results in smoother, higher quality veneer. The heated blocks are then conveyed to the veneer lathe. To maximize veneer yield, each block is gripped on its ends at its geometric center. While rotating at high speed, the block is fed against a stationary knife parallel to its length. Veneer is peeled from the block in a continuous, uniformly thin sheet, much like unwinding a roll of paper towels, but at speeds of up to 800 lineal feet per minute.

Depending on its intended use, the veneer may range in thickness from 1/16 to 3/16 inches. After being peeled down to a diameter anywhere from 5 to 2 1/2 inches, the peeler core is ejected from the lathe. Peeler cores may be sawn into 2x4s, used for fence posts and landscape timbers, or chipped for use as pulp chips or fuel.

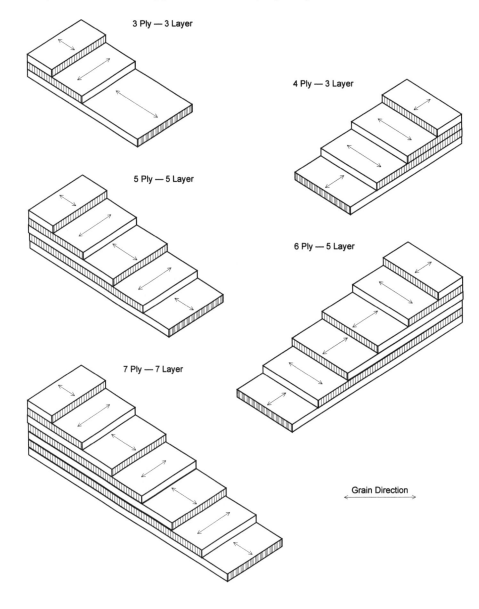

Figure 1. Typical plywood construction.

The continuous sheet of veneer is then transported by conveyor to a clipping station where it is clipped into usable widths and defects are cut out. The veneer, which is still wet or green, is then sorted by width and grade. Green veneer is usually rough-graded as either A-B or C-D, though other grades such as fishtail—veneer good only on one end—or utility—very low grade veneer—are also sorted out.

The wet veneer is then dried to an average moisture content of about 5 percent. Since it is critical that veneer moisture content be low at the time adhesive is applied, each sheet is metered as it exits the dryer. Pieces overly wet or dry are rerouted to be redried or reconditioned, respectively. Properly dried veneer is then sorted into one of as many as 15 to 20 different grades according to the size and number of knots and other natural and processing defects. Each grade has a specific use, with some requiring special processing before being assembled into plywood. After grading and/or processing, the veneer is taken to the lay-up area.

Adhesive—almost always a waterproof phenol-formaldehyde—is applied to the veneers in the lay-up area by spraying, curtain coating, roller coating, extrusion and more recently, by foaming. With the first method, liquid adhesive is simply sprayed onto the veneer as its passes under one or more spray heads. In the curtain coating technique, the veneer is coated as it travels through a "waterfall" of adhesive. Adhesive is applied to both sides of the veneer in the roller coating method by feeding it between adhesive-coated rollers. As the term suggests, narrow ribbons of adhesive are extruded onto the veneer in extrusion application. With the newest method, adhesive foamed to a shaving cream-like consistency is applied to the veneer in a manner similar to extrusion. With the exception of roller coating, adhesive is applied to one side of the veneer only.

Veneer is laid-up into plywood by hand, machine, or a combination of both. Hand lay-up is the oldest method and in some applications, still the only practical way of making plywood. With this method, face, back and center veneers are hand-placed by workers called sheet turners. After being coated on both sides with adhesive, the alternating core plies are placed by hand or machine. The lay-up process is almost completely automated in newer plywood plants, though the narrow strips used for cores may still be placed manually. Before being laid-up, narrow strips sometimes are joined together into full width sheets with hot melt adhesive-coated fiberglass thread so that they can be handled by machine. Also, veneers may be upgraded by punching out knots and other defects and replacing them with wood plugs or patches.

Once assembled, panels are conveyed from the lay-up area to the pressing area. Panels are first given a cold prepressing to flatten the veneers and transfer the adhesive to uncoated sheets, then hot pressed. The time that elapses between spreading the adhesive on the veneers and applying pressure to them in the hot press is called the assembly time. Maintaining the assembly time within certain limits is critical to ensuring a good bond between veneers. Enough time must be allowed for the adhesive to begin to penetrate into the wood and for some of the moisture in the adhesive to evaporate into the air or disperse into the wood. If too much time passes, however, the adhesive may dry out or pre-harden before hot pressing, resulting in a poor quality bond prone to delamination. Panels are hot pressed under moderate pressures (100 to 200 psi) and high temperatures (about 300 °F) to bring the veneers into intimate contact and cure the adhesive. With today's multiopening presses, between 20 and 50 panels are produced per press load. Pressing time varies according to panel thickness, and ranges anywhere from 3 minutes to about 10 minutes.

After hot pressing, the panels are solid-piled or hot stacked to ensure complete curing of the adhesive, then sawn to size. Panels are then graded with regard to the product standard under which they were manufactured. Knotholes and splits on the faces and backs of some panels may be repaired with wood plugs, or with synthetic patches by filling them with what is essentially liquid plastic that quickly hardens. Those that do not meet the specification are downgraded or rejected. Panels needing further processing are sent to the finishing area where, depending on their intended use, they may be sanded to thickness, profiled with tongue and groove edges, surface textured, scarf- or finger-jointed, oiled and edge-sealed or given other treatments. Panels are then ready for shipping.

Quality Assurance

Model building codes in the United States stipulate that plywood used for structural applications like subflooring and sheathing must meet the requirements of certain Department of Commerce standards. *Voluntary Product Standard PS 1-95 Construction and Industrial Plywood* and *Voluntary Product Standard PS 2-92 Performance Standard For Wood-Based Structural-Use Panels* (2) spell out the ground rules for manufacturing plywood and establishing its properties. These standards have evolved over time from earlier documents, and represent a consensus opinion of the makers, sellers and users of plywood products as well as other concerned parties. In addition, model building codes require that the manufacturers of plywood be inspected by and their products certified for conformation to *PS 1-95* or *PS 2-92* by independent third-party qualified agencies on a periodic unannounced basis.

Under *PS 1-95*, plywood panels intended for structural uses may be certified or rated using either prescriptive- or performance-based criteria. Because *PS 2-92* applies to all structural use wood-based panels including plywood, oriented strand board and waferboard, it is strictly performance-based.

With *PS 1-95*, as long as a plywood panel is manufactured using the veneer grades, adhesive and construction set out in the standard's prescriptive requirements, it is by definition acceptable. In order for so-called formula-made plywood to meet the span rating requirements of *PS 1-95*, it must be assembled so that the proportion of wood with the grain perpendicular to the panel's face grain is not less than 33 percent or more than 70 percent of the panel's thickness. In panels with 4 or more plies, the combined thickness of the inner layers must equal 45 percent or more of the panel's thickness. Generally speaking, for panels of the same thickness and made with the same face and back veneer species, stiffness and strength increase as the thickness of the face and back veneers increase. All other things being equal, the stiffness and strength of plywood also increases as panel thickness increases.

Plywood manufactured for structural uses which is rated by performance-based testing under *PS 1-95* or *PS 2-92* or *TECO PRP 133* (3) for instance, must pass tests that demonstrate that its strength, stiffness and durability meet the stated criteria. Termed Performance Rated Panels or PRP, these panels must be either EXPOSURE 1 or EXTERIOR exposure durability class. Those tested are selected from panels in the lot with near-minimum grade characteristics and near-minimum thickness. The panels are subjected to concentrated static- and impact-bending tests in both the dry and wet condition, and to a uniform load test in which the load is applied by atmospheric pressure as a vacuum is drawn on the panel's underside. In all tests, panel deflection and ultimate load are recorded. At least 90 percent of the panels tested must deflect no more than the specified maximum. All of the panels tested in each lot must support the specified minimum ultimate load.

On the basis of these tests, a manufacturing specification containing information regarding the panel's construction, and bending stiffness and strength is written for the mill and control values are established. The specification serves as the basis for quality assurance testing by both the mill's in-plant technicians and the independent testing and inspection agency. Control values established during the initial evaluation of the panel are used as the basis for quality assessment of all subsequent production of that particular panel. To ensure consistent panel quality, all plywood products qualified by testing undergo quarterly re-examination by the qualified agency who inspects the plywood manufacturer. Plywood certified by a qualified inspection and testing agency will bear the grade mark of the agency.

Plywood Classification and Grades

Plywood is classified by both exposure durability class and by grade. Exposure durability class refers to a panel's ability to resist the damaging effects of exposure to the weather or to moisture. Panel grades are either names that describe the panel's intended use—underlayment or concrete form, for example—or letters that identify the grades of the face and back veneers such as A-B.

Veneer Grades

The veneers from which plywood is made are visually graded according to the size, number and location of natural and processing defects that affect their strength and appearance. Knots, decay, splits, insect holes, surface roughness, number of repairs and other defects are considered. More repairs—familiar as those boat-shaped wood patches, for example—and bigger knots are allowed in the lower veneer grades. Veneers are graded as N, A, B, C,

C-Plugged and D. N-grade or natural finish veneers are virtually blemish-free, and contain only a few minor surface repairs. A and B veneers have solid surfaces with neatly made repairs and small, tight knots. Knotholes up to 1 inch in diameter are allowed in C veneers, while D veneers may have knotholes as large as 2 1/2 inches across. Because their appearance is usually of secondary importance, panels meant for sheathing and other structural uses are made mostly from C and D grade veneers. N, A and B veneers are reserved for panels where appearance is the primary consideration in such uses as exterior trim and soffits, interior paneling, doors and cabinets.

Plywood Exposure Durability Class

Plywood is made in only two exposure durability classes—interior type and exterior type. Interior type panels are bonded either with a water-resistant interior-use adhesive and identified as INTERIOR in the grade stamp, or with a waterproof exterior-use adhesive and designated EXPOSURE 1. All interior type panels may contain D grade veneer. INTERIOR plywood is meant only for dry indoor applications where the panel is permanently protected from moisture. EXPOSURE 1 panels are intended for uses where long delays in construction or exposure to high moisture in service is possible. Though there is also a provision for using an intermediate adhesive to produce EXPOSURE 2 panels, it is seldom done. These panels are intended for protected applications and where only moderate construction delays are foreseen. EXTERIOR grade panels are the only panels appropriate for permanent outdoor exposure. All veneers in EXTERIOR plywood are C grade or better and bonded with a waterproof exterior-use adhesive. The veneers in EXTERIOR panels will remain bonded even under conditions of severe and cyclic wetting.

Plywood Grades

There are many, many plywood grade names (Tables 1 and 2). In addition to the 30 or so generic names listed in *PS 1-95*, each agency that inspects plywood mills and certifies their products has coined its own trademarked grade names. Panels intended for use as single-layer flooring (combined subfloor and underlayment) made by manufacturers certified by TECO, for example, are called Floorspan®, while those made by APA-The Engineered Wood Association-certified mills are named Sturd-I-Floor®. Though the trademarked names may be different, the minimum stiffness and strength properties of the panels are not. With the exception of custom-order panels, plywood is strictly a commodity product; panels of the same grade and thickness conforming to either *PS 1-95* or *PS 2-92* are interchangeable among manufacturers.

Span Rating

The more than 70 species of wood used for making softwood plywood (including some hardwoods) are classified into five groups according to their stiffness and strength (Table 3). The strongest woods, like Douglas-fir and southern pine, are in Group 1; the weakest, in

Table 1. Grade Names for Interior Plywood Grades (1).

PANEL GRADE DESIGNATIONS	MINIMUM	VENEER	QUALITY	SURFACE
	FACE	BACK	INNER PLIES	
N-N	N	N	C	Sanded 2 sides
N-A	N	A	C	Sanded 2 sides
N-B	N	B	C	Sanded 2 sides
N-D	N	D	D	Sanded 2 sides
A-A	A	A	D	Sanded 2 sides
A-B	A	B	D	Sanded 2 sides
A-D	A	D	D	Sanded 2 sides
B-B	B	B	D	Sanded 2 sides
B-D	B	D	D	Sanded 2 sides
Underlayment	C Plugged	D	C & D	Touch-sanded
C-D Plugged	C Plugged	D	D	Touch-sanded
Structural I C-D				Unsanded
Structural I C-D Plugged, Underlayment				Touch-sanded
C-D	C	D	D	Unsanded
C-D with exterior glue	C	D	D	Unsanded

Table 2. Grade Names for Exterior Plywood Grades (1).

PANEL GRADE DESIGNATIONS	MINIMUM FACE	VENEER BACK	QUALITY INNER PLIES	SURFACE
Marine, A-A, A-B, B-B, HDO, MDO				See regular grades
Special Exterior, A-A, A-B, B-B, HDO, MDO				See regular grades
A-A	A	A	C	Sanded 2 sides
A-B	A	B	C	Sanded 2 sides
A-C	A	C	C	Sanded 2 sides
B-B (concrete form)				----
B-B	B	B	C	Sanded 2 sides
B-C	B	C	C	Sanded 2 sides
C-C Plugged	C Plugged	C	C	Touch-sanded
C-C	C	C	C	Unsanded
A-A High Density Overlay	A	A	C Plugged	----
B-B High Density Overlay	B	B	C Plugged	----
B-B High Density Concrete Form Overlay	B	B	C Plugged	----
B-B Medium Density Overlay	B	B	C	----
Special Overlays	C	C	C	----

Group 5. Today, almost all plywood intended for structural uses is not marked with a species group number, but with a two-number span rating like 32/16 instead. As with softwood lumber allowable design values, plywood span ratings were developed by breaking thousands of full-size panels of varying construction and thickness. The number on the left represents the maximum recommended on-center spacing for framing when the panel is used as roof sheathing. The right-hand number is the maximum recommended on-center spacing of framing when the panel is used as subflooring. Panels intended for use as single-layer flooring (combined subfloor and underlayment) have only one span rating number—24 OC, for example. In all cases, the panels are meant to be installed with their length perpendicular to framing and across three or more supports. Again, panels of the same grade and span rating can be substituted for one another regardless of who made or certified them.

Allowable Design Values

Except in special engineering applications like diaphragms and earthquake-resistant shear walls for instance, knowledge of a plywood panel's allowable design values is not necessary. The span ratings alone ensure that the panels will perform well under building code-required roof and floor loadings when properly fastened to framing at the correct spacing. When needed, design values can be found in APA-The Engineered Wood Association's *Plywood Design Specification* (4) or in its *Design Capacities of APA Performance-Rated Structural-Use Panels Technical Note N375* (B) (Table 4). Panels graded STRUCTURAL I are usually the best choice for engineered applications.

Allowable design stresses for plywood are based on a panel being 24 or more inches wide across the direction of the grain of its face. The effect of defects permitted in the specific panel grade on plywood strength must be taken into consideration whenever the application calls for strips narrower than 24 inches. In this case, the allowable stresses must be reduced proportionately from 100 percent at a width of 24 inches to 50 percent at a width of 8 inches in any application where failure could pose a risk to persons or property. Plywood in widths of less than 8 inches has performed well, but always should be chosen to be as free of defects as possible.

Plywood Dimensions

Plywood panels are normally available in widths of 4 feet or 5 feet, and in lengths of 5 feet to 10 feet in one-foot increments. Other sizes can be special ordered. The most common sizes are 4 feet by 8 feet and 4 feet by 10 feet. In response to builders' complaints that when properly spaced, 4x8 panels do not line up with framing after several sheets have been laid end to end, manufacturers now offer sized-for-spacing panels 47 7/8 inches by 95 7/8 inches that do line up with framing. Longer plywood panels, and always those over 12 feet, may be scarf- or finger-jointed.

Plywood is available in almost any thickness from about 3/16 inches to 1 1/2 inches or more. Since surface smoothness and uniformity of thickness from panel to panel are important in some applications—underlayment, for example—panels can be ordered with

Table 3. Wood species permitted for use in softwood plywood are grouped according to their stiffness and strength. The strongest are in Group 1; the weakest, in Group 5 (1).

Group 1	Group 2	Group 3	Group 4	Group 5
Apitong	Cedar, Port Orford	Alder, Red	Aspen	Basswood
Beech, American	Cypress	Birch, Paper	Bigtooth	Poplar, Balsam
Birch	Douglas-fir [2]	Cedar, Alaska	Quaking	
Sweet	Fir	Fir, Subalpine	Cativo	
Yellow	Balsam	Hemlock, Eastern	Cedar	
Douglas-fir 1	California Red	Maple, Bigleaf	Incense	
Kapur	Grand	Pine	Western	
Keruing	Noble	Jack	Red	
Larch, Western	Pacific Silver	Lodgepole	Cottonwood	
Maple, Sugar	White	Ponderosa	Eastern	
Pine	Hemlock, Western	Spruce	Black	
Caribbean	Lauan	Redwood	(Western Poplar)	
Ocote	Almon	Spruce	Pine	
Pine, Southern	Bagtikan	Engelmann	Eastern	
Loblolly	Mayapis	White	White	
Longleaf	Red Lauan		Sugar	
Shortleaf	Tangile			
Slash	White Lauan			
Tanoak	Maple, Black			
	Mengkulang			
	Meranti, Red			
	Mersawa			
	Pine			
	Pond			
	Red			
	Virginia			
	Western White			
	Spruce			
	Black			
	Red			
	Sitka			
	Sweetgum			
	Tamarack			
	Yellow Poplar			

1. *Douglas-fir trees grown in the states of Washington, Oregon, California, Idaho, Montana, Wyoming and the Canadian Provinces of Alberta and British Columbia.*

2. *Douglas-fir trees grown in the states of Nevada, Utah, Colorado, Arizona and New Mexico.*

Table 4. Allowable stresses for plywood (psi) are based on normal duration of load, and on common structural applications where panels are 24 inches or greater in width (4).

Type of Stress		Species Group of Face Ply	Grade Stress Level				
			S-1		S-2		S-3
			Wet	Dry	Wet	Dry	Dry Only
EXTREME FIBER STRESS IN BENDING (F_b)	F_b	1	1430	2000	1190	1650	1650
TENSION IN PLANE OF PLIES (F_t) &		2,3	980	1400	820	1200	1200
Face Grain Parallel or Perpendicular to Span (At 45° to Face Grain Use 1/6 F_t)	F_t	4	940	1330	780	1110	1110
COMPRESSION IN PLANE OF PLIES		1	970	1640	900	1540	1540
Parallel or Perpendicular to Face Grain	F_c	2	730	1200	680	1100	1100
		3	610	1060	580	990	990
(At 45° to Face Grain Use 1/3F_c)		4	610	1000	580	950	950
SHEAR THROUGH THE THICKNESS		1	155	190	155	190	160
Parallel or Perpendicular to Face Grain	F_v	2,3	120	140	120	140	120
(at 45° to Face Grain Use 2 F_v)		4	110	130	110	130	115
ROLLING SHEAR (IN THE PLANE OF PLIES)		Marine & Structural I	63	75	63	75	----
Parallel or Perpendicular to Face Grain (At 45° to Face Grain Use 1-1/3 F_s)	F_s	All Other	44	53	44	53	48
MODULUS OF RIGIDITY (OR SHEAR MODULUS)		1	70,000	90,000	70,000	90,000	82,000
Shear in Plane Perpendicular to Plies (Through the Thickness)	G	2	60,000	75,000	60,000	75,000	68,000
(At 45° to Face Grain Use 4G)		3	50,000	60,000	50,000	60,000	55,000
		4	45,000	50,000	45,000	50,000	45,000
BEARING (ON FACE)		1	210	340	210	340	340
Perpendicular to Plane of Plies F_c ⊥		2, 3	135	210	135	210	210
		4	105	160	105	160	160
MODULUS OF ELASTICITY IN BENDING IN PLANE OF PLIES		1	1,500,000	1,800,000	1,500,000	1,800,000	1,800,000
	E	2	1,300,000	1,500,000	1,300,000	1,500,000	1,500,000
Face Grain Parallel or Perpendicular to Span		3	1,100,000	1,200,000	1,100,000	1,200,000	1,200,000
		4	900,000	1,000,000	900,000	1,000,000	1,000,000

unsanded, touch-sanded or sanded faces. The standard nominal thickness of unsanded panels ranges from 5/16 inches to 1 1/4 inches in increments of 1/8 inch for panels more than 3/8 inches thick. Sanded panels are manufactured in nominal thicknesses of 1/4 inches through 1 1/4 inches or more in 1/8-inch increments. Custom-ordered plywood can be made in virtually any thickness. Actual thickness can vary from nominal thickness by +/-1/32 inches for unsanded plywood no more than 13/16 inches thick, or by 5 percent of the nominal thickness for panels over 13/16 inches. The tolerance for sanded plywood is +/-1/64 inches for panels up to 3/4 inches thick, and +/-3 percent of the nominal thickness for panels over 3/4 inches.

Characteristics

Although plywood is an engineered wood product itself, it is also used as a component in other engineered wood products and systems in applications such as wood I-joist webs, box beams, stressed-skin panels and panelized roofs. Plywood has high strength-to-weight and strength-to-thickness ratios, and more equal stiffness and strength in width and length than solid wood. Plywood has excellent dimensional stability along its length and across its width (6). Its minimal edge swelling makes it perhaps the best choice for glued tongue and groove joints, even where some wetting is expected. Because the alternating grain direction of its layers significantly reduces splitting, plywood is an excellent choice for uses which call for fasteners to be placed very near a panel's edges. In uses where internal knotholes and voids may pose a problem, such as in small pieces, plywood can be ordered with solid core and center veneers.

Grade Mark

Panel grade marks contain mandatory information about the panel's grade, span rating or species group number, exposure durability class, and thickness, as well as the name or logo of the qualified inspection agency and the product standard to which it conforms (Fig. 2). The name or number of the producing mill and other optional information such as that acknowledging recognition of the product for use in federally-funded construction projects (HUD UM-40C for Housing and Urban Development Use of Material Bulletin 40C) may be included as well.

Specialty Plywood Panels

Some plywood panels are designed for special uses. What follows is a partial listing of some of the specialty plywood panels available, their typical uses and the specific requirements of the panel grades.

Marine

These panels must meet the requirements of EXTERIOR plywood, and as the name implies, often find use in boat building and other severe exposure applications. Only two species of veneer may be used in Marine plywood—Douglas-fir 1 and western larch. Panel grades may be A-A, A-B, B-B, High Density Overlay or Medium Density Overlay. A-grade faces are

May 1996   Volume No. 2, Issue No. 1

How to Read a Plywood Gradestamp

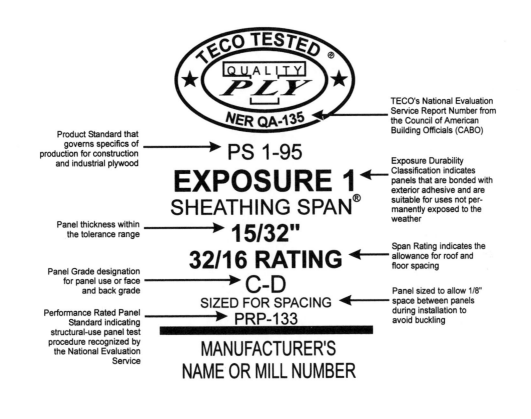

Product Standard that governs specifics of production for construction and industrial plywood → **PS 1-95**

EXPOSURE 1 ← Exposure Durability Classification indicates panels that are bonded with exterior adhesive and are suitable for uses not permanently exposed to the weather

SHEATHING SPAN®

Panel thickness within the tolerance range → **15/32"**

32/16 RATING ← Span Rating indicates the allowance for roof and floor spacing

Panel Grade designation for panel use or face and back grade → **C-D**

SIZED FOR SPACING ← Panel sized to allow 1/8" space between panels during installation to avoid buckling

Performance Rated Panel Standard indicating structural-use panel test procedure recognized by the National Evaluation Service → **PRP-133**

TECO's National Evaluation Service Report Number from the Council of American Building Officials (CABO)

NER QA-135

MANUFACTURER'S NAME OR MILL NUMBER

For Additional Information About Panel Products, Contact TECO Toll Free at 1-800-628-1763

Figure 2. A typical plywood grade mark.

limited to a total of 9 single repairs in a 4x8 sheet. All wood repairs are bonded with exterior-use adhesive and are set with a method using both heat and pressure. All inner plies are B grade or better and are full length and width. Edge or end splits and core or center gaps cannot exceed 1/8 inch in width.

Decorative

Decorative panels have special face treatments—rough sawn, brushed or grooved, for example—and find use as paneling, store fixtures and exterior trim and siding. Except for the treatment of the faces these panels meet all of the requirements of *PS 1-95*. These special faces may include butt jointed veneers.

Underlayment

These panels have touch-sanded surfaces and are designed to go directly under finish floor coverings. The face veneers are at least 1/10 inch thick. The veneer under the face ply is C grade or better with no knotholes over 1 inch across the grain, unless the face veneer is at least 1/6 inch thick. When the face veneer is 1/6 inch or thicker, the veneer adjacent to it may be D grade with open defects limited to 2-1/2 inches across the grain. In C-C Plugged grade, open defects in the veneer adjacent to the face may be up to 1-1/2 inches across the grain when the face veneer is 1/6 inch or thicker.

Concrete Form

Both faces of concrete form panels are always from the same species group and are B grade or better. Produced in Class I or Class II, concrete form is sanded on both sides and oiled and edge-sealed unless otherwise agreed upon by the buyer and seller. In Class I panels faces may be of any Group 1 species, the cores may be of any Group 1 or 2 species, and centers may be of any Group 1, 2, 3, or 4 species. For Class II, faces may be of any Group 1 or 2 species, and the cores and centers of any Group 1, 2, 3, or 4 species. Group 3 faces are permitted if the face veneer is at least 1/8 inch thick and the core is limited to Group 1, 2, or 3 species.

Structural I

Structural I panels are designed for engineered applications such as roof, floor and shear wall diaphragms and other structural components where design properties including compression, tension, shear and cross-panel flexural properties, or nail bearing are important. Panels are bonded with exterior-use adhesive, and special limitations are placed on defect size and type, size of repairs and panel construction.

Special Exterior

Except for species, these panels meet all of the requirements for Marine plywood, and can be produced in A-A, A-B, B-B, High Density Overlay and Medium Density Overlay grades. They find use as signs, and as exterior siding and trim.

Overlaid Panels

Plywood is sometimes overlaid with other non-veneer materials to impart certain surface characteristics. Unless agreed upon by the buyer and seller, all overlaid plywood is overlaid on both sides. If only one side is overlaid, the exposed back is C grade or better. Grade designations such as A-A HDO (High density overlay) refer to the veneer directly beneath the overlay.

High Density Overlay—High density overlay or HDO panels are usually covered with one or more phenolic-impregnated cellulose-fiber sheets that contain at least 45 percent resin solids. Other resins may be used. The overlay on each face is not less than 0.012 inches thick and does not weigh less than 60 pounds per 1000 ft.^{2} The overlay's surface is such that further finishing by paint or protective coating is unnecessary. These panels are used in applications such as industrial work surfaces, concrete forms, signs, and industrial and agricultural bins.

Medium Density Overlay—With medium density overlays (MDO) the resin-treated faces are uniformly smooth, and are intended as a base for decorative and protective finishes in signs, store fixtures, paneling and shelving. Medium density overlays consist of one or more resin-treated sheets of cellulose-fiber containing not less than 17 percent resin solids for beater loaded sheets, or 22 percent solids for impregnated sheets. The overlay weighs at least 58 pounds per 1000 ft.^{2} and is at least 0.012 inches thick.

Special Overlays—Other overlays are also available. Fiberglass-reinforced plastic overlays, for example, are applied to panels for use in truck bodies, shipping containers, walk-in coolers and other applications where tough, abrasion-resistant surfaces are needed. Panels are EXTERIOR grade. Panels with other types of special overlays or finishes may be custom ordered.

Treated Plywood
As all treating of plywood with preservatives and fire retardants is done by others outside of the plywood industry, there are no formal grades of treated plywood. Plywood is easily pressure-treated with waterborne preservatives and fire retardants, and is readily available for use where such protection is needed. Plywood for foundations, for example, is typically treated to a retention of 0.60 pounds of preservative per cubic foot of wood. Standards regulating the treatment of plywood with preservatives and fire retardants are maintained by the American Wood-Preservers' Association (7). Since treatment of plywood with some fire retardant formulations reduces its stiffness and strength, the manufacturer of the fire retardant should be contacted to obtain the appropriate adjustment factors.

Storing, Handling and Installing Plywood

Storage
At the job site, plywood should be stored flat and kept dry until it is put in use. Bundled plywood should be elevated off of the ground on stringers, with one placed under the middle of the bundle and another about one foot in from each end. The bundle must be

protected from direct wetting with a "breathable" tarp loosely draped to provide ample air circulation around its bottom and sides. Although some panels may check, warp or suffer other minor damage from extended exposure to the elements, waterproof exterior-use adhesives are not affected by moisture.

Handling

Reasonable care should be taken in handling plywood. Although it is very strong, plywood can be damaged when handled roughly. Corners or edges may be crushed or broken, making the panels more difficult to handle, resulting in unnecessary repair work.

Installation

Though substantially more dimensionally stable than sawn lumber, plywood panels are typically much drier (6 to 10 percent moisture content) when sold, and should be expected to expand in length and width when exposed to high relative humidity, dew, rain or snow during construction. An expansion gap of at least 1/8 inch should be left between the ends and edges of all panels during installation (Fig. 3). Otherwise, the edges of tightly-butted (and thus improperly installed) panels will be restrained from swelling laterally. To accommodate the expansion, the panel will buckle outward from the framing, resulting in a wavy and uneven surface that is unsightly in a roof and sure to squeak when walked on in a floor. The H-clips placed between the edges of plywood panels on roofs space panels just about right.

Whenever possible, subflooring and single-layer flooring panels should be both nailed and glued. This creates a partial composite T-beam action between the plywood and the framing that stiffens the floor and virtually eliminates nail pops and squeaks as well.

The fastener-holding power of plywood is excellent when nails, staples or screws are inserted through its face. Though fastener type, size and spacing differ with the application and the thickness of the panel, in most situations roof, floor and wall sheathing is attached with 6d nails spaced 6 inches on-center at the panels' edges and 12 inches apart in the field (Fig. 4). Longer fasteners and closer spacing may be needed for special engineered applications, or where plywood is used on buildings located in high wind or seismic zones.

Specifying Plywood

Plywood can be purchased by the sheet or the boxcar load. Before ordering plywood, it is necessary to be sure of the specific requirements of the intended application, especially with regard to appearance, stiffness and strength, and exposure to the elements. When ordering plywood, use of a formal, written specification is the best way to avoid misunderstanding between the buyer and seller.

May 1995   Volume No. 1, Issue No. 2

Spacing, Storage and Handling of Panels

Spacing of Panels

Panels bonded with exterior adhesive generally are shipped from the plant at 2 to 6 percent moisture content. In-use conditions may raise the moisture content to 12 to 15 percent higher. Panels expand as wood normally does when moisture content increases. That is why it is necessary to allow spacing between nailed panels. If panel edge clips are required for certain roof sheathing installations, they may also serve to maintain the recommended spacing.

Recommended Panel Spacing as Shown Below:

Allow 1/8" spacing between EDGE joints.

Allow 1/8" spacing between END joints.

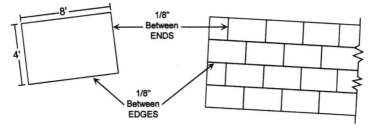

Storage

Warehouse storage is the best way to give carpenters clean, easy-to-handle panels. If the panels must be stored outdoors, protect the panels by covering them with tarps or plastic. The panels should be placed on stickers or stringers to keep them from direct contact with the ground. A minimum of 4 inches is recommended.

We recommend that you use three supports to accomplish the 4 inch, aboveground spacing. One support should be placed in the middle of the load and one about 12 inches from each end. To help prevent panel distortion, keep loads level. Provide for ample air circulation around sides and bottom of the panels.

Warping, checking or other minor damage may result from extended exposure to the elements. Exterior glue will not be affected by dampness.

Handling

Handle panels with reasonable care. Battered corners and edges cause unnecessary extra nailing and repair work.

For Additional Information About Panel Products, Contact TECO Toll Free at 1-800-628-1763

Figure 3.   To prevent buckling, the ends and edges of plywood panels should always be spaced by 1/8 inch.

Plywood

Recommended Minimum Fastening Schedules

Roof, Wall and Subfloor Sheathing (Sheathing Span®)

Panel Thickness (in.)	Nailing*		
	Size	Panel Edges	Intermediate
5/16	6d	6 o.c.	12 o.c.
3/8	6d	6 o.c.	12 o.c.
7/16, 15/32, 1/2	6d	6 o.c.	12 o.c.
19/32, 5/8, 23/32, 3/4, 7/8, 1	8d	6 o.c.	12 o.c.**
1-1/8	8d or 10d	6 o.c.	12 o.c.**

* Other code approved fasteners may be used.
** For spans 48 inches or greater, nail 6 inches o.c. at all supports.

Combination Subfloor-Underlayment (Floorspan®)*

Span Rating (Maximum Joist Spacing) (in.)	Panel Thickness (in.)	Nail Size and Type	Spacing (in.)		
			Supported Panel Edges Glue-Nailed	Supported Panel Edges Nailed Only	Intermediate Supports
16	19/32, 5/8, 21/32	6d ring—or screw shank	12 o.c.	6 o.c.	12 o.c.
20	19/32, 5/8, 23/32, 3/4	6d ring—or screw shank	12 o.c.	6 o.c.	12 o.c.
24	11/16, 23/32, 3/4	6d ring—or screw shank	12 o.c.	6 o.c.	12 o.c.
	7/8, 1	8d ring—or screw shank	6 o.c.	6 o.c.	12 o.c.
48	1-1/8	8d ring—or screw shank	6 o.c.	6 o.c.	6 o.c.

* Applicable building codes may vary from the above recommendations.

For Additional Information About Panel Products, Contact TECO Toll Free at 1-800-628-1763

Figure 4. To take full advantage of the racking resistance and diaphragm action afforded by plywood sheathing, panels must be secured to framing with the proper size fasteners at the correct spacing.

When specifying a sanded grade of plywood like A-C, designate the number of sheets; the grade; the exposure durability class; the species by either group number or name; the number of plies; the thickness after sanding; panel width and length; the applicable product standard; and any special requirements. For example, 100 sheets; A-C; Exterior; Group 1; 5-ply; sanded to 1/2 inch; 48 inches by 96 inches; agency-certified to *PS 1-95*; solid cores and center.

A specification for unsanded grades such as C-D sheathing should include the number of sheets; the grade; the exposure durability class; the number of plies; the span rating; the nominal thickness; panel width and length; and any special requirements. For instance, 100 sheets; C-D; Exposure 1; 5-ply; 32/16 span rating; 15/32 inch; 47 7/8 inches by 95 7/8 inches; agency-certified to *PS 1-95*; Structural I. Any other special requirements, such a specific number of layers, for example, should be noted.

It is important to remember that a span rating does not refer to a panel of a specific thickness, but only to the allowable span. If plywood of a certain thickness is needed, perhaps to match panels already in place, then the thickness and the span rating must be specified. If not, the panel delivered may thinner or thicker than what is wanted. This is because span ratings account for both the species group and panel thickness. Both a 3/8-inch-thick Group 1 panel and a Group 2 or 3 panel 1/2 inches thick, for instance, are span-rated for framing 24 inches on-center.

As a rule, plywood mills are willing to make panels meeting virtually any special requirements of the buyer. In some cases this may add to their cost, especially if only a small quantity is wanted, it takes extra time to manufacture them, or there is no market for the overrun. Certain mills are both more amenable and more adaptable to manufacturing custom panels than others. These mills can be found by contacting one of the plywood inspection and testing agencies.

References

1. National Institute of Standards and Technology. 1995. Voluntary Product Standard PS 1-95 Construction and Industrial Plywood. United States Department of Commerce. Gaithersburg, Maryland.

2. National Institute of Standards and Technology. 1992. Voluntary Product Standard PS 2-92 Performance Standard for Wood-Base Structural-Use Panels. United States Department of Commerce. Gaithersburg, Maryland.

3. TECO. 1991. TECO PRP-133 Performance Standards and Policies For Structural-Use Panels. TECO. Madison, Wisconsin.

4. APA, The Engineered Wood Association. 1995. Plywood Design Specification. APA. Tacoma, Washington.

5. APA, The Engineered Wood Association. Design Capacities of APA Performance-Rated Structural-Use Panels Technical Note N375 B, June 1995. APA. Tacoma, Washington.

6. Forest Products Laboratory. 1987. Wood Handbook: Wood as an Engineering Material. Agriculture Handbook No. 72. USDA Forest Service Forest Products Laboratory. Madison, Wisconsin.

7. American Wood-Preservers' Association. 1995. Book of Standards. AWPA. Woodstock, Maryland.

Chapter 3

Metal Plate Connected Wood Trusses

Steven M. Cramer, Ph. D.
Department of Civil and Environmental Engineering
University of Wisconsin
Madison, Wisconsin

and

Ronald W. Wolfe
USDA Forest Service, Forest Products Laboratory
Madison, Wisconsin

Ideally, a truss is an assembly of structural members connected by pins that form a rigid framework comprising a network of triangles. When loads are applied, a truss responds with axial resisting forces within its members—an extremely efficient way to resist loads. From a technical viewpoint, a truss is truly an engineering marvel that provides a means of spanning an opening much wider than the length of the truss's longest member without incurring large bending stresses.

Metal plate connected (MPC) wood trusses approach the ideal truss configuration in their general behavioral characteristics. The major differences are that some members extend continuously through joints, and the connections are made with metal plates whose teeth are embedded in the intersecting wood members. The connection details in a MPC wood truss do not closely resemble the frictionless pinned connections of the ideal truss. As a result, the rotational restraint arising from member continuity and the metal plate connections induces bending forces in MPC wood truss members that do not occur in the ideal truss. Despite these differences, the similarities dominate. MPC wood trusses have a very high strength-to-weight ratio and are extremely efficient in sustaining loads in the plane of the truss. Lumber—usually 2x4s or 2x6s—is used efficiently in a MPC truss, and can result in significant savings of wood—25 percent or more—over conventional 2x8 or 2x10 rafter construction. All factors considered, the MPC wood truss is one of the most efficient structural engineered wood products used today.

Truss terminology is unique (Fig. 1). The members that form the outline of a truss are called chords. Members spanning between the top and bottom chords are webs. A joint or panel point in a MPC wood truss normally comprises two or more members held together in the same plane by metal plate connectors, with one plate on each side of the joint. Plates are usually located symmetrically with respect to the joint's center.

Heavy timber trusses were used in the United States for over 200 years prior to the development of the metal plate connector in the 1950s that spurred the widespread use of dimension lumber. Truss applications in the 18th and 19th centuries were limited primarily to larger public buildings, churches, mills and bridges. Railroad engineers are often credited with advancing the design process for wood trusses from an intuitive art to an engineering-based science with the advent of the trussed timber bridges necessary to maintain the gentle grades on the "steel highway" that stretched across the continent in the 1800s. In the late 19th and early 20th centuries, heavy timber trusses were replaced by steel trusses. During World War II, thousands of roofs were built with light frame trusses connected with bolts, or nailed metal or plywood gusset plates. It was not until the early 1950s though, when Ohio-born architect A. Carroll Sanford developed the first punched metal plate connected wood truss, that wood trusses became popular as an engineered building component in light-frame construction.

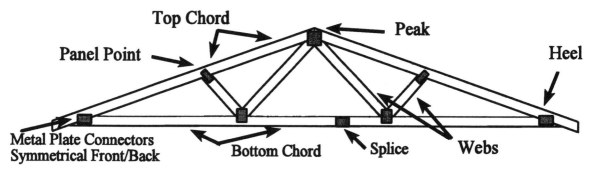

Figure 1. Truss terminology.

By 1960, several companies were providing connector plates, pressing equipment and engineering services to the fabricators of light-frame wood trusses. The industry was growing, and these companies realized the need for industry-wide standards to guide the design, fabrication and testing of wood trusses. That same year the Truss Plate Institute (TPI) was formed to develop and maintain these standards. Today, the governing standard for MPC wood truss design is *ANSI/TPI 1-1995 National Design Standard for Metal Plate Connected Wood Truss Construction* (1). TPI initially served the interests of both the metal plate connector manufacturers and the truss fabricators. In 1983, truss fabricators formed a second association—the Wood Truss Council of America (WTCA)—to focus on quality control, marketing and training for truss fabricators. Today, these independent organizations work closely together to maintain a strong, stable MPC wood truss industry. Both have offices in Madison, Wisconsin.

MPC wood trusses have grown rapidly in popularity, as they have reduced the cost of buildings with long, clear spans and complex roof designs. Initially, the market for trusses was residential pitched roofs, but in the last 20 years they have been used increasingly in parallel chord configurations for floors and flat roofs in commercial as well as residential structures. Clear spans of 30 feet and more are easily achieved in residential structures. In light commercial and agricultural applications, spans of 60 feet and more are not uncommon. The Wood Truss Council of America estimates that MPC wood trusses are used in over 75 percent of all new residential roofs constructed in the United States.

A new application for parallel chord wood trusses currently being studied is their use in bridges on secondary and rural roads (2, 3). Designs under consideration include stress-laminated truss bridge decks and laminated truss girders which support a transverse wood bridge deck. The stress-laminated decks consist of numerous trusses separated with lumber spacers that are compressed together with post-tensioned steel rods inserted through the trusses and spacers that react against steel plates along the deck's edges. A number of these bridges have been built recently, and are currently being monitored to establish their long term performance.

Materials Used in MPC Wood Trusses

Wood

To keep costs down and quality consistent, MPC wood truss manufacturers most commonly use softwood species groups including southern pine, SPF (spruce-pine-fir), hem-fir (western hemlock and western fir) and Douglas fir. Species preferences are often regional. While the majority are made with chords and webs of 2x4 dimension lumber, trusses are fabricated with lumber as large as 2x12 and timbers as large as 4x10 when the application requires it. Glued-laminated timber, laminated veneer lumber (LVL) and parallel strand lumber (PSL) are gaining acceptance for use in special trusses.

All lumber used in MPC wood trusses has been graded or stress-rated either visually or by machine to establish its allowable stresses for structural design. As the term implies, visual grading involves a trained lumber grader making a rapid visual assessment of a board's suitability for structural use on the basis its growth characteristics—growth rings per inch, percent summerwood, slope of grain, size and location of knots and shake—as well as its manufacturing characteristics such as planer skips, wane and warp. Grades for dimension lumber are uniformly applied in all regions of the United States for commercial softwood species under the direction of the American Lumber Standard Committee and the National Grading Rule Committee (4).

Machine stress rated (MSR) lumber is also visually graded to limit growth and manufacturing characteristics, but is distinguished from visually stress-rated lumber by the addition of a nondestructive test in which its modulus of elasticity (MOE) is measured directly. Known correlations between a species' MOE and strength permit a more accurate assessment of the stiffness and strength properties of each board. New machine-based techniques for grading lumber are continuing to be developed. Machine evaluated lumber (MEL) is an increasingly popular alternative to visual or MSR grading methods, and offers the opportunity for using a variety of machine-based techniques to assess lumber quality.

While all engineered applications of lumber require stress-rated material—visual, MSR or MEL—the light-frame wood truss industry is the biggest user of MSR lumber. The higher allowable stresses, combined with a lower percentage of unsuitable pieces, make MEL or MSR lumber the best choice for many truss fabricators.

Truss fabricators rarely find it economical to inventory more than three or four different grades of lumber. Culls—downgraded lumber originally purchased for chords—are often crosscut to shorter lengths and used for webs. In many cases, this means that lumber visually graded as No. 1 or No. 2 is used for webs. In the process, defects like knots and wane—bark or wood missing from the corners, edges or faces of a board sawn to include portions of the surface of the log—that limit the effective connector plate/clear wood area at the joint and the load that can be transferred into the webs are removed. As a result, webs are often of a higher quality than is needed for the forces to be carried.

Dimensional instability and susceptibility to decay, insects and fire are often cited as the primary disadvantages of using wood in structural applications. But for each of these potential problems, well-known and effective control strategies exist. Decay, insects and substantial dimensional change normally can be avoided by keeping wood moisture content below 19 percent, and by preventing wide fluctuations in ambient relative humidity. Chemical treatments can be used to improve wood's resistance to decay and fire, but it is still important to keep moisture content low. Proper construction detailing offers the best protection against fire. Fire-resistant truss assemblies make use of gypsum board sheathing as a fire barrier, and can provide 1- and 2-hour fire resistance ratings.

Over the past 20 years, attention has been drawn to dimensional instability problems in truss lumber containing juvenile wood and compression wood. Juvenile wood is formed for the first 5 to 20 years of a tree's growth. It is distinguished from mature wood, which is formed in the later years of a tree's growth, by its lower specific gravity, lower tensile strength and greater dimensional change with changing moisture content. Compression wood is abnormal wood formed on the underside of leaning or crooked trees. Like juvenile wood, it shrinks 5 to 10 times as much along the grain as mature wood does.

Dimensional instability associated with some lumber used in trusses occasionally creates a problem for truss manufacturers, contractors and homeowners alike—the formation of cracks in the corner joints of drywall at ceiling-interior partition junctions. Though "truss uplift" or "truss rising," as it is called, is routinely blamed, it is only one of the many possible causes of a problem that occurs in both truss-framed and stick-built roofs known generically as ceiling-floor partition separation (CFPS) (20). CFPS is most often caused by excessive shrinkage of framing lumber, foundation settlement or heaving, and poor construction technique. In those cases where "truss rising" is responsible, the problem occurs during the heating season when the wood in the bottom chord of a roof truss dries out as a result of being against a warm ceiling and covered by insulation. The truss's top chord may actually pick up moisture as warm, moist air from the living space rises into the attic and condenses on the cold framing and sheathing. Expansion of the top chord and shrinkage of the bottom chord causes a truss to arch upward and lift the ceiling away from non-loading-bearing interior partitions. The longitudinal shrinkage of lumber containing juvenile wood and/or compression wood is much greater than that for mature wood and thus exacerbates the problem. Truss uplift is a cosmetic problem, not a structural one, and can be avoided by creating a floating connection between the truss's bottom chord and the top of interior partitions. Where rigid connections between trusses and partitions already exist, the best fix is to simply conceal the movement with a cornice molding attached only to the ceiling.

Metal Connector Plates

Metal plates with punched teeth are used to hold the chord and web members together in a wood truss. A metal connector plate is placed on the front and back of the lumber in each connection to ensure a balanced structural response.

Connector plates are made from galvanized sheet steel or, in special applications, from stainless steel, and must meet the requirements found in *ANSI/TPI 1-1995* (1). The majority of plates are made using hot-dipped galvanized steel. Electrolytic zinc coatings, while used on some heavier gauge plates, are not as resistant to rust and corrosion as hot-dipped coatings. When trusses with galvanized plates are to be used in a corrosive environment, the plates must be painted with special coatings. There have been some attempts to use aluminum/zinc paints to provide added resistance in marine environments, but these are rarely used. Stainless steel plates are available for especially corrosive environments, but are prohibitively expensive for common applications. Trusses used in certain special facilities such as hospitals, must have stainless steel plates.

The steel may range in thickness from 20 gauge to 14 gauge (0.036 inches to 0.071 inches), and must have a minimum yield stress of 33,000 psi. Teeth are punched out of the plate, and remain attached to it at their bases. Teeth are typically 0.375 to 0.5 inches in length, and in some designs, are given a slight twist. The teeth may be aligned or staggered; each pattern has its potential advantages.

A metal connector plate acts as an array of short nails attached to a common head—the plate from which they were punched. Connector plates are designed to transfer forces between truss members in the plane of the plate. Neither the plate nor its teeth are intended to be subjected to withdrawal forces—loads that act perpendicular to the plane of the plate and cause its teeth to pull out of the wood. The short teeth, however, are very effective in resisting lateral forces—like tension and compression—that act in the plane of the plate. The lateral resistance of a connector plate is a function of the characteristics of the plate and its teeth, as well as the specific gravity and other properties of the wood in which it is embedded.

Standards for evaluating truss plate lateral strength were originally developed by TPI (22). Today, TPI continues to develop standards regarding the testing of metal plate connectors using the consensus procedures of the American National Standards Institute (ANSI) (1). The lateral resistance of metal connector plates embedded in the wide face of lumber members is species-specific, and is measured with four different tension tests in which the load is applied (Fig. 2):

1. p**A**rallel to the length of the plate and p**A**rallel to the wood grain (AA orientation);

2. p**E**rpendicular to the length of the plate and p**A**rallel to the wood grain (EA orientation);

3. p**A**rallel to the length of the plate and p**E**rpendicular to the wood grain (AE orientation); and

4. p**E**rpendicular to the length of the plate and p**E**rpendicular to the wood grain (EE orientation).

Since plates may be rectangular or square, plate length refers to the dimension of the plate that is parallel to the slots created when the teeth are punched during fabrication.

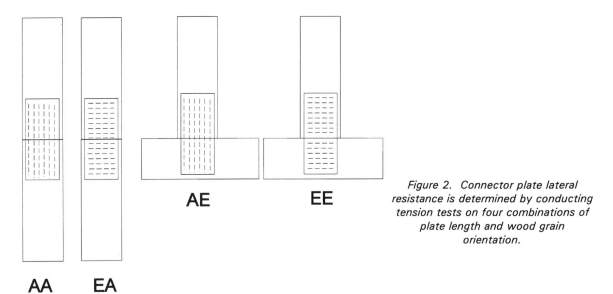

AE   EE

AA   EA

Figure 2. Connector plate lateral resistance is determined by conducting tension tests on four combinations of plate length and wood grain orientation.

A minimum of five test specimens for each condition is required to be tested to establish lateral resistance. Allowable design values are taken as the lesser of either the ultimate load divided by 3.2 or the load at 0.03 inches of joint displacement divided by 1.6 (1). Design values may be based on the plate's gross area, in which case all of the teeth of the wood/metal contact area are included, or on its net area, where teeth within 0.25 inch of the wood member's edge and 0.5 inches of its end are not counted. Plates are also tested for tensile strength along their length and across their width, and for shear strength under six different combinations of plate orientation and applied load.

There are currently fewer than a dozen manufacturers of metal plate connectors in the United States; several of these have international affiliations. Each company has its own patented plate configuration and proprietary design values.

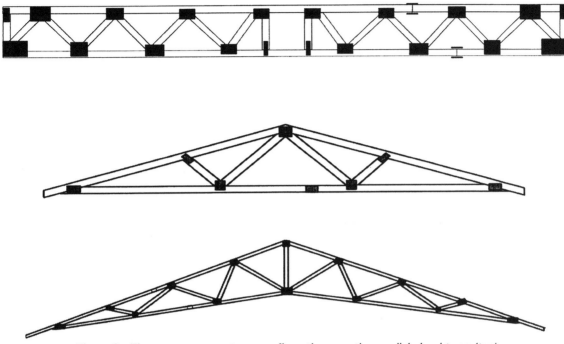

Figure 3. The most common truss configurations are the parallel chord truss (top), the pitched chord truss (center) and the scissors truss (bottom).

Truss Configuration and Load-Resisting Behavior

Truss Configuration
Trusses are sold in a wide variety of sizes and shapes. The design process is robust enough to allow trusses to be sold as both a mass-produced commodity item and as a unique one-of-a-kind design. Three common configurations—the parallel chord truss, the pitched chord truss, and the scissors truss—encompass the majority of designs (Fig. 3). The number of configurations is virtually endless, providing an abundance of architectural possibilities limited only by the designer's imagination (Fig. 4).

How Trusses Resist Load
The load-carrying efficiency of a truss is achieved only when loads are applied parallel to the plane defined by the axes of the chords, that is, when loads are applied in-plane (Fig. 5). The great stiffness and strength of a truss is a result of its vertical depth and the triangulation of its chords and webs. In a simplistic way, a simply-supported truss acts like a deep, narrow beam. When loadings are in-plane, the top chord of a simply-supported

3 - 69

TRUSS TYPES

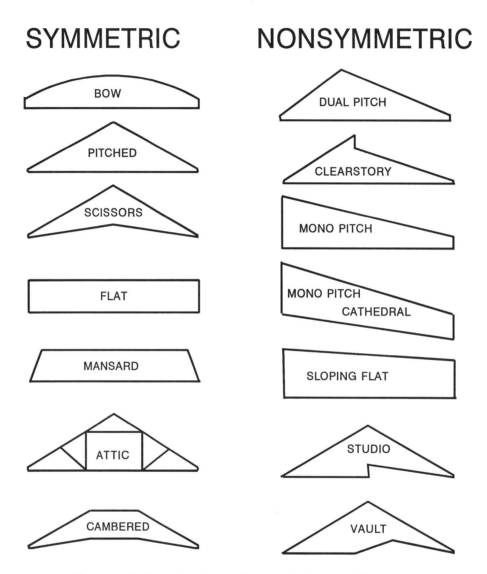

SYMMETRIC

BOW

PITCHED

SCISSORS

FLAT

MANSARD

ATTIC

CAMBERED

NONSYMMETRIC

DUAL PITCH

CLEARSTORY

MONO PITCH

MONO PITCH CATHEDRAL

SLOPING FLAT

STUDIO

VAULT

Figure 4. Roofs of virtually any shape can be framed with trusses.

truss will be in compression and the bottom chord in tension, just like the flanges of a wood or steel I-beam (Fig. 6).The opposing tensile and compressive forces in the top and bottom chords, respectively, and the usually large distance between them, impart bending resistance to the truss. Depending on the truss's configuration, web members may be in either tension or compression under load, and serve to carry the shear force induced in the truss.

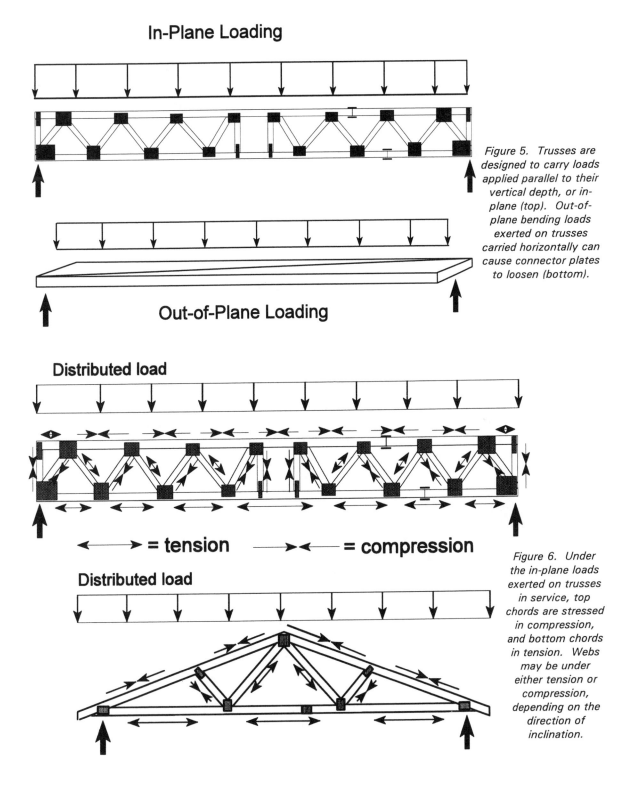

In-Plane Loading

Out-of-Plane Loading

Figure 5. Trusses are designed to carry loads applied parallel to their vertical depth, or in-plane (top). Out-of-plane bending loads exerted on trusses carried horizontally can cause connector plates to loosen (bottom).

Distributed load

←———→ = tension   ———►◄—— = compression

Distributed load

Figure 6. Under the in-plane loads exerted on trusses in service, top chords are stressed in compression, and bottom chords in tension. Webs may be under either tension or compression, depending on the direction of inclination.

Out-of-plane or sideways loadings cause the truss to bend about a lesser depth equal only to the width of its members. The structural advantage of the wide spacing between the top and bottom chords is lost under such circumstances, and the bending resistance of the truss is dramatically reduced. Controlling out-of-plane loading is critical in achieving satisfactory truss performance and avoiding loosened plates and possible catastrophic failure. Out-of-plane loading can occur during transport, handling and erection if trusses are carried horizontally rather than vertically, as is recommended. To understand how in-plane and out-of-plane loadings affect truss performance, take the example of a 17.5-foot-long parallel chord truss 12 inches deep supported at its ends. When oriented vertically, this truss will deflect only about 0.02 inches under its own weight. If the truss is laid flat, however, it will deflect by just over 0.5 inches, or almost 30 times as much. This means that a load applied during handling or erection that generates even 0.25 inches of deflection in-plane could produce as much as 7 inches of deflection when applied out-of-plane, and likely damage the truss. When transporting trusses, it is often impossible to avoid handling them flatwise. To ensure that damage does not occur due to out-of-plane loading while the truss is in the vulnerable flatwise position, trusses are typically bundled tightly together with steel or plastic bands so that they act as a unit of increased depth out-of-plane.

The long, slender chords and webs commonly found in roof trusses are susceptible to buckling failure caused by compressive and/or bending forces. Consideration of this instability is especially important during truss installation. The seemingly low loads applied by workers walking on trusses during installation, as well as the self-weight of the trusses, can be critical if the trusses are not sufficiently braced. The full design capacity of a truss is not achieved until the truss is tied into the rest of the building's structural framework, and sheathing or purlins have been fully connected to its top chords.

Truss Deflection
While wood members and metal connector plates are sized during design to provide an adequate margin of safety to avoid collapse under the anticipated loadings, deflection of the truss must also be limited by design to avoid serviceability problems. Interior doors that do not open, and annoying vibrations in a limber, sagging floor are two serviceability problems that can arise from excessive truss deflection. Truss deflection is a combination of the elongation of the wood members under load, and axial, shear and rotational displacements at the connections between them. It has been shown with finite element analysis that for a 17.5-foot-long parallel chord truss 12 inches deep subject to design loadings, approximately 85 percent of the truss's deflection is due to elongation of the members and 15 percent is associated with deformation of the connections. As the design load increases, the connections account for a greater percentage of the deflection.

Long-term deflection of MPC wood trusses due to creep—time-dependent progressive deflection under sustained constant load—can be two to three times the initial deflection under self-weight. Increases in ambient temperature or wood moisture content, and especially cyclic moisture content changes, can greatly increase creep.

MPC Wood Truss Analysis and Design

Professional Roles in the Design Process

Trusses are specified by architects, engineers and other building designers by providing to truss fabricators basic geometry and use details such as truss type, on-center spacing, span, bearing conditions, overhang dimensions, and special loading or environmental exposures (5). The building designer does not design the truss. This is done by a structural engineer working for either the truss fabricator or the connector plate manufacturer. The truss fabricator chooses a truss design that meets the general architectural requirements proposed by the building designer. A truss placement plan may also be prepared by the truss fabricator for use by the contractor who will install the trusses. The building designer must review the truss design and placement plan to ensure that they meet the needs of the building's design. The building designer specifies the permanent bracing that is needed to tie the trusses to the building's structural framework. Temporary bracing for the trusses and other parts of the building is usually determined and installed by the builder or contractor.

Good communication and a clear understanding of the responsibilities of each party involved in the design and construction process is important for a successful building project. A breakdown of professional responsibilities is provided in WTCA's *WTCA 1-1995 Standard Responsibilities in the Design Process Involving Metal Plate Connected Wood Truss Construction* (6) and in TPI's *Commentary & Appendices to ANSI/TPI 1-1995 National Design Standard for Metal Plate Connected Wood Truss Construction* (7). It is not necessary for the building designer, contractor or owner to know all of the details of the MPC wood truss design process to specify and use trusses in building designs. The general design process and key considerations are none-the-less important, and are explained herein.

Design of MPC Wood Trusses

The procedure for designing MPC wood trusses in the United States is specified in *ANSI/TPI 1-1995 National Design Standard for Metal Plate Connected Wood Truss Construction* (1). The standard was developed by and is maintained by TPI as an American National Standard with the American National Standards Institute. The design process involves determining internal truss member forces through a structural analysis, computing combined stress indices for each member from the forces determined, selecting wood member sizes and grades, and sizing plates for connections. A MPC wood truss is a complex structure. Structural analysis of trusses can become quite complicated as the analysis model selected more closely simulates the real situation.

In general, the first step in performing a structural analysis of a truss involves creating a mathematical model that approximates the conditions of the real structure. Models of varying complexity are employed for analyzing MPC wood trusses, and the level of complexity chosen for one situation may not be appropriate for another. Interestingly, the choice of a particular model may or may not dramatically influence the results of the structural analysis and the resulting truss design. Use of a particular analysis method does not guarantee that an appropriate structural model has been chosen; this aspect of structural engineering is a skill that is achieved only through experience. The suitability of the model chosen should be verified. For example, if a model is used to compute forces for sizing members, then it should be confirmed that it is adequate for the task of predicting forces. Often, truss analysis models are verified by comparing computed deflections with measured deflections made on actual trusses. Many times it is assumed that if a structural analysis model yields the correct deflection, then all other aspects of the results—member forces, for example—must also be correct. Such a practice is not recommended, particularly if the experiments are limited in replications, load cases and support conditions. Structural types should include the entire range of intended uses. The investigation should also include experimental stress analyses that allow for free body checks of forces, moments and shears in the critical members.

ANSI/TPI 1-1995 provides some guidance for choosing a mathematical model for typical design situations. Aspects of MPC wood trusses that warrant consideration in selecting or developing a mathematical model for structural analysis include:

1. the geometry and properties of the wood members

2. the truss's loading and support conditions

3. the size, placement and lateral resistance characteristics of metal plate connectors

4. the alignment of wood members at joints

In designing a truss that will perform satisfactorily, the forces developed in each member by the anticipated loads are first determined in a structural analysis. Each force in each member is then resolved in to a stress—force per unit area or force per connector tooth— and compared with the strength of the grade of wood or the lateral resistance of the metal plate connectors, respectively, to determine the needed grade and size of lumber and connector plate. Since stresses in chords and webs can result from both bending and axial forces, a combined stress index is used to account for both.

Metal plate connectors are sized on the basis of a combination of engineering, fabrication and handling considerations. Connectors are sized not only to ensure that they will safely hold the wood members together under the expected loadings, but also to resist out-of-plane loadings that inevitably occur during assembly, handling and erection. Both the plate contact area—the number of square inches of the lumber covered by the connector—and the number of teeth and their length are important. Contact area calculations may be based on either the plate's gross area, or on its net area, and include adjustments for plate misplacement. Those made with the net area method also assume a limited contribution from teeth located within 0.25 inches of a member's edges and 0.5 inches of its end. Under load, joints in a truss may be subject to tension, compression or shear, or a combination thereof. For joints under compression—the peak of a pitched roof truss, for example—plates are sized to carry half the force; the wood-to-wood bearing area is assumed to carry the rest. Where joints are subject to tension—the splice in the bottom chord of a floor truss, for instance—plates are sized to carry the entire force.

Engineering design considerations assume that tooth forces within the contact area are equal, and that they are the result of only the axial force in the wood member. In reality, tooth forces are not uniform. While this is especially true when bending moments occur, it is also true for larger plates under only axial load. Underlying the presumption of equal tooth forces is the assumption that all deformation in the joint arises from tooth slip. In fact, stretching or strain in the wood beneath the plate and of the plate itself also contributes to joint deformation. Finite element analysis of splice joints in chords suggests that tooth slip makes up the vast majority of joint deformation in connections with small plates, and validates the design assumption. But as the connection becomes larger, steel- and wood-deformation make a larger contribution to joint deformation than does tooth slip (Fig. 7). The different plate misplacement allowances and handling criteria set by different truss fabricators also influence the minimum plate size required for each joint.

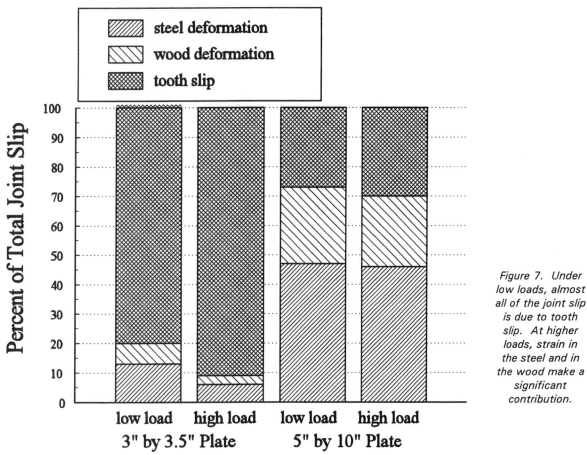

Figure 7. Under low loads, almost all of the joint slip is due to tooth slip. At higher loads, strain in the steel and in the wood make a significant contribution.

TPI Analysis Methods for MPC Wood Truss Design

ANSI/TPI 1-1995 provides two alternatives for mathematical modeling of MPC wood trusses. The first is an empirical analysis and design method provided for use by experienced truss design engineers that can be conducted manually without the aid of a structural analysis computer program. With this method, axial forces in truss members are found based on the assumption that all members are connected by pins. Bending moments are estimated using the simple beam moment formula, with modifiers applied to the length of the beam

$$M = \frac{w\,(QL)^2}{8}$$

where: M = design moment (ft.-lb.)
w = distributed design load per unit length of wood member (lb./ft.)
Q = factor to adjust the length for computing moments
L = nominal panel length of truss chords used to compute bending moment (ft.)

Although the pin-joined truss model is not a realistic analog of any MPC wood truss, in many cases the axial forces determined with it are close to those determined with more sophisticated models. Likewise, design moments determined with the empirical method are approximate, and usually conservative.

In the second truss analysis method specified in *ANSI/TPI 1-1995*, truss chords and webs are modeled as two-dimensional plane frame members (Fig. 8). This method is favored by most truss design engineers. Chords are modeled as continuous members pinned at their ends. At heel joints, chords may be considered as connected by fictitious or virtual members to simulate the rotational rigidity imparted by the plate connectors. Webs are modeled as pinned members that carry only axial force. In the truss analog model, the webs are pinned at the interior joint locations, but the chords are not (Fig. 9). For simplicity, the lateral resistances of the connections in this analog model are designated as being either pinned or fixed; elongation, shear and rotation of the metal plate connectors is ignored.

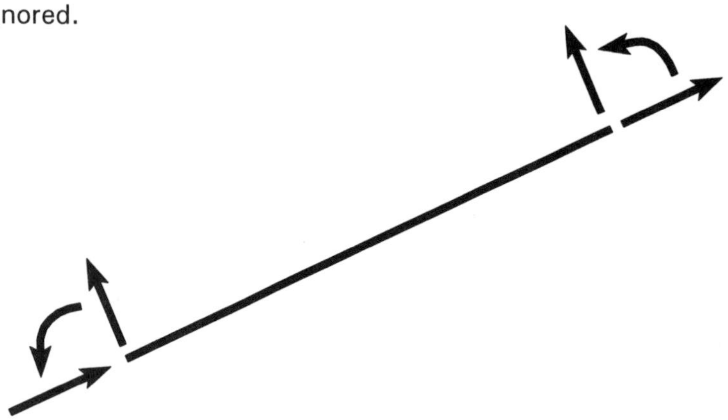

Figure 8. Truss chord modeled as a two-dimensional plane frame member with six degrees of freedom.

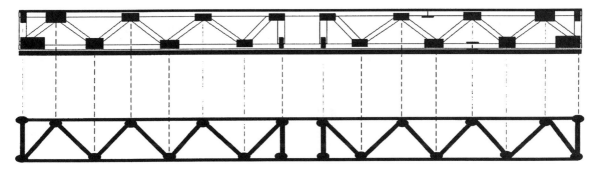

Figure 9. Analog model of a parallel chord floor truss used in structural analysis.

ANSI/TPI 1-1995 describes this second approach as an *exact* model, though no structural model is exact in the literal sense. *Exact* as used here does not guarantee that the forces are identical to those in real trusses; instead, it simply means that the mathematics of the model satisfies the basic rules of structural mechanics. The analysis can be conducted using any one of the many commercially available structural analysis computer programs that possess two-dimensional plane frame elements. The Purdue Plane Structures Analyzer (PPSA), for example, is a well-respected program that has been used widely for designing trusses (8, 9). In addition to having two-dimensional plane frame elements for use in analyzing the truss members, PPSA can also determine the buckling lengths of members and compute the combined stress index for each member to aid in lumber selection. Each truss plate manufacturer has sophisticated truss design programs that are leased to truss designers. With these programs, a designer can analyze and design a truss, and produce a fabrication drawing and a lumber cut list in less than a minute.

Advanced Truss Analysis Models
The TPI truss analysis models have been used for designing millions of trusses that have displayed acceptable performance. Several aspects of the models are not completely realistic and, as with any structural analysis model, refinements can be made to provide more accurate predictions of truss performance. Increased realism may be desirable for research and development or for analysis of unique trusses, even if the extra sophistication is not warranted for everyday truss design. Several computer programs that allow for more sophisticated analysis with advanced mathematical models have been developed and provide additional insight into truss behavior. In many instances use of these models can lead to significantly different results than those yielded by the more simple models. Unlike the TPI approaches, these advanced models account for the eccentricity of web and chord members in a connection and the non-rigid, nonlinear lateral resistance offered by metal plate connectors.

Members of MPC wood trusses often carry large axial loads. Eccentricity, or the lack of alignment of the centerlines of webs and chords in a joint, can cause members to act as lever arms for the axial forces, and can produce substantial bending moments that must be accounted for in some situations (Fig. 10).

Likewise, the lateral resistance offered by metal plate connectors produces forces at the ends of members that are in reality different from those computed with a simple hinged-web analysis model (12). The importance of these differences depends on many factors relating to how the results of the truss analysis will be used. Also, as the force exerted on a connector plate exceeds the design loads, its load-displacement and moment-rotation lateral resistances become nonlinear. The plate's nonlinear behavior is important when computing moments and forces within a truss whenever applied loads significantly exceed design loads.

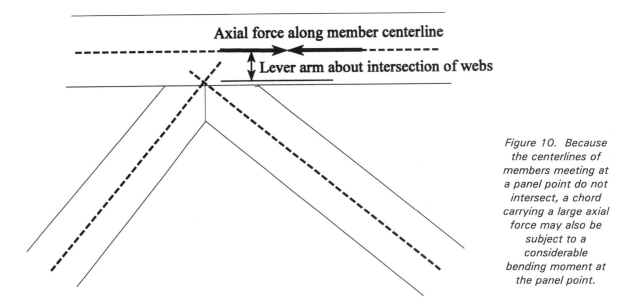

Figure 10. Because the centerlines of members meeting at a panel point do not intersect, a chord carrying a large axial force may also be subject to a considerable bending moment at the panel point.

One advanced model provided the first rational treatment of joint eccentricity and the nonlinear lateral resistance characteristics of connector plates, and set the stage for further developments (10). The model also accounted for plate buckling because of gaps between members in joints under compression. These features were later incorporated into an enhanced version of PPSA called PPSAFT (Purdue Plane Structures Analyzer Foschi-Triche) (11).

Another advanced model built upon these innovations and significantly reduces the computation time associated with modeling the wood/metal contact areas (12). It has the capability to account for large truss displacements that exceed several percent of the truss's length. In addition, a truss assembly can be analyzed as a series of two-dimensional truss models connected by sheathing. Plywood, oriented strand board or other structural sheathing fastened to the trusses' top chords is modeled in two ways. First, it is treated as a series of linear, elastic beams that cross the trusses and distributes loads among them. Secondly, the sheathing is modeled with special elements that account for the partial composite action as a result of it being nailed, and in the case of floor trusses, glued to the top chords (13). The sheathing and top chord act like a T-beam that is stiffer and stronger than the top chord itself. This model assumes that the connection between the sheathing and the wood is linear and elastic; that there is no friction between the two; that the truss deflections are small; and that there are small gaps between sheathing panels. Compared with the simpler models, analyses done with this approach more closely reflect the truss's true performance as measured in laboratory tests.

Truss Fabrication

The fabrication of MPC wood trusses involves four operations—material preparation, truss layout, plate pressing and preparation for shipment. Each may have an effect on a truss's performance. Special equipment and training of personnel is required to ensure consistent quality and load-carrying capacity among trusses. Wood members must be precisely cut and aligned before being joined, plates must be properly placed and pressed, and care must be exercised in handling and preparing trusses for shipment. By necessity, trusses are manufactured under controlled conditions in accordance with restrictive fabrication specifications and tolerances set forth in *ANSI/TPI 1-1995* (1).

Material Preparation
Dimension lumber is cut to length, and angles cut on its ends to fit specific joint configurations using computer-controlled saws. This often involves making two angled cuts on each end to precise tolerances to provide the needed tight-fitting joints. If a joint in compression contains an unacceptably wide gap, the plates may buckle at design load. *ANSI/TPI 1-1995* permits a maximum gap of 0.125 inches for all chord/chord joints except compression splices, which are limited to 0.0625 inches. Interior web/chord joints may have gaps as large as 0.25 inches. When wider gaps are present, potential problems are avoided by oversizing plates so that they cover the entire joint area (Fig. 11).

Truss Layout
To ensure that all truss dimensions meet those prescribed by the design drawing, a template or jig to guide member and plate placement is set up on a layout table. Accurate positioning of the template or jig is critical. Fabrication quality standards require that the truss's actual length deviates from the design length by a tolerance of 0.5 inches or less for trusses up to 30 feet long. Truss height may vary by no more than 0.25 inches for trusses up to 5 feet tall. For trusses longer than 30 feet or taller than 5 feet, the respective tolerances increase by 0.25 inches. Precut chords and webs are positioned according to the template's configuration, and connector plates are placed on both sides of each joint. Depending on the type of press used, connector plates may be either fully or partially pressed into the wood while the truss is on the layout table. In the latter case, the truss is carefully lifted from the layout table and passed through a roller press for final pressing.

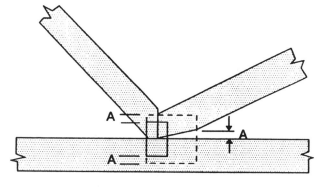

A=1/4 inch

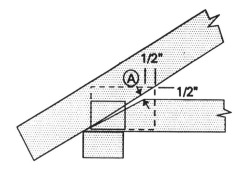

A=1/8 inch

Figure 11. When gaps in joints exceed allowable tolerances, oversize plates are applied to compensate.

Connector Plate Pressing

Three types of presses are used in truss fabrication—hydraulic, C clamp and roller. Pressures required to fully embed plates in wood range from 1000 to 1500 psi. With plates for light-frame trusses ranging in size from 2 square inches to 130 square inches, pressing forces of up to 200,000 lb. are needed. The machines capable of exerting these loads are stationary. The portable presses used to make field connections and repairs are typically limited to about 10,000 lb. capacity. These light-duty presses embed plates in steps, pressing about 5 to 10 squares inches at a time.

A hydraulic press usually consists of a set of heavy steel platens up to 16 feet long, controlled by hydraulic rams (Fig. 12). With some systems, the truss is passed between stationary platens; in others, the platen mechanism rolls along the truss's length on a floor-mounted track. In both cases, the pressing operation is a stop-and-start process. The platens close on the truss only where the plates are located, and the pressing force is parallel to the length of the plate's teeth.

*Figure 12. The platens of this hydraulic press close on the trusses
only where the plates are located as the press moves down the layout table.*

Layout tables are not used with a C clamp press. With this system, chords and webs are laid on top of carefully positioned pedestals, with each joint falling over a pedestal. A hydraulically-controlled C clamp press is suspended from a gantry by a cable or chain hoist so that it can be moved easily around the truss from joint to joint. These presses can exert from 20,000 to 100,000 lb. of force. Since they do not have the capacity of the larger stationary presses, C clamp presses are sometimes used as a first-pass press prior to final pressing in a roller press.

A roller press comprises a set of parallel rollers 12 to 14 feet long which embeds plates as a truss passes between them (Fig. 13). Plates are partially embedded using either a hammer or a gantry press before being passed through the roller press. The primary advantage of a roller press is that its continuous pressing motion speeds truss fabrication beyond the stop-and-start hydraulic presses. The fact that the roller force is applied at an angle to the plate's teeth, rather than parallel to them, however, means that there is the potential for some teeth to be bent over as they are pressed into the wood. Opinions are mixed as to the effect this has on joint strength. When plates are fully embedded using a stationary, single-pass roller press, *ANSI/TPI 1-1995* requires that a design adjustment factor, Q_R, that accounts for reductions in joint capacity associated with single-pass pressing, be applied to truss designs.

Figure 13. With roller pressing, the truss may be lifted from the layout table and passed between stationary rollers —as shown here— or an overhead roller may travel along the length of the layout table.

Truss Shipment

Exercising care in handling trusses is important at all times. These structural engineered wood products are designed to carry loads oriented parallel to the plane of their chords and webs or in-plane, and have a low capacity for resisting out-of-plane or sideways loadings. Trusses carried flat can experience excessive out-of-plane bending forces that can cause plates to pull out of the wood. As most trusses are stored flat during fabrication, they are supported on closely-spaced blocking to prevent them from bending.

To minimize out-of-plane bending during shipment, trusses are solid-piled, then banded. Metal bands are placed close to the panel points to prevent bending of the joints. The bands and the friction they induce between trusses impart composite action which stiffens the entire bundle and facilitates its handling without causing excessive out-of-plane displacement.

ANSI/TPI 1-1995 provides criteria for marking trusses with cautionary tags prior to shipment to minimize installation errors. Because parallel chord trusses may be cambered, or have higher grade lumber on their tension edges, they must be marked to indicate to the installer which edge should be up. If a truss is designed to bear at points other than at its heels, these locations must be clearly marked so that trusses are not reversed end for end. Long web or chord members that must be permanently braced to prevent them from buckling must also be marked.

Handling, Installing and Bracing MPC Wood Trusses

Handling

Handling of trusses during installation potentially presents the most critical stresses a truss will see in its lifetime. The best way to prevent handling-caused problems in trusses, of course, is to minimize the number of times they are handled. Problems can be avoided simply by following the procedures for handling, installing and bracing trusses recommended in TPI's *HIB-91 Commentary and Recommendations for Handling Installing & Bracing Metal Plate Connected Wood Trusses* (14).

Improper handling, including out-of-plane bending and/or large concentrated loads exerted by the weight of workers or construction materials, may damage joints or members. In almost all cases, fabricators oversize plates to accommodate handling stresses, and will increase them further if recurrent problems exist for a particular truss design. *HIB-91* suggests that the stresses exerted on plates in a truss bent out-of-plane with a lateral deflection of more than 3 inches in 10 feet should be considered excessive, and may result in a reduction in joint capacity. This much deflection can give rise to lateral plate forces exceeding 700 lb., as well as tooth withdrawal forces. The result is a tendency for the plate to back out of the wood. Trusses subjected to out-of-plane bending because of mishandling should be inspected prior to installation for plate embedment gaps and crushing of the wood around the teeth.

Installation

As prefabricated engineered wood products, trusses are constructed to tight tolerances. Proper installation requires that the supporting structure be constructed to the same tolerances to avoid installation problems and to ensure that the truss's structural performance is as expected.

The first step in any truss installation is to inspect the supporting structure. Bearing walls must be properly designed and constructed to adequately support the trusses. The distance between bearing points in the structure must match those of the trusses. Headers and lintels intended to support trusses should be securely attached to the building. All framing anchors and tiedowns should be accurately located and permanently fastened in place prior to installing the trusses.

Trusses should be scheduled for delivery on the day they are to be installed. If they must be stored, they should be supported off of the ground on blocking spaced to prevent them from bending excessively. If stored vertically, the bundle should be braced to prevent it from toppling. For long term storage, the bundle should be covered with a water repellent tarp to protect the trusses from the weather. TPI recommends placing the truss bundle as close to the erection site as possible upon delivery.

Trusses are placed either by hand, or with a crane. The proper lifting strategy depends on the truss's length. Small trusses—those with less than a 30 foot span—can usually be lifted by hand upside down onto the bearing seats, and then rotated into position with little problem. When hoisting trusses by crane, lifting cables should be attached at the top chord's quarter points (Fig. 14). If the truss's span is over 30 feet, a spreader bar must be used, with the cables from the bar to the top chord toeing inward to prevent the truss from buckling. For trusses longer than 60 feet, a rigid strongback should be fastened to the truss at 10-foot intervals. In all cases, cables should not be removed until the truss's heels are securely fastened in place, and all temporary bracing has been installed.

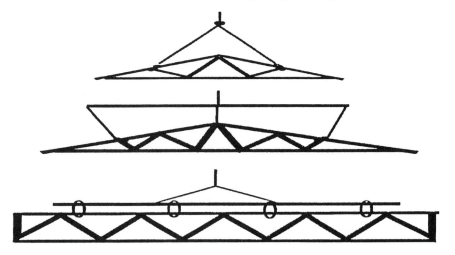

Figure 14. To avoid damaging trusses when hoisting them by crane, slings are attached only at panel points. A spreader bar is needed when trusses exceed 30 feet in length.

As their span increases, trusses become more flexible and harder to handle. It is sometimes advantageous to join several longer trusses into a subassembly on the ground, then lift it in place. The subassembly, which is cross-braced and sheathed, can be lifted as a rigid unit, practically eliminating problems with out-of-plane flexibility.

Sometimes, truss height exceeds highway clearance limits. In these cases, trusses are shipped in sections that are spliced or piggybacked in the field (Fig. 15). Splices can be made on the ground or, with the aid of temporary shoring, after the bottom or supporting section has been installed. When erecting piggybacked trusses, the supporting section should be completely installed and securely fastened and braced prior to adding the top or supported section.

Also, the top chord bearing extensions on a top-chord-bearing parallel chord truss are designed to carry one-half of the design load as a shear force. To minimize the effect of this shear load on the bending stresses present in the bearing extension, the intersection point of the truss's end web and top chord should be located within 0.5 inches of the inner edge of the bearing seat.

Once installed, it is important for subsequent construction that all trusses be properly spaced and aligned, both vertically and horizontally. Spacing of trusses should be within 0.25 inches of specification, and bow in the truss should not exceed the lesser of either the span divided by 200 (L/200) or 2 inches, as measured from a line stretched between the bearing supports. It is equally important that trusses be plumb. At any point along the length of the truss, a plumb line attached to the top chord should be within 1/50 of the depth of the truss at that point, as measured from the bottom chord (1).

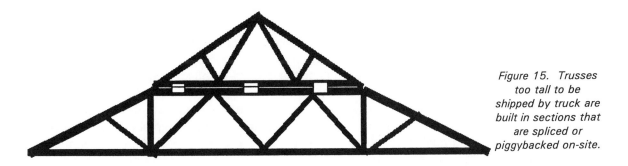

Figure 15. Trusses too tall to be shipped by truck are built in sections that are spliced or piggybacked on-site.

Truss chords and webs should never be cut or notched during erection of the trusses or during installation of utilities or other building components. If even one member is cut, the load-resisting capability of the truss can be drastically reduced, and the truss's design is no longer valid. If, for whatever reason, a truss is damaged during installation, the truss manufacturer should be notified so that a truss design engineer can propose a repair strategy.

Bracing

The bracing of trusses is critical to ensure worker safety and to avoid toppling accidents during erection. Temporary lateral and crossbracing is used to hold trusses in line and to maintain framing system stability until permanent bracing—which includes the sheathing—is installed. Trusses are most vulnerable to toppling during installation, and pose the risk of serious injury to workers should they fall. Properly designed temporary or erection bracing holds the trusses in a vertical position, keeps loads in-plane, and virtually eliminates the risk of collapse. Temporary bracing usually includes ground bracing, continuous lateral struts or ties, and diagonal and crossbracing. Each type of temporary bracing plays a specific role in stabilizing the trusses and providing support, and the presence of some, but not all of the needed bracing may give workers a dangerous false sense of safety. *ANSI/TPI 1-1995* provides minimum requirements for truss installation and bracing. The design of temporary bracing is addressed in TPI's *DSB-89 Recommended Design Specification for Temporary Bracing of Metal Plate Connected Wood Trusses*, an essential reading for professionals involved in designing and constructing truss-framed buildings (15).

When installing trusses, it is extremely important to securely brace the first truss in a vertical orientation, as all subsequent trusses will be braced against it. This is done using ground braces which run from the truss's top chord to a ground anchor outside the building, or to one attached to the floor below. Lateral bracing is then attached to the top and bottom chord of each truss as it is installed to ensure its proper alignment and the stability of the entire assembly. Lateral bracing includes members applied perpendicular to the span as well as at an angle to it. It must be emphasized that lateral bracing by itself will not prevent a domino-like toppling of multiple trusses. In addition to the lateral bracing applied to the chords, truss-to-truss crossbracing also is installed against the webs to improve stability, maintain alignment and assist in distributing vertical loads in the finished structure.

Permanent bracing includes diagonal chord and web bracing, roof sheathing, purlins and other members that connect the trusses to the building's structural framework. It is normally designed and specified by the engineer of record or building designer. Permanent bracing ensures worker safety during construction and enhances the performance of the truss assembly over the life of the structure by distributing loads to other parts of the framework. Temporary lateral bracing applied to the top chord is replaced by sheathing, which also serves to stabilize the truss assembly and promote load-sharing. Web cross bracing and lateral bracing applied to the top of the bottom chord is permanent and helps to stiffen the assembly against lateral and gravity loads.

Performance-Related Issues in Buildings

Constructed With MPC Wood Trusses
Buildings constructed with MPC wood trusses represent an engineering advance from intuitively designed light-frame stick-built assemblies of the past. Improved confidence in the increased strength and stiffness of fabricated trusses over that of site-built dimension lumber systems permits a savings in materials and labor in the construction of floor and roof assemblies. While trusses have increased design flexibility and reduced costs, they also have introduced new performance issues for designers, contractors and building owners regarding strength, system redundancy, vibration characteristics and fire endurance (21). And though MPC wood trusses have a proven track record of nearly 40 years in residential and commercial buildings, designers and contractors still ask "How well do MPC wood trusses really perform?"

Strength
Tests of both full-scale truss- and conventionally-framed roof assemblies conducted at the Forest Products Laboratory in Madison, Wisconsin, have shown that MPC wood truss roof assemblies have a greater inherent safety than dimension lumber rafter roof assemblies (16, 17). Dimension lumber rafter roofs have been used for over 100 years with little evidence of structural failure due to design gravity loads. Static analysis of the lateral shear forces at the bearing point—where a rafter is normally nailed to a ceiling joist with six or fewer nails—suggests possible inherent weakness in roofs with slopes of less than 6 in 12 built in Northern (snow load) climates. In tests of full-scale rafter roofs, heel connections exhibited lateral displacements ranging from 0.06 inches to 0.14 inches when the rafters were loaded to design limits. The displacement was primarily plastic, so little recovery took place when the load was removed. Maximum loads for rafter systems were less than 1.4

times design loads. Truss-framed roofs, on the other hand, exhibited little plastic deformation under loads up to 1.5 times their design limits. Maximum loads ranged from 1.5 to over 2.0 times design loads. Part of the difference may be attributable to the 15 percent increase in allowable load awarded to a dimension lumber rafter for assembly interaction effects. Truss elements are permitted a 15 percent increase for bending stress, but this normally translates to less than a 5 percent increase in the truss's load capacity.

System Redundancy

The many trusses in a roof or floor assembly are typically closely spaced—most often 24 inches on-center—and interconnected by sheathing. This system redundancy sets the stage for increased safety whenever structural wood members of different grades, stiffnesses and strengths are connected together. Typically, the safety of such assemblies will depend not on the strength of any one member as assumed in design, but instead on the collective action of all of the members in the assembly. Trusses are designed on an individual member basis in which wood member strength is assumed to be less than that expected for 95 percent of the members of the same grade and species, and by assuming that the loads on the entire assembly are distributed in proportion to a presumed tributary area assigned to each truss. In reality, the trusses in an assembly interact. Loads are transferred among trusses based on the flexural rigidity of each truss in relation to the rigidity of its neighbors, and that of the sheathing as well. More importantly in the case of trusses, there is considerable variability in individual wood member strength and in the amount of force that is directed to any one member. The greater the variability, the more likely it is that when a low-strength member fails there will be higher strength members nearby that can assume the broken member's share of the load without failing. Because a redundant system by definition has a series of interconnected repetitive members, the loads carried by an unusually limber or weak member have a strong possibility of being transferred to stronger adjacent members, and potential collapse of the assembly is avoided. Two characteristics of roof and floor truss assemblies thus contribute to greater safety than is assumed in the design of individual trusses—the redundancy in the assembly and the statistical distribution of wood member and connection strength in each truss in the assembly.

Vibration Characteristics

The vibration characteristics of truss-framed assemblies vary with their stiffness, span, mass, damping characteristics and boundary conditions (18). In light-frame structures, unwanted vibrations in floor systems present the greatest design challenge. While avoiding this problem has always required more than simply checking a floor's static deflection, vibration problems have become more common with the increased spans that accompanied the development of light-weight structural engineered wood products like floor trusses and wood I-joists. It is clear that limiting the static load deflection using the common criterion of span divided by 360 (L/360) will not guarantee acceptable vibrational performance in a floor. Exactly what constitutes acceptable or unacceptable vibrational performance is determined largely by personal perceptions and preferences. In addition, it is known that preferences can take on regional variations as well. Thus, a floor acceptable in one part of the country may not be acceptable in another. Part of the vibrational response of a floor has to do with the relationship between the width and depth of the framing members. If member width remains constant, member depth must be increased as the span increases to maintain similar stiffness. Deep, narrow, long-span members are subject to torsional as well as in-plane vibration. Lateral blocking is often needed with long-span parallel chord floor trusses to inhibit torsional vibration.

Fire Endurance

Fire endurance is an important design consideration with light-frame wood trusses due to the relatively high surface-area-to-volume ratio of their 2x4 chords and webs. In a fire, dimension lumber of smaller cross-sectional area will heat up and burn faster than more massive members. Also, connection failure can occur in a truss if charring of the members removes enough of the wood surrounding the teeth of the metal plate connector. However, connector plates both reflect radiant heat away from wood members and accelerate the conduction of heat into them (19). The former effect usually offsets the latter. Removal of plates from trusses which burned through in fire tests showed that the wood under the plates was clean, bright and unaffected. The best means of achieving fire endurance in roof and floor truss assemblies is to apply fire-resistant protective coverings such as gypsum board to the bottom chords to inhibit the spread of fire into the assembly. When combined with proper firestopping and draftstopping, this will yield a model building code-approved method for providing an effective barrier to fire growth and spread. Standard configurations of gypsum board sheathing offer fire-protected assemblies that are rated to endure one hour of standard fire exposure. This allows more time for people to exit the building and more time for firefighters to save it. Other designs employ heat-sensing sprinkler systems to quickly suppress a fire should it occur.

Specifying Metal Plate Connected Wood Trusses

A specification for trusses for a simple gable roof includes the type and number of each truss needed, span, pitch, top-chord overhang, soffit return details, and any special loading requirements such as a slate roof or HVAC equipment to be mounted in the attic. Regardless of the complexity of the roof or floor system, the architect, designer or builder needs to provide to the truss fabricator a building framing plan and any special loading requirements. Using this information, the trusses are designed by computer using sophisticated engineering software most often provided by the connector plate manufacturer.

References

1. Truss Plate Institute. 1995. ANSI/TPI 1-1995 National Design Standard for Metal Plate Connected Wood Truss Construction. TPI. Madison, Wisconsin.

2. Triche, M., M. Ritter, S. Lewis and R. Wolfe. 1994. Design and Field Performance of a Metal Plate Wood Truss Bridge. Pages 1310-1315 *in* ASCE Structures Congress 12 Proceedings, Vol. 2.

3. Dagher, H., H. Caccese, F. Altimore, Y. Hsu, R. Wolfe and M. Ritter. 1995. Using Lightweight MPC Wood Trusses in Bridges. Pages 9-12 *in* ASCE Structures Congress 13 Proceedings, Vol. 1.

4. United States Department of Commerce. 1994. Voluntary Product Standard PS 20-94 American Softwood Lumber Standard. USDC. Washington, D. C.

5. Smulski, S. 1994. All About Roof Trusses. Fine Homebuilding. 89:40-45.

6. Wood Truss Council of America. 1995. WTCA 1-1995 Standard Responsibilities in the Design Process Involving Metal Plate Connected Wood Trusses. WTCA. Madison, Wisconsin.

7. Truss Plate Institute. 1995. Commentary & Appendices to ANSI/TPI 1-1995 National Design Standard for Metal Plate Connected Wood Truss Construction. TPI. Madison, Wisconsin.

8. Triche, M. and J. Richardson. 1994. Design of Wood Structures Using PPSA. Frame Building News. 6(5):74-88.

9. Suddarth, S. and R. Wolfe. 1984. Purdue Plane Structures Analyzer II - A Computerized Wood Engineering System. General Technical Report FPL-GTR-40. USDA Forest Service Forest Products Laboratory. Madison, Wisconsin.

10. Foschi, R. 1977. Analysis of Wood Diaphragms and Trusses Part II: Truss Plate Connections. Canadian Journal of Civil Engineering. 4:353-362.

11. Triche, M. and S. Suddarth. 1988. Advanced Design of Metal Plate Connector Joints. Forest Products Journal. 38(9):7-12.

12. Cramer, S., D. Shrestha and P. Mtenga. 1993. Computation of Member Forces in Metal Plate Connected Wood Trusses. Structural Engineering Review. 5(3):209-217.

13. Warner, J. and D. Wheat. 1986. Analysis of Structures Containing Layered Beam-Columns with Interlayer Slip. Unpublished report. Civil Engineering Department. University of Texas. Austin, Texas.

14. Truss Plate Institute. 1991. HIB-91 Commentary and Recommendations for Handling Installing & Bracing Metal Plate Connected Wood Trusses. TPI. Madison, Wisconsin.

15. Truss Plate Institute. 1989. DSB-89 Recommended Design Specification for Temporary Bracing of Metal Plate Connected Wood Trusses. TPI. Madison, Wisconsin.

16. Wolfe, R. and M. McCarthy. 1989. Structural Performance of Light-Frame Roof Assemblies I. Truss Assemblies with High Stiffness Variability. Research Paper FPL-RP-492. USDA Forest Service Forest Products Laboratory. Madison, Wisconsin.

17. Wolfe, R. and T. LaBissoniere. 1991. Structural Performance of Light-Frame Roof Assemblies II. Conventional Truss Assemblies. Research Paper FPL-RP-499. USDA Forest Service Forest Products Laboratory. Madison, Wisconsin.

18. Kalkert, R., D. Dolan and F. Woeste. 1995. Wood-Floor Vibration Design Criteria. Journal of Structural Engineering. 121(9):1294-1297.

19. White, R., S. Cramer and D. Shrestha. 1993. Fire Endurance Model for a Metal-Plate-Connected Wood Truss. Research Paper FPL-RP-522. USDA Forest Service Forest Products Laboratory. Madison, Wisconsin.

20. Percival, D. 1991. Separation Between Ceiling/Floor and Partition Walls. Wood Design Focus. 2(2):3-6.

21. Callahan, E. 1995. Metal Plate Connected Wood Truss Handbook. Wood Truss Council of America. Madison, Wisconsin.

Chapter 4

Wood I-joists

Sherman Nelson, P. E.

TrusJoist MacMillan
Boise, Idaho

Though first presented in the 1920s, the concept of configuring wooden structural bending members using a wood panel product web and sawn lumber flanges was not fully developed until the 1940s, when it was driven by war-related research on wooden aircraft (9-13). Members were conceived as box- and I-shaped in cross section, with the presumption that they would be custom designed and fabricated to meet the specific requirements of the job.

The first commercial product appeared in 1968, when Trus Joist Corporation, Boise, Idaho, began marketing a proprietary engineered wood product with an I-shaped cross section that was manufactured in a continuous process. The company provided tables of section properties and load/span information to help designers incorporate the product into various building applications. This marked the onset of the prefabricated wood I-joist industry (20, 21). Today more than a dozen companies in North America manufacture wood I-joists. The industry is also developing, but to a lesser extent, in both Europe and the Pacific Rim. The exceptional growth of the wood I-joist industry, and the rapid acceptance of its products in the marketplace, has been driven by the need for a high-quality, dimensionally consistent and stable, lightweight framing member with reliable capacity and predictable performance. The availability of long lengths for both clear span and multiple span applications, extensive product distribution networks and engineering design and technical support, as well as in-field service, have all contributed to this record of marketplace success. It is anticipated that the current estimated production of over 400 million lineal feet of wood I-joists annually will rise to nearly 900 million lineal feet by the year 2005 (1).

The many series, sizes, and depths of wood I-joists available today reflects their numerous applications and the variety of raw materials from which they are made (Fig. 1). Though these products are used in a wide range of structural applications, the term "joist" is appropriate because their predominant use is as an alternative to sawn lumber floor joists in repetitive light-frame construction (Fig. 2). They are particularly useful where long, clear spans are needed, and give designers flexibility in floor plans. Wood I-joists with large cross sections are often used as heavily-loaded, non-repetitive carrying members and might more properly be called I-beams. Wood I-joists are also used as roof joists, headers, and in other structural applications such as concrete forming (Fig. 3).

Figure 1. Wood I-joists are available in numerous depths and flange widths, reflecting their many applications.

Figure 2. Increasingly popular in residential floor systems, wood I-joists should be braced prior to installing subflooring to prevent them from toppling.

Figure 3. Deep wood I-joists are
frequently used in commercial
roof systems.

Materials

I-joist flanges may be single or laminated pieces of visually graded or machine stress rated sawn lumber, or laminated veneer lumber (LVL). One manufacturer has proposed a fiber-reinforced sawn lumber flange. Another has suggested using small logs from forest thinning operations for flanges.

4 - 93

Webs are predominately structural use plywood or oriented strand board (OSB). At least two I-joist producers utilize sawn dimension lumber for webs. While most I-joists have a single web, one manufacturer makes an insulated double-webbed I-joist header by sandwiching rigid foam between the webs. In Europe, webs of light-gauge corrugated steel and medium density hardboard have been used.

The adhesives used to bond webs and flanges are exclusively of the exterior water-resistant type. Most conform to *ASTM D2559 Standard Specification for Adhesives for Structural Laminated Wood Products for Use Under Exterior (Wet Use) Conditions* (18) or *CSA 0112-M Standards for Wood Adhesives* (19). Other adhesives not included in either of these standards can be used, provided it can be shown that their performance is equivalent to those referenced. The configuration of the web-to-flange connection—a groove in the flange into which the web is inserted—varies among manufacturers, as does the web-to-web connection used to make the webs continuous.

Most manufacturers offer several series of wood I-joists, each with numerous depths. While most have parallel flanges and lack camber, at least one manufacturer offers a tapered-depth product that provides, for instance, both roof drainage and a flat ceiling. Wood I-joists currently manufactured vary in depth from 9 1/4 inches to 38 inches, and are available in lengths up to 80 feet. Flanges may range from 1 1/2 inches by 1 1/2 inches to 4 5/8 inches by 2 5/8 inches in cross section, while webs may be from 3/8 inches to 7/8 inches thick.

Manufacturing

Like the proprietary products they produce, the processes for manufacturing wood I-joists vary considerably throughout the industry. High-volume residential series I-joists are usually fabricated in a fully-automated continuous production line at speeds of 350 feet per minute or more. The product is literally extruded from an assembly machine that accepts flanges and webs at one end and dispenses the finished product on the fly at the other. At the other end of the production scale are custom hand lay-up processes which are more typically used for the heavier commercial or industrial product lines.

In a typical fabrication process, sawn lumber or LVL is ripped to width into flanges, which, if required, are then finger-jointed end-to-end (Fig. 4). A profiled groove is routed into one face of each flange along its length, and the mating tongue routed onto the edges and ends of webs cut to width in a prior operation. Adhesive—typically phenol resorcinol formaldehyde—is applied in the groove just before the flanges and webs enter the assembly machine, where they are pressed together. After exiting the assembler, knockouts are punched into the web, and the I-joists cut to length and passed through an oven to cure the adhesive. The finished product is inspected and bundled for shipment.

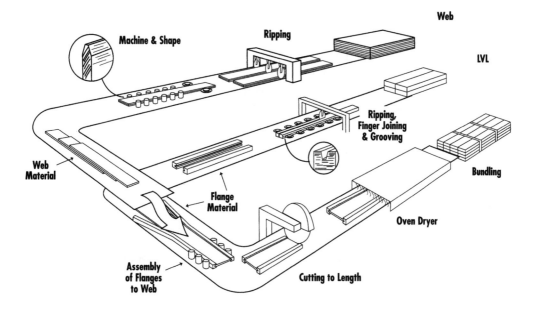

*Figure 4. The majority of wood I-joists are made in a continuous process;
custom sizes are often laid-up by hand.*

Quality Assurance

As required by the model building code acceptances, all wood I-joist manufacturers must be inspected on a regular, unannounced basis by an independent third-party inspection agency. Each must have a manual detailing its manufacturing standards and in-plant quality control testing procedures and records, which the inspection agency uses as the basis for verification of compliance. With any changes, modifications or variances in raw materials or processes, a manufacturer is required to be re-qualified for acceptance by the model building codes.

Product Standardization

Because the wood I-joist industry is still relatively young, and there is a wide range of raw materials and processes used in making the available products, its first 30 years have offered little in terms of product standardization. In effect, the industry is still "settling in". Product innovation, development and optimization continue at a relatively fast pace. Though there are high-volume applications for wood I-joists—residential floor systems, for example—in which it appears that the products offered by three or four different manufacturers are interchangeable, each of these products is in fact unique. Each has different performance characteristics, such as load capacity, fire- and sound-transmission ratings, system warranties or other building code-accepted proprietary features.

The producers and distributors of these proprietary products play an important role in providing the assurances and technical information necessary to ensure their proper application and use. Although there are some general design considerations that apply to all wood I-joists, designers, specifiers and users of these products are encouraged to seek the services, design assistance and technical literature provided by the actual manufacturer or authorized supplier.

Industry Product Standards and Building Code Acceptance

As the wood I-joist industry grew from one manufacturer to several, representatives from these companies met with other interested parties from the larger wood products industry and related regulatory agencies to develop industry standards for their products. This led ultimately to the formation of the Wood I-Joist Manufacturers Association in 1984. WIJMA regularly holds open meetings to address issues of common interest to the manufacturers of wood I-joists. Its primary focus has been the development of performance-based standards for wood I-joists. The standards require that a product's performance first be established in qualification testing programs, then verified through continuous quality assurance testing at the manufacturing level overseen by an independent third-party inspection agency. If a product's performance falters, its allowable design values are automatically reduced. Conversely, continued improvement in performance can result in increases in its allowable design values.

The first wood I-joist industry performance standard, *AC14 Acceptance Criteria For Prefabricated Wood I-Joists*, was accepted by the International Conference of Building Officials in 1987, and is still in effect (2). WIJMA was also instrumental in creating *ASTM D5055 Standard Specification for Establishing and Monitoring Structural Capacities of Prefabricated Wood I-Joists* in 1990 (3). Sponsored by ASTM committee D07 Committee on Wood, the standard is periodically updated and revised in accordance with ASTM procedures. Both *ASTM D5055* and its Canadian counterpart *CSA 086.1-M94 Engineering Design in Wood (Limit States Design) A National Standard of Canada* (22) are referenced by the model building codes in North America.

The standards by which wood I-joists are evaluated overseas are similar to those in North America. In Europe, for example, each country presently has its own evaluation criteria, however, most plan to eventually adopt *Eurocode 5 Design of Timber Structures* (23). Each country will develop a *National Application Document* which will become part of *Eurocode 5*. In the interim, a proponent seeking approval for the use of wood I-joists must apply directly to each country or agency. For the most part, the reviewing bodies are government agencies:

Europe	UK	British Board of Agrément
	France	Centre Scientifique et Technique du Bâtiment (CSTB); several building control agencies, including Bureau Veritas and SOCOTEC, are also building code enforcement authorities, and should also be consulted
Asia	Japan	Ministry of Construction (MOC) Article #38
Australia		Australian Building Systems Appraisal Council (ABSAC)

It may also be necessary to consult with other agencies in other countries that do not accept the approvals of those listed above.

Due to the proprietary nature of its products, each wood I-joist manufacturer must gain building code acceptances for the use of its products individually. This is done by demonstrating that products meet the acceptance criteria of the model building codes, the Canadian Construction Materials Center and the international building code agencies. State, county and local building code jurisdictions may also have specific requirements related to the use of wood I-joists. The acceptances issued by these organizations serve as the basis for the design and use of these product lines. Designers and specifiers should obtain copies of the acceptance criteria from wood I-joist manufacturers to ensure proper compliance.

Establishing the Strength of Wood I-joists

Manufacturers use either empirical (testing-based), rational (engineering theory-based), or combined empirical/rational analysis procedures to establish the bending stiffness, moment capacity (essentially, bending strength) and shear strength of wood I-joists. Originally, rational analysis procedures were more convenient because I-joists were made with lumber flanges and plywood webs whose properties were well established (27, 28). As the wood I-joist industry evolved, substantial research in the form of full-scale testing was accomplished, via both a daily quality control basis and as ad hoc testing programs designed to evaluate the performance of specific I-joist configurations. In addition, various types of proprietary oriented strand board panels began to be used for webs, while flange materials expanded to include special grades of both sawn lumber and proprietary structural composite lumber. Eventually, the original rational analysis procedures were replaced by combined empirical/rational methods, and in some cases, by strictly empirical methods, with rigid ties to quality assurance testing. As a result, most manufacturers today use empirical or combined empirical/rational procedures such as those outlined in *ASTM D5055*, in which full-size I-joists are loaded to destruction. Bending stiffness and strength, and shear strength are calculated directly from load-deflection data collected during the tests. Allowable design values are then assigned based on these data.

In the following example, a rational analysis procedure is used to determine the section properties for 14-inch-deep wood I-joist whose web is made of Structural I-grade plywood with a 0.125-inch-thick inner ply running parallel to the I-joist's length (Fig. 5). The allowable shear-through-the-thickness stress, v, is 250 psi for an effective plywood thickness of 0.371 inches as per the then-current allowable design values (27). The allowable rolling shear stress, s, at the web/flange interface is 75 psi. (The typical 50 percent reduction does not apply because the web is confined inside the rout cut into the flange.) The flange lumber has an allowable axial stress, f_b, of 2000 psi and an MOE of 2.2 million psi.

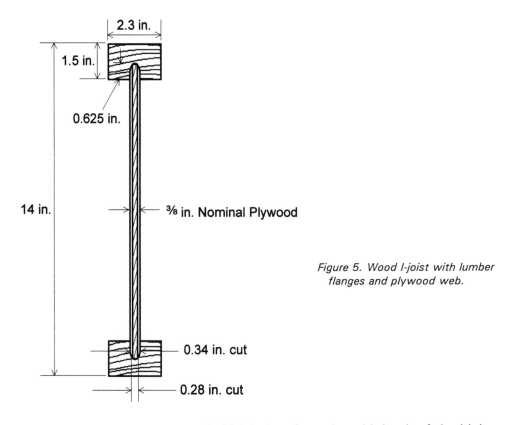

Figure 5. Wood I-joist with lumber flanges and plywood web.

The centroid, c, of the trapezoidal rout is 5.802 inches from the mid-depth of the I-joist:

$$c = \left(\frac{0.625}{3}\right)\left(\frac{2\,(0.34)+0.28}{0.28+0.34}\right) = 0.323$$

c = (0.625 - 0.323) + 5.5 = 5.802

The area, A, of the rout is 0.194 square inches:

$$A = \left(\frac{0.34 + 0.28}{2} \right) 0.625 = 0.194$$

The section properties for one-half of the I-joist are

element	A	y	Ay	Ay^2	+	I$_o$
flange	3.450	6.250	21.56	134.77		0.65
rout	-0.194	5.802	-1.12	-6.52		--
web	0.766	3.063	2.35	7.18		2.39
Σ	4.022		22.79	138.47		
Σ less web	3.256		20.44	128.89		

where: A = area (in.^{2})
  y = distance from mid-depth of I-joist to centroid of element (in.)
  Ay = static moment of element around mid-depth of I-joist (in.^{3})
  Ay^2 = moment of inertia of element around mid-depth of I-joist (in.^{4})
  I$_o$ = moment of inertia of element around its own centroid (in.^{4})

The section properties for the entire I-joist are

  I$_s$ = 2 (138.47) = 276.94
  I$_b$ = 2 (128.89) = 257.78
  Q$_P$ = 22.79
  Q$_{RS}$ = 20.44

where: I$_s$ = gross moment of inertia (in.^{4})
  I$_b$ = net flange moment of inertia (in.^{4})
  Q$_P$ = total static moment of I-joist around its own centroid (in.^{3})
  Q$_{RS}$ = static moment for rolling shear (in.^{3})

The bending moment, shear and rolling shear capacities of the I-joist are:

bending moment in flange

$$M = \frac{f_b\, I_b}{C} = \frac{2000\,(257.78)}{7\,(12)} = 6137 \text{ ft.-lb.}$$

shear-through-the-thickness in web

$$V_P = \frac{v\, I_s\, b}{Q_P} = \frac{250\,(277)(0.371)}{22.79} = 1127 \text{ lb.}$$

rolling shear for web inside rout

$$V_{RS} = \frac{s\, n\, I_s\, h}{Q_{RS}} = \frac{75\,(2)(277)(0.625)}{20.44} = 1270 \text{ lb.}$$

where: C = distance to mid-depth of I-joist (in.)
       b = effective thickness of web (in.)
       n = 2 sides of rout
       h = depth of rout (in.)

The allowable bending moment for this I-joist is 6137 ft.-lb. Since the horizontal shear-through-the-thickness force in the plywood web is less than the rolling shear force for the web inside the rout, shear-through-the-thickness controls the design for shear.

Guidelines for Designing With Wood I-joists

WIJMA's *Technical Bulletin No. 1 Design Guidelines* (8) describes the various design features that must be considered when designing and building with wood I-joists. Reprinted in its entirety on the following pages, this comprehensive document explains the state-of-the-art design considerations regarding wood I-joists including, among other things, deflection, moment and shear checks; duration of load and creep effects; bearing details; and connections. The detail in *Technical Bulletin No. 1* may appear somewhat overwhelming, however, most wood I-joist manufacturers offer computer-assisted design support as well as the technical support necessary to properly specify their products.

TECHNICAL BULLETIN No. 1   **DESIGN GUIDELINES**

Wood I-Joist Manufacturers Association   **November 1994**

**WOOD I-JOIST
DESIGN GUIDELINE**

The Wood I-Joist is similar to conventional lumber in that it's based on the same raw materials, but differs in how the material is composed. For this reason, design practices compatible with conventional lumber are not always compatible with the unique configurations and wood fiber orientation of the Wood I-Joist. To avoid deficiencies, designers using Wood I-Joists should develop solutions in accordance with the following guidelines.

DESIGN SPAN:

The **design span** used for determining critical shears and moments is defined as the clear span between the faces of support plus one-half the minimum required end bearing on each end (see Figure 1). For most Wood I-Joists, the minimum required end bearing length varies from 1 1/2" to 3 1/2" (adding 2" to the clear span dimension is a good estimate for most applications). At locations of continuity over intermediate bearings, the **design span** is measured from the centerline of the intermediate support to the face of bearing at the end support, plus one-half the minimum required bearing length. For interior spans of a continuous joist, the **design span** extends from centerline to centerline of the intermediate bearings.

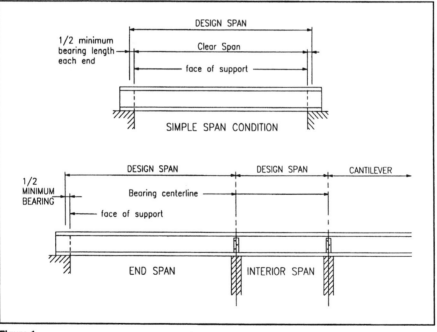

Figure 1

DURATION OF LOAD:

When the working stress design methodology is used, Wood I-Joists can be designed using the same strength adjustments for **duration of load** allowed for sawn lumber. Using the provisions spelled out in appendix B of the 1986 edition of *National Design Specification for Wood Construction*, critical combinations of loads and durations can easily be found. The following conditions are examples of the various **duration of load** combinations that may need to be checked:

1) All dead loads at 90% duration
2) All floor live loads plus dead loads at 100% duration
3) All roof snow loads plus floor live loads plus dead loads at 115% duration
4) All roof live loads (often referred to as construction loads) plus floor live loads plus dead loads at 125% duration
5) Any other combinations required by local building codes or special conditions (i.e.: 133% wind or seismic loading)

Note: Heavily insulated roofs or heavy snow load areas may not qualify for duration of load increases due to the potential for longer term loadings. This condition is typical in very heavy snow load regions (example: snow load greater than 60 PSF) where 2 months accumulated duration at design load over the life of the structure is exceeded.

All duration of load combinations need to be checked to determine the worst case for strength determination. To find this worst case, first determine the magnitude of each load and accumulate subtotals of combination loads at or below each duration of load adjustment level. Next, divide each combination of loads by the highest considered duration adjustment. The result after division having the highest value is the critical combination and **duration of load**. An example procedure for assessing the critical combination requires a check of each **duration of load** as follows:

1) Actual Unit stress (DL) less than or = 0.90 (Design Value)
2) Actual Unit stress (DL + LL) less than or = 1.0 (Design Value)
3) Actual Unit stress (DL + LL + SL) less than or = 1.15 (Design Value)
4) Actual Unit stress (DL + LL + SL + WL) less than or = 1.33 (Design Value)

For reference, this procedure is detailed in the *National Design Specification for Wood Construction* published by the National Forest Products Association.

DESIGN LOADS CASES:

Most building codes require consideration for the critical distribution of loads. Due to the long length and continuous span capabilities of the Wood I-Joist, these code provisions have particular meaning. Considering a multiple span member, the following design load cases might apply:

FLOOR MEMBERS

<u>Residential Applications</u>

1) All spans with total loads

2) Alternate span loading

3) Adjacent span loading

4) Partial span loading (joists with holes)

5) All load durations for each special load type i.e.: point; triangular

<u>Commercial Applications</u>

1) All spans with total loads

2) Alternate span loading

3) Adjacent span loading

4) Partial span loading (joists with holes)

5) All load durations for each special load type i.e.: point; triangular

6) Concentrated loading provisions ("Safe Loads")

ROOF MEMBERS

1) All spans with total loads
2) Alternate or adjacent span loading
   (optional for some snow load conditions)
3) Partial span loading (joists with holes)
4) All load durations for each load type

For each of these loadings, the worst case shears, moments, deflections, and reactions need to be identified. The worst case in each of these categories at all critical locations should be used in the final member design. When using a Load and Resistance Factor Design (LRFD) methodology which utilizes factored loads, there are no load cases involving duration of load. Additionally, with LRFD, to properly consider member deflection, un-factored load combinations will need to be checked. This is especially important with multiple span applications. A basic description of each of these load cases follows:

Total loads on all spans — This load case involves placing the actual loads on all spans. For example, if a design load of 40 PLF Live Load/20 PLF Dead Load was needed on a 3 span continuous member, this load case would place the full design load on the length of all 3 spans simultaneously.

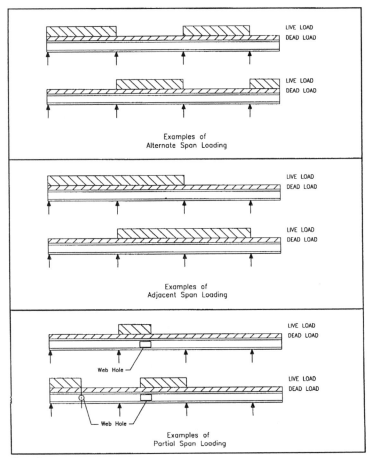

Examples of
Alternate Span Loading

Examples of
Adjacent Span Loading

Examples of
Partial Span Loading

Figure 2

Alternate span loading — This load case places the live load portion of the design loads on every other span and can involve two loading patterns. The first pattern results in the removal of the live loads for all even numbered spans. The second pattern removes live loads for all odd numbered spans. For roof applications, some building codes require removal of only a portion of the live loads from odd or even numbered spans. The alternate span load case usually generates maximum end reactions, mid-span moments, and mid-span deflections. Illustrations of this type of loading are shown in Figure 2.

Adjacent span loading — This load case (see Figure 2) removes live loads from all but two adjoining spans. All other spans, if they exist, are loaded with dead loads only. Depending on the number of spans involved, this load case can lead to a number of load patterns. All combinations of adjacent spans become separate loadings. This load case is usually used for floor applications to develop maximum shears and reactions at internal bearing locations.

Partial span loading — This load case, often referred to as unbalanced loading, involves applying live loads to less than the full length of a span (see Figure 2). For Wood I-Joists with web holes, this case is used to develop maximum member shears at hole locations. When this load case applies, uniform live load is applied only from the closest bearing location to the furthest edge or centerline of a hole location (exact location dependent upon the hole size). The loading is also repeated from the opposite direction. For each hole within a given span, there are two corresponding load cases. Live loads other than the uniform application load, located within the span containing the hole, are also applied simultaneously. This includes all special loads such as point or tapered loads.

Concentrated load provisions — Again, most building codes have a concentrated load (live load) provision in addition to standard application design loads. This load case considers this concentrated load to act in combination with the system dead loads on an otherwise unloaded floor. Usually, this provision applies to non-residential construction. An example is the 2000 lb. concentrated load over a 2 1/2 square foot area ("Safe" loading) required for office floors. This load case helps insure the product being evaluated has the required shear and moment capacity throughout its entire length and should be considered when analyzing the effect of web holes.

Combined with the various duration of load checks, a properly designed multiple span member requires numerous load case evaluations. Most Wood I-Joist producers have developed computer programs, load and span tables, or both, that take these various load cases into account.

DESIGN VALUES:

The **design values** for Wood I-Joists are often developed from extensive empirical test data and therefore may not agree with values developed solely through rational engineering calculations. For this reason, the latest Model Building Code Agency evaluation reports are generally a reliable source for Wood I-Joist **design values**. These reports list accepted **design values** for shear, moment, stiffness, and minimum bearing. In addition, these Evaluation Reports usually note the limitations on web holes, concentrated loads, and requirements for web stiffeners.

Each Wood I-Joist producer develops their own proprietary design values. The derivation of these values are monitored by the applicable building code authorities. Since materials, manufacturing processes, and product evaluations may differ between the various producers, selected **design values** are appropriate only for the intended product and application.

ENVIRONMENT AND TREATING EFFECTS:

The design values listed in the Evaluation Reports are generally applicable to dry conditions of use. **Environmental effects**, such as high moisture conditions, or pressure impregnated chemical treatments, may result in strength and stiffness adjustments different from those used for sawn lumber. Individual Wood I-Joist producers should be consulted for appropriate adjustments for unusual environmental conditions or treated applications.

SHEAR DESIGN:

At end bearing locations, the critical shear is the vertical shear at the end of the design span. The practice of neglecting all uniform loads within a distance from the end support equal to the joist depth, commonly used for other wood materials, is not applicable to Wood I-Joists. At locations of continuity, the critical shear location for several Wood I-Joist types is located a distance equal to the depth of the joist from the centerline of bearing (uniform loads only). A cantilevered portion of a Wood I-Joist is generally not considered a location of continuity (unless the cantilever length exceeds the joist depth) and vertical shear at the cantilever bearing is the critical shear. Individual producers, or the appropriate Evaluation Reports, should be consulted for reference to **shear design** at locations of continuity.

Often, the allowable shear value is based on other considerations such as bottom flange bearing length or the installation of web stiffeners or bearing blocks. Care must be taken to make sure that the allowable shear values used in the design are appropriate for the intended application and installation. Loads imposed upon a Wood I-Joist at a bearing location can undermine the members shear capacity, requiring attention to the bearing design and details.

MOMENT DESIGN:

Where joists are arranged in compliance with the qualifications for repetitive member design (i.e.: 3 or more adjacent members spaced 24" on center or less joined by a transverse load distributing decking capable of supporting the design loads), the allowable bending moment may be increased beyond single member design values. The **moment design** strength increases are based on the statistical strength variability of the specific flange material selected.

Joists with flanges made from laminated veneer lumber (LVL) or parallel strand lumber (PSL) usually can be increased 4% when the repetitive member design criteria is met. Joists with MSR lumber flanges can use an increase of 7% while joists with visually graded lumber flanges are allowed a repetitive member increase of 15%.

Because the flanges of the Wood I-Joist are highly stressed, field notching of the flange is not allowed because it will reduce the member's **moment design** capacity. Similarly, excessive flange nailing or the use of improper nail sizes can cause flange splitting that will also reduce capacity.

DEFLECTION DESIGN:

Wood I-Joists, due to their efficient utilization of wood fiber, are susceptible to the effects of shear deflection, usually insignificant in the design of sawn lumber members. This component of deflection can account for as much as 15% to 30% of the total deflection. For this reason, both bending and shear deflection should be considered in the **deflection design**. The general form for deflection calculations of Wood I-Joists follows:

Simple span uniform loads:

$$\text{Deflection} = \underbrace{\frac{5\,W\,L^4}{384\,E\,I}}_{\substack{\text{bending} \\ \text{component}}} + \underbrace{\frac{K\,W\,L^2}{8\,A_v\,G}}_{\substack{\text{shear} \\ \text{component}}}$$

For other loads and span conditions, an approximate answer can be found by using conventional bending deflection equations adjusted as follows:

$$\text{Deflection} = \left(\text{Bending Deflection}\right)\left(1 + \frac{384\,E I\,K}{40\,A_v GL^2}\right)$$

W	=	Uniform load in pounds per lineal inch
L	=	Design span in inches
EI	=	Joist moment of inertia times flange modulus of elasticity
K	=	Shear deflection coefficient
A_v	=	Effective joist section shear area
G	=	Shear modulus for the joist's web material

The values for use in these equations can be found by contacting an individual producer or from their Evaluation Reports.

Since Wood I-Joists have the inherent capability to span farther than conventional lumber, the model building code maximum live load deflection criteria may not be appropriate for many floor applications. Many Wood I-Joist producers recommend using stiffer criteria, such as L/480 for residential floor construction and L/600 for public access commercial applications like office floors. The minimum code required criteria for storage floors and roof applications is normally adequate.

FLOOR PERFORMANCE:

Designing a floor system to meet the minimum requirements of a building code may not always provide acceptable performance to the end user. Although these minimum criteria help assure a floor system can safely support the imposed loads, the system ultimately must perform to a level that provides satisfaction to the end user. Since expectancy levels may vary from one person to another, designing a floor system becomes a subjective issue requiring judgment as to the sensitivity of the intended occupant.

Joist deflection is often used as the sole means for designing in floor performance. Although deflection is a factor, there are other equally important variables that can influence the performance of a floor system. A glue-nailed floor system will generally have better deflection performance than a nail only system. Selection of the decking materials is also an important consideration. Deflection of the sheathing materials between joists can be reduced by placing the joists at a closer on center spacing or increasing the sheathing thickness.

Proper installation and job site storage are important considerations. All building materials, including the Wood I-Joists, need to be kept dry and protected from exposure to the elements. Proper installation includes correct spacing of the sheathing joints, care in fastening of the joists and sheathing, and providing adequate and level supports. All of these considerations are essential to the system performance.

Vibration may be a design consideration for floor systems that are stiff and where very little dead load (i.e.: partition walls, ceilings, furniture, etc.) exists. Vibrations can generally be damped with a ceiling system directly attached to the bottom flange of the Wood I-Joists. Effective bridging or continuous bottom flange nails (i.e.: 2x4 nailed flat-wise and perpendicular to the joist and tied to the end walls) can also help to minimize the potential for vibration in the absence of a direct applied ceiling.

BEARING DESIGN:

Bearing design for Wood I-Joists requires more than consideration for perpendicular to grain bearing values. The minimum required bearing length takes into account a number of considerations. These include: cross grain bending and tensile forces in the flanges, web stiffener connection to the joist web, adhesive joint locations, strength and durability, and perpendicular to grain bearing stresses. The model building code evaluation reports provide a source for **bearing design** information, usually in the form of minimum required bearing length.

Usually, published bearing lengths are based on the maximum allowable shear capacity of the particular product and depth. Bearing lengths for Wood I-Joists are most often based on empirical test results rather than a calculated approach. Each specific producer should be consulted for information where deviations from published criteria are desired.

To better understand the variables involved in a Wood I-Joist bearing, it's convenient to visualize the member as a composition of pieces, each serving a specific task. For a typical simple span joist, the top flange is a compression member, the bottom flange is a tension member, and the web resists the vertical shear force. Using this concept, shear forces accumulate in the web member at the bearing locations and must be transferred through the flange to the support structure. This transfer involves two critical interfaces: between the web and flange materials and between the flange and support member.

Starting with the support member, flange to support bearing involves perpendicular to grain stresses. The lowest design value for either the support member or flange material is usually used to develop the minimum required bearing area. This minimum bearing area is seldom the control for determining the minimum required bearing length.

The second interface to be checked is between the lower joist flange and the bottom edge of the joist web, assuming a bottom flange bearing condition. This connection, usually a routed groove in the flange and a matching shaped profile on the web, is a glued joint secured with a waterproof structural adhesive. The contact surfaces include the sides and bottom of the routed flange.

In most cases, the adhesive line stresses at this joint control the bearing length design. The effective bearing length of the web into the flange is approximately the length of flange bearing onto the support plus an incremental length related to the thickness and stiffness of the flange material.

Since most Wood I-Joists have web shear capacity in excess of the flange to web joint strength, connection reinforcement is often required. The most common method of reinforcement is the addition of web stiffeners (also commonly referred to as bearing blocks). Web stiffeners are vertically oriented wood blocks positioned on both sides of the web tight to the bearing flange at bearing locations and beneath heavy point loads within a span (snug to the bottom of the top flange). Figure 3 shows a typical end bearing assembly.

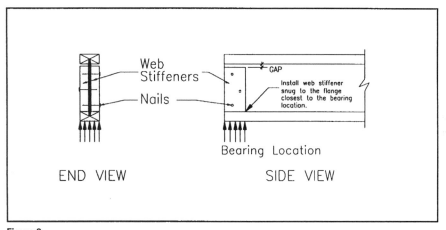

Figure 3

WEB STIFFENERS:

When correctly fastened to the joist web, web stiffeners transfer some of the load from the web into the top of the bottom flange. This reduces the loads on the web to flange joint. A pair of web stiffeners (one on each side) is usually mechanically connected to the web with nails or staples loaded in double shear. For some of the higher capacity Wood I-Joists, nailing and supplemental gluing with a structural adhesive is required. The added bearing capacity achievable with web stiffeners is limited to allowable bearing stresses where they contact the bearing flange, and the mechanical connection to the web.

Web stiffeners also serve the implied function of reinforcing the web against buckling. Since shear capacity usually increases proportionately with the depth, web stiffeners are very important for deep Wood I-Joists. For example, a 30" deep Wood I-Joist may only develop 20 to 30 percent of its shear and bearing capacity without properly attached web stiffeners at the bearing locations. This is especially important at continuous span bearing locations, where reaction magnitudes can exceed simple span reactions by an additional 25 percent.

Wood I-joists

For shallow depth joists, where relatively low shear capacities are required, web stiffeners may not be needed. When larger reaction capacities are required, web stiffener reinforcement may be needed, especially where short bearing lengths are desired.

Web stiffeners should be cut short so as not to contact the opposite joist flange. If they are cut too long and force fit, the inherent prying action can fracture the critical adhesive joint between the flange and web. When properly installed, the gap created by cutting them short is positioned opposite of the imposed load or bearing. Figure 4 illustrates the bearing interfaces.

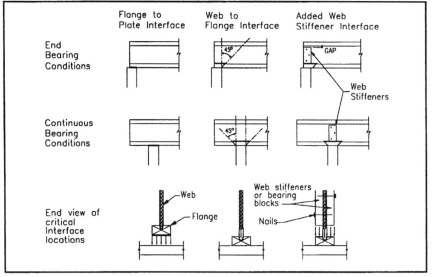

Figure 4

SLOPED BEARING CONDITIONS:

Sloped bearing conditions require design considerations that are different from conventional lumber. An example is a birdsmouth bearing cut (notches in the bottom flange — see Figure 5). This type of bearing should only be used on the low end bearing for Wood I-Joists. Another example is the use of metal joist support connectors that attach only to the web area of the joist and do not provide a bottom seat in which to bear. In general, this type of connector is not recommended for use with Wood I-Joists without consideration for the resulting reduced capacity.

The birdsmouth cut is a good solution for the low bearing when the slope is steep and the tangential loads are high (loads along the axis of the joist member). This assumes the quality of construction is good and the cuts are made correctly and at the right locations. This type of bearing cut requires some skill and is not easy to make, particularly with the wider flanged joists. The bearing capacity, especially with high shear capacity members, may be reduced as a result of the cut since the effective flange bearing area is reduced. The notched cut will also reduce the member's shear and moment capacity at a cantilever location.

An alternative to a birdsmouth cut is a beveled bearing plate matching the joist slope or special sloped seat bearing hardware manufactured by some metal connector suppliers. These alternatives also have special design considerations when used with steep slope applications. As the member slope increases, so does the tangential component of reaction, sometimes requiring additional flange to bearing nailing or straps to provide resistance. Figure 5 shows some examples of acceptable low end bearing conditions.

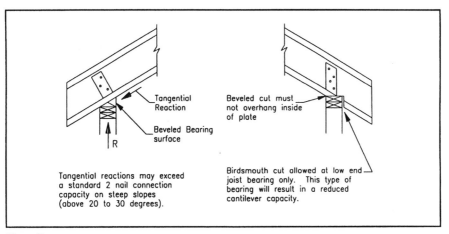

Figure 5

For the high end support, bottom flange bearing in a suitable connector or on a beveled plate is recommended. When slopes exceed approximately 30°, straps or gussets may be needed to resist the tangential component of the reaction.

Support connections to the web area of a Wood I-Joist, especially at the high end of a sloped application, are not generally recommended. Since a Wood I-Joist is made up of a number of pieces, joints between web sections occurring near the end of the member may reduce the joist's shear capacity when not supported from the bottom flange.

When a Wood I-Joist is supported from the web only, the closest web to web joint from the end may be stressed in tension. This could result in a joint failure with the web section pulling out of the bottom flange. Locating these internal joints away from the end of the member or applying joint reinforcements are potential remedies, but generally are not practical in the field.

The best bearing solution is to provide direct support to the joist's bottom flange to avoid reductions in capacity. Figure 6 shows typical high end bearing conditions.

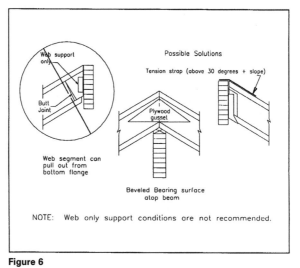

Figure 6

Wood I-joists

Beveled end cuts, where the end of the joist is cut on an angle (top flange does not project over the bearing, much like a fire cut), also require special design consideration. Again the severity of the angle, web material, location of web section joints, and web stiffener application criteria affect the performance of this type of bearing condition. The specific Wood I-Joist producers should be consulted for limits on this type of end cut.

It is generally accepted that if a Wood I-Joist has the minimum required bearing length, and the top flange of the joist is not cut beyond the face of bearing (measured from a line perpendicular to the joist's bottom flange), there is no reduction in shear capacity. This differs from the conventional lumber provision that suggests there is no decrease in shear strength for beveled cuts of up to an angle of 45°. The reason involves the composite nature of the Wood I-Joist and how the member fails in shear and/or bearing. Figure 7 provides an illustration of the beveled end cut limitation.

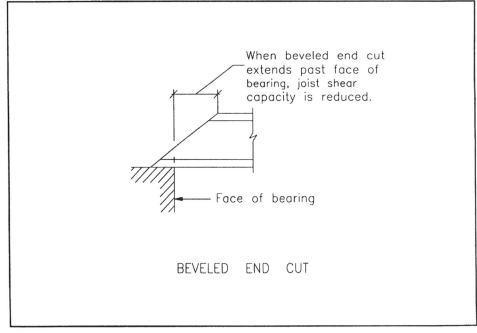

When beveled end cut extends past face of bearing, joist shear capacity is reduced.

Face of bearing

BEVELED END CUT

Figure 7

CONNECTOR DESIGN/JOIST HANGERS:

Although there are numerous hangers and connectors available that appear compatible with Wood I-Joists, many are not. Hangers developed for conventional lumber or glulam beams often use large nails and space them in a pattern that will split the joist flanges and web stiffeners. Hanger selection considerations for Wood I-Joists should include nail length and diameter, nail location, Wood I-Joist bearing capacity, composition of the supporting member, physical fit, and load capacity. For example, hangers appropriate for a Wood I-Joist to glulam beam support may not be compatible for a Wood I-Joist to Wood I-Joist connection.

In general, nails into the flanges should not exceed the diameter of a 10d common nail, with a recommended length no greater than 11/2". Nails into web stiffeners should not exceed the diameter of a 16d common nail. Nails through the sides of the hanger, when used in combination with web stiffeners, can be used to reduce the joist's minimum required bearing length. Nails help transfer loads directly from the joist web into the hanger, reducing the load transferred through direct bearing in the bottom hanger seat.

Hangers should be capable of providing lateral support to the top compression flange of the joist. This is usually accomplished by a hanger flange that extends the full depth of the joist. As a minimum, hanger support should extend to at least mid-height of a joist used with web stiffeners. Some connector manufacturers have developed hangers specifically for use with Wood I-Joists that provide full lateral support without the use of web stiffeners. Figure 8 illustrates lateral joist support requirements for hangers.

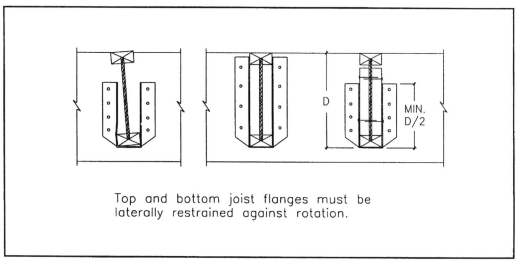

Top and bottom joist flanges must be laterally restrained against rotation.

Figure 8

When top flange style hangers are used to support one joist from another, especially the wider flanged Wood I-Joists, web stiffeners need to be installed tight to the bottom side of the support joists to flange. This prevents cross grain bending and rotation of the top flange. Figure 9 shows top flange hanger considerations.

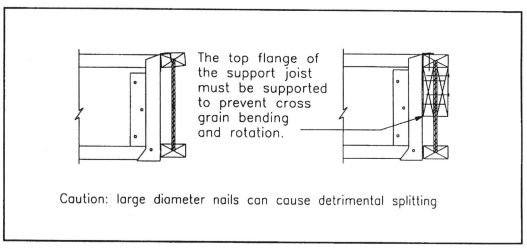

The top flange of the support joist must be supported to prevent cross grain bending and rotation.

Caution: large diameter nails can cause detrimental splitting

Figure 9

Wood I-joists

When face nail hangers are used for joist to joist connections, nails into the support joist should extend through and beyond the web element. Filler blocks should also be attached sufficiently to provide support for the hanger. Again, nail diameter should be considered to avoid splitting the filler block material.

Multiple joists need to be adequately connected together to achieve desired performance. This requires proper selection of a nailing or bolting pattern and attention to web stiffener and blocking needs. Considering that most framers carry only 10d and 16d nails in their aprons, nailing together multiple joists wider than 2 1/2" can be a problem.

For a double joist member loaded from one side only, the minimum connection between members should be capable of transferring at least 50% of the applied load. Likewise, for a triple member loaded from one side only, the minimum connection between members must be capable of transferring at least 2/3 of the applied load. The actual connection design should consider the potential slip and differential member stiffness. Many producers recommend limiting multiple members to 3 joists, 2 for 3 1/2" wide joists.

The low torsional resistance of most Wood I-Joists is also a design consideration for joist to joist connections. Eccentrically applied side loads, such as a top flange hanger hung from the side of a double joist, create the potential for joist rotation. Bottom flange restraining straps, blocking, or directly applied ceiling systems may be needed on heavily loaded eccentric connections to resist rotation. Figure 10 shows additional joist connection considerations for use with face nail hangers.

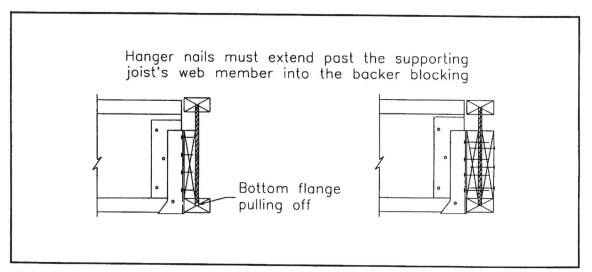

Figure 10

LOAD TRANSFER DESIGN:

Bearing loads originating above the joists at the bearing location require blocking to transfer these loads around the Wood I-Joist. This is typically the case in a multi-story structure where bearing walls stack and platform framing is used. Usually, the available bearing capacity of the joist is needed to support its reaction, leaving little if any excess capacity to support additional bearing wall loads from above.

The most common type of blocking uses short pieces of Wood I-Joist, often referred to as blocking panels, positioned directly over the lower bearing and cut to fit in between the joists. These panels also provide lateral support for the joists and an easy means to transfer lateral diaphragm shears.

The ability to transfer lateral loads (due to wind, seismic construction loads, etc.) to shear walls or foundations below is important to the integrity of the building design. Compared with dimension lumber blocking, which usually is toe-nailed to the bearing below, Wood I-Joist blocking can develop higher diaphragm transfer values because of a wider member width and better nail values.

Floor sheathing material, cut in strips equal to the joist depth, can also be used as a rim joist to support the loads from above. This solution, without additional attachment detailing, may not provide sufficient diaphragm boundary nailing where lateral loads are a specific design concern. Hence, blocking is often specified at corners of the building to provide for lateral load transfer through the floor structure.

A third method uses vertically oriented short studs, often called squash or cripple blocks, on each side of the joist and cut to a length slightly longer than the depth of the joist. This method should be used in combination with some type of rim joist or blocking material when lateral stability or diaphragm transfer is required.

The use of horizontally oriented sawn lumber as a blocking material is strongly discouraged. Wood I-Joists generally do not shrink in the vertical direction due to their panel type web, creating the potential for a mismatch in height as sawn lumber shrinks to achieve equilibrium. When conventional lumber is used in the vertical orientation, shrinkage problems are not a problem because changes in elongation due to moisture changes are minimal. Figure 11 shows a few common methods for developing vertical load transfer. [**Author's note**: Although used extensively in the past, both the single layer plywood rim joist detail (left) and the cripple block without rim joist detail (center) shown in Figure 11 are now discouraged by most wood I-joist manufacturers and building code agencies because of the difficulty in ensuring these connections' lateral capacity. In both cases, manufacturers should be contacted for recommended alternatives.]

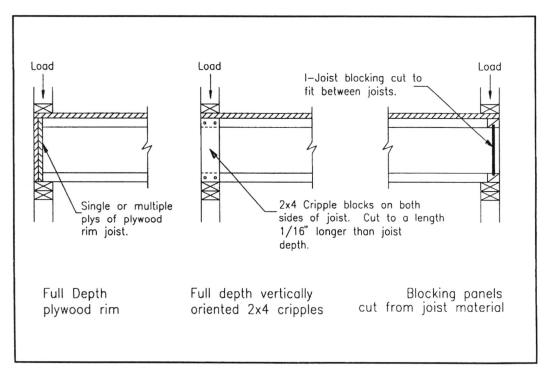

Figure 11

WEB HOLE DESIGN:

Holes cut in the web of a Wood I-Joist affect the member's shear capacity. Usually, the larger the hole, the greater the reduction in shear capacity. For this reason, holes are generally located in areas where shear loads are low. This explains why the largest holes are generally permitted near mid-span of a member. The required spacing between holes and from the end of the member is dependent upon the specific materials and processes used.

The allowable shear capacity of a Wood I-Joist at a hole location is influenced by a number of variables. These include: percentage of web removed, proximity to a vertical joint between web segments, the strength of the web to flange glue joint, flange stiffness, and the shear strength of the web material. Since Wood I-Joists may be manufactured using different processes and materials, each producer should be consulted for the proper **web hole design.**

The methodology used to analyze the application loads is important in the evaluation of web holes. All load cases should be considered that will develop the highest shear at the hole location. Usually, for members resisting simple uniform design loads, the loading condition that develops the highest shear loads in the center area of a joist span involves partial span loading.

Web holes do contribute somewhat to increased deflection. The larger the hole, the larger the contribution. Provided there are not too many holes involved, the contribution is negligible. In most cases, using a producer's recommended hole criteria and limiting the number to three or less per span, the additional deflection does not warrant consideration.

LATERAL STABILITY:

The design values contained in the Evaluation Reports assume continuous lateral stability of the joist's compression edge and lateral torsional restraint at the support locations. This stability is provided generally by diaphragm sheathing or bracing at 16" on center or less (based on 11/2" width joist flange) nailed to the joist's compression flange.

Applications without continuous lateral bracing will generally have reduced moment design capacities. The reduced capacity results from the increased potential for lateral buckling of the joist's compression flange. Consultation with individual producers is recommended for all applications without continuous lateral bracing.

SPECIAL LOADS OR APPLICATIONS:

Wood I-Joists are configured and optimized to act primarily as joists to resist bending loads. Applications that result in significant axial tension or compression loads, requiring web holes, special connections, or other unusual conditions should be evaluated only with the assistance of the individual Wood I-Joist producer.

Other Design Considerations

Computer Design Programs

In recent years there has been a proliferation of programs for computer-aided structural design in wood. Some include rather sketchy attempts to account for applications of wood I-joists. Caution should be exercised when using these generic design programs for wood I-joists because of the somewhat complex design considerations and the unique requirements and properties of these proprietary products (16). The designer or specifier is advised to seek design support directly from the manufacturers of wood I-joists, who typically have engineers on call specifically for this purpose.

Fire

The thinner webs and smaller flanges of the lighter series of wood I-joists are arguably vulnerable during direct exposure to fire, as are the smaller sizes of sawn lumber, and for that matter, light gauge steel framing. These and other fire- and heat-susceptible structural members ought to be shielded from direct exposure to flame. Although building codes may not require such protection in single family dwellings, a layer of fire-resistant material— such as gypsum board—can easily be applied to the bottom of wood I-joists (7). Such protection can isolate the fire below the members and significantly extend the amount of time occupants have to evacuate the building. This often allows firefighters to extinguish the flames before structural damage occurs.

Fire-rated floor/ceiling systems constructed with wood I-joists that meet the criteria of *ASTM E119 Standard Test Methods for Fire Tests of Building Construction and Materials* (24) and *CAN/ULC-S101-M89* (25) are specified in either the building code acceptances or in published certified listings for these products. Fire-rated systems include 45-minute, 1-hour and, in some cases, 2-hour rated protection. To ensure compliance, the designer or specifier must strictly adhere to the specified materials and construction details. Substitute materials may not provide the same fire resistance. Good workmanship in installing materials is key in maximizing the fire safety of these systems. Research on the fire performance of wood I-joist floor/ceiling systems, including full-scale fire tests and fire modeling, is on-going. WIJMA offers an informational video on the topic, *I-Joist Fire Video Reference Guide*.

Fire Sprinklers

Automatic fire suppression is the latest trend in modern fire protection design. The recent improvements in fire sprinkler design, performance and economy ought to be considered when designing any wood-frame structure. Though some wood I-joist manufacturers offer details for attaching sprinkler hardware and piping to their products, the only standard that addresses the location and method for installing sprinklers in structures is the National Fire Protection Association's *NFPA 13 Standard for the Installation of Sprinkler Systems* (14). Provisions for wood I-joists, as well as other approved structural systems, are contained in Chapter 4 of this consensus standard, which is published every three years. NFPA's Fire

Sprinkler Subcommittee is responsible for reviewing the standard and making recommendations for action to the Main Sprinkler Committee, who then prepares a draft document for public comment.

Sound Transmission

Reducing the transmission of sound through wood-frame floor/ceiling systems has become increasingly important, especially in condominiums and multi-family housing. When used in conjunction with sound-deadening construction methods, the dimensional consistency and stability of wood I-joists can help reduce the transmission of both airborne sound and sound created when a floor is set into vibration by impacts like footfalls. Several wood I-joist manufacturers include techniques for creating both sound transmission class- and impact insulation class-rated floor/ceiling systems in their building code acceptances and technical literature. As with fire performance, material selection and good workmanship are vital in limiting sound transmission.

Creep

Concern has been expressed about creep—the progressive deflection of a structural material under long term loading—in wood I-joists, particularly for those with OSB webs. Research has shown that the creep performance of wood I-joists is on a par with that of sawn lumber joist systems (4, 5, 6). However, the designer or specifier is encouraged to require in the product specification that web material with a high shear modulus be used.

Bridging

The primary purpose of bridging between sawn lumber joists is to promote load-sharing among the members. The greater the variability in strength and stiffness among the members, the greater the need for load-sharing and bridging. For most wood I-joist systems, the variability in structural performance among members is very small. As a result, the building code acceptances have deemed bridging between wood I-joists to be unnecessary. Tests of full-scale floor systems have confirmed that conventional bridging offers little or no benefit to the system's structural performance and reliability. However, some wood I-joist manufacturers provide specific bridging details for the purpose of enhancing floor performance by reducing annoying floor vibrations (17).

Job Site Concerns

Accustomed to using commodity products like sawn lumber and plywood, builders tend to assume equivalence among all wood I-joists because of their similar appearance. But because wood I-joists are proprietary products, this is not the case. Upon receiving wood I-joists at the job site, builders should verify that they bear the manufacturer's name; the product series or grade; the date of manufacture; the relevant building code evaluation service report number; and the quality mark of the approved inspection agency. The presence of these marks indicates to the local building officials that the product is approved for use in their jurisdiction. While these identifications are seemingly minimal assurances, there have been numerous instances where their absence created unnecessary problems and delays during framing inspections.

The manufacturer's installation instructions are typically provided with the delivered product. In some cases this may include custom layout drawings that give specific cut-to-length instructions and identify where each wood I-joist is to be installed. In other cases, the installation instructions may simply contain suggestions and warnings related to the proper storage and handling of the product; layout drawings are provided by the designer or specifier.

Storage
Like all wood and wood-based products, wood I-joists should be protected from the elements while stored on site. Bundled wood I-joists should be kept upright at all times (webs vertical), and stored off the ground on an adequate number of stickers and covered with a loosely draped tarp to protect them from rain or snow.

Bracing
Wood I-joists tend to be laterally unstable during handling and erection because of their long lengths and thin webs. Manufacturers' instructions for properly bracing wood I-joists during erection must be followed (Fig. 6) (15). Otherwise, there is a potential danger for wood I-joists to buckle laterally or roll over when walked on, until they are finally stabilized by attaching the sheathing. Builders tend to take undue risks, and there have been far too many accidents and injuries due to buckling and roll over.

Attachment of Sheathing
Sheathing must be attached to wood I-joists in accordance with the diaphragm design, when applicable, as well as with the requirements of the governing building code, and the sheathing and I-joist manufacturers. Most wood I-joist manufacturers publish minimum on-center nail spacings and nail row spacings for each series or type of wood I-joist they offer. Spacings must not be infringed—missed or improperly driven fasteners can result in squeaks and increase the transmission of sound. Specifications often call for sheathing to be both glued and nailed because this increases the floor system's stiffness. The diaphragm design for seismic resistance and special load considerations, especially in commercial construction, may require special methods of sheathing attachment. Most wood I-joist manufacturers provide technical assistance for such cases.

Holes
Under no circumstances should holes or notches ever be cut in the flanges of a wood I-joist; doing so may seriously compromise its strength. The webs of wood I-joists routinely contain regularly spaced circular knockouts for running utilities. Holes can be cut elsewhere in the web of an I-joist, however, their size and placement is limited by their location along the member's length. Most wood I-joist manufacturers publish illustrated guides to assist electricians, plumbers and heating contractors in determining the permissible hole size and placement.

TYPICAL INSTALLATION INFORMATION

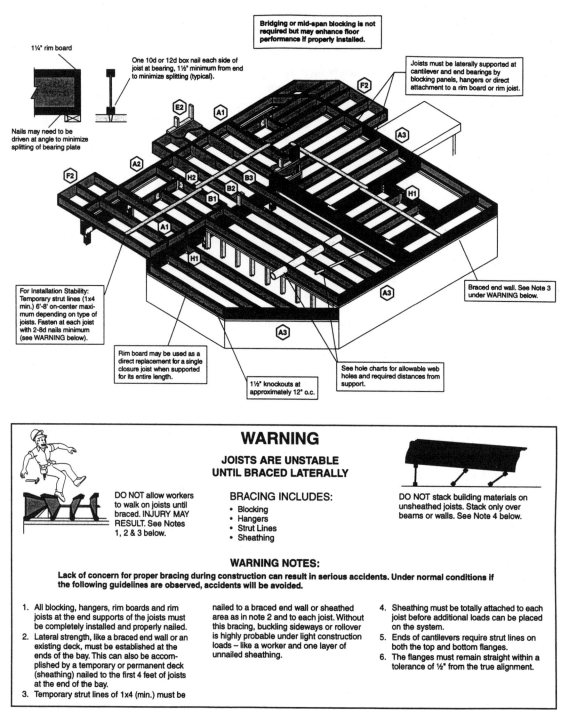

Bridging or mid-span blocking is not required but may enhance floor performance if properly installed.

1¼" rim board

One 10d or 12d box nail each side of joist at bearing, 1½" minimum from end to minimize splitting (typical).

Joists must be laterally supported at cantilever and end bearings by blocking panels, hangers or direct attachment to a rim board or rim joist.

Nails may need to be driven at angle to minimize splitting of bearing plate

For Installation Stability: Temporary strut lines (1x4 min.) 6'-8' on-center maximum depending on type of joists. Fasten at each joist with 2-8d nails minimum (see WARNING below).

Braced end wall. See Note 3 under WARNING below.

Rim board may be used as a direct replacement for a single closure joist when supported for its entire length.

1½" knockouts at approximately 12" o.c.

See hole charts for allowable web holes and required distances from support.

WARNING

JOISTS ARE UNSTABLE
UNTIL BRACED LATERALLY

DO NOT allow workers to walk on joists until braced. INJURY MAY RESULT. See Notes 1, 2 & 3 below.

BRACING INCLUDES:
- Blocking
- Hangers
- Strut Lines
- Sheathing

DO NOT stack building materials on unsheathed joists. Stack only over beams or walls. See Note 4 below.

WARNING NOTES:

Lack of concern for proper bracing during construction can result in serious accidents. Under normal conditions if the following guidelines are observed, accidents will be avoided.

1. All blocking, hangers, rim boards and rim joists at the end supports of the joists must be completely installed and properly nailed.
2. Lateral strength, like a braced end wall or an existing deck, must be established at the ends of the bay. This can also be accomplished by a temporary or permanent deck (sheathing) nailed to the first 4 feet of joists at the end of the bay.
3. Temporary strut lines of 1x4 (min.) must be

nailed to a braced end wall or sheathed area as in note 2 and to each joist. Without this bracing, buckling sideways or rollover is highly probable under light construction loads – like a worker and one layer of unnailed sheathing.

4. Sheathing must be totally attached to each joist before additional loads can be placed on the system.
5. Ends of cantilevers require strut lines on both the top and bottom flanges.
6. The flanges must remain straight within a tolerance of ½" from the true alignment.

Figure 6. Literature explaining the methods for safely and properly installing wood I-joists is available from most wood I-joist manufacturers and WIJMA.

Connectors

Wood I-joists are often face-mounted on girders of sawn timber, glued laminated timber or structural composite lumber using metal hangers fastened with nails (26). Most wood I-joist manufacturers publish guidelines to help builders choose the proper type and size connectors, as well as the correct fasteners. These guidelines, as well as those presented in WIJMA's *Technical Bulletin No. 1 Design Guidelines* are especially useful when wood I-joists are used as roof joists that bear on a structural ridge beam because the beveled end cuts often complicate matters beyond a builder's experience with sawn lumber rafters .

Suggested Specification

The specification for wood I-joists should state that the product must meet the requirements of the governing industry or product standard—*ASTM D5055* in the United States or *CSA 086.1-M94* in Canada—and the quality assurance provisions therein. The product must have a current acceptance from the governing building code agency. Wood I-joists should be clearly marked with the name of the manufacturer, the product series or type, the date of manufacture, the building code evaluation service report number, and the quality mark of the third-party inspection agency. When required, the engineering shop drawings must be available from the manufacturer, otherwise, the manufacturer's technical literature showing installation details and load/span capacities must be available.

As wood I-joists are proprietary products, most manufacturers have engineers on staff to assist architects, designers and builders in writing specifications and selecting the correct product(s) for the application.

References

1. Guss, L. 1995. Engineered Wood Products: The Future is Bright. Forest Products Journal. 45(7/8):17-24.

2. ICBO Evaluation Service, Inc. 1988. AC14 Acceptance Criteria for Prefabricated Wood I-Joists. ICBO. Whittier, California.

3. American Society For Testing and Materials. 1990. ASTM D5055 Standard Specification for Establishing and Monitoring Structural Capacities of Prefabricated Wood I-Joists. ASTM. West Conshohocken, Pennsylvania.

4. Leichti, R. 1986. Assessing The Reliability of Wood Composite I-Beams. Ph. D. dissertation. Auburn University. Auburn, Alabama.

5. Leichti, R. and R. Tang. 1984. Composite I-Beam Compares Favorably With Traditional Solid Sawn Lumber. Highlights of Agricultural Research. Alabama Agricultural Experiment Station. Auburn University. Auburn, Alabama. 31(2):4.

6. Leichti, R. and R. Tang. 1986. Creep Analysis of Wood Composite I-Beams. Pages 484-489 *in* Proceedings Southeastern Conference on Theoretical and Applied Mechanics XIII. University of South Carolina. Columbia, South Carolina.

7. Canadian Wood Council. 1991. Wood Reference Handbook. CWC. Ottawa, Ontario, Canada.

8. Wood I-Joist Manufacturers Association. 1994. Technical Bulletin No.1 Design Guidelines. WIJMA. Madison, Wisconsin.

9. Forest Products Laboratory. 1943. Design of Plywood Webs for Box Beams. Report 1318. USDA Forest Service Forest Products Laboratory. Madison, Wisconsin.

10. Lewis, W. and E. Dawley. 1943. Stiffeners In Box Beams and Details of Design. Report 1318-A. USDA Forest Service Forest Products Laboratory. Madison, Wisconsin.

11. Lewis, W., T. Heebrink, W. Cottingham and E. Dawley. 1943. Buckling in Shear Webs of Box and I-Beams and the Effect Upon Design Criteria. Report 1318-B. USDA Forest Service Forest Products Laboratory. Madison, Wisconsin.

12. Lewis, W., T. Heebrink, W. Cottingham and E. Dawley. 1944. Additional Tests of Box and I-Beams to Substantiate Further the Design Curves for Plywood Webs In Box Beams. Report 1318-C. USDA Forest Service Forest Products Laboratory. Madison, Wisconsin.

13. Lewis, W., T. Heebrink and W. Cottingham. 1944. Buckling and Ultimate Strengths of Shear Webs of Box Beams Having Plywood Face Grain Direction Parallel or Perpendicular to the Axis of the Beams. Report 1318-D. USDA Forest Service Forest Products Laboratory. Madison, Wisconsin.

14. National Fire Protection Association. 1994. NFPA 13 Standard for the Installation of Sprinkler Systems. NFPA. Quincy, Massachusetts.

15. Eck, C. 1995. Wood I-Joist Do's and Don'ts. Journal of Light Construction. 13(12):34-37.

16. Nelson, S. 1994. Design Considerations for Structural Composite Lumber and Prefabricated Wood I-Joists. Wood Design Focus. 5(1):8-13.

17. Chui, Y. 1994. Vibrational Performance of Wood Floor Systems: Optimization of Performance and Retrofitting. Wood Design Focus. 5(3):8-11.

18. American Society for Testing and Materials. 1992. D2559 Standard Specification for Adhesives for Structural Laminated Wood Products for Use Under Exterior (Wet Use) Conditions. ASTM. West Conshohocken, Pennsylvania.

19. Canadian Standards Association. 1977. CSA O112-M Standards for Wood Adhesives. CSA. Rexdale, Ontario, Canada.

20. Leichti, R., R. Falk and T. Laufenberg. 1990. Prefabricated Wood Composite I-Beams: A Literature Review. Wood and Fiber Science. 22(1):62-79.

21. Leichti, R., R. Falk and T. Laufenberg. 1990. Prefabricated Wood I-Joists: An Industry Overview. Forest Products Journal. 40(3):15-20.

22. Canadian Standards Association. 1994. CSA O86.1-M94 Engineering Design In Wood (Limit States Design) A National Standard of Canada. CSA. Rexdale, Ontario, Canada.

23. European Committee for Standardization. 1995. Eurocode 5 Design of Timber Structures. CEN. Brussels, Belgium.

24. American Society for Testing and Materials. 1992. E119 Standard Test Methods for Fire Tests of Building Construction and Materials. ASTM. West Conshohocken, Pennsylvania.

25. Underwriters Laboratories, Inc. 1989. CAN/ULC-S101-M89. Fire Endurance Tests of Building Construction and Materials. Northbrook, Illinois.

26. Maly, J. 1990. Special Design Considerations for Wood I-joists. Wood Design Focus. 1(1):12-15.

27. American Plywood Association. 1968. Plywood Design Specification Supplement No. 2 Design of Plywood Beams. APA. Tacoma, Washington.

Chapter 5

Oriented Strand Board and Waferboard

John Lowood, P. E.

Structural Board Association
Willowdale, Ontario, Canada

Oriented strand board or OSB is an engineered structural use panel manufactured from thin wood strands bonded together with waterproof resin under heat and pressure. Used extensively for roof, wall and floor sheathing in residential and commercial construction, OSB is actually a second generation panel that evolved from the original waferboard, a structural use panel developed in 1954 by Dr. James d'Arcy Clarke, an internationally-respected wood scientist. An early environmentalist, Clarke was looking for a way to use the "weed" species left in the forests of the northwestern United States after harvesting the more valuable Douglas-fir, true firs, spruces and pines, as well as slabs, edgings and other sawmill "waste". At the time, aspen—a fast-growing hardwood—and these other species were not considered suitable for lumber, veneer and pulp.

Familiar with nonstructural chipboard, particleboard and hardboard, Clarke felt he could make a panel with structural properties by utilizing the strength of long aspen fibers rather than by cutting or breaking them into short lengths. He discovered that the shavings or wafers produced by slicing freshly harvested aspen logs along the grain—as one would whittle a piece of wood with a knife—could then be bonded together with a phenolic resin and pressed into a panel that had many of the characteristics of construction grade plywood. Thus, waferboard was born. Impressed by his invention, Clarke's employer constructed a small waferboard mill near Sand Point, Idaho, and sold the panels locally.

Encouraged by the abundance of aspen in the forests of northern Canada, a group of businessmen in Saskatchewan purchased Clarke's patent in 1961, and formed Wisewood Limited to manufacture waferboard. The first mill was built on the edge of Canada's boreal forest in northeastern Saskatchewan in the town of Hudson Bay. Wishing to strengthen the economy of this marginal farming region, the provincial government allocated to the mill an abundance of good quality wood fiber.

Sensing a threat, distributors loyal to the plywood interests refused to stock waferboard, leaving Wisewood to sell to small builders and farmers in Saskatchewan. The fact that many of the barns, grain bins and fences made with this product are still in use today is strong evidence of the durability of waferboard and its exterior grade resin. With a limited market and a lack of building code approval, Wisewood soon faced bankruptcy.

In 1963, the Saskatchewan government sold its interest in Wisewood to MacMillan Bloedel Limited, a large Canadian forest products company with pulp, newsprint, lumber and plywood interests, who was looking for a lower cost panel product to complement its large softwood plywood production. With its national distribution system and the resources to carry out product research and obtain building code approval, MacMillan Bloedel successfully restarted the mill, which contained one 14-opening press 4 feet by 16 feet. The press, dryers, resin blenders and forming line were modified particleboard equipment, while the waferizer was a large horizontal chipper that sliced rather than chipped the 2-foot-long log blocks fed to it. Renamed Aspenite, the product became an overnight success because it was strong, durable and cost less than plywood.

MacMillan Bloedel marketed Aspenite in central Canada for roof, wall and floor sheathing in barns, cattle sheds and garages. Other uses included grain bins, fences, packaging and hoarding. MacMillan Bloedel's researchers developed grooved panel siding, underlayment and concrete forming panels. Its technical field staff successfully presented Aspenite to architects, engineers, designers and builders because it was priced lower than plywood. Many of the buildings constructed in the 1960s with Aspenite are still used today. Eventually, Aspenite became a generic term for waferboard much like Masonite had earlier become the generic term for hardboard.

In 1973, a second waferboard mill opened in Timmins, Ontario to exploit the aspen resource in the spruce and pine forests in north central Ontario. The Waferboard Corporation marketed Malette Waferboard through the national distribution arm of Canadian Forest Products Ltd. Canfor Building Materials Division. Like MacMillan Bloedel, Canfor used the Malette product to supplement its plywood sales.

Throughout the 1970s, other waferboard mills were constructed in Canada, and the first mills built in the boreal forest areas of the United States. The first true OSB mill was not constructed until 1982, although mills producing oriented waferboard were in operation prior to this.

The Raw Material

The original waferboard product followed the Clarke patent and was manufactured from aspen which was abundant in central Canada and in the north central United States. However, when the industry expanded into the southern United States in the late 1970s southern yellow pine began to be used. With the conversion from waferboard to OSB in the 1980s, and expansion of the industry, other species such as white birch, red maple, sweetgum and yellow-poplar were found to be suitable. Other hardwoods could also be added to the mix, but only in small quantities. In Canada, OSB has been successfully made with eastern white pine and spruce, while at least one western mill is using a mixture of aspen and jack pine. Others use balsam poplar and white birch. With the opening of plants in Scotland and France in the mid-1980s, Scots pine and maritime pine began to be used. The newest mill in Chile uses radiata pine. Plants under construction in Asia and Australia will likely use rubberwood and eucalyptus.

The Manufacturing Process

The principle of reconstituting wood fiber into panels was well-known when Clarke invented waferboard. Up to that time, however, no one had attempted to make a panel entirely out of thin wafers of wood. Chipboard—which is often confused with waferboard because the coarse particles of wood in its core are overlaid with thin, chips of wood—had been produced in Europe for several years. Particleboard and hardboard, which are made from coarse particles and wood fibers, respectively, had been around for many years. The only true structural use panel suitable for exterior use at the time of Clarke's discovery was Douglas-fir plywood.

In a generic manufacturing process for waferboard or OSB, debarked logs are heated in soaking ponds, then sliced into thin wood elements. The wafers or strands are dried, blended with resin and wax, and formed into thick, loose mats which are pressed under heat and pressure into large panels. The panels are then sawn into 4-foot by 8-foot sheets, and solid-piled or hot stacked for 12 to 48 hours before being shipped (Fig. 1).

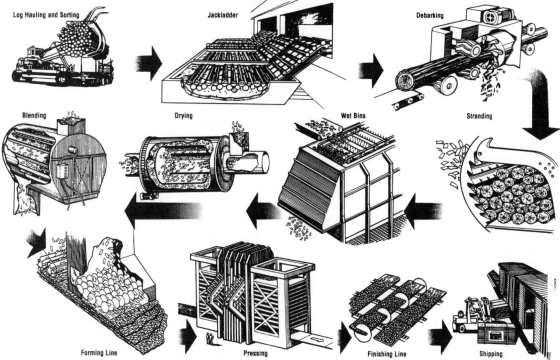

Figure 1. The computer-controlled process for making oriented strand board is highly automated; most plants operate round-the-clock.

Aspen logs must be heated in large tanks or soaking ponds of hot water to soften the wood prior to slicing. Early ponds were heated by direct steam injection, but today heat exchangers using hot oil or direct-fired coil heaters are used. Mills using southern yellow pine and mixed hardwoods do not need to heat the wood, however, they are gradually installing soaking ponds because heating the logs significantly improves the slicing process and wafer and strand quality.

The Manufacture of Waferboard

Early waferboard mills resembled particleboard mills except for the wafer preparation section. This section contained equipment to thaw frozen logs in winter and heat logs year-round prior to debarking and waferizing. Also found here was a saw to cut the approximately 8-foot-long logs into blocks 28 to 32 inches long.

To produce the long-fiber wafers that give waferboard its strength, the waferizer was designed specifically to slice wafers of a predetermined size and geometry from green logs. This required a disc-type chipper which sliced the wood along the grain rather than chipping it across the grain as did a conventional chipper. The waferizer resembled a horizontal disc chipper, except that the log blocks were fed lengthwise against knives embedded in the face of the rotating disc rather than butt first, so that wafers would be sliced from the block, not chipped. The early waferizers were fed log blocks held in a vertical chute so that they were held against the disc by gravity. In later machines, the discs were mounted vertically. Log blocks were forced against them by a chain mechanism whose spikes grabbed each end of the blocks as the chains moved them towards the rotating knife disc.

Wafer geometry varied, but generally wafers were roughly rectangular—about 1 inch wide, up to 1.5 inches in length and 0.03 inches thick.

Green wafers were stored in bins temporarily, then dried in a triple-pass dryer heated with steam, natural gas or a direct-fired unit. The dried wafers were held in dry bins until needed, then passed through a rotating blender where they were sprayed with resin and wax before being sent to the forming line. Here, wafers were dropped onto a moving conveyor belt into a loose mat, which under heat and pressure, was pressed into a panel. Like particleboard, a three-layer panel was produced. No attempt was made to orient the wafers, so the product was called "random" waferboard. Later developments in mat forming gave some orientation to the wafers, which increased the panel's strength in one direction. Hence, "oriented" waferboard.

The Manufacture of Oriented Strand Board

Oriented strand board is a second generation panel that evolved from the original waferboard. The first true OSB panel was produced in 1982 at the Edson OSB Division of Pelican Sawmills Limited in Alberta, Canada. Having strength and stiffness equivalent to plywood, OSB was marketed as being superior to waferboard and as an alternative to plywood. OSB differs from waferboard in that it is made from long, narrow strands, with the strands of each of its layers aligned parallel to one another, but perpendicular to those in adjacent layers, like the cross-laminated veneers of plywood. It is this perpendicular orientation of different layers of aligned strands that gives OSB its unique characteristics and allows it to be engineered to suit different uses. OSB mills are highly automated, large-volume producers that often operate 24 hours a day. Most North American mills produce the equivalent of 28,000 to 35,000 4-foot by 8-foot by 3/8-inch thick panels every day, while the newest mills produce over 45,000 panels daily from 100 truckloads or about 84,750 ft^3 of logs.

Stranding

Whole trees, with tops and branches removed, are delivered to the mill. Most often they are slashed into 8-, 16- or 24-foot lengths for processing, then fed into the mill by fast-moving log haulers or giant track-mounted overhead cranes. Typically, logs are debarked then sent either to the soaking ponds or directly to the strander. Three types of stranders are used. Of the traditional block strander, the long log disc strander and the long log ring strander, the latter is the most common. Since 1982, ideal strand geometry has evolved from a width of 0.5 inches and length of 3 inches to a length ranging from 4.5 inches to 6 inches. Strand thickness has been reduced from 0.03 inches to 0.023 inches to 0.027 inches.

Drying

Green strands are stored in wet bins and then sent to dryers, which may be the traditional triple-pass dryer, a single-pass dryer, a combination triple-pass/single-pass dryer or the latest innovation, a three-section conveyor dryer. The introduction of new drying techniques allows the use of longer strands, reduces surface inactivation of strands and lowers dryer outfeed temperatures. Lower outfeed temperatures permit strands to exit the dryer at a higher moisture content. At the same time, they reduce the amount of volatile organic compounds driven off from the strands that must be handled by air emission controls. After drying, strands are screened to remove under- and oversize strands, and to sort strands by size for strategic placement on the panels' faces and core. Sorted strands are sent to dry bins.

Blending

The blending of strands with resin and wax is a highly controlled operation, with separate rotating blenders used for face strands and core strands. During blending, emulsified or slack wax is sprayed onto the strands ahead of the resin. Different resin formulations are used for face and core strands. Face resins may be liquid or powdered phenolics, while core resins may be phenolics or isocyanates. The use of isocyanate resins for core strands is growing because they cure at lower temperatures, and therefore faster than phenolics. Mills are increasing the number of blenders to give flexibility in resin choice and to simplify resin changeover. Spinning disc resin applicators adapted from the automobile finishing industry have revolutionized resin application, however, additional research is required to accurately measure resin coverage.

Mat Forming

The mat forming process for OSB has also changed. The advent of strand orientation, for instance, complicated mat forming machines. Early-on electrostatic alignment of strands was experimented with. This method proved inefficient, complex and expensive. The most reliable method developed is also the most simple, and is still used today. Resembling a farmer's disc harrow, it utilizes a combination of spinning discs to align strands along the panel's length, and star-type cross-orienters to position them across its width. Both use the geometry of the strand—long and narrow—to place it between the spinning discs or let it fall into a trough before it is ejected onto a moving screen or conveyor belt below the forming heads. Oriented layers of strands within the mat—face, core, face, for example—are dropped sequentially, each by a different forming head. Mat density is continuously measured with a nucleonic device to ensure that the forming machine is felting a uniform mat. Most forming lines are nominally 8 feet wide, however, with the growing offshore market, 9- and 12-foot lines are being installed. These widths satisfy Japan's need for 3-foot by 6-foot panels and allow for lower forming speeds when running thin panels. Modern mat formers use wire screens laid over a moving conveyor belt to carry the mat into the press, or they may use a screenless system in which the mat lies directly on the conveyor belt.

Hot Pressing

All this careful preparation comes together in the hot press, where the loose mat of strands is compressed and the resin cured to form a structural use panel. As many as sixteen 12-foot-wide by 24-foot-long panels may be formed simultaneously in today's multiple-opening presses. The press must compact and consolidate the mat and raise its internal temperature high enough—between 350 and 400 °F—to cure the resin, all within 3 to 5 minutes. Previously the resin cure time and temperature was dictated by its manufacturer. However, the need for OSB manufacturers to shorten press cycles, while maintaining or improving mechanical and physical properties, has prompted a major study of press cycles and resin cure time. Today's OSB products often have nonstandard density profiles through their thickness. The need to reduce thickness swelling means that the panel's faces should be compressed less, which in turn, reduces panel stiffness. These trade-offs are of major importance. To help manufacturers, researchers and press operators sort them out, new measuring and recording equipment has been developed which allows press performance to be simulated in the laboratory before it is put into practice. The increase in press size from a nominal width of 8 feet to 12 feet also brings changes in heat transfer and press venting practices. Press manufacturers have also increased the daylight—the space between the platens—and the number of platens from 12 to 16. The larger press size has increased the presses' nominal annual production capacity from 300 million square feet based on a 3/8 inch panel thickness to 550 million square feet.

Finishing

After being ejected from the press, an OSB master panel is sawn into several 4-foot by 8-foot panels, which may then be face-sanded and profiled with tongue and groove edges. The interleaved strands on its surface give OSB a basket weave effect, which after sanding, takes on a marbleized appearance. The raised screen pattern on one face that makes panels less slippery underfoot in roofing applications is actually pressed into the face during hot pressing. Ultrasonic devices detect panels with internal defects, which are culled. Grade stamps are applied, and while still hot, panels are solid-piled (hot stacked) for 12 to 48 hours to complete curing of the resin. After being bundled into units and labeled, the panels' edges are sprayed with a low-permeability coating that retards moisture absorption. When required by the application or the buyer, mills may also cut panels to custom sizes, mark them with nailing lines, and notch tongues to allow the drainage of pooled water. Some proprietary floor panels have modified edge coatings; special panels are manufactured for use as the faces of structural insulated building panels and as webs for wood I-joists.

Environmental Controls

In compliance with clean air regulations, OSB mills have sophisticated particulate collection systems and VOC (volatile organic compounds) removal equipment at both the drying and pressing sections. Mills are designed so as to eliminate wastewater discharges from resin mixing and cleaning operations, collect log yard run-off and to utilize all of the wood fiber in the delivered logs. Bark, strander fines, panel trim, sawdust and other processing residues are burned to generate heat for dryers, presses, soaking ponds and for heating the plant in winter. Reject panels are used for dunnage during shipment.

The Future of OSB Manufacturing

Changes in manufacturing techniques and the development of new products is accelerating as OSB moves to become a world class structural use panel. It is expected that online mechanical and physical property measurements such as machine stress rating will become common. These measurement systems will likely evolve into machine control systems. The use of computerized equipment to make measurements and control each step of the process is growing. Plant operators will be able to adjust processes easily without reducing quality, and avoid downtime from major upsets. New OSB products will compete with all other structural and nonstructural wood-based panels. Lower dryer temperatures, improved resins and upgraded in-plant ventilation systems will ensure a safer workplace.

North American Production and Markets

Since the early 1980s, the production of OSB has expanded rapidly in both the United States and Canada, though waferboard was still the dominant product in Canada until late in the decade. The faster growth of OSB in the United States was due to mills being built closer to larger and growing communities, and to its lower overall manufacturing costs. In 1993, mills in the United States produced approximately 265 million ft.^{3} of OSB structural use panels, while those in Canada followed with 88 million ft.^{3} Estimates are that by 1997, the United States' production will climb to 388 million ft.^{3} and Canada's to 212 million ft.^{3} It is expected that at least 15 percent of the total volume will be exported. In 1996, 36 OSB mills were operating in the United States, with 8 more under construction. Canada has 17 producing mills, 2 under construction, and 3 in the planning stages. At least one OSB mill is in operation in Mexico, Scotland, France and Russia. A mill is being built in both Ireland and Chile. Luxembourg, Poland, the Czech Republic, Austria, Thailand and Australia are all considering constructing OSB mills.

Opportunities for OSB in Asia and Oceania

In September 1994, the international Finnish forest products consulting company Jaakko Pöyry predicted an annual increase in the demand for all types of wood-based panels of 3 percent per year. Demand for OSB was seen growing at 5.7 percent per year. According to Jaakko Pöyry, new markets and mills in Asia and Oceania could likely both create and meet a significant amount of this demand because OSB has moderate raw material costs, improved cost competitiveness when compared with solid wood products and a wide range of uses.

Quality Assurance

Quality assurance procedures and product standards for OSB structural use panels have evolved in step with changes in the product and manufacturing process, and continue to do so. The original standards set down in 1988 were *ANSI A-208.1 American National Standard for Mat-Formed Particleboard* (4) and *CSA O188.1 Mat Formed Wood Particleboard and Waferboard* (5). The basis for quality assurance testing is *ASTM D1037 Standard Methods of Evaluating the Properties of Wood-Base Fiber and Particle Panel Materials* (6), though some of its procedures have been modified to suit the unique nature of OSB. The current test procedures are outlined in *PS 2-92 Performance Standard for Wood-Based Structural-Use Panels* (1) and *CSA O325 Construction Sheathing* (2), both of which are performance-based standards, and in *CSA O437 OSB and Waferboard* (3), a modified product standard. OSB manufacturers are required to ensure that their panels meet the performance criteria of one of these standards, and indicate that by stamping panels with a quality mark identifying the standard. Under *PS 2-92* and *CSA O325* a manufacturer is required to enter into an agreement with an accredited testing agency to demonstrate that its panels conform with the chosen standard's requirements. The manufacturer must also maintain an in-plant quality control program in which panel properties are regularly checked, backed by an independent third-party-administered quality assurance program. The third party agency must visit the mill on a regular unannounced basis, and confirm that the in-plant quality control program is being maintained and that panels meet the minimum requirements of the two standards.

Standards Development and Building Code Acceptance

When waferboard was first offered in the marketplace in the 1950s, model building codes in the United States and Canada did not contain provisions for its use. Because of its newness, it did not fit under the "conventional construction" category. Consequently, during the 1960s and through most of the 1970s, each waferboard maker had to seek individual approval for use of its product in residential construction from local building officials in each jurisdiction where it wished to sell its product under the building codes "alternate" materials provisions.

At the time, most waferboard manufacturers were members of the National Particleboard Association, and waferboard was considered to be a type of particleboard. In 1976 Canadian manufacturers formed the Waferboard Association—now called the Structural Board Association—for the purpose of developing product standards that could be referenced in the model building codes in Canada and the United States. With the assistance of NPA, the Waferboard Association created *ANSI A 208.1 American National Standard for Mat-Formed Wood Particleboard* (4), the first standard for structural use panels made from wafers and exterior use resins. The standard was later referenced in the United States in ICBO's *Uniform Building Code* (7), BOCA's *National Building Code* (8), SBCCI's *Standard Building Code* (9) and CABO's *One and Two Family Dwelling Code* (10). In Canada, the Canadian Standards Association developed *CSA O188.1 Mat Formed Wood Particleboard and Waferboard* (5), which expanded the approval for use of waferboard in Canada when it was referenced in the 1980 edition of the *National Building Code of Canada* (11).

In 1978, the first oriented structural use panel was produced and soon recognized by the American Plywood Association (APA)—now called APA-The Engineered Wood Association—as having equivalent performance to plywood in most uses. The panel was included in APA's performance-rated panel standard *APA PRP 108 Performance Standards and Policies for Structural-Use Panels* (12). Shortly thereafter, another quality assurance agency—TECO—included OSB in its *TECO PRP-133 Performance Standards for Structural Use Panels* (13). The Canadian Standards Association developed *CSA O437 OSB and Waferboard* in 1985 and *CSA O325 Construction Sheathing* in 1987. The latter covers both OSB and plywood and closely matches *APA PRP-108* and *TECO PRP-133*.

In 1992, as a requirement of the Canada/US Free Trade Agreement, Canadian and American structural use panel standards were harmonized through the cooperative efforts of APA-The Engineered Wood Association, the Council of Forest Industries and the Structural Board Association, encouraged and supported by the United States and Canadian governments. A new United States standard, *Voluntary Product Standard PS 2-92 Performance Standard for Wood-Based Structural-Use Panels*, was published by the Department of Commerce. Today, OSB manufactured to the harmonized standards *PS 2-92* and *CSA O325* is quality-certified by three agencies—APA-The Engineered Wood Association, Pittsburgh Testing Laboratories and PFS/TECO Corporations.

OSB has full building code acceptance in North America. Standards are in place in Japan and Europe, but the product has not yet been fully accepted by all building code officials in Japan. In Europe, standards pertaining to OSB must be adopted by the member countries of the European Economic Community. However, OSB manufacturers in Canada and the United States are now obtaining approval for use on a country-by-country basis.

Engineering Design with OSB in North America

The initial design information for OSB in the United States came from APA-The Engineered Wood Association's *Design Capacities of APA Performance Rated Structural-Use Panels Technical Note N375* (17). First published in 1988 and updated in 1993, the document provides engineering design values for plywood and modification factors which are applied to them to obtain design values for OSB. In 1988, the Structural Board Association commenced work on an OSB engineering design standard for Canada. Through a comprehensive testing program, a series of OSB panel strength levels or classes was established, which allows a manufacturer to have a design rated product suited to its manufacturing process. To qualify as design rated under *CSA O452 Design Rated OSB* (18), a panel must meet or exceed the 95th percentile for strength and stiffness established for its class when tested at 68 °F and 80 percent relative humidity. Design rated OSB is now referenced in *CSA O86.1 Engineering Design in Wood (Limit States Design) A National Standard of Canada* (19) which allows its use where humidity levels will not produce a wood moisture content higher than 15 percent. Like plywood, design values for OSB are further modified for duration of load and other long term performance effects. In the United States, design values are being established for OSB independent of plywood and will be published in a joint Canadian/American supplement to the American Society of Civil Engineers' *AF&PA/ASCE 16-95 Load and Resistance Factor Design Standard for Engineered Wood Construction* (20).

Uses for OSB

OSB can be used in virtually any structural or nonstructural application where a large, thin, dimensionally stable panel is needed. As all wood-based panels expand when exposed directly to high humidity or rain over long periods, unfinished and unfaced OSB should be used only in protected construction or for interior uses. Because it is an engineered wood product, OSB's properties can be custom-designed for all suitable end uses by the manufacturer provided there is a sustainable market. OSB is used in a myriad of both structural and nonstructural applications:

packaging and crating	dry storage pallets	furniture frames
chair seats and backs	industrial tabletops	decorative wall panels
hardwood flooring core	finished flooring	furniture panel core
bins and tanks	hoarding and barriers	floor, wall and roof sheathing
concrete forms	decks and platforms	trailer walls
shutters	stress skin panels	shelving and display racks
I-joist webs	structural insulated panels	

Characteristics of OSB

OSB is a unique panel product which is often confused with particleboard and chipboard (Table 1). The main difference is that OSB is a structural use panel made with a waterproof,

Table 1. The basic properties of oriented strand board conforming to PS 2-92 or CSA 0325 and CSA 0437.0. Strength and stiffness values are average ultimate test values, not working stresses for design purposes.

Property	PS 2-92 (or CSA 0325)	CSA 0437.0 (Grade O-2)
Thickness tolerance	+/- 1/32" (+/- 0.8 mm)	+/- 0.03" (+/- 0.75 mm)
Length and width tolerance (maximum deviation from nominal)	+0", -1/8" (+/-0, -3.2 mm)	+0", -5/32" (+/-0, -4 mm)
Squareness tolerance (maximum deviation from square)	1/64 in/ft of width (1.3 mm/m)	5/32" (4 mm)
Straightness tolerance (maximum deviation from straight line)	1/16" corner to corner (1.6 mm)	1/16" corner to corner (1.5 mm)
Minimum modulus of rupture parallel perpendicular	N/A (not applicable) N/A	4200 psi (29.0 MPa) 1800 psi (12.4 MPa)
Minimum modulus of elasticity parallel perpendicular	N/A N/A	800,000 psi (5500 MPa) 225,000 psi (1500 MPa)
Minimum internal bond	N/A	50 psi (0.345 MPa)
Maximum linear expansion oven dry to saturated	N/A N/A	0.35% parallel 0.50% perpendicular
one sided wetting (or 50-90% relative humidity)	0.30% along major axis 0.35% across major axis	N/A N/A
oven dry to vacuum pressure soak	0.50%	N/A
Minimum thickness swell (24 hour soak)	25% (one sided wetting)	15% for 1/2" thick or less 10% for greater than 1/2"
Bond durability (minimum modulus of rupture) 6 hour cycle	50% retention	N/A
2 hour boil - parallel - perpendicular	N/A N/A	2100 psi (14.5 MPa) 900 psi (6.2 Mpa)
Minimum lateral nail resistance		400t lb (70t N) [t = thickness, in. (mm)]

heatproof and boilproof resin. It is also a multilayer panel in which the surface strands are aligned with the panel's long dimension, while the core strands are oriented perpendicular to them. Other characteristics of OSB include:

1. High value for the price.

    OSB has a high strength-to-weight ratio, is easy to handle and install using conventional carpentry tools, and costs less than comparable wood-based structural use panels.

2. No voids, knotholes or delamination.

    The manufacturing process precludes the formation of internal voids and knotholes in OSB panels. The resins and pressing techniques used virtually eliminate the possibility of delamination, and online devices detect and cull any defective panels before they leave the plant. In addition, OSB panels must meet stringent internal bond strength criteria.

3. Strength comparable to plywood.

    The flexural (bending), tensile, compressive, and bearing strengths of OSB structural use panels are equal to or better than those for plywood of the same thickness.

4. Higher shear strength than plywood.

    Because of its homogeneous composition, OSB has higher horizontal and rolling shear strengths than plywood of the same thickness.

5. Low environmental impact.

    OSB is made from small-diameter, fast-growing trees and trees that have low commercial value as sawlogs or veneer logs. Modern mills are self-sufficient in meeting their heating energy needs and are equipped with state-of-the-art pollution control devices to meet stringent clean air requirements.

6. Uniform construction.

    Both surfaces of OSB panels have the same quality and characteristics (smoothness, hardness, appearance, etc.).

7. Flexibility in panel size.

    Made in master panels as large as 12 feet by 24 feet, OSB can be supplied in a wide range of smaller sizes tailored to meet specific end uses.

8. Wide range of thicknesses.

   OSB is available in thicknesses ranging from 1/4 inch (actual) to 1.5 inches. The most common thicknesses are 3/8 inch, 7/16 inch, 15/32 inch, 19/32 inch, 23/32 inch, 7/8 inch and 1 1/8 inches.

9. Machineable.

   OSB can be machined with regular woodworking tools; carbide-tipped saw blades are recommended. It can be punched, bored and profiled with clean edges. Depending on the panel's use, tiny voids between strands on its edges may need to be filled.

10. No measurable release of formaldehyde.

    The phenol formaldehyde and isocyanate resins used for OSB are completely cured during the pressing and hot stacking processes. Therefore, there is no off-gassing of free formaldehyde from OSB panels.

11. Fire resistant.

    OSB has flame spread properties and fire resistance equal to or higher than plywood of the same thickness, and equivalent to solid wood of the same density. The thermosetting adhesive does not melt, but does char at the same rate as wood during fire exposure.

In-service Performance of OSB

Storage
Like all wood and wood-based products, OSB should be stored off the ground and out of the weather under a loosely draped tarp. Although it has an Exposure 1 durability rating—which means the panel will maintain its integrity during long construction delays where it may be exposed to high humidity and rain—direct exposure to moisture for prolonged periods may cause the panel's edges to swell or its surfaces to roughen. Tests have proven that edge swelling and surface roughness have little affect on the panel's structural performance, however, its appearance is degraded.

Workability
OSB structural use panels are easy to saw, drill, plane, file or sand with normal carpentry tools. Carbide-tipped saw blades are recommended, as is the use of blades designed specifically for cutting wood-based panels.

Fastening
The interleaved layers of strands developed during the OSB forming process create panels with excellent fastener-holding properties. When nails or staples are driven though its face,

OSB has fastener-holding properties in direct withdrawal and nail head pull-through equal to or better than other wood-based structural use panels. Fastener-holding strength is considerably reduced when a panel's surface is damaged by overdriven fasteners shot from pneumatic tools. Fasteners driven into the edges of an OSB panel are prone to withdrawal, and cannot be relied upon for structural connections. Cyclic racking tests simulating earthquake loading have shown that OSB has the same excellent performance as plywood under these conditions.

For normal use, panels 1/2 inch thick or less should be fastened with 6d common smooth- or spiral-shank nails, while 8d nails should be used to fasten thicker panels. In both cases, fasteners are spaced 6 inches on-center along the panel's edges, and 12 inches on-center in the field. Fasteners should be placed at least 3/8 inches from the panel's edges.

Closer fastener spacing is required when OSB is used in regions of high wind or seismic activity. At a minimum, fastener spacing should be reduced in the field to 6 inches on-center. However, even closer spacing and longer nails may be necessary in high wind areas. The local building official should be consulted.

The Span Rating System
The span rating for OSB is established by testing the panel under various loading conditions prescribed in *PS 2-92* and *CSA O325*. For OSB structural sheathing tested under *PS 2-92*, the span rating consists of two numbers separated by a slash—24/16, for example. The number on the left is the maximum recommended on-center spacing of framing (in inches) when the panel is used as roof sheathing. The right-hand number indicates the maximum span when used as floor sheathing. In each case the edges of this 7/16-inch thick panel must either fall over the framing or be supported by blocking or H clips. Floor sheathing panels must be covered by an additional layer of structural material such as underlayment, wood strip flooring applied across the joists or concrete topping. For OSB single layer flooring—that is, combined subfloor and underlayment—the span rating is given as a single number such as 20 OC. The number indicates the maximum recommended on-center spacing of framing (in inches).

OSB structural sheathing evaluated under *CSA O325* also uses a numerical span rating system. For each span number, the CSA system identifies both the use and the edge or surface treatment required, as in 1R24/2F16. The left-side designation means that the panel may be installed on a roof (R) without edge support (1) at a maximum span of 24 inches. The right side indicates that the panel may be applied on a floor (F) over a maximum span of 16 inches, provided that a structural overlay system (2) is placed over the panel. As before, the overlay may be underlayment, wood strip flooring or concrete.

Performance Under High Humidity Conditions
Like all wood and wood-based products, OSB is hygroscopic. It absorbs water vapor from the air and swells in dimensions when ambient relative humidity is high, and releases water vapor and shrinks when relative humidity is low. However, OSB is considerably more dimensionally

stable than sawn lumber and timber because of its plywood-like cross-layering of strands. Since OSB leaves the mill at about 2 percent moisture content, it is much drier than the average equilibrium moisture content of 8 to 12 percent found inside most heated buildings. This means that its dimensions will increase a little after installation. Though the wax added to the strands and the coating applied to the panel's edges provide resistance to the absorption of moisture, an expansion gap of 1/8 inch should always be left between panels.

According to North American product standards, OSB must maintain its strength and stiffness under normal humidity conditions—also referred to as standard conditions—of 68 °F and 65 percent relative humidity. These conditions are typical of protected construction applications—sheathing under siding, for instance—and produce in OSB a moisture content of 8 to 9 percent compared with 12 percent for solid wood. The lower equilibrium moisture content for OSB stems from a lessening of its hygroscopicity due to exposure to high temperatures during pressing. In addition, standards require OSB to maintain its strength and stiffness when exposed directly to the weather during long construction delays. A special condition is placed on OSB panels certified as design rated. The stated design values for these panels are determined after exposing OSB to 68 °F and 80 percent relative humidity, which produces in OSB a moisture content of 12 to 13 percent, which is lower than the 16 percent moisture content that solid wood would achieve under the same conditions.

For dry service conditions—that is, when the ambient relative humidity produces in solid wood an average equilibrium moisture content of no more than 19 percent—tabulated design values for OSB have been adjusted for duration of load effects by a factor similar to that for plywood, sawn lumber and glued-laminated timber.

An exception is made for Design Rated OSB manufactured in accordance with *CSA O452* used in structures that may be subject to permanent loads in excess of 50 percent of their design strength capacity (a heavy-duty warehouse floor, for instance). If the structure is protected from direct exposure to moisture, but subjected intermittently to high temperature and humidity, then OSB's strength values have to be adjusted by a duration of load factor of 0.45.

When OSB panels are subject to permanent loads in excess of 50 percent of their design strength capacity, serviceability design for creep—deflection due to long term loading—should be considered. Limited data indicates that deflection due to creep may be taken as two times the elastic or normal deflection under dry conditions and six times normal deflection for conditions where the sustained OSB moisture content is 16 percent or higher due to prolonged exposure to 85 percent or greater relative humidity.

Under nonpermanent loads and conditions leading to high environmental extremes, such as may be found in some roof sheathing applications, repeated exposure to moisture—whether high humidity or condensation—may lead to creep. Like all untreated wood products, all structural use panels are susceptible to mildew and mold growth with prolonged exposure to

80 percent or higher relative humidity. OSB panels should not be exposed to these conditions for long periods. Adequate roof ventilation must be provided, and other measures taken, including preservative treatment, to prevent degradation of the panels whether they are OSB or plywood.

The Phenomenon of Roof Ridging

Roofs sheathed with wood products occasionally exhibit ridges or depressions. This phenomenon is especially noticeable after a frost or when the sun is low in the sky, and worsened when roof shingles are thin or lightweight. Roof ridging, as it is called, can occur regardless of whether the roof is sheathed with OSB, plywood or shiplap lumber, though it is usually most noticeable with OSB and plywood. It is caused by the build-up of excessive moisture in the attic due either to inadequate ventilation or to moisture-laden air entering into the attic from the living space through the attic hatch or other unsealed penetrations, or by improperly venting a clothes dryer or bath exhaust fan into the attic. Panel edges swell as they absorb moisture, and may cause the outline of the panel to telegraph through the shingles. Panels restrained from swelling laterally by their neighbors bow upward or downward instead. Evidence of excessive moisture in the attic will be found as rust on the tips of roofing nails, as rust spots on the insulation below, or as mildew and mold on sheathing and framing. Proper ventilation practice calls for an attic to have a net free vent area equal to 1/300 of the ceiling area for roof slopes over 3/12 pitch and 1/150 of the ceiling area for pitches of 3/12 or less. For best results, half of the net free vent area should be at the eave and half at the ridge. Experience has shown that the most effective system combines a continuous soffit vent with a continuous ridge vent. Modern ridge vents are designed to prevent the entry of rain and snow into the attic.

OSB under Hardwood Flooring

Recent tests have confirmed the suitability of OSB panels 23/32 inches or thicker as a base for hardwood flooring (16). The results have been accepted by both the National Oak Flooring Manufacturers Association and the National Wood Flooring Association, provided that the panels have a 48/24 span rating or are designated for use as single layer flooring over a maximum span of 24 inches on-center.

Exposed Uses

Oriented strand board structural use panels are suitable for exposed use on walls under certain conditions. A minimum gap of 1/8 inch must be maintained between adjacent panels and where panels abut window and door openings. All edges must be primed, caulked or covered by battens. Exposed surfaces must be protected against direct wetting with a top quality acrylic latex paint and companion primer designated by the manufacturer as stain blocking or stain resistant. Though other types of exterior coatings also work well on OSB, solid color stains, semi-transparent stains and water repellents do not offer the same protection from rain and sun as paints do. Some lifting of the surface strands may occur if these finish types are used.

Fire Performance

Tests of OSB's performance under fire conditions have been carried out by a number of agencies. Although fire performance also depends on the wood species and manufacturing process, OSB panels generally have a surface flame spread rating of approximately 150 and meet the C classification. OSB wall sheathing has successfully passed fire endurance tests. In one trial, the wall section consisted of 3/8 inch OSB sheathing, fiber glass insulation between load-bearing studs, and 1/2 inch type C gypsum wallboard, with the flame against the wallboard. In another test, OSB and plywood were mounted directly against the test furnace. Flame penetration through the OSB was equal to or slower than that for plywood of the same thickness. In recognition of this, Underwriters Laboratories has approved the use of OSB in wall systems where plywood has been previously approved.

Formaldehyde Emission

As the phenol formaldehyde and isocyanate resins used in OSB are waterproof, heatproof and boilproof, there is no measurable off-gassing of formaldehyde from OSB panels once the binder is fully cured. Mills normally solid-pile or hot stack panels immediately out of the press for 12 to 48 hours before shipment to ensure complete cure of the resin. Yet, full-size OSB panels are routinely tested for formaldehyde emissions using the ASTM large chamber test method (15).

Permeability

The permeability of OSB to water vapor is measured in accordance with *ASTM E96 Standard Test Method for Water Vapor Transmission of Material in Sheet Form* (14). Panels with a permeability of 1.0 perm or less are considered to act as a vapor retarder. Those with a perm rating of 2.0 or more are considered to pass sufficient water vapor such that a wall cavity with a high moisture load because of the use of green studs or leakage of free water will eventually dry out. Permeability is a function of thickness; thinner panels have a higher perm rating than thicker panels. A panel 3/8 inches thick, for example, has a perm rating of about 2.5, while the rating for a 5/8-inch-thick panel is about 1.1.

Specifying OSB

Product Standards

Oriented strand board is an engineered structural use panel with unique mechanical and physical properties and behavioral characteristics. It can be engineered to meet the requirements of the most demanding customer. When used as a sheathing panel in the United States, it must meet the performance criteria contained in the Department of Commerce's *Voluntary Product Standard PS 2-92 Performance Standard for Wood-Based Structural-Use Panels*. In Canada, panels must comply with the Canadian Standards Association's *CSA O325 Construction Sheathing* or its *CSA O437 OSB and Waferboard*. All three standards set maximum values for deflection under load, thickness swell and linear expansion, and minimum values for strength, stiffness, and lateral nail loads.

When specifying OSB, the designer must indicate the panel's:

1. type or grade—Standard, Structural 1 or Proprietary
2. use—roof, wall or floor sheathing, single layer flooring or underlayment
3. thickness and span rating
4. length and width
5. durability rating—Exposure 1 or Exterior
6. edge treatment—tongue and groove or square edge
7. unsanded or sanded faces
8. special treatment—preservative or fire retardant

Current Research

OSB structural use panels are commodity products in North America. Their primary market is in residential and commercial construction and renovation. Thus, OSB output fluctuates with the availability of low interest rate mortgages and the number of housing starts. In periods of reduced construction activity, the markets for OSB quickly shrink. Mills are faced with falling returns that barely cover production costs. The result is a contraction of the OSB industry. However, the contraction is usually of short duration, and followed by a period of industry expansion which typically causes an oversupply of panels and highly competitive prices. Little action was taken in the past to remedy the supply and demand volatility because OSB manufacturers realized that the makers of competitive structural use panels like plywood were continuously facing raw material shortages and significantly higher materials and production costs. OSB manufacturers simply waited, assuming that "The market would always return".

Remembering recent history and expecting a major expansion in OSB production capacity, the OSB industry realized that pro-active measures were required to sustain OSB's popularity and avoid repeating past mistakes. A strong market-driven research program was thought to be the best way to make this happen. In 1992, the Structural Board Association formed an alliance with the Alberta Research Council and Forintek Canada Corporation, two of Canada's largest wood research organizations, to carry out research on OSB. Funded at over $1.4 million annually, the program is managed by the Structural Board Association and now includes other major research organizations and many universities in North America. The program addresses projects initiated by both market needs and OSB manufacturers. The program has not only carried out significant research, but has also encouraged the OSB industry's suppliers and equipment manufacturers to upgrade their products. Press size, for example, has been increased from 4 feet by 16 feet to 12 feet by 24 feet as a result.

Each year research projects are chosen from among many submissions and prioritized by a management committee. Those addressing the most important needs or showing the best potential return are funded. The following is a summary of some recently completed and on-going projects.

Long term performance

Because OSB structural use panels have a relatively short history of use—about 20 years—manufacturers and others have sought ways to ensure their long term performance in all types of construction. A research project focusing on OSB's long term performance commenced in 1994. The project developers realized that it was necessary to accommodate the changing wood species, resins and manufacturing technology that characterizes today's OSB industry. Their objectives are to first develop a short-duration test method to predict the long term duration of load and creep performance of OSB, and secondly, to obtain approval for the test method from the appropriate standards-writing organizations in North America, Europe and Japan. Researchers have two challenges. The first is to develop a test that can be conducted quickly in-plant to identify panels likely to fail over time because of, for example, a change in the wood raw material, resin, or manufacturing process. The second is to create a more statistically precise method for screening the behavior of a group of panels. The latter will be useful in establishing adjustment factors for design values for duration of load and creep of OSB under various loads and varying levels of humidity. This would allow a manufacturer to test its panels in-plant and advise a prospective customer about their expected performance.

Optimization of pressing parameters

This project evaluated a number of key materials and manufacturing variables including strand thickness, resin content, strand alignment, panel density, and compression strategy. A set of experimental panels was produced. The data generated were used to create a computer model that will allow OSB product developers to determine how a change in one of the variables will affect OSB's mechanical and physical properties.

Thickness swell reduction

This study examined how water soaking time and the distance of the measuring device from the panel's edge affected the measured value for thickness swell of OSB. The study also evaluated the usefulness of edge sealers, using a modified version of the kitchen cabinet edge wicking test method (21). Also, uncoated, hand-sealed and factory-sealed test specimens were subjected to simulated rain, and their thickness swell compared with that of controls.

Preservation of OSB

This project assessed the effectiveness of borate compounds in improving the decay-, insect- and fire-resistance of OSB. Ten series of experimental panels were prepared to evaluate the effect of zinc borates on the properties of OSB (5 with novolac-type phenol formaldehyde resin, and 5 with resole phenol formaldehyde resin with polyethylene glycol as a flowing agent). Results showed that OSB panels could be effectively treated with borate preservatives, which could open new markets for OSB.

OSB surface quality improvement

Accelerated tests which reproduce surface staining in OSB were developed to identify wood species responsible for the staining, and to evaluate coatings or treatments to control or eliminate the bleed-through of extractives from OSB into vinyl flooring. Various methods of reproducing the staining were examined. The effect of wood species and tissue types within a species on the occurrence of staining was evaluated. Various coatings, overlays and treatments to control bleed-through were evaluated, both in terms of effectiveness and cost. Upon completion, this project should increase the market for OSB underlayment.

Product stewardship

This project examined the environmental impact of discarding, reusing and burning OSB manufacturing residues. Tests were conducted to determine the recyclability of OSB panel trim; the leachability of aspen wood and OSB panel trim; and the combustibility of OSB and plywood panels.

Machine stress rating of OSB

This project evaluated several online mechanical and physical property measurement systems. The objective was to establish specifications for installing a prototype machine stress rating system in an OSB mill using data developed in earlier tests, and to determine the scope of the modifications to existing machine stress rating devices needed to make them useful for nondestructive testing of OSB panels.

Optimization of the strander operation

For this project, experimental data and mill records and information relating to the strander operation were reviewed to determine the optimal conditions that are necessary to maximize wood recovery from the log and minimize the variation in strand geometry.

Strand alignment factors in the production of OSB

The objective of this project was to analyze the forming equipment utilized by the OSB industry to identify both its limitations and the opportunities for improving strand alignment. The findings support the prospect of improving OSB's strength-to-weight ratio and maximizing the usage of processed strands. Several techniques for measuring strand alignment, including computer-driven digital image analysis, were identified.

Resin and wax distribution

This project's objectives included assessing the usefulness of fluorescence microscopy and digital image analysis for measuring the amount of resin and wax on commercial strands, determining wood species effects, identifying the components needed for such an imaging system, and evaluating the system under production conditions. A computer-driven prototype was successfully demonstrated using various wood species, strands, resins and waxes.

Volatile organic compounds released from OSB

Volatile organic compound emission tests were conducted on OSB, plywood, particleboard and medium density fiberboard bonded with both phenol formaldehyde and isocyanate resins. Results revealed no significant amount of chemicals from the benzene, ethylbenzene, toluene and xylene family of compounds in the panels' emissions. A limited study of pressing parameters showed that longer press times and higher press temperatures slightly reduced emissions released naturally from the wood.

Samples of indoor air were collected in an OSB mill at different times, from different work areas, and by different employees. Samples were analyzed in a gas chromatograph and a mass spectrometer. Air inside the mill easily met workplace standards, however, mill location and the type of wood, wax and resin were found to have an effect on indoor air quality. In a complementary study, the Alberta Research Council looked at wood dust and resin particles and their concentrations, and developed a strategy for reducing airborne particulates inside OSB mills.

Summary

Oriented strand board and its predecessor, waferboard, have been used as structural use panels in building construction for over four decades. The OSB product has continuously evolved in quality, performance, adaptability, and acceptance by a growing community of users. This has occurred because OSB is an engineered wood panel which can be custom-designed and modified to suit the needs of its customers, from the high-volume commodity builder to the most sophisticated end user. As a relatively new product, its performance has been supported by more research and testing than traditional wood products. As this testing and research is ongoing, OSB will continue to evolve to meet the needs of new manufacturing techniques and new markets.

References

1. National Institute of Standards and Technology. 1992. Voluntary Product Standard PS 2-92 Performance Standard for Wood-Based Structural-Use Panels. U. S. Department of Commerce. Washington, D. C.

2. Canadian Standards Association. 1992. CSA O325 Construction Sheathing. CSA. Rexdale, Ontario, Canada.

3. Canadian Standards Association. 1993. CSA O437 OSB and Waferboard. CSA. Rexdale, Ontario, Canada.

4. National Particleboard Association. 1989. ANSI A208.1 American National Standard for Mat-Formed Wood Particleboard. NPA. Gaithersburg, Maryland.

5. Canadian Standards Association. 1978. CSA O188.1 Mat Formed Wood Particleboard and Waferboard. CSA. Rexdale, Ontario, Canada.

6. American Society for Testing and Materials. 1993. D1037 Standard Methods of Evaluating the Properties of Wood-Base Fiber and Particle Panel Materials. ASTM. West Conshohocken, Pennsylvania.

7. International Conference of Building Officials. 1994. Uniform Building Code. ICBO. Whittier, California.

8. Building Officials & Code Administrators International, Inc. 1996. National Building Code. BOCA. Country Club Hills, Illinois.

9. Southern Building Code Congress international. 1994. Standard Building Code. SBCCI. Birmingham, Alabama.

10. Council of American Building Officials. 1995. One and Two Family Dwelling Code. CABO. Falls Church, Virginia.

11. Canadian Commission of Fire and Building Codes. 1985. National Building Code of Canada. National Research Council. Ottawa, Ontario, Canada.

12. American Plywood Association. 1991. APA PRP-108 Performance Standards and Policies for Structural-Use Panels. APA. Tacoma, Washington.

13. TECO. 1989. PRP-133 Performance Standards for Structural Use Panels. TECO Corporation. Madison, Wisconsin.

14. American Society for Testing and Materials. 1980. E96 Standard Test Method for Water Vapor Transmission of Material in Sheet Form. ASTM. West Conshohocken, Pennsylvania.

15. American Society for Testing and Materials. 1985. E1333 Standard Test Method for Determining Formaldehyde Release from Wood Products Under Defined Test Conditions Using a Large Chamber. ASTM. West Conshohocken, Pennsylvania.

16. Lang, E., T. McLain and J. Loferski. 1992. Performance of Wood Floor Systems Under Fluctuating Moisture Changes. Final Technical Report to National Oak Flooring Manufacturers Association. Virginia Tech. Blacksburg, Virginia.

17. American Plywood Association. 1991. Design Capacities of APA Performance Rated Structural-Use Panels Technical Note N375. APA. Tacoma, Washington.

18. Canadian Standards Association. 1994. CSA O452 Design Rated OSB. CSA. Rexdale, Ontario, Canada.

19. Canadian Standards Association. 1994. CSA O86.1 Engineering Design in Wood (Limit States Design) A National Standard of Canada. CSA. Rexdale, Ontario, Canada.

20. American Society of Civil Engineers. 1995. AF&PA/ASCE 16-95 Load and Resistance Factor Design Standard for Engineered Wood Construction. ASCE. New York, New York.

21. Kitchen Cabinet Manufacturers Association. 1990. ANSI/KMCA A161.1-1990 Recommended Performance and Construction Standards for Kitchen and Vanity Cabinets. KCMA. Reston, Virginia.

Chapter 6

Structural Composite Lumber

Sherman Nelson, P. E.

Trus Joist MacMillan
Boise, Idaho

Structural composite lumber (SCL) is a generic term that describes a family of engineered wood products that combine veneer sheets or strands or other small wood elements with exterior structural adhesives to form lumber-like structural products. An important characteristic common to SCL products like laminated veneer lumber (LVL), parallel strand lumber (PSL) and laminated strand lumber (LSL) is that the grain of the wood elements is aligned essentially parallel with the member's length to optimize its structural properties. Also, LVL, PSL and LSL all use wood fiber much more efficiently than sawn lumber and timber (Fig. 1). These lumber-like products are used for the same structural applications as the sawn lumber and timber for which they substitute—girders, beams, headers, joists, studs and columns.

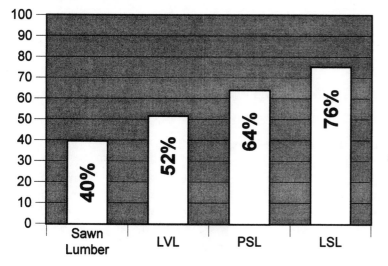

Figure 1. The wood fiber contained in a log is used more efficiently when it is converted into structural composite lumber than into sawn lumber.

Though other engineered wood products are also made by bonding together wood elements with adhesives, they are not considered to be SCL. Glued-laminated timbers, for example, are not SCL because their dimension lumber laminations are much, much larger than the small wood elements that define SCL products. And even though plywood and oriented strand board are made from veneers and strands, respectively, neither is thought of as SCL. In both, the wood elements are cross-laminated, and formed into panels that are used as sheathing, not as structural framing.

In some sense, a product is defined as SCL if the manufacturer wants to call it that and it meets the performance criteria of *ASTM D5456 Standard Specification for Evaluation of Structural Composite Lumber Products* (1) or other industry standards that apply to SCL.

While SCL products first appeared in the marketplace in the early 1960s, the concept of SCL is not new. Though not named so at the time, SCL had its beginnings in the early days of the aircraft industry prior to World War II. Taking advantage of wood's high strength-to-weight ratio, engineers parallel-laminated spruce veneers with adhesive for use as wing spars and other structural members in airplanes.

In some cases, the veneers were first impregnated with adhesive, then parallel-laminated at high temperature to cure the adhesive. Sometimes the veneers were compressed while heated to form highly densified laminated veneer products called compreg. Uncompressed products were referred to as impreg. This SCL-like technology was used during World War II in both the United States and Europe for such things as airplane propellers to further the war effort (2, 3, 4). Impregnating and parallel-laminating the veneers both strengthened the product and markedly improved its dimensional stability. Additional military applications considered or used included flight decks, floor supports in naval magazines and cold storage spaces, molded sections for aircraft, dielectric structures, and ablation cooling materials for hypervelocity vehicles. This technology later led to the evolution of molded parts of plastic-modified wood and paper products—a long stretch from today's commercial SCL products.

Recently, impregnated, laminated veneer SCL has been employed in solving two structural problems. In one case, the technology was used to create a high-strength connector for splicing long-span wood truss chords. In the second, Douglas-fir veneer reinforced with fiberglass and epoxy was used to make 120-foot-long wind turbine blades fatigue-resistant.

Today's Structural Composite Lumber Products

There are doubtless numerous applications of earlier versions of what could be termed SCL, many of which may continue today. However, this chapter is directed towards those products meeting the more specific definition of the SCL industry of today given in *ASTM D5456* and other standards. These products comprise a family of engineered wood products that combine wood fiber with exterior structural adhesives to form large billets which are then ripped into smaller members for specific applications.

Laminated Veneer Lumber

Laminated veneer lumber (LVL) was the first type of SCL commercially produced for the marketplace. It consists of layers of wood veneers—Douglas-fir and southern pine, for example—laminated together with the grain of each veneer aligned primarily with the length of the finished product (Fig. 2). In a typical LVL manufacturing process, rotary-peeled veneers about 0.125 inches thick are dried, then graded ultrasonically for stiffness and strength (Fig. 3). After being coated with a waterproof structural adhesive—usually phenol formaldehyde—the veneers are laid-up such that lower grade veneers are placed in the core, and higher grade veneers on the faces. Veneers are fed into a hot press where they are formed into a solid billet under heat and pressure. LVL is manufactured to either a fixed length using a stationary or staging press, or to an indefinite length in a continuous press. Billets exiting the press may be up to 3.5 inches thick, and made even thicker in a secondary gluing operation. Produced in widths up to 4 feet, billets are typically ripped into numerous narrow strips. LVL is available in lengths up to the shippable maximum of 80 feet.

Figure 2. Laminated veneer lumber (LVL) is made by gluing together multiple plies of rotary-peeled veneer such that the grain of each is parallel to the product's length.

In the early 1960s, Weyerhaeuser Corporation developed Lamineer® LVL, which it produced on a prototype continuous press. The company marketed a limited amount of the product for several years, but the venture did not succeed past the pilot operation and was eventually discontinued.

In 1968 Trus Joist Corporation developed and produced Microllam™ LVL using a proprietary continuous press. This product line continues to be manufactured at six plants in North America. The company is now a joint venture of TJ International and MacMillan Bloedel,

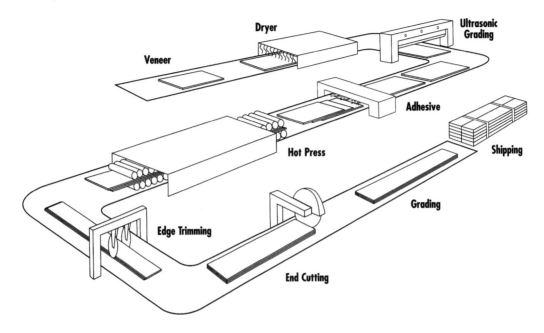

Figure 3. Ultrasonic grading allows the stiffest and strongest veneers to be placed on the product's faces, contributing to LVL's high allowable design values.

managed by the former under the name Trus Joist MacMillan. The company produces the majority of the LVL manufactured in North America as well as other SCL and engineered wood products.

In the 1970s researchers at the Forest Products Laboratory in Madison, Wisconsin, conducted research on a LVL concept they called Press-Lam (5). Although significant progress was made on the Press-Lam product, including construction of an experimental bridge, no commercial development was pursued.

The next entry into the LVL industry was Finnforest OY in 1975. This Finnish company started a pilot manufacturing operation for LVL made of Norway spruce in one of their plywood mills. The first full-scale manufacturing line began production in 1980 in Lohja, Finland. Approximately half of their production is exported to North America through McCausey Lumber Company in Roseville, Michigan, and marketed under the Master Plank® Beam trademark. The remainder is distributed in Europe under the trade name Kerto.

There are currently many producers of LVL worldwide, including Tecton Laminates, South Coast, Louisiana-Pacific, Willamette Industries, Boise Cascade, and Georgia-Pacific in the United States; Tembec in Canada; Forwood, Engineered Timber Industries, and Hancocks in Australia; Jyuken in New Zealand; and Keyo in Japan.

Advantages of LVL

LVL has many potential advantages over sawn lumber and timber in strength, predictability of performance, available sizes, dimensional consistency, dimensional stability, and treatability.

The use of veneers in making LVL results in a re-distribution of the knots, slope of grain and other natural defects that occur in the log. Consequently, these and other strength-reducing defects are harmlessly dispersed throughout the product's volume. Further, each veneer is graded both visually and mechanically with non-destructive ultrasonic and density measuring equipment (6). This permits fabricators to strategically place higher grade veneers where strength is needed—usually on the product's faces—and lower grade veneers in its core. It also allows the development of specific lay-up patterns—including mixed species—to match application requirements. The opportunity to grade and lay-up veneers in specific patterns enhances both LVL's strength and predictability of performance. Also, it makes the most efficient use of the wood resource, as low grade logs are significantly upgraded relative to the strength of the lumber and timber sawn from the same logs. Furthermore, the coefficient of variation in strength and stiffness for LVL typically ranges between 10 and 15 percent, compared with 25 to 40 percent for structural grades of sawn lumber and timber. As a result, the allowable design stresses for most grades of LVL are higher than those for sawn lumber and timber.

LVL billets exit the press with consistent dimensions and a relatively low and consistent moisture content of about 10 percent. Although LVL will change in dimensions with changes in its moisture content, it is more dimensionally stable than sawn lumber and timber. When framing systems employ both LVL (minimal shrinkage) and sawn lumber and timber (significant shrinkage), designers and builders must use framing techniques that compensate for the difference in shrinkage. And while sawn lumber and timber may bow, crook, twist and cup, the only warpage in LVL is the potential for cupping across its width. Thicker pieces are much less susceptible to cupping than thinner ones. Some manufacturers minimize this characteristic by overlaying its faces with a water barrier or by cross-laminating subsurface veneers. Since the size of LVL is not limited by the size of the logs from which the veneers were peeled, the long lengths, wide widths and heavy thicknesses in which it is available offer advantages over sawn lumber and timber. Because of the consistency among pieces, there is little reason to re-grade LVL at the job site. On the contrary, the wide variability among pieces of sawn lumber and timber increasingly forces re-grading on-site, with some pieces down-graded or culled.

The lathe checks that open in the veneer during peeling and other ports-of-entry built-in during lay-up, make LVL easily treatable with preservatives and fire retardants in conventional pressure-treating processes. Even LVL of large cross section is fully penetrated by the treatment, whereas some species of sawn lumber and timber require incising to achieve only limited subsurface penetration.

Disadvantages of LVL

Although LVL has many advantages over sawn lumber and timber, raw logs must first of all be peelable. This places limitations on log size and quality, and on some wood species as well. Also, the pressing operations used in making LVL offer little opportunity for significant densification of the wood, so enhancement of strength and stiffness through densification is minor. Cupping across the width can be a problem when LVL is improperly laid directly on the ground during storage, or when thin pieces are used in applications where the moisture environment is different for each surface. As an engineer must be hired to select the proper size and grade LVL for certain applications, builders are sometimes discouraged from using LVL because of the additional expense. Finally, the high capital investment and relatively low production rates for LVL result in economics that demand higher value-added applications in order for operations to be profitable.

Parallel Strand Lumber

In the early 1970s MacMillan Bloedel Ltd. of Vancouver, Canada, began research on a production process for an SCL product which was presented to the marketplace in 1984 under the trade name Parallam® PSL. In 1991 the joint venture agreement between MacMillan Bloedel and TJ International resulted in the transfer of this technology to Trus Joist MacMillan for its management. Known generically as parallel strand lumber, Parallam® PSL is the only PSL product currently available (Fig. 4). It is produced at plants in Vancouver, British Columbia; Colbert, Georgia; and Buckhannon, West Virginia.

Figure 4. Parallel strand lumber's (PSL) unique appearance arises from the use of thin strips of veneer.

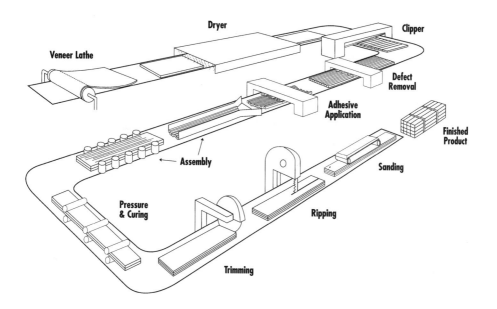

Figure 5. PSL is manufactured in huge billets which are then ripped into smaller sizes.

As with LVL, the manufacture of PSL begins with rotary-peeled and graded veneer about 0.125 inches thick (Fig. 5). Veneer sheets are clipped into strands approximately 0.75 inches wide, thus permitting the use of roundup, fishtail and other pieces of less-than-full-width veneer. The wood fiber in these veneers is mostly clear sapwood from the outer portion of the tree and is higher-than-average in strength than the rest of the wood fiber in the log, and represents material that is not usable in the LVL process. Presently, PSL is made from Douglas-fir, western hemlock, southern pine and yellow-poplar.

After a waterproof, structural adhesive—typically phenol resorcinol formaldehyde—is applied, the strands are fed into a continuous press to form a mat of highly consistent density. The continuous pressing operation allows for greater densification of the wood than is achieved in pressing LVL. The adhesive is cured using microwaves which, in effect, cure the billet from the inside out. Thus, the cross section of the billet—typically 11 inches by 19 inches—is greater than that for LVL where heat is transferred from the outside in. Billets, which are up to 66 feet long, are then ripped into smaller members. If needed, PSL can be bonded together into T-beams and other structurally-efficient shapes in secondary gluing operations.

Advantages of PSL
PSL enjoys all of the advantages noted for LVL, with the exception of the opportunity for layering veneer strands by grade. Strength is enhanced instead by increasing the amount of densification of the wood. The large cross section of the billet minimizes the need for secondary gluing in applications requiring a large cross section. In addition, PSL accepts

preservative and fire retardant treatments more readily than LVL. Furthermore, PSL makes an even greater use of wood fiber than LVL (Fig. 1). The synergism created by combining PSL and LVL production lines in the same plant offers an even greater opportunity for increasing wood fiber utilization.

Disadvantages of PSL

As with LVL, the PSL technology is limited to peelable logs. The need to hire an engineer to determine the proper size and grade PSL for a certain application may deter some contractors. Also, PSL is heavier than the same size sawn or glued-laminated timber. Its adhesive is more abrasive to saws and drills. Because of its typically large size, field connections must often be made with metal plates and through-bolts rather than with nails. Like LVL, PSL production lines are capital-intensive; steady production and an end product suited for value-added applications are a necessity.

Laminated Strand Lumber

As part of the 1991 Trus Joist MacMillan joint venture, TJ International also acquired a MacMillan Bloedel-conceived laminated strand lumber (LSL) technology. The first LSL plant came on-line shortly thereafter in Deerwood, Minnesota. A second plant is now operating in Kentucky. The product is marketed as TimberStrand® LSL in North America and Intrallam™ LSL in Europe (Fig. 6).

Figure 6. Based on long, thin strands, laminated strand lumber (LSL) is the latest structural composite lumber product to appear in the marketplace.

To some extent, LSL is an extrapolation of oriented strand board (OSB) technology in which the whole log, excluding the bark, is processed through the rotating knives of a stranding machine (Fig. 7). In the case of LSL, however, the 12-inch-or-so-long strands are significantly longer than the 3- to 6-inch lengths used for OSB, but about the same thickness—0.03 to 0.05 inches. Their greater length is the key to LSL's longitudinal strength and to orienting the strands during mat formation so that they will be essentially parallel to the finished product's length. Undesirable strands are screened out beforehand and used as fuel for the production process. Two features unique to LSL technology are the use of a polymeric diphenylmethane diisocyanate adhesive which is sprayed onto the strands as they tumble inside a rotating drum, and curing of the adhesive in a stationary steam injection press. Eight-foot-wide billets up to 5.5 inches thick and 48 feet long have been made with this technology.

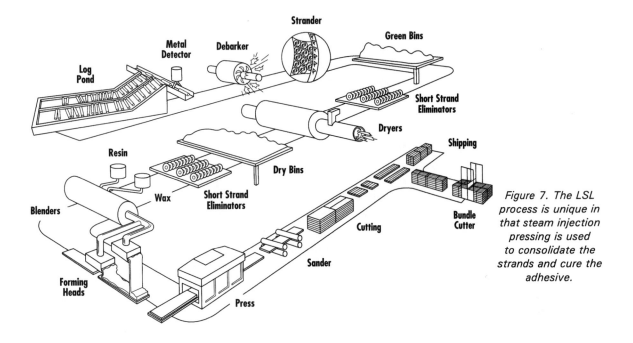

Figure 7. The LSL process is unique in that steam injection pressing is used to consolidate the strands and cure the adhesive.

Advantages of LSL
Unlike LVL and PSL, the raw material for LSL is not limited to peelable logs of preferred species. Small logs and crooked logs of many species, including aspen, yellow-poplar and other underutilized, fast-growing species are acceptable. Hence, LSL technology uses wood fiber more efficiently than any other SCL product (Fig. 1). The unique steam injection pressing process permits significant enhancement of LSL's strength through densification of the wood. Strategic lay-up of the strands in the LSL manufacturing process results in a product with improved transverse strength and limited cupping potential. Preservative treatments are accomplished in-process by treating the strands prior to pressing, rather than in a secondary operation as is required with other SCL products and sawn lumber and timber. LSL demonstrates excellent fastener-holding power and mechanical connector performance. Virtually all of the other advantages of LVL and PSL are also found in LSL.

Disadvantages of LSL
Even with steam injection curing of the adhesive, the dimensional stability of LSL—particularly thickness swelling—is not as good as that of LVL and PSL. This is because the

greater densification of the wood in LSL versus LVL and PSL results in more swelling with changes in its moisture content. As with all SCL products, there are significant capital investment requirements for LSL production lines.

Other Structural Composite Lumber Products

A registered trademark of APA-The Engineered Wood Association, COM-PLY® is a composite of an OSB core overlaid with veneer or LVL on its edges or faces. Currently manufactured as a sheathing panel with veneer faces, it therefore does not meet the definition of SCL. However, a plant in Roxboro, North Carolina once produced a COM-PLY® SCL with LVL on its edges for use as joists, headers and rafters. Called Arrowood, the product is no longer available. Much of the research behind both COM-PLY® technologies was conducted at the USDA Southeastern Forest Experiment Station in Athens, Georgia (7).

Scrimber is a whole-log SCL technology formerly utilized by Scrimber International of Mount Gambier, South Australia (8). The process involves first crushing lengthwise, then scrimming—forming bundles of interconnected and aligned strands that maintain the original orientation of the grain—small diameter trees and thinnings to produce a mat with a reported 85 percent wood fiber utilization. The scrimmed mat is then dried. After adhesive is added, the mat is formed into the desired shape and pressed as the adhesive is cured by radio frequency energy. Though Scrimber is no longer produced, Georgia-Pacific is currently evaluating this technology for making SCL from southern pine thinnings.

Oriented strand lumber (OSL) is a concept utilizing OSB technology and processes to produce an SCL product from strands up to 6 inches long. Several OSB manufacturers are examining the technology at the present time.

Applications for Structural Composite Lumber

Applications for SCL are becoming nearly as numerous and varied as those for sawn lumber and timber. Originally directed at structural uses, there are an increasing number of non-structural applications. The current estimated production of SCL is approaching 30 million ft.^{3} annually, and is projected to reach 70 million ft.^{3} annually in the next decade (9).

One of the incentives driving the development and production of SCL has been the decline in the availability of high-grade sawn lumber and timber. LSL is used for studs, blocking, rim joists and light-duty headers in residential construction (Fig. 8). LVL and PSL are used extensively for framing members such as girders, beams, joists, headers, lintels and columns in light-frame construction where stiffness, strength and predictability of performance are needed (Figs. 9, 10). Substantial quantities of both are also employed for concrete forming (Fig. 11) and electric utility structures. A large percentage of LVL is used as flanges for wood I-joists, as well as for the chords of proprietary wood-and-metal trusses (Fig. 12). LVL has been used extensively as scaffold plank (Fig. 13). In an early application of some note, LVL was used to create a 400-foot clear span barrel arch roof over an athletic stadium at the University of Idaho at Moscow (Fig. 14) (10). The structure was recognized by the American Society of Civil Engineers as "The Outstanding Structural Engineering Achievement of 1976".

Figure 8. LSL studs are making inroads into the residential framing market.

Figure 9. High stiffness and strength contribute to LVL's use as headers, beams and girders.

Figure 10. Offering the highest stiffness and strength of all structural composite lumber products, PSL performs well in non-repetitive uses such as girders.

Figure 11. PSL often finds use in concrete forming applications.

Figure 12. The flanges of these proprietary wood- and-metal trusses are LVL.

Figure 13. Most scaffold plank used in the United States is now LVL.

Figure 14. LVL was used in the roof of the 400-foot clear span arena at the University of Idaho.

Figure 15. PSL is being used increasingly where both strength and appearance are important.

Figure 16. Heavy metal plates and through-bolts secure PSL members in this structure.

There have been many heavy timber applications of SCL in the form of PSL, including long span trusses, structural ridge beams, columns and post-and-beam type structures (Figs. 15, 16). Because it is easily treated with preservatives, PSL is increasingly being used in both highway and pedestrian bridges (Fig. 17) (11, 12).

Figure 17. PSL has figured prominently in the recent revival of wooden bridges on secondary roads in the United States.

Other applications for SCL include truck beds; flooring in transoceanic shipping containers; railroad ties; outer laminations for glued-laminated timbers; snow ski and diving board cores; furniture, door and window frames; keels, ribs and other structural members in naval mine sweeper construction; kiln stickers; caskets; and structural members such as T-beams that require secondary gluing. The use of Kevlar® and other reinforcements, such as glass fibers to create even higher strength SCL composites is being explored.

Product Standards and Building Code Acceptance of Structural Composite Lumber

For several years, the manufacturers of the various proprietary SCL products in North America met with wood industry groups, building code officials, construction industry representatives and other interested parties, under the auspices of the American Society for Testing and Materials (ASTM) committees D07 Committee on Wood and D07.02 Subcommittee for Lumber and Engineered Wood Products for the purpose of developing an appropriate industry standard for these products. The first version of *ASTM D5456 Standard Specification for Evaluation of Structural Composite Lumber Products* was published in 1993. This is the primary product standard for the SCL industry, and is referenced extensively in the model building codes. The standard covers the requirements for qualification testing, determination of allowable design values, quality assurance and independent inspection requirements. The committees continue to update the standard through the procedures of ASTM.

The International Conference of Building Officials (ICBO) publishes *AC47 Acceptance Criteria for Structural Composite Lumber* (13). *AC47* references *ASTM D5456* and gives further requirements for acceptance of SCL products used in ICBO's jurisdictions, as well as a procedure for evaluating the performance of fasteners in SCL.

C33-93 Standard for Preservative Treatment of Structural Composite Lumber by Pressure Processes, a commodity treating standard for LVL and PSL, is published by the American Wood-Preservers' Association (14).

In 1995 the American Association of State Highway and Transportation Officials (AASHTO) released *Interim Specifications for Highway Bridges* (15), an amendment to its *Standard Specifications for Highway Bridges* (16), that includes SCL as a structural wood-based material and references *ASTM D5456*. Additionally, AASHTO will soon reference SCL in its material specifications *M-133* and *M-168* (17).

Under its Committee 05, the American National Standards Institute (ANSI) recently developed a draft standard titled *Structural Composite Lumber in Utility Structures* (18). ANSI already publishes *ANSI 10.8 American National Standard for Construction and Demolition Operations - Scaffolding - Safety Requirements* (19) whose appendix serves as a basis for LVL scaffold plank applications. Additional acceptances of LVL scaffold plank include reference to the government specification *MIL-L-19140E* (20) for fire retardant treated plank and *Directive No. 100-31* (21) for OSHA acceptance.

The American Institute of Timber Construction's *ANSI/AITC A190.1 Structural Glued-laminated Timber* (22) and *AITC 402-90 Standard for Laminated Veneer Lumber (LVL) Used in Structural Glued Laminated Timber*—which is found in *AITC 200-92 Inspection Manual for Structural Glued Laminated Timber (23)*—permit the use of LVL for the outer laminations of glued-laminated timber. A task force of ASTM's D07 Committee on Wood is working on a provision for including LVL in *ASTM D3737 Standard Method for Establishing Stresses for Structural Glued-laminated Timber (Glulam)* (24).

SCL is expected to be added to Clause 13 of *CSA 086.1 Engineering Design in Wood (Limit States Design) A National Standard of Canada* (25) by the end of 1996, with reference made to *ASTM D5456*.

Two standards for windows, doors and millwork that make reference to the use of SCL are Canadian Standards Association *CAN/CSA-A440-M90 Windows* (26) and the National Wood Window and Door Association standards *I.S. 4* (27) and *I.S.1-A Architectural Wood Flush Doors* (28).

In Japan there are two standards applicable to SCL, *Nourin Suisansho Kokuji #1494* (29) for LVL, and the acceptances of proprietary PSL and LSL under *Article #38* (30). In Australia and New Zealand, standard *DR94434 Structural Laminated Veneer Lumber* (31) is under development.

Building Code Acceptance of Structural Composite Lumber

All SCL products are proprietary and unique. As a result, each manufacturer of SCL has pursued acceptance for its proprietary products directly from the model building code organizations. These products cannot be interchanged because no industry-wide common grades have been established to serve as a basis for equivalence. Although some products may seem similar because of their presentation in the marketplace, equivalence should never be assumed. Thus, the manufacturer or model building code organization must be contacted to obtain the specific acceptance criteria for each SCL product.

Designing With Structural Composite Lumber

Two determinations must be made when using SCL products before beginning the design process:

1. What industry product standards and/or building code acceptances govern this particular application?

2. What specific proprietary SCL product is going to be used in this particular application?

It would be wrong, for example, to use a product standard or building code acceptance that relates to the use of SCL in buildings if the application is scaffolding, concrete forming or bridges. It would also be wrong to assume equivalence among all SCL products, because each is proprietary and unique. In fact, a manufacturer may offer several SCL product lines or grades within each line. Simply put, there is no commodity SCL. When sizing framing members for instance, it is also wrong to assume that any SCL product is an appropriate substitute for the sawn lumber and timbers cited in the conventional construction provisions of the model building codes, even if the allowable design stresses for the SCL are higher than those of the acceptable sawn products.

Design provisions in the *National Design Specification for Wood Construction* (NDS) (32) should not be presumed to apply to SCL unless the acceptances for the specific proprietary SCL product indicates so. Design provisions for connectors—nails, through-bolts, lag screws, shear plates, split rings, etc.—in the *NDS* have been developed for sawn lumber and timber and may not be appropriate for a particular SCL product. This caveat also applies to metal connector plates, joist hangers and other connectors available in the marketplace.

SCL is not sawn lumber and timber, and sawn lumber and timber is not SCL. Each SCL product is unique. The manufacturer of each SCL product is obligated to provide technical information and test results to ensure the proper application of its proprietary products. While all manufacturers provide technical literature, some also furnish computer software to assist designers and specifiers in designing with their products.

Member Orientation

The structural performance of SCL depends on the direction of the applied load relative to the member's orientation because of the alignment and/or strategic placement of wood elements in the manufacturing process. LVL, for example, can be used as either a joist or a plank, with load applied parallel or perpendicular, respectively, to its width. For this reason the building code acceptances for SCL products designate the allowable design values for both vertical and horizontal orientations.

Size or Volume Effect

All structural materials, including SCL, exhibit size or volume effects. That is, there is a different apparent stress performance or strength depending on the cross-sectional area and length of the member being tested. In theory, this relates to the probability of failure and the presence of a weak link in the chain of finite elements composing the member. Both the number of links (member size) and the variability in the strength among the links (statistical coefficient of variation) contribute to the member's strength. Because they have more links and a wider range of link strengths, larger members typically have a lower apparent strength. The converse is true for smaller members.

SCL has a significantly lower coefficient of variation in strength among members than that for structural grades of sawn lumber and timber. Research has shown that the size or volume effect theory holds true for SCL (33). The design adjustment factors for the size or volume (length, width and depth) of structural members follow the generalized equation:

$$k = \left(\frac{V_1}{V_2} \right)^m$$

Here k is the adjustment factor multiplier applied to the basic allowable design stress; m relates to the variability of the material; and V_1 and V_2 represent the volumes of the two members being considered.

Importantly, the adjustment factors for each SCL product are unique. They are also smaller than those for sawn lumber and timber. The correct size or volume effect design adjustment factors can be found in the manufacturer's design literature and in the specific SCL product building code acceptance.

Duration of Load

Like sawn lumber and timbers, SCL products exhibit duration of load effects. The load that a member can safely support, either continuously or intermittently, depends not only on its magnitude, but also on how long the load is maintained. The duration of load design adjustment factors commonly applied in designing with sawn lumber and timber may or may not be appropriate for specific SCL products (34). SCL products are reconstituted wood-based products made from various materials in different manufacturing processes. These parameters may affect their long term performance relative to duration of load. Building code acceptances for individual SCL products consider this design adjustment factor.

Deflection

The design value reported for the modulus of elasticity (MOE) in bending for sawn lumber and timber is typically the mean apparent MOE. That is, the value includes the effect of deflection due to shear. Since the amount of shear deflection depends on the span-to-depth ratio, the apparent MOE is actually a presumed span-to-depth ratio mean apparent MOE. Unfortunately, this issue is further complicated by the fact that MOE is orientation-dependent—joist versus plank—and that deflection is also sensitive to wood moisture content (35, 36). The manufacturers of SCL products and standards-writing committees recognize that many of the structural applications of SCL—non-repetitive use and heavily loaded, for example—are more likely to be optimized in design. They have chosen, therefore, to present the deflection characteristics of SCL products such that bending and shear deflections are accounted for separately by the designer.

Camber

Unlike glued-laminated timber, SCL is provided to the marketplace without camber. Camber is achievable in SCL only when members are bonded together in a secondary manufacturing process. The designer must consider if and how the lack of camber may affect each particular application.

Creep

Creep—the time-related deflection of a structural member under long term load—is generally less for a wood-based product whose moisture content at installation and in-service is near the equilibrium moisture content of the environment in which it will be used. Because SCL products are manufactured at a moisture content of 10 to 12 percent, they creep much less than sawn lumber and timber which is usually at 19 percent moisture content or higher when installed. However, creep should be considered whenever SCL products are used in high humidity environments and where limited deflection is critical, such as for headers over sliding or folding doors. The SCL manufacturer should be consulted for creep performance characteristics of the specific SCL product.

Moisture Content

An increase in moisture content generally decreases the strength and stiffness of all wood-based products. SCL products have building code-accepted allowable design values which are already adjusted to a moisture condition under which sawn lumber and timber will achieve an equilibrium moisture content of 12 percent. This relates to dry conditions of use. The moisture content design adjustment factors provided in the building codes and product standards for sawn lumber and timber are generally appropriate for SCL products as long as 12 percent moisture content is used as the starting basis. Most SCL product building code acceptances are limited to interior use; the manufacturer should be consulted for special considerations under exterior use.

Repetitive Member Design Adjustment

Building codes and product standards typically provide adjustment factors for increasing allowable design values in applications where repetitive members are closely spaced, such as in rafter and joist systems. The basis for these factors is somewhat obscure, but presumably, it relates to the probability of stronger members sharing loads transferred from adjacent weaker members. Thus, the statistical variability in strength and stiffness among the repetitive members becomes important. Since SCL has a lower coefficient of variation for strength than sawn lumber and timber, it does not deserve as large a repetitive member adjustment factor. That is the logic behind the building codes and product standards that have assigned repetitive member increase factors to SCL that are only about one-half of those for sawn lumber and timber. The issue of what design stresses the increases apply to—bending, tension, compression, shear, etc.—varies somewhat depending on which building code governs the application (37).

Preservative Treatment

Some pressure processes for introducing waterborne preservatives, as well as some preservatives, may adversely affect the strength of both sawn lumber and timber and SCL products. This is less of an issue with oilborne preservatives. The manufacturer of the SCL product must be consulted for any strength reduction factors that may apply.

Fire Retardant Treatment

Even after being treated with a fire retardant, all wood and wood-based products—including SCL—are still combustible. However, flame spread and char rates are greatly reduced. In recent years, fire retardant treatments for all wood products have been under scrutiny because of numerous field problems with certain chemical types. Interactions among the fire retardant, the temperature to which the treated product is exposed, the duration of exposure, and the wood moisture content have resulted in the rapid degradation of some treated lumber and plywood, especially in roof systems (38). There have been many failures and numerous legal claims. A designer or specifier is advised to exercise caution prior to recommending that any wood-based product be treated with a fire retardant. Specialized expertise or consultants and the fire retardant treatment company should be contacted before specifying these treatments. Research results and technical advisories regarding the use of fire retardant treated wood and wood-based products are available from the Forest Products Laboratory in Madison, Wisconsin (39).

Fire Resistance

The rate of flame spread and charring of untreated sawn lumber and timber and SCL depends on many factors including the wood species, density and moisture content, and the member's cross-sectional area. The use of fire-resistant gypsum panels to enclose wood-based framing, firestopping and other techniques for creating fire-resistant constructions are well known. Provisions in building codes and product standards regarding fire resistance for sawn lumber and timber should not be used for SCL products unless specifically designated in the building code acceptances for these products. Again, the SCL manufacturer should be consulted for information on the fire resistance of its products. There has been concern expressed by some designers and specifiers that the adhesive in SCL may melt in a fire. The concern is both unfounded and chemically incorrect. Under fire exposure, the thermosetting adhesives used in SCL char at essentially the same rate as the bonded wood.

Temperature

The effect of temperature on the strength of SCL generally follows that for sawn lumber and timber. However, in applications involving extraordinary temperatures (above 150 °F), such as in freezers, hot plenums or kilns, the SCL manufacturer should be consulted for any strength reductions that might apply.

Connectors

As with sawn lumber and timbers, the orientation of the grain of the wood elements into which a fastener is inserted dictates the connector's performance in SCL. For example, the allowable design values for nails depend not only on the direction of loading, but on whether the nail is driven into the edge, face or end of the member. Similarly, the allowable spacing between connectors such as through-bolts depends on the orientation of the grain of the veneers or strands. Connectors in SCL products perform uniquely according to the product and its grade, and possibly differently than in sawn lumber and timber.

Side Loading of Multiple-Ply Structural Composite Lumber

It is common to use multiple members of SCL side-by-side for girders, beams, headers and other bending members. In many cases, a load is applied to only one side of the multiple member by joists or other framing members mounted on its face. The designer is advised to consider the requirements for the connections between the plies—nails, through-bolts, lag screws—as well as the torsional effects that one-side-loading exerts on the composite member.

Notches and Holes

Depending on their size, shape and location, notches and holes can have a significant effect on the performance of SCL structural members, just as they do in sawn lumber and timber. Indeed, the effect may be magnified because of localized stress risers, and the fact that SCL members are often heavily loaded and non-repetitive. SCL structural members are usually designed with these considerations in mind, and there is no reason to think that they would perform differently. Some manufacturers have conducted limited research on this subject and present guidelines for allowable notches and holes. When in doubt, contact the manufacturer.

Installation

Due to their higher allowable design stresses and cost, designs using SCL typically are more optimized than those based on sawn lumber and timber. As a result, SCL members are more likely to be heavily loaded, and used in non-repetitive framing systems. Because of the optimization of their use in designs, SCL products can be less forgiving of the abuses of poor workmanship during installation. Joints and connections between members, for instance, must be made in accordance with the manufacturer's recommendations and the designer's specifications and tolerances. Proper storage and handling of these products during shipping and at the job site is essential. Additionally, inspection of the framing system during the construction process and after completion of the structure is critical. Manufacturers typically provide guidelines and warnings to assist builders in properly storing, handling and installing SCL products.

Suggested Specification

The specification for SCL applications should include reference to the governing industry or product standards, the quality assurance provisions therein, and the building code acceptance for the product selected. Builders and contractors are strongly motivated to minimize costs, and do not necessarily recognize fully the differences between products, particularly if they look the same. The specification should also reference the requirement for third party inspection of the manufacturer and importantly, the proper marking and identification of the product. Most manufacturers of these proprietary products have engineers in-house to assist architects, designers and builders in writing specifications and selecting the correct product(s) for the application.

References

1. American Society for Testing and Materials. 1993. ASTM D5456 Standard Specification for Evaluation of Structural Composite Lumber Products. ASTM. West Conshohocken, Pennsylvania.

2. Forest Products Laboratory. 1987. Wood Handbook: Wood as an Engineering Material. Agriculture Handbook No. 72. USDA Forest Service Forest Products Laboratory. Madison, Wisconsin.

3. Stamm, A. and R. Seborg. 1960. Forest Products Laboratory Resin-Treated, Laminated, Compressed Wood (Compreg). Report No. 1381 (revised). USDA Forest Service Forest Products Laboratory. Madison, Wisconsin.

4. Stamm, A. and R. Seborg. 1962. Forest Products Laboratory Resin-Treated Wood (Impreg). Report No. 1380 (revised). USDA Forest Service Forest Products Laboratory. Madison, Wisconsin.

5. FPL Press-Lam Research Team. 1977. Press-Lam: Progress in Technical Development of Laminated Veneer Structural Products. Research Paper FPL 279. USDA Forest Service Forest Products Laboratory. Madison, Wisconsin.

6. Pieters, A. 1979. Preprint 3534 Ultrasonic Energy: A New Method for Veneer Grading. ASCE Annual Convention and Exposition. Boston, Massachusetts.

7. Koenigshof, G. 1986. Strength and Stiffness of Composite Floor Joists. Forest Products Journal. 36(9):66-70.

8. Jordan, B. no date. Scrimber: The Leading Edge of Timber Technology. Scrimber International. Mount Gambier, Australia.

9. Guss, L. 1995. Engineered Wood Products: The Future is Bright. Forest Products Journal. 45(7/8):17-24.

10. Nelson, S. 1976. Preprint 2800 University of Idaho Stadium. ASCE Annual Convention and Exposition. Philadelphia, Pennsylvania.

11. Meyer, C. and M. Ritter. 1995. Stress-Laminated Bridges of Structural Composite Lumber. Wood Design Focus. 6(2):20-23.

12. Meyer, C. Laminated Veneer Lumber Bridges: A Case History. Wood Design Focus. 1(4):8-9.

13. ICBO Evaluation Service, Inc. 1995. AC47 Structural Composite Lumber. ICBO Evaluation Service. Whittier, California.

14. American Wood-Preservers' Association. 1995. C33 Standard for Preservative Treatment of Structural Composite Lumber by Pressure Process. AWPA. Woodstock, Maryland.

15. American Association of State Highway and Transportation Officials. 1995. Interim Specifications for Highway Bridges. AASHTO. Washington, D. C.

16. American Association of State Highway and Transportation Officials. 1991. Standard Specifications for Highway Bridges. AASHTO. Washington, D. C.

17. American Association of State Highway and Transportation Officials. 1995. Standard Specifications for Transportation Materials and Methods of Sampling and Testing. AASHTO. Washington, D. C.

18. American National Standards Institute. ANSI 05 Draft Standard for Structural Composite Lumber in Utility Structures. ANSI. New York, New York.

19. American National Standards Institute. 1977. ANSI 10.8 American National Standard Safety Requirements for Scaffolding. ANSI. New York, New York.

20. Department of Defense. 1984. MIL-L-19140E Military Specification-Lumber and Plywood, Fire Retardant Treated. DOD. Washington, D. C.

21. Occupational Health and Safety Administration. 1975. OSHA Directive No. 100-31 Laminated Scaffold Planks. OSHA. Washington, D. C.

22. American Institute of Timber Construction. 1992. ANSI/AITC A190.1 Structural Glued-laminated Timber. AITC. Englewood, Colorado.

23. American Institute of Timber Construction. AITC 200-92 Inspection Manual. AITC. Englewood, Colorado.

24. American Society for Testing and Materials. 1995. ASTM D3737 Standard Method for Establishing Stresses for Structural Glued-laminated Timber (Glulam). ASTM. West Conshohocken, Pennsylvania.

25. Canadian Standards Association. 1994. CSA 086.1 Engineering Design In Wood (Limit States Design) A National Standard of Canada. CSA. Rexdale, Ontario, Canada.

26. Canadian Standards Association. 1994. CAN/CSA-A440-M90 Windows A National Standard of Canada. CSA. Rexdale, Ontario, Canada.

27. National Wood Window and Door Association. 1991. NWWDA IS-4. NWWDA. Des Plaines, Illinois.

28. National Wood Window and Door Association. 1991. NWWDA IS 1-A Architectural Wood Flush Doors. NWWDA. Des Plaines, Illinois.

29. Japan Plywood Inspection Company. 1994. Nourin Suisansho Kokuji #1494 JAS Structural LVL Standard. JPIC. Tokyo, Japan.

30. Building Center of Japan. 1990. Article #38 The Building Standard Law of Japan. BCJ. Tokyo, Japan.

31. Standards Australia and Standards New Zealand. 1994. Australia/New Zealand DR94434. Homebush, Australia and Wellington, New Zealand.

32. American Forest & Paper Association. 1991. National Design Specification for Wood Construction. AF&PA. Washington, D. C.

33. Sharp, D. and S. Suddarth. 1981. Volumetric Effects in Structural Composite Lumber. International Timber Engineering Conference. London, England.

34. Wood, L. 1951. Relation of Strength of Wood to Duration of Load. Report No. R1916. USDA Forest Service Forest Products Laboratory. Madison, Wisconsin.

35. Skaggs, T. and D. Bender. 1991. Shear Deflection of Composite Wood Beams. Paper No. 91-4543. American Society of Agricultural Engineers.

36. Bolduc, W. 1991. The Importance of Young's Modulus for High Strength Structural Wood Products. 1991 International Timber Engineering Conference London, England.

37. Sharp, D. and D. Gromala. 1988. Concepts of Wood Structural System Performance. International Timber Engineering Conference.

38. Levan, S. and J. Winandy. 1990. Effects of Fire Retardant Treatments on Wood Strength: A Review. Wood and Fiber Science. 22(1):113-131.

39. Levan, S. and M. Collet. 1989. Choosing and Applying Fire-Retardant-Treated Plywood and Lumber for Roof Designs. General Technical Report FPL-GTR-62. USDA Forest Service Forest Products Laboratory. Madison, Wisconsin.

Chapter 7

Fire Protection Design and Engineered Wood Products

Michael J. Slifka, P. E.

PFS Corporation
Madison, Wisconsin

In 1961 the then-National Forest Products Association (NFoPA)—now the American Forest & Paper Association—conducted a comparative fire test on side-by-side exposed wood and steel members supporting a roof deck carrying a simulated load (1). The wood members were 4-inch by 14-inch sawn lumber; steel members were 14-inch-deep open web joists. Both were sized to accommodate the design load placed on them. The purpose of the test was to determine whether sawn lumber joists designed to carry the same load as comparable steel joists would survive in a fire at least as long as the steel members.

To that end, the test was a success. By the time the test furnace had raised the temperature inside the chamber to approximately 1300 °F 13 minutes into the test, the steel joists had deflected 18 inches. Shortly after the furnace was turned off, the steel-supported section of the roof deck collapsed. In contrast, the wood joists maintained their structural integrity throughout the fire test with minimal deflection—about 1/2 inch, and though their surfaces were heavily charred, 80 percent of their cross section was unaffected. They continued to safely carry the simulated roof load after the furnace was turned off.

For all the eagerness that NFoPA put into this comparative test, the last sentence in its report makes the telling point about this and most of the other fire tests and related data developed by the wood industry to date. "It is evident, from the results, that unprotected and untreated wood joists have substantially more fire resistance than unprotected steel joists." Despite this convincing demonstration, model building codes still allow only limited occupancy use and limited building size for both unprotected wood- and steel-framed structures.

The technical record of fire testing of wood and wood-based products is replete with these one-of-a-kind comparative tests of unprotected wood versus other unprotected structural materials. The results of these tests have had little bearing on resolving real world design issues for design professionals who wish to include wood and wood-based products in their proposed designs. One reason is that despite retaining their structural integrity in fires, flames typically spread rapidly across the surfaces of wood members. Today, however, more and more wood and wood-based structural members and components—especially engineered wood products—are being utilized because of the increasing use of fire-protected design approaches that allow wood-frame buildings with a wider occupancy use and greater height and floor area. Fire safety in these buildings is ensured through the creation of fire-rated—also referred to as fire-protected or sheathed—wall, floor/ceiling, and roof/ceiling assemblies in which wood members are shielded with fire resistant materials.

Wood-frame Structures and Building Codes

Being a carbon-based, cellulosic material, wood will combust, pyrolize or otherwise burn when subjected to either sufficient radiant energy (as from a fire a short distance away) or sufficient direct heat (as from a flame in direct contact). The wood design and technical literature abounds with reports of attempts to brush, spray, dip, immerse and pressure-treat wood with a variety of chemicals to alter its combustibility. While these methods represent effective treatments for reducing the spread of flames across the surface of wood, they do not make wood fireproof. Given enough heat and time, even fire retardant treated wood members and assemblies will char and ultimately fail under fire attack. Fire retardant treated wood, however, does not contribute fuel to encourage fire growth.

Given untreated wood's known combustibility, it is not difficult to understand the model building codes' traditional approach regarding wood—minimize its use to a few occupancies, primarily residential and other low hazard types, and to structures that are limited in height or small in area. This limit-the-use-of-wood approach has evolved over the last two centuries as the building codes' purpose has changed from preventing entire cities built with wood from suffering a conflagration, to preventing more than one city block from burning, to preventing a fire from escaping from the structure of origin, to preventing a fire from leaving the floor of origin, to preventing a fire from leaving the area or room of origin. With this ever more exacting attempt to either allow for only small fires in highly compartmentalized construction, or to prevent ignition from taking place altogether, wood is only reluctantly recognized by the model building codes for limited use.

Currently, the model building codes either severely limit the size—height and area—of buildings built with wood, or require that wood structural members be protected if a larger structure is to be erected. In building code terminology, "protected" refers to wood-frame structures in which the wooden members have been either sheathed with a non-combustible or limitedly combustible material like gypsum board or metal lath and plaster, or insulated with a thermal barrier of fireproofing material, or treated with chemicals that inhibit combustion, as is the case with fire retardant treated lumber. The fire resistance afforded by both load-bearing and non-load-bearing protected assemblies is most often expressed in terms of the minimum time they can be expected to survive in a fire—1-hour rated or 2-hour rated, for example—before burn through or collapse will occur. "Unprotected" describes structures in which no additional sheathing, insulating or treating of wood has taken place in order to reduce its combustibility or temporarily shield it from fire.

The three model building codes in use in the United States—ICBO's Uniform Building Code (2), BOCA's National Building Code (3) and SBCCI's Standard Building Code (4)—reflect the limited recognition of unprotected structures built with wood-frame load-bearing walls (Table 1). Examples of structures subject to the size limitations of Table 1 include fast-food restaurants, convenience stores, small office buildings and filling stations.

Table 1. Maximum allowable building size for unprotected wood construction.

	Maximum Number of Occupied Stories	Maximum Building Height (ft.)	Maximum Single Floor Area (sq. ft.)
National Building Code	2	35	7,200
Standard Building Code	2	40	10,000
Uniform Building Code	2	40	12,000

In contrast, by providing one hour of fire protection to the structural members and loading-bearing components and assemblies in a wood-frame structure by means of sheathing, insulation or treatment, the same building codes allow the increases in height and area shown in Table 2. Structures regulated as per Table 2 include office buildings, apartments, and small office/warehouse combinations, as long as activities in the latter do not involve hazardous operations or materials.

Table 2. Maximum allowable building size for protected wood construction.

	Maximum Number of Occupied Stories	Maximum Building Height (ft.)	Maximum Single Floor Area (sq. ft.)
National Building Code	3	40	15,300
Standard Building Code	3	50	15,000
Uniform Building Code	3	50	21,000

Where fire-protected wood-frame interior partitions and floor and roof assemblies are used in structures with masonry or other 2-hour rated exterior bearing walls, the model building codes permit even larger structures (Table 3). The size restrictions of Table 3 apply to larger apartment and office buildings, motels and mid-size warehouses; hazardous processes or materials are again prohibited.

Table 3. Maximum allowable building size for protected wood construction with masonry or other 2-hour rated exterior bearing walls.

	Maximum Number of Occupied Stories	Maximum Building Height (ft.)	Maximum Single Floor Area (sq. ft.)
National Building Code	4	50	19,000
Standard Building Code	4	65	24,000
Uniform Building Code	4	65	27,000

Since protected wood construction permits significantly greater story height and floor area than unprotected construction in certain residential, business and mercantile occupancies, it is utilized in most cases. As seen in Tables 1, 2 and 3, the maximum allowable number of stories increases by up to 100 percent, building height by up to 62 percent, and floor area by up to 164 percent when fire-protected wood assemblies are utilized. As the maximum building size may vary depending on the specific occupancy and use, the design professional should carefully review the pertinent model building code to determine the actual allowable maximums. Clearly, the use of fire-protected wall, floor and roof assemblies gives the design professional the greatest flexibility when considering the use of wood and wood-based products in small to medium size structures.

Wood and Fire

In their report *The Performance of Wood in Fire* (6), investigators at the Forest Products Laboratory in Madison, Wisconsin, summarized their findings from decades of research on wood and fire. "The property of wood which enables it to burn at a moderate rate, through a slow process of pyrolytic decomposition, followed by charring and flaming, is one of its important characteristics. It is intimately related with man's oldest uses for nature's versatile material. On the one hand, for shelter and protection, and on the other, for fuel..."

The report goes on to point out that the direct burning of wood is rare. Rather, the more correct term is pyrolysis, a process in which the wood decomposes when subjected to heat and gives off flammable gases and tars, leaving behind a char residue. Pyrolysis of wood is both temperature-sensitive and temperature-driven. At temperatures below 520 °F, it is slow in occurring and requires the external application of heat to sustain it. At or above 520 °F, pyrolysis is rapid and heat is released as a byproduct. After flammable gases given off by the wood as a byproduct of pyrolysis mix with sufficient oxygen, flaming combustion can occur. Sometimes a pilot flame is needed to ignite the flammable gases, though high temperature alone can also cause ignition. If the rate of heating the wood is twice or more as great as that required for pilot ignition, spontaneous ignition is possible.

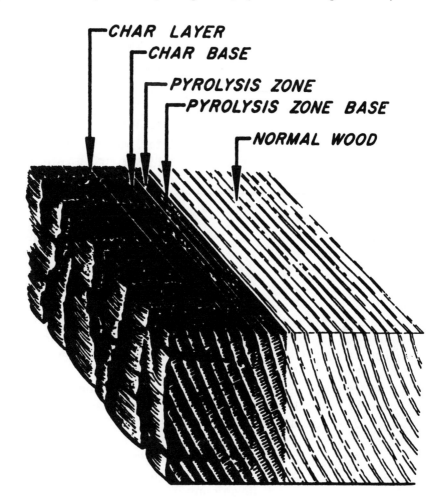

Figure 1. During fire exposure, wood chars at a rate of 3/4 to 1-1/2 inches per hour, depending on its moisture content and density (FPL M 130 020).

Due to wood's poor thermal conductivity, high specific heat and the insulating layer of char formed on its surface, the pyrolysis reaction cannot quickly penetrate into a wood member (Fig. 1). Rather, it will slowly build up the layer of char on its surface. Rates of char formation are typically in the 3/4 to 1-1/2 inches per hour range. When the flammable gases are spent, oxygen reaching the char layer will cause it to burn by glowing combustion, like charcoal in a barbecue grille. This occurs only at temperatures in excess of

1200 °F. Flaming combustion and glowing combustion are independent processes. The ignitibility of a wood member depends on its moisture content, density, and time and temperature of heating, as well as its mass and geometry (6, 16) (Table 4).

Table 4. Typical range of ignition temperatures for wood (6, 16).

spontaneous ignition	650 to 800 °F[a]
exothermic heating point	445 to 465 °F[b]
pilot flame ignition	315 to 385 °F for untreated wood[c]
	290 to 500 °F for treated wood[d]
	608 to 660 °F for softwoods[e]
	590 to 740 °F for hardwoods[f]

[a]small wood samples only   [d]40 minutes pre-heating
[b]untreated wood   [e]4 to 6-1/2 minutes pre-heating
[c]40 minutes pre-heating   [f]4 to 6-1/2 minutes pre-heating

Flame Spread

A dimensionless quantity, the flame spread of wood and wood-based materials is most often determined using *ASTM E84 Standard Test Method for Surface Burning Characteristics of Building Materials* (7). Traditionally, flame spread was simply a comparison of the rate of propagation of a flame over the surface of the material being tested with the established rates of 0 (zero) for cement asbestos board and 100 for red oak flooring. However, red oak is no longer used as a standard in *ASTM E84*. Flame spread is now determined in tests in which the furnace is first calibrated with a standard noncombustible material. Often confused with fire resistance, flame spread ratings do not necessarily relate to a material's ability to resist destruction by fire, nor can they be used to predict a material's fire performance. Flame spread relates only to a material's surface burning characteristics. Interior finish materials—wood flooring, wall paneling and gypsum board, for example—are classified according to their flame spread rating (Table 5). The most resistant to the spread of flames, Class A or I finishes have a rating of 0-25. Flame spread ratings for Class B or II finishes are 25-75, and for Class C or III, 76-200 (10).

Fire Penetration

Since the cross-sectional area of a structural wood member determines its load-carrying capacity, the rate at which its surface chars during a fire determines how long it will safely support a load before collapsing (6, 16). The rate of charring of wood during fire exposure ranges from 1/30 to 1/50 of an inch per minute, or an average of about 1-1/2 inches per hour for untreated wood, and is reduced as either its moisture content or density increases.

Table 5. Typical flame spread ratings for various wood and wood-based products.

	flame spread rating
sawn lumber and plywood	75-135
oriented strand board	135-160
structural insulation board	46-170
medium density fiberboard	97-144
hardboard	87-119
particle board	83-106
fire retardant treated wood panels	<25-75

Fire Retardant Treatment

While dimension lumber and plywood pressure-impregnated with fire retardants is widely available, engineered wood products with such treatments are available only upon request. These proprietary chemical formulations do not render wood and wood-based products fireproof; they simply inhibit the spread of flames across their surfaces. Some fire retardants may reduce the strength of wood and wood-based products after treatment (25). Designers must account for this loss of strength when using fire retardant treated structural members, and should contact the manufacturer of the fire retardant, as well as the manufacturer of the engineered wood product, to obtain the appropriate strength adjustment factors (26).

Engineered Wood Products and Fire

Fire Research Needs

In its *National Engineered Lightweight Construction Fire Research Project Literature Search & Technical Analysis* (8), the National Fire Protection Research Foundation (NFPRF) reported "There is very little test data available on the fire endurance performance of [wood] I-joists. Unsheathed (unprotected) testing is limited to non-standardized and semi-standardized ad hoc tests that can only shed limited light on fire performance characteristics of these products. From this testing, though, it can be surmised that [wood] I-joists will perform less well under fire conditions than an equivalent sized solid-sawn member. This is intuitively obvious, given the differences in the cross sections of each. Solid-sawn sections have more "fat" to burn through. To gain fire performance information that will provide the needed information for firefighting tactics, only standardized testing should be performed." Similar concerns have been raised regarding the fire endurance of metal plate connected wood trusses, which are typically made with 2x4 chords and webs (14, 22).

NFPRF also noted that "The standardized comparative testing of unsheathed assemblies to date is limited to 2x10 joists, metal plate connected wood trusses, and steel C-joists... There are no tests available for wood I-joists, metal web trusses, PECS web trusses, and steel bar joists. Standardized comparative tests do exist for protected assemblies for all lightweight components, due to model code requirements."

It is apparent that the model building codes, by prohibiting sizable wood-frame structures, do not require any testing to determine the fire resistance of unprotected wood structures or their component assemblies. In its necessarily conservative approach, building codes treat unprotected structures, their component assemblies and the wood members that make up the components as having no fire resistance.

Today, there is an increased emphasis on firefighter life safety issues. If further research and testing is to be conducted on the fire resistance of unprotected wood members, assemblies or structures, a new protocol may have to be created that goes beyond the current method—*ASTM E 119 Standard Test Methods for Fire Tests of Building Construction and Materials* (9)—used for unprotected structures. At this time, however, there is no call for developing a new protocol, no existing data base, and no expectation for new fire test data to be developed for unprotected wood components, assemblies and structures. As such, firefighters must exercise extreme caution when dealing with fires in both unprotected wood-frame and steel-framed structures.

Adhesives in Engineered Wood Products

The phenol formaldehyde, resorcinol formaldehyde, phenol resorcinol-formaldehyde and isocyanate adhesives used in making engineered wood products are thermoset polymers that do not soften or melt or lose their strength or adhesion under fire conditions. Researchers have shown that phenol-resorcinol-formaldehyde bondlines remain intact even in charred wood (23). During fire exposure, glued-laminated timbers perform no differently than sawn timbers of the same size. To date, there is no evidence to suggest that engineered wood products like laminated veneer lumber and parallel strand lumber will behave any differently in a fire than the sawn lumber and timbers they replace.

Principles for Achieving Fire Resistance

Whether structural members of sawn lumber and timber or engineered wood products are used individually or in an assembly, they will eventually char and burn under fire attack. Model building codes drive design professionals to create wood-frame buildings with fire-protected or sheathed assemblies. As engineered wood products behave under fire conditions similar to sawn lumber and timber, more and more manufacturers of engineered wood products have sponsored proprietary fire tests using their products and the same protective sheathing techniques successfully used for years with sawn products.

Harmathy's Rules

The techniques used for designing and constructing fire-rated (protected) wall, floor/ceiling and roof/ceiling assemblies are based fundamentally on ten principles for achieving fire resistance first enunciated by renowned fire researcher Tibor Z. Harmathy (24).

> *Rule 1. The "thermal" fire endurance of a construction consisting of a number of parallel layers is greater than the sum of the "thermal" fire endurance characteristics of the individual layers when exposed separately to fire.*

In other words, the whole is greater than the sum of its parts. For example, 1/2 inch gypsum board has a fire endurance rating of 15 minutes. But two layers of 1/2 inch gypsum board have an estimated endurance rating not of 15 + 15 = 30 minutes, but of about 40 minutes. It is the creation of a small air space between the layers of material fastened together that increases the fire resistance of the assembly.

> *Rule 2. The fire endurance of a construction does not decrease with the addition of further layers.*

Just as adding more insulation to an already insulated attic will further reduce heat loss, adding more fire resistant material to an existing fire resistive design will further increase its fire resistance.

> *Rule 3. The fire endurance of constructions containing continuous air gaps or cavities is greater than the fire endurance of similar constructions of the same weight, but containing no air gaps or cavities.*

Again, air is a good insulator. The presence of air gaps or cavities between framing members inside a wall or floor/ceiling assembly adds to its fire resistive value when compared with a similar assembly without air pockets.

> *Rule 4. The farther an air gap or cavity is located from the exposed surface, the more beneficial its effect on the fire endurance.*

As fire attacks the exposed surface of a wall or floor/ceiling assembly, heat is conducted into its interior. Air gaps inside an assembly are effective in resisting the further advance of conductive heat flow. The farther away the air gap is from the flame, the more protection it provides. As a result, a wall assembly with an air gap 2 inches behind its surface will perform better in fire resistance tests than one with an air gap only 1/2 inch behind its surface. Once the air gap is exposed to direct flames, its insulating ability is lost.

Rule 5. The fire endurance of an assembly cannot be increased by increasing the thickness of the completely enclosed air layer.

As air cavities formed by studs and joists become deeper than 4 inches, convection currents will form and defeat the insulative effectiveness of the air gap.

Rule 6. Layers of materials of low thermal conductivity are better utilized on the side of the construction on which fire is more likely to happen.

Simply put, placing the most insulative materials closest to the fire produces the best results.

Rule 7. The fire endurance of asymmetrical constructions depends on the direction of heat flow.

Wall and floor/ceiling assemblies built with different materials on each face will have a different fire endurance rating depending on which face is exposed to the fire. If an assembly is asymmetric, a fire applied to the side with the poorer insulative materials will produce a failure faster than if the fire were applied to the side with the better insulative materials.

Rule 8. The presence of moisture, if it does not result in explosive spalling, increases the fire endurance.

In short, high moisture content increases an assembly's fire resistance. The greater the amount of moisture in an assembly under fire attack, the more heat energy that will be absorbed in driving the moisture off. As a result, the pyrolysis reaction is prolonged and flaming combustion delayed. Concrete is an exception. Excessive moisture in it will be converted to steam under fire attack, and can cause explosive spalling.

> *Rule 9. Load-supporting elements, such as beams, girders and joists, yield higher fire endurance when subject to fire endurance tests as parts of floor, roof or ceiling assemblies than they would when tested separately.*

Under fire conditions, the overall fire resistance of a structure or assembly made up of many wood members will be greater than that of any individual member because of load-sharing among the members.

> *Rule 10. The load-supporting elements (beams, girders, joists, etc.) of a floor, roof or ceiling assembly can be replaced by such other load-supporting elements, which, when tested separately, yielded fire endurance not less than that of the assembly.*

Building code officials will accept a substitute structural member for use in an assembly that achieved a 30-minute fire endurance rating if, for example, the substitute member demonstrated a 30-minute rating when tested alone.

Designing Fire-Protected Assemblies

Component Additive Method

Harmathy's rules are also given in AF&PA's *Component Additive Method (CAM) for Calculating and Demonstrating Assembly Fire Endurance* (13). The CAM method has been adopted or is being reviewed for adoption by many building codes, including the three model building codes. The CAM method is available for use by design professionals for calculating fire ratings for unique structural assemblies using either sawn lumber and timber or engineered wood products not already accepted by building codes. With the CAM method, the calculated fire resistance of an assembly takes into account the fire endurance of the exposed shielding and the time to failure of the framing members, as well as any extra protection afforded by cavity insulation (Tables 6, 7 and 8).

Table 6. Fire resistance time assigned to protective membranes before failure (burn through or collapse) will occur (13).

Description of Finish	Time (min.)
3/8 inch Douglas fir plywood, phenolic bonded	5
½ inch Douglas fir plywood, phenolic bonded	10
5/8 inch Douglas fir plywood, phenolic bonded	15
3/8 inch gypsum board	10
½ inch gypsum board	15
5/8 inch gypsum board	20
½ inch Type X gypsum board	25
5/8 inch Type X gypsum board	40
Double 3/8 inch gypsum board	25
½ + 3/8 inch gypsum board	35
Double 1/2 inch gypsum board	40

Notes:

1. On walls, gypsum board shall be installed with the long dimension parallel to framing members with all joints finished. However, 5/8 inch Type X gypsum wallboard may be installed horizontally with the horizontal joints unsupported.

2. On floor/ceiling or roof/ceiling assemblies, gypsum board shall be installed with the long dimension perpendicular to framing members and shall have all joints finished.

Table 7. Fire resistance time assigned to wood-frame components before failure (burn through or collapse) will occur (13).

Description of Frames	Time (min.)
Wood studs, 16 inches on center	20
Wood joists, 16 inches on center	10
Wood roof and floor truss assemblies, 24 inches on center	5

Table 8. Fire resistance time assigned for additional protection before failure (burn through or collapse) will occur (13).

Description of additional protection	Time (min.)
Add to the fire endurance rating of wood stud walls if the spaces between the studs are filled with rockwool or slag mineral wood batts weighing not less than 1/4 lb./sq. ft. of wall surface.	15
Add to the fire endurance rating of non-load bearing stud walls if the spaces between the studs are filled with glass fiber batts weighing not less than 1/4 lb./sq. ft. of wall surface.	5

Using Approved Fire-Rated Assemblies

In lieu of calculating the fire resistance of a structural assembly, the design professional can also draw from the sizable library of protected assemblies already tested under *ASTM E119* (9) that were developed by the manufacturers of engineered wood products. Some of the assemblies tested are proprietary in nature and available to the design professional only from the manufacturer or supplier of the specific engineered wood product. Others using commodity wood products have been made public via directory listings of fire-rated assemblies published by nationally recognized fire testing laboratories and listing agencies, such as Underwriters Laboratories and Factory Mutual Research Laboratories (Figs. 2 and 3). (Note that the examples shown in Figures 2 and 3 are for illustration purposes only and do not contain all the fastening and material specifications needed to construct them.) In addition, accepted designs for protected wood-frame assemblies are readily available in the research and industry association literature (5, 11, 12, 15, 17-21).

The benefit to the design professional in specifying a fire-rated assembly that is already tested is that acceptance by the building code authority having jurisdiction is achieved quickly. Development of a unique protected assembly via the CAM method or by demonstrating its effectiveness through full-scale fire testing is possible, however, the time and cost to achieve regulatory acceptance via this latter route may be significant.

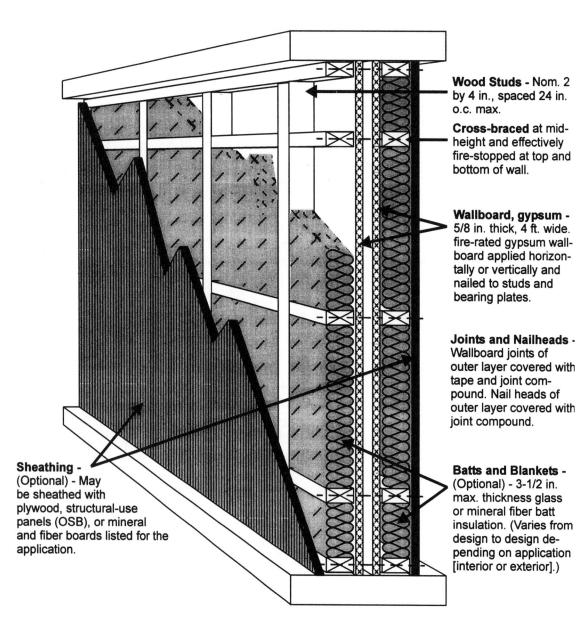

Wood Studs - Nom. 2 by 4 in., spaced 24 in. o.c. max.

Cross-braced at mid-height and effectively fire-stopped at top and bottom of wall.

Wallboard, gypsum - 5/8 in. thick, 4 ft. wide. fire-rated gypsum wallboard applied horizontally or vertically and nailed to studs and bearing plates.

Joints and Nailheads - Wallboard joints of outer layer covered with tape and joint compound. Nail heads of outer layer covered with joint compound.

Batts and Blankets - (Optional) - 3-1/2 in. max. thickness glass or mineral fiber batt insulation. (Varies from design to design depending on application [interior or exterior].)

Sheathing - (Optional) - May be sheathed with plywood, structural-use panels (OSB), or mineral and fiber boards listed for the application.

Figure 2. Example of a 1-hour fire-rated wall assembly (adapted from 28).

Flooring - 4 by 8 ft. by 23/32 in. thick interior plywood with exterior glue and T & G long edges. Installed perpendicular to joists with end joists centered over joists and staggered. Some fire assemblies may use OSB in lieu of plywood.

Wood Joists - Nom. 2 by 10 in., spaced 24 in. o.c. max, fire-stopped.

Cross Bridging - Nom. 1 by 3 in. or nom. 2 by 10 in. solid blocking.

Rafters - Nom. 2 by 6 in., spaced 24 in. o.c. max, bridged laterally with solid blocking 7 ft. o.c. max.

Batts and Blankets - (Optional) - 3-1/2 in. max. thickness glass or mineral fiber batt insulation located mid-height or higher up in extended space.

Wallboard, gypsum - 5/8 in. thick, 4 ft. wide. Wallboard or lath applied horizontally or vertically and nailed to studs and bearing plates 7 in. o.c..

Light fixture - (optional) - Installed per requirements of the listing of the fire-rated assembly.

Sheathing - (Optional) - Varies depending upon assembly that was fire tested. May be plywood, OSB or mineral and fiber board.

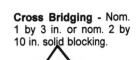

Figure 3. Example of a 1-hour fire-rated floor/ceiling assembly (adapted from 28).

Sprinklers

Automatic sprinkler systems are also an effective means of providing fire protection in wood-frame structures. The National Fire Protection Association's *NFPA 13 Standard for the Installation of Sprinkler Systems* (27) gives guidelines for properly locating sprinklers in structures framed with sawn lumber and timber, as well as engineered wood products such as metal plate connected trusses and wood I-joists. The additional load imposed on structural members by sprinkler piping and the water contained in it, as well as the sprinkler/framing connection details, must be considered during the building design phase. The manufacturer of the specific engineered wood product should be consulted for instructions for attaching sprinkler pipes and heads to its products.

Summary

While engineered wood products are relatively new to the design community, their performance under fire exposure and the fire protection methods for using them safely in building designs mirror the tried-and-true methods already developed for creating fire-protected assemblies for buildings framed with sawn lumber and timber.

The designer seeking to enhance the fire resistance of a structure or assembly built with either sawn wood or engineered wood products can employ several techniques, including:

1. sheathing the assembly with a non-combustible or limitedly combustible layer of material such as gypsum board or metal lath and plaster

2. coating members with approved fireproofing materials, or using fire retardant treated sawn wood and engineered wood products

3. combining sheathing and treatment to achieve higher levels of fire resistance (2 to 3 hours); adding insulation, firestopping and draftstopping at critical locations in an assembly to create air gaps

4. installing a sprinkler system

References

1. American Forest & Paper Association. 1961. Technical Report No. 1 Comparative Fire Test on Wood and Steel Joists. AF&PA. Washington, D. C.

2. International Conference of Building Officials. 1994. Uniform Building Code. ICBO. Whittier, California.

3. Building Officials & Code Administrators International, Inc. 1996. National Building Code. BOCA. Country Club Hills, Illinois.

4. Southern Building Code Congress International, Inc. 1994. Standard Building Code. SBCCI. Birmingham, Alabama.

5. Building Officials & Code Administrators International, Inc. 1994. Chapter 7 Fire Resistance of Archaic Materials and Assemblies *in* Guidelines for Determining Fire Resistance Ratings of Building Elements. BOCA. Country Club Hills, Illinois.

6. Forest Products Laboratory. 1960. The Performance of Wood in Fire. Report No. 2202. USDA Forest Service Forest Products Laboratory. Madison, Wisconsin.

7. American Society for Testing and Materials. 1996. ASTM E84 Standard Test Method for Surface Burning Characteristics of Building Materials. ASTM. West Conshohocken, Pennsylvania.

8. National Fire Protection Research Foundation. 1992. National Engineered Lightweight Construction Fire Research Project Literature Search & Technical Analysis. NFPRF. Quincy, Massachusetts.

9. American Society for Testing and Materials. 1995. ASTM E119 Standard Test Methods for Fire Tests of Building Construction and Materials. ASTM. West Conshohocken, Pennsylvania.

10. American Forest & Paper Association. 1991. Design for Code Acceptance Series No. 1. Flame Spread Performance of Wood Products. AF&PA. Washington, D. C.

11. American Forest & Paper Association. 1991. Design for Code Acceptance Series No. 2. Design of Fire-Resistive Exposed Wood Members. AF&PA. Washington, D. C.

12. American Forest & Paper Association. 1991. Design for Code Acceptance Series No. 3. One-Hour Fire-rated Exterior Wood-Frame Walls. AF&PA. Washington, D. C.

13. American Forest & Paper Association. 1991. Design for Code Acceptance Series No. 4 Component Additive Method (CAM) for Calculating and Demonstrating Assembly Fire Endurance. AF&PA. Washington, D. C.

14. Schaffer, E. 1988. How Well Do Wood Trusses Really Perform During a Fire? Fire Journal. 82(2):57-63.

15. White, R. 1993. Enhancements to Performance: Design for Fire Resistance. Pages 63-67 *in* Proceedings 47329 Wood Products for Engineered Structures: Issues Affecting Growth and Acceptance of Engineered Wood Products. Forest Products Research Society. Madison, Wisconsin.

16. Forest Products Laboratory. 1987. Fire Safety in Wood Construction *in* Wood Handbook: Wood as an Engineering Material. Agriculture Handbook No. 72. USDA Forest Service Forest Products Laboratory. Madison, Wisconsin.

17. Schaffer, E. 1992. Fire-Resistive Structural Design. Pages 47-60 *in* Proceedings International Seminar on Wood Engineering. University of Denver. Denver, Colorado.

18. APA-The Engineered Wood Association. 1995. Design/Construction Guide Fire-Rated Systems. APA. Tacoma, Washington.

19. Gypsum Association. 1992. Fire Resistance Design Manual GA-600-92. GA. Washington, D. C.

20. American Forest & Paper Association. 1991. Improved Fire Safety: Design of Firestopping and Draftstopping for Concealed Spaces. AF&PA. Washington, D. C.

21. United States Gypsum Company. 1992. Gypsum Construction Handbook. USGC. Chicago, Illinois.

22. Mittendorf, J. 1988. Joist-Rafter Versus Lightweight Wood Truss. Fire Engineering. 141(7):48-50.

23. Schaffer, E. 1968. A Simplified Test for Adhesive Behavior in Wood Sections Exposed to Fire. Research Note FPL-0175. USDA Forest Service Forest Products Laboratory. Madison, Wisconsin.

24. Harmathy, T. 1965. Ten Rules of Fire Endurance Rating. Fire Technology. 1(2):93-102.

25. Levan, S. and J. Winandy. 1990. Effect of Fire Retardant Treatments on Wood Strength: A Review. Wood and Fiber Science. 22(1):113-131.

26. Levan, S. and M. Collet. 1989. Choosing and Applying Fire-Retardant-treated Plywood and Lumber for Roof Designs. General Technical Report FPL-GTR-62. USDA Forest Service Forest Products Laboratory. Madison, Wisconsin.

27. National Fire Protection Association. 1994. NFPA 13 Standard for the Installation of Sprinkler Systems. NFPA. Quincy, Massachusetts.

28. NAHB Building Systems Councils, 1992. Fire Rated Assemblies for System Built Housing. Washington, D.C.

Chapter 8

Long Term Performance and Durability of Engineered Wood Products

Joseph R. Loferski, Ph. D.

Department of Wood Science and Forest Products
Virginia Tech
Blacksburg, Virginia

Engineered wood products have many advantages over traditional sawn wood products and offer new architectural opportunities such as longer spans to provide large unobstructed rooms. Because these products are made from a renewable resource that includes younger, smaller-diameter and plantation-grown trees, they will be available far into the future. Furthermore, as advances in materials science are made, more types of engineered wood products will appear in the marketplace. Innovations in architecture will dictate new uses and new building construction systems. Because engineered wood products are economical, make the most efficient use of the wood resource, have low material property variability and can be produced in a wide range of sizes and shapes, they will be the primary wood-based structural materials of the future.

As with all building materials, wood and wood-based products must be used correctly to ensure their proper performance. While some engineered wood products have a long history of use—plywood and glued-laminated timber, for example—others such as wood I-joists and structural composite lumber are relatively new. Therefore, many questions arise from designers and users regarding their long term performance characteristics including creep, duration of load, moisture content and dimensional stability, resistance to decay fungi and insects, and durability of gluelines. Because these engineered products are made from wood, most of the considerations related to their durability are similar to those for promoting long-lived structures constructed with sawn lumber and timber.

Whether made of wood, steel or concrete, buildings represent a huge capital investment. It is important to protect this investment from deterioration, otherwise the current and future owners will be faced with the cost of unnecessary repairs that could have been avoided if proper design and construction details had been used. The cost of building and owning a long-lived, low-maintenance wood-frame structure can be minimized by paying attention to details during the design and construction phases that promote water-shedding and minimize water infiltration and within-building condensation.

Effects of Time

Wood is a rheological material. (Rheology is the study of the deformation and flow of materials.) This means that some of its properties are time-dependent. When solid wood products are loaded continuously for long periods of time, they can exhibit creep and duration of load effects. Because engineered wood products are manufactured from wood elements like lumber, veneer and strands that are bonded together with a structural adhesive, they too, exhibit creep and duration of load behavior. Time-dependent effects are complex, and caused primarily by changes in the molecular organization of the three polymers of which wood is mainly composed—cellulose, hemicellulose and lignin. The adhesives used in engineered wood products can have time-dependent properties as well. Furthermore, the microscopic interface between the wood and the adhesive where stresses are transferred and distributed among the composing elements can also influence long term performance.

Creep

Creep—the progressive deformation of a structural material under a long term sustained load—is a highly complex process. The creep phenomenon is familiar to anyone who has seen a heavily loaded wooden bookshelf sag between its supports over time. The longer the shelf remains loaded, the more it sags. Wood and wood-based products are generally considered to be viscoelastic. That is, they slowly "stretch out" or creep over time under a continuously applied load. Their creep behavior has been characterized in creep, creep recovery, and stress relaxation experiments (11, 12, 21). Researchers studying creep in wood and wood-based products have created mathematical models to describe the phenomenon (3, 10). Some have developed theoretical approaches to explain creep that include deformation kinetics, time-temperature equivalency and molecular theory. Most studies have been conducted on solid wood; only a few have looked at the creep behavior of engineered wood products (27).

Most creep experiments are conducted using small or full-size beams loaded in bending. The beam is loaded with a constant force, and its downward deflection is monitored over a long time. Creep accrues relatively fast at first, but usually slows down to an almost imperceptible rate. The creep properties of a wood product are estimated from a plot of creep deflection versus time (Fig. 1). As with solid wood, creep in engineered wood products is affected by moisture content, temperature, stress level and time under load. The rheological properties of the adhesive also play a role. Experiments have shown that the rate and amount of creep is accelerated when the moisture content of solid wood or an engineered wood product alternates cyclically between wetter and drier values (9).

The results of a simple creep experiment on a wooden beam loaded in bending are shown in Figure 1. Here, the load history and centerline deflection are plotted against time. Upon application of the load, the beam bends downward, and experiences an instantaneous elastic deflection. The elastic deflection is used in conjunction with the applied load to compute beam's modulus of elasticity or MOE. This is essentially what is done in assigning an E or stiffness value to machine stress rated lumber. The instantaneous deflection is totally elastic; the beam will immediately recover to its original shape if the load is immediately removed. If the load is maintained, however, the beam will continue to deflect

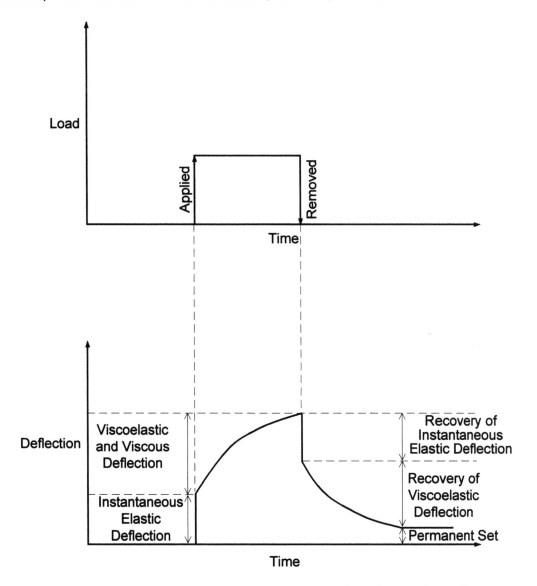

Figure 1. Load/time and creep deflection/time behavior of wood (adapted from 3).

or creep downward. The additional deflection that occurs after the initial elastic deflection is referred to as viscoelastic deflection. In a sense, the molecules of the wood are being slowly stretched over time. Upon removing the load, the beam springs back, instantly recovering the elastic part of the deformation. As time passes, it starts to recover the viscoelastic deformation, and depending on its properties, may or may not fully recover to its original shape. In the latter case, the member is permanently deformed.

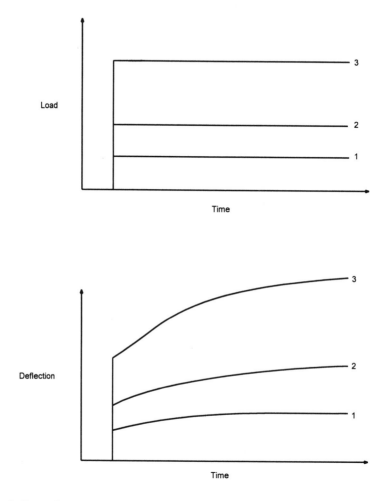

Figure 2. Rate of creep deflection increases as applied load increases (adapted from 3).

Under constant ambient temperature and relative humidity, the rate of creep, or how fast the member sags over time, is related to the applied load and the level of stress it induces in the member (Fig. 2). Low levels of stress produce only primary creep in which the creep rate decreases as time goes on. Moderate levels of stress cause secondary creep. In this case, the creep rate remains constant over time. High levels of stress lead to tertiary creep. Here, the member deflects at an increasing rate, and is in imminent danger of failing. The creep response curve for a highly stressed beam that eventually fails by creep-rupture shows all three stages of creep (Fig. 3).

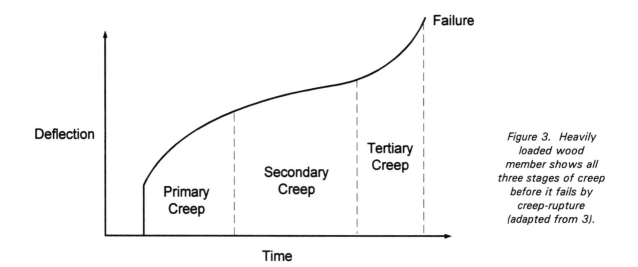

Figure 3. Heavily loaded wood member shows all three stages of creep before it fails by creep-rupture (adapted from 3).

When a solid wood member under a bending load is exposed to widely fluctuating environmental conditions that cause its moisture content to cyclically alternate between high and low, a phenomenon known as mechanosorptive creep occurs (Fig. 4). With each cycle of wetting and drying, the creep deflection of the member increases beyond that which would occur if its moisture content were constant. After a large number of cycles, the member can fail catastrophically even at low stresses that would not have produced failure under constant moisture conditions.

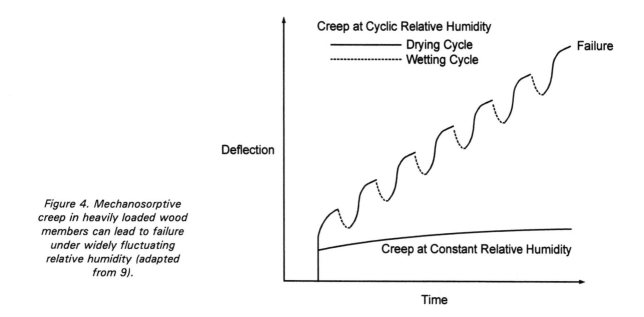

Figure 4. Mechanosorptive creep in heavily loaded wood members can lead to failure under widely fluctuating relative humidity (adapted from 9).

Engineered wood products can also experience mechanosorptive creep if subjected to cyclic moisture content changes (26). Products used in exterior environments, as well as those in interior applications where relative humidity varies widely—swimming pool enclosures and ice rinks, for example—must be suitably protected by flashings, finishes or other means to minimize cyclic changes in their moisture content.

In designing wood structures, designers must size solid wood and engineered wood products such that when loaded, the stresses induced will produce only primary creep in them. This is analogous to ensuring that structural members are not stressed beyond their allowable design values, or in other words, stressed only within the range of elastic behavior. In some engineered wood products, the anticipated amount of creep is first estimated using a rule of thumb which involves applying a magnification factor to the dead load deflection. With glued-laminated timber, for example, the immediate deflection caused by the dead load and the permanently sustained live load is computed, then multiplied by 1.5 to produce an estimate of the creep deflection as a result of permanent loading (2). The total deflection is computed by adding the creep deflection to the deflection due to the short term component of the design load (snow and wind loads, for example). Creep for other engineered wood products is calculated in a similar fashion using the appropriate creep adjustment factor supplied by the manufacturer. Often, adjustment factors are related to the expected in-service equilibrium moisture content of the product—dry (19 percent or less), exposed (28 percent) and ground contact or saturated (above 28 percent).

More sophisticated approaches to creep analysis can also be conducted by applying the mathematical models in published research results (3, 10). These models may be useful in estimating creep-induced changes in the geometry of columns, arches and domes, all of which rely on elastic stability for structural safety. For example, shallow arches and domes can fail by "snap-through buckling"—which is what happens when you push your thumb into a tennis ball—if excessive creep deflection forces their geometry into an unstable configuration.

Generally, excessive creep deflection in beams causes a serviceability problem rather than a catastrophic failure. Symptoms include sloping floors, cracked drywall, out-of-square door and window openings, and sagging roofs. In most situations, the level of stress is not sufficient to induce the tertiary creep that leads to failure in wood and wood-based materials. Besides, the excessive sagging is an easily recognized warning that something is structurally amiss. Designers utilizing engineered wood products must be knowledgeable regarding the creep characteristics of the products they are using. This information is available from the manufacturer.

In those cases where a designer anticipates a large creep deflection, some types of engineered wood products can be manufactured with a slight built-in arch or camber to offset the deflection that will occur when loads are applied. Builders apply this principle when they install sawn floor joists "crowned edge up." The top or bottom surface of cambered beams is always marked so that the member is oriented correctly during placement. After installation, the dead weight of the member and what it supports, as well as the live loads, cause the member to flatten and create a flat floor with no sag.

Most wood and wood-based materials are connected together with mechanical fasteners such as nails, through-bolts, lag screws, and toothed metal plates. Metal clips, brackets, hangers and other types of framing anchors fastened with nails, screws or bolts are also common. Joints constructed with mechanical fasteners typically exhibit creep when monitored over a long time. This means that the long term deformation of wood-frame structures can be governed by creep in the connections, whereas short term deformation is dominated by creep in the wood and wood-based structural members, especially those loaded in bending (13). Therefore, consideration of the creep response of both wood and wood-based structural members and their connections is important in ensuring acceptable long term performance.

Duration of Load

Another time-dependent property of wood and wood-based products is duration of load (3, 21). The load that a wood or wood-based member can safely support, either continuously or intermittently, depends not only on its magnitude, but also on how long the load is maintained. In essence, the apparent strength of wood and wood-based products depends on how large the load is and how long the member has to carry it. The relationship between apparent wood strength and time under load was originally described by researchers at the Forest Products Laboratory in Madison, Wisconsin (Fig. 5) (30). The so-called Madison Curve was adopted in the *National Design Specification for Wood Construction (NDS)*, and is used for adjusting all material properties of wood and wood-based products and the connections between them, except for MOE and compression strength perpendicular to the grain (2). Wood and wood-based products have higher apparent strength under short term loading, and lower apparent strength under long term or permanent loading.

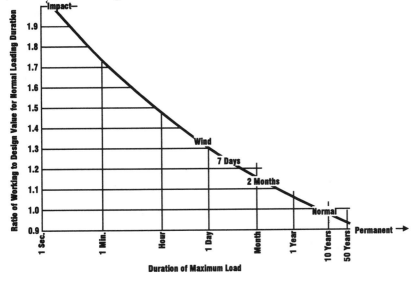

Figure 5. All material properties of sawn wood and engineered wood products, except for modulus of elasticity and compression perpendicular to the grain, must be adjusted to account for duration of load effects (adapted from 2).

The published allowable design stresses for wood and wood-based products are based on a 10-year cumulative load duration (2, 21). That is, over the lifetime of the structure members will be loaded at their allowable design value for a total of 10 years. The majority of the time, of course, they are loaded at much lower levels. When designing a wooden structure, the estimated duration of each load—wind and snow, for example—is taken from the appropriate building code or standard and the allowable stresses are adjusted according to the load duration factors given by the Madison Curve. For example, if designing for a snow load which has a cumulative maximum duration of two months in the life of a structure, the allowable tabulated stresses are increased by 15 percent to reflect the two-month load duration. For many engineered wood products and the connections between them, allowable stresses are adjusted in a similar manner. When designing glued-laminated timber, for example, the procedure for adjusting allowable stresses is identical to that for sawn lumber and timber. Because the adhesive bond between wood elements in some engineered wood products may affect both the duration of load and creep response of the product, it may or may not behave in a manner similar to solid wood. Creep and duration of load effects could be lessened or magnified relative to solid wood. As such, the designer should consult the manufacturer to obtain the appropriate duration of load adjustment factors.

Effects of Moisture

All wood and wood-based products are hygroscopic, meaning that they have an affinity for water in both the liquid and vapor phases. In the living tree, wood is saturated with water. During the manufacture of both sawn lumber and timber and engineered wood products, the majority of the water originally in the wood is removed by kiln drying. The as-manufactured moisture content is about 2 percent for oriented strand board, for example, 8 to 10 percent for wood I-joists, and 12 to 15 percent for glued-laminated timber, compared with 16 to 19 percent for sawn lumber. Drying of the raw wood is desirable and required because lower moisture content results in wood products that are stronger and stiffer. Also, many adhesives used for engineered wood products bond well only when applied to wood at low moisture content. Finally, decay fungi and most insects will not attack dry wood; and drying wood to the anticipated equilibrium moisture content of the service environment preshrinks products to their in-service dimensions. Once installed, however, wood and wood-based products may be exposed to environmental conditions that cause changes in their moisture content and dimensions, and increase their susceptibility to insects and decay fungi as well.

Dimensional Stability

Wood and wood-based products shrink and swell only when their moisture content is below the fiber saturation point, which is about 30 percent for most species. At the fiber saturation point, the cell walls are fully swollen, but the cell cavities are empty, and wood is at its maximum dimensions. When wood's moisture content is between 30 and 0 percent, it shrinks (or swells) in approximately direct proportion to the amount of moisture lost (or gained). During periods of low ambient relative humidity wood releases water vapor to the air and shrinks in dimensions. When relative humidity is high, it absorbs moisture and swells. The relative amount of shrinking and swelling with changes in moisture content is a measure of wood's dimensional stability.

The shrinkage coefficients for solid wood are directly related to the orientation of the wood fibers in the tree relative to the longitudinal (along the fibers), radial (across the growth rings), and tangential (around the growth rings) directions (Fig. 6). For example, the shrinkage coefficients for oak which dries from the fiber saturation point to the oven-dry condition (0 percent moisture content) are approximately 8 percent in the tangential direction, 4 percent in the radial direction and 0.1 percent in the longitudinal direction. The shrinkage coefficients are different for each species, and are tabulated in many sources (21).

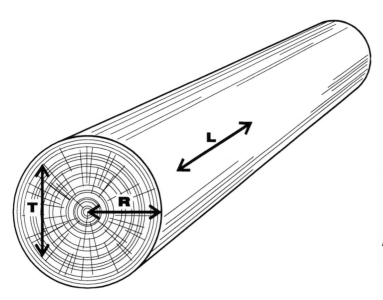

Figure 6. There are three principal material directions in logs and in the lumber sawn from them. The longitudinal plane, L, is parallel to the grain. The radial plane, R, is perpendicular to the growth rings, while the tangential plane, T, is parallel to the growth rings.

The longitudinal shrinkage coefficient for "normal" wood is much smaller than that for juvenile wood—wood produced by trees during the first 5 to 20 years of life—and reaction wood—wood produced in branches and in leaning trees. In both of these kinds of abnormal wood, longitudinal shrinkage may approach 1 to 2 percent. Excessive longitudinal shrinkage of dimension lumber containing juvenile wood or compression wood leads to bowing, crooking and twisting, and may contribute to "truss uplift" as well (31, 32, 39). Because engineered wood products are often made from younger trees, they may contain a large percentage of juvenile wood. This may lead to dimensional instability and warpage problems.

Engineered wood products like oriented strand board (OSB) and laminated strand lumber (LSL) are made from thin wood strands sprayed with adhesive that are pressed together under high pressure and compressed to a specified thickness. Upon absorbing moisture in-service, the densified strands may swell irreversibly in thickness, leading to performance problems like edge swelling and fastener head pull-through. The edges of an OSB panel, for example, will absorb moisture from humid air more quickly than its center, causing the edges to increase in thickness. This may cause the outline of OSB floor sheathing panels to become faintly visible through vinyl or linoleum floor coverings. Likewise, the edges of OSB roof sheathing panels may telegraph through shingles. Manufacturers now minimize thickness swelling by applying coatings such as waxes and pigmented paints that retard moisture absorption by the panels' edges (4, 16). Site cut edges should be similarly re-sealed during installation.

If plywood or OSB floor, wall and roof sheathing panels are tightly butted during installation and subsequently exposed to moisture, they will swell in-plane. If no expansion joint is present, out-of-plane buckling will occur. Buckling can cause fastener withdrawal or head pull-through, leading to a wavy, squeaky floor. All structural use wood panels should be installed with a 1/8 to 1/4 inch space between them to minimize buckling problems (15).

Shrinkage of sawn floor joists can cause a gap to open between the top of the framing and the bottom of subfloor panels. Squeaks occur when occupants walk on the floor because the panel rubs against the shank of the nail. This annoying problem can be avoided by applying an elastomeric construction adhesive directly to the tops of the joists during construction. The subfloor panels are then nailed to the joists. After the adhesive cures, it keeps the joists and panels in contact and eliminates squeaky floors. Because wood I-joists do not shrink appreciably after installation, shrinkage-caused floor squeaks usually do not occur with this product. However, designers and builders must use framing techniques that account for the difference in shrinkage between sawn lumber joists (significant) and wood I-joists and other engineered wood products (minimal) when both products are used in the same framing system, to avoid sloping and humped floors, cracked drywall, and other shrinkage-related problems (33).

The amount of shrinkage or swelling caused by moisture content changes in wood below the fiber saturation point can be estimated using:

$$\Delta D = D_i \, S \frac{\left(MC_s - MC_f\right)}{FSP}$$

where: ΔD = change in dimension
D_i = initial dimension
S   = shrinkage coefficient (decimal equivalent)
MC_s = starting moisture content (percent)
MC_f = final moisture content (percent)
FSP = fiber saturation point (approximately 30 percent)

For example, to estimate the change in the width of a 48-inch-wide oriented strand board panel with a shrinkage coefficient of 0.5 percent as it increases from an installed moisture content of 6 percent to 10 percent:

$$\Delta D = 48 \left(0.005\right)\left(\frac{10-6}{30}\right) = 0.032 \text{ in.}$$

This equation can be used to estimate the dimensional changes that will occur in engineered wood products as long as the shrinkage coefficient is known. This can be obtained from the manufacturer.

The shrinking and swelling of engineered wood products that are densified during manufacture—OSB, LSL, and parallel strand lumber (PSL), for example—is often not completely reversible when the products are exposed to cyclic moisture conditions. Slight, but permanent changes in thickness, width, and even length can occur, the magnitude of which is determined by many factors including the wood species, the degree of densification and the difference between the as-manufactured and in-service moisture content. Like sawn lumber and timber, engineered wood products restrained from shrinking and swelling by fasteners or the method of construction, especially if moisture content changes are large, may check, split, warp or buckle.

Effects of Temperature

Mechanical Properties

The stiffness and strength of wood decrease as its temperature is raised, and increase as its temperature is lowered (21). Below about 200 °F the immediate effects of short term exposure are fully reversible. Prolonged exposure of wood to temperatures above 150 °F, however, can produce irreversible strength loss because of thermally-driven chemical changes that take place in the wood. The magnitude of strength loss is affected by wood moisture content, temperature, time of exposure, heating medium (air versus water, for example), wood species and member size. Because of a synergistic effect between moisture content and temperature, strength loss is greater and occurs faster in wood of high moisture content exposed to high temperature. In general, member bending strength is reduced more than bending stiffness, and impact resistance reduced more than bending strength.

Occasionally, structural wood products are exposed to extraordinary temperatures in use. Glued-laminated timber bridges in northern climates may experience extreme cold, while LVL or PSL framing may be subject to hot air escaping from ovens or kilns in industrial processes. Allowable design values given in the *NDS* are "applicable to members used under ordinary ranges of temperature and occasionally heated in use to temperatures of up to 150 °F" (2). The *NDS* advises that design values may have to be adjusted for each 1 °F difference in temperature from a reference value of 68 °F "when wood structural members are cooled to very low temperatures at high moisture content, or heated to temperatures up to 150 °F for extended periods of time". Though the effect of temperature on engineered wood products is most likely the same as it is for solid wood, the manufacturer should be consulted for specific recommendations.

Coefficient of Thermal Expansion
Like most materials, wood expands when heated, and contracts when cooled. The coefficient of thermal expansion of ovendry wood parallel-to-the-grain is independent of specific gravity, and ranges from 0.0000017 to 0.0000025 per °F for both softwoods and hardwoods. Coefficients in both the radial (α_r) and tangential directions (α_t), however, are affected by specific gravity (SG), and are considerably higher. The across-the-grain coefficients for ovendry wood are estimated as (21):

$$\alpha_r = (18SG + 5)\ (0.000001)\ \text{per °F}$$

$$\alpha_t = (18SG + 10.2)\ (0.000001)\ \text{per °F}$$

Wood that contains moisture, however, does not behave the same as ovendry wood does when heated or cooled. When heated, for example, wet wood (greater than 5 percent moisture content) will expand initially because of the increase in temperature. But, it will also eventually contract because of a loss of moisture. Since contraction of the wood due to moisture loss is much, much greater than expansion due to heating, the net result is that wet wood shrinks upon being heated. For this reason, dimensional change in wood due to changing temperature is rarely important.

Weathering

The surfaces of engineered wood products exposed to the environment will slowly weather and erode due to the combined actions of sunlight, water and biological organisms. Unprotected surfaces will soon discolor from yellowish to a light gray, dark brown or black because of ultraviolet light-induced changes in the wood's chemical components and the action of mildew. Repeated swelling and shrinking associated with cyclic wetting and drying of the wood from exposure to sunlight, rain, dew, and high relative humidity causes mechanical damage to its surfaces. Cyclic shrinking and swelling opens microscopic fissures in the wood cell walls that eventually develop into macroscopic cracks and checks in the product's surfaces. In addition, grain raising, loosened fibers, thickness swelling, warping and fastener loosening can result from the effect of cyclic moisture changes in wood products in unprotected exterior exposures. While non-film-forming water repellents and semi-transparent stains will slow the process of weathering, opaque film-forming finishes such as paints and solid color stains that screen out ultraviolet light are very effective at preventing weathering altogether (5). Finishes are not wood preservatives. Regardless of its type, a finish cannot control or eliminate biodeterioration because it protects only the surface of the product. Therefore, unless the product has been manufactured specifically for exterior use and treated with an appropriate preservative, it should be utilized only in environments where it is protected from excessive moisture and direct wetting. Guidance from the manufacturer should be obtained before engineered wood products are utilized in an exterior environment.

Biodeterioration

Wood consists of three organic polymers—cellulose, hemicellulose, and lignin—which are remarkably similar in all timber species. While these chemicals are extremely stable and durable, some biological organisms, under the right environmental conditions, can attack and degrade wood. Because engineered wood products are also composed of wood, the conditions under which they are attacked by organisms and the severity of the damage, are virtually identical to those for sawn lumber and timber.

Deterioration caused by mildew, mold, decay fungi, insects and other biological organisms is probably the single most serious problem that affects the long term performance of wood and wood-based building products. Biological deterioration is quiet, relatively slow, and often goes unnoticed for years before being detected. In almost every case, biodeterioration in wood-frame buildings is the result of design flaws, poor workmanship, neglected maintenance or inappropriate use of products.

Decay Fungi

All wood and wood-based products are susceptible to attack by decay fungi. Primitive plants that lack chlorophyll, decay fungi derive their metabolic energy by breaking down the wood cell walls into their constituent molecules which are readily digested. From an economic viewpoint, decay fungi cause far more damage to wood and wood-based products in buildings than do insects.

Before decay fungi can invade wood, there must be an adequate supply of oxygen, temperatures in the 40 to 100 °F range, a food source, and most importantly, sufficient moisture. Since oxygen and temperature conditions are almost always favorable, and the food is the wood itself, controlling wood moisture content is the critical factor in preventing decay. Wood moisture content must be at least 30 percent, and liquid water must also be present, before decay fungi can infect wood. Once established, some fungi can continue their attack at a moisture content as low as 20 percent. Below 20 percent, however, all fungal activity ceases. This is one reason why dimension lumber is routinely dried to 19 percent moisture content or less. Since the average equilibrium moisture content inside heated buildings ranges from about 6 to 16 percent annually, wood inside buildings is not likely to decay. But wood on the exterior of buildings, and wood inside buildings that is wetted by roof and plumbing leaks or condensation is still susceptible (29, 35). Since fungal spores are everywhere, no wood product that is wet enough is safe from infection. But, by simply keeping wood and wood-based products dry, decay fungi cannot attack. Furthermore, drying products already infected with decay fungi below approximately 20 percent moisture content causes most fungi to become dormant. No further damage is done, and if the product still has sufficient strength, a partially decayed member may still be serviceable and may have acceptable performance indefinitely. However, if the wood again becomes wet in the future, the fungi will quickly reactivate and continue to slowly destroy the product.

Two broad classes of decay fungi attack wood and wood-based products in buildings—brown rots and white rots. Both are recognized by the way their attack changes wood's appearance and color.

Brown rot fungi usually attack softwoods and destroy primarily the cellulose component of the cell wall. They leave behind the lignin, which is dark brown in color. Hence, the name brown rot. Wood attacked by brown rot is identified by its brown color, sunken surfaces and the characteristic cross-grain cracks and cubical checking that give infected wood a charred appearance (Fig. 7). A special type of brown rot known as water-conducting fungi are often referred to by the misnomer dry-rot. Able to transport water over long distances through root-like rhizomorphs, water-conducting fungi attack seemingly dry softwoods and hardwoods. These fungi are relatively rare.

Figure 7. Brown-rotted wood in an advanced state of decay shows characteristic cubical checking (courtesy of S. Smulski).

White rot fungi prefer hardwoods, but will attack softwoods as well. These fungi decompose both lignin and cellulose. White-rotted wood appears whitish, grayish or yellowish in color, often with black streaks that delineate the zone of decay. In the advanced stages of white rot decay, the wood is spongy and has a stringy texture.

In its incipient and early stages, decay is difficult to detect. Later, masses of fungal filaments called mycelia and fruiting bodies (mushrooms) that release spores will appear on wood products with advanced decay whether caused by white or brown rot fungi.

The most important effect that decay fungi have on wood and wood-based products is an immediate and substantial loss of strength. Studies show that for even a small loss in weight—5 to 10 percent of the original weight—a piece of wood infected with decay in its early stages loses as much as 80 percent of its impact bending strength (23). With engineered wood products, the loss of strength should be taken very seriously, and may create a potentially hazardous situation. Because these products are often used as non-repetitive members and stressed near their allowable design limits, any degradation of a product could drastically affect its performance. The loss of strength could lead to a catastrophic collapse should the degradation go unnoticed for a sufficiently long time. Therefore, controlling wood moisture content and minimizing the infiltration of water into a building are critical to the long term performance of these materials.

Non-decay Fungi
Mildew, molds, and staining fungi are types of non-decay fungi that feed on starches and sugars stored inside wood cells rather than on the cell wall itself. Though discoloration of wood by staining fungi happens almost exclusively in logs and freshly sawn lumber during processing, mildew and mold can affect wood and wood-based products anywhere, any time (14). They discolor the surface of products with a wide range of colors from bright yellow to blue-green to black, but do not cause them to decay. Mildew and mold require less water than decay fungi, and can live in wood with only 20 percent moisture content. Although they are of concern primarily from a cosmetic viewpoint, their presence in wooden structures signals excessive moisture and potentially the perfect environment for decay fungi or insects or both.

Insects
The main insects of concern in wood-frame buildings are termites, carpenter ants, powderpost beetles and old house borers (24, 28). In the United States, most insect damage is done by subterranean termites which require direct soil contact and abundant moisture. Subterranean termites not only excavate tunnels in wood called galleries, but eat it as well. No species of wood or kind of wood-based product is immune. Termites usually enter buildings through foundation cracks below grade, but will build shelter tubes up the sides of a foundation to reach the wood above. Rarely seen, termites will hollow out the interior of a piece of wood until its strength is compromised.

The recently-introduced Formosan termite is a voracious organism that attacks both dry and wet wood above and below ground. This newcomer is difficult to control because the soil treatments which work well for subterranean termites are ineffective on Formosan termites due to their above-ground mode of entry into buildings. Fumigation of the entire building may be needed to eliminate Formosan termites.

Carpenter ants use wood for nesting only. They tunnel into wood and eject excavated shavings called frass outside of their tunnels. Extensive tunneling can seriously weaken structural members. Carpenter ants forage for food outside of the nest. Because they do not digest wood, carpenter ants can live inside wood which has been treated with some preservatives that are toxic to other wood-inhabiting insects.

Both subterranean termites and carpenter ants prefer to colonize moist or wet wood, but will attack wood at virtually any moisture content. Because engineered wood products are manufactured with dry wood at less than 15 percent moisture content, the potential for subterranean termite and carpenter ant infestations can at least be minimized by simply keeping them dry.

Several types of wood-boring insects are capable of infesting new wood products even in a relatively dry condition. Powderpost beetles—lyctids and anobiids—and the old house borer are the main offenders. Adults of all three insects lay their eggs in checks and irregularities in the surfaces of wood and wood-based products. After they hatch, larvae tunnel extensively inside the wood seeking stored sugar and starch. In doing so, they reduce the wood to a fine, powdery frass, hence the name powderpost beetles. While the larvae of most species remain in the wood for only a few months, some species may feed for up to 12 years before they metamorphose into adults and emerge through exit holes they bore in its surface.

Lyctids prefer new, freshly-milled hardwoods and often infest recently-processed lumber. They can attack engineered wood products manufactured from hardwoods like glued-laminated timber and oriented strand board. Anobiid beetles attack hardwoods and softwoods, and engineered wood products made from either. Visible on the surfaces of infested wood, powderpost beetle exit holes are up to 1/8 inch in diameter. It usually takes many generations of powderpost beetle activity to remove enough wood to produce a significant strength reduction in the affected product.

Despite its name, the old house borer prefers new softwood products. Adult beetles gnaw large, oval exit holes, with distinctive ripplemarks lining the walls. A larva of this insect can live in a wood product for years before exiting as an adult.

Old house borers and powderpost beetles are difficult to control once they have established themselves in a building. Most infestations are inadvertently built into a structure during construction by using infested products. Infestations often start in improperly stored materials, especially if they are left unprotected for a long time before use. Anobiid beetles, however, are more likely to enter existing buildings from the outside, and are especially attracted to damp crawl spaces and basements.

Because the wood from which engineered wood products is made is kiln dried at high temperature during manufacture, the larvae and eggs of wood-boring insects in infected raw material are usually killed. The drying process has a general sterilizing effect, and kills decay fungi and non-decay fungi as well. If engineered wood products are improperly stored after manufacture, however, they may become infested and can harbor insects that will subsequently infest the building. Because the wood-boring insects create galleries hidden inside the wood, their presence may go unnoticed for years until frass and exit holes are discovered. Chemicals are used to eradicate infestations because these insects can live in dry wood. Fumigation is one method that has been used successfully to eradicate powderpost beetles and old house borers. Other methods may be available. The local cooperative extension service agency should be contacted to determine the acceptable methods at the time treatment is needed.

Preservative Treatment

Preservative treatment is required to provide long term protection wherever wood and wood-based products cannot be kept dry. Engineered wood products can be treated with a variety of chemicals to enhance their resistance to decay fungi and insects. In the United States, these restricted-use pesticides are under continuous review by the Environmental Protection Agency (EPA). Designers should verify that the chemicals being specified for a given project are currently approved for that use.

Naturally durable wood is produced only in the heartwood of some tree species. The durability is provided by toxic extractives deposited in the cell walls which deter decay fungi and insects. Because engineered wood products are made using the entire cross section of a tree, and often made from small and young trees which have a higher percentage of non-durable sapwood, the amount and toxicity of extractives is insufficient to protect the product against decay fungi or insects. Therefore, preservative treatments which utilize a chemical to poison the wood is the preferred way of extending the service life of wood and wood-based products in environments conducive to insects and decay fungi.

Protecting wood from biodeterioration with chemicals has historically been accomplished with one of two basic methods—pressure impregnation, and topical application by brushing, spraying, dipping and soaking. Recently, water diffusible preservatives based on borates have been introduced. These compounds are capable of migrating by diffusion throughout a piece of wood which has received a brush, spray or dip treatment.

Pressure treating is an industrial process, and is the most effective method of applying preservatives to wood and wood-based products. The product is placed in a large treating cylinder and a vacuum is drawn to remove the air from inside the wood cell cavities. The cylinder is then flooded with preservative and subjected to high pressure to force the chemical deep into the wood cell walls. After treatment, a vacuum is applied to remove excess preservative from the cell cavities as well as the wood surface. The amount of chemical retained by the wood is an indication of the level of protection afforded, and is determined by the wood species, and pressure and time in the cylinder. Retention levels—expressed in pounds of preservative per cubic foot of wood (pcf)—for all types of preservatives and treated products are regulated by industry standards published by the American Wood-Preservers' Association (AWPA) (34).

Except in refractory (hard-to-treat) species, nearly one hundred percent of the cross section of thinner wood products like dimension lumber is treated with preservative in the pressure-treating process. With larger members, however, pressure-treating provides a shell of treated wood surrounding an untreated core. Therefore, when pressure-treated wood is cut or drilled, untreated wood may be exposed. This wood is susceptible to deterioration by insects and decay fungi unless it is treated in the field with preservative. Some engineered wood products readily accept preservatives, or as is the case with glued-laminated timber, can be made from lumber already treated with preservative. For example, parallel strand lumber, laminated veneer lumber and plywood are all available as preservative-treated products.

Three types of wood preservatives are available—creosote, oilborne and waterborne formulations (35). Both creosote and oilborne preservatives impart water repellency properties to the treated product. This property tends to reduce the shrinking and swelling of the product with exposure to liquid water, and extends its service life by minimizing weathering-related checking and cracking as well.

Creosote, which has been used for more than a century to treat railroad crossties, bridge timbers and utility poles, should not be used inside buildings because of its toxicity and odor. Oilborne pentachlorophenol is likewise restricted to similar industrial uses. The chemical is extremely toxic, and products treated with it should not be used in residential structures or livestock buildings. Both creosote and pentachlorophenol have excellent field performance. Glued-laminated timber used for bridges and utility structures is about the only engineered wood product that is treated with creosote and pentachlorophenol.

During the past 20 years, wood and wood-based products treated with waterborne preservatives have become commonplace in the United States. The main waterborne preservative used today is chromated copper arsenate or CCA. CCA-treated products are safe to use inside buildings because the preservative chemically bonds to the wood cell wall after treatment. Once the wood has dried, the chemical becomes insoluble in water and will not leach out of the wood. Water repellent finishes can be used on CCA-treated wood products to minimize shrinking and swelling, and surface checking caused by weathering. Plywood treated with CCA to a retention of 0.60 pcf is available for below-ground use in wood foundations. Wood and wood-based products for ground contact uses are treated to 0.40 pcf, and for above-ground uses, to 0.25 pcf. Each piece of preservative-treated wood should bear the quality stamp or tag of an independent third-party inspection agency accredited by the American Lumber Standard Committee such as PFS Corporation or Timber Products Inspection that indicates the preservative type, level of retention, exposure category and other information.

Care should be taken when handling and machining treated wood products. Avoid breathing the sawdust and minimize skin contact with treated products. Burying treated wood scraps at an approved landfill is usually the best disposal method. Treated wood should never be burned; the smoke and ashes are toxic. EPA-approved consumer information sheets which discuss the proper use and handling of treated wood products are available from the retailers of treated products and AWPA.

In addition to creosote, pentachlorophenol and CCA, a wide variety of other proprietary chemicals is used for treating wood; each provides varying degrees of decay and insect resistance. Wood preservation is an area of active research by government, university, and industrial laboratories. New preservatives and methods of treatment are continually emerging under various trade names. Designers and specifiers should contact the preservative manufacturer for specific recommendations.

Fire Retardant Treatment
Fire retardant treatments for wood and wood-based products are proprietary chemical formulations. They do not render wood products fireproof, but instead substantially slow the rate at which flames spread across their surfaces. Some fire retardants may reduce the strength of the product after treatment (36). This reduction must be considered when designing buildings utilizing fire retardant treated wood products (37). Designers and users should contact the manufacturer of the fire retardant to obtain the appropriate strength reduction factors.

Adhesive Durability

Only waterproof, structural adhesives that meet the rigorous strength and durability requirements of *ASTM D2559 Standard Specification for Adhesives for Structural Laminated Wood Products for Use Under Exterior (Wet Use) Exposure Conditions* are used to manufacture engineered wood products (38). Under *ASTM D2559*, adhesives must meet minimum criteria for shear strength, resistance to delamination during accelerated exposure to wetting and drying, and resistance to deformation (creep) under static load. The phenol formaldehyde, resorcinol formaldehyde, phenol resorcinol-formaldehyde and isocyanate adhesives used in making engineered wood products have an excellent record of long term performance and durability in the field—over 50 years in the case of plywood and glued-laminated timber. Because these adhesives are waterproof, laminated veneer lumber and parallel strand lumber can be pressure-treated with waterborne preservatives after manufacture. Glass-like when cured, these adhesives are not attacked by biological organisms, do not emit formaldehyde or other vapors, and do not soften or melt even when exposed to direct flame. Since the strength of adhesion between these adhesives and wood is greater than the cohesive strength of the wood itself, test blocks bonded with these adhesives routinely show over 75 percent wood failure when loaded to destruction. During the manufacture of engineered wood products, bondline quality is continuously monitored, and strength and durability tests conducted daily on samples taken directly from production.

Architectural Details that Minimize Deterioration

Architectural details that promote water-shedding contribute to the longevity of buildings constructed with wood and wood-based products primarily by restricting and minimizing situations which cause them to become and remain wet (1, 7, 8, 17, 18, 20, 22). Probably 90 to 95 percent of all durability problems in wood-frame buildings have to do with water infiltration. Controlling the entry and retention of moisture is of paramount importance to the long term performance of buildings. Wood buildings get wet in many ways. The four most common sources of moisture are ground water, piped water, condensation and exposure to dew, rain and snowmelt (25).

Ground Water
Entry of ground water into buildings is controlled by site drainage, soil slopes and foundation waterproofing, as well as by the use of gutters and downspouts (Fig. 8). Properly installed perimeter drain systems will minimize ground water infiltration into the foundation and floor slab of the building. These systems utilize a perforated pipe in a gravel bed near the footings of the foundation to direct water to either daylight or to an appropriate sump. Foundation walls should be coated on the outside with an approved waterproofing material or drainage membrane so that water contacting the foundation will flow downward into the perimeter drain. Because ground water will wick through concrete and masonry, building codes require that preservative treated wood be used wherever wood is in contact with concrete and masonry. A metal shield inserted between wood and concrete or masonry is an effective capillary break. A vapor retarder should be placed under the floor slab to prevent both water vapor and radon released from the underlying soil from entering into the basement. The soil around the building should be graded so that it slopes away from the foundation for at least 8 to 10 feet at approximately 1/4-inch per foot. This will provide positive drainage of rain and snowmelt away from the structure.

A vapor retarder should always be installed over exposed soil in crawl spaces to minimize the evaporation of moisture from the ground into the crawl space where it is subsequently absorbed into wood and wood-based framing and floor sheathing products. The vapor retarder can be 4- or 6-mil polyethylene sheeting laid over the soil and lapped onto the foundation walls. Taping of seams is not needed, as the primary benefit is achieved simply by covering most of the exposed soil. Many building codes in the United States do not require a perimeter drainage system with crawl space construction. However, the benefits of providing drainage as is done with a full basement is well worth the slight additional cost during construction.

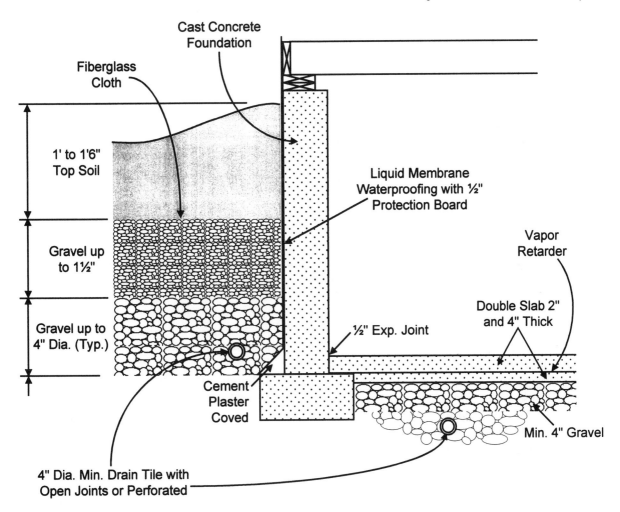

Figure 8. Each of the many elements of a foundation drainage system plays an important role in preventing the entry of ground water into a basement.

Piped Water

Buildings contain a network of water pipes for plumbing and heating needs that have the potential to leak, and can provide the cold surfaces upon which condensation can occur. Because large leaks are usually detected and repaired quickly, they seldom contribute to the long term degradation of wood and wood-based products. However, slow, persistent leaks which directly wet wood and wood-based materials often go unnoticed for years, and lead to degradation and decay. Cold water pipes in humid basements or crawl spaces present a cold surface upon which condensation may form and subsequently drip onto and wet wood and wood-based products. Unchecked, this can provide the perfect environment for decay fungi and insects. Insulating cold water lines will eliminate condensation-caused problems.

It is the responsibility of the building's owner to identify and correct in a timely manner leaking pipes or condensation problems. However, the designer of the building needs to be aware of these issues, and should locate water pipes in accessible areas to accommodate future repairs.

Condensation

Wetting of wood and wood-based products by condensation occurs when warm, moist air is cooled to its dew point temperature, usually by contacting a cold surface. Though happening most commonly on windows, condensation can also occur inside exterior wall cavities, and in basements and attics (25). The water vapor that causes condensation inside walls, basements and attics can be carried there by air currents, or it can pass through permeable building products. In wooden structures, condensation can cause cyclic shrinking and swelling problems, as well as mildew, mold and decay. Constructing buildings with properly applied vapor retarders, sealing potential airflow paths, and reducing the level of interior moisture by proper ventilation and by regulating interior temperature and relative humidity will eliminate most condensation problems.

Many construction materials are "transparent" to water vapor. Because the water molecule is so small, it can find pathways directly through seemingly solid materials and will pass through them in a process known as diffusion. In contrast, droplets of liquid water are relatively large and can be repelled by coating surfaces with water repellents, paints or overlays such as vinyl. When warm, moist indoor air migrates through joints between finish materials or through utility cutouts in a wall, floor or ceiling and is cooled to its dew point, condensation will occur. Therefore, wood products hidden inside walls, basements and attics can be exposed directly to liquid water. The situation is exacerbated because walls are not ventilated, and the ventilation in attics is often insufficient to dry the products below the 20 percent moisture content threshold at which fungal activity stops.

Condensation can occur in wood-frame buildings in both cold and warm climates. In cold climates, moisture in warm interior air may condense onto cold framing and sheathing inside walls, floors, and ceilings as it attempts to escape to the outside. In warmer climates where air conditioning is commonly used, warm, moist air outside the building will migrate through exterior walls towards the interior and can condense on framing and drywall surfaces cooled below the dew point (19). Framing and floor sheathing in crawl spaces under air conditioned rooms can be routinely wetted as a result.

Vapor retarders prevent hidden condensation by restricting the movement of water vapor by diffusion, and when sealed at their edges, can also keep moisture-laden air from migrating into walls, floors and ceilings (25). Examples include polyethylene sheeting, kraft-paper-faced batt insulation, metallic foils, rigid foam insulation and special paints. Vapor retarders should be installed according to local building code requirements, and are always installed on the warm side of the wall. In most parts of the United States, this means on the interior of the wall, typically underneath the gypsum wallboard.

Wetting by Weather
All wood and wood-based products that are exposed to the weather should be protected from direct wetting by rain. Adequate roof overhangs can protect doors, windows, trim and siding by partially shielding them from direct exposure to the weather. Extending the roof to provide a 12- to 18-inch-wide eave overhanging the exterior walls is an excellent way to reduce weathering effects on building exteriors. Gutters and downspouts should be used to collect roof runoff and direct it away from the foundation or into a drain or sump. Buildings which lack rain gutters often have a basement or crawl space moisture problem because of the large volume of water that falls from the roof onto the ground next to the foundation. Siding and trim near the ground can be wetted and subjected to premature deterioration by roof runoff splashing from the ground onto the building. All wood and wood-based products should be at least 8 to 10 inches above the finished grade to minimize wetting by splashing. Flashings should be installed around all windows, doors and architectural details that project beyond the siding to restrict the flow of liquid water under and behind siding and trim, where it may enter into the walls. All wood and wood-based siding and trim should be finished on the front, back, edges and ends with exterior coatings that minimize the absorption of water and protect exposed surfaces against degradation caused by ultraviolet light. Preservative-treated products should be used wherever the needed protection against wetting by water cannot otherwise be provided.

Serviceability Problems

Other problems can occur in structures built with engineered wood products. These are referred to as serviceability problems because they affect primarily the function of the building, rather than the safety of the occupants. The gap that opens at the wall/ceiling junction because of truss uplift, and the sliding patio door that does not open because the designer did not account for creep in the header are two examples of serviceability problems. Annoying vibrations in floors framed with wood I-joists or parallel chord trusses is another.

Because wood I-joists are lightweight and can span greater distances than sawn dimension lumber, some buildings have experienced floor vibration problems. One reason for this is that residential floors traditionally have been designed to conform to a deflection criterion based on relatively short spans (about 15 feet). For example, the value obtained by dividing the span (in inches) by 360 (L/360) has been used as the maximum allowable deflection for residential buildings and many commercial structures. However, when spans become longer, this deflection limit may not be appropriate because the amount that a floor will deflect under this criterion increases to the point where annoying vibrations may occur. Such problems are related to the natural fundamental frequency of vibration of the floor joists—whether they are wood I-joists, trusses or sawn dimension lumber—and the supporting girder. Researchers have shown that floor vibration problems are subjective, and are interpreted differently by different people. A floor acceptable to one person may be annoying to another.

A recently proposed design criteria requires that the fundamental frequency of vibration of the individual joists and of the girder, and their combined fundamental frequency both be greater than 15 Hertz (6). In most cases, this will yield, from a vibration standpoint, a satisfactory floor. The fundamental frequency of a joist or girder is based on its material properties and geometry, as well as the applied load:

$$F = 1.57 \sqrt{\frac{386\ EI}{WL^3}}$$

where: F = fundamental frequency of vibration (Hertz)
          E = modulus of elasticity (psi)
          I = moment of inertia (in.^{4})
          W = total supported permanent load (lb./in.)
          L = span (in.)

The fundamental frequency of the joists is affected by the vibration characteristics of the girder. The combined fundamental frequency of vibration of the floor system is:

$$F = \sqrt{\frac{F^2 \text{ joist } (F^2 \text{ girder})}{F^2 \text{ joist} + F^2 \text{ girder}}}$$

At present, these equations are based on laboratory experiments and in-situ tests of floor systems in buildings, and may be modified in the future.

Solving floor vibration problems in existing buildings is more difficult than designing floors to avoid them. Many times the finished floor or ceiling surfaces must be removed to perform repairs, adding to the expense. Several solutions are available to reduce floor vibration problems. In some cases, the problem is minimized by simply rearranging the furniture. This redistributes the mass on the floor in such a way that it shifts the frequency of vibration into an acceptable range.

An effective solution that worked on floors with excessive vibration is the addition of another layer of plywood or OSB over the existing subfloor. This effectively increases the floor's stiffness without adding much to its mass. The new layer should be secured with both construction adhesive and nails or screws. Though often done, installation of additional cross-bracing or blocking between wood I-joists has proven less effective.

Recently, the manufacturers of engineered wood products have addressed the floor vibration problem. Designers should consult the manufacturer of the product because their design criteria to minimize floor vibrations are usually more strict than those required by the building code, which deals primarily with life safety issues. A simple design guideline for reducing floor vibrations, for example, might require that the deflection be limited to the span divided by 480 (L/480) or 600 (L/600).

Summary

Buildings properly designed and constructed with engineered wood products should provide excellent performance and durability indefinitely. Time tends to magnify defects in designs, materials and methods of construction which can lead to excessive creep, biodeterioration and serviceability problems. Proper design and construction of a wood-frame building requires that strict attention be paid to details that encourage water-shedding and minimize the infiltration of water and within-building condensation. Such details will provide the simplest and least expensive means for promoting the longevity of wood and wood-based building products.

Two famous wood scientists have summarized the most important considerations for ensuring the longevity of sawn lumber and timber, and they apply to engineered wood products as well:

1. Keep wood dry.
2. Don't let wood get wet.
3. Don't let water contact wood.

Designers and builders who follow these simple guidelines will create wood-frame buildings with few problems and long lives.

References

1. Aho, A. 1988. Wood, Water, and Wisdom: Designing Structures for Moisture Control. Pages 89-98 *in* Proceedings No. 47358 Wood Protection Techniques and the Use of Treated Wood in Construction. Forest Products Research Society. Madison, Wisconsin.

2. American Forest & Paper Association. 1991. National Design Specification for Wood Construction. AF&PA. Washington, D. C.

3. Bodig, J. and B. Jayne. 1982. Mechanics of Wood and Wood Composites. Van Nostrand Reinhold Company. New York, New York.

4. Carll, C. 1983. Edge Treatment Effects on Edge Degradation on Aspen Waferboard in Simulated Weathering. Pages 313-323 *in* Proceedings of the 17th International Particleboard/Composite Materials Symposium. Washington State University. Pullman, Washington.

5. Cassens, D. and W. Feist. 1991. Exterior Wood in the South Selection, Applications, and Finishes. General Technical Report FPL-GTR-69. USDA Forest Service Forest Products Laboratory. Madison, Wisconsin.

6. Dolan, J. and R. Kalkert. 1994. Overview of Proposed Wood Floor Vibration Design Criteria. Wood Design Focus. 5(3):12-15.

7. Dost, W. and E. Botsai. 1990. Wood: Detailing for Performance. GRDA Publications. Mill Valley, California.

8. Freas, A. 1982. Evaluation, Maintenance and Upgrading of Wood Structures. American Society of Civil Engineers. New York, New York.

9. Hearmon, R. and J. Paton, J. 1964. Moisture Content Changes in Creep of Wood. Forest Products Journal. 14(8):357-359.

10. Holzer, S., J. Loferski and D. Dillard. 1989. A Review of Creep in Wood: Concepts Relevant to Develop Long term Behavior Predictions for Wood Structures. Wood and Fiber Science. 21(4):376-392.

11. LeGovic, C. 1994. Creep of Wooden Structural Components: Testing Methods. Pages 109-116 *in* Creep in Timber Structures. P. Morlier, ed. E&FN Spon. London, England.

12. Morlier, P. and L. Palka. 1994. Basic Knowledge of Creep. Pages 9-39 *in* Creep in Timber Structures. P. Morlier, ed. E&FN Spon. London, England.

13. Morlier, P. 1994. Time-Dependent Slip of Joints in Timber Engineering. Pages 98-107 *in* Creep in Timber Structures. P. Morlier, ed. E&FN Spon. London, England.

14. Oatman, L., and C. Lane. 1988. Mold and Mildew in the Home. NR-FO-3397. Cold Climate Housing Information Center. University of Minnesota. St. Paul, Minnesota.

15. O'Halloran, M. 1981. Predicting Buckling Performance of Plywood Composite Panels for Roofs and Floors. Research Report No. 144. American Plywood Association. Tacoma, Washington.

16. Price, E. 1984. Proceedings of a Workshop on the Durability of Structural Panels. General Technical Report SO-53. USDA Forest Service Southern Forest Experiment Station. New Orleans, Louisiana.

17. Scheffer, T. and A. Verrall. 1979. Principles for Protecting Wood Buildings from Decay. Research Paper FPL-190. USDA Forest Service Forest Products Laboratory. Madison, Wisconsin.

18. Trechsel, H. (editor). 1994. Manual on Moisture Control in Buildings. MNL 18. American Society for Testing and Materials. West Conshohocken, Pennsylvania.

19. TenWolde, A. and H. Mei. 1986. Moisture Movement in Walls in a Warm, Humid Climate. Pages 570-582 *in* Proceedings Thermal Performance of Exterior Envelopes of Buildings. American Society of Heating, Refrigerating, and Air Conditioning Engineers. Atlanta, Georgia.

20. USDA Forest Service. 1986. Wood Decay in Houses: How to Prevent and Control It. Home and Garden Bulletin No. 73. US Government Printing Office. Washington, D. C.

21. Forest Products Laboratory. 1987. Wood Handbook: Wood as an Engineering Material. Agriculture Handbook No. 72. USDA Forest Service Forest Products Laboratory. Madison, Wisconsin.

22. Verrall, A. and T. Amburgey. 1975. Prevention and Control of Decay in Homes. IAA-25-75. US Government Printing Office. Washington, D. C.

23. Wilcox, W. 1978. Review of Literature on the Effects of Early Stages of Decay on Wood Strength. Wood and Fiber. 9(4):252-257.

24. Williams, L. 1988. Wood-Inhabiting Insects and Their Control: Producer and User Viewpoints. Pages 67-76 *in* Proceedings No. 47358. Wood Protection Techniques and the Use of Treated Wood in Construction. Forest Products Research Society. Madison, Wisconsin.

25. Lstiburek, J. and J. Carmody. 1991. Moisture Control Handbook Principles and Practices for Residential and Small Commercial Buildings. Van Nostrand Reinhold. New York, New York.

26. Johnson, A. and G. Klein. 1993. Case Study: Moisture-Related I-Joist Deflections in an Apartment Complex. Wood Design Focus. 4(1):3-6.

27. Chen, G., R. Tang and E. Price. 1989. Effect of Environmental Conditions on the Flexural Properties of Wood Composite I-beams and Lumber. Forest Products Journal. 39(2):17-22.

28. Smulski, S. 1992. Wood-Destroying Insects. Journal of Light Construction. 10(12):35-39.

29. Smulski, S. 1993. Wood Fungi Causes and Cures. Journal of Light Construction. 11(8):22-28.

30. Wood, L. 1951. Relation of Strength of Wood to Duration of Load. Report R1916. USDA Forest Service Forest Products Laboratory. Madison, Wisconsin.

31. Gorman, T. 1985. Juvenile Wood as a Cause of Seasonal Arching in Trusses. Forest Products Journal. 35(11/12):35-40.

32. Quarles, S. and R. Erickson. 1987. Mechanism of Floor-Ceiling Partition Separation. Forest Products Journal. 37(9):33-39.

33. Smulski, S. 1993. Detailing for Wood Shrinkage. Fine Homebuilding. 81:54-59.

34. American Wood-Preservers' Association. 1995. Book of Standards. AWPA. Woodstock, Maryland.

35. Zabel, R. and J. Morrell. 1992. Wood Microbiology Decay and Its Prevention. Academic Press, Inc. New York, New York.

36. Levan, S. and J. Winandy. 1990. Effect of Fire Retardant Treatments on Wood Strength: A Review. Wood and Fiber Science. 22(1):113-131.

37. Levan, S. and M. Collet. 1989. Choosing and Applying Fire-Retardant-Treated Plywood and Lumber for Roof Designs. General Technical Report FPL-GTR-62. USDA Forest Service Forest Products Laboratory. Madison, Wisconsin.

38. American Society for Testing and Materials. 1992. ASTM D2559 Standard Specification for Adhesives for Structural Laminated Wood Products for Use Under Exterior (Wet Use) Exposure Conditions. ASTM. West Conshohocken, Pennsylvania.

39.   Wood Truss Council of America. 1995. Partition Separation Brochure D-PS. WTCA. Madison, Wisconsin.

Chapter 9

Quality Assurance in the Manufacture of Engineered Wood Products

Larry A. Beineke, Ph. D., P. E.

PFS Corporation
Raleigh, North Carolina

Engineered wood products can be thought of as those wood products which require structural engineering input in both their design and use. In the widest sense, these products include metal plate connected wood trusses, stamped metal web wood trusses, tubular metal web wood trusses, glued-laminated timber, wood I-joists, structural composite lumber, and structural use panels. A generic term, structural composite lumber encompasses laminated veneer lumber (LVL), parallel strand lumber (PSL), and laminated strand lumber (LSL). Structural use panels comprise oriented strand board (OSB) and plywood.

Engineered wood products are differentiated from commodity wood products like sawn lumber in that they require special consideration not only in their design and manufacture, but also in their storage, handling, and erection. The advice of a structural engineer is often necessary to ensure these products' adequate performance in their intended application; skilled, knowledgeable carpenters are needed to see that the design is executed properly.

Because engineers must rely on the design values assigned to engineered wood products by their manufacturers, and because life and property are potentially at risk because of their structural applications, precise control over the manufacturing process and the resulting product quality are paramount. How process control and quality control are achieved and maintained in the manufacture of engineered wood products is the focus of this chapter.

Influence of Building Codes

All engineered wood products are used in structural applications which directly affect life safety and protection of property. Thus, these products come under the purview of model, state, and local building codes.

Building codes have adopted certain combinations of building materials and methods of construction as "conventional construction" because of decades of successful performance. As long as this prescriptive outline for construction is followed, the results are by definition, acceptable. For example, under "Nailing and Stapling Requirements" the *Standard Building Code* (13) states "The number and size of nails or staples connecting wood members shall not be less than those specified in Table 2306.1." Table 2306.1 lists about fifty different types of connections (such as "Joist to Band Joist, Face Nail"), as well as the size ("16d Common Nail") and number of fasteners to be used ("3"). Thus, if a carpenter drives three 16d common nails through the face of a lumber band joist into the end of a lumber floor joist, the connection automatically "meets code" and will be accepted by the local building inspector.

In order not to discourage the development and use of new, innovative building products and techniques, building codes also provide for the use of "alternate" building materials and methods of construction. Engineered wood products fall into this category. Rather than being prescriptive in nature, as is the case for conventional construction, acceptance of alternate materials and methods by the building codes is performance-based. That is, the demonstrated performance of the product or technique is used to determine its usefulness and appropriateness for a given application. Product performance is based on the results of standardized tests in which properties such as strength and stiffness, fire resistance, durability, long term performance, behavior under fluctuating temperature and moisture conditions, fastening requirements, and thermal and acoustical performance are evaluated. The structural properties of most types of engineered wood products are established under separate standards. However, common standards such as *ASTM E119 Fire Tests for Building Construction and Materials* (7) may be relied upon for testing other more general properties.

As part of the building code acceptance procedures, a manufacturer of engineered wood products is required to maintain a quality assurance program which includes follow-up inspections at the manufacturing facility by a qualified (inspection) agency. For example, ICBO's *AC47 Acceptance Criteria for Structural Composite Lumber* (8) states that "Quality control inspections shall be performed by an independent quality control agency..." The quality assurance program is embodied in a quality control manual and a manual of production standards. The quality control manual is a collaborative effort among the manufacturer, the qualified agency, and the model building code organization, and empowers an in-plant quality control department with the responsibility of and authority to ensure the manufacture of products that meet or exceed the mechanical and physical properties established for them during the initial qualification and certification process.

The quality control manual sets out specifications and inspection procedures for incoming raw materials, materials in process and finished goods. It also spells out quality assurance sampling and testing procedures and frequencies, along with calculation methods and target values for quality control tests. Finally, it establishes administrative and record keeping procedures to ensure independence of the in-plant quality control function and to preserve a paper trail of all quality control department actions.

With certain exceptions, most quality control programs are proprietary, but may include a few prescriptive requirements taken from the building codes or from standards published by others. Whatever form it takes, the quality control program must be acceptable to both the qualified agency and the building code authorities.

The manual of production standards contains mostly proprietary information related to the hands-on activities required to produce acceptable products. Each manufacturer has its own special way of making its product. These proprietary process controls are unique to each plant and must be maintained within specific tolerances. While these parameters and their tolerances are important to the quality and acceptability of the finished product, they are the province of the production department and are thus in a separate document. When an undesirable shift in product quality or properties is detected, the quality control technician notifies the production personnel who then adjust the manufacturing variables accordingly.

Qualified Agencies
The building code and the building official who enforces it are just two parts of an interdependent system which also includes the seller (manufacturer), the buyer (distributor, builder, contractor, owner), the qualified agency (independent third party), and the engineer. The building code is at the system's hub (Fig. 1). The relationships among the various parties are shown by their placement around the hub. In one way or another, all contribute to ensuring product quality. For example, the building official interacts directly with the buyer and the qualified agency. Likewise, both the buyer and the seller interact directly with the engineer. Less direct relationships among the parties are influenced by the building code. For example, the building official interacts with the seller and engineer through the influence of or screening of the building code.

The roles of the building codes, building officials, and seller (manufacturer) are the well-understood and obvious parts of the quality assurance framework. Less well recognized are the roles of the buyer (distributor, builder, contractor, owner) and the engineer. Their importance becomes clear when it is understood that these parties are responsible for design, application, handling, and installation of engineered wood products. These functions at the beginning (design and application) and end (handling and installation) of the construction process determine the quality of the finished project as much as the building material manufacturing process does. Both groups are equally important to the successful utilization of engineered wood products.

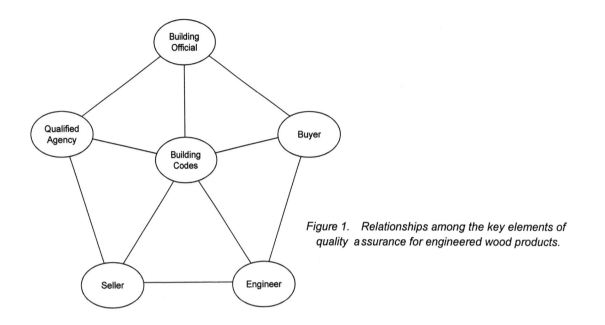

Figure 1. *Relationships among the key elements of quality assurance for engineered wood products.*

Perhaps the least understood role in the quality assurance framework is that of the qualified agency. As defined in *ASTM D5055 Specification for Establishing and Monitoring Structural Capacities of Prefabricated Wood I-joists* (5) and *ASTM D5456 Standard Specification for Evaluation of Structural Composite Lumber Products* (6), a qualified agency has four characteristics:

1. it has personnel trained to inspect engineered wood products manufacturing facilities and their quality control records to determine compliance with the applicable codes and standards and conformance with the quality control manual

2. it has internal procedures to be followed in conducting quality control audits of engineered wood products manufacturing facilities

3. it has no financial interest in or dependence on any single engineered wood products client

4. it must be accepted as a qualified agency by state and local building code authorities in whose jurisdictions the engineered wood products are to be used

The qualified agency is an independent third party that monitors the manufacturer's in-plant quality assurance procedures by conducting unannounced inspections of its facility, production process, quality assurance process, and quality control records a predetermined number of times annually. All findings are compared with the requirements of the quality control manual for that facility to judge compliance.

In turn, the qualified agency authorizes the manufacturer to apply the agency's trademarked logo to products which meet the requirements of the applicable standards and quality control program (Fig. 2). Along with the building code evaluation service acceptance report number, the presence of the qualified agency's trademark on an engineered wood product indicates to the local building official that the product complies with the building code requirements of the local jurisdiction. This smoothes the regulatory process and facilitates the introduction of new products into the marketplace.

PFS ✓ ®

PS 2-92 PRP-133
HUD-UM-4OC
EXPOSURE 1
SHEATHING SPAN®
3/8" 24/0 RATING
SIZED FOR SPACING

Manufacturer Name

MILL OOOO

CONSTRUCTION SHEATHING
2R24/W24
9.5 mm
CSA 0325

↑ **STRENGTH AXIS THIS DIRECTION** ↓

Figure 2. The presence of a trademarked logo of a qualified agency on an engineered wood product is evidence that the manufacturer is under contract with the agency for testing, certification, trademarking and inspection services.

The contractual relationship between the manufacturer and the qualified agency incorporates the quality control manual by reference and sets out the rules for the use of the qualified agency's trademark on material which complies with the require-ments of the quality control manual. It also defines the authority of the qualified agency. The qualified agency has no police power. It cannot force the manufacturer to discontinue production, nor can it impede production in any way. The power of the qualified agency resides in its contractual authority to disallow the use of its trademark if circumstances warrant. The trademark is important because it is the only independent evidence to the building official on the job site that the product meets the provisions of the local building code. Without the trademark, the product is not acceptable to the vast majority of building code jurisdictions in North America. It is to the obvious benefit of the manufacturer to comply with the quality control procedures if it wishes to market its products in regions of the country which are protected by building codes.

Five qualified agencies in the United States have wood product testing laboratories accredited by the National Institute of Standards and Technology (NIST) under its National Voluntary Laboratory Accreditation Program (NVLAP): PFS Corporation, Madison, Wisconsin; TECO/PFS, Eugene, Oregon; National Particleboard Association, Gaithersburg, Maryland; Pittsburgh Testing Laboratories, Eugene, Oregon; and APA-The Engineered Wood Association, Tacoma, Washington. Through this program, NIST certifies the capabilities of third-party inspection laboratories for national and international accreditation purposes.

Summary
In the fast-moving climate of engineered wood products, the one constant is the need for consistently high quality. In the widest sense, quality assurance of engineered wood products is a joint effort among the manufacturer, the building official, the engineer, the buyer, and the qualified agency. These are the people and parties involved day-to-day in establishing and maintaining the quality of engineered wood products. At the forefront of the effort, however, is the qualified agency which must be knowledgeable, practical, and flexible. Performance-based quality systems provide a framework in which changing raw materials, raw material quality, and production processes can be managed to produce products which meet the requirements of the application, are competitive with other materials, and are environmentally friendly and wood-efficient.

Metal Plate Connected Wood Trusses

Metal plate connected (MPC) wood trusses are one of the most intensely engineered structural wood products. Surprisingly, this engineered wood product is fabricated from a commodity product—sawn lumber—and proprietary metal connector plates. Though a considerable amount of testing has been done to establish design values for the lumber and connector plates, little on-going testing of the completed truss or its components is performed. As is the case with glued-laminated timber, virtually no quality control testing is done on assembled trusses. Rather, quality control programs focus on the inspection of connector plate dimensions, orientation and placement; lumber grades and sizes; joint tolerances and other fabrication characteristics that influence a truss's performance. These and other parameters must equal or exceed those specified on a design drawing of the truss prepared by a registered professional engineer. The Truss Plate Institute (TPI), Madison, Wisconsin; PFS Corporation, Madison, Wisconsin; Timber Products Inspection, Conyers, Georgia; and others provide third-party quality control programs for the nation's truss fabricators.

TPI Quality Assurance Program

Because TPI is made up primarily of truss plate producers, who are also the primary truss engineers, its quality assurance program and manufacturing standards are oriented towards ensuring the structural safety of trusses. The TPI program sets out specifications and tolerances for metal plate connectors and truss assembly. Most of the quality assurance program's criteria are based on TPI's new truss standard, *ANSI/TPI 1-1995 National Design Standard for Metal Plate Connected Wood Truss Construction* (14). Among other things, the standard provides technical information and specifications for MPC wood truss design and fabrication. Part of the document is devoted to quality assurance issues both in the manufacture of metal connector plates and in the assembly of trusses. This is because some of the assumptions underlying truss design and analysis are based on the expected quality of the plates and truss fabrication. For example, the design calculations for connector plate size assume that the plate's teeth are fully embedded into clear wood. If the teeth are not fully embedded, they are not as effective as assumed. The quality assurance inspector must count the number of partially embedded teeth, measure the embedment gaps, and determine whether or not the required number of effective teeth has been met, or whether repairs are warranted.

The first step in ensuring truss quality is the proper design and analysis of the truss by a qualified, registered professional engineer. The truss design drawing must carry the engineer's seal. The drawing shows the lumber sizes and grades; plate sizes and positions; and the location of bearing points and special bracing as well as other engineering parameters. All quality control functions of the truss fabricator and the independent inspector are referenced to this sealed engineered drawing.

In general, the TPI quality control mandates for trusses and plates take the form of requirements or tolerances on items which have been shown by test, experience, or engineering judgment to be important to the performance of the truss as built when compared with its expected performance based on the engineered design.

Among other things, the quality control mandates address truss design and analysis, chord and web lumber, special markings such as bearing or bracing locations, connector plates, joint fit, and acceptable corrective actions. *ANSI/TPI 1-1995* fixes the allowable fabrication tolerances which either singly or in combination will not encroach on the truss's structural performance or lessen the built-in factor of safety.

TPI maintains a quality control inspection program for truss fabricators based on *ANSI/TPI 1-1995*. A disinterested inspection agency (that is, an independent third party) makes periodic unannounced visits to the truss manufacturer to monitor the quality of fabrication of trusses in process as well as that of trusses stored in the yard. The inspector uses the sealed engineered drawing as a basis for comparison of the trusses as-designed and as-built.

Trusses found in non-compliance must be repaired in accordance with the engineer's recommendations. While TPI has no direct policing authority, it can remove its trademark from non-compliant trusses, and revoke its future use by the fabricator, thereby effectively preventing the fabricator from selling trusses in regions where building codes require the TPI quality mark.

WTCA In-Plant Quality Control Program

The Wood Truss Council of America (WTCA) is a trade association representing the interests of the fabricators of MPC wood trusses that administers a newly-introduced hands-on, this-is-how-you-do-it quality control program used by the fabricator's in-plant quality control personnel. The WTCA program differs from the TPI program in two respects. First, it focuses on process control rather than product control, and secondly, it does not require third-party inspections. It is well-coordinated with the TPI program, so there are few, if any, instances where TPI's tolerances and requirements cannot be achieved in the real world truss manufacturing environment. Included in WTCA's program are quality control forms for in-plant use in inspecting plates, lumber, and truss assembly. Most important, however, is the inclusion of computer software that permits a fabricator to set up and maintain a quality control data base for monitoring manufacturing performance over time.

Currently, there are no requirements in the WTCA quality control program for monitoring process control parameters. While the program does provide limits for go-no-go decision-making, there are no mechanisms or guidelines for determining when the truss fabricating process is out of control. The data bases created with the WTCA software will logically lead to the development of such guidelines, but at present they have not been promulgated by the truss industry.

Connector Plate Quality Control

While most building code jurisdictions in North America require that truss fabricators' quality control programs be monitored by an independent third party, they do not require third-party inspection of the manufacturers of metal connector plates. However, some far-sighted connector plate producers have installed such programs because they realize the benefits that accrue. Others have set up similar programs on a self-monitored basis.

Most of these programs have provisions that parallel and incorporate the metal connector plate quality control requirements of *ANSI/TPI 1-1995*. The requirements address the steel's specifications; the chemical, physical, and structural properties of the steel; properties of the anti-corrosion coatings; and mill test reports. Also covered are various manufacturing parameters, measurements, and observations; steel master coil-to-finished plate tracking requirements; and record keeping functions. All plate manufacturers who are members of TPI participate in TPI's Voluntary Steel Verification Program.

In addition to these measurement- and observation-oriented requirements, some proprietary programs also require tension testing of steel coupons and tension testing of wood-to-wood joints made with plates sampled from production. This testing produces the definitive indication of plate quality and performance. Though such programs are expensive and time-consuming, they yield dividends useful in setting die maintenance schedules and provide tangible evidence of the consistent production of plates with acceptable plate design values over time. At the discretion of the plate manufacturer, the programs can require a monthly unannounced inspection by an independent third party agency to monitor current and past production and to check quality control records.

Summary

ICBO's *Uniform Building Code* (9) states "Each truss manufacturer shall retain an approved agency having no financial interest in the plant being inspected to make nonscheduled inspections of truss fabrication and delivery and operations." BOCA's *National Building Code* (16) has a similar language, but SBCCI's *Standard Building Code* (13) has no requirement that truss manufacturers be third-party inspected. Although two of the model building codes require quality assurance programs for truss fabricators, enforcement is up to local jurisdictions. Since only a few localities actually enforce the requirements, less than a third of the nation's truss fabricators have a third-party-monitored quality control program. The situation may change when the proposed *International Building Code* (17) is published in the year 2000.

On the other hand, building codes do not require the manufacturers of metal connector plates to maintain independently-administered quality control programs. Most do, however, because they realize that it is in their economic best interest to produce a consistent, high-quality product and, given today's litigious business environment, perhaps out of a sense of self-preservation as well.

Wood I-joists

The simplistic appearance of a wood I-joist belies its complexity in both manufacture and structural behavior. The key to its performance lies in the adhesive joints between the web and flanges and between web segments. Properly formed and glued joints are critical to performance; flange and web material quality are secondary. As is the case with all engineered structural components—whether wood or non-wood—both the materials and the processes determine the quality of the finished product.

Raw Materials

The three components of wood I-joists—adhesive, web stock and flange stock—are checked continuously by production personnel, and periodically by in-house quality control technicians to ensure that they posses certain physical and mechanical properties before being admitted into the production process.

The type, temperature and viscosity of the adhesive is determined before it is unloaded from the vendor's tanker. Certification of compliance *with ASTM D2559 Specification for Adhesives for Structural Laminated Wood Products for Use Under Exterior (Wet Use) Exposure Conditions* (4) is also required.

At a minimum, the web stock—either oriented strand board (OSB) or plywood—is checked on a lot, truckload, or carload basis for grade, thickness, and squareness before being accepted. Some I-joist manufacturers also measure the density, shear strength through the thickness, and linear expansion and thickness swell of the panels before they go into the production process. Plywood is also examined for core gaps, and face/back veneer defects. The extent of checking and testing of the incoming web stock depends on the I-joist manufacturer's philosophy. On the one hand, the incoming material is presumed to be adequate, so a minimal number of checks are performed. Any bad stock will be discovered during the post-manufacturing inspection of the finished I-joists. On the other hand, the assumption is that it is better to cull unacceptable web stock before it is processed into a finished product. Whether more money is spent testing web stock or scrapping unacceptable I-joists is debatable. Acceptable end product is produced under both philosophies.

I-joist manufacturers employ two kinds of flange materials—laminated veneer lumber (LVL) and sawn lumber that may or may not be finger-jointed. In either case, an initial check is made for grade, dimensions, and visible defects such as blows or delamination in LVL and oversize knots or excessive wane in sawn lumber.

LVL flange stock must also be tested periodically by the in-house quality control technicians for bending stiffness or modulus of elasticity (MOE) and tensile strength. Also, if LVL is ripped into strips—two 2x3's from a 2x6, for example—then the wider material must also meet certain criteria to ensure that the strips do not contain defects that could jeopardize their performance. In addition, samples of finger-jointed sawn lumber flanges are tested to destruction in tension by the in-house quality control technicians to establish compliance with both minimum and running average strength requirements.

In Process

During the manufacturing process, production line workers make many observations and measurements of the materials and processing parameters. Adhesive temperature and viscosity, flow rate, and ratio of resin to hardener are observed continuously; measurements are made periodically as specified in the guidelines set out in the plant's quality control manual. The quality control manual is most often written by the manufacturer, and accepted by the qualified agency and the model building code organizations after review.

Plywood and OSB web stock is checked periodically for dimensions, squareness, and voids on exposed edges. After being cut to size, a profile is machined on its long edges. As the profile must fit snugly into a groove plowed into the flange, it is measured against a standard groove profile. The profile on web-to-web joints is also compared with a standard. Profile checks are always made after the cutterhead assembly is changed.

The grade and general physical condition of LVL and lumber flange stock is continuously noted. Flanges are regularly measured for dimensions and groove location. The groove's profile is periodically gauged against a standard, especially after the cutterhead or other machining parameters are changed.

I-joists are visually inspected for camber, plumbness, flange/web fit, web/web fit, and adhesive squeeze-out at web/web and flange/web joints as they emerge from the assembly machine. I-joist depth is measured periodically. These observations are particularly important after adjustments are made to the assembly machine setup.

Finished Goods
A final inspection of the I-joists is made by the shipping department. Dimensions; plumbness; the presence, legibility, and spacing of identification and certification marks; splits in the flange at the groove; and gaps in the web/web or flange/web joints are noted, and members culled if needed. Prior to shipment, I-joists are bundled and their ends are sprayed with a sealant to reduce moisture gain during transit and while on site. Lastly, bundled I-joists are wrapped with a vapor-permeable housewrap-like material to protect them from direct wetting.

Tests
In addition to testing incoming materials and materials in process, short lengths of full size I-joists are also tested by the in-house quality control technicians. Shear tests are the most important because they address the critical adhesive joints securing the web and flanges. A specimen 6 to 8 feet long is selected from production at random after each assembly machine setup change and periodically from each shift, after a certain lineal footage of I-joists is produced, or on some other time- or production-related basis. The specimen is loaded so that it is forced to fail in shear. The shear strength must meet a certain minimum value—usually a multiple of the design value for that particular I-joist configuration—which is given in the plant's quality control manual. A certain running average for shear strength, based on the most recent week's production, for example, must also be maintained.

When an I-joist's moment capacity design value (a measure of its bending strength) is based on qualification tests rather than calculations, *ASTM D5055* requires that moment testing for quality control be performed on a sample whose length is at least 20 times its depth. As with shear strength, certain minimum values and running averages of moment capacity must be maintained. The test is expensive to conduct because of the amount of material needed to monitor a typical day's production. While some manufacturers perform the test because it can yield somewhat higher moment capacity design values when compared with the calculation method, most feel that the expense and difficulty of handling the large specimens (40 foot length for a 24-inch deep I-joist, for example) outweigh the potential benefits of higher design values.

Retests

All I-joists are held in storage until the results of the required daily quality control tests show that they have passed. If a retest is called for because some requirement is not met, the retest samples are chosen at random from the production lot represented by the failed sample. With the more sophisticated product tracking systems, samples can be pulled sequentially both ahead of and behind the failed sample. This is done to define the extent of the problem, and helps in identifying its cause.

Qualified agency

Under *ASTM D5055*, the qualified agency is required to make periodic, unannounced visits to the production facility to monitor the process and review the quality control records. The standard does not stipulate a set number of visits; this is negotiated between the manufacturer and the agency. However, visits are made at least 12 times per year. The qualified agency is also charged with approving the in-plant quality control manual. The manual becomes the standard by which the performance of the plant, in terms of the quality of its products, is judged.

Summary

The quality control plan in wood I-joist plants is implemented in a three-phase system of overlapping continuous observations, frequent measurements, and periodic testing of randomly chosen samples. While it is not possible to measure and test all the properties of all I-joists on a continuous basis, the general approach taken in these quality control programs provides assurance that the product shipped meets or exceeds the model building codes' requirements for alternate building materials.

Structural Composite Lumber

The production of structural composite lumber (SCL)—laminated veneer lumber (LVL), parallel strand lumber (PSL) and laminated strand lumber (LSL)—presents many challenges to quality control personnel. SCL products and their manufacturing processes are complex and dynamic. The array of controllable variables that impacts the properties and performance of SCL products is daunting. For example, fluctuations in products are made—take place on two levels. First, the inherent variability of the wood itself must be considered. This is familiar territory for wood technologists and poses no particular problems. In fact, SCL was invented to take advantage of the fact that gluing together veneers or strands of wood narrows the natural variability among different pieces of wood, thereby improving the predictability and performance of the finished product. The perfection of furnish grading machines allows producers to fine-tune furnish grades and grade mixes at any time not only to produce SCL with the desired properties, but also to make the most efficient use of the wood on hand.

Secondly, and more significantly, the wood resource is changing. Supplies of the high-grade wood needed to make high-grade LVL and PSL—southern pine and Douglas-fir— are dwindling. At the same time, the number of plants producing these products has increased dramatically, and shows no signs of slowing. As a result, the shrinking pool of high quality wood must be divided among more plants. Consumer demand for LVL and PSL is steadily rising, adding more pressure on the wood resource. All of these factors have combined to cause occasional industry-wide wood shortages, production slow-downs, and difficulties in maintaining consistent quality in these products.

To remedy the situation, SCL producers are utilizing new species of wood, mixing wood species, and using lower grades of the preferred species. This has led to increased production of the lower grades of SCL. At present, the higher grades of SCL—those with an allowable bending stress (F_b) of 2900 psi or more and a modulus of elasticity (MOE) of 1.9 million psi or more—still predominate. But increasing quantities of SCL with an F_b of 2600 psi or less and an MOE of 1.6 million psi or less are being introduced into the marketplace.

Quality control programs must be flexible in order to accommodate these and other variations in materials, processes and products. Prescriptive quality control programs such as those outlined in *Voluntary Product Standard PS 1-95 Construction and Industrial Plywood* (10), in which adherence to a rigid production recipe ensures an acceptable product, often cannot be adjusted fast enough to keep pace with the changing realities of the SCL manufacturing environment. To stay in step with variations in materials, processes and products—some of which can occur daily—quality control programs for SCL are instead, performance-based. That is, they ensure a certain level of performance exists in finished products made from a variety of raw materials under changing manufacturing conditions.

Raw Material

All SCL manufacturers have an in-house program for monitoring the quality of incoming raw materials. Species, grade, moisture content, dimensions, and visual appearance of the wood furnish is checked by lot, truckload or carload. Likewise, adhesives are checked on a lot or truckload basis for type, temperature, viscosity, and the manufacturer's certification that it meets certain industry standards.

In Process

The in-process quality control inspection requirements vary according to the product being manufactured. The inspection process generally includes noting the quality of the wood furnish entering the process and measuring its moisture content; measuring the adhesive's temperature, viscosity, and spread rate; and monitoring pressing time, temperature, and pressure cycles.

Finished Goods

The quality control protocols for finished SCL products usually include visual inspection for blows and delaminations, and measurement of dimensions. Finished products must also pass certain physical and mechanical property tests before they can be shipped.

Variable Selection

In a performance-based quality control plan, selection of the variables or properties to be monitored depends upon the material's intended uses. For example, if an SCL product will be stressed only in tension in use; there is little reason, from a quality control standpoint, to test it in compression unless the compression test is easier or less expensive to perform, and a strong correlation exists between the material's compressive and tensile strengths.

In the case of SCL, many different properties are important in use, they and others must be monitored in the quality assurance program. Since SCL is most often used to resist bending loads; its bending properties are of primary importance. In the manufacture of SCL, different grades or species of veneer sheets, veneer strands, or wood strands may be positioned in different layers through the thickness of the finished product. Thus, SCL may have different bending properties depending on how its cross section is oriented when in use. This, in turn, leads to a specific quality control regimen, not only for each type of SCL, but for each product line within each type.

In making LVL, for instance, lower grade veneers are placed in the core, and higher grade veneers on the faces. In service, however, LVL can be installed with its wide face oriented either vertically or horizontally. The first case—wide face positioned vertically— is known as edgewise or beam-and-header or joist orientation. The second case—wide face positioned horizontally—is referred to as flatwise or plank orientation. Most beam-and-header stock is manufactured at 1.75 inches thick, so two pieces side-by-side equal the 3.5-inch-thickness of a 2x4 stud wall. Most plank stock is 1.5 inches thick, and used for scaffold planks or I-joist flanges. Since the two thicknesses are rarely interchanged in use, a rational quality control plan may call for testing the bending properties only in the edgewise orientation for beam-and-header LVL and only in the flatwise orientation for plank LVL. It may be desirable to perform confirmation testing in the opposite orientation for each product type, perhaps on a weekly or monthly basis, to ensure that those properties are being maintained should there ever be a need, for example, for a 1.75-inch thick plank. Quality control test requirements for PSL and LSL are likewise based in part on the products' intended uses.

Bending strength and stiffness control most SCL designs; therefore, they are critical to the performance of SCL structural members. Quality control tests of these properties usually are conducted at least once per shift. The decision whether or not to ship the product is based on the results of these pass/fail tests. Otherwise, these properties may not be as high as assumed by the building designer, and the integrity of the structure may be at risk.

Properties of lesser importance such as compression parallel and perpendicular to the grain, and shear parallel to the grain are also less sensitive to the SCL manufacturing process. They may be tested once a week or even less often, and are not useful in pass/fail decision-making. The purpose of these tests is simply to track the values over time employing statistical methodologies to ensure that the design values for these properties are being maintained.

Glue Line Durability

The durability of glue lines is very important to the long term performance of SCL. However, because of the length of time needed to conduct glue line durability tests, they may be done infrequently and are not generally used for pass/fail decisions. In fact, there is controversy among the users of the adhesives as to whether the tests are necessary at all. Most adhesive-related defects in SCL that are detected with durability tests—pre-hardened glue lines, blows and delaminations—are also visibly obvious to production and quality control personnel monitoring the manufacturing process. Also, the samples taken for glue line durability testing are so small that the likelihood of including a defect not previously found during manufacture is small. In addition, constant checks are made to ensure that the adhesive mix and spread rate and the wood furnish moisture content and other factors which influence bond formation and adhesion, and therefore, glue line durability, are correct and within the adhesive manufacturer's specifications. Thus, some argue that vacuum-pressure-soak-dry and boil tests such as those described in *PS 1-95* or *ASTM D2559* are redundant and unnecessary. On the other hand, many SCL manufacturers prefer having the hard evidence proving good glue lines that the relatively easy to conduct durability testing provides.

Density

The density of an SCL product generally correlates well with its bending strength and stiffness. With some SCL products and wood species, a certain amount of consolidation or densification of the wood during pressing is necessary to achieve the desired level of performance. The as-manufactured density of SCL can be estimated by dividing the weight of a small sample by its volume. This property is used only for process control purposes and is not useful for making pass/fail decisions.

Quality Control Test Procedures

Once the material properties and process parameters to be monitored have been selected, the appropriate test methods are easily chosen. Most are based on ASTM standards. *ASTM D5456*, for example, specifies the tests required for qualification, certification, and design value determination for SCL. Many of these same tests are used for daily or periodic quality control functions as well. The necessary equipment ranges from a viscometer to a drying oven to a universal testing machine or even specialized tension and bending testers which automatically calculate strength and stiffness. All SCL producers have well-equipped quality control testing laboratories in which they carry out physical and mechanical property tests for their full range of products.

Setting Acceptance Criteria

Establishing pass/fail acceptance criteria includes balancing the costs of rejecting too much acceptable material and accepting too much material unsuitable for structural applications.

In general, SCL producers are concerned primarily with products whose properties are at or below the minimum acceptable limits of performance. While products with properties well above these thresholds may be considered as wasting good raw material, the consequences of selling exceptional products are not as harsh as those of selling marginal products. Though it behooves producers to watch the high end to keep costs under control, the low end determines whether or not products are shipped and whether or not problems occur in service.

The typical sample mean and range control charts (X and R charts) of statistical process control in which the average performance of test samples and the range of those test results, respectively, are plotted versus time are generally not used by SCL manufacturers. Rather, a process which monitors minimums, averages and running averages is used. In most cases all test values for a given production lot or shift must exceed a minimum value and meet or exceed a target value for their average as well. The target value is generally a multiple of the design value for the property under consideration. For example, a quality control sample for an LVL production lot usually consists of a certain length, say 10 feet, of a 4-foot wide billet. The sample may be cut into five edgewise bending specimens, and into specimens for other tests as well. Each of the five bending specimens must be stronger than the specified minimum value, and the average bending strength of the five must equal or exceed the target value. This ensures that the LVL is adequately strong and that the variation in strength among pieces is within acceptable limits. In addition, a running average of the properties of the five to ten most recent production lots must also be above certain limits. This allows the producer to track trends in the production process.

Finally, *ASTM D5456* requires an annual recalculation of design values based on the previous year's quality control test data. If the design value so calculated is below the published value for that property, the design value must be reduced, or the plant must go through a complete requalification/recertification process.

Resampling and Retesting

When quality control limits are not met, a scheme of resampling and retesting against an adjusted pass/fail criterion is put in motion for all products associated with the failed quality control sample. The procedures that must be followed to determine the extent and cause of the problem are outlined in the plant's quality control manual. All manufacturers hold material represented by the quality control sample until quality control test results are received so that the material is available for resampling should retests be called for. Some operations resample from the production lot on a random basis; those with more sophisticated product tracking capabilities often sample forward and backward from the failed sample to more accurately pinpoint the extent and cause of the problem.

Depending on the breadth of the manufacturer's product line, material from a production lot which fails the retest requirements of the quality control program can be downgraded to a grade which the tests show it meets. If no such grade exists, the material can be re-assigned to non-certified, non-structural uses. Pass/fail criteria for retests are adjusted upward in most programs so that the final average of the original tests and the retests is a greater multiple of the design value. This ensures a high level of confidence in the performance of the shipped product.

Out-of-specification material must be marked and disposed of according to the provisions of the quality control manual. Disposal includes ripping the material into kiln stickers or dunnage, hogging it into fuel chips, or machining it into pieces for non-structural, industrial uses such as truck and freight car flooring. Documentation of the resampling and retesting results, disposal of the substandard product, and actions to remedy the problem must be available for review by the qualified agency.

Qualified Agency Inspection

ASTM D5456 sets out the general requirements for quality control of SCL production. Unannounced inspection visits by representatives of qualified agencies (independent third parties) are required, but the frequency of inspections and inspection procedures are left to be negotiated between the producer and the agency.

Because SCL is often used in non-repetitive, primary load-carrying applications, consistency of quality is paramount. Thus, most SCL plants are visited by an agency inspector twice monthly. The primary purpose of these inspections is to audit the in-plant quality control program records to verify conformance with the procedures described in the quality control manual. The inspector does not perform a quality control inspection per se; the inspector simply reviews the work done by the in-plant quality control and production staffs to determine whether the provisions of the quality control manual have been followed. During the visit, the inspector may also observe the production processes, the activities of the in-plant quality control technicians, and the performance of quality control tests. Particular attention is paid to quality control records, especially those having to do with resampling and retesting, substandard material, and other problems that arose during the course of production since the previous visit.

Summary

Quality cannot be inspected into or tested into SCL products. It must be manufactured into them. With that in mind, the quality control plans employed by SCL manufacturers are designed to ensure that quality raw materials are fed into controlled production processes. In-plant inspection and testing provide the proof. Audits by qualified agen-cies provide independent verification of the performance of the entire system.

Structural Glued-laminated Timber

The requirements for manufacturing, inspecting, testing, and certifying structural glued-laminated timbers are contained in *ANSI/AITC A190.1-1992 American National Standard for Wood Products—Structural Glued-laminated Timbers* (2) sponsored by the American Institute of Timber Construction (AITC). AITC, APA-The Engineered Wood Association and PFS/TECO Corporations and others administer quality control programs for the producers of glued-laminated timber. Since these programs are based on the same standard, only the AITC program is discussed.

ANSI/AITC A190.1-1992 sets down the minimum requirements for the production of glued-laminated timber including sizes and tolerances, lamination grades and combinations, adhesives, and manufacturing guidelines and limitations. The standard also references *AITC 200-92 Inspection Manual for Structural Glued-laminated Timber* (1). This document describes the requirements for the quality control system for the laminating facility and explains the duties and responsibilities of the qualified agency. The quality control program is concentrated in five areas: facilities, personnel, materials, testing, and independent inspection. Unlike those for other engineered wood products, the requirements for glued-laminated timber are highly specific and described in detail in both *ANSI/AITC A190.1-1992* and *AITC 200-92*.

Facilities

While *AITC 200-92* does not purport to dictate the kinds of equipment necessary to make glued-laminated timbers, it does provide guidelines and general requirements for the capabilities of the production equipment needed to produce finished goods which meet the requirements of *ANSI/AITC A190.1-1992*.

Protected storage space is addressed because of the importance of maintaining the moisture content of the dimension lumber laminating stock within the range recommended by the adhesive manufacturer. A typical manufacturing process comprises grading and cutting lumber to remove certain defects; ripping and planing lumber; end- and edge-gluing lumber, and face-gluing lumber to form the final product. These operations require precision saws, planers, glue mixers and applicators, and presses which must be carefully maintained.

Quality control laboratory space is also addressed. Of course, space must be available within the plant to house the test equipment and store the quality control samples and records required by *AITC 200-92*. Equipment ranges from a simple magnifying glass to aid in gauging glue line thickness to sophisticated instruments to measure glue line temperature or pressure within the glue lines.

Personnel

Because of the tight tolerances required in the gluing operations, trained and experienced personnel are needed to supervise adhesive mixing and spreading stations in the manufacturing process. Likewise, personnel responsible for the lumber grading and quality control functions must be properly trained and qualified.

Lumber graders must be approved by AITC or certified by the American Lumber Standard Committee (ALSC) (3). They are responsible for grading dimension lumber laminating stock under grade descriptions and provisions contained in ALSC-certified grading rules such as those published by the Southern Pine Inspection Bureau (12) and the Western Wood Products Association (15). The performance of the lumber graders is checked periodically by the grading agency.

Quality control personnel are directed by a supervisor responsible for managing and maintaining the quality control system. All quality control personnel must have the training, experience, and integrity to inspect the materials, processes and products, and to keep accurate, up-to-date records of the quality control process. It is the responsibility of the quality control staff to make the final inspection of the finished goods and to apply the certification marks on products which comply with *ANSI/AITC A190.1-1992* and with the terms of the licensing agreement between the laminator and the qualified agency.

Materials

The adhesives and lumber used in making glued-laminated timbers must meet certain requirements and standards. The adhesives used for most of the glued-laminated timber manufactured in North America meet the requirements for exterior exposure set out in *ASTM D2559*. In addition, the adhesives must be qualified for use in each plant for end-, edge-, and face-bonding. Qualification tests include glue line shear tests on edge- and face-bonded samples based on strength and percent wood failure, and for durability and delamination resistance after a vacuum-pressure-soak-dry (VPSD) cycle. New lots of previously qualified adhesive must be tested for shear strength and percent wood failure prior to use.

The same shear strength, percent wood failure and delamination tests used to qualify an adhesive for use in glued-laminated timber are also used by the laminator in conducting in-house quality control tests. Samples are taken on a daily basis. Limits are set for shear strength and percent wood failure as well as for the percentage of the length of the glue line that can delaminate after VPSD exposure. Other adhesive-related checks made during the assembly process include adhesive type, mix ratio, viscosity, spread rate, cure temperature, wood surface condition, and clamping pressure.

The lumber used for making glued-laminated timber must pass several visual checks during the manufacturing process. Proper grading is key. In addition, the temperature and condition of lumber surfaces are noted prior to the application of adhesive. Excessive squeeze-out from edge or end joints may require that the lumber be resurfaced so that face-bonding is not affected. As laminations are laid up, end joint spacing among laminations is checked to be sure that it meets the requirements of the beam's grade. The positioning of different grades of lumber throughout the cross section and along the beam's length is also verified.

Inspection of the finished product includes measuring the member's moisture content, dimensions, camber, and thickness of its glue lines, and noting its appearance grade and the quality and location of end joints. The member is then stamped with the appropriate grade, certification, and identification marks.

Tests
AITC 200-92 lists all sixteen tests required by *ANSI/AITC A190.1-1992*. Those most important in daily quality control concern adhesive joint strength and durability. Because of their size, it is impractical and uneconomical to test full size glued-laminated timbers as part of a quality control program. The design procedures for glued-laminated timber are well established, and are based on anticipated loadings, lumber grades, and the creation of sound glue lines between laminations. As is the case with metal plate connected wood trusses, quality assurance programs for glued-laminated timber focus on ensuring the integrity of the connections between pieces of lumber—in this case the glue lines between laminations. Quality control tests that can be performed quickly and easily are thus made on small specimens so that judgments concerning the acceptability of the finished product can be made in a timely fashion.

Independent Inspection
The qualified agency must approve each plant's quality control and production procedure manuals. In addition, its representatives must be present during the testing which qualifies the adhesives and joints that are to be used in manufacturing the product.

After qualification, the qualified agency makes periodic, unannounced inspections of the production facility. The frequency of the visits is not stipulated in *ANSI/AITC A190.1-1992* or in *AITC 200-92*; it is worked out between the manufacturer and the agency. The independent inspector observes the production process and reviews the quality control records. The inspector verifies that the provisions of the quality control manual are being met and that the finished goods meet the requirements of *ANSI/AITC A190.1-1992*, *AITC 200-92*, and the trademark licensing agreement.

Summary
Structural glued-laminated timbers are usually designed for long-span, heavy-load applications in residential, commercial and institutional buildings; highway and pedestrian bridges; and other structural situations where quality and reliability are of critical importance. The quality assurance program outlined in *ANSI/AITC A190.1-1992* provides assurance to the architects, building designers and engineers who design, specify and build with glued-laminated timber and to the public that the structures built with products manufactured in conformance with *ANSI/AITC A190.1-1992* will perform safely and as intended for the life of the structure.

Structural Use Panels

Structural use panels like plywood and oriented strand board (OSB) represent a rapidly evolving and growing segment of engineered wood products. The excellent in-service performance of structural use panels was vividly demonstrated in the aftermath of Hurricane Andrew that struck Florida in 1992 and the Northridge Earthquake that rattled California in 1994. In both of these natural disasters, buildings with properly fastened structural use panels consistently performed better than neighboring buildings where panels were improperly fastened or not used at all. The strength and rigidity of light-frame wood buildings depends to a large degree on the bracing and diaphragm action afforded by structural use panels used as wall, roof, and floor sheathing.

The original structural use panel, plywood is also one of the oldest engineered wood products. While now considered a commodity product, plywood was originally invented to satisfy the need for large, strong, dimensionally stable wood panels for use in the furniture and construction industries. These assets were engineered into the product by first carefully preparing and grading veneers, then cross-laminating them under the watchful eye of a quality control program.

OSB is the newest member of this class of engineered wood products. Like plywood, it is thought of most often as a commodity product, but has the potential to be the most highly engineered of all of the engineered wood products. The number of possible combinations of wood species; strand size, shape, and orientation within a layer; number, thickness and orientation of layers; panel thickness and density; adhesives and additives; and pressing time, temperature and pressure is seemingly limitless.

Even though they differ in construction and appearance, plywood and OSB share common applications and compete for the same markets. As they are also manufactured and tested under a common product standard, they are discussed together, with differences between them pointed out along the way.

Product Standards

Two standards govern the production of structural use panels, *Voluntary Product Standard PS 1-95 Construction and Industrial Plywood* (10) and *Voluntary Product Standard PS 2-92 Performance Standard for Wood-Based Structural-Use Panels* (11). In its original edition as *PS 1-66*, *PS 1-95* was strictly a prescriptive standard for softwood plywood made for construction and industrial applications. It described the veneer grades, combinations of veneer grades in a lay-up, and adhesive types acceptable for use in making various permitted grades of plywood. Also described was the testing required for certification of the plywood produced by each mill. By definition, plywood manufactured according to the recipe contained in the standard using properly graded veneers and permitted adhesive was acceptable for certification under *PS 1-66*. As long as the recipe was followed, the manufacturer would make good plywood. The character of the standard remained unchanged in the 1972 edition. The 1983 edition, and the latest edition—*PS 1-95*—broke with this tradition. Both allow manufacturers to use performance-based testing to demonstrate the suitability of veneers of various wood species, particularly the tropical hardwoods, for making plywood.

The advent of non-veneered wood panels in the form of particleboard, waferboard, and OSB drove the creation of *PS 2-92*. Under this performance-based standard, any wood-based structural use panel can be considered for certification as long as it can be shown that the panel meets the specified end use requirements. Because of the general move away from prescriptive standards towards performance-based standards, the requirements of *PS 2-92* are discussed here, with reference made to *PS 1-95* only to highlight important differences.

PS 2-92

PS 2-92 sets forth the requirements for determining the acceptability of wood-based structural use panels based on their performance in tests of adhesive bond durability, and panel dimensional stability and load-carrying capacity, as well as specifications and tolerances for wood furnish, panel construction, panel dimensions, and other physical and mechanical properties.

In addition, a general framework for the tests and procedures of a quality certification program is described in which inspections, sampling, and testing is performed by a qualified, independent agency. The amount of testing and frequency of inspections is left to policies set by the qualified agency.

The standard approach by qualified agencies is to assign a representative who visits a mill on a periodic basis and observes mill procedures, reviews mill quality control records, and collects samples to be sent to a central laboratory for confirmation testing. The in-plant quality control technicians perform primarily visual inspections of the product for glue line-related properties. The tests conducted at the central laboratory confirm the in-house visual checks and provide information on panel strength and stiffness as well. The drawback to this system is that several days can pass before test results are sent to the mill, during which time the product represented by the test samples may have already been shipped. Occasionally, this leads to field inspections and/or call backs; however, the in-plant program is generally sufficient to ensure that the panels will perform as intended.

Under some quality assurance plans a representative of the qualified agency actually works in the mill daily, functioning essentially as its quality control technician. The inspector has an in-house laboratory with the appropriate equipment to do the required daily testing, data analysis and reporting. Periodically, specimens are sent to the qualified agency's central laboratory to verify in-plant results. The advantage of having an independently-run quality control program in-plant is that the fast turnaround of test results allows mill personnel to respond immediately to changes in materials and manufacturing conditions that affect panel quality.

Small specimens are used for the glue line quality and durability tests performed in the mill. Tests conducted in the central laboratory are more extensive, require larger specimens, and assess the strength, stiffness, and other mechanical and physical properties of the panels in relation to the requirements of *PS 2-92* or *PS 1-95*.

A recent innovation in panel testing has enhanced a mill's ability to do pass/fail quality control testing of structural use panels based on the criteria of *PS 2-92* and the mill's own quality and production standards. An automated, computer-controlled test machine can test samples up to approximately 4 feet by 8 feet in bending over three supports. The large size is more reflective of typical use conditions, and corresponds more closely to the intent of *PS 2-92*. The machine is calibrated to the performance limits for concentrated load and stiffness set out in *PS 2-92*. If the samples from a production lot pass this test, and the glue line quality and durability tests as well, the lot is certified for shipment. Reliance on testing conducted in a remote laboratory is reduced; and the immediate, in-plant structural testing of a large specimen increases the manufacturer's confidence that the product will perform adequately in its intended application.

Whereas *PS 1-95* essentially allows a manufacturer to certify a panel to a specific grade simply by using veneers of a certain grade for its face, back, and core, and then bonding them with certain adhesives, *PS 2-92* permits the use of virtually any veneer or other wood furnish. As long as the panel meets the grade's requirements for stiffness, strength, racking resistance, fastener holding and dimensional stability, as well as those for glue line quality and durability, the panel construction may be certified for that grade under *PS 2-92*.

Certification

The two main steps to panel certification under *PS 2-92* are qualification and evaluation. During qualification, samples of the product are tested according to the battery of tests listed in *PS 2-92*. The results are then compared with the required values for the grade designation being sought. Once the grade for a particular panel construction has been established, the same production lot is sampled again and tested. The objective of this evaluation round of tests is to establish statistically-determined control points for average, minimum (strength, for example), and maximum (deflection, for example) performance under specific tests. The control points then serve as the basis for the quality control program. The qualified agency's program also incorporates the control points and utilizes them in its independent, central-laboratory-testing of products sampled from the mill.

The manufacturing process used to produce the test lot is written into a mill specification for that particular product. Whenever that product is manufactured, this specification is followed and panels of comparable structural capacity and quality should be made. That determination, of course, is made based on the quality control test results.

While *PS 2-92* is quite specific about which test and control points are to be used in a quality control program, it is silent on quality control program policies and procedures. It leaves to the qualified agency the task of writing operational policies and the procedures to be followed for initial sampling, resampling, retesting, and other inspection-related functions. In response, qualified agencies have developed detailed policies and procedures to be followed by the mills under their certification programs. Most make use of statistical concepts for sampling and data analysis. Also provided are detailed procedures for inspection visits and mill program review, all within the framework established by *PS 2-92*.

Summary

Voluntary product standards *PS 1-95* and *PS 2-92* for structural use panels help this industry provide more consistently reliable building materials than ever before. Manufacturers are recognizing that even with products shipped to commodity markets, the cost of a good quality control program is more than offset by the reduction in money spent settling claims of poor performance.

Conclusion

Quality is an over-used word, almost a cliché. In spite of that, the importance of the concept of quality cannot be over-emphasized—especially when applied to the structural engineered wood products used in homes, public buildings and other structures. Natural and man-made disasters from time-to-time point out graphically the need for quality in all aspects of building construction with all materials. More and more, consumers demand that quality be real, and not just a marketing gimmick; they are justifiably outraged when the lack of promised quality results in the unnecessary loss of life or property.

Engineered wood products answer the demand for a more efficient use of the world's wood resources. At the same time, their manufacturers shoulder the responsibility of producing safe and reliable structural materials capable of performing as promised over time. It is no accident that quality assurance programs are a top priority among the manufacturers of engineered wood products. Poor performance caused by poor product quality will not be tolerated by consumers and likewise, is unacceptable to the industry. Effective quality assurance programs have helped drive consumer acceptance of engineered wood products and will continue to support their growing use.

References

1. American Institute of Timber Construction. 1992. ITC 200-92 Inspection Manual for Structural Glued-laminated Timber. AITC. Englewood, Colorado.

2. American Institute of Timber Construction. 1992. NSI/AITC A190.1-1992 American National Standard for Wood Products—Structural Glued-laminated Timber. AITC. 1992. Englewood, Colorado.

3. American Lumber Standard Committee. 1996. ALSC Agencies Typical Grade Stamps. ALSC. Germantown, Maryland.

4. American Society for Testing and Materials.1992. D2559-92 Standard Specification for Adhesives for Structural Laminated Wood Products for Use Under Exterior (Wet Use) Exposure Conditions. ASTM. West Conshohocken, Pennsylvania.

5. American Society for Testing and Materials. 1995. D5055-95a Standard Specification for Establishing and Monitoring Structural Capacities of Prefabricated Wood I-joists. ASTM. West Conshohocken, Pennsylvania.

6. American Society for Testing and Materials. 1993. D5456-93 Standard Specification for Evaluation of Structural Composite Lumber Products. ASTM. West Conshohocken, Pennsylvania.

7. American Society for Testing and Materials. 1988. E119-88 Standard Test Methods for Fire Tests for Building Construction and Materials. ASTM. West Conshohocken, Pennsylvania.

8. International Conference of Building Officials. 1996. AC47 Acceptance Criteria for Structural Composite Lumber. ICBO. Whittier, California.

9. International Conference of Building Officials. 1994. Uniform Building Code. ICBO. Whittier, California.

10. National Institute of Standards and Technology. 1995. Voluntary Product Standard PS 1-95 Construction and Industrial Plywood. United States Department of Commerce. Gaithersburg, Maryland.

11. National Institute of Standards and Technology. 1992. Voluntary Product Standard PS 2-92 Performance Standard for Wood-Base Structural-Use Panels. United States Department of Commerce. Gaithersburg, Maryland.

12. Southern Pine Inspection Bureau. 1991. Standard Grading Rules for Southern Pine Lumber. SPIB. Pensacola, Florida.

13. Southern Building Code Congress International. 1994. Standard Building Code. SBCCI. Birmingham, Alabama.

14. Truss Plate Institute. 1995. ANSI/TPI 1-1995 National Design Specification for Metal Plate Connected Wood Truss Construction. TPI. Madison, Wisconsin.

15. Western Wood Products Association. 1991. Western Lumber Grading Rules. WWPA. Portland, Oregon.

16. Building Officials & Code Administrators International, Inc. 1996. National Building Code. BOCA. Country Club Hills, Illinois.

17. International Code Council. (undated). International Building Code. ICC. Whittier, California.

Chapter 10

Building Codes and Engineered Wood Products

J. Robert Nelson, P. E.

PFS Corporation
Los Angeles, California

Building codes are important to the manufacturers of wood I-joists, laminated veneer lumber, parallel strand lumber and other engineered wood products because, being relatively new, these products are still considered to be somewhat different than conventional sawn dimension lumber and timbers. Though it may sometimes seem otherwise, building codes are designed to regulate building materials and methods of construction, not prevent the introduction of new ones. However, to the manufacturer wanting to introduce a new product or building technology into the marketplace, it often seems that there is one regulatory roadblock after another. By design, building codes are not intended to prevent the use of any material or method of construction not specifically cited. They do, however, require proof that new products and technologies are at least equal in performance to those already allowed. As a result, it may appear to some that new materials and methods of construction are at a disadvantage. As will be shown, this is not the case.

Building Codes

Building codes are documents that set forth the minimum requirements regarding the design and construction of buildings and other structures. Their purpose is to establish regulations, that if met or exceeded, will help ensure the safety and health of the building's occupants and users.

Though building codes set minimum standards to which structures are to be built, the standards do not represent a lower threshold of construction quality which, if not met, means the building is automatically unsafe or unserviceable. Instead, the standards represent a compromise in which safety, serviceability and economics are considered. Building codes regulate not only the materials and methods used in constructing a building, but also specify the allowable occupancy or activities that may take place inside the structure. In general, building codes are most concerned with ensuring a building's structural integrity and providing for the prevention and suppression of fire—the same concerns that are paramount to the manufacturers of engineered wood products.

Model Building Codes
Three organizations in the United States—the International Conference of Building Officials (ICBO), the Building Officials & Code Administrators International, Inc. (BOCA) and the

Southern Building Code Congress International (SBCCI)—publish model building codes. Each is a nonprofit service organization whose voting membership is made up of the local building officials in each city, county or state that has adopted its building code (Fig. 1). ICBO's *Uniform Building Code* (1) has been adopted by almost all of the states west of the Mississippi River. BOCA's *National Building Code* (2) is used primarily in the mid-Atlantic states, and in New England as well. States in the southeastern U. S. have adopted SBCCI's *Standard Building Code* (3).

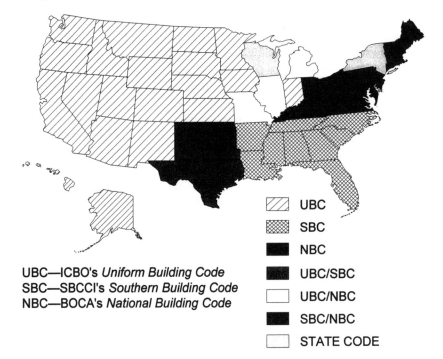

UBC—ICBO's *Uniform Building Code*
SBC—SBCCI's *Southern Building Code*
NBC—BOCA's *National Building Code*

UBC
SBC
NBC
UBC/SBC
UBC/NBC
SBC/NBC
STATE CODE

Figure 1. Current areas of model building code use.

Formed in 1972, the Council Of American Building Officials (CABO) is a nonprofit association made up of the three model building code organizations. CABO represents the interests of all three in matters of national importance. One outgrowth of this combined effort is the *One and Two Family Dwelling Code* (4). Though the document has not met with much success in the western U.S., it has been adopted in many jurisdictions in the Midwest and east.

None of the model building codes, or any other building code-related document, has legal authority until it has been formally adopted by a particular city, county or state. Once adopted, it becomes law and imbues the local building official with the police powers of a law enforcement officer. A "building official" is the officer or other designated authority charged with the administration and enforcement of the provisions in the building code. In the course of enforcing building code regulations, a building official can order construction to be stopped, deny occupancy permits, condemn structures as unsafe, and fine builders, owners and other violators.

Changing the Building Code

All three of the model building codes have procedures that allow anyone—a building products manufacturer who feels that the building code does not address its products correctly or that it does not reference its products at all, for instance—to propose changes or amendments. Changes are carefully reviewed in public hearings by experts in building construction, and fire- and life-safety, as well as building officials. Proposed changes are processed every year; those approved are published in annual supplements to the model building codes. Though only building officials that are members of the particular model building code organization may vote on proposed changes, all interested parties are given ample time to air their views. Updated editions of the model building codes are issued every three years.

Common Building Code Format

The three model building code organizations recently reformatted the order of arrangement of their building codes so that similar provisions are located in the same designated chapters in all three. This is a great improvement and convenience for architects, building designers, engineers, contractors and others who must work with more than one of the model building codes. In addition, newer editions of the building codes include both English units and "soft" metric equivalents.

ICBO's *Uniform Building Code*, for instance, is now published in three volumes to help architects, building designers, plans examiners, building inspectors and others quickly locate those provisions applicable to their field (Fig. 2). *Volume 1* (33) contains the administrative, fire- and life-safety, and field inspection provisions. Included are all nonstructural provisions, as well as those structural provisions necessary for field inspections. Provisions for structural engineering design, including those formerly found in the *Uniform Building Code Standards* (36) are now in *Volume 2* (34). The structural standards have been incorporated into the applicable chapter as divisions of the chapter. *Volume 3* (35) contains all remaining material. The testing and installation standards previously found in the *Uniform Building Code Standards* are now located here. A cross-reference directory that indexes the 1991 format to the 1994 common code format is also available from ICBO.

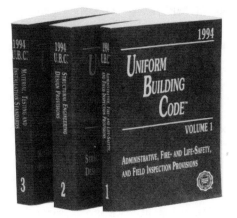

Figure 2. Published in three volumes, ICBO's Uniform Building Code *is organized in the same format as BOCA's* National Building Code *and SBCCI's* Standard Building Code.

The present three-code system has created considerable difficulties for architects, building designers, engineers, contractors, manufacturers and others who design, build and/or sell products in more than one model building code jurisdiction. The burgeoning number of amendments to the three model building codes written by local municipalities has further complicated things. The change to a common format is the first step towards the creation of a common national building code and may lead to the formation of a single model building code organization as well. Though this has been discussed for years, no action was taken until 1994 when representatives from the three model building code organizations formed the International Code Council (ICC). Its goal is to develop a single, unified model building code for use nationwide. The proposed *International Building Code* (5) is planned to be published in the year 2000.

Prescriptive or Performance-Based

Today, building codes may be prescriptive, performance-based or both. In prescriptive building codes, permitted materials and methods of construction are clearly spelled out, much like the ingredients and mixing instructions in a cookbook recipe. On the other hand, performance-based building codes simply specify the acceptance criteria which a product or construction technique must meet in order to be approved for use in a specific application. For example, a prescriptive building code might state that subfloor panels must be ½-inch-thick C-C Group 1 plywood when joists are spaced 16 inches on-center. A performance-based building code would say only that subfloor panels must meet certain load-carrying capacity and deflection requirements. This opens the door for the use of plywood or oriented strand board or any other structural use panel of any thickness, as long as its meets the specific performance criteria.

Prescriptive building codes acknowledge the use of certain traditional materials and methods of construction as "conventional construction". As long as a building is assembled using the materials and methods explicitly stated in the building code, the results are by definition, acceptable.

So as not to deter the introduction and use of new products and techniques, prescriptive building codes also have provisions that permit the use of "alternate" materials and methods of construction. If, for example, a builder wishes to use a novel structural product not mentioned in the conventional construction provisions, the builder must produce justification for its use in the form of technical literature, test results or structural calculations usually provided by the product's manufacturer. Ultimately, the manufacturer must show that the product's performance is at least equal to that of the materials already allowed under the conventional construction provisions. Sawn dimension lumber floor joists, for instance, are classified as conventional construction, while wood I-joists are considered as alternate construction. As such, proof of performance is needed before they will be approved for use.

Building codes empower a building official to approve any alternate material or method of construction, provided the official finds it to be at least equivalent to that prescribed in the building code. As such, it has to have the same or better suitability, strength, effectiveness, fire resistance, durability, safety, sanitation, etc. for the intended purpose. For example, section 104.2.8 of the *Uniform Building Code* (1) "Alternate Materials, Alternate Design and Methods of Construction" indicates that the building official shall require that sufficient evidence or proof be submitted to substantiate any claims that may be made regarding the product's use. Section 104.2.9, "Tests", explains that all testing of the product performed to substantiate the product's suitability shall be done by an approved agency (also referred to as a qualified agency). It also stipulates that if the building code does not specify what tests are to be conducted, then the building official shall determine the appropriate test procedures. An "approved agency" is an established and recognized entity regularly engaged in conducting tests or furnishing inspection services that has demonstrated its competency to and been accepted by the building code officials. In building codes, "approved" means accepted by the building official. Inspectors and plans examiners also have the power to approve because they are the building officials' duly authorized representatives.

Model Building Code Evaluation Service Reports

The need for a building products manufacturer to submit test data to receive approval from the building officials in every city, county and state where its product or technique will be used is impractical. As a solution, the model building code organizations created "evaluation services". The evaluation service is a subsidiary corporation of the model building code organization which reviews test data submitted by manufacturers, grants recognition when warranted, and publishes technical documents called Evaluation Service reports that verify the product's suitability and acceptance for use by the model building code organization. Though the review and approval process often takes up to a year, it is far more efficient than the manufacturer of a building material or method of construction having to obtain individual approval from every local jurisdiction in which it would like to market its products. The Evaluation Service reports also give manufacturers a way to gain the recognition they need at a reasonable cost.

The underlying concept is to give local building officials the advantage of having a staff of knowledgeable engineers whom they could consult, and to relieve them of having to review large amounts of test data submitted by building products manufacturers. Local building departments often do not have the expertise, manpower or time to review product test data to make decisions concerning the suitability of new products and technologies. When questions arise concerning the suitability or acceptance of a material or method of construction, a local building official most often will request a model building code Evaluation Service report to substantiate its approval for use.

The procedures a manufacturer must follow before an evaluation service will issue a report certifying its products' or techniques' acceptance are set by each model building code organization. Though the following describes the procedures of the ICBO Evaluation Service, those used by BOCA's and SBCCI's evaluation services are similar.

First, an application form is filed, accompanied by the basic fee, which in 1996, is around $4700.00. There are extra charges for additional items and for evaluation service reports more than one page long. A renewal fee of about $5500.00 must be paid every two years to keep the report active.

A description of the test procedures used and a complete set of test data must be submitted with the application. When periodic inspections by a quality control inspection service or "qualified agency" are deemed necessary, the manufacturer must also furnish to the Evaluation Service an in-plant quality control manual. Both the testing and inspections must be performed by a qualified agency approved by the model building code organization. If the product is prefabricated, like a wood I-joist or laminated veneer lumber (LVL), for example, production of the samples to be tested must be witnessed by the qualified agency. The application is processed and assigned to one of the Evaluation Service staff engineers for review. After considering the evidence submitted, the engineer writes a report which includes a description of the product or technique and a conclusion or findings. During the initial evaluation, the engineering staff commonly has questions and comments that must be resolved before the Evaluation Service report is finalized. These concerns may or may not call for additional testing. Once the concerns have been resolved, the Evaluation Service report is published.

The Evaluation Service staff has the authority to accept products or techniques that comply with the requirements of the building code. If the Evaluation Service report concerns a product not specifically mentioned in the building code, then it must be voted on by the Evaluation Committee. Composed of building officials appointed by the organization's board of directors, the Evaluation Committee holds quarterly public hearings and provides input to the Evaluation Service engineering staff. Those who do not agree with a decision made by the Evaluation Service staff may request an appeal hearing before the Evaluation Committee. All actions of the Evaluation Committee are published in the form of Evaluation Service Acceptance Criteria (Fig. 3). ICBO, for example, has developed more than 60 Acceptance Criteria, covering everything from structural sandwich panels to walking decks. Once an Acceptance Criteria is established, the Evaluation Service staff may approve similar products as long as the manufacturer submits the specified data. Both ICBO's *AC14 Prefabricated Wood I-Joists* (27) and *AC47 Structural Composite Lumber* (28) apply to engineered wood products.

Once the Evaluation Service report is accepted, it is published and distributed to all members of the model building code organization (approximately 2,400 local building code jurisdictions, architects, engineers and others for ICBO). An index of the reports is published bimonthly and sent to over 12,500 subscribers (Fig. 4). Some model building code organizations also maintain computerized data bases such as ICBO's Product Information Retrieval System.

ICBO Evaluation Service Acceptance Criteria

Evaluation reports issued by ICBO Evaluation Service, Inc. (ICBO ES), are based on performance features of the *Uniform Building Code™*, ICBO's *Uniform Mechanical Code™* and related codes. The following acceptance criteria provide guidelines on required performance features for various products and systems in evaluation reports. The criteria were developed and adopted in conjunction with public hearings conducted by the ICBO ES Evaluation Committee. These criteria may be revised from time to time through the same public hearing process. Unless mentioned otherwise, the criteria are in effect.

Copies of the criteria are available on request from ICBO Evaluation Service, Inc., 5360 Workman Mill Road, Whittier, California 90601-2299. Notices of future public hearings conducted by the Evaluation Committee concerning revisions to acceptance criteria will be mailed to interested parties known to ICBO ES. Hearing notices will be mailed to others requested in writing to be included on the mailing list for copies of specific acceptance criteria. Acceptance criteria available are as follows:

★ AC78   ACQ Wood Preservative Treatment—July 1994
• AC58   Adhesive Anchors in Concrete and Masonry Elements—April 1995
• AC100   Air-conditioning Equipment Pads—April 1994
• AC38   Alternate Water-resistance Test Method for Nonpaper-based Weather-resistive Barriers—September 1990
• AC64   Aluminum Siding—July 1991
• AC67   Ceiling Systems Incorporating Decorative Foam Plastic Molding—September 1991
• AC110   Cellular (Foamed) Thermoplastic Trim Molding—January 1995
• AC11   Cementitious Exterior Wall Coatings—April 1994
• AC28   Class 5 Ducts Conveying Nonflammable Corrosive Fumes and Vapors—April 1990
• AC29   Cold, Liquid-applied, Below Grade, Exterior Dampproofing and Waterproofing Materials—January 1994
• AC111   Composite Rubber Hose and Fittings for Use in Hydronic Heating Systems—July 1995
• AC65   Concrete and Clay Tile Fasteners—July 1991
• AC15   Concrete and Concrete Masonry Wall Systems—June 1987
• AC08   Concrete Tile Underlayment on Spaced Sheathing—January 1989
• AC32   Concrete with Synthetic Fibers—July 1993
★ AC30   Construction Joint Systems—January 1992
• AC99   Corrugated Stainless Steel Interior Gas Piping System—September 1994
• AC112   Cross-linked Polyethylene (PEX) Tube and Fittings for Use in Hydronic Heating Systems—July 1995
• AC86   Determining Limiting Heights of Composite Walls Constructed of Gypsum Board and Steel Studs—July 1995
★ AC102   Development of Propriety Design Formulas for Plastic-reinforced Glued-laminated Beams—July 1994
★ AC59   Direct-applied Exterior Finish Systems (DEFS)—September 1992
★ AC62   Disodium Octaborate Tetrahydrate Wood Preservative Treatment by Pressure Processes—September 1995
• AC41   Ductile Connectors in Precast Concrete Special Moment Resisting Frames—January 1995
• AC01   Expansion Anchors in Concrete and Masonry Elements—January 1993
• AC26   Extended Set Control Chemical Admixture System—June 1990
• AC24   Exterior Insulation and Finish Systems—January 1993
• AC90   Fiber Cement Panels for Use as Exterior Wall Siding—September 1993
★ AC107   Fire-retardant-treated Wood Roof Systems—April 1995
• AC101   Flexible Enclosure Systems for Grease Ducts—April 1994
• AC97   Foam Plastic Insulated Garage Doors—September 1994
• AC12   Foam Plastic Insulation—January 1996
• AC91   Foamed-Cement Wall Systems—September 1993
• AC68   Glass Block Masonry Construction—April 1993
★ AC96   Grading of White Spruce, Black Spruce and Lodgepole Pine Tapersawn Shakes—January 1996
• AC35   Grease Duct Enclosure Systems—January 1991
• AC81   Insul-Cot Cotton Batt Insulation—January 1993
★ AC13   Joist Hangers and Similar Devices—August 1966 (Revised January 1990)
★ AC89   Laboratory Accreditation—September 1995
★ AC75   Membrane Roof-covering Systems—July 1992 (Corrected April 1994)
• AC25   Metal-faced, Plastic Core Wall Panels on Noncombustible Exterior Walls—January 1992
• AC49   Molded Polyolefin-Plastic Pad Footings—September 1990
• AC87   Mortar with Admixtures—January 1996 (Effective January 1, 1997)
★ AC108   Nonload-bearing Wall Assemblies Containing Combustible Components Using the Intermediate-scale, Multistory Test Apparatus—January 1996
• AC82   Phenolic Gypsum Core Panels Used as Exterior Wall Coverings—September 1992
• AC83   Plastic Panels for Walls of Water Closet Compartments and Showers—September 1993
• AC16   Plastic Skylights—January 1989
• AC92   Polymer-Modified FRP Panels Used as Exterior and Interior Wall Cladding—September 1993
• AC70   Power-driven Fasteners in Concrete, Steel and Masonry Elements—September 1995 (Effective April 1, 1996)
• AC51   Precast Stone Veneer—June 1988 (Corrected February 1991)
• AC34   Prefabricated Fireboxes—January 1990
★ AC14   Prefabricated Wood I-Joists—July 1993
★ AC94   Product Specific Wood Shake and Shingle Roof Systems—April 1994
★ AC09   Quality Control Agencies for Wood Shake and Shingle Grading—April 1995 (Corrected December 1995)
★ AC98   Quality Control Agency Accreditation—January 1996
★ AC10   Quality Control Manuals—April 1995
★ AC66   Quality Control of Fire-retardant-treated Lumber—September 1991

(Continued)

★ *Applies to wood products*

Figure 3. All three model building code organizations publish lists of acceptance criteria that spell out the required performance features for a wide range of materials and methods of construction.

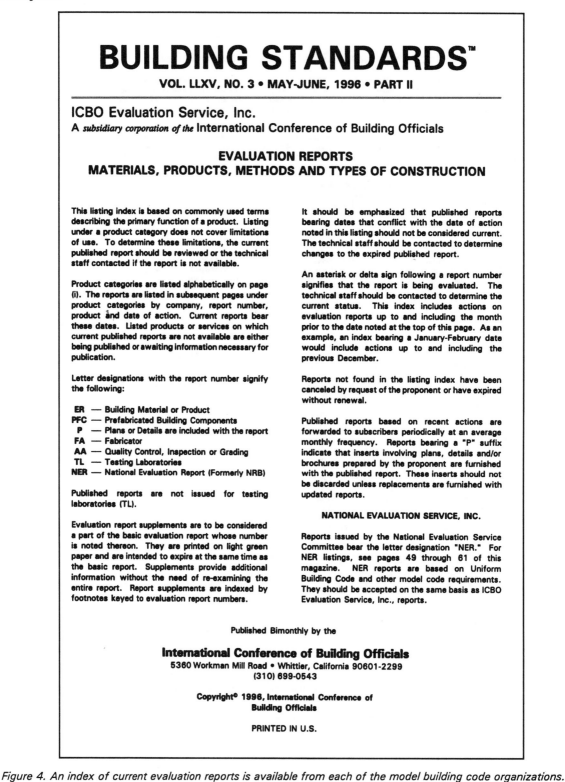

BUILDING STANDARDS™

VOL. LLXV, NO. 3 • MAY-JUNE, 1996 • PART II

ICBO Evaluation Service, Inc.
A *subsidiary corporation of the* International Conference of Building Officials

EVALUATION REPORTS
MATERIALS, PRODUCTS, METHODS AND TYPES OF CONSTRUCTION

This listing index is based on commonly used terms describing the primary function of a product. Listing under a product category does not cover limitations of use. To determine these limitations, the current published report should be reviewed or the technical staff contacted if the report is not available.

Product categories are listed alphabetically on page (i). The reports are listed in subsequent pages under product categories by company, report number, product and date of action. Current reports bear these dates. Listed products or services on which current published reports are not available are either being published or awaiting information necessary for publication.

Letter designations with the report number signify the following:

ER — Building Material or Product
PFC — Prefabricated Building Components
P — Plans or Details are included with the report
FA — Fabricator
AA — Quality Control, Inspection or Grading
TL — Testing Laboratories
NER — National Evaluation Report (Formerly NRB)

Published reports are not issued for testing laboratories (TL).

Evaluation report supplements are to be considered a part of the basic evaluation report whose number is noted thereon. They are printed on light green paper and are intended to expire at the same time as the basic report. Supplements provide additional information without the need of re-examining the entire report. Report supplements are indexed by footnotes keyed to evaluation report numbers.

It should be emphasized that published reports bearing dates that conflict with the date of action noted in this listing should not be considered current. The technical staff should be contacted to determine changes to the expired published report.

An asterisk or delta sign following a report number signifies that the report is being evaluated. The technical staff should be contacted to determine the current status. This index includes actions on evaluation reports up to and including the month prior to the date noted at the top of this page. As an example, an index bearing a January-February date would include actions up to and including the previous December.

Reports not found in the listing index have been canceled by request of the proponent or have expired without renewal.

Published reports based on recent actions are forwarded to subscribers periodically at an average monthly frequency. Reports bearing a "P" suffix indicate that inserts involving plans, details and/or brochures prepared by the proponent are furnished with the published report. These inserts should not be discarded unless replacements are furnished with updated reports.

NATIONAL EVALUATION SERVICE, INC.

Reports issued by the National Evaluation Service Committee bear the letter designation "NER." For NER listings, see pages 49 through 61 of this magazine. NER reports are based on Uniform Building Code and other model code requirements. They should be accepted on the same basis as ICBO Evaluation Service, Inc., reports.

Published Bimonthly by the

International Conference of Building Officials
5360 Workman Mill Road • Whittier, California 90601-2299
(310) 699-0543

PRINTED IN U.S.

Figure 4. An index of current evaluation reports is available from each of the model building code organizations.

When a product or technique is specified on a building's plans or installed in the field, usually all that is necessary for it to be accepted by a building official is the inclusion of the Evaluation Service report number. The number must be stamped on the product, along with the name or logo of the approved inspection agency, if third-party inspections are required by the model building codes (Fig. 5). Manufacturers of engineered wood products must be inspected periodically on an unannounced basis by a qualified agency.

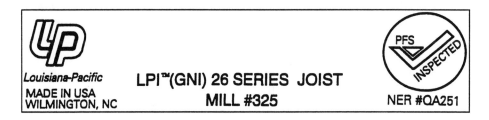

Figure 5. In addition to the stamps of the manufacturer and the qualified agency, engineered wood products are also marked with the relevant evaluation service report number.

Types of Evaluation Service Reports

There are three types of evaluation service reports. The first simply states that a product or technique conforms to the provisions of the building code. The second kind confirms that a product or technique is accepted by the building code as an alternate to conventional construction. The third type verifies that the company identified therein is certified to perform third-party testing, inspection and quality control functions.

The first type of evaluation service report is the simplest and easiest for a building products manufacturer to obtain (Fig. 6). In this case, a manufacturer wishes to show that its product or technique conforms to a standard or standards referenced in the model building codes. The manufacturer needs only to submit independent laboratory test results demonstrating the properties or performance of its product or technique. A description of the product or technique is submitted, along with a statement of the conclusion that is being requested. As an example, suppose that a manufacturer wants to show that a novel floor system conforms with the building code's required one-hour fire rating. Since the model building codes have adopted *ASTM E119 Standard Test Methods for Fire Tests of Building Construction and Materials* (29) as the standard for fire testing of floor and roof systems, the test must be performed in accordance with *ASTM E119*. The manufacturer must provide a written description of the floor system and, since it is load-bearing, submit data that substantiate the characteristics of the structural members and show that the fire test was conducted with the test-specified design load applied.

The second kind of evaluation service report is sought when a manufacturer seeks acceptance of a product or technique as an alternate to that specified in the building code. Obtaining this approval is more complicated due to the fact that there are no standard tests referenced by the building code against which the product or technique can be judged. It then becomes necessary to satisfy the concerns of the Evaluation Service engineering staff and Evaluation Committee by proving that the product or technique conforms to the intent of the building code and/or its design and performance requirements rather than to its prescriptive provisions. For example, when wood I-joists and laminated veneer lumber (LVL) were first introduced about 25 years ago, there were no prescriptive building code requirements and no nationally-recognized performance-based standards pertaining to them. Producers of I-joists and LVL obtained Evaluation Service reports by working in cooperation with the Evaluation Service staff engineers and the qualified testing and inspection agencies. This effort produced test data and in-plant quality assurance programs that convinced the Evaluation Service staff that these new structural engineered wood products would perform as well as the sawn dimension lumber and timbers for which they were seeking status as an alternate. This was done not by simply arguing that these products were just as good as sawn lumber, but instead by providing convincing and appropriate certification test data and daily quality control test records, and by performing periodic unannounced third-party inspections on a more frequent basis than was the norm. The acceptance process was repeated more recently with the advent of parallel strand lumber (PSL) and laminated strand lumber (LSL).

Today, the acceptance process for engineered wood products is much simpler because standards have been created for both wood I-joists—*ASTM D5055 Standard Specification for Establishing and Monitoring Structural Capabilities of Prefabricated Wood I-Joists* (14) —and structural composite lumber—*ASTM D5456 Standard Specification for Evaluation of Structural Composite Lumber* (15)—and are referenced in the model building codes (Fig. 6).

The third type of evaluation service report is used to evaluate or verify the qualifications of agencies engaged in third-party inspection, testing and/or quality control assurance programs. The procedures used are similar to those described for the first type, though each model building code evaluation service has a unique set of rules for granting acceptance. The ICBO Evaluation Service, for instance, certifies testing laboratories and quality control agencies under *AC89 Laboratory Accreditation* (30) and *AC98 Quality Control Agency Accreditation* (31), respectively.

National Evaluation Service
Rather than seek individual acceptance from each of the three model building code evaluation services, a manufacturer who plans to distribute a product or technique nationwide will usually apply to the National Evaluation Service (NES). Since the NES consists of representatives from all three model building code organizations, the evaluation service report bears the names of all three, and will be accepted locally by all three memberships. The NES approval process is somewhat cumbersome and more time consuming, however, because the manufacturer has to deal with all three Evaluation Service staffs at the same time, and must satisfy the concerns of each before moving on to the next step. Also, the fees are about triple that paid for securing acceptance from one model building code organization. NES reports are distributed by each model building code organization in the same fashion as they disseminate their own reports (Fig. 7).

National Evaluation Service, Inc.

SECRETARIAT		
BOCA Evaluation Services, Inc.	ICBO Evaluation Service, Inc.	SBCCI-Public Safety Testing and Evaluation Services, Inc.
4051 West Flossmoor Road Country Club Hills, Illinois 60478-5795 (708) 799-2305	5360 Workman Mill Road Whittier, California 90601-2299 (310) 699-0541	900 Montclair Road, Suite A Birmingham, Alabama 35213-1206 (205) 591-1853

NATIONAL EVALUATION REPORT

Copyright © 1993, National Evaluation Service, Inc.

Report No. NER-450
Reissued January 1, 1993
THIS REPORT IS SUBJECT TO
RE-EXAMINATION IN ONE YEAR

AI-23, AI-24 AND AI-44 WOOD I-BEAMS
AMERICAN I-BEAM CORPORATION
5523 BROADWAY, S.E.
ALBUQUERQUE, NEW MEXICO 87105

I. SUBJECT: AI-23, AI-24 and AI-44 Wood I-Beams.

II. PROPERTY FOR WHICH EVALUATION IS SOUGHT: Structural Wood Members (joists and rafters).

III. DESCRIPTION: A. General: The wood I-beams are used in lieu of solid wood joists and rafters to support superimposed roof and floor loads. The I-beams have structural wood flanges and webs of oriented strand board (OSB), waferboard or plywood. The web sections are installed as minimum 4-foot panels and the full thickness V-joint edge is glued to form a continuous web. The web-flange glued connection is made by inserting the web into a groove in the center of the wider flange face.

The AI-23, AI-24 and AI-44 I-beams range in depth from 9$^1/_2$ to 16 inches, 12 to 24 inches and 16 to 30 inches, respectively.

B. Material Composition: Flanges: Flanges for the AI-23 consist of 2 by 3 lumber members ripped from 2 by 6, 2100f- 1.8 E MSR lumber regraded to comply with the plant quality control manual and assigned an allowable tensile stress of 1,400 psi. Flanges for the AI-24 are 2 by 4 MSR lumber complying with the code. Flanges for the AI-44 consist of two nominal 2 by 4 MSR lumber members laminated together. The glulam flange material is of LC-10 or LC-12 grade lumber, as noted in NER-267. MSR lumber complies with Section 52.00 of the "Western Grading Rules 88," published by Western Woods Products Association. Allowable stresses for the flanges are the same as noted in the code or a current evaluation report. Flanges containing finger-end joints are proof stressed and qualified under AITC 200-86. Moisture content of the flange at time of fabrication is between 7 and 15 percent. Design stresses are permitted to be increased for duration of load in accordance with the code. When qualifying for repetitive member use, an increase in moment capacity of 4 and 7 percent for I-beams with glulam and MSR lumber flanges, respectively, is permitted.

Webs: Webs are a minimum $^3/_8$-inch, $^1/_2$-inch, $^5/_8$-inch or $^3/_4$-inch-thick OSB or plywood conforming to Exposure 1 performance-rated panels, as noted in National Evaluation Report NER-108. Plywood meets Structural I specifications.

Adhesives: Exterior-type adhesives complying with AITC 200-86 are required for the flange face and end joint. An Exterior-type adhesive complying with ASTM D 2559-84 is required for flange-web and web-web joints.

C. Design: 1. Intermediate web stiffeners are not required. Bearing stiffeners are required for I-beams exceeding a 14-inch depth with $^3/_8$-inch-thick webs, exceeding a 16-inch depth with $^1/_2$-inch-thick webs, and exceeding a 20-inch depth with $^5/_8$-inch or $^3/_4$-inch webs. Field installed 2 by 4 stiffeners must conform to Figure No. 1. Plant installed (glued-on) stiffeners comply with Figure No. 2. Web stiffeners are installed at concentrated loads as required. A wall running perpendicular to and supported by joists, would be one example. Circular web holes are allowed in uniformly loaded beams as indicated in Figure No. 3.

2. The compression flange shall be laterally supported in accordance with the design and I-beams ends restrained to prevent rotation. Diaphragm sheathing attached to the top flange and to an end wall or shear transfer panel capable of transferring a minimum force of 50 pounds per foot provide the required lateral restraint. In lieu of diaphragm sheathing, blocking or cross-bracing providing a minimum lateral restraint force of 50 pounds per foot is permitted.

3. Allowable design properties for the AI-23, AI-24 and AI-44 I-beams are noted in Tables Nos. I, II and III, respectively. Tabulated allowable shear values assume a 2-inch minimum bearing length for the AI-23 and AI-24 I-beams, and a 2$^1/_2$-inch minimum bearing length for the AI-44 I-beams. Bending and shear deflections are calculated as follows:

For bending deflection use standard engineering formulae.

For shear deflection use 8M/K.

Example (Uniformly loading):

$$\Delta = \frac{5WL^4}{384EI} + \frac{8M}{K} = \frac{5WL^4}{384EI} + \frac{WL^2}{K}$$

Example (Concentrated load at midspan):

$$\Delta = \frac{PL^3}{48EI} + \frac{8M}{K} = \frac{PL^3}{48EI} + \frac{2PL}{K}$$

W = Uniform load in pounds per lineal inch.
L = Effective span in inches.
EI = Moment of inertia times modulus of elasticity.
K = Shear deflection coefficient.
M = Bending moment in inch-pounds.
P = Concentrated load in pounds.

IV. INSTALLATION: Plans and structural calculations, signed and sealed by a registered engineer where required by state statutes, shall be furnished to the local building official, verifying that American Wood-I beams comply with this report and the applicable building code.

V. IDENTIFICATION: Each I-beam is identified with the manufacturer's name, the quality control agency, PFS Corporation (NER-QA251), the evaluation report number and the product line designation. The lumber flanges are stamped with a grade mark to identify the grade of the flange material.

Page 1 of 3

Figure 6. *This evaluation service report indicates that this product conforms to the provisions of the model building code. Additionally, this evaluation service report for an engineered wood product confirms acceptance by the model building codes of these products as an alternate to "conventional" construction.*

VI. EVIDENCE SUBMITTED: 1. Computer printout of Wood-I joist properties dated August 27-29, 1990, submitted with application dated January 22, 1991. Included in the analyses are results of full-scale load tests conducted on joists with web holes.

2. Report covering full-scale load tests (certification testing), dated August 17, 1990, prepared by J. Robert Nelson, P. E., representing PFS Corporation.

3. Quality control manual for Albuquerque, New Mexico, I-beam plant, revised August, 1990, prepared by PFS Corporation (NER-QA251).

VII. CONDITIONS OF USE: The National Evaluation Service Committee finds that the American Wood-I Beams described in this report are acceptable alternative materials, products or methods of construction to those specified in the 1990 BOCA National Building Code with 1992 Accumulative Supplement, the 1991 Standard Building Code with 1992 Revisions and the 1991 Uniform Building Code with 1992 Supplement, subject to the following conditions:

1. I-beams are produced at the Albuquerque, New Mexico, facility with quality inspections by PFS Corporation (NER-QA251).

2. Loading conditions, calculations and other design details for each project, verifying that the I-beams comply with this report and the appropriate building code, shall be available to the local building official, upon request. Engineering calculations and drawings, sealed by a registered professional engineer or architect, are to be provided when required by the applicable code.

3. Cutting or notching of the flanges is not permitted and web holes must conform with Figure No. 3.

4. Moisture content of the material does not exceed 19 percent at end use conditions.

TABLE NO. I—DESIGN PROPERTIES FOR AI-23 JOISTS[1]

DESCRIPTION	OVERALL DEPTH (Inches)	ALLOWABLE MOMENT (Ft.-Lbs.)	ALLOWABLE SHEAR (Pounds)	EI (x 10^6)	K (x 10^6)
1.5 by 2.5 MSR	9.5	2,870	900	240	4.5
Flanges	11.875	3,830	1,160	405	5.7
3/8-inch OSB	14	4,700	1,380	590	6.7
Web	16	5,520	1,600	800	7.7
1.5 by 2.5 MSR	9.5	2,790	1,000	240	5.8
Flanges	11.875	3,720	1,280	400	7.4
1/2-inch OSB	14	4,550	1,530	580	8.7
Web	16	5,350	1,760	790	9.9
1.5 by 2.5 MSR	9.5	2,800	680	260	2.6
Flanges	11.875	3,730	860	450	3.3
15/32-inch Ply-	14	4,580	1,020	680	3.9
wood Web	16	5,370	1,170	940	4.5

[1]The allowable moment and shear values are for normal duration loading and are permitted to be increased for load duration in accordance with Section 2.2.5 of the National Design Specification (1986 edition).

TABLE NO. II—DESIGN PROPERTIES FOR AI-24 JOISTS[1,2]

DESCRIPTION	OVERALL DEPTH (Inches)	ALLOWABLE MOMENT (Ft.-Lbs.)	ALLOWABLE SHEAR (Pounds)	EI (x 10^6)	K (x 10^6)
1.5 by 3.5 MSR	12	4,560	1,180	640	5.9
Flanges	14	9,160	1,390	905	6.9
2400f–2.0E	16	10,760	1,610	1,220	8
3/8-inch OSB	18	12,370	1,830	1,590	9
Web	20	13,980	2,040	2,000	10
	22	15,600	2,260	2,470	10.9
	24	17,210	2,470	2,990	11.9
1.5 by 3.5 MSR	12	7,400	1,300	630	7.7
Flanges	14	8,960	1,540	900	9
2400f–2.0E	16	10,530	1,780	1,210	10.4
1/2-inch OSB	18	12,090	2,020	1,570	11.6
Web	20	13,670	2,260	1,990	12.9
	22	15,240	2,460	2,460	14.2
	24	16,810	2,730	2,970	15.4
1.5 by 3.5 MSR	12	7,200	1,790	620	9.5
Flanges	14	8,700	2,120	880	11.1
2400f–2.0E	16	10,220	2,440	1,190	12.7
5/8-inch OSB	18	11,740	2,630	1,550	14.2
Web	20	13,260	2,630	1,960	15.8
	22	14,780	3,410	2,420	17.3
	24	16,310	3,730	2,930	18.8
1.5 by 3.5 MSR	12	7,430	890	690	3.4
Flanges	14	8,990	1,050	990	4
2400f–2.0E	16	10,560	1,210	1,360	4.6
15/32-inch Ply-	18	12,140	1,360	1,800	5.2
wood Web	20	13,710	1,510	2,310	5.8
	22	15,290	1,660	2,890	6.4
	24	16,880	1,810	3,550	7

[1]The allowable moment and shear values are for normal duration loading and are permitted to be increased for load duration in accordance with Section 2.2.5 of the National Design Specification (1986 edition).

[2]Other MSR flanges shall only be used when the allowable shear value and K value are used and the allowable moment and EI value are factored as follows:
allowable moment by actual Ft/1925
EI by actual E/2.2

TABLE NO. III—DESIGN PROPERTIES FOR AI-44 JOISTS[1,2]

DESCRIPTION	OVERALL DEPTH (Inches)	ALLOWABLE MOMENT (Ft.-Lbs.)	ALLOWABLE SHEAR (Pounds)	EI (x 10^6)	K (x 10^6)
LC-10 (DF)	16	11,860	2,250	1,470	12.1
3.0 by 3.375	18	13,950	2,580	1,950	13.7
Flanges	20	16,060	2,730	2,510	15.3
5/8-inch OSB	22	18,170	3,230	3,140	16.9
Web	24	20,300	3,560	3,840	18.5
	26	22,430	3,880	4,620	20
	28	24,570	4,200	5,480	21.5
	30	26,720	4,520	6,420	23.1
LC-10 (DF)	16	11,700	2,700	1,460	14.3
3.0 by 3.375	18	13,750	3,090	1,940	16.2
Flanges	20	15,810	3,480	2,490	18
3/4-inch OSB	2	17,890	3,870	3,110	19.9
Web	24	19,980	4,260	3,820	21.7
	26	22,070	4,640	4,590	23.5
	28	24,170	5,030	5,450	25.3
	30	26,270	5,410	6,380	27.1

[1]The allowable moment and shear values are for normal duration loading and are permitted to be increased for load duration in accordance with Section 2.2.5 of the National Design Specification (1986 edition).

[2]LC-12 flange material is permitted to be substituted for the LC-10.

Figure 6. Page 2 of National Evaluation Report.

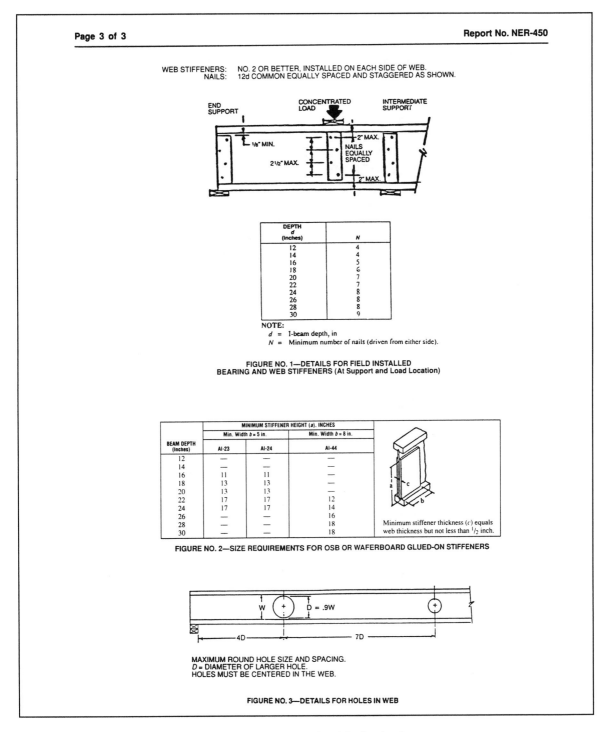

WEB STIFFENERS: NO. 2 OR BETTER, INSTALLED ON EACH SIDE OF WEB.
NAILS: 12d COMMON EQUALLY SPACED AND STAGGERED AS SHOWN.

DEPTH d (Inches)	N
12	4
14	4
16	5
18	6
20	7
22	7
24	8
26	8
28	8
30	9

NOTE:
d = I-beam depth, in
N = Minimum number of nails (driven from either side).

FIGURE NO. 1—DETAILS FOR FIELD INSTALLED
BEARING AND WEB STIFFENERS (At Support and Load Location)

BEAM DEPTH (Inches)	MINIMUM STIFFENER HEIGHT (a), INCHES		
	Min. Width b = 5 in.		Min. Width b = 8 in.
	AI-23	AI-24	AI-44
12	—	—	—
14	—	—	—
16	11	11	—
18	13	13	—
20	13	13	—
22	17	17	12
24	17	17	14
26	—	—	16
28	—	—	18
30	—	—	18

Minimum stiffener thickness (c) equals web thickness but not less than $1/2$ inch.

FIGURE NO. 2—SIZE REQUIREMENTS FOR OSB OR WAFERBOARD GLUED-ON STIFFENERS

MAXIMUM ROUND HOLE SIZE AND SPACING.
D = DIAMETER OF LARGER HOLE.
HOLES MUST BE CENTERED IN THE WEB.

FIGURE NO. 3—DETAILS FOR HOLES IN WEB

Figure 6. Page 3 of National Evaluation Report.

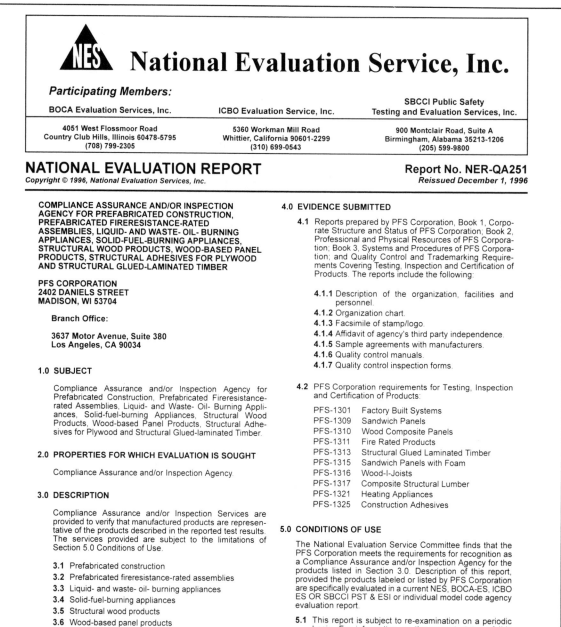

National Evaluation Service, Inc.

Participating Members:

BOCA Evaluation Services, Inc.

ICBO Evaluation Service, Inc.

SBCCI Public Safety
Testing and Evaluation Services, Inc.

4051 West Flossmoor Road Country Club Hills, Illinois 60478-5795 (708) 799-2305	5360 Workman Mill Road Whittier, California 90601-2299 (310) 699-0543	900 Montclair Road, Suite A Birmingham, Alabama 35213-1206 (205) 599-9800

NATIONAL EVALUATION REPORT

Copyright © 1996, National Evaluation Services, Inc.

Report No. NER-QA251
Reissued December 1, 1996

COMPLIANCE ASSURANCE AND/OR INSPECTION
AGENCY FOR PREFABRICATED CONSTRUCTION,
PREFABRICATED FIRERESISTANCE-RATED
ASSEMBLIES, LIQUID- AND WASTE- OIL- BURNING
APPLIANCES, SOLID-FUEL-BURNING APPLIANCES,
STRUCTURAL WOOD PRODUCTS, WOOD-BASED PANEL
PRODUCTS, STRUCTURAL ADHESIVES FOR PLYWOOD
AND STRUCTURAL GLUED-LAMINATED TIMBER

PFS CORPORATION
2402 DANIELS STREET
MADISON, WI 53704

Branch Office:

3637 Motor Avenue, Suite 380
Los Angeles, CA 90034

1.0 SUBJECT

Compliance Assurance and/or Inspection Agency for
Prefabricated Construction, Prefabricated Fireresistance-
rated Assemblies, Liquid- and Waste- Oil- Burning Appliances, Solid-fuel-burning Appliances, Structural Wood
Products, Wood-based Panel Products, Structural Adhesives for Plywood and Structural Glued-laminated Timber.

2.0 PROPERTIES FOR WHICH EVALUATION IS SOUGHT

Compliance Assurance and/or Inspection Agency.

3.0 DESCRIPTION

Compliance Assurance and/or Inspection Services are
provided to verify that manufactured products are representative of the products described in the reported test results.
The services provided are subject to the limitations of
Section 5.0 Conditions of Use.

3.1 Prefabricated construction

3.2 Prefabricated fireresistance-rated assemblies

3.3 Liquid- and waste- oil- burning appliances

3.4 Solid-fuel-burning appliances

3.5 Structural wood products

3.6 Wood-based panel products

3.7 Structural adhesives for plywood

3.8 Structural glued-laminated timber

4.0 EVIDENCE SUBMITTED

4.1 Reports prepared by PFS Corporation, Book 1, Corporate Structure and Status of PFS Corporation; Book 2,
Professional and Physical Resources of PFS Corporation; Book 3, Systems and Procedures of PFS Corporation; and Quality Control and Trademarking Requirements Covering Testing, Inspection and Certification of
Products. The reports include the following:

4.1.1 Description of the organization, facilities and
personnel.

4.1.2 Organization chart.

4.1.3 Facsimile of stamp/logo.

4.1.4 Affidavit of agency's third party independence.

4.1.5 Sample agreements with manufacturers.

4.1.6 Quality control manuals.

4.1.7 Quality control inspection forms.

4.2 PFS Corporation requirements for Testing, Inspection
and Certification of Products:

PFS-1301	Factory Built Systems
PFS-1309	Sandwich Panels
PFS-1310	Wood Composite Panels
PFS-1311	Fire Rated Products
PFS-1313	Structural Glued Laminated Timber
PFS-1315	Sandwich Panels with Foam
PFS-1316	Wood-I-Joists
PFS-1317	Composite Structural Lumber
PFS-1321	Heating Appliances
PFS-1325	Construction Adhesives

5.0 CONDITIONS OF USE

The National Evaluation Service Committee finds that the
PFS Corporation meets the requirements for recognition as
a Compliance Assurance and/or Inspection Agency for the
products listed in Section 3.0. Description of this report,
provided the products labeled or listed by PFS Corporation
are specifically evaluated in a current NES, BOCA-ES, ICBO
ES OR SBCCI PST & ESI or individual model code agency
evaluation report.

5.1 This report is subject to re-examination on a periodic
basis. For information on the current status of this
report, contact one of the participating members of the
NES.

Page 1 of 1

*Figure 7. Since the National Evaluation Service consists of representatives from
BOCA, ICBO and SBCCI, this report will be accepted in all three jurisdictions.*

Special Provisions By Local Building Jurisdictions

Even when presented with a model building code Evaluation Service report or National Evaluation Service report, officials in some jurisdictions occasionally have additional questions or concerns regarding a product's properties or performance. Some fire service officials, for example, have expressed concern about whether lightweight engineered wood products like metal plate connected wood trusses and wood I-joists will safely support firefighters during the latter stages of a fire. As a result, some cities have threatened to ban the use of these products. In response to such reactions, the National Fire Protection Research Foundation researched the problem and published its findings as the *National Engineered Lightweight Construction Fire Research Project Literature Search & Technical Analysis* (32). In addition, fabricators of the affected products conducted extensive fire testing and have implemented a national plan of education and fire safety to address the concerns.

Other jurisdictions may require proof beyond the evaluation service reports that materials or methods of construction will perform adequately. The City of Los Angeles, for instance, requires manufacturers of new building products to obtain approval for use through its own in-house research department. Likewise, the City of New York requires that the proponents of products or techniques not specified in the building code request a variance and appear before its appeals board to earn acceptance.

Special requirements may be imposed at the state level as well. The State of Florida and its Dade County, for example, also ask for special approval of certain building products because of local natural phenomena—hurricanes, in this case. California's State Architect, who has jurisdiction over public schools and hospitals, does not allow the use of oriented strand board (OSB) webs in wood I-joists in either type of buildings. Officials are concerned that OSB will not provide the same resistance to moisture that plywood does. Even though several wood I-joist and OSB producers submitted weathering data showing otherwise, the decision has not been changed. Considered in California to be "Factory-Built Housing Components", structural sandwich panels are therefore regulated by the State rather than the local building official. The panels must be approved by a state-accepted Design Approval Agency and inspected by a state-accepted Quality Assurance Agency. Panels that arrive at the building site with a state insignia must be accepted by the local jurisdiction.

At least one of the model building code organizations is concerned about the effect of duration of load on certain engineered wood products. As a result, manufacturers of structural composite lumber—LVL, PSL and LSL, for example—are being asked to submit data that substantiates their performance under long term loading even though it was the opinion of the governing ASTM committee that the performance of these products would be equal to or better than that of sawn lumber and timbers.

Standards in Model Building Codes

Many of the numerous regulations printed in the model building codes and evaluation service reports are actually excerpts from standards published by nationally recognized technical or trade associations. An even larger number of nationally recognized standards are adopted "by reference". The building code simply says that as long as the material or method of construction meets the criteria set forth in a certain standard written by a certain association, then it is acceptable. What follows is a description of some of the more important standards that affect building code acceptance of engineered wood products.

American Forest & Paper Association

A nonprofit association of lumber and paper producers, the American Forest & Paper Association (AF&PA) was formerly known as the National Forest Products Association. AF&PA's *National Design Specification for Wood Construction* (11) documents the recommended practices for designing and building with structural lumber, glued-laminated timber, timber piles and the connections for each. Its supplement, *National Design Specification Supplement Design Values for Wood Construction* (12) contains tabulated design values for sawn lumber and glued-laminated timber. Both documents are cited extensively in building codes.

American Institute of Timber Construction

The American Institute of Timber Construction (AITC) is the national nonprofit technical trade association for the structural glued-laminated timber industry. Its members design and fabricate glued-laminated timbers, supply connectors and related hardware, and erect and/or design wood structural systems. AITC publishes the *Timber Construction Manual* (6), a reference book for architects, building designers, engineers, contractors and others in the wood design and construction communities, as well as many standards. Design values and other relevant information for softwood glued-laminated timber is given in *AITC 117 Standard Specifications for Structural Glued Laminated Timber of Softwood Species* (7). Similar specifications for members made from hardwoods are found in *AITC 119 Standard Specifications for Hardwood Glued Laminated Timber* (8). Provisions for the preservative treatment of glued-laminated timbers are specified in *AITC 109 Standard for Preservative Treatment of Structural Glued Laminated Timber* (9), while manufacturing requirements are spelled out in *ANSI/AITC A190.1-1992 American National Standard for Wood Products— Structural Glued Laminated Timber* (10). AITC also administers a third-party quality control and inspection program for fabricators of glued-laminated timber.

American National Standards Institute

The American National Standards Institute (ANSI) is both a standards development system and a federation of standards developers. ANSI acts as a coordinator for the voluntary standards development system, and sets the principles of openness, balance of interests, due process, public review and consensus among all parties directly and indirectly affected by existing or proposed standards. Examples of standards developed under the ANSI protocol and referenced in building codes include *ANSI/AITC A190.1-1992 American National*

Standard for Wood Products—Structural Glued Laminated Timber (10) and *ANSI/TPI 1-1995 National Design Standard for Metal Plate Connected Wood Truss Construction* (20).

American Society of Civil Engineers

The objective of the American Society of Civil Engineers (ASCE) is to advance the science and profession of engineering to enhance the welfare of mankind. In 1980, the Board of Direction approved rules governing the writing and maintenance of standards developed by ASCE. Its standards are created through a consensus process that includes balloting by a standards committee made up of both members and non-members, as well as balloting by ASCE's entire membership and the public. *ASCE 7-93 Minimum Design Loads for Buildings and Other Structures* (13), for instance, is used to establish the minimum values for floor and roof live loads, wind loads, snow loads and other loadings specified in the model building codes.

American Society for Testing and Materials

The American Society for Testing and Materials (ASTM) is the world's largest source of voluntary consensus standards. A nonprofit organization, ASTM provides a forum in which producers, users, consumers and other interested parties meet on common ground to discuss and write consensus standards for building materials, systems and services. Standards in ASTM's multiple-volume *Annual Book of ASTM Standards* typically address sampling procedures, test methods, instrumentation, definitions of terms, practices, classifications and specifications. Most standards applicable to wood products are under the purview of committee D07 Committee on Wood and subcommittee D07.02 Subcommittee for Lumber and Engineered Wood Products. D07.02 is the most important standards-writing body for engineered wood products, having recently produced *ASTM D5055 Standard Specification for Establishing and Monitoring Structural Capabilities of Prefabricated Wood I-Joists* (14) and *ASTM D5456 Standard Specification for Evaluation of Structural Composite Lumber Products* (15).

American Wood-Preservers' Association

The American Wood-Preservers' Association (AWPA) is the principal standards-writing organization for the wood preserving industry in the United States. An international, nonprofit, technical society founded to promote the exchange of information, AWPA provides a forum for technical interchange between industry, research and the users of preservative- and fire-retardant treated wood. Increasingly, building codes are requiring the use of wood treated with a preservative or a fire retardant in specific applications. For example, both AWPA's *C20-93 Structural Lumber—Fire-Retardant Treatment by Pressure Processes* (16) and *C27-93 Plywood—Fire-Retardant Treatment by Pressure Processes* (17) are referenced by the model building codes.

APA-The Engineered Wood Association

APA-The Engineered Wood Association is a nonprofit trade association whose members manufacture structural use wood-base panels produced in the United States, as well as a percentage of those made in Canada. APA conducts quality inspections and testing of structural use panels for its members, performs basic research on panels, and promotes their use worldwide. Though not a standards-writing body, some of APA's technical publications such as the *Plywood Design Specification* and its supplements (39) are cited in some state and local building codes.

Canadian Standards Association

Chartered in 1919, the Canadian Standards Association (CSA) is an independent, not-for-profit organization that develops consensus standards and related certification, testing and quality registration programs for building materials, consumer goods and other products. Its more than 1700 standards spell out the requirements or guidelines for the safety, performance and/or quality of products, processes, systems and services. CSA is a Nationally Recognized Testing Laboratory in the United States, which enables it to test and certify products as meeting U. S. standards. CSA standards referenced in the model building codes include *CSA O325 Construction Sheathing* (37) and *CSA O437 OSB and Waferboard* (38).

National Fire Protection Association

Founded by the people in the business of insuring property owners against loss due to fire, the National Fire Protection Association (NFPA) today is a nonprofit association of insurers, firefighters, fire prevention specialists and fire protection engineers. Minimum fire safety requirements and other provisions published in *NFPA 101 Life Safety Code* (18) and other standards published by NFPA have found their way into the model building codes. *NFPA 13 Standard for the Installation of Sprinkler Systems* (19), for instance, has been widely adopted.

Truss Plate Institute

The Truss Plate Institute, Inc. (TPI) is an association of manufacturers engaged in the production of metal connector plates for the wood truss industry, of the fabricators of metal plate connected wood trusses, and of individuals or firms engaged in related activities. TPI establishes methods of design and construction for wood trusses, as well as recommendations for their storage, handling, installation, and temporary and permanent bracing. *ANSI/TPI 1-1995 National Design Standard for Metal Plate Connected Wood Truss Construction* (20) details truss design and analysis methods, fabrication requirements, and specifies how to test truss plates and full size trusses as well. TPI administers a voluntary third-party quality control inspection program for truss fabricators.

United States Department of Commerce

As specified in the *Code of Federal Regulations* (21), the United States Department of Commerce develops voluntary product standards for the purposes of establishing nationally-recognized requirements for products, and for providing all concerned parties with a common basis for understanding their characteristics. The National Institute of Standards and Technology (NIST) — formerly the National Bureau of Standards (NBS) — administers the program as a supplement to the activities of the private sector standards-writing organizations. Examples of voluntary product standards cited in the model building codes include *PS 1-95 Construction and Industrial Plywood* (22) and *PS 2-92 Performance Standard for Wood-Based*

Structural-Use Panels (23) for plywood and oriented strand board, respectively, and *PS 20-94 American Softwood Lumber Standard* (24) for structural softwood lumber. The National Voluntary Laboratory Accreditation Program (NVLAP) administered by NIST certifies the capabilities of third-party inspection laboratories for national and international accreditation purposes. Five third-party wood product testing laboratories in the United States are NVLAP-accredited: PFS/TECO Corporations, Madison, Wisconsin; PFS/TECO Corporations, Eugene, Oregon; National Particleboard Association, Gaithersburg, Maryland; Pittsburgh Testing Laboratories, Eugene, Oregon; and APA-The Engineered Wood Association, Tacoma, Washington.

Underwriters Laboratories

Underwriters Laboratories, Inc. (UL) is one of the largest nonprofit independent fire-testing organizations. Its laboratories examine and test materials, devices and systems to determine their relation to life, fire, and casualty hazards, and crime prevention. UL establishes its own in-house standards that specify test methods and acceptance criteria for numerous products, including some based on wood. Many of them, including *UL 790 Test Standard for Determining the Fire Retardancy of Roof-Covering Materials* (25), have been adopted by the model building codes as fire performance standards. UL's in-house standards are not generally considered as consensus standards; however, many of them have been accepted as such after being reviewed under the ANSI consensus standard development process.

Wood I-Joist Manufacturers Association

The Wood I-Joist Manufacturers Association (WIJMA) is a nonprofit organization composed of the producers of wood I-joists and other allied parties. While WIJMA does not write or publish standards, it actively participates in other standards-writing bodies such as ASTM. Members also work on solving common problems faced by fabricators and users, and promote the use of engineered wood products as well. WIJMA publishes informational documents such as *Technical Bulletin No. 1 Design Guidelines* (26), which explains among other things, how wood I-joists are designed, installed, braced and fastened.

Summary

The manufacturer of a new building material or method of construction has many hurdles to jump before its product or technique is accepted for use under the model building codes. Even after building code recognition is received, a manufacturer must monitor the various model building codes and local jurisdictions to ensure that its product or technique is given due consideration and treated fairly. A manufacturer who is not aware of proposed changes to the building codes that affect its products and techniques may miss out on the opportunity to participate in the decision-making process. Once made, changes to the model building codes are often difficult to reverse.

There is no doubt that the model building code organizations and their evaluation services provide a critical service, without which there would be turmoil in the construction industry.

Though the approval process may prove tedious to manufacturers, it is necessary to ensure that all building materials and methods of construction are structurally adequate, safe, and will perform as intended. The evaluation service arms of the model building code organizations not only provide the needed forum from which to receive product recognition, they also provide the "level playing field" necessary for fair competition among the manufacturers of engineered wood products and other building materials alike.

References

1. International Conference of Building Officials. 1994. Uniform Building Code. ICBO. Whittier, California.

2. Building Officials & Code Administrators International, Inc. 1996. National Building Code. BOCA. Country Club Hills, Illinois.

3. Southern Building Code Congress International. 1994. Standard Building Code. SBCCI. Birmingham, Alabama.

4. Council of American Building Officials. 1995. One And Two Family Dwelling Code. CABO. Falls Church, Virginia.

5. International Code Council. (Undated). International Building Code. ICC. Whittier, California.

6. American Institute of Timber Construction. 1994. Timber Construction Manual. AITC. Englewood, Colorado.

7. American Institute of Timber Construction. 1993. AITC 117 Standard Specification for Structural Glued Laminated Timber of Softwood Species. AITC. Englewood, Colorado.

8. American Institute of Timber Construction. 1985. AITC 119 Standard Specifications for Hardwood Glued Laminated Timber. AITC. Englewood, Colorado.

9. American Institute of Timber Construction. 1990. AITC 109 Standard for Preservative Treatment Of Structural Glued Laminated Timber. AITC. Englewood, Colorado.

10. American Institute of Timber Construction. 1992. ANSI/AITC A190.1 Structural Glued Laminated Timber. AITC. Englewood, Colorado.

11. American Forest & Paper Association. 1991. National Design Specification for Wood Construction. AF&PA. Washington, D. C.

12. American Forest & Paper Association. 1991. National Design Specification Supplement Design Values for Wood Construction. AF&PA. Washington, D. C.

13. American Society of Civil Engineers. 1993. ASCE 7-93 Minimum Design Loads for Buildings and Other Structures. ASCE. New York, New York.

14. American Society for Testing and Materials. 1995. ASTM D5055 Standard Specification for Establishing and Monitoring Structural Capacities of Prefabricated Wood I-Joists. ASTM. West Conshohocken, Pennsylvania.

15. American Society for Testing and Materials. 1993. ASTM D5456 Standard Specification for Evaluation of Structural Composite Lumber Products. ASTM. West Conshohocken, Pennsylvania.

16. American Wood-Preservers' Association. 1995. C20 Book Of Standards. AWPA. Woodstock, Maryland.

17. American Wood-Preservers' Association. 1995. C27 Book Of Standards. AWPA. Woodstock, Maryland.

18. National Fire Protection Association. 1994. NFPA 101 Life Safety Code. NFPA. Quincy, Massachusetts.

19. National Fire Protection Association. 1994. NFPA 13 Standard for the Installation of Sprinkler Systems. NFPA. Quincy, Massachusetts.

20. Truss Plate Institute. 1995. ANSI/TPI 1-1995 National Design Standard for Metal Plate Connected Wood Truss Construction. TPI. Madison, Wisconsin.

21. Office of The Federal Register. 1995. Code of Federal Regulations. Part 10 Title 15 OFR. Washington, D. C.

22. National Institute of Standards and Technology. 1995. Voluntary Product Standard PS 1-95 Construction and Industrial Plywood. NIST. Gaithersburg, Maryland.

23. National Institute of Standards and Technology. 1992. Voluntary Product Standard PS 2-92 Performance Standard for Wood-Based Structural-Use Panels. NIST. Gaithersburg, Maryland.

24. National Institute of Standards and Technology. 1994. Voluntary Product Standard PS 20-94 American Softwood Lumber Standard. NIST. Gaithersburg, Maryland.

25. Underwriters Laboratories, Inc. 1983. UL 790 Test Standard for Determining the Fire Retardancy Of Roof-Covering Materials. UL. Northbrook, Illinois.

26. Wood I-Joist Manufacturers Association. 1994. Technical Bulletin No.1 Design Guidelines. WIJMA. Madison, Wisconsin.

27. ICBO Evaluation Service, Inc. 1993. AC14 Prefabricated Wood I-Joists. ICBO Evaluation Service. Whittier, California.

28. ICBO Evaluation Service, Inc. 1995. AC47 Structural Composite Lumber. ICBO Evaluation Service. Whittier, California.

29. American Society For Testing and Materials. 1995. ASTM E119 Standard Test Methods for Fire Tests of Building Construction and Materials. ASTM. West Conshohocken, Pennsylvania.

30. ICBO Evaluation Service, Inc. 1995. AC89 Laboratory Accreditation. ICBO Evaluation Service. Whittier, California.

31. ICBO Evaluation Service, Inc. 1995. AC98 Quality Control Agency Accreditation. ICBO Evaluation Service. Whittier, California.

32. National Fire Protection Research Foundation. 1992. National Engineered Lightweight Construction Fire Research Project Literature Search & Technical Analysis. NFPRF. Quincy, Massachusetts.

33. International Conference of Building Officials. 1994. Uniform Building Code Volume 1 Administrative, Fire- and Life-Safety, and Field Inspection Provisions. ICBO. Whittier, California.

34. International Conference of Building Officials. 1994. Uniform Building Code Volume 2 Structural Engineering Design Provisions. ICBO. Whittier, California.

35. International Conference of Building Officials. 1994. Uniform Building Code Volume 3 Material, Testing and Installation Standards. ICBO. Whittier, California.

36. International Conference of Building Officials. 1994. Uniform Building Code Standards. ICBO. Whittier, California.

37. Canadian Standards Association. 1992. CSA O325 Construction Sheathing. CSA. Rexdale, Ontario, Canada.

38. Canadian Standards Association. 1993. CSA O437 OSB and Waferboard. CSA. Rexdale, Ontario, Canada.

39. APA-The Engineered Wood Association. 1995. Plywood Design Specification. APA. Tacoma, Washington.

Chapter 11

Load and Resistance Factor Design

David S. Gromala, P. E.

Weyerhaeuser
Tacoma, Washington

Load and resistance factor design (LRFD) formats are rapidly replacing the traditional allowable stress design (ASD) formats as the predominant structural design basis around the world. In the United States, steel and concrete design specifications are available either optionally or exclusively in the LRFD format (1, 2). In Canada, only a limit states design format is supported for all materials (3).

Until recently, design specifications for engineered wood construction—which includes both structural sawn lumber and structural engineered wood products—were available in only the ASD format. In 1996 the first LRFD standard for engineered wood construction was published by the American Society of Civil Engineers. *AF&PA/ASCE 16-95 Load and Resistance Factor Design Standard for Engineered Wood Construction* (4) embodies the work of virtually the entire wood products industry, supported by a major commitment from experts in the field of reliability-based design (of which LRFD is a part). *AF&PA/ASCE 16-95* represents over a decade of development, refinement and trial use, and is the basis for the American Forest & Paper Association's (AF&PA) *Load and Resistance Factor Design Manual for Engineered Wood Construction* (5). The *LRFD Manual* complements the provisions of *AF&PA/ASCE 16-95* by providing explanatory information, design examples and product-specific design values.

The wood products industry intends to continue to support both the ASD and LRFD formats for the foreseeable future (6, 7). In this way, LRFD can take its place in engineered wood design on its own merits by being used when prescribed by building code provisions, when preferred by individual designers or when it demonstrates economic or other benefits.

One advantage of *AF&PA/ASCE 16-95* that users will quickly note is that its scope is virtually complete across the spectrum of structural wood products and their connections. Unlike the familiar ASD specifications of today in which different product types are covered individually—the *National Design Specification for Wood Construction* (*NDS*) (8), for example, has separate sections for lumber, glued-laminated timber and generic connections—*AF&PA/ASCE 16-95's* procedures cover the entire range of both commodity and proprietary wood products. Thus, the architect, designer or engineer who chooses to use dimension lumber roof framing and wood I-joist floor framing connected with proprietary hangers to either glued-laminated timber or structural composite lumber beams will find that all of these products are covered in *AF&PA/ASCE 16-95* and the *LRFD Manual*.

With the recent introduction of the LRFD method, one question that lingers in the minds of many architects, designers and engineers is "Why change at all?" These practitioners may be comfortable designing with the ASD method and see no reason to undertake the time and expense of switching to LRFD. "If fit ain't broke, don't fix it." is the recurring theme.

While some proponents of LRFD might argue that ASD is indeed "broke," a more common notion is that ASD, while adequate, is simply not as useful as it once was. Changes in structural design philosophy, exemplified by today's computer-assisted design software that creates designs that are pushed closer to the allowable stress limits than the older, more approximate design techniques, have removed part of the historical margin of design conservatism. This trend has been accelerated by increased competition among design firms that often forces designers to abandon the "arbitrary" conservatism they might have once added to their designs. Similarly, the introduction of new and improved structural materials continually stretches the system of codes and standards by which allowable design stresses are derived.

In theory, LRFD provides an improved design system that can better accommodate such changes. The statistical procedures used in LRFD were developed for precisely these types of conditions; that is, where comprehensive changes force a rethinking of the entire design process. LRFD brings rigor to this process by forcing the quantification of important design-related parameters in a consistent and unbiased manner (9, 10, 11).

Design Formats

Allowable Stress Design
The ASD method is based on the concepts of design loads and allowable stresses. Design loads are assumed to be large enough to reasonably represent the most severe loads that will be imposed on a structure during its lifetime. Allowable stresses induced in structural materials by applied loads are assumed to be low enough such that the materials will behave in a linear elastic manner. The combination of high design loads and low allowable stresses is presumed to provide an acceptably large margin of safety.

For a given structural configuration, the ASD process usually includes three steps:

1. assignment and placement of loads

2. structural analysis (apportioning loads and computing stresses/forces on members and connections)

3. member selection and connection detail design

Building code requirements and standard engineering practices usually define most of the variables for the designer. For typical buildings:

1. the magnitude and placement of design loads is specified in the applicable building code documents

2. structural analysis techniques are well-known, especially for common frame-type buildings

3. member selection and connection detailing techniques are widely available for the major structural materials

Because the ASD method has dominated structural engineering throughout history, the designer accepts the relationships between applied loads and member strength as having appropriate levels of safety built into this design system.

Load and Resistance Factor Design
LRFD is based on the concepts of factored load effects and factored resistance effects, which are analogous to ASD's design loads and allowable stresses, respectively. As long as the resistance effects (material strength) equal or exceed the load effects (induced stresses), a member or structure is assumed to be safe.

When the American Concrete Institute introduced in 1963 the concept of factored loads for the ultimate strength design method, it effectively launched a new design process (12). The ultimate strength design method permitted a designer to analyze a structure at a higher state of stress than the ASD method permitted. This offered distinct advantages for structures in which the material or members' behavior is significantly different (when compared with linear elastic analysis) at high levels of stress. *ACI 318-63 Building Code Requirements for Reinforced Concrete* and *ACI 318R-63 Commentary* specified the magnitude of the load factors (greater than 1.0, applied to design loads) and the resistance factors (less than 1.0, applied to material strengths). When used to analyze a member stressed to near its ultimate capacity, the provisions of *ACI 318-63* were assumed to provide an acceptably large margin of safety.

The appearance of *ANSI A58.1-1972 Minimum Design Loads for Buildings and Other Structures* (13) formalized the concept of load factors into a nationally-recognized standard that could be applied across a range of structural materials. In retrospect, it was the introduction of consensus-based load factors and load combinations in *ANSI A58.1-1972* that sparked the development of LRFD standards for each structural material. Since the model building codes historically had used *ANSI A58.1-1972* as the basis for many of their design loads, it was inevitable that factored load combinations would eventually find their way into ICBO's *Uniform Building Code* (14), BOCA's *National Building Code* (15) and SBCCI's *Standard Building Code* (16).

Differences Between ASD and LRFD

The differences between ASD and LRFD are often portrayed on the basis of a supposed difference between deterministic (discrete values) and probabilistic (variable values) design methods. While this explanation is not entirely wrong, it is misleading; ASD and LRFD differ primarily in their underlying bases and design formats.

Underlying Basis

The difference in the underlying bases of ASD and LRFD lies not in the deterministic versus probabilistic argument, but in the manner by which the probabilistic concepts used in both are treated.

In ASD, the magnitude of the design loads is determined based on the judgment of the loads committees of the model building code organizations. The committees rely heavily on standards such as *ASCE 7-93 Minimum Design Loads for Buildings and Other Structures* (17), and commonly establish the magnitude of design loads on the same basis. The choice of design loads is generally probabilistic. Wind and snow loads, for instance, are based on a 50-year mean recurrence interval or a 2 percent annual probability of exceedance. Similarly, the magnitude of allowable design stresses for a specific structural material is determined by judgment; in this case, by the appropriate standards committee. ASTM Committee D07, for example, determines design stresses for wood. The judgment embodied in the various ASTM standards for structural lumber includes a probabilistic estimate of strength—the lower 5 percent exclusion limit of a strength versus frequency distribution—and a reduction factor of 2.1 that provides safety in use. When viewed in this light, the magnitudes of the design loads and the allowable design stresses in ASD are generated in a probabilistic manner, but the reduction factor is based on engineering judgment.

In LRFD, the magnitude of the nominal loads and resistances is first determined in virtually the same manner as in ASD. Then, a target reliability index is determined. The target is determined by examining a range of design cases that, in the judgment of the standards committee, provide an adequate level of safety. Whether the target is chosen as the average or minimum of these cases is based on the committee's judgment. It is during the next step—in which load factors and resistance factors are established to "smooth" the computed reliability across the various design cases—that LRFD begins to deviate from ASD. Some design cases receive an increase in capacity (relative to ASD), while others receive a decrease. It is in the establishment of the load and resistance factors that LRFD relies more on probabilistic analysis than ASD.

Design Formats

Once the basic design parameters are established (design loads and allowable stresses in ASD; load factors, resistance factors, and nominal strengths in LRFD), the design is performed in the same manner in both formats. Though a designer uses predetermined values for each of the design parameters, this does not mean that the design is deterministic. In fact, depending on one's definition of "deterministic," either both ASD and LRFD are deterministic, or neither is deterministic.

Similarities Between ASD and LRFD

Despite their differences, ASD and LRFD also have certain similarities. For example, both formats start with design checking equations that require a comparison of load effects with the capacity of the member or connection.

Take the case of a flexural member under a combination of dead load and live load. For simplicity, it is assumed that the proper engineering units are already included in the parameters and that all material adjustment factors (with the exception of load duration) are embedded in the adjusted material design values. The general form of a simple design checking equation for a flexural member requires that the moment resistance supplied by the member meets or exceeds the applied moment exerted by the load:

$$M_{applied} \leq M_{supplied}$$

In ASD, the specific notation is:

$$D + L \leq C_D F_b S_{ASD}$$

where D and L are the design dead load moment and design live load moment, respectively; C_D is the load duration factor; F_b is the allowable bending stress; and S_{ASD} is the section modulus.

In LRFD, the notation is similar, yet different:

$$1.2D + 1.6L \leq \lambda \phi R_n S_{LRFD}$$

Here, λ is the time effect factor; ϕ is the resistance factor; R_n is the nominal bending strength; and S_{LRFD} is the section modulus.

From a format standpoint, the equations are essentially the same. The only significant differences are the introduction of load factors 1.2 and 1.6 on the left side of the LRFD equation, and the resistance factor ϕ on its right side. The notation is also slightly changed from load duration factor C_D to time effect factor λ and from allowable stress F_b to nominal strength R_n.

11 - 279

When a design checking equation is viewed as a balance between applied loads and member or connection resistances, the primary difference between ASD and LRFD is one of scale (Fig. 1). While each design checking equation still balances loads and stresses, the LRFD equation is based on much larger numerical values.

Advantages of LRFD
LRFD offers three advantages not available with ASD.

Load factoring—The ability to set safety factors on a sliding scale across various load ratios and load combinations based on their relative predictability permits LRFD to smooth safety levels across a range of design cases. A side benefit is that the load factors are explicitly stated in the load standard rather than hidden within an obscure reduction factor.

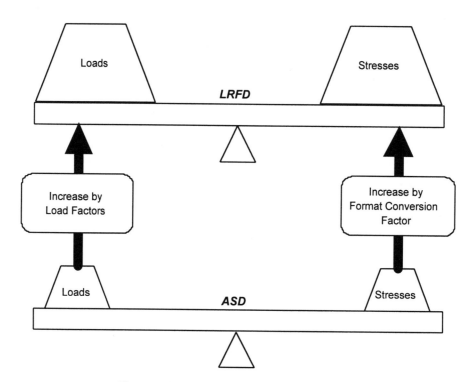

Figure 1. Scaling differences in ASD versus LRFD.

Design strength resembles material strength—This is a perception issue that is best illustrated with an example. Assume that a designer uses a lumber grade with an allowable bending stress of 1500 psi. The designer then learns that the average bending strength of this grade of lumber exceeds 6000 psi. Even though other critical pieces of information are missing—coefficient of variation, adjustment factors, etc.—the designer perceives (wrongly) a safety factor of 4 in the member's design strength. Experience has shown that there is a subconscious tendency to believe that allowable design values are overly conservative, especially in those areas of application that are part technical and part marketing. The misconception disappears in LRFD, because the design values are nearly identical to the strength values. As with load factoring, this change from hidden to explicit factors can only improve a designer's instincts.

Easier to teach—A handicap faced by the wood products industry is that civil engineering curricula at colleges and universities have severe time constraints imposed on their course offerings. Since most structural engineers are expected to design major structures in steel and concrete, these materials receive the most attention. With LRFD, more of the design process is actually material-independent. This means that students who learn LRFD already understand most of the concepts needed to design wood structures using LRFD without having to take an additional course dedicated to wood.

LRFD for Engineered Wood Construction

The transition from ASD to LRFD is illustrated here with a two-step example. The first part provides an overview of the LRFD system, focusing on where the familiar factors of safety come from and where they are repositioned. The second gives a closer view of the details of the system in which elementary beam, wall stud and bolted connection design examples are computed in both ASD and LRFD formats.

Repositioning of Factors of Safety

ASD is based on the premise that the actual in-service stresses induced in a structure are limited to arbitrarily low levels, and therefore provides an adequate margin of safety. LRFD, on the other hand, is based on calculation of member stresses at a factored, and therefore higher, load. The difference is sometimes portrayed as being extremely significant. Under this line of thinking, ASD is successful because it limits the response of the structure to very low, and thus, linear stress-strain conditions. This thinking continues with the belief that LRFD forces the designer to consider "ultimate strength behavior," with the implication that linear analysis is too simplistic for use with the LRFD format.

In reality, the scaling differences between ASD and LRFD are better described as differences in style than as differences in substance. Consider the following hypothetical design example:

A structural product is designed using the "Traditional Design System" (TDS), in which the permissible stress, F, is computed by dividing the average test strength, M, by a factor of safety of 4 ($F = M/4$). Design load under this system is also traditional, and uses conservative estimates of dead load, D, and live load, L, on the structure. TDS limits the permissible stress to be less than or equal to the sum of the applied loads,

$$F \leq D+L$$

which is the same as saying $M/4 \leq D+L$.. This system thus limits stresses to safe, linear levels.

The same product is then designed using the "Radical Design System" (RDS). Here, the design strength value, R, is taken as the average ultimate test strength, M. No safety factor is applied, so R=M. Design load under RDS is based on the concept of load factoring. Based on statistical analysis, the load factors for both dead, D, and live loads, L, are established as 4.0. The design equation is:

$$R \leq 4D + 4L$$

Note that the computed stresses under RDS are in the range of ultimate strengths at the design limit state. Does this mean that all material or geometric nonlinearity must be taken into account to accurately depict structural performance? The answer is found in the following calculations, where M = 4000 kip-ft., D = 200 kip-ft. and L = 800 kip-ft. (1 kip = 1000 lb.).

For TDS:

$$F = M/4 = 4000/4 = 1000 \text{ kip-ft.}$$
$$D+L = 200+800 = 1000 \text{ kip-ft.}$$

Since the permissible stress, F, does not exceed the sum of the applied loads, D+L, the design is acceptable (member is loaded to 100 percent of TDS capacity).

For RDS:

$$R = M = 4000 \text{ kip-ft.}$$
$$4D + 4L = 4(200) + 4(800) = 4000 \text{ kip-ft.}$$

Since member ultimate strength R does not exceed the sum of the factored loads, 4D+4L, the design is acceptable (member is loaded to 100 percent of RDS capacity).

Is the design stress condition actually different between TDS and RDS, or are the differences simply an alternative way of viewing structural design and safety levels? If a TDS structure is built next to a RDS structure, and each is subjected to the same applied loads, will there be a difference in the actual member stresses in each structure on any given day?

Mathematically, there is no difference between a divisor of 4 placed on the left side of an equation (TDS) and a multiplier of 4 on the right side (RDS). This shows that the two design systems are simply alternative ways of viewing the same design condition. Thus, the side-by-side structures will experience the same actual in-service stresses despite the differences in the design equations chosen to describe them.

This exercise does not prove that one system is better than the other; it simply illustrates that there are alternative ways of achieving the same design goals. What then, is the advantage of RDS that makes it worthy of the time and effort required to change formats? The answer to this question is best answered by examining the underpinnings of both design systems.

While TDS (that is, ASD) has had a successful history over many years, it has a major flaw that limits its ability to keep pace with the need for continuing refinements in design. The flaw is the "lumping" of the entire safety factor as a hidden divisor in the design stress (F = M/4). One problem with TDS is that the actual safety level is the same regardless of whether most of the load is highly predictable (as with dead loads) or only poorly predictable (as with live loads like snow and wind). Another is that the magnitude of the safety factor is hidden from the daily calculations of most designers, with the potential effect that the actual level of safety may be somewhat obscure.

RDS (that is, LRFD), on the other hand, exposes the hidden safety factor by making it an explicit multiplier on the design load. A feature found in "real" RDS, but not included in this simple hypothetical example, is the use of different load factors for different loads. In this way, higher or lower factors are imposed as required to maintain a constant level of safety across all designs. Finally, the addition of resistance factors to the design equation means that the former all-in-one safety factor is split, with part applied to the resistance effects and the remainder to the load effects.

Design Examples

Beam
A glued-laminated timber floor beam 3.125 in. wide must resist a total applied moment of 230 kip-in. (46 kip-in. dead load and 184 kip-in. live load). It has an allowable bending stress F_b of 2400 psi (ASD) (Table 1), and a nominal bending strength R_n of 6.1 ksi (LRFD) (Table 2) (1 ksi = 1000 lb. per in.^{2}). All size/volume effects are the same for ASD and LRFD, and are included in the basic design value. No other design adjustments are required because the member will be used at "reference conditions" (dry-use, untreated, etc.). What is the required depth of the beam?

The basic design equation for the ASD case is:

$$C_D F_b S_{ASD} \geq D + L$$

where C_D is the load duration factor, F_b is the allowable bending stress and S_{ASD} is the required section modulus. For this example, $C_D = 1.00$ (floor load) as per *NDS*, and:

$$S_{ASD} = \frac{D+L}{C_D\, F_b} = \frac{46+184}{1.00\,(2400)} = 95.8 \text{ in.}^3$$

11 - 283

Solving $S_{ASD} = (b\,d^2)\,/\,6$, where b and d are the width and depth of the beam, respectively, indicates a member 13.5 inches deep is needed.

The corresponding design equation for the LRFD case is:

$$\lambda\,\phi_b M \;\geq\; 1.2D + 1.6L$$

As per *AF&PA/ASCE 16-95*, $\lambda = 0.80$ and $\phi_b = 0.85$, and

$$M = \frac{1.2D + 1.6L}{\lambda\,\phi_b} = \frac{1.2\,(46) + 1.6\,(184)}{0.80\,(0.85)} = 514.1 \text{ kip - in.}$$

For a member with a nominal bending strength of 6.1 ksi, the required section modulus is $M/R_n = 514.1/6.1 = 84.3$ in^3. The corresponding LRFD design depth of 12.7 inches represents a 7 percent savings in material relative to the ASD-derived depth. (For ease of use, the *LRFD Manual* has beam design tables wherein the tabulated moment values already include λ and ϕ_b built in as the product $\lambda\,\phi_b M$.)

Note that in Tables 1 and 2 the design modulus of elasticity is 1.8 million psi for both the ASD and LRFD cases. Thus, if the deflection criteria were sufficiently stringent to control this design, both formats would yield the same required member depth.

Table 1. Allowable stress values for ASD (8).

Description	Size / Grade	Species	Design Properties	
Glued-laminated timber	3-1/8 in. wide	Douglas-fir	F_b = 2400 psi	E = 1.8 million psi
Wall stud	2x4 / Stud	spruce-pine-fir	F_b = 675 psi	E = 1.2 million psi
Bolt	5/8-in. diameter	southern pine framing	Z = 1870 lb.	

Table 2. Reference strength values for LRFD (5).

Description	Size / Grade	Species	Design Properties	
Glued-laminated timber	3-1/8 in. wide	Douglas-fir	R_n = 6.1 ksi	E = 1800 ksi
Wall stud	2x4 / Stud	spruce-pine-fir	R_n = 1.71 psi	E = 1200 ksi
Bolt	5/8-in. diameter	southern pine framing	$\lambda \phi_z Z$ = 3.23 kip	

Wall Stud
A 2x4 wall stud loaded laterally by the wind is subject to an applied moment M of 2990 in.-lb. It has an allowable bending stress F_b of 675 psi (ASD) (Table 1); a nominal bending strength R_n of 1.71 ksi (LRFD) (Table 2); and a section modulus S of 3.06 in.^{3} Again, all size/volume effects are the same for ASD and LRFD, and are included in the basic design value. No other design adjustments are required because the member will be used at reference conditions. What is the ratio of member capacity to required capacity?

The design equation for the ASD case is:

$$C_D F_b S \geq M$$

where C_D is the load duration factor, F_b is the allowable bending stress and S is the section modulus. As per *NDS*, C_D = 1.6 (wind load) and:

$$M = C_D F_b S = (1.6)(675)(3.06) = 3304 \text{ in.-lb.}$$

The ratio of member capacity to required capacity is 3304/2990 = 1.11, and the capacity supplied exceeds the capacity required by 11 percent.

The design equation for LRFD for this case is:

$$\lambda \phi_b M \geq 1.3W$$

where W is the applied moment caused by wind loading. As per *AF&PA/ASCE 16-95*, λ = 1.0 and ϕ_b = 0.85. The required moment resistance is:

$$M = \frac{1.3\,W}{\lambda\,\phi_b} = \frac{1.3\,(2.99)}{1.0\,(0.85)} = 4.58 \text{ kip - in.}$$

For a member with a nominal bending strength of 1.71 ksi, and a section modulus S of 3.06 in.^{3}, the member capacity is R_n S = (1.71) (3.06) = 5.23 kip-in., which exceeds the required capacity by 14 percent ([5.23 / 4.58] = 1.14).

Bolted Connection
A bolted splice in the chord of a roof truss made from southern pine will be subjected to a total pure tensile force parallel to the grain of 6000 lb. (1500 lb. dead load and 4500 lb. snow load). The main member is 3 in. thick, and each side member, 1.5 in. thick. The design capacity, Z, of the 5/8-in. diameter bolts to be used is 1870 psi (ASD) (Table 1), and their factored capacity, $\lambda\,\phi_z$ Z, is 3.23 kips (LRFD) (Table 2). Members have adequate edge and end distances, the requirements for which are the same for both ASD and LRFD. Size/volume effects are also the same for ASD and LRFD, and are included in the basic design value. No other design adjustments are required because the member will be used at reference conditions. How many bolts are required?

The basic design equation for the ASD case is:

$$Z_{ASD} \geq 6000 \text{ lb.}$$

The design connection capacity Z_{ASD} is the product of n, the number of bolts, and Z, the design capacity of a single bolt.

Based on experience, it is assumed that one row of three bolts will be required. *NDS* provides a conservative estimate for the group action factor C_g for three bolts of 0.97. The load duration factor C_D is 1.15 (snow load) as per *NDS*. On this basis, the design capacity of the connection is:

$$Z_{ASD} = nZC_DC_g = (3)\,(1870)\,(1.15)\,(0.97) = 6258 \text{ lb.}$$

Since the design capacity exceeds the required capacity (6258/6000 = 1.04), the design is acceptable.

The corresponding equation for the LRFD case is:

$$\lambda \, \phi \, Z \geq 1.2D + 1.6L = 1.2(1.5) + 1.6(4.5) = 9.0 \text{ kips}$$

As before, it is assumed that one row of three bolts will be required. The design strength of the connection Z_{LRFD} is:

$$Z_{LRFD} = n \, \lambda \, \phi \, ZC_g = (3) \, (3.23) \, (0.97) = 9.4 \text{ kips}$$

Again, the design capacity exceeds the required capacity (9.4/9.0 = 1.04), so the design is acceptable.

Design Provisions of the AF&PA/ASCE 16-95 Standard for Engineered Wood Construction

AF&PA/ASCE 16-95 governs the use of LRFD procedures for building design in the United States. It uses *ASCE 7-93 Minimum Design Loads for Buildings and Other Structures* (17) for load factors and load combinations, and requires that reference strength values be established in accordance with *ASTM D5457-93 Standard Specification for Computing the Reference Resistance of Wood-Based Materials and Structural Connections for Load and Resistance Factor Design* (18). Finally, it retains behavioral equation consistency with *NDS*.

Several items within *AF&PA/ASCE 16-95* are worthy of special note, either because they are new in the LRFD method or because their provisions differ from those of *NDS*.

General Provisions and Reliability Methodology
General provisions for the LRFD standard are provided in *AF&PA/ASCE 16-95* Chapter 1. Several introductory concepts are described in detail in the commentary to Chapter 1.

The LRFD notation used in *AF&PA/ASCE 16-95* for wood products differs from that used for steel. The differences are in the terms "required," "design," and "nominal" which are used to modify the word "strength." *AF&PA/ASCE 16-95* describes the problem:

> "In steel LRFD, the term "required strength" is used to denote the force on the member due to factored loads. Similarly, the term "design strength" is used to denote the factored member capacity—which is a product of the resistance factor and another term called the "nominal strength." Thus, steel

LRFD uses notation that sometimes includes applicable factors and some-times does not."

"This problem is compounded for wood LRFD for two reasons. First, designers must often "track" both unadjusted and adjusted strength quan-tities. This alone would confound a simple notation system. A second source of confusion lies in the need to publish not only member strengths (i.e., moment capacity) but also material properties (i.e., the LRFD equivalent of allowable stresses). This need to define both unadjusted (called "reference") and adjusted quantities of both member and material parameters forced the wood LRFD notation down a slightly different track than steel. A description of the notation and its rationale follows."

"In this standard, the term "resistance" is used to refer to member capacities (i.e., moment resistance, compression resistance, etc.). This is distinct from the term "strength" which refers to limit state material properties—con-ceptually a "factored allowable stress." As mentioned previously, the devi-ation from steel LRFD notation was needed because it is anticipated that designers of wood products will track not only the forces due to factored loads (called "required" resistance in steel LRFD), but also both reference (i.e., unadjusted) and adjusted resistance and sometimes reference and adjusted member strength."

Chapter 1 introduces the "handbook" resistance factors, ϕ, for each stress mode, which are presented in *AF&PA/ASCE 16-95* Table 1.4-1 (Table 3). The resistance factors are higher for the least variable properties and lower for the most variable properties. This hierarchy of resistance factors applies to all engineered wood products. Since product-specific differences in computed reliability are handled in the design value derivation, there are no product-specific reliability adjustment factors to further burden the designer.

Table 3. AF&PA/ASCE 16-95 *Table 1.4-1. Resistance factors, ϕ (4).*

Application	Symbol	Value
compression	ϕ_c	0.90
flexure	ϕ_b	0.85
stability	ϕ_s	0.85
tension	ϕ_t	0.80
shear/torsion	ϕ_v	0.75
connections	ϕ_z	0.65

Chapter 1 also introduces the time effect factor λ for each load combination. The time effect factor is the LRFD equivalent of the familiar ASD load duration factor. It is derived in a completely different manner than the load duration factor, and is numerically scaled differently as well. In essence, the time effect factor accounts for time-related differences in the computed reliability between the reference condition and the design condition being examined. A specific value for the time effect factor is coupled to each load combination; it is not tied to any definitive period of time under load. The commentary to Chapter 1 further describes the time effect factor:

> "It is significant from a designer's perspective that the time effect factor is identical for the gravity load cases of floor live, snow and roof live, in contrast to the different factors used in allowable stress design. As discussed above, this is because, when measured on a reliability basis, the factor used for floors in ASD is conservative. Conversely, the factor used for roof live load was judged to be close enough to the other two cases that the same value could be used. The end result is that time effect factors more closely align with standards of other countries, in which relatively short-term loads receive a 1.0 factor (relative to short term test values), intermediate duration loads receive a 0.80 factor and long-term loads receive the lowest factor."

The time effect factors are to be used with load combinations as indicated in *AF&PA/ASCE 16-95* Table 1.4-2 (Table 4). In general, the time effect factor is 1.0 for load combinations that are controlled by wind or earthquake loads; 0.8 for load combinations controlled by typical gravity loads on roof or floor systems; and 0.6 for permanent loads. Exceptions to this general rule—impact loads and storage floor loads, for example—are noted in *AF&PA/ASCE 16-95*. Further discussion regarding the derivation of the time effect factor can be found in references 19 and 20.

Table 4. AF&PA/ASCE 16-95 Table 1.4-2. Time effect factors, λ (4).

Load Combination	Time Effect Factor (λ)
1.4D	0.6
1.2D + 1.6L + 0.5(L_r or S or R)	0.7 when L is from storage 0.8 when L is from occupancy 1.25 when L is from impact[a]
1.2D + 1.6(L_r or S or R) + (0.5L or 0.8W)	0.8
1.2D + 1.3W + 0.5L + (L_r or S or R)	1.0
1.2D + 1.0E + 0.5L + 0.2S	1.0
0.9D - (1.3W or 1.0E)	1.0

[a]For connections, λ = 1.0 when L is from impact.

Behavioral Equations

Aside from those noted here, users will find few significant differences between the behavioral equations in *AF&PA/ASCE 16-95* and those found in *NDS*.

LRFD design equations typically are in the general form of:

$$\text{(Supplied)} \quad \lambda \, \phi \, R' \; > \; R_u \quad \text{(Applied)}$$

where R' is the adjusted member resistance and R_u is the required member resistance. This format differs from the ASD format in that:

1. the time effect factor λ is always a separate factor applied to the adjusted member resistance, whereas in ASD a reduction to "normal" load duration is embedded in the adjusted design stress

2. the resistance factor ϕ is always a separate factor, whereas in ASD reduction factors are embedded in the allowable design stress

3. the "applied" side of the equation includes factored loads, whereas in ASD the loads are unfactored, with this component of the "safety factor" embedded in the allowable design stress

In addition to the general reformatting due to the introduction of the resistance factors, several other items are worthy of note.

Compression—The column slenderness ratio equation (*AF&PA/ASCE 16-95* Equation 4.3-2) has been reformatted into the familiar "$P/P_{critical}$" format. Users may wonder why terms related to member stability include a divisor of λ. This is because these terms are supposed to be independent of the time effect factor, and because the general design equation includes multiplication by λ. Thus, stability terms must be "pre-divided" by λ to cancel the latter effect.

Another change relative to *NDS* is an enhanced description of the resistance of notched columns (*AF&PA/ASCE .16-95* Section 4.3.3). The improvement includes a specific definition of how to determine the critical portion of a notched column, depending on whether the notch is in a critical or noncritical location.

Provisions related to tapered columns (*AF&PA/ASCE 16-95* Section 4.3.4) include an expanded table of coefficients by which the location of the critical section can be determined for a wider variety of support conditions.

Bending—The beam slenderness ratio equation (*AF&PA/ASCE 16-95* Equation 5.2-5) also has been reformatted into a format similar to the "P/P$_{critical}$" format used for columns. This requires the addition of separate equations for the critical buckling moment as a function of the beam stiffness and its lateral slenderness ratio. While this may appear to add complexity to the calculation, the equations are relatively straightforward to apply.

Other differences from *NDS* include specific provisions for a composite action factor to be applied to the computed stiffness of members in assemblies, and an expanded list of load sharing factors (*AF&PA/ASCE 16-95* Section 5.3).

Combined axial and bending loads—*AF&PA/ASCE 16-95* contains many changes relative to *NDS* regarding members subject to combined axial and bending loads. Some are simple expansions of the concepts in the *NDS* equations, such as the expansion of the stability equations to include both strong and weak axis effects. Others, however constitute major additions to wood design procedures—the calculation of second-order stability effects, for instance—that were adopted from steel design procedures. Designers who must consider combined axial and bending loads in their designs are advised to review *AF&PA/ASCE 16-95* Section 6.3 and its commentary.

Connections—Many of the connection provisions are fully consistent with *NDS*. Since the implementation of the European Yield Model in *NDS* was concurrent with its introduction into the LRFD standard, the two are highly consistent.

One difference from *NDS* is an equation-based method for computing the withdrawal resistance of nails and spikes ($Z_W = 4.5\ 9DG^{2.5}\ pn_f$) and wood screws ($Z_W = 9.47\ DG^2$ pn_f). Another is found in *AF&PA/ASCE 16-95* Equation 7.4-12 that limits connection forces at an angle, α, to the wood surface:

$$\frac{Z_u \cos \alpha}{\lambda \phi_z Z'} + \frac{Z_u \sin \alpha}{\lambda \phi_z Z_W} \leq 1.0$$

Here, α is the angle between the load and the wood surface ($0° < \alpha < 90°$); Z_u is the connection force due to factored loads; λ is the time effect factor (Table 4); ϕ_z is the resistance factor for connections (0.65) (Table 3); Z' is the adjusted lateral resistance; and Z_W is the adjusted withdrawal resistance.

Ponding—*AF&PA/ASCE 16-95* Appendix A3 includes specific provisions for checking designs for the ponding of rainwater.

Summary

After over a decade of development, a load and resistance factor design format is available for engineered wood construction in the United States. *AF&PA/ASCE 16-95* provides a comprehensive set of design procedures that covers virtually all wood-based products and connections for structural design. This standard is augmented by the *LRFD Manual*, which includes explanatory information, design examples and product-specific design values.

While the LRFD format is slightly different in appearance than the ASD format, it is easy to learn due to its similarity to the current design format. As the design examples presented here showed, there is compatibility between the two formats.

Both the ASD and LRFD formats will be acceptable for use in engineered wood construction design for the foreseeable future; architects, designers and engineers can choose the format that best suits their needs. Reliability-based design expert Bruce Ellingwood (21) highlights the benefits of LRFD:

> "Applying partial factors of safety to the load and strength terms makes the sources of design uncertainty more apparent and better accounts for variability. Practicing engineers who are uncomfortable with wood as a construction material may be convinced to change their view of it, now that there is a sound technical basis for the provisions. LRFD has narrowed the range of reliabilities in practice and, as a result, economies in design can be realized without sacrificing safety and performance. Finally, LRFD is easier to teach. This will facilitate the introduction of wood design into engineering curricula; in the long term, this will do more to enhance the use of wood in building construction than any other measure."

During the next decade, design professionals will decide whether these advantages are compelling enough to warrant the switch from ASD to LRFD.

References

1. American Concrete Institute Committee 318. 1992. ACI 318-92 Building Code Requirements for Reinforced Concrete and ACI 318R-92 Commentary. ACI. Detroit, Michigan.

2. American Institute of Steel Construction. 1994. Load and Resistance Factor Design Specification for Structural Steel Buildings, Second Edition. Chicago, Illinois.

3. Canadian Standards Association. 1994. CSA-O86.1 Engineered Design in Wood (Limit States Design). CSA. Rexdale, Ontario, Canada.

4. American Society of Civil Engineers. 1995. AF&PA/ASCE 16-95 Load and Resistance Factor Design Standard for Engineered Wood Construction. New York, New York.

5. American Forest & Paper Association. 1996. Load and Resistance Factor Design Manual for Engineered Wood Construction. AF&PA. Washington, D. C.

6. Gromala, D., D. Sharp, D. Pollock and J. Goodman, J. 1990. Load and Resistance Factor Design for Wood: The New U.S. Wood Design Specification. *In* Proceedings of the 1990 International Timber Engineering Conference. Tokyo, Japan.

7. Gromala, D., D. Pollock and T. Williamson. 1994. Development and Implementation of a Load and Resistance Factor Design System in the United States. *In* Proceedings of the 1994 Pacific Timber Engineering Conference. Queensland University. Brisbane, Australia.

8. American Forest & Paper Association. 1991. National Design Specification for Wood Construction. AF&PA. Washington, D. C.

9. Harr, M. 1987. Reliability-Based Design in Civil Engineering. McGraw-Hill. New York, New York.

10. Shooman, M. 1968. Probabilistic Reliability: An Engineering Approach. McGraw-Hill, New York, New York.

11. Thoft-Christensen, P. and Baker, M.J. 1982. Structural Reliability Theory and Its Applications. Springer-Verlag. New York, New York.

12. American Concrete Institute Committee 318. 1963. ACI 318-63 Building Code Requirements for Reinforced Concrete and ACI 318R-63 Commentary. ACI. Detroit, Michigan.

13. American National Standards Institute. 1972. ANSI A58.1-1972 Minimum Design Loads for Buildings and Other Structures. New York, New York.

14. International Conference of Building Officials. 1994. Uniform Building Code. ICBO. Whittier, California.

15. Building Code & Administrators International, Inc. 1996. National Building Code. BOCA. Country Club Hills, Illinois.

16. Southern Building Code Congress International. 1994. Standard Building Code. SBCI. Birmingham, Alabama.

17. American Society of Civil Engineers. 1993. ASCE 7-93 Minimum Design Loads for Buildings and Other Structures. New York, New York.

18. American Society for Testing and Materials. 1993. ASTM D5457 Standard Specification for Computing the Reference Resistance of Wood-Based Materials and Structural Connections for Load and Resistance Factor Design. West Conshohocken, Pennsylvania.

19. Ellingwood, B. and D. Rosowsky. 1991. Duration of Load Effects in LRFD for Wood Construction. Journal of the Structural Division. American Society of Civil Engineers. 117(2):584-599.

20. Hendrickson, E., B. Ellingwood and J. Murphy. 1987. Limit State Probabilities of Wood Structural Members. Journal of Structural Engineering. American Society of Civil Engineers. 113(1):88-106.

—A—

Appendix

Part 1 - Section 3

BUILDING COMPONENTS

Listing by BCAR

Building components are listed under a service designated as "Listing by Building Components Acceptance Report" ("BCAR"). The description of product(s) or construction and information are referenced in the current BCAR. The PFS certification mark and/or NER-QA251 identified on the PFS stamp on the said product(s) is evidence that the manufacturer is under contract for trademarking and follow-up inspection service.

The building components are certified to a model building code standard and/or product standards.

[1]Indicates manufacturers who are also active in the "California Factory-Built Housing Program" and the "California Mobilehomes, Commerical Coaches, Special Purpose Commercial Coaches and Recreational Vehciles Program" and who require PFS' service as either a Quality Assurance Agency (QAA) or as a Design Agency Approval (DAA), or both, under these California programs.

(Look for this Certification Mark)

Advanced Connector Systems
3335 East Broadway
Phoenix, AZ 85040
Pho: (602) 243-5161
Fax: (602) 243-4212

PFS #739
Mill #435
Welded Joist Hangers/WR

Amwood Building Components
dba E.S. Homes
Highway 30 West
P.O. Box 338
Toledo, IA 52342
Pho: (515) 484-5166
Fax: (515) 484-5182

PFS #860
Mill #463
Trusses/MR

Ariel Truss Company, Inc.
616 NW 139th Street
Vancouver, WA 98685
Pho: (360) 574-7333
Fax: (360) 574-7334

PFS #851
Mill #464
UBC Truss/WR

Automated Building Components
P.O. Box 666
Long Lake, MN 55356
Pho: (612) 473-7376
Fax: (612) 473-2918

PFS #451
Mill #210
Trusses/MR

Automated Building Components
1111 8th Street
Chetek, WI 54728
Pho: (715) 924-4867
Fax: (715) 924-2585

PFS #128
Mill #211
Trusses/MR

Automated Building Components
200 Old Factory Road
PO Box 532
Sharon, WI 53585-0532
Wat: (800) 232-1466
Fax: (414) 736-6655

PFS #903
Mill #478
Trusses/MR

Automated Products
1812 Karau Drive
P.O. Box 808
Marshfield, WI 54449
Pho: (715) 387-3426
Fax: (715) 387-6588

PFS #822
Mill #227
Trusses/MR

Butler Manufacturing Co.
P.O. Box 419917
Kansas City, MO 64141
Pho: (816) 968-3000
Fax: (816) 968-3630

Corporate Headquarters

Plant Locations:

Lester Building Systems
Div. Butler Mfg. Co.
P.O. Box 9
Charleston, IL 61920
Pho: (217) 348-7676
Fax: (217) 345-4016

PFS #710
Mill #451
Trusses/MR

Lester Building Systems
Div. Butler Mfg. Co.
P.O. Box 37
Lester Prairie, MN 55354
Pho: (612) 395-2531
Fax: (612) 395-2969

PFS #70
Mill #202
Stress Skin Panels/MR
Trusses/MR

Lester Building Systems
Div. Butler Mfg. Co.
Rt. 1, P.O. Box 25
Clear Brook, VA 22624
Pho: (540) 665-0182
Fax: (540) 665-0109

PFS #710
Mill #341
Trusses/MR

Cascade Truss Company
213 East Reserve St.
Vancouver, WA 98661
Pho: (360) 735-9001
Fax: (360) 735-9006

PFS #1019
Mill #537
UBC Truss/WR

Cleveland Steel Specialty Co.
14430 Industrial Ave., South
Cleveland, OH 44137
Pho: (216) 475-7660
Wat: (800) 251-8351
Fax: (216) 475-7664

PFS #717
Mill #397
Welded Truss Hangers/SER

Consolidated Lumber & Truss Co., Inc.
P.O. Box 219
Santa Maria, CA 93456-0219
Pho: (805) 922-8441
Fax: (805) 922-7363

PFS #479
Mill #306
UBC Truss/WR

Darrington Truss Company
45616 Hwy 530 NE
P.O. Box 1176
Darrington, WA 98214
Pho: (360) 436-7242
Wat: (800) 840-7242
Fax: (360) 436-1320

PFS #995
Mill #524
Trusses/WR

Enduro Products, Inc.
930-A East Orangethorpe
Anaheim, CA 92801
Pho: (714) 526-5898
Fax: (714) 526-6511

PFS #892
Mill #497
Deck Covering/WR

FCP, Inc.
Excelsior Industrial Park
P.O. Box 99
Blandon, PA 19510-0099
Pho: (610) 926-0100
Fax: (610) 926-9232

PFS #668
Mill #404
Components/CO

Hi-Tek Forest Products, Inc.
234 North Sherman Avenue
P.O. Box 1720
Corona, CA 91720
Pho: (909) 735-7070
Fax: (909) 735-7075

PFS #841
Mill #455
UBC Truss/WR

Hi-Tek Forest Products, Inc.
1006 Southeast 9th
Bend, OR 97702
Pho: (503) 389-8000
Fax: (503) 389-4486

PFS #794
Mill #345
UBC Truss/WR

Homan Lumber Mart, Inc.
1650 West Lusher
P.O. Box 818
Elkhart, IN 46515
Pho: (219) 293-6596
Pho: (219) 522-4700
Fax: (219) 522-0338

PFS #901
Mill #476
Trusses/MR

International Homes of Cedar
21704 - 87th Avenue, S.E.
P.O. Box 886
Woodinville, WA 98072
Pho: (206) 668-8511
Fax: (206) 668-5562

PFS #640
Mill #374
Thermo-Lam Wall Timbers/WR

Mobil Chemical Company
158 Capitol Lane
Winchester, VA 22602
Pho: (540) 678-8100
Fax: (540) 678-8139

PFS #915
Mill #486
Composite Lumber/SER

North American Forest Products, Inc.
69708 Kraus Road
P.O. Drawer AC
Edwardsburg, MI 49112
Pho: (616) 663-8506
Fax: (616) 663-2073

PFS #983
Mill #513
Trusses/MR

Oregon Dome/Design Pacific
3215 Meadow Lane
Eugene, OR 97402
Pho: (541) 689-3443
Fax: (541) 689-9275

PFS #796
Mill #431
Wood Panels/WR

Oregon Truss Company, The
17900 Southeast Wallace Road
Dayton, OR 97114
Pho: (503) 868-7922
Wat: (800) 441-7922
Fax: (503) 868-7871

PFS #641
Mill #373
UBC Truss/WR

Pittsville Homes, Inc.
Hwy. 80 South, Box C
Pittsville, WI 54466
Pho: (715) 884-2511
Fax: (715) 884-2136

PFS #431
Mill #249
Trusses/MR

Premier Industries
 dba System 3
1019 Pacific Avenue
Suite 1501
Tacoma, WA 98402
Pho: (206) 572-5111
Fax: (206) 387-7100

Corporate Headquarters

Plant Locations:

Premier Building Systems[1]
 dba System 3
3434 West Papago
Phoenix, AZ 85009
Pho: (602) 269-7266
Fax: (602) 269-8407

PFS #930
Mill #408
FBH Components/WR
Sandwich Panels/WR

Premier Building Systems[1]
 dba System 3
4609 70th Avenue, East
Puyallup, WA 98371
Pho: (206) 735-5709
Fax: (206) 926-3992

PFS #930
Mill #506
FBH Components/WR

Robbins Engineering, Inc.
P.O. Box 280055
Tampa, FL 33682-0055
  UPS: 10500 University Ctr Dr
      Tampa, FL 33612
Pho: (813) 972-1135
Fax: (813) 971-6117

Corporate Headquarters

Plant Locations:

Robbins Engineering, Inc.
13025 N. Nebraska Avenue
Tampa, FL 33612
Pho: (813) 971-3030
Fax: (813) 975-0511

PFS #969
Mill #517
Truss Connector Plates/SER

Robbins Engineering, Inc.
3616 South Road, C-2
Mukilteo, WA 98275
Pho: (206) 513-5835
Wat: (800) 532-9404
Fax: (206) 347-5828

PFS #969
Mill #520
Truss Connector Plates/SER

Seven D Industries, Inc.
Truss Division
R.D. #5, Box 73-A
Tyrone, PA 16686
Pho: (814) 684-5160
Fax: (814) 684-1585

PFS #1034
Mill #540
Trusses/NR

Silver Metal Products
2150 Kittyhawk Road
Livermore, CA 94550-9611
Pho: (510) 449-4100
Fax: (510) 373-9213

PFS #798
Mill #433
Welded Joist Hangers/WR

Southside Lumber Company
21901 Industrial Boulevard
Rogers, MN 55374
Pho: (612) 428-4112
Fax: (612) 428-2971

PFS #138
Mill #212
Trusses/MR

Superior Walls of America, Ltd.
Route 322 West
P.O. Box 427
Ephrata, PA 17522
Pho: (717) 626-9255
Fax: (717) 626-7319

PFS #570
Mill #328
Foundations/NR

Surface Decking Company
6320 Clara Street
Bell Gardens, CA 90201
Pho: (310) 927-1361
Fax: (310) 927-4469

PFS #893
Mill #485
Deck Covering/WR

Truss Components of Washington, Inc.
5102 Lambskin Street
Tumwater, WA 98502
Pho: (360) 753-0057
Fax: (360) 956-3109

PFS #858
Mill #490
UBC Truss/WR

Truss Components, Inc.
P.O. Box 468
Cornelius, OR 97113
Pho: (503) 357-2118
Fax: (503) 359-5242

PFS #644
Mill #377
UBC Truss/WR

Tualatin Valley Builders
P.O. Box 1138
Lake Oswego, OR 97034
Pho: (503) 635-7731
Fax: (503) 635-5947

PFS #646
Mill #378
UBC Truss/WR

Universal Forest Products
3153 Three Mile Road, N.E.
Grand Rapids, MI 49505
Pho: (616) 364-6161
Fax: (616) 361-7534

Corporate Headquarters

Plant Locations:

Universal Forest Products
15 Walnut Street
P.O. Box 389
Windsor, CO 80550-0389
Pho: (303) 686-9655
Fax: (303) 686-9670

PFS #934
Mill #505
Trusses/MR

Universal Forest Products
50415 Herbert
P.O. Box 129
Granger, IN 46530-0129
Pho: (219) 277-7670
Fax: (219) 277-0547

PFS #601
Mill #290
Trusses/MR

Universal Forest Products
149 Bay Road
P.O. Box 945
Belchertown, MA 01007-0945
Pho: (413) 323-7247
Fax: (413) 323-5780

PFS #523
Mill #293
Trusses/MR

Universal Forest Products
Plant #232
1570 East Highway 101
Shakopee, MN 55379
Pho: (612) 496-3080
Wat: (800) 949-1440
Fax: (612) 496-0085

PFS #985
Mill #521
Trusses/MR

Universal Forest Products
P.O. Box 1635
Salisbury, NC 28144
  UPS: 358 Woodmill Road
          Salisbury, NC 28144
Pho: (704) 855-1600
Fax: (704) 855-2130

PFS #664
Mill #339
Trusses/MR

Universal Forest Products
Royer Street, P.O. Box 31
Gordon, PA 17936-0031
Pho: (717) 875-2811
Fax: (717) 875-4072

PFS #786
Mill #292
Trusses/MR

Universal Forest Products
Hwy. 81 South
P.O. Box 447
Grandview, TX 76050-0447
Pho: (817) 866-3306
Fax: (817) 866-2834

PFS #523
Mill #299
Trusses/MR

VanderPol Building Components
841 East Badger Road
Lynden, WA 98264
Pho: (360) 354-5883
Fax: (360) 354-1584

PFS #797
Mill #393
UBC Truss/WR

Wausau Homes, Inc.
P.O. Box 8005
Wausau, WI 54402-8005
  UPS: Hwy. 51 South
          Rothschild, WI 54474
Pho: (715) 359-7272
Fax: (715) 359-2867

Corporate Headquarters

PFS #194
Mill #61
Closed Panel/MR

Plant Location:

Wausau Homes, Inc.
731 Alternate 27 North
P.O. Box 308
Lake Wales, FL 33853-0308
Pho: (813) 676-9390
Fax: (813) 676-7961

PFS #379
Mill #340
Trusses/SER

ENGINEERED WOOD PRODUCTS

Listing by BCAR

Engineered wood products are listed under a service designated as "Listing by Building Components Acceptance Report" ("BCAR"). Engineered wood products include laminated veneer lumber (LVL), parallel strand lumber (PSL), laminated strand lumber (LSL), wood I-joists and glue-laminated beams. The description of product(s) or construction and information are referenced in the current BCAR. The PFS certification mark and/or NER-QA251 identified on the PFS stamp on the said product(s) is evidence that the manufacturer is under contract for trademarking and follow-up inspection service.

LVL, PSL and LSL are evaluated for conformance under ASTM D5456, "Standard Specification for Evaluation of Structural Component Lumber Products". Wood I-joists are evaluated for conformance under ASTM D5055, "Standard Specification for Establishing and Monitoring Structural Capacities of Prefabricated Wood I-Joists". Glue-Laminated Beams are tested for conformance with ANSI/AITC Standard A190.1-1983 for "Structural Glue-Laminated Timber".

(Look for this Certification Mark)

Boise Cascade Corporation 1155 Antelope Road P.O. Box 2400 White City, OR 97503-0400 Pho: (503) 826-1470 Wat: (800) 232-0788 Fax: (503) 826-0219	PFS #716 Mill #412 I-Joists/WR LVL/WR

Georgia-Pacific Corporation
P.O. Box 3190
Roxboro, NC 27573
  UPS: 1000 North Park Drive
         Roxboro, NC 27573
Pho: (910) 599-1000
Fax: (910) 597-8660
	PFS #925
	Mill #498
	I-Joists/SER
	LVL/SER

Louisiana-Pacific Corporation 1 L-P Drive Samoa, CA 95564 Pho: (707) 443-7511 Fax: (707) 443-0522	Corporate Headquarters

Plant Locations:

American Laminators aka Fiber Technologies P.O. Box 858 Drain, OR 97435 Pho: (541) 836-2026 Fax: (541) 836-7144	PFS #466 Mill #541 LVL/SER
Louisiana-Pacific Corporation Reading & Tyler Roads P.O. Box 629 Red Bluff, CA 96080 Pho: (916) 527-4343 Fax: (916) 527-9271	PFS #735 Mill #437 Wood I-Joists/WR
Louisiana-Pacific Corporation 2706 Highway 421 North Wilmington, NC 28401 Pho: (910) 762-9878 Wat: (800) 444-9105 Fax: (910) 763-8178	PFS #584 Mill #325 I-Joists/SER LVL/SER

Louisiana-Pacific Corporation
325 Industrial Drive
Fernley, NV 89408
Pho: (702) 575-5564
Wat: (800) 223-5647
Fax: (702) 575-6803

PFS #883
Mill #466
I-Joists/SER
LVL/SER

Superior Wood Systems, Inc.
1301 Garfield Avenue
P.O. Box 1208
Superior, WI 54880
Pho: (715) 392-1822
Fax: (715) 392-3484

PFS #718
Mill #395
I-Joists/SER

Tecton Laminates Corporation
Highway 20 West
P.O. Box 587
Hines, OR 97738
Pho: (503) 573-2312
Fax: (503) 573-6474

PFS #643
Mill #376
I-Joists/WR
LVL/WR

Tembec, Inc.
48 Rue Boivin
Box 1178
Ville-Marie, QC J0Z 3W0
Canada
Pho: (819) 629-2543
Fax: (819) 629-3133

PFS #1029
Mill #538
LVL/MR

TrimJoist Corporation
P.O. Drawer 2286
Columbus, MS 39704-2286
   UPS: 5146 Highway 182 E
           Columbus, MS 39701
Pho: (601) 327-7950
Fax: (601) 329-4610

PFS #955
Mill #510
Wood Trusses/SER

Trus Joist MacMillan
200 E. Mallard Drive
Boise, ID 83706
Pho: (208) 364-1200
Fax: (208) 364-1300

Corporate Headquarters

Plant Locations:

Trus Joist MacMillan   PFS #515
Claresholm Industrial Airport   Mill #527
P.O. Box 1060   I-Joists/WR
Claresholm, AB T0L 0T0
Canada
Pho: (403) 625-4414
Fax: (403) 625-3778

Trus Joist MacMillan   PFS #515
1272 Derwent Way   Mill #481
Annacis Island, BC V3M 5R1   PSL/WR
Canada
Pho: (604) 526-4665
Fax: (604) 526-3157

Trus Joist MacMillan   PFS #515
5088 Edison Avenue   Mill #280
P.O. Box 786   Trusses/WR
Chino, CA 91708
Pho: (909) 627-7331
Fax: (909) 591-8924

Trus Joist MacMillan   PFS #515
Rt. 2, Box 4   Mill #482
Colbert, GA 30628   PSL/WR
Pho: (404) 788-3551
Fax: (404) 788-3657

Trus Joist MacMillan   PFS #515
410 Clay Road   Mill #282
P.O. Box 5326   I-Joists/WR
Valdosta, GA 31603-5326   LVL/WR
Pho: (912) 333-7000
Fax: (912) 333-7665

Trus Joist MacMillan   PFS #515
New Products Plant   Mill #277
2610 East Amity Road   I-Joists/WR
Boise, ID 83707
Pho: (208) 333-7771
Fax: (208) 343-8166

Trus Joist MacMillan   PFS #515
Hwy 15 & N. Pads Branch Road   Mill #528
P.O. Box 7897   LSL/WR
Hazard, KY 41701
Pho: (606) 436-8787
Fax: (606) 436-0802

Trus Joist MacMillan Route 3, Box 1385 Nachitoches, LA 71457 Pho: (318) 357-1424 Fax: (318) 352-2033	PFS #515 Mill #283 I-Joists/WR LVL/WR
Trus Joist MacMillan Country Road 102 P.O. Box 460 Deerwood, MN 56444 Pho: (218) 546-8114 Fax: (218) 546-7178	PFS #515 Mill #483 LSL/WR
Trus Joist MacMillan 200 Colomett P.O. Box 357 Delaware, OH 43015 Pho: (614) 363-1317 Fax: (614) 369-1154	PFS #515 Mill #281 Trusses/WR
Trus Joist MacMillan Willamette Valley Office 3930 Cross Street Eugene, OR 97402 Pho: (541) 689-9000 Fax: (541) 689-7637	PFS #515 Mill #274 I-Joists/WR LVL/WR
Trus Joist MacMillan 550 South Bailey Hillsboro, OR 97123 Pho: (503) 648-6641 Fax: (503) 640-2322	PFS #515 Mill #276 Trusses/WR
Trus Joist MacMillan 93747 Highway 99 South Junction City, OR 97448 Pho: (503) 998-3900 Fax: (503) 998-1518	PFS #515 Mill #275 LVL/WR
Trus Joist MacMillan 2345 West Deschutes Drive Stayton, OR 97373 Pho: (541) 796-7676 Fax: (541) 769-4413	PFS #515 Mill #284 I-Joists/WR LVL/WR

Trus Joist MacMillan
100 TJM Drive
Route 1, Box 107-10
Buckhannon, WV 26201
Pho: (304) 472-8564
Fax: (304) 472-7395

PFS #515
Mill #528
LVL/WR
PSL/WR

Universal Forest Products
50415 Herbert
P.O. Box 129
Granger, IN 46530-0129
Pho: (219) 277-7670
Fax: (219) 277-0547

PFS #1026
Mill #539
Wood I-Joists/MR

Wadena Lumber Products & Technology
P.O. Box 109
Wadena, MN 56482
Pho: (218) 631-2607
Wat: (800) 982-4863
Fax: (218) 631-2607

Corporate Headquarters

PFS #918
Mill #491
Wood I-Joists/MR

Plant Location:

American I-Joist Corp.
5523 Broadway, S.E.
Albuquerque, NM 87105
Wat: (800) 873-4255
Fax: (505) 873-4444

PFS #953
Mill #507
Wood I-Joists/MR

Weyerhaeuser Company
2509 Aspen Drive
Edson, AB T7E 1F8
Canada
Pho: (403) 723-6963
Fax: (403) 723-7195

PFS #1015
Mill #1015
OSB/CO

Weyerhaeuser Company
4111 West Four Mile Road
Grayling, MI 49738
Pho: (517) 348-2881
Fax: (517) 348-2319

PFS #1014
Mill #1014
OSB/CO

PFS #1018
Mill #1018
OSB/CO

Weyerhaeuser Company
P.O. Box 487
Sutton, WV 26601
  UPS: U.S. Hwy 19
          Heaters, WV 26627
Pho: (304) 765-4220
Fax: (304) 765-4283

Part 1 - Section 13

HUD MANUFACTURED HOME TRUSS PROGRAM

Listing by Report

HUD Manufactured Home Trusses are listed under a service designated as "Listing by Report". The description and information concerning testing and follow-up inspection are referenced in document PFS-1305. The PFS label affixed to each bundle on said product(s) is evidence that the manufacturer is under contract for trademarking and follow-up inspection service.

(Look for this Certification Mark)

Alpine Engineered Products, Inc.   Corporate Headquarters
2820 N. Great Southwest Parkway
Grand Prairie, TX 75050-6472
Pho: (214) 660-4422
Pho: (214) 660-3217
Fax: (214) 660-4994

Franchisees:

Chassis, Inc. - Truss Division   PFS #609
Highway 286 West   Mill #350
P.O. Box 1207   Trusses/SR
Conway, AR 72032
Pho: (501) 327-0770
Fax: (501) 329-9139

Hi-Tek Forest Products, Inc.
234 N. Sherman Avenue
P.O. Box 1720
Corona, CA 91720
Pho: (909) 735-7070
Fax: (909) 735-7075

PFS #609
Mill #455
Trusses/SR

Hi-Tek Forest Products, Inc.
200 N. Cloverdale
Boise, ID 83704
Pho: (208) 323-1447
Fax: (208) 323-1384

PFS #609
Mill #462
Trusses/SR

Hi-Tek Forest Products, Inc.
1006 Southeast 9th
Bend, OR 97702
Pho: (503) 389-8000
Fax: (503) 389-4486

PFS #609
Mill #345
Trusses/SR

North American Forest Products, Inc.
69708 Kraus Road
P.O. Drawer AC
Edwardsburg, MI 49112
Pho: (616) 663-8506
Fax: (616) 663-2073

PFS #609
Mill #513
Trusses/SR

Pre-Cuts, North Carolina Division
325 McKay Street
P.O. Box 729
Laurinburg, NC 28352
Pho: (919) 277-0358
Fax: (919) 276-1540

PFS #609
Mill #353
Trusses/SR

Automated Products
1812 Karau Drive
P.O. Box 808
Marshfield, WI 54449
Pho: (715) 387-3426
Fax: (715) 387-6588

PFS #822
Mill #227
Trusses/MR

Consolidated Lumber & Truss
100 River Road
P.O. Box 310
Parker, PA 16049
Pho: (412) 399-2992
Fax: (412) 399-2480

PFS #534
Mill #303
Trusses/NR

Homan Lumber Mart, Inc.
1650 West Lusher
P.O. Box 818
Elkhart, IN 46515
Pho: (219) 293-6596
Pho: (219) 522-4700
Fax: (219) 522-0338

PFS #902
Mill #477
Trusses/MR

Seven D Industries, Inc.
Truss Division
R.D. #5, Box 73-A
Tyrone, PA 16686
Pho: (814) 684-5160
Fax: (814) 684-1585

PFS #707
Mill #396
Trusses/NR

Universal Forest Products
3153 Three Mile Road, N.E.
Grand Rapids, MI 49505
Pho: (616) 364-6161
Fax: (616) 361-7534

Corporate Headquarters

Plant Locations:

Universal Forest Products
6878 W. Chandler Blvd.
Chandler, AZ 85226
Pho: (602) 961-0833
Fax: (602) 961-4816

PFS #881
Mill #468
Trusses/MR

Universal Forest Products
15 Walnut Street
P.O. Box 389
Windsor, CO 80550-0389
Pho: (303) 686-9655
Fax: (303) 686-9670

PFS #934
Mill #505
Trusses/MR

Universal Forest Products
50415 Herbert
P.O. Box 129
Granger, IN 46530-0129
Pho: (219) 277-7670
Fax: (219) 277-0547

PFS #523
Mill #290
Trusses/MR

Universal Forest Products
149 Bay Road
P.O. Box 945
Belchertown, MA 01007-0945
Pho: (413) 323-7247
Fax: (413) 323-5780

PFS #523
Mill #293
Trusses/MR

Universal Forest Products
330 McKay Street
P.O. Box 99
Laurinburg, NC 28352
Pho: (919) 277-0358
Fax: (919) 277-9929

PFS #906
Mill #480
Trusses/MR

Universal Forest Products
P.O. Box 1635
Salisbury, NC 28144
   UPS: 358 Woodmill Road
            Salisbury, NC 28144
Pho: (704) 855-1600
Fax: (704) 855-2130

PFS #664
Mill #339
Trusses/MR

Universal Forest Products
Royer Street, P.O. Box 31
Gordon, PA 17936-0031
Pho: (717) 875-2811
Fax: (717) 875-4072

PFS #786
Mill #292
Trusses/MR

Universal Forest Products
Hwy. 81 South
P.O. Box 447
Grandview, TX 76050-0447
Pho: (817) 866-3306
Fax: (817) 866-2834

PFS #523
Mill #299
Trusses/MR

STRUCTURAL USE PANELS

Listing by Trademarking

Structural use panels are listed under a service designated as "Listing by Trademarking". This section includes plywood, waferboard, oriented strand board (OSB) and composite panels. The technical description of structural use panels is in the U.S. Department of Commerce NIST Voluntary Product Standard PS 2, "Performance Standard for Wood-Based Structural Use Panels." Structural use panels are evaluated for conformance under either NIST PS 2 and/or PRP 133.

The PFS clients shown below, in addition to being listed by name and address, include each client's mill number and "recipes" (which are the current range and type of structural use panels produced by each client).

The PFS certification mark identified on the PFS stamp on the said products is evidence that the manufacturer is under contract for testing, certification, trademarking and inspection services.

(Look for this Certification Mark)

(Sample Grademark)

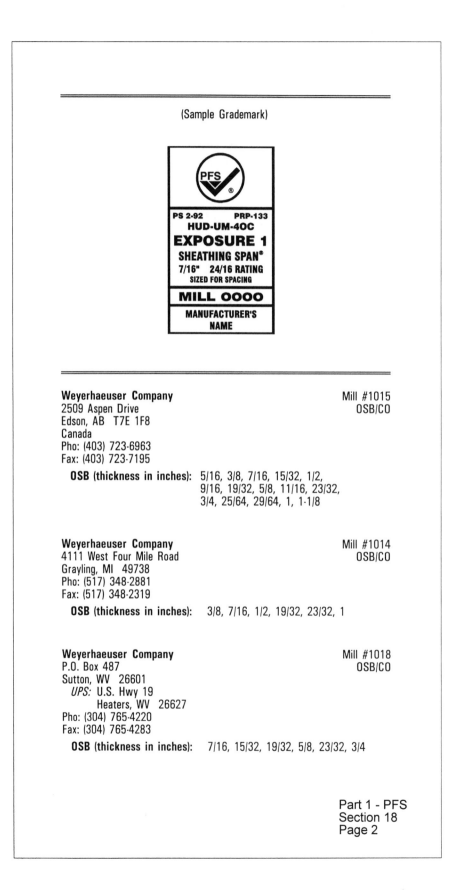

Weyerhaeuser Company   Mill #1015
2509 Aspen Drive   OSB/CO
Edson, AB   T7E 1F8
Canada
Pho: (403) 723-6963
Fax: (403) 723-7195

   OSB (thickness in inches): 5/16, 3/8, 7/16, 15/32, 1/2,
9/16, 19/32, 5/8, 11/16, 23/32,
3/4, 25/64, 29/64, 1, 1-1/8

Weyerhaeuser Company   Mill #1014
4111 West Four Mile Road   OSB/CO
Grayling, MI   49738
Pho: (517) 348-2881
Fax: (517) 348-2319

   OSB (thickness in inches):   3/8, 7/16, 1/2, 19/32, 23/32, 1

Weyerhaeuser Company   Mill #1018
P.O. Box 487   OSB/CO
Sutton, WV   26601
  UPS: U.S. Hwy 19
      Heaters, WV   26627
Pho: (304) 765-4220
Fax: (304) 765-4283

   OSB (thickness in inches):   7/16, 15/32, 19/32, 5/8, 23/32, 3/4

Part 2 - Section 1

PLYWOOD

Listing by Trademarking

Plywood is listed under a service designated as "Listing by Trademarking". This section includes construction and industrial use plywood. The technical description of plywood is found in the U.S. Department of Commerce National Institute of Standards and Technology (NIST) Voluntary Product Standard PS 1-95 "Construction and Industrial Use Plywood". Plywood is evaluated for conformance under NIST PS 1 and/or PS 2.

The TECO clients shown below, in addition to being listed by name and address, include each client's mill number and "recipes" (which are the current range and type of plywood panels produced by each client).

The TECO certification mark and/or NER-QA135 identified on the TECO stamp on the said products is evidence that the manufacturer is under contract for testing, certification, trademarking and inspection services.

(Look for this Certification Mark)

TECO TESTED®

(Sample Grademarks)

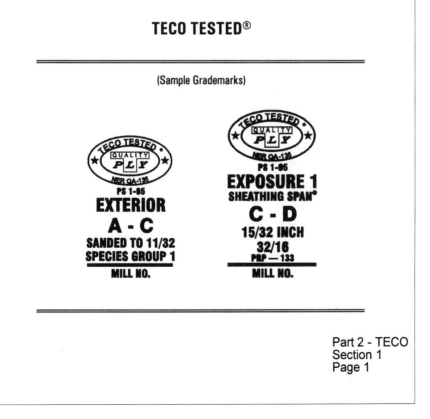

How to Read a Plywood Gradestamp

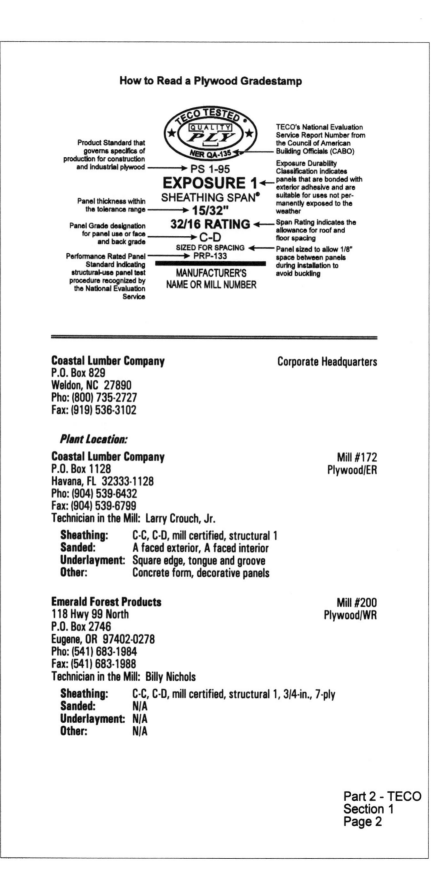

Product Standard that governs specifics of production for construction and industrial plywood → PS 1-95

TECO's National Evaluation Service Report Number from the Council of American Building Officials (CABO)

EXPOSURE 1 ← Exposure Durability Classification indicates panels that are bonded with exterior adhesive and are suitable for uses not permanently exposed to the weather

SHEATHING SPAN®

Panel thickness within the tolerance range → **15/32"**

Panel Grade designation for panel use or face and back grade → **32/16 RATING** ← Span Rating indicates the allowance for roof and floor spacing

C-D

Performance Rated Panel Standard indicating structural-use panel test procedure recognized by the National Evaluation Service → SIZED FOR SPACING **PRP-133** ← Panel sized to allow 1/8" space between panels during installation to avoid buckling

MANUFACTURER'S NAME OR MILL NUMBER

Coastal Lumber Company
P.O. Box 829
Weldon, NC 27890
Pho: (800) 735-2727
Fax: (919) 536-3102

Corporate Headquarters

Plant Location:

Coastal Lumber Company
P.O. Box 1128
Havana, FL 32333-1128
Pho: (904) 539-6432
Fax: (904) 539-6799
Technician in the Mill: Larry Crouch, Jr.

Mill #172
Plywood/ER

Sheathing:	C-C, C-D, mill certified, structural 1
Sanded:	A faced exterior, A faced interior
Underlayment:	Square edge, tongue and groove
Other:	Concrete form, decorative panels

Emerald Forest Products
118 Hwy 99 North
P.O. Box 2746
Eugene, OR 97402-0278
Pho: (541) 683-1984
Fax: (541) 683-1988
Technician in the Mill: Billy Nichols

Mill #200
Plywood/WR

Sheathing:	C-C, C-D, mill certified, structural 1, 3/4-in., 7-ply
Sanded:	N/A
Underlayment:	N/A
Other:	N/A

Lane Plywood, Inc.
65 Bertelsen Road North
Eugene, OR 97402-5301
Pho: (503) 342-5561
Fax: (503) 343-8102

Mill #71
Plywood/WR

Sheathing:	C-C, C-D, mill certified, structural 1
Sanded:	A faced exterior, A faced interior, B faced exterior, B faced interior
Underlayment:	Limited to 1-1/8", square edge, tongue and groove
Other:	Concrete form, marine plywood, siding

MacMillan Bloedel Packaging, Inc.
Highway 10
Box 336
Pine Hill, AL 36769
Pho: (334) 963-4391
Fax: (334) 963-4414

Mill #164
Plywood/ER

Sheathing:	C-D
Sanded:	N/A
Underlayment:	Square edge, tongue and groove
Other:	N/A

Martco Partnership
P.O. Box 1110
Alexandria, LA 71309
Pho: (318) 445-1973
Fax: (318) 473-2624

Corporate Headquarters

Plant Location:

Martco Partnership
1695 Hwy 490
Chopin, LA 71447
Pho: (318) 379-2855
Fax: (318) 379-2861

Mill #220
Plywood

  Sheathing: C-C, C-D, mill certified, structural 1
  Sanded: N/A
  Underlayment: Square edge, tongue and groove
  Other: N/A

Omak Wood Products, Inc.
729 S. Jackson Street
Route 2, Box 54
Omak, WA 98841-9609
Pho: (509) 826-1460
Fax: (509) 826-2905

Mill #210
Plywood/WR

  Sheathing: C-C, C-D, mill certified, structural 1
  Sanded: N/A
  Underlayment: Square edge, tongue and groove
  Other: N/A

The Springfield Group
72B Centenial Loop, Suite 1
Eugene, OR 97401
Pho: (541) 344-4886
Fax: (541) 741-4672

Corporate Headquarters

Plant Locations:

Fitzgerald Forest Products
240 Peachtree Road
PO Box 278
Fitzgerald, GA 31750-0278
Pho: (912) 424-0294
Fax: (912) 424-0424
Technician in the Mill: Charlie Welch

Mill #143
Plywood/ER

  Sheathing: C-C, C-D, mill certified, structural 1
  Sanded: N/A
  Underlayment: N/A
  Other: N/A

Springfield Forest Products　　　　　　　　　　Mill #10
1651 South "F" Street　　　　　　　　　　　　　　Plywood/WR
P.O. Box 719
Springfield, OR 97477-0119
Pho: (541) 726-2124
Fax: (541) 741-4672
Technician in the Mill: Gary McBride

    Sheathing:　　C-C, C-D, mill certified, structural 1
    Sanded:　　　　N/A
    Underlayment: Square edge, tongue and groove
    Other:　　　　 Siding

Weyerhaeuser Company　　　　　　　　　Corporate Headquarters
810 Whittington Ave.
P.O. Box 1060
Hot Springs, AR 71902
Pho: (501) 624-5631
Fax: (501) 624-8323

   Plant Locations:

Weyerhaeuser Company　　　　　　　　　　Mill #164
Hwy 96 East　　　　　　　　　　　　　　　　　Plywood/ER
P.O. Box W
Millport, AL 35576
Pho: (334) 596-3311
Fax: (334) 596-1204

    Sheathing:　　C-C, C-D, mill certified
    Sanded:　　　　N/A
    Underlayment: N/A
    Other:　　　　 N/A

Weyerhaeuser Company　　　　　　　　　　Mill #161
U.S. Hwy 70　　　　　　　　　　　　　　　　　Plywood/ER
P.O.Box 38
Dierks, AR 71833
Pho: (501) 286-2281
Fax: (501) 286-2329

    Sheathing:　　C-C, C-D, mill certified
    Sanded:　　　　A faced exterior, B faced exterior
    Underlayment: Square edge, tongue and groove
    Other:　　　　 Decorative panels, siding

Weyerhaeuser Company　　　　　　　　　　Mill #162
P.O. Box 7　　　　　　　　　　　　　　　　　 Plywood/ER
Mountain Pine, AR 71956-0007
Pho: (501) 767-7232
Fax: (501) 767-7363

    Sheathing:　　C-C, C-D, mill certified, structural 1
    Sanded:　　　　B faced exterior
    Underlayment: Square edge, tongue and groove
    Other:　　　　 Decorative panels, siding

Weyerhaeuser Company
Dweese Road
P.O. Box 708
Philadelphia, MS 39350
Pho: (601) 650-7200
Fax: (601) 650-7295

Mill #163
Plywood/ER

    Sheathing: C-C, C-D, mill certified
    Sanded: N/A
    Underlayment: N/A
    Other: N/A

Weyerhaeuser Company
West Main Street Extension
P.O. Box 787
Plymouth, NC 27962
Pho: (919) 793-8111
Fax: (919) 793-8865

Mill #165
Plywood/ER

    Sheathing: C-C, C-D, mill certified
    Sanded: B faced exterior
    Underlayment: Square edge, tongue and groove
    Other: N/A

Weyerhaeuser Company
HC 74, Box 100
Wright City, OK 74766-9701
Pho: (405) 981-2211
Fax: (405) 981-1244
Technician in the Mill: Jesse Corcoran

Mill #160
Plywood/ER

    Sheathing: C-C, C-D, mill certified, structural 1
    Sanded: A faced exterior, B faced exterior
    Underlayment: Square edge, tongue and groove
    Other: N/A

Corporate Headquarters

Willamette Industries
Atlantic Division
452 Lakeshore Pkwy, #120
Rock Hill, SC 29730
Pho: (803) 328-3838
Fax: (803) 328-6146

Willamette Industries
Southern Division Headquarters
603 Reynolds Drive
P.O. Drawer 1100
Ruston, LA 71273
Pho: (318) 255-6258
Fax: (318) 251-9589

Corporate Headquarters

Plant Locations:

Willamette Industries   Mill #202
Emerson Division   Plywood/ER
101 Columbia, 14W
Emerson, AR 71740-0286
Pho: (501) 547-2955
Fax: (501) 547-2920

    Sheathing: C-C, C-D, mill certified, structural 1
    Sanded: A faced exterior, B faced exterior
    Underlayment: Limited to 1-1/8", square edge, tongue and groove
    Other: Concrete form

Willamette Industries   Mill #100
P.O. Box 158   Plywood/ER
Zwolle, LA 71486-0158
Pho: (318) 645-6124
Fax: (318) 645-7434

    Sheathing: C-C, C-D, mill certified, structural 1
    Sanded: N/A
    Underlayment: Limited to 1-1/8", square edge, tongue and groove
    Other: N/A

STRUCTURAL USE PANELS

Listing by Trademarking

Structural use panels are listed under a service designated as "Listing by Trademarking". This section includes plywood, waferboard, oriented strand board (OSB) and composite panels. The technical description of structural use panels is in the U.S. Department of Commerce NIST Voluntary Product Standard PS 2, "Performance Standard for Wood-Based Structural Use Panels." Structural use panels are evaluated for conformance under either NIST PS 2 and/or TECO PRP 133.

The TECO clients shown below, in addition to being listed by name and address, include each client's mill number and "recipes" (which are the current range and type of structural use panels produced by each client).

The TECO certification mark and/or NER-QA135 identified on the TECO stamp on the said products is evidence that the manufacturer is under contract for testing, certification, trademarking and inspection services.

(Look for this Certification Mark)

TECO TESTED®

(Sample Grademark)

```
TECO
TESTED® OSB
NER-QA 135

PS 2-92          PRP-133
EXPOSURE 1
SHEATHING SPAN®
7/16"   24/16 RATING
SIZED FOR SPACING

MANUFACTURER'S
NAME

MILL NO.
```

How to Read an OSB Gradestamp

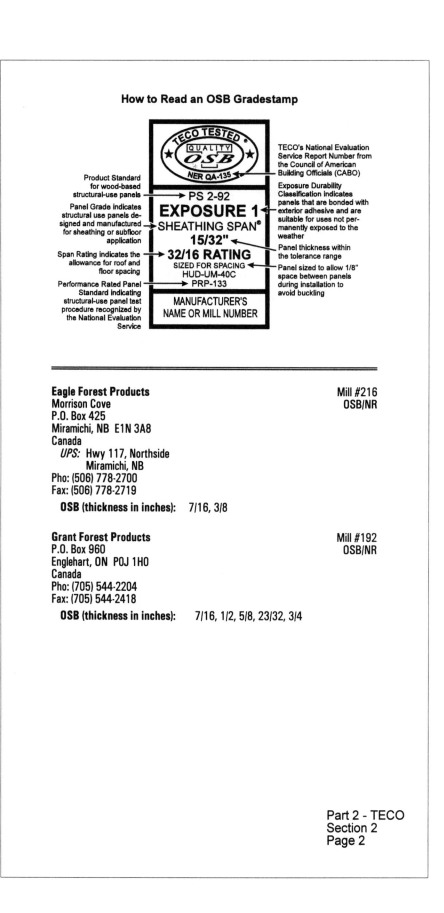

TECO's National Evaluation Service Report Number from the Council of American Building Officials (CABO)

Product Standard for wood-based structural-use panels → PS 2-92

Panel Grade indicates structural use panels designed and manufactured for sheathing or subfloor application → EXPOSURE 1 SHEATHING SPAN® 15/32"

Exposure Durability Classification indicates panels that are bonded with exterior adhesive and are suitable for uses not permanently exposed to the weather

Span Rating indicates the allowance for roof and floor spacing → 32/16 RATING

Panel thickness within the tolerance range

SIZED FOR SPACING HUD-UM-40C

Panel sized to allow 1/8" space between panels during installation to avoid buckling

Performance Rated Panel Standard indicating structural-use panel test procedure recognized by the National Evaluation Service → PRP-133

MANUFACTURER'S NAME OR MILL NUMBER

Eagle Forest Products
Morrison Cove
P.O. Box 425
Miramichi, NB E1N 3A8
Canada
  UPS: Hwy 117, Northside
          Miramichi, NB
Pho: (506) 778-2700
Fax: (506) 778-2719

Mill #216
OSB/NR

   OSB (thickness in inches):   7/16, 3/8

Grant Forest Products
P.O. Box 960
Englehart, ON P0J 1H0
Canada
Pho: (705) 544-2204
Fax: (705) 544-2418

Mill #192
OSB/NR

   OSB (thickness in inches):   7/16, 1/2, 5/8, 23/32, 3/4

Jager Strandboard   Mill #214
PO Box 530   OSB/NR
Wawa, ON P0S 1K0
Canada
Pho: (705) 856-2771
Fax: (705) 856-2791

   OSB (thickness in inches):   7/16, 23/32, 15/32, 19/32, 1/2

Langboard, Inc.   Mill #207
Highway 84   OSB/ER
P.O. Box 837
Quitman, GA 31643
Pho: (912) 263-8943
Fax: (912) 263-5535

   OSB (thickness in inches):   3/8, 7/16, 15/32, 1/2, 19/32, 5/8, 23/32

Longlac Wood Industries, Inc.   Mill #132
Katamaki Road   Waferboard/NR
P.O. Bag 2000
Longlac, ON P0T 2A0
Canada
Pho: (807) 876-2257
Fax: (807) 876-4604

   Waferboard (thickness in inches):   3/8, 7/16, 3/4, 1/2

MacMillan Bloedel, Ltd.   Corporate Headquarters
925 W. Georgia Street
Vancouver, BC V6C 3L2
Canada
Pho: (604) 661-8000
Fax: (604) 661-8377

Plant Location:

SASKFOR Products, Inc.　　　　　　　　　　　Mill #89
OSB Division　　　　　　　　　　　　　　　　　OSB/NR
HWY 9 South & Airport Road
P.O. Box 460
Hudson Bay, SK SOE OYO
Canada
Pho: (306) 865-1700
Fax: (306) 865-2610

OSB (thickness in inches):　　3/8, 7/16, 1/2, 5/8, 3/4

Malette, Inc.　　　　　　　　　　　　　Corporate Headquarters
P.O. Box 1100
Timmins, ON P4N 7H9　　　　　　　　　　　Mill #137
Canada　　　　　　　　　　　　　　　　　　OSB/NR
Pho: (705) 268-1462
Fax: (705) 360-1229

OSB (thickness in inches):　　7/16, 15/32, 19/32, 5/8, 23/32

Plant Location:

Panneaux Malette OSB, Inc.　　　　　　　Mill #187
P.O. Box 40　　　　　　　　　　　　　　　OSB/NR
Grand-Mere, QC G9L 5K7
Canada
Pho: (819) 538-0735
Fax: (819) 538-0595

OSB (thickness in inches):　　7/16, 15/32, 1/2, 19/32, 5/8, 3/4

Martco Partnership　　　　　　　　　　Corporate Headquarters
P.O. Box 1110
Alexandria, LA 71309
Pho: (318) 445-1973
Fax: (318) 473-2624

Plant Location:

Martco Partnership　　　　　　　　　　Mill #198
P.O. Box 70　　　　　　　　　　　　　　　OSB/ER
Morrow, LA 71356-0070
Pho: (318) 346-7217
Fax: (318) 346-4197

OSB (thickness in inches):　　3/8, 7/16, 15/32

THE
IMPEACHERS

THE
IMPEACHERS

*The Trial of Andrew Johnson
and the Dream of a Just Nation*

BRENDA
WINEAPPLE

RANDOM HOUSE

NEW YORK

Published in the United States by Random House, an imprint and division
of Penguin Random House LLC, New York.

RANDOM HOUSE and the HOUSE colophon are registered trademarks
of Penguin Random House LLC.

Library of Congress Cataloging-in-Publication Data
Names: Wineapple, Brenda, author.
Title: The impeachers : the trial of Andrew Johnson and the dream of a
just nation / Brenda Wineapple.
Description: First edition. | New York : Random House, [2019] | Includes
bibliographical references and index.
Identifiers: LCCN 2018034980| ISBN 9780812998368 | ISBN 9780812998375 (ebook)
Subjects: LCSH: Johnson, Andrew, 1808–1875—Impeachment. | United States—
Politics and government—1865–1869.
Classification: LCC E666 .W59 2019 | DDC 973.8/1092—dc23 LC record
available at https://lccn.loc.gov/2018034980

Printed in the United States of America on acid-free paper

randomhousebooks.com

2 4 6 8 9 7 5 3 1

First Edition

Book design by Jo Anne Metsch

Frontispiece: "The Senate as a Court of Impeachment for
President Andrew Johnson," as sketched by Theodore R. Davis.

Endpapers: The impeachment of Andrew Johnson: spectators applaud loudly at
the close of Representative Bingham's speech. From a sketch by James E. Taylor.

For Michael Dellaira,
always

. . . The cease of majesty
Dies not alone; but, like a gulf, doth draw
What's near it with it: it is a massy wheel,
Fix'd on the summit of the highest mount,
To whose huge spokes ten thousand lesser things
Are mortised and adjoin'd; which, when it falls,
Each small annexment, petty consequence,
Attends the boisterous ruin.

—WILLIAM SHAKESPEARE, *Hamlet*, III, 3

"Men in pursuit of justice must never despair."

—THADDEUS STEVENS

Contents

Dramatis Personae

The Impeachment Trial of President Andrew Johnson

Presiding: Chief Justice of the Supreme Court Salmon P. Chase

House of Representative "Managers" Prosecuting Impeachment of President Andrew Johnson for High Crimes and Misdemeanors

Benjamin F. Butler of Massachusetts, chief prosecuting attorney, Radical Republican

John A. Bingham of Ohio, Republican

George S. Boutwell of Massachusetts, Radical Republican

John A. Logan of Illinois, Radical Republican

Thaddeus Stevens of Pennsylvania, Radical Republican

Thomas Williams of Pennsylvania, Republican

James F. Wilson of Iowa, Republican

Attorneys Defending President Andrew Johnson Against Impeachment

Henry Stanbery, former attorney general, lead counsel, Republican

Benjamin Robbin Curtis of Massachusetts, former Supreme Court justice, nominally unaffiliated

William M. Evarts, New York attorney, Republican

William S. Groesbeck, Ohio attorney, Republican

Thomas A.R. Nelson, Tennessee judge, Republican

NOTABLE PERSONS IN THE JOHNSON ADMINISTRATION

McCulloch, Hugh (1808–1895). Treasury secretary, Republican. Served also in the Lincoln administration.

Seward, William (1801–1872). Secretary of state, Republican. Served also in the Lincoln administration.

Stanbery, Henry (1803–1881). Attorney general, Republican. Replaced James Speed. Resigned to serve as Johnson's chief counsel during the impeachment trial.

Stanton, Edwin M. (1814–1869). Secretary of war, Republican. Served also in the Lincoln administration.

Welles, Gideon (1802–1878). Secretary of the navy, Republican. Served in the Lincoln and the Johnson administrations.

NOTABLE PERSONS IN THE THIRTY-NINTH AND FORTIETH U.S. CONGRESS

House of Representatives

Ashley, James (1824–1896). Radical Republican, Ohio.

Bingham, John (1815–1900). Republican, Ohio.

Boutwell, George S. (1818–1905). Radical Republican, Massachusetts.

Butler, Benjamin F. (1818–1893). Radical Republican, Massachusetts; later, Democrat.

Stevens, Thaddeus (1792–1868). Radical Republican, Pennsylvania.

Washburne, Elihu (1816–1887). Republican, Illinois.

Senate

Fessenden, William Pitt (1806–1869). Republican, Maine.

Grimes, James (1816–1872). Republican, Iowa.

Ross, Edmund G. (1826–1907). Republican, Kansas; later, Democrat.

Sumner, Charles (1811–1874). Radical Republican, Massachusetts.

Trumbull, Lyman (1813–1896). Republican, Illinois; later, Democrat.

Wade, Benjamin (1800–1878). Radical Republican, Ohio.

NOTABLE PERSONS, MILITARY

Grant, Ulysses S. (1822–1885). Republican. General. Eighteenth President of the United States, Republican.

Sheridan, Philip (1831–1888). Republican. Major-general. Military governor of Texas and Louisiana.

Sherman, William Tecumseh (1820–1891). Republican. Major-general during war, promoted general of the army.

NOTABLE PERSONS OUTSIDE GOVERNMENT

Blair, Montgomery (1813–1883): Republican/Democrat. Postmaster general during Lincoln administration. Brother of **Francis Preston Blair, Jr.**, Democratic vice-presidential candidate, 1868.

Downing, George T. (1819–1903). African American activist, businessman, entrepreneur, and restauranteur.

Phillips, Wendell (1811–1884). Radical Republican. Orator.

Ream, Lavinia (Vinnie) (1847–1914). Sculptor.

Whitman, Walt (1819–1891). Poet. Anti-slavery Democrat before the war.

NOTABLE JOURNALISTS

Ames, Mary Clemmer (1831–1884). Republican. Author of "Woman's Letter from Washington" for *The Independent* (Radical).

Briggs, Emily Edson (1830–1910). Pseudonym, Olivia. Radical Republican, writing for the *Washington Chronicle* and *The Philadelphia Press*, who asked would "all this trouble have come upon the land if the men had stayed at home managing business and the women had done the legislating?"

Clemenceau, Georges (1841–1929). Radical. Anonymous journalist for *Le Temps* in Paris; later, twice premier of France.

Douglass, Frederick (c.1817–1895). Radical Republican. Founder and publisher of *The North Star*. Also, orator, author, diplomat.

Greeley, Horace (1817–1872). Republican. Editor and publisher of the

New-York Tribune; later Liberal Republican presidential candidate (1872).

Marble, Manton (1834–1917). Democrat. Proprietor and editor of the leading Democratic newspaper, the *New York World*.

Raymond, Henry (1820–1869). Republican. Editor and publisher of *The New York Times*; also U.S. representative and chairman of the Republican National Committee.

Twain, Mark (1835–1910). Yes, *the* Mark Twain, né Samuel Clemens of Missouri.

FINALLY

Johnson, Andrew (1808–1875). Democrat. Seventeenth President of the United States. Military governor of the Union-held portion of Tennessee during the war (1862–1865); Vice President under Lincoln.

Johnson, Eliza McCardle (1810–1876). First Lady. Outlived her husband by nearly six months.

Prologue

February 25, 1868, Washington, D.C.

A cold wind blew through the city, and the snow was piled in drifts near the Capitol, where gaslights flickered with a bluish light. Throngs of people, black and white, waited anxiously outside or pressed into the long corridors and lobbies.

At quarter past one o'clock in the afternoon, the doorkeeper of the U.S. Senate announced the arrival of Pennsylvania Representative Thaddeus Stevens.

Carried aloft in his chair because he'd been weakened by illness, Stevens was helped to stand upright, and after taking a moment to gain his balance—born with a clubfoot, he wore a specially made boot—he linked arms with Representative John Bingham, of Ohio, who had accompanied him to the Senate. The two men strode with slow dignity down the main aisle of the chamber.

The jam-packed galleries were so hushed that there was no mistaking what Stevens, emaciated but inexorable, had come to say. He formally greeted Benjamin Wade, the Senate's presiding officer, and then pulled a paper from the breast pocket of his dark jacket and read aloud, each word formed with precision. "In obedience to the order of the House of Representatives, we have appeared before you in the name of the House of Representatives and of all the people of the United States.

"We do impeach Andrew Johnson, President of the United States, of high crimes and misdemeanors in office."

Just the day before, the House of Representatives had voted overwhelmingly, 126 to 47, to undertake this extraordinary step: the impeachment, the first ever, of the President of the United States. No one dared to speak.

Stevens had been pushing hard for Andrew Johnson's impeachment for over a year, but previous attempts had failed. Now congressional Republicans believed they no longer had a choice: impeachment was the only way to stop a President who refused to accept the acts of Congress, who usurped its prerogatives, and who, most recently, had violated a law that he pretended to wave away as unconstitutional. But for people like Thaddeus Stevens, the specific law that President Andrew Johnson had violated—something called the Tenure of Office Act—was merely a legal pretext; Johnson should have been impeached by the House and brought to trial by the Senate much earlier, and he had been lucky to have escaped this long.

That is why Thaddeus Stevens was considered inexorable. Then again, so was Andrew Johnson, who had been heard to say, *"This is a country for white men, and, by G—d, as long as I am president it shall be a government for white men."* That offended Stevens to the core. He and fellow impeachers believed that the war to preserve the Union had been fought to liberate the nation once and for all from the noxious and lingering effects of slavery. "If we have not been sufficiently scourged for our national sin to teach us to do justice to all God's creatures, without distinction of race or color," Stevens had declared at war's end, "we must expect the still more heavy vengeance of an offended Father."

"'All men are created free and equal' and 'all rightful government is founded on the consent of the governed,'" Stevens insisted in 1867. "Nothing short of that is the Republic intended by the Declaration." Thaddeus Stevens had fought to create a world where blacks and whites lived in harmony and equal citizenship. Discovering that the place he had chosen for his burial would not inter black men or women, he immediately sold the plot and bought one in an integrated cemetery. He then wrote his own epitaph: "Finding other cemeteries limited by charter rules as to race, I have chosen this that I might illustrate in death the principles which I advocated through a long life, Equality of man before his Creator."

But Andrew Johnson had sought to obstruct, overthrow, veto, or challenge every attempt of the nation to bind its wounds after the war or to create a just republic from the ashes of the pernicious and so-called "peculiar institution" of slavery. Recently eradicated, to be sure, by proclamation, by war, and by constitutional amendment, its malignant effects stalked every street, every home, every action, particularly but not exclusively in the South. "Peace had come, but there was no peace," a journalist would write.

Stevens continued to read from the paper he'd pulled from his coat pocket. The House would provide the Senate—and the country—with specific articles of impeachment in the coming days but in the meantime "we demand of the Senate that it order the appearance of said Andrew Johnson to answer said impeachment."

"The order will be taken," Senator Wade replied.

It sounded like a death sentence, an onlooker observed, though not to the young Washington correspondent Mark Twain. "And out of the midst of political gloom," Twain rejoiced, "impeachment, that dead corpse, rose up and walked forth again!"

"ANDREW JOHNSON WAS the queerest man who ever occupied the White House," one of his colleagues remembered. As Lincoln's Vice President, thrust into the presidency after Lincoln's assassination, Johnson earned the hatred and opprobrium of most Republicans, particularly those members of Lincoln's party in Congress who initially hoped that he had become one of them. Although he had been a Democrat, he'd been Lincoln's running mate, after all. But just six weeks after the assassination, Johnson swerved away from what many considered to be Lincoln's program for reconstruction and the fruits of a hard-fought, unthinkably brutal war.

Still, *impeachment?* That was new territory even for a reviled President, and certainly other chief executives had been reviled: Franklin Pierce, old John Quincy Adams, and on occasion Lincoln himself. Yet never before had Congress and the country been willing to grapple directly with impeachment, as defined in the Constitution. Then again, never before had the country been at war with itself, with more than 750,000 men dead, at the very least, during its Civil War, and countless men and women, black and white, still dying, and murdered, in Memphis, in New Orleans, in other cities and in the countryside, in Mississippi, Georgia, South Carolina, Florida, Texas, Alabama.

So in 1868 Congress and the public would have to consider the definition of a high crime and the meaning of a misdemeanor. It was bewildering. "The multitude of strangers were waiting for impeachment," Twain observed. "They did not know what impeachment was, exactly, but they had a general idea that it would come in the form of an avalanche, or a thunder clap, or that maybe the roof would fall in."

For no one knew what the first-ever impeachment of the President of the United States would look like or what sufficient grounds, legal or otherwise, were necessary. No one knew partly because the U.S. Constitution provides few guidelines about impeachment beyond stipulating, in Article II, Section 4, that a federal officer can be impeached for treason, bribery, or a high crime or misdemeanor. The House of Representatives shall have the sole power of impeachment, the Constitution says, and a simple majority of members can vote to impeach. The Senate shall then have the sole power to try all impeachments, and if there is a trial of the U.S. President, the chief justice of the Supreme Court shall preside over it. No person shall be convicted without the concurrence of two-thirds of the members of the Senate present. A conviction requires the person be removed from office. As for further punishment, the convicted person may or may not be prosecuted by law. That's pretty much it.

And if the President—the President of the United States—was to be impeached for treason, bribery, or a high crime or misdemeanor, then the country had to define "high crime." Originally, the crime warranting impeachment was "maladministration," but James Madison had objected; the term was hazy. Yet "high crimes and misdemeanors" is fuzzy too. In *Federalist* 65, Alexander Hamilton clarified—sort of: a high crime is an abuse of executive authority, proceeding from "an abuse or violation of some public trust." Impeachment is a "national inquest into the conduct of public men." Fuzzy again: are impeachments to proceed because of violations of law—or infractions against that murky thing called public trust?

But surely if the only crimes that were impeachable were "high," then the Founders must have meant "high misdemeanors" as well. For a misdemeanor is a legal offense, ranked below that of a felony. Was a President to be impeached for any misdemeanor—like stealing a chicken—or did it have to be something, well, "higher"?

Yet the fact remains that the Founding Fathers had anticipated the possible need for an impeachment. Of that, there can be no doubt. A man in a position of power must be held accountable for his actions. And so they outlined a way to adjudicate accountability—to provide, in other words, a way to maintain a responsible and good government, which is to say to preserve the promise of a better day.

Still, the impeachment of a President seemed no less revolutionary, no less confusing, and no less terrifying for that. Impeachment was the democratic equivalent of regicide, for Benjamin Franklin had said that without impeachment, assassination was the only way for a country to rid itself of a miscreant chief executive who acted like a king. And murder was of course out of the question.

President Andrew Johnson's utterly unprecedented impeachment thus presented knotty constitutional issues—and at a very specific, very difficult time in American history. The ink on the Appomattox peace agreement was barely dry, and the country was seeking moral clarity or, more particularly, the restoration of the Union in a country facing the consequence of war, a reconstruction half done, and a popular if unreadable general, Ulysses S. Grant, waiting in the wings to be elected the next chief executive. Driven by some of the most arresting characters in American history—

Charles Sumner, Wendell Phillips, Benjamin Butler, Secretary of War Edwin Stanton, and especially Thaddeus Stevens—it was one of the most significant moments in the nation's short history, occurring as it did when it did.

For there were concrete, burning questions to be answered about the direction the country would take: Under what terms would the eleven seceded Southern states of the former Confederacy be allowed to re-enter the Union? Should the states that had waged war against the Union be welcomed back into the House and the Senate, all acrimony forgotten, all rebellion forgiven, as if they had never seceded? President Johnson argued that the eleven states had never left; the Constitution forbade secession, and so the Union had never been dissolved. As a consequence, to his way of thinking, these Southern states should resume their place in the Union, their former rights and privileges restored, as soon as their governments could be deemed loyal—mostly by their renouncing secession, accepting slavery's abolition, and swearing allegiance to the federal government. In theory, such a speedy restoration would swiftly repair the wounds of war.

Yet what about the condition of four million black men and women, recently freed but who had been deprived during their lives of literacy, legitimacy, and selfhood? Shouldn't this newly free population be able to control their education, their employment, their representation in government? Were these black men and women then citizens, and if so, could they vote? In 1865, just after the war ended, the white delegates to the South Carolina state convention would hear none of that. As a northern journalist reported in disgust, to them "the negro is an animal; a higher sort of animal, to be sure, than the dog or the horse."

Would the nation then reinstate the supremacist status quo for whites? "Can we depend on our President to exert his influence to keep out the Southern States till they secure to the blacks at least the freedom they now have on paper?" a Union general worried. Allowing white Southerners to rejoin the Union quickly while at the same time denying the black man the vote seemed to many

Republicans, black and white, "replanting the seeds of rebellion," as Thaddeus Stevens said, "which, within the next quarter of a century will germinate and produce the same bloody strife which has just ended."

In a South where houses had been burned, crops had failed, and the railroads had been destroyed, soldiers were hobbling home from the front in gray rags, seeking paroles, jobs, and government office. Thousands of people, both black and white, were dying of starvation. Around Savannah, about two thousand persons had to live on charity. Black men and women in the hundreds had been turned off plantations with little or no money and maybe a bushel of corn.

Visitors from the North frequently found white Southerners smoldering, aggrieved, and intransigent; white Southerners had tried to protect their homes, believing they'd fought for the unassailable right of each state to make its own laws and preserve its own customs. And they wouldn't surrender such rights easily, having lost the war. "It is our duty," said South Carolina planter Wade Hampton, "to support the President of the United States so long as he manifests a disposition to restore all our rights as a sovereign State." Union General Philip Sheridan, renowned for unrelenting aggression during the war, alerted his superiors that planters in Texas were secretly conspiring "against the rights" of the freedmen. In New Orleans, a visitor was stunned to find a picture of Lincoln hanging next to one of John Wilkes Booth, and above them both, a huge portrait of Robert E. Lee.

All through the South, ex-Confederates were vilifying the black population, and one legislature after another had been passing "black codes," ordinances designed to prevent freedmen and -women from owning property, traveling freely, making contracts, and enjoying any form of civil rights or due process. "People had not got over regarding negroes as something other than human," said a journalist traveling through the South. Meanwhile, Andrew Johnson, the Tennessean occupying the White House, had acted quickly. While Congress was in recess, he singlehandedly re-established Southern state governments by executive proclamation.

He subsequently issued pardons to former Confederates on easy terms and at an astonishing rate. He later nudged out of the Freedmen's Bureau those who disagreed with his position and tried to shut down that Bureau by vetoing legislation that would keep it running. He vetoed civil rights legislation as unfair to whites and attempted to block passage of the Fourteenth Amendment, which guaranteed citizenship to blacks. He turned a cold eye on the violence directed toward the freedmen, and he emphatically staked out a position he sought to maintain, saying, "Everyone would and *must* admit that the white race is superior to the black."

Yet on December 4, 1865, at the opening session of the Thirty-Ninth Congress, the clerk at the House of Representatives had omitted from the roll call the names of Southern congressmen.

Battle lines were being drawn, albeit without a bayonet or rifle.

The four-year period between the death of Lincoln in the spring of 1865 and the inauguration of Ulysses S. Grant in March of 1869 seems a thicket of competing convictions, festering suspicions, and bold prejudice. Yet oddly, for years and years, the intensely dramatic event—the impeachment of the U.S. President—has largely been papered over or ignored. For years, we've sidestepped that ignominious moment when a highly unlikeable President Johnson was brought to trial in the Senate, presumably by fanatical foes. The whole episode left such a bitter aftertaste, as the eminent scholar C. Vann Woodward said more than four decades ago, that historians often relegated the term "impeachment" to the "abysmal dustbin" of never-again experiences—like "secession," "appeasement," and "isolationism."

The year before Woodward's pronouncement, though, Michael Les Benedict had brilliantly scrutinized the political dimensions of Johnson's impeachment, thus breaking with the long tradition of embarrassment, outrage, or silence. Regardless, that tradition has persisted—despite David O. Stewart's careful study, a decade ago, of how dark money may have influenced the final vote. And though Stewart, a practiced lawyer, is no friend of Andrew Johnson, he too concludes, albeit sadly, that the whole affair was a "political and legal train wreck."

But to reduce the impeachment of Andrew Johnson to a mistaken incident in American history, a bad taste in the collective mouth, disagreeable and embarrassing, is to forget the extent to which slavery and thus the very fate of the nation lay behind Johnson's impeachment. "This is one of the last great battles with slavery," Senator Charles Sumner had said. "Driven from these legislative chambers, driven from the field of war, this monstrous power has found refuge in the Executive Mansion, where, in utter disregard of the Constitution and laws, it seeks to exercise its ancient far-reaching sway."

Impeachment: it was neither trivial nor ignominious. It was unmistakably about race. It was about racial prejudice, which is not trivial but shameful. That may be a reason why impeachment and what lay behind it were frequently swept under the national carpet. Then too the whole idea of impeachment does not fit comfortably within the national myth of a democratic country founded in liberty, with abundant space, opportunity, and resources available to all. Impeaching a President implies that we make mistakes, grave ones, in electing or appointing officials, and that these elected men and women might be not great but small—unable to listen to, never mind to represent, the people they serve with justice, conscience, and equanimity. Impeachment suggests dysfunction, uncertainty, and discord—not the discord of war, which can be memorialized as valorous, purposeful, and idealistic, but the far less dramatic and often squalid, sad, intemperate conflicts of peace, partisanship, race, and rancor. Impeachment implies a failure—a failure of government of the people to function, and of leaders to lead. And presidential impeachment means failure at the very top.

In 1868, the highly unlikeable President Johnson was impeached and then brought to trial in the Senate by men who could no longer tolerate the man's arrogance and bigotry, his apparent abuse of power, and most recently, his violation of law. Johnson's impeachment was thus not a plot hatched by a couple of rabid partisans—notably the powerful congressional leader Thaddeus Stevens and his counterpart in the Senate, Charles Sumner. For both Stevens and Sumner were unswerving champions of abolition and civil rights—and yet both were long considered malicious and vindictive zealots, cold and maniacal men incapable of compassion or mercy.

Yet Senator Sumner, the regal advocate of human dignity and political equality, more or less came into his own thanks to historian David Herbert Donald's two biographies of him, one that earned a Pulitzer Prize in 1961; the other bore the title "The Rights of Man." As for Thaddeus Stevens, in the Pulitzer Prize–winning *Profiles in Courage* of 1956, John F. Kennedy called him "the crippled, fanatical personification of the extremes of the Radical Republican movement, master of the House of Representatives, with a mouth like the thin edge of an ax." Kennedy's depiction of Stevens was derived in part from the diabolical portrayal of Stevens in D. W. Griffith's controversial movie *Birth of a Nation*. In 2012, in the film *Lincoln*, Steven Spielberg mercifully updated the record, with the actor Tommy Lee Jones playing a more likeable person. But Thaddeus Stevens still lurks in the shadows of history, a fiendish figure whose clubfoot was said to be a sign of the devil, and a man vengefully bent on destroying the South.

Kennedy also applauded the "courage" of the senators who voted against the conviction of Andrew Johnson, ostensibly because they put the best interests of the country above career and politics. Singling out Edmund G. Ross of Kansas, Kennedy soft-pedaled the fact that Ross may have been bribed to acquit Johnson—or if he wasn't exactly bribed, he successfully importuned Johnson for favors, perks, and position shortly after his apparently courageous vote.

And then there is President Andrew Johnson. Lambasted as "King Andy" in one of Thomas Nast's biting political cartoons, Johnson was a self-made man, born in a log cabin, who, though raised in poverty, rose after Lincoln's assassination to the topmost position in the land. In his youth, Johnson had been a tailor with a taste for stump oratory and politics, and in 1829, at the age of twenty-one, he was elected alderman in Greeneville, Tennessee, where he was living with his wife and children. He then became mayor, then legislator, then state senator, and he was subsequently elected to the U.S. House of Representatives. He served in Congress for ten years before being elected governor of Tennessee, and he eventually landed in the U.S. Senate as a fierce states' rights Democrat but also a staunch Unionist.

Johnson's heroic, lonely stand against secession—he was the only senator from a Confederate state to oppose it—earned him an appointment as military governor of Tennessee during the war and then the vice-presidential slot when President Lincoln ran for re-election in 1864.

With a Southern War Democrat on the Republican ticket, Peace Democrats could not easily tag Lincoln as anti-Southern. Johnson also helped Lincoln appeal to the working class, especially the Irish, for Johnson did not approve of the common prejudice against Catholics. Yet his tenure as Vice President began badly. Presumably suffering from a nasty cold, he had medicated himself with a concoction that included some fortifying shots of alcohol. Whatever he drank, Johnson arrived at Lincoln's second inauguration reeking of whiskey, and after muttering something not quite comprehensible about his being a plebeian and a man of the people, he bent over and planted a sloppy kiss on the Bible. Secretary of the Navy Gideon Welles shifted uncomfortably in his seat and said to Secretary of War Edwin Stanton, who would play a key role in the impeachment, that Johnson must be either drunk or crazy.

Regardless, after the dust of impeachment had mostly settled, Johnson was credited as being the valiant public servant whose plan for reconstruction had been temperate, fair-minded, constitutional, and intrepid. One writer, in the 1920s, anticipating Kennedy's portrayal, christened Johnson a "profile in courage" whom future generations would regard as an "unscathed cross upon a smoking battlefield." Johnson was seen for a time as a populist, a champion of democracy and of the beloved Constitution; as a man of principle, flawed perhaps, but honest, upright, brave.

Perhaps he had been brave—if, that is, one can separate mettle from mulishness. For in the end, Andrew Johnson assumed powers as President that he used to thwart the laws he didn't like. He disregarded Congress, whose legitimacy he ignored. He sought to restore the South as the province of white men and to return to power a planter class that perpetuated racial distrust and violence.

Still, Andrew Johnson had once vowed to penalize the traitorous, secessionist South. "The American people must be taught—if they do not already feel—that treason is a crime and must be punished," he had said just days after Lincoln's assassination. At the same time, he argued, as he always had, that since secession was illegal, only people could be traitors, not states. His position was that as long as rebels applied to him for pardons, which they amply did, he would amply grant them. A traitor, to Johnson, then became anyone he disliked—mostly Republicans, and especially men like Thaddeus Stevens and Charles Sumner.

Convinced by the summer of 1866 that congressional Republicans were out to get him, Johnson toured the North and West and in a set of speeches remarkable for their vituperation, he shouted out to the crowd that he hadn't been responsible for recent riots, such as had occurred in Memphis or New Orleans. Blame Charles Sumner; blame Thad Stevens; blame Congress or anyone dubious about the Southern governments he had put into place, crackpot fanatics who wanted to give all people the vote, even in some cases women, regardless of color. Don't blame him.

The years right after the war were years of blood and iron: bloody streets, iron men, oaths of allegiance, as they were called, in which former rebels swore their loyalty to the Union. But to what kind of Union government were they promising to be loyal? For these were years in which the executive and the legislature struggled to define, or redefine, the responsibilities of a representative government— and the question of who would be fairly represented. These were years of sound and fury, of fanaticism and terror, of political idealism and mixed motives, of double-dealing and high principle—and of racism, confusion, and fear. It was a time of opportunism, paranoia, pluck, and tragedy: tragedy for the nation, to be sure, and for individuals, often nameless, who lost their lives in the very, very troubled attempts to remake the country and to make it whole.

The nation was at a crossroads, and at the very center of that crossroads was impeachment.

Part One

BATTLE LINES
OF PEACE

The United States Capitol dome, under construction, 1865.

Mars

April 15, 1865, Washington, D.C.

Secretary of War Edwin Stanton leaned over the bedside of his good friend, Abraham Lincoln, and, tears spilling down his cheeks, spoke the memorable phrase: now he belongs to the angels—or the ages. No one is quite sure which word, "angels" or "ages," Stanton uttered, but each works poignantly well.

Many were likely surprised by Stanton's sobs. And his eloquence. Most knew him as hard, implacable, and gruff. He barked out orders to his inferiors, he kept the lamps burning in the War Department all through the night, and he'd organized the Union army with precision. His long beard trailed down to the middle of his chest, as if he had no time to bother with a barber, and he took exercise by standing at his high desk for as many as fifteen hours a day. He was so devoted to the War Department, in fact, that people were likely not surprised, three years later, when Stanton assumed center stage during the impeachment controversy.

Of all people, though, President Lincoln might have understood best what motivated his secretary of war. For if Stanton had ever unburdened himself, it would have been to his chief executive.

These two men—Lincoln, tall and lean and genial; Stanton, shorter, squatter, and far more volatile—were friends. Wrapped in a plaid shawl and with his hat pulled down over his forehead, during the war Lincoln would walk over to the War Department and sit in the small room next to Stanton's office, where Lincoln kept a desk. He and Stanton waited, each of them anxious, for telegraph dispatches from the many fields of battle. Sometimes they relaxed together, occasionally driving north of the city to the leafy retreat known as the retired soldiers' home, where the secretary of war, like Lincoln and his family, escaped from summer heat. These men truly loved each other, said Representative Henry Dawes, who knew them both.

Edwin Stanton had also shared with Lincoln grief of a more personal sort. Like Lincoln's boy Willie, Stanton's young son had also died in 1862. But Stanton mainly sought relief in work, and unlike Lincoln, always appeared to be on guard, shouldering sorrows that acquaintances only sometimes glimpsed. After Stanton's father, a well-liked physician, had died suddenly in 1827, the thirteen-year-old Stanton took charge of the Steubenville, Ohio, household that included his mother, his brother, and his two sisters. He completed only one year at Kenyon College but studied law in the office of his guardian, becoming the sort of brilliant attorney on whom nothing was lost—and who left nothing to chance. He prepared cases with a meticulous, even furious, attention to detail, and he argued with aggressive often insolent vigor. He might insult a witness or a judge, or tell the opposing counsel to quit whining. A stocky, broad-shouldered man with brown, sharp eyes under steel-rimmed spectacles that he often wiped, he was not an easy person to like, and there were a great many people who did, in fact, dislike him.

As Henry Dawes would recall, Edwin Stanton was also "prone to despond." When he was twenty-two, he married Mary Lamson, and after the burial of their firstborn daughter, Stanton disinterred the child and placed her remains in a metal box that he kept on the mantelpiece. When his wife died not long afterward—Stanton was thirty—he stopped eating and sleeping and in the night would rush from room to room, lamp in hand, crying out, "Where is Mary?" Not long after that, Stanton, learning that his brother Darwin had cut his own throat, ran to Darwin's house, where blood was pooling on the floorboards. He then raced out into the freezing cold in such a hurry that friends, fearing for his life, coaxed him back and stayed with him until he calmed down. Stanton took responsibility for Darwin's family but never seemed to recover. "I feel indifferent to the present, careless of the future—" he said, "in a state of bewilderment the end of which is hidden."

Yet Stanton's law practice was thriving. He moved to Pittsburgh, where he argued on behalf of the state of Pennsylvania before the Supreme Court to prevent a bridge from being built across the Ohio River because, Stanton claimed, it would prevent tall steamboats from traveling under it and thereby restrict interstate commerce. The case dragged on for almost a decade, and though Stanton technically lost, steamboat travel continued. Then in 1856, Stanton married Ellen Hutchison, a woman from a wealthy Pittsburgh family and Stanton's junior by sixteen years. Though Lincoln's secretary John Hay described her "as white and cold and motionless as marble, whose rare smiles seemed to pain her," the marriage seems to have been happy in spite of Stanton's working long hours—and his even longer absences.

Attorney General Jeremiah S. Black had appointed Stanton as special U.S. counsel to inspect alleged Mexican land grants in California. During his protracted stay in the West—almost a year— Stanton immediately learned Spanish to gather the documents scattered througout the state, or that were allegedly lost, and he exposed several bogus land grant deals, one of which actually claimed ownership of San Francisco. In early 1859, he returned to Washington, where he had moved his family, and built an impressive brick house, three stories high, on the north side of K Street. He was a prosperous, sought-after man in a country about to break apart.

He was also involved in legal spectacles, serving on the defense team for Daniel Sickles, the Democratic congressman from New

York who had recently shot and killed District Attorney Philip Barton Key. There was no doubt as to Sickles' guilt, but the trial was something of a circus, featuring two of Washington's well-known political creatures, the flamboyant Sickles and the deceased Philip Key. Sickles had served as James Buchanan's secretary when Buchanan was minister to the Court of St. James's during the Franklin Pierce administration. The good-looking District Attorney Key was the son of Francis Scott Key, composer of "The Star-Spangled Banner." He also happened to be the lover of Sickles' wife.

Along with six other lawyers, Edwin Stanton defended Sickles before a packed Washington courtroom eager for salacious details about the affair. Sickles admitted he'd killed Key but pleaded not guilty by reason of "temporary insanity," the first time such a plea had been offered in the United States. Sickles had to be insane, his lawyers contended; what man wouldn't be driven crazy by his wife's infidelity? The all-male jury voted to acquit Sickles, another triumph for Edwin Stanton.

The next year, 1860, during the last days of his presidency, James Buchanan reshuffled his cabinet and appointed Stanton as attorney general. But unlike President Buchanan, who dithered over how to handle the threat of secession, Stanton was firm. America was the only democracy in the world, Stanton asserted more than once, and he was committed to its preservation—even if that meant leaking information to Republican Senator William H. Seward about President Buchanan's intentions toward a besieged Fort Sumter in 1860. Little wonder that among his enemies, Stanton earned a reputation as disingenuous, if not downright duplicitous.

When Lincoln appointed Edwin Stanton his secretary of war, there were many people who still distrusted him. During the war many men distrusted many other men, but Stanton was a favorite villain: he could be satirical, contemptuous, impatient, and just plain rude. One biographer described his "pantherlike pursuit of the evildoer." John Hay thought Stanton an energetic "man of administrative scope and executive tact," but Hay also said he'd rather "make a tour of a smallpox hospital" than ask Stanton for a favor.

Still, Stanton's assistant in the War Department, Charles Anderson Dana, said Stanton was far more than an aggressive patriot. He was a student of the Bible, of history, and of literature; he read every book he could find on Napoleon and he adored Charles Dickens. During the war, he kept Dickens' *Pickwick Papers* near his bed because it never failed to soothe him. His library contained over 2,500 volumes.

Although Stanton, a former Democrat, was now a Republican, Democratic friends praised him as an honest man sworn to protecting the country from extremists of any stripe. He hated both abolition *and* secession. And though as a child Stanton had reportedly sat on abolitionist Benjamin Lundy's knee, or so a colleague wishfully recollected, the adult Stanton had steered clear of the abolitionists. He did maintain for many years his friendship with Salmon Chase, the celebrated fugitive slaves' lawyer, but refused to join the abolitionist cause. Yet in Washington, Stanton frequently visited the home of Gamaliel Bailey, editor of *The National Era*, which had published *Uncle Tom's Cabin* in serial form. Slowly his moderate views—if they *had* been moderate—about slavery and emancipation changed. Or, perhaps more likely, he started to express views long held but that he'd kept to himself. It's hard to know—he was always canny. "Stanton is a character such as Plutarch would have liked to describe," political scholar Francis Lieber said.

While in Lincoln's cabinet, Stanton encouraged the deployment of black troops; he supported the Emancipation Proclamation; he endorsed the Thirteenth Amendment, outlawing slavery. His detractors perceived these positions as disloyal because they seemed to contradict his earlier allegiance to the Democratic party and called into question his earlier contempt for abolitionists. They began branding Stanton a traitor. "Such hostility should, however, be accounted a crown of honor," Representative James G. Blaine observed.

Stanton's friend Jeremiah Black initially rose to Stanton's defense. "My own personal knowledge," Black said, "does not enable me to accuse him of any mean or disgraceful act." Later, Black would reconsider. If Stanton had been merely posing as an anti-abolitionist, good states' rights Democrat—if he was a man to "run with the hare and hunt with the hounds"—then Edwin Stanton was nothing more than an oily, beady-eyed trickster of the most unscrupulous sort.

Were there two different Stantons? A Democrat who didn't much like him would say that there were. Or were Democrats and Republicans just duking out their differences, using the war secretary as their foil? Surely Stanton had been torn between loyalty to Democrats like Buchanan and Jeremiah Black and his growing recognition that slavery was an unpardonable sin—and that secession, as a way to preserve slavery, was an unpardonable error. Perhaps that's why he drove himself so hard. Asthmatic since boyhood, his attacks at times had become so severe that he would double over, wheezing and gasping. He smoked cigars to open up his bronchial passages. (He wasn't the only one who thought this would help.) He pretended to take fresh air in order to pacify his friend the surgeon general, who begged him to relax. "Keep me alive till this rebellion is over," Stanton replied, "and then I will take a rest!" He added, a bit more seriously, "A long one, perhaps."

Certainly Edwin Stanton was the most enigmatic man in Lincoln's cabinet, and, during Andrew Johnson's administration, the ultimate thorn in Johnson's side. Yet Stanton never defended himself publicly against those who traduced him, even when his critics were George McClellan and William Tecumseh Sherman. Then again he may have deliberately appeared to seem all things to all men. Later, he would characterize himself as "in-betweenity." But whether as Democrat or as newly minted Republican, Stanton wanted to protect the law of the land—the Constitution—even when he seemed to take the law into his own hands. A clerk in the War Department thought that Stanton prosecuted the war as if it were a case he was arguing in court: "He seemed to regard himself as holding a brief for the Government and to be bent on bringing his client out successful, leaving everybody else to look out for himself and to get in the way at his peril."

Brilliant and prickly, Edwin McMasters Stanton was secretary
of war during the Lincoln and Johnson administrations; but
resisting Johnson's attempts to subvert Reconstruction laws,
"Stanton is coming to be regarded as the champion of Congress," colleagues observed just before Johnson dismissed him.

Yet if he perplexed or antagonized people, he also inspired them.
"He was the bulwark of confidence to the loyal North," one of his
secretaries declared. "In the dark hours he was the anchor which
held fast the destiny of the republic." For despite the trappings of
success—the huge house, the large receptions—and his crusty, well-
defended exterior, Stanton possessed an endearing humility. Each
day he walked over to the general market, a basket on arm, to banter
with Confederate sympathizers, from whom he picked up information as well as fruit or bread from their stalls. If a Union man was
selling produce, Stanton gently provided a scrap of encouraging
news. Secretary of State William Seward's daughter once commented on the "merry twinkle" in Stanton's eye. When her father

was severely injured in a carriage accident in 1865, Stanton tenderly bathed Seward's face "like a woman in the sickroom," she said. "He loved those he trusted, and he trusted without question those he loved." One of General Meade's aides, terrified to meet Stanton, reported that he found the secretary of war "mild as drawn butter."

He could also throw an inkstand at you; he could dismiss you as an imbecile, which was his early estimation of Lincoln, although Stanton rapidly changed his mind (he could do that too) and considered the President in all ways his superior. The two men had met as early as 1855, when Stanton was already a prominent attorney and Lincoln a backwoods lawyer, or so Stanton thought, and they were briefly brought together in a patent infringement case. Stanton snubbed Lincoln and according to one journalist referred to him as a "giraffe." But Lincoln admired Stanton, and in 1862 chose him to succeed the ineffective and scandal-ridden Simon Cameron as war secretary. In all likelihood his appointment was promoted by Lincoln's secretary of state, William Seward, who remembered that Stanton had divulged intelligence about cabinet decisions during the Fort Sumter crisis. It was a very small world.

The instant that Stanton took over the unvarnished war office in 1862, with its odor of stale tobacco and panic, he rolled up his sleeves. "As soon as I can get the machinery of the office working," he said, "the rats cleared out, and the rat-holes stopped, we shall move," he declared. He did not mince words. Nor stop. Stories of Stanton's capacity for work are legion. He promptly read as much as possible about the administration of armies, for he had to raise a huge one. With an efficiency bordering on genius, he consolidated control over the telegraph lines, tightly censoring war information, and from time to time he tried to censor the newspapers. He oversaw the standardization of extensive railroad track; he updated the signal systems. During the day, in order to rest, he might lock the door to his office, lie down on his couch, and scan British newspapers sympathetic to the Confederacy. "I consider him one of the heroic elements in our war," Francis Lieber declared.

He drove subordinates as hard as he drove himself. "He was

prone to be suspicious of those who did not work as he did," Henry Dawes noted. His dark eyes were rimmed with weariness. Trails of gray ran down his long, full beard; his lips folded into a grimace. A web of lines appeared on his once-smooth face because for all his thunder and granite, Stanton was painfully sensitive to the responsibility he bore for hurling men, hundreds of thousands of them, into battle. Yet he followed the rules with rigidity, believing as he did in organization and discipline. One afternoon, after coldly turning down a family's heartrending pleas for clemency for a soldier who had deserted, Stanton walked into his office and, according to his clerk, broke down. "God help me to do my duty," he cried. "God help me to do my duty!"

When the administration took the remarkable step of suspending habeas corpus, Stanton acted as its front man. He was excoriated as a tyrant, a ruffian, a dictator, an ogre. Supposedly he had withheld reinforcements from his former friend General George McClellan, causing McClellan's devastating defeat in the Peninsula campaign. There was also the matter of his decision to shut down recruiting offices in the summer of 1862. Wrongly, he had thought victory near—and that he would not have to deliver more men to their deaths. But always Lincoln firmly backed his war secretary, whom he called his "Mars." To President Lincoln, Stanton was the rock "against which the breakers dash and roar, dash and roar without ceasing."

"I do not see how he survived," Lincoln added, "why he is not crushed and torn to pieces."

General Ulysses S. Grant, a man not given to overstatement, and not always fond of the secretary, nonetheless praised Stanton as "one of the great men of the Republic."

During the election of 1864, Stanton was bedridden for three weeks, and he may have recovered sooner had he been appointed to the Supreme Court that fall. It was the only position Edwin Stanton really wanted, but Lincoln said he could not manage without him. After Lee surrendered, when Stanton wanted to resign from the cabinet, Lincoln asked him to remain. "It is not for you to say when you will no longer be needed here," the President said to him. So Stanton stayed, and he stayed, and he stayed. It may be accurately said that, after the war, Edwin Stanton was but one more casualty of it.

ON APRIL 14, 1865, Edwin Stanton had been undressing for bed when he heard a loud knocking at the front door. His wife hurried into the room, incredulous. Lincoln had been shot. Secretary of State William Seward had been stabbed. Suddenly the Stanton house was teeming with people. Someone begged the secretary not

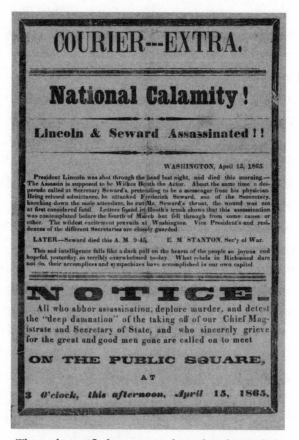

The early terrified rumors in the wake of Lincoln's
assassination suggested Secretary of State
Seward had died as well.

to go out—someone else said a man was outside lurking in the shadows—but Stanton had to go to Bill Seward's home, where he found Seward barely conscious on bloody bedsheets.

Seward's son Frederick too had been severely wounded, as was George Robinson, the army nurse who'd been assigned to Seward after Seward's recent carriage accident. Stanton tried to soothe Mrs. Seward. He ordered a soldier to guard the premises, and he posted sentries at the homes of other cabinet members. Gideon Welles, the secretary of the navy, arrived, and Stanton and Welles drove together to the Peterson house, across from Ford's Theater, where Lincoln lay.

The city was already in an uproar. Soldiers everywhere were patrolling, alert, frightened, angry.

The next morning, in a dull and misty rain, the dazed capital city began to wrap itself in black crepe. Government offices did not open. Drinking establishments closed. Theaters canceled performances. Pictures of Lincoln appeared in store windows. Men and women, black and white, milled in front of the White House. There were some arrests of former rebels. The homes of cabinet officers remained guarded. Police had banged on the door of a Washington boardinghouse, where they had been told conspirators may have secretly met. Wagons filled with produce were turned away from the city, and cavalry watched for suspicious persons: there may have been more assassins sneaking about, waiting to strike.

Stanton took charge. He needed to apprehend the persons behind the murder of Lincoln and the attempt on Secretary of State Seward. How many officials had been targeted, and how many assassins were involved? He would bring them to justice. He dispatched detectives, instructing them to dig up as much evidence as possible. He ordered more soldiers to fan out over the city. He sent for General Grant, who had gone to Philadelphia instead of joining President Lincoln the night before. He closed Ford's Theater and arranged the funeral ceremonies. He oversaw Lincoln's burial attire, choosing to dress him in the Brooks Brothers suit Lincoln had worn at the second inaugural.

Convinced that he too had been a target, Stanton was certain that somehow Jefferson Davis, the President of the Confederacy, was implicated.

Rumors flew around Washington, around the North, throughout the South.

It would have been reassuring to prove a conspiracy of Southerners—that would have made sense. Southerners might want to extend the war, not rupture the early peace. Generals Lee and Grant had already met at Appomattox, and General Lee had surrendered, but peace was not going to come easy. In Iowa, one woman was jubilant about Lincoln's assassination; while in South Carolina, a Union soldier, learning of Lincoln's death, confided to his diary that "God will punish & forgive, I suppose; but men never can."

BY TEN O'CLOCK in the morning on the day that Abraham Lincoln died, Edwin Stanton and several other members of the Lincoln cabinet had gathered at the Kirkwood House, a five-story hotel on Pennsylvania Avenue at 12th Street, where Vice President Andrew Johnson lived in a two-room suite on the second floor. They had come to witness the swearing-in of Johnson as the President of the United States.

Salmon Chase, by then chief justice of the Supreme Court, administered the oath of office. "May God support, guide, and bless you in your arduous duties," Chase concluded the brief ceremony.

This was a very different scene from the one that had taken place a little more than a year earlier when, during his inauguration as Vice President, Johnson gestured extravagantly and delivered such a long, incoherent speech that Senator Zachariah Chandler groaned. "I was never so mortified in my life," he said. "Had I been able to find a hole I would have dropped through it out of sight."

This time, Andrew Johnson rose to the occasion. He reassured members of the government and the press first of all by his deportment. Reporters described him as dignified, composed, and sober.

He promised continuity: he would keep the members of Lincoln's cabinet as his own. He reassured Republicans, particularly the more radical wing of the party, that he was "clearly" of the opinion "that those who are good enough to fight for the Government are good enough to vote for it; and that a black heart is a more serious defect in an American citizen than a black face."

Although Johnson had been a slave-state Democrat, to George Julian, a Republican representative from Indiana, the new President "would prove a godsend to the country." After all, Johnson had emphatically declared that "robbery is a crime; rape is a crime; murder is a crime; *treason* is a crime; and *crime* must be punished." Johnson had been referring mainly to Lincoln's assassins, but former Confederates seemed to be put on notice. George Julian was satisfied.

So too was Ohio Senator Benjamin Wade, who wasted no time meeting with fellow Republicans to discuss how to bolster the President's cabinet.

Secretary of State Seward had to go, of course. He had been seriously injured, but more than that, Republicans like Benjamin Wade never trusted the waffling secretary. No one mentioned replacing Secretary of War Edwin Stanton. For whatever anyone had previously thought of Andrew Johnson, if they thought of him at all, many people expressed relief that in this sad hour, there was the warhorse Edwin Stanton, battered but unbowed. "Thank God Stanton lives," said Cincinnati lawyer William Dickson.

"The country cannot spare you," the historian George Bancroft wrote Secretary Stanton. If Stanton still considered retiring, he must banish the thought. "Stand your ground," he was told. "Don't resign. There is work for you yet to do."

CHAPTER TWO

Magnificent Intentions

"Our whole system is like molten wax,
ready to receive an impression."

—CHARLES SUMNER

The marble of the U.S. Capitol sparkled in the sunlight. It was still under construction, the extensions enlarging it half done, and the monument to George Washington, unfinished and underfunded, reached only partway to the sky. Washington: a city of magnificent intentions, Charles Dickens had said. "There is incompleteness wherever the eyes rest," a visitor to the city observed years after Dickens came and went.

Incomplete buildings symbolized the state of the country after four long years of war, division, and death—four years during which the city daily watched those plain pine coffins being loaded into open hearses; four years of hunger and privation and of burning cities, of thousands of refugees, white and black, without shelter or means of support. Nothing and no one could go back to the way things were, and there were so many unanswered questions. How would the nation fulfill its mission of liberty and equality, begun a century earlier with the Declaration of Independence? And could a nation so recently divided pull itself together, finally indivisible, or would it remain shattered, shaken, and in pieces?

By the late spring of 1865, some 40,000 freed blacks had arrived in Washington looking for work. A number of them found jobs and homes in Maryland or Virginia, thanks in large part to the ministrations of the Freedmen's Bureau, which was set up to provide just that: work, education, assistance, even in some cases land. Four hundred acres in Arlington had been divided into small lots for rent. But many people were housed in shanties, stables, cellars, or improvised homes knocked together with tarpaper, and they had no wood, no blankets in winter, no means of subsistence.

They lived in the shadow of marble government buildings and of the Executive Mansion, itself dingy after those four years of war. Washington in summer was hot; and in winter, the streets and open spaces were thick with black mud or slush and snow — and "dead horses, dead dogs, cats, rats, rubbish, and refuse of all kind," journalist Jane Swisshelm noted. Pigs rooted in people's yards. "I have even heard its inhabitants tell stories of nightly pig-hunts in the streets," a British visitor said, "and of the danger of tumbling over a cow on the pavement on a dark night." Near the White House were brothels and gambling houses and saloons, where

After the war, emancipated men and women flocked to
the country's capital, where they often lived in impoverished
conditions, largely ignored by Washington politicians.

more than one congressman drank too much, and not far away
was the street known as Newspaper Row, where harried journalists
scribbled news.

There was no industry in Washington—none except politics.
And yet the white marble buildings glistened in the April light of
1865, and the city's broad avenues possessed a gracious elegance
that visitors liked to associate with the South. The actress Charlotte
Cushman, visiting the city, noted how people with great fortunes
had settled in Washington. Often they were Southerners, she observed, who intended to "get back the political ascendancy dear to
every Southern heart."

To them, Andrew Johnson actually did seem a godsend in this
confusing time, when the country seemed half-finished, the peace
rocky, and the state of the Union unclear. Should the South be
punished, more than war had already punished it, for its disloyalty?
Should the Southern states that rebelled be allowed to come back
into the Union without being further penalized for having left? And
what about the fate of the former Southern slave who, before the
war, had been counted as three-fifths of a person, per the compromise written into the Constitution? (Apportioning representation,
the compromise had given the North a net gain—but had also provided slave-holding states a commensurate reduction in federal
taxes, which were based on eligible inhabitants.) Now free, the former slave would be counted as a full person. That would increase
the number of representatives from the Southern states in the
House of Representatives—quite unfairly, if persons of color were
denied the vote.

After Appomattox, General William Tecumseh Sherman leaped
into the fray. Brilliant and irascible, though something of an amoral
pragmatist, the leathery Sherman had known devastation firsthand;
his army had caused much of it. But he hated war, which he waged
with fury, and he wanted to bring Southerners into the Union on
their old footing as soon as possible, hoping magnanimous terms
would produce law and order. Far exceeding his authority, Sherman presented Confederate General Joseph Johnston with terms of

surrender stunningly more lenient than what General Grant had offered Robert E. Lee.

Sherman's so-called "general amnesty" included official recognition of existing state governments in the South, home rule (jurisdiction over state policies and practices), and the restoration of property and political rights in the former Confederate states. However, he did not insist that the former Confederates recognize the Emancipation Proclamation; critics quickly noted that a restoration of their property could be understood as a return of their slaves. And Sherman's amnesty would easily allow rebellious Southerners—"the worst men of the South," as Sherman's brother John, an Ohio senator, called them—to reinstate their state organizations, which would endanger the welfare of freed blacks and those whites who'd been loyal to the Union.

Edwin Stanton was apoplectic.

Unlike Stanton, General Sherman assumed that Southern leaders would accept the results of the war and, if left alone, cultivate their own gardens. Simple, generous, impulsively naïve to many, not just to Stanton, General Sherman was seen as selling out the freed men and women, the Unionists, and the Republican party. Even Sherman's brother cringed. General Sherman's terms were "inadmissible," Senator Sherman acknowledged while defending the general, whom he said had merely taken a "simple military view" of the situation.

War had honed General William Tecumseh Sherman to a thin, wiry point; he was tenacious and temperamental—and exceptional. "No one could be with him half an hour and doubt his greatness," a journalist once said. Raised by Ohio Senator Thomas Ewing after Sherman's father died, he attended West Point, married Ewing's daughter Ellen, and then resigned from the army in 1853 to seek his fortune elsewhere. His stint as a banker in San Francisco left him disillusioned and impoverished, so in 1859 he took a position as head of a new military college in Louisiana. After Louisiana seceded from the Union, Sherman left the college and in 1861 received an appointment as a Union infantry colonel.

Called insane when he insisted that 200,000 troops were necessary to suppress the rebellion in Kentucky, he refurbished his reputation by becoming an inspired soldier, devoted to the Union. Grant admired him hugely, and Sherman completely trusted Grant. "He stood by me when I was crazy and I stood by him when he was drunk," Sherman drily noted when someone tried to denigrate Grant, "and now, sir, we stand by each other always."

At a hastily convened cabinet meeting, with General Grant attending, President Johnson had acted swiftly to reject the Sherman agreement, partly because it might suggest that the general had little faith in Johnson's abilities. The press had hinted that Sherman was eyeing the President's job, though General Sherman immediately quashed the preposterous rumor. "Gossip of my having presidential aspirations is absurd and offensive to me," he told Grant, "and I would check it if I knew how." Sherman loathed Washington politics, never sought political office, and in 1884 famously refused a presidential run: "I will not accept if nominated," he declared, "and will not serve if elected."

Secretary of War Stanton loudly censured General Sherman in the press, which sparked a nasty public quarrel between the two men. Senator John Sherman begged the angry Stanton to back down. The last thing the country needed was a spat between its secretary of war and one of its most revered generals. Do not drive General Sherman into the ranks of the so-called Copperheads, John Sherman added, using the common nickname for Southern-sympathizing Peace Democrats.

General Sherman wasn't a Democrat, he wasn't a Copperhead, and he claimed that he was just following Lincoln's lead when he sought to befriend white Southerners after the war. This was the position of many other moderate Republicans as well, for as early as 1863, Lincoln had been laying plans to reunify the country. To that end, he'd issued a "Proclamation of Amnesty and Reconstruction," which included full pardons to any ex-Confederate seeking amnesty, provided that he hadn't been in the Confederate government or served as a high-ranking officer in its army. The proclamation also included the restoration of property (except slaves) to those same ex-Confederates if they also swore to defend the Constitution and all the laws of the United States, including the Emancipation Proclamation. Once ten percent of the prewar electorate in a formerly seceded Southern state took this oath, they could re-establish a new and loyal state government. Those new loyal governments would be entitled to representation in Washington—if Congress approved, naturally, since it had the right to determine the qualifications of its own members.

Lincoln had not said anything about voting or civil rights. But his amnesty proclamation was a wartime measure intended, in 1863, to lure Southerners back into the Union while making sure that slaves stayed free. No one knew with certainty what Lincoln's reconstruction policies, after the war, would actually have been, which is why his last speech was—and continues to be—parsed over and over again. For just days before his assassination, from the balcony of the White House, Lincoln had addressed a large black and white audience on the lawn. Declaring that "we, the loyal people" were not of one mind about what he called reconstruction, or the "re-inauguration of the national authority," he reminded the audience that reunification could be "fraught with great difficulty." And he said he was amenable to plans other than his own.

He also said he was open to enfranchising black men who were "very intelligent" or who had served "our cause as soldiers."

While Lincoln lay in state in the East Room of the White House, his cabinet had met, and on Easter Sunday April 16, a dutiful Edwin Stanton read to them a draft of the interim reconstruction plan he'd presented at Lincoln's last cabinet meeting, which he had revised, per Lincoln's instructions. Since some Southern states, like Tennessee, were already under the jurisdiction of a military governor loyal to the Union, and since Virginia already had a loyal governor, Stanton suggested putting other states, like North Carolina, whose government was in shambles, under the jurisdiction of a temporary military marshal. That marshal could order the election of new and loyal government officials. The proposal was but a sketch, of course, hastily pulled together, and intended first and foremost to prevent bedlam in the South. It left open the question of voting rights for blacks.

That evening, before the fireplace in his office at the War Department, Stanton again presented the reconstruction plan, this time to a group of Republicans that included Massachusetts Senator Charles Sumner, Indiana Representative Schuyler Colfax, and several other members of Congress. Sumner pounced: Stanton had not included a provision for negro suffrage—giving the black man the vote.

Exhausted, Stanton explained he had not wanted to divide the Republican party, which he knew he would, by including suffrage. Sumner insisted. "This is a moment for changes," he said. "Our whole system is like molten wax, ready to receive an impression."

Sumner's ideas about reconstruction included full civil and political rights for all black men, and he was not alone. Just days before Lincoln's assassination, Chief Justice of the Supreme Court Salmon Chase, who'd been Lincoln's treasury secretary, told Lincoln it would be a crime and a folly "if the colored loyalists of the rebel states shall be left to the control of restored rebels, not likely in that case to be either wise or just." The editor of *Harper's Weekly* similarly noted that if "the political power in the late insurrectionary State be intrusted exclusively to the whites, the colored population will be left entirely at the mercy of those who have always regarded them with contempt, and who doubtless feel bitterly toward them as the real cause of the war which has desolated the South." Think of it: without the right to vote, the freedpeople might be denied the right to testify in court, to sit on juries, to bear arms, to attend church, even to learn how to read.

Abolitionist leader Frederick Douglass, a former slave, put the issue succinctly: "Slavery is not abolished until the black man has the ballot."

Frederick Douglass, Charles Sumner, Thaddeus Stevens, and Chief Justice Chase were some of those lumped together as "Radicals," or "Radical Republicans," a somewhat loose designation generally intended as a slur and one that referred mostly to policies vis-à-vis the South. (The epithet "radical" seems to have originated in the earlier label "radical abolitionist," which the Democrat press in particular, but not exclusively, had applied with contempt.) Though Radical Republicans were not necessarily a cohesive group—few groups are—generally speaking, they had believed that the Civil War should be fought first and foremost to emancipate the slaves; after the war, they championed civil rights for blacks and alleged that a reconstruction policy overly lenient to the former Confederate states would unquestionably return the freedmen and -women to a condition like slavery. Radical Republicans had feared that outcome in 1864, while the war raged, and they feared it more now that the war was over. And so they clamored for black voting rights. Many of them argued that the states formerly in rebellion should not be readmitted into Congress until they guaranteed suffrage.

And so at Charles Sumner's urging, Edwin Stanton revised his blueprint for reconstruction yet again, including in it a proviso for giving black men the vote. In this, Stanton may have appeared to be a Radical Republican. Yet certain moderate Republicans—and even a number of Democrats—backed granting black men some form of suffrage if certain qualifications were met, like the ability to read and write. These Republicans often thought such a requirement should be levied on white voters too.

The Democratic *New York Herald* supported qualified black suffrage, mainly because it seemed expedient. "The radical abolition faction of the North, slavery being abolished, have mounted their new hobby of negro suffrage, and they threaten to 'ride it rough shod' over the Southern States, and over the administration if it shall presume to stand in the way," the paper noted. Since the population of the cotton states was at least one-half freed blacks, the *Herald* suggested that "upon some fair system of restrictions, we would urge them to incorporate negro suffrage into their new State constitutions." Suffrage would undercut the platform of Northern radicals by hastening the readmission of Southern states into Congress, and the readmission of Southern states into Congress would presumably bring Democrats back into control of it.

Intent on making sure that Congress—and Congress alone—handled matters of reconstruction, Thaddeus Stevens claimed that the executive branch of government had already accumulated too much power, particularly during the war, when Lincoln appropriated authority rightly belonging to the legislature. As a result, Schuyler Colfax and several other congressional leaders asked President Johnson to convene a special session of Congress as soon as possible, Congress not being due to convene until December 1865, almost eight months after the assassination.

In no rush to reduce the presidential power that Lincoln had wielded, Andrew Johnson said he was too busy. By nature a suspicious man always looking over his shoulder, Johnson well knew that a bullet, not the ballot, had placed him in the Executive Mansion. He was the Accidental President. And conscious that his accidental presidency could disappear without an electoral mandate, he was reluctant at first to show his hand. But since he had despised secession with every fiber of his being, his hatred of it only strengthened his intention to make the Union whole again and to heal its wounds while he, Andrew Johnson, emerged unequivocally as the nation's leader. He believed that providence had chosen him to consummate this most sacred task of healing—and to keep his sacred office.

THE NEW PRESIDENT seemed "dignified, urbane, and self-possessed," said the diarist George Templeton Strong, who had earlier thought Andrew Johnson a boor. Johnson positively glowed with republican simplicity and goodness. "I rejoice in having such a plain man of the people to rule over us," declared the unshakable abolitionist Lydia Maria Child. When the prominent merchants and bankers of New York purchased a magnificent carriage and span of horses for him, the new President straightaway refused the gift. "Those occupying high official positions," he explained politely, must "decline the offerings of kind and loyal friends." He was roundly praised for his integrity.

Delegations from New York and North Carolina, from Massachusetts and Louisiana, and from Illinois and Virginia said he combined Lincoln's honesty with Andrew Jackson's grit, and that although he came from the South, he hated the Southern aristocracy. "We plebeians, the majority of the U.S. have great confidence in your ability and sympathy," a Philadelphia man wrote to Johnson. "You were once one of us who toil."

White Southerners feared that Johnson might prove a man who would "out Herod, Herod," as one planter worried, meaning he'd cruelly punish the South, but many black community leaders voiced hope, "knowing you to be A friend of our 'race.'" The editor of the New Orleans *Black Republican* declared that "as colored men, we have entire confidence in President Johnson." Hadn't Andrew Johnson, just the year before, stood on the steps of the Capitol in Nashville at dusk, and declared to the cheering crowd that he'd be the black man's Moses, leading them to freedom?

Johnson also impressed Charles Sumner enough for Sumner to tell a friend that *"in the question of colored suffrage the President is with us."* The matter of voting rights for black men remained dear to Senator Sumner's heart, and he blithely assumed that Johnson agreed with him, although Johnson had said nothing. As one of Sumner's biographers observes, "Sumner had too often taken silence for consent."

Other people shared Sumner's great expectations. "Johnson, we have faith in you," said tough-minded Ohio Senator Benjamin Wade. His declaration of faith in Johnson became a mantra, demonstrating to skeptics that Wade, the bluntest member of the most radical wing of the Republican party, approved of the new President. Or at least Wade wanted to believe that even if there wasn't a program yet in place, Johnson wouldn't fritter away the fruits of war or obstruct the Republican program for the creation of a more perfect Union.

In the wake of Lincoln's death, Andrew Johnson correctly judged the public mood as one combining grief and fury. During his first weeks in office, he continued to proclaim, as he'd done during the war, that treason was odious, criminal, a capital offense. He offered substantial cash rewards for the apprehension and arrest of such traitors as Confederate President Jefferson Davis as well as several other rebel officials. And on May 1, 1865, Johnson authorized a military trial for the eight persons arrested and then accused of conspiring with John Wilkes Booth to assassinate President Lincoln, Vice President Johnson, Secretary of State Seward, and General Grant.

Booth had managed to escape from Ford's Theater and cross the Potomac to hide in a tobacco barn in Virginia, where a skittish soldier shot him through a hole in the wall. That left seven men and one woman held in irons at the Old Arsenal Penitentiary. With the civil courts in Washington open, there was no constitutional reason for a military trial, and the controversial decision to authorize one offended the public to such an extent that Johnson instructed his attorney general, James Speed, to defend it: because Lincoln, as President, was commander in chief and thus a military personage, his assassination was considered a military crime.

Just as controversial was the decision to hold the trial behind closed doors. Reporters were not to be allowed into the courtroom; the proceedings would be communicated by one man, the presiding judge, Stanton's friend General Joseph Holt, to a single representative of the press at the end of each day. This too seemed unconstitutional, a muzzling of the freedom of the press in a country no longer at war. The ruling was reversed, but not before it deeply worried Democrats, who condemned such executive interference in the courts.

Montgomery Blair, once Lincoln's postmaster general, was quick to reassure fellow Democratic leaders: President Johnson had authorized the military tribunal merely to dupe the Radical Republicans. "He will break with them soon on the fundamental question of states rights and negro suffrage," Blair soothed. "Foreseeing this, he probably means for the *present* to be stiff on the punishment of traitors. . . . There is no principle involved in that."

The trial lasted fifty days, during which 360 witnesses told the truth as they had seen or remembered it. Twenty-nine of them were former slaves who testified both for and against the defendants. But whatever anyone—black or white—alleged, or whatever the presumed innocence or guilt of the defendants, the Northern public wanted convictions, particularly because for those fifty days, the public heard about a lot more than the night of the assassination. They heard tales of vials of smallpox smuggled over the border in suitcases by Confederate agents hoping to release them in Northern cities; they heard of attempts to kill President Lincoln with infected clothing. They heard of the horrific conditions at two notorious prisons, Libby in Richmond and Andersonville in Georgia. At the latter, in just one year, 13,000 Yankees had starved or died of dysentery, gangrene, and scurvy, if they hadn't been lucky enough to be killed quickly by a bullet.

The eight defendants who shuffled into the makeshift courtroom, initially wearing hoods over their heads (except for the woman, Mary Surratt) to isolate or humiliate them, were thus accused of more than conspiring to kill the President; they were guilty of war crimes. All eight were found guilty. Three of them were sentenced to life in prison; one of them, the man who presumably readied Booth's horse for his escape from Ford's Theater, to six years in prison. The rest, including George Atzerodt, who was supposed to kill Andrew Johnson (but got cold feet), and Mrs. Surratt, were summarily hanged with twenty-four hours' notice. Later it was alleged that several of the judges petitioned President Johnson to convert Mary Surratt's sentence to life imprisonment. He insisted he never saw the paperwork. Johnson did, however, grant executive pardons to three of the men with life sentences in early 1869, just before he left office.

OUT OF RESPECT for the grieving Mrs. Lincoln, Johnson had delayed moving into the White House for six weeks—his family was not arriving from Tennessee until August—and he set up a temporary office in the Treasury Building, where he hung the flag that had been suspended over Lincoln's box at Ford's Theater. Mary Todd Lincoln, who didn't like Johnson, complained that he failed to pay his respects, but she took some comfort in his administration following her husband's without a hitch. "It was a remarkable illustration," said reporter Noah Brooks, "of the elasticity and steadiness of our form of government that its machinery moved on without a jar, without tumult, when the head was suddenly stricken down."

In recognition of the deep sorrow afflicting the nation, with hundreds of thousands of its citizens killed and its President murdered, Johnson also called for a national day of mourning, initially slated for the end of May. After that, he hoped the country could move forward—and look forward to a future of reunion and amity.

It was wishful thinking. The political jockeying over the fate of the nation had begun. Actually, it had never stopped.

CHAPTER THREE

The Accidental President

"In what new skin will the old snake come forth?"

—FREDERICK DOUGLASS

May, 1865

The city flags were again flying at full mast by the end of May and the dreary black crepe had been removed from buildings. The city was jammed. Spectators were standing on roofs or craning out of windows while the crowds on the street below threw flowers at the triumphant soldiers, come to Washington to celebrate the Union victory in a two-day grand parade. Their rifles flashing in the brilliant sunlight, these soldiers trotted on horseback down Pennsylvania Avenue—a marvelous sight, said the graying poet Walt Whitman, who watched sun-bronzed men, heroes all, and troops decorated with scarves of scarlet. Artillery, ambulances, army wagons participated in a pageant meant to cheer the public into peace. The black regiments had not been invited.

The new President was poised and solemn. Impeccably dressed, Andrew Johnson stood erect on a large covered platform located in front of the Executive Mansion, and straight as a doorpost, his hair tucked under his ears, he saluted the passing armies as they lowered their regimental flags—many of them tattered and pierced with bullet holes—or shook the outstretched hands of the victors. No

An eloquent leader of the abolitionist and civil rights movements, Frederick Douglass had escaped from slavery to become a gifted lecturer, writer, and political journalist—and a withering critic of Andrew Johnson.

longer did he seem the boozy backwoodsman who slobbered over the Bible during his inauguration the previous March. One newspaper alleged that Johnson hadn't been drunk; the Confederates had obviously poisoned him.

"We have an era of good feeling now," George Templeton Strong noted with hope. Yet many Republicans, particularly Radicals, had grown anxious. "Johnson talks first rate," Senator Ben Wade said, "but don't just say the word." The word was "suffrage."

"There is no guarantee for personal civil liberty, but that of political liberty—universal suffrage," said another Radical. Did President Johnson understand this?

Men willing to shoulder the muskets of the republic should be allowed to "carry its ballots," a group of black men from New Bern, North Carolina, petitioned Johnson. It would be patently unfair, they said, to enfranchise the white men who'd fought against the country while denying the vote to black men who'd fought for it. Johnson said little, allowing for a while his self-appointed advisers to believe what they wanted to believe. But when a delegation of black ministers called on him at the White House, he told them with galling condescension that too many former slaves loaf around, looking to the government for handouts.

"They seem to think that with freedom every thing they need is to come like manna from heaven," Johnson said.

The petitioners didn't need hectoring, and they certainly didn't need freedom defined for them. They needed a voice in government, they needed representation, they needed to vote.

"In what new skin will the old snake come forth?" Frederick Douglass then pointedly asked. To him, as he made clear, the snake was slavery. Or Andrew Johnson. The honeymoon with Johnson, if honeymoon it had been, was coming to an end.

ON MAY 9, 1865, Andrew Johnson, President for less than a month, issued an executive order that restored Virginia as a loyal state and established Unionist Francis H. Pierpont as its provisional governor. Pierpont would be "aided by the Federal Government," President Johnson declared, "in the lawful measures which he may take for the extension and administration of the State government."

Thaddeus Stevens was troubled. "I see the President is precipitating things," he gloomily exclaimed. "Virginia is recognized! I fear before Congress meets he will have so bedeviled matters as to render them incurable."

Stevens tactfully reminded Johnson that "reconstruction is a very delicate question." And that Congress understood reconstruction to be a legislative, not an executive, prerogative. More directly, Stevens then added, "how the executive can remoddle [*sic*] the States in the union is past my comprehension. I see how he can govern them through military governors until they are reorganized. The forcing [of] governor Pierpont, chosen by a thousand votes on the million inhabitants of Virginia as their governor and call[ing] it a republican form of government may provoke a smile, but can hardly satisfy the judg[men]t of a thinking people. Had you made him a military govr. it were easily understood."

He too advised Johnson to convene an extra session of Congress—lest many assume "the Executive was approaching usurpation" of legislative authority.

Charles Sumner was also troubled. "The Pierpont govt is nothing but a sham," Sumner told the outspoken orator Wendell Phillips.

Johnson did not heed the advice or the warnings of these Republicans. At the end of May, he issued two proclamations. In the first, he decriminalized former citizens of the Confederacy willing to take an oath of allegiance to the federal government, as long as they hadn't been high-ranking officers in the Confederate government or military, and as long as they didn't possess a taxable net worth of more than $20,000. But former high-ranking officers or wealthy planters might apply directly to him for a presidential pardon.

Almost immediately Washington was teeming with ex-Confederate soldiers, con men, and conspirators, all seeking a presidential dispensation. Women too: Walt Whitman, working as a clerk in the attorney general's office, saw throngs of white Southern women, young and old, dressed in coal black, come on behalf of husbands or sons or brothers. By summer's end, Johnson had approved about 2,700 pardons. Eager to strip the wealthy planter class of its former privileges, Johnson was just as eager to earn their thanks.

Though Thaddeus Stevens was leery about admitting any former Confederates back into the government, whether or not they had been pardoned and no matter what kind of oath of allegiance they swore, Johnson ignored him. Rather, in his second proclamation, the President appointed a former secessionist, William H. Holden, as the provisional governor of North Carolina, "with all the powers necessary and proper to enable such loyal people of the State of North Carolina to restore said State to its constitutional relations to the Federal Government." Johnson also gave Holden authority to appoint mayors, judges, sheriffs, and constables. And Holden was not obligated to set aside any of the laws discriminating against blacks passed before the war—laws that prevented free blacks from testifying against a white person, for instance, or laws restricting the movement or the employment of free blacks.

The governor was also to supervise the election of delegates to a state convention whose purpose was to create a new constitution for North Carolina. This new constitution was required only to repudiate slavery, the ordinances of secession, and the Confederate debt. The citizens eligible to vote were citizens, now deemed loyal, who'd been on the voter rolls of 1860. That obviously excluded the freedmen—and did include many of the men who'd served the Confederacy.

"Better, far better, would it have been for Grant to have surrendered to Lee," Wendell Phillips quipped, "than for Johnson to have surrendered to North Carolina."

"Is there no way to arrest the insane course of the President?" Thaddeus Stevens asked Charles Sumner. "If something is not done the President will be crowned king before Congress meets." Congress would not reconvene until December, six months away. "I see our worthy president fancies himself a sovereign power—His North Carolina proclamation sickens me," Stevens told another friend.

When Johnson appointed the planter William Sharkey as provisional governor of Mississippi, some moderate Republicans were finally shaken. "I am not well satisfied with the way things are going on," said Charles Eliot Norton, the editor of the conservative *North American Review*. "Mr. Johnson is making mistakes the consequences of which will be dangerous, & hard to undo." Even more disturbing was Johnson's appointment of Benjamin Perry as provisional governor of South Carolina, for Perry had been in the Confederate legislature during the war.

Johnson continued to cold-shoulder Congress. "Nothing since Chancellorsville," Charles Sumner cried, "has to my mind been so disastrous to the National Cause."

For Johnson not only ignored black suffrage, he hinted that he would favor sending blacks to Africa, "a clime and country suited to you, should it be found that the two races cannot get along together."

The President then appointed James Johnson (no relation) provisional governor of Georgia and proceeded to issue similar proclamations for the remaining unreconstructed states. (Acting as a wartime President, not a peacetime one, Lincoln had already appointed provisional governors in Tennessee, Louisiana, and Arkansas.) "Among all the leading Union men of the North with whom I have had intercourse," Stevens warned Johnson in July, "I do not find one who approves your policy." Chief Justice Salmon Chase called Johnson's policy "a moral, political & financial mistake."

Of course there were no precedents for any of this, and there was something improvised about these lurchings into peace. Yet as far as Johnson was concerned, certain *individuals* may have rebelled against the Union; the *states* had not. He repeated himself: the eleven states of the Confederacy had never actually been out of the Union because they did not have the legal right to secede. (That's like saying a murderer could not kill because killing was against the law, Thaddeus Stevens acidly remarked.) According to Johnson, since these states hadn't seceded, they had not relinquished their right to govern themselves as they wished.

"There is no such thing as reconstruction," he added. "These States have not gone out of the Union, therefore reconstruction is unnecessary. I do not mean to treat them as inchoate States, but merely as existing under a temporary suspension of their government, provided always they [now] elect loyal men."

Johnson also insisted that his policy was based on Lincoln's point of view: the "erring" sister states hadn't left the Union. Ignoring Lincoln's further statement that the question about the legal right of secession was academic, he could allege that he was fulfilling the mission of the great martyred President.

Charles Sumner vehemently differed with Johnson. By passing ordinances of secession, Sumner said, the rebel states had forfeited their status as states. They had committed suicide. The rebel states could no longer exist as states because they had been *"vacated"* — as Sumner put it — "by all local governments we are bound to recognize."

Thaddeus Stevens thought Johnson's position absurd. "The theory that the rebel states, for four years a separate power and without representation in Congress, were all the time here in the Union," he said, "was a good deal less ingenious and respectable than the metaphysics of [Bishop] Berkeley, which proved that neither the world nor any human being was in existence."

Because the rebel states were tantamount to conquered provinces — even Lincoln had treated Louisiana, Arkansas, and Tennessee as such — Stevens proposed they be "held in a territorial condition until they are fit to form State constitutions, republican in fact and in form, and ask admission into the Union as new States."

But Johnson's ally Gideon Welles, the fusty secretary of the navy whom Lincoln called Old Neptune, wanted to let the sister states back into the Union as soon as possible, and Welles had no use for a black man voting. He made his position clear when Johnson took a straw vote in the cabinet. War Secretary Edwin Stanton might have wanted suffrage to be part of the President's proclamations; Welles did not.

Secretary of State William Seward hadn't been able to vote — he was still at home, recovering from the wounds he had received on the night of Lincoln's assassination. Sympathetic to Seward, whose fractured jaw had been fitted with some sort of metal contraption, Gideon Welles nonetheless considered Seward a turncoat temporizer who cared less for states' rights than a strong federal government—and a complicated man who could slyly adapt to any situation he couldn't control.

Welles assumed that Seward wouldn't support suffrage—but Welles also assumed that when Seward came back into the cabinet, he'd be aiming to control Andrew Johnson.

WILLIAM HENRY SEWARD was a genial, pliable optimist—and a survivor. He'd survived President Buchanan and the Buchanan administration, he'd survived the pressure of the Radicals, he'd survived an attempt on his life.

Raised in upstate New York, Seward had been an outspoken anti-slavery Whig before the war as well as a state senator and the

Secretary of state under Presidents Lincoln and Johnson, the very complicated William H. Seward so loyally supported Johnson that he was called the President's "ill-genius."

governor of New York; in 1849 he'd been elected to the U.S. Senate. But during the secession crisis, Seward broke with the Republican platform, which forbade extending slavery into the territories, and he tried to conciliate the South with a plan that would have approved it. He also proposed that the country should consider a constitutional amendment forever forbidding congressional interference with slavery in the states where it already existed. Smacking of appeasement, the proposal appalled many Republicans, who viewed it as a sop to the secessionists. "God damn you Seward," a Republican senator shouted on the floor. "You've betrayed your principles and your party."

Seward had been working to reconcile North and South. Regardless, or maybe because of this, Lincoln had placed him in the cabinet as his secretary of state. Assuming he knew more than the President, Seward was certain that Lincoln would do what he told him, and during the first overwrought days of that administration, he told Lincoln not to buck the Confederates of South Carolina but rather to surrender Fort Sumter to pacify them. He then leaked information to them that Sumter would be evacuated, which of course it was not.

He had also advised Lincoln to provoke an international crisis, believing that a war with Spain and France would prevent war at home. Lincoln did not adopt Seward's plans, which, if anything, revealed Seward's Machiavellian tendencies. But as historians have persuasively argued, Seward helped collect Democratic votes for the Thirteenth Amendment in exchange for a reconstruction policy lenient toward the South and the promise of a new political party, a Union party, composed of conservative Republicans like himself and willing Democrats. But hardline Democrats loathed Seward almost as much as they disliked Edwin Stanton, and they wanted Johnson to remove both Seward and Stanton immediately from the cabinet in return for their support.

Radical Republicans too distrusted the shifty Seward. Johnson's decision to welcome back into the Union those whom he'd called traitors bore Seward's mark, they thought. "Seward entered into him," Thaddeus Stevens said, "and ever since, they have been running down steep places into the sea." Carl Schurz, the noted German refugee who had recently served as a Union general, agreed that Johnson's recent policy toward the South reeked of Seward.

Having mostly recovered from the wounds he'd received on the night of Lincoln's assassination, though still swollen around the jaw, Seward soon returned to his office as secretary of state and promptly became Johnson's staunch ally. They too were an odd couple: William Seward was cultured, conniving, and a wily strategist enormously sensitive to the political climate, while Andrew Johnson was uncultured, stubborn, and frequently off marching to his own drummer. Yet both of them wanted to curb the power of the federal government, or so they claimed.

At sixty-four, the ebullient Seward was showing some signs of age. His hair was gray, his eyebrows frizzled, his chin almost nonexistent, his nose long and droopy. He spoke well, and he liked to speak. In July, the scar on his face from the assassination attempt quite visible, Seward addressed an audience in his upstate New York hometown. Praising President Johnson as a man of integrity and bravery, a man without personal caprice or selfishness, and a man who merely wanted to heal the breach caused by war, Seward also suggested that it was he, William Seward, who'd been masterbuilder of the President's policy of reconciliation. (Enemies called him Mephistopheles.) He reminded his audience that the terms now on the table had already been worked out by Lincoln and his cabinet—namely, again, by William Seward. Who could argue with the wisdom of Lincoln, the great national martyr? Andrew Johnson merely wanted the same things: reconciliation and peace. We can now trust each other, North and South, Seward repeated; we are again friends.

The radical *National Anti-Slavery Standard* labeled Seward's speech an act of cowardice. Charles Sumner hated it. By trusting former Confederates, Sumner declared, "we give them political power, including the license to oppress loyal persons, whether white or black, and especially the freedmen. For four years we have met them in battle; and now we rush to trust them, and to commit into their keeping the happiness and well-being of others. There is peril in trusting such an enemy."

Charles Sumner, at one extreme, and Navy Secretary Gideon Welles, at another, weren't the only ones who mistrusted Seward. Longtime Democrats, the dynastic Blair family had no use for him. Montgomery Blair, who seemed to have Johnson's ear, thought Seward an underhanded liar. Formerly Lincoln's postmaster general, and before that an accomplished lawyer who had argued before the Supreme Court that the former slave Dred Scott was free because he resided in free territory, Blair firmly opposed giving black men the vote. Any hint of racial equality repulsed him, and fearing miscegenation above all, he hoped to rid the country of blacks by deporting them. Before the election of 1864, Radical Republicans demanded Lincoln remove Montgomery Blair from the cabinet, which Lincoln did.

Blair was at first enthusiastic about Andrew Johnson, and the Blairs had been good to the Tennessean. After Johnson's embarrassing performance at his vice-presidential inauguration, his friend former New York senator Preston King stowed Johnson at the Blairs' Maryland home, where the Blairs hospitably provided him with cover and circulated a plausible reason—illness—for his drunken blathering. Once Johnson was President, the Blairs believed he had deftly hoodwinked the Radicals when he ordered the trial of the accused Lincoln assassination conspirators, noting that, in the end, "there will be but few [Southerners] punished after all." Montgomery Blair also assured Democratic power-brokers that Johnson had promised the federal government would not interfere with the states. If Democrats dawdled, or withheld their support from Johnson, "there may be mischief done."

But Democratic power-brokers were lukewarm on Johnson. By summer, he still hadn't tossed Edwin Stanton or William Seward out of the cabinet. "Public events have shown, ever since Johnson's ascension, that he is entirely in the hands of Stanton and Seward," fumed George Ticknor Curtis, the government commissioner fa-

mous for hurling the fugitive Thomas Sims back into slavery in
Georgia in the 1850s. "His [Johnson's] adoption of the military
trial," Curtis referred to the Lincoln conspirators' case, "and his execution of the victims have clearly rendered his retreat from their
[Radical] control an impossibility." Johnson then kept Montgomery
Blair waiting so long in the antechamber of his office that Blair
never saw the President that day. "What chance at conservative
ideas to the mind of Johnson," Curtis wondered, "if he keeps thus at
arm's length a man who is presumed to be his personal friend and
is one of the leading politicians of the country?"

"Seward & Stanton are jubilant," former Congressman Samuel
Sunset Cox, himself a conservative leader, warned his Democratic
friends about Johnson. "There is the best of reasons for believing
that all our efforts to help him would be met with a lecture on our
derelictions as Dems."

Johnson's proclamations therefore concerned Democrats as
much as they upset the Radical Republicans, although for different
reasons. "He is nominally a President of a republic, but in reality an
absolute ruler issuing *decrees* (not executing *laws*), and carrying
them out by naked military force. This seems to me to be his present attitude," jurist William Shipman declared. Johnson was acting
autocratically, exercising war powers when the war was over. "I shall
be glad to see him change his position, and disavow both by word
and deed the monstrous assumptions of executive power," Shipman
continued. "If he does not do so, then in the struggle which is to
come between him and the radicals, we must take care that we do
not commit ourselves to his support."

These Democrats actually preferred black suffrage to presidential tyranny: "Now while the President would doubtless appoint better men, he would do it by the exercise of a power utterly inconsistent
with free institutions. The negroes would elect them by ballot, at
least in formal harmony with the principles upon which our government, state and national, are founded."

Andrew Johnson was gradually alienating almost everyone in the
North.

CHAPTER FOUR

Moses

"I care not whence the blows come. And some will find, before
this thing is over, that while there are blows to be given,
there will be blows to receive."

—ANDREW JOHNSON

In 1860, and in the months just before the outbreak of war, no one had seemed braver than Tennessee Senator Andrew Johnson. When indignant secessionists in South Carolina wanted to sever ties with the United States, he had boldly defied them. "I am opposed to secession," Johnson had declared, not mincing words, on the floor of the Senate just a month after Abraham Lincoln's election. "He that is unwilling to make an effort to preserve the Union," Senator Johnson thundered, "or, in other words, to preserve the Constitution, I think is unworthy of public confidence, and the respect and gratitude of the American people." On these points, preserving the Union and the Constitution, Andrew Johnson never wavered.

Andrew Johnson lived for and by the U.S. Constitution, and during that secession winter of 1860, he reminded colleagues again and again that the Constitution makes no provision for a state ever to leave the Union. About this, he was clear. And he said he'd cling to the Constitution "as the ship-wrecked mariner clings to the last plank, when the night and the tempest close around him."

Senator Johnson was also very clear about his position on slavery. The U.S. Constitution guaranteed its protection, including its spread into the territories. If Lincoln and his fellow Republicans were to be stopped from tampering with slavery—which they must be—Johnson said they must be stopped from *inside* the government, not outside it.

Mississippi Senator Jefferson Davis shook his head in disgust.

Burned in effigy from one end of Tennessee to another, Andrew Johnson was blasted as a traitor to the South. "Hanging is too good for such a degraded old wretch," said a Georgia newspaper. Johnson had to be an ally of that repulsive abolitionist Benjamin Wade, it was alleged. Or he was the tool of an underhanded William Seward, then senator from New York. Anyway, what could anyone really expect of Andy Johnson, whom Southern planters disdained as a "scrub": a gauche, backwoods Tennessee tailor who by the age of twenty couldn't even recite the alphabet. What could a scrub know about the Constitution? Soon it was also rumored that Andy Johnson had challenged Texas Senator Louis Wigfall to a duel over secession, but Wigfall didn't duel anymore—which was lucky for Andy, his detractors snorted, since Wigfall was a damned good shot.

Yet Andrew Johnson had taken his stand, and he held his ground. Still, he couldn't stem the South's slide into secession.

For months, he'd been pleading with Southern friends and colleagues not to secede, and he'd even proposed amendments to the Constitution that might please them. He suggested that the President and Vice President be elected directly by popular vote and that half of the Supreme Court justices be selected from slave-holding states. He proposed a permanent line be drawn between slave and free states and that slavery be protected in the slave states. Most important, he declared that these amendments should be unamendable. If they were passed, he insisted, there'd be no need for secession. The proposals went nowhere. On December 20, 1860, church bells in Charleston celebrated South Carolina's leaving the Union, and by February 1861, seven states had passed secession ordinances.

Again Johnson protested. He invoked the specter of his beloved hero President Andrew Jackson, born in poverty, like Johnson himself; a committed Democrat, like himself; a committed Unionist, also like himself; and a self-proclaimed man of the people, like himself. President Jackson had trusted the yeoman farmer and the hardworking mechanic and men who weren't members, as Andrew Johnson put it, of an "upstart, swelled-headed, iron heeled, bob-tailed aristocracy."

"If Andrew Jackson were President of the United States, this glorious Union of ours would still be intact," Johnson chastised fellow Southerners. Andrew Jackson had chided his own Vice President, John C. Calhoun, when Calhoun insisted that a state possessed the right to veto, or nullify, any federal law it found unconstitutional. In 1832, the South Carolina legislature had declared a federal tariff to be null and void—and it also claimed that the federal government's failure to uphold the state's decision on nullification was grounds for secession. But President Jackson had argued that the Constitution established a national government, not a series of independent, strutting states that could ignore the federal laws they had all made together.

This was essentially the same case that Andrew Johnson made about secession in the Senate two days before Lincoln's inauguration. It didn't fly. Immediately charged with pandering to the North, Johnson hotly replied that to him the Northern abolitionist was as fanatical as the Southern secessionist—wild extremists bent on destroying the very best government on earth. And if those extremists wanted to attack him, go ahead, Johnson dared his Senate colleagues. "I care not whence the blows come," he cried. "And some will find, before this thing is over, that while there are blows to be given, there will be blows to receive; and that while others can thrust, there are some who can parry. They will find that it is a game that two can play at."

The galleries erupted in applause. That pleased Johnson. He said he'd always placed his faith in the people. The people would defend the Constitution, and they'd stand behind him. Together,

Andrew Johnson, the seventeenth American President and the first ever to be impeached, had earlier defied his Southern colleagues when he bravely stood up in the Senate and denounced secession, but after the war, Johnson just as proudly was heard to say, "This is a white man's government."

Andrew Johnson and the people would protect the country; it was self-serving politicians who made all the trouble.

Wasn't Johnson a politician, Senator Wigfall shot back; hadn't Andrew Johnson been a professional politician most of his life?

Johnson was unfazed. "These two eyes of mine never looked upon anything in the shape of mortal man that this heart feared," he shouted.

"Three cheers for Andy Johnson," someone in the galleries yelled.

Johnson was blunt, he was brash, he was tenacious, and he represented the common folk—which is how newspapers, especially in the North, depicted him. It was also the way he liked to characterize himself before, during, and after the war. "He was free from ostentation and the honors heaped upon him did not make him forget to be kind to the humblest citizen," an acquaintance recalled. During a political career that by 1861 had already spanned three decades—he *was* a career politician—Johnson consistently delivered speech after stump speech in praise of "the people," those unsung (white) laborers who struggled to survive every day and who could not parade "family distinctions on account of superior blood." "The aristocracy in this district know that I am for *the people*," Johnson proudly announced in 1845 when defending his seat in the House of Representatives. To him, the aristocracy was any well-born or connected group, like lawyers, that earned their bread "by fatiguing their ingenuity" rather than by the sweat of their brows.

Why did you allow your sons to become lawyers, a friend baited Johnson. "Because they had not sense enough to be mechanics," he snapped back.

Johnson's scrappy populism appealed to those men and women who resented plutocrats who, as Johnson reminded them, possessed unmerited privileges beyond the reach of you and me. Pulling out his plain silver pocket watch, he dangled it in front of the crowd, roaring that his rival owned a timepiece made of pure gold. He said he took his cues from a higher power, which he represented in the same way he represented plain people. *"The voice of the people,"* he summed up, *"is the voice of God."* Such platform histrionics appalled sober politicians who didn't dangle watches or divinities, and they called Johnson a demagogue. Even Democrats took offense.

Early in his career, Johnson also lashed out against the electoral college, legislative prerogatives, and cabals that rigged political conventions. He fiercely advocated homestead legislation that would give federal land in the western territories to the poor and landless, either at low cost or for nothing, as long as they built a dwelling and lived there for five years. In fact, he'd been pushing a homestead bill since 1846—and he never stopped pushing it even when South-

erners and members of his own party tried to block it. Southerners
called it the handiwork of Northerners and abolitionists, for they
feared that a homestead act would eventually lead to the admission
of more free states into the Union. Not Johnson: in 1858, he was
quoting Thomas Jefferson on the virtues of agrarianism—large cities are sores on the body politic—and conjuring Andrew Jackson's
image of an independent farmer as the country's heart and soul.
Land for the landless meant remuneration for one's toil, and it
stirred the patriotic soul. "When a man has a home," Johnson said,
"he has a deeper, a more abiding interest in the country, and he is
more reliable in all things that pertain to the Government."

Now, in 1861, Johnson was berating Southern secessionists.
"Were I President of the United States," he exclaimed, "I would
have them arrested and tried for treason; and if convicted, by the
Eternal God, I would see that they suffer the penalty of law at the
hands of the executioner." On his way home to Tennessee from
Washington that April, Johnson clashed with the mobs that inevitably poured onto the railroad platform at almost every stop. A knot of
men blocked his train at the Lynchburg, Virginia, station, and when
Johnson drew his gun, the conductor swiftly stepped forward and
convinced the men to let the train proceed. At Abingdon, Johnson's
hat was ripped from his head and torn to pieces, and at Bristol another throng of men wanted to lynch him.

Delegates from the seceded states had met in Montgomery, Alabama, and had elected Jefferson Davis as provisional president of
the newly formed Confederate States of America. Davis had to deal
with more than a difficult scrub from East Tennessee. At four-thirty
in the morning on April 12, 1861, General Pierre-Gustave Toutant
de Beauregard of those Confederate States gave the order for gun-
ners to fire on the federal garrison at Fort Sumter, in Charleston
Harbor. As a Confederate state, South Carolina had demanded that
the United States of America evacuate the fort. Two days later, on
April 14, 1861, Fort Sumter surrendered to the Confederates, and
the Civil War had begun.

SIX YEARS LATER, in the spring of 1867, as the seventeenth President of the United States, Andrew Johnson triumphantly returned to Raleigh, North Carolina, the city of his birth. The occasion was the dedication of a monument, a tomb, in honor of his father—a ten-foot red limestone structure built to replace the original, small headstone on which only two initials, "JJ," had been rudely carved.

It was quite a homecoming for a local boy who'd had no schooling, prospects, or fancy connections. But Andrew Johnson had always believed that democracy was the political equivalent of Jacob's ladder and that any man born in the United States—Johnson meant any *white* man—could climb that ladder, rung by rung, to the very top, despite whatever disadvantages he may have earlier endured, such as poverty. And Andrew Johnson had been climbing that ladder for a lifetime, pulling himself away from the misery of his boyhood.

Glancing at his father's towering tomb, he disdainfully asked, where are they now? Where is Raleigh's upper crust? Neither Johnson nor his father had been a member, for Jacob Johnson had worked as a janitor, constable, and stable-keeper. He had been the sexton who rang the only bell in town—and who'd rung that bell after rescuing three men from an overturned canoe and carrying them to shore. He'd rung the bell but, exhausted, just a few days later, he'd suffered a fatal heart attack.

Andrew Johnson never forgot—he'd never been allowed to forget—where he came from, a family of poor whites rebuffed by the bankers, judges, lawyers, and politicians whose clothes his mother sewed and washed and for whom his father had sacrificed his life.

Born on December 29, 1808 in the kitchen of an inn where his parents then worked, Andrew Johnson grew up in a log cabin and thus shared with Lincoln the privations of a hardscrabble youth. But the comparison between the two men ends there. Lincoln was flexible and kind and brilliant—with a deft, manipulative mind whose point of view kept enlarging over time; Johnson was a brave but obstinate man whose convictions, over time, calcified into a creed.

After the death of his father, his mother, Mary (Polly) Johnson, had remarried but soon farmed out her two sons to a local tailor as indentured servants, or "bound-boys," as they were called. "Though she sent me out penniless and friendless and did not afford me advantages which you now enjoy," Johnson softly commented at the foot of his father's tall monument, "I can say whatever may have been her delinquencies, she is my mother and I love her still."

Bound-boys had to work twelve hours a day until they turned twenty-one, at which time they'd be set free. Since education was a condition of indenture, they were supposedly taught to read and write. But it's not clear what Johnson learned in James Selby's tailoring shop, although Johnson long remembered listening to men who, waiting for their clothes, read aloud. He must have loved those readings, for later he said he'd missed his vocation. If he'd been educated, he once lamented, he'd have been a schoolteacher—or a chemist. "It would have satisfied my desire to analyze things, to examine them in separate periods and then unite them again to view them as a whole," Johnson claimed. He also said that as a chemist or a teacher, he wouldn't have had to "play the hypocrite and indulge in heroics." Yet though he never seemed to be faking, whether on the stump, in the Senate, or in the White House, Johnson did enjoy something like heroics, for he saw himself as a lone spirit fighting for the good and the right. Andrew Johnson was cut from a martyr's cloth, one of his cabinet members would say.

While he sewed at the tailor shop, a clerk named William Hill read to young Johnson, whose favorite book was *The American Speaker*, a compilation of speeches containing sections from *Hamlet* and Edmund Burke as well as George Washington's farewell address, the inaugural address of Thomas Jefferson, and several speeches by the chief of the Seneca nation. It was thrilling stuff. Johnson so loved the book that Bill Hill gave it to him, and Johnson said he could read it before he learned to spell. In the White House, he recited sections of it. And he could not have forgotten the book's preface, which claimed that by studying these speeches, the young reader would almost certainly travel on the royal "road to distinction," or climb that wonderful ladder.

Still, servitude is servitude, and whatever Andrew Johnson dreamed as he sat in the tailor shop, for the rest of his life he remained exquisitely sensitive to slights, real or perceived. The high-and-mighty planters who sat on the top rung of Johnson's ladder were his enemies, but so too were the slaves and free blacks whom he considered below him—and whom he feared might clamber up a rung or two and knock him to the ground.

In the spring of 1824, when Johnson was fifteen, his face freckled and his hair golden brown, he and his brother ran away from Selby's place. There's no record of where they went or how far; Selby did offer a reward for their capture, much as if the boys had been fugitive slaves. When Johnson returned to Raleigh three years later, he offered to buy out his contract as well as reimburse Selby for time lost. Selby apparently demanded more money than Johnson could afford, so Johnson left town again, no doubt further embittered against the man and the class that demeaned him. This time, his mother and stepfather joined him, all headed west for Tennessee, in a two-wheeled wooden car pulled by a blind horse. They settled in the rural village of Greeneville in the eastern part of the state, where Johnson met Eliza McCardle, the daughter of a local shoemaker. The young couple married. Johnson was eighteen and Eliza a little over sixteen, and his worldly possessions were said to consist of that blind horse, a cot, and five dollars.

At the time Johnson was rather handsome. He was five foot ten; his eyes were dark, intense, and, according to one friend, "sparkling." His cheekbones were high, his mouth firm and not yet locked into a perpetual frown. Unfortunately, very little is known about Eliza McCardle Johnson, an only child apparently educated at the local school, who disappeared from public view once Johnson became President. She suffered from poor health after the birth of their fifth child in 1852—but gossips heard that Eliza Johnson lived apart from her husband, who treated her badly. He spent long periods separated from her, both when he went to Nashville as a young legislator and after he was elected to the U.S. Senate. Years later, Eliza Johnson's prospective biographer concluded that "in the end, I did not know whether she loved Andrew or hated him."

Eliza Johnson did prove herself to be made of strong stuff, particularly during the early days of war when Johnson was in Washington. East Tennessee had remained Unionist after the rest of the state seceded in June of 1861, and so the Confederates naturally considered the Johnsons to be enemy aliens. They seized the Johnson home in Greeneville, removed their slaves, and smashed or

First Lady Eliza McCardle Johnson was seldom seen
during the Johnsons' White House years.

sold their possessions. Forced to leave town, Eliza Johnson and her ten-year-old son traveled on rugged, desolate roads to cross Confederate lines, sleeping beside railroad tracks when no one would offer shelter. But Andrew Johnson expected from his family no less than he expected of himself. "We must hold out to the end, this rebellion is wrong and must be put down let cost what it may in the life and treasure—" he would instruct his wife. "You & Mary [their daughter] must not be weary, it is our fate and we Should be willing to bear it cheerfully—" he added. "Impatience and dissatisfaction will not better it or shorten the time of our suffering."

When Johnson entered the White House, Mrs. Johnson's sickroom was located across the hall from the library. The President could hear his wife cough or moan, and Johnson's private secretary recalled that he could hear the First Lady weeping in her bedroom. Johnson's bodyguard circumspectly noticed that she had seemed "far more content when her husband was an industrious young tailor." In those days, Eliza Johnson had helped Andrew with his writing, or so it was rumored. (Johnson's spelling was atrocious.) And the couple had prospered. Johnson was known to create stylish clothes, and young men from the nearby college so admired his coats and pants that he hired a staff of tailors to keep up with the orders. He himself always dressed simply in black broadcloth, though in later life he wore dark brocade waistcoats to match his black doeskin trousers, and to keep his linen crisp, he changed it more than once a day.

He also developed a taste for public performance. "He was naturally and inherently disputatious, cautious, and pugnacious, and opposition was his delight," a contemporary remembered. Evidently at his wife's urging, Johnson joined a debating society at the local college and on Friday nights walked the four miles from his home in order to compete. It was said that he was initially timid and his voice weak. That changed fairly soon when he realized people were listening. He ran for office. In 1829, he was elected alderman, then town mayor, and in 1835 was sent to the state legislature after a blistering campaign during which he typically called his rivals ghouls, hyenas, and carrion crows. His foes—there was an ever-growing number—said he catered to the prejudices of whatever crowd he addressed. If they liked, he liked; if they hated, he hated more.

But in a slave-holding state, the exercise of manual labor was considered beneath the dignity of a white person, and as one historian has noted, the tailor's profession was regarded as effeminate. Plying a needle as you sat cross-legged on a table or fitting clothes to another man's body was not the same as splitting rails, and Johnson, alert to any form of ridicule, also cultivated a reputation for scrappiness and physical strength. And since success included, for him, the ownership of others, when serving in the state legislature in Nashville in 1835, Johnson bought a fourteen-year-old girl named Dolly. In all, Johnson would own about nine slaves, and after the war he proudly claimed more than once that he never sold a single one of them. Mainly, he was proud to have acquired them in the first place. It was another rung on that ladder.

Dolly recalled that she'd been for sale at auction when it was she who spotted Johnson. Liking his looks, she asked him to buy her, which he did. Whether Dolly's account is true or not, it does suggest there may have been attraction between them—or that Dolly preferred a story in which she was not passive. Whatever happened, by the laws of the day Johnson was her owner, the master. Years later a rumor circulated to the effect that Johnson had fathered at least one, if not all three, of Dolly's light-skinned children—although it was also said that Johnson's son Robert had fathered Dolly's youngest. Such allegations would surprise no one, then or later. It's also true that political enemies often accused one another of miscegenation.

But Johnson could brag that he'd climbed out of illiteracy, poverty, and Greeneville. Having successfully invested in real estate, the penniless apprentice was now as successful as the local gentry, even if the gentry wouldn't embrace him. As if in retaliation, Johnson constantly referred to that success, flaunting his bleak persistence to anyone who might condescend to him. He thus converted grievances into political advantage. Johnson was a champion of the underprivileged, the enemy of snobbery and affectation, a plain person, without frills, earthy and ungilded. What you saw was what you got. Or what he wanted you to see.

Johnson lost only one election, and that was to the Tennessee statehouse in 1837, and he returned to the state legislature two years later. "He was always a candidate for Something," a Tennessee congressman reminisced. Johnson served in the U.S. House of Representatives from 1843 to 1853, where he opposed government spending; he even argued against a resolution to pave the muddy streets of Washington. Similarly, he fought federal support for railroads, which he foresaw as ruining the livelihood of those who ran wayside inns or depended on wagons to bring their goods to market. In this, he nurtured an idyllic view of the countryside, one partly shared by such eastern writers as Ralph Waldo Emerson: "We build railroads, we know not for what or for whom," Emerson warned in 1844, "but one thing is certain, that we who build will receive the very smallest benefit." For Johnson, the nostalgic dream of the country as small, white, and mythically pastoral was to a large extent his fantasy about the childhood he never had. Later, one of his favorite books was *The Lost Cause Regained*, a jeremiad, written just after the war, about the South's return to its former lily-white glory.

A states' rights defender who rigorously championed the institution of slavery and a Democrat wary of executive privilege or power, Johnson did support the President's right to veto bills, a right Johnson would exercise years later when he reached the White House. The contradiction did not bother him. Unsurprisingly, he did not see eye to eye with all Democrats. "Party, to him, as to most politicians, was valuable because it enabled him to mount upon the shoulders of his followers and thus rise to power," noted a Greeneville judge. Fellow Tennessee Democrat and former President James K. Polk never liked Johnson, complaining that "he is very vindictive and perverse in his temper and conduct." Johnson had supported Polk's war with Mexico, just as he firmly opposed the

Wilmot Proviso, which would prohibit slavery in any of the territories annexed as a result of that war.

When redistricting in Tennessee made it obvious that he could not win another election to the House of Representatives, Johnson ran successfully for governor, and he ran for governor again in 1855, bitterly attacking the American, or "Know-Nothing," party. With his talent for the stump, as well as his willingness to cut deals with Whigs, Johnson won a surprising victory. By then he was forty-seven years old, heavier, his hair slightly thinning, his brow wrinkled. Two years later, he was elected to the U.S. Senate.

In Washington, he kept mainly to himself. Jefferson Davis later recalled that Johnson used his "plebeian origins as a bar to warm social relations." A friend recalled that Johnson "had no sense of humor." One of his White House secretaries said he saw Johnson smile only once, and though he seemed polite enough at official receptions, his eye "lacked the luster of a light heart." In fact, there was nothing light about him. A zealous autodidact, he larded his speeches with quotations from the Bible, Shakespeare, and John Milton, and he so admired Thomas Gray's "Elegy Written in a Country Churchyard" that he often recited it. He read Alexander Pope with pleasure, quoting,

> "Unlearned, he knew no schoolman's subtle art,
> No language but the language of the heart.
> By nature honest, by experience wise,
> Healthy by temperance and exercise. . . ."

He often returned to Joseph Addison's 1713 tragedy *Cato*, committing much of the play to memory. Like Cato resisting the imperial Caesar, Johnson said that after the war, he wanted only to "restore the commonwealth to liberty," and during his impeachment trial, he told his secretary that "Cato was a man who would not compromise with wrong but being right, died before he would yield."

Though he easily took offense, while campaigning he could brush aside most slurs. When Parson William G. Brownlow called him a toady whose father was indicted for pilfering poultry—and that he came "from as mean a family as any rake who ever came from North Carolina"—Johnson shrugged it off. When vilified as an atheist and a Roman Catholic, Johnson sharply countered that no one could be a Catholic and an infidel at the same time. The only smear that bothered him was the charge that he was born a bastard.

He avoided organized religion, but during his impeachment trial, he started attending St. Patrick's Church in Washington to hear the sermons of Bernard Maguire, the Irish-born president of Georgetown College, whom he admired. Overall, though, he said his "faith" was "based on the eternal principles of right"—which he felt he could ascertain himself. If he needed to refer to a Bible, he turned to the Constitution. Politics was his religion. "The passion of his life was the desire of power," an acquaintance reminisced.

In the Senate, Johnson often dreamed of occupying the Executive Mansion. And why shouldn't he? A clairvoyant had whispered to him that Old John Brown, the raider of Harper's Ferry, sent word from Hell, where Brown now lived, that said Andrew Johnson would be nominated President. The clairvoyant may have bungled the message a bit, but Johnson heard what he wanted to hear, for the White House was the highest rung on his ladder, and by 1860, it may have seemed in reach.

At the State Democratic convention in Nashville, Tennessee, he maneuvered allies hoping to secure enough delegates to nominate him for President at the national convention, but he hadn't reckoned on Democrats spinning out of control. When the party met nationally in Charleston the issue was slavery, the issue was secession, the issue was the Republicans. Southern Democrats marched out of the national convention. Reconvening in Baltimore, those Democrats who hadn't bolted the party nominated Stephen Douglas for President; the rest proceeded to nominate John Breckinridge. Realizing he didn't stand a chance, Johnson withdrew his name and without much enthusiasm endorsed Breckinridge. He was not optimistic about the future of the country.

TENNESSEE GOVERNOR ISHAM Harris once said that if Andy Johnson was a snake, he'd bite the heels of rich men's children. Like Johnson, Harris was an outspoken, raucous man, but unlike Johnson, he was an unapologetic secessionist who slammed Lincoln as a bloody tyrant. When Lincoln told Governor Harris that he needed soldiers to crush the rebellion, the Tennessee governor instead instructed the state legislature to adopt an ordinance of secession, which would be submitted to the voters for ratification in early June.

Andrew Johnson, who hated Harris as much as he loathed secession, spoke against secession at a Unionist convention in Knoxville, even though he'd been told he'd be beheaded if he dared to open his mouth. Johnson was unafraid. When a nearby brass band noisily tried to drown him out, Johnson just raised his voice louder and kept talking. Even his critics admired his guts. But by the late spring of 1861, it was all too late, and when Johnson returned to Washington, he rode out of Tennessee just ahead of the secessionists hoping to assassinate him.

Back in Washington, Johnson was appointed to the joint congressional committee tasked with overseeing the conduct of the war. That July, Congress approved his and Senator Crittenden's resolution that war be waged only to restore the Union, not to abolish slavery. Thaddeus Stevens did not vote for the resolution, but most congressmen did.

Johnson continued railing against the secessionists: in seeking to break up the Union, this handful of rabid traitors had usurped the will of the people, and these traitors must be defeated. "My wife and children have been turned in to the street," he said. "My house has been turned into a barracks, and for what? Because I stand by the Constitution." But after these miserable traitors were defeated, the Southern states could return to the Union because, according to Johnson, the Constitution stipulated that the states could never leave, guns and cannons notwithstanding.

AFTER THE WAR, he did not change his tune. There was something remarkably consistent about Andrew Johnson, although in his case, and as it turned out, consistency was no virtue.

On February 23, 1862, Nashville citizens gathered along the riverbank to greet General Don Carlos Buell and the Union army, which had forced the Confederates in Tennessee out of the city. That same day, Abraham Lincoln appointed Andrew Johnson military governor of Tennessee.

Unsure of what exactly he was supposed to do beyond serving at the President's pleasure, Johnson was presumably to form a provisional government in Nashville, one sturdy enough to succeed the Confederate government (now situated in Memphis) if and when Union troops removed it. So his assignment was not only vague, it was dangerous, since rebels controlled the western part of the state. "Let Andrew Johnson beware," they said. "He may find a Corday in every woman he meets; he may expect at every corner, in every crowd, the ball that is to send him to his Maker's presence, unshrived of his odious crimes."

Johnson immediately denounced traitors by name, appointed loyal men to government posts, and imprisoned any city official who refused to take an oath of allegiance to the Union; that included the mayor of Nashville and eminent clergymen. Enemies accused him of inaugurating a reign of terror, but he was impervious to criticism. He sent General A. C. Gillem into the hills of East Tennessee to rout the guerillas who'd been murdering men and women throughout the state. Newspaper publishers sympathetic to the Confederacy could find themselves in jail, and he levied monthly assessments on rebel-sympathizers on behalf of the wives, widows, and children reduced to poverty. By spring, he was boasting to Lincoln that he had arrested more than seventy rebels. Johnson gave Southerners a chance to pledge their allegiance, and by paroling offenders, he conducted a covert policy of conciliation. "I hardly ever got my hands on a rebel stock of supplies," said Union General Grenville Dodge, "that I did not find Johnson trying to pull them off."

Johnson was adamant about fortifying East Tennessee—and Nashville—and kept pestering Stanton, Lincoln, and General Buell for military assistance. He disliked the cautious Buell, who planned to leave Nashville utterly undefended in the summer of 1862. Johnson threatened to burn Nashville to the ground before he'd surrender it to the legendary Confederate General Nathan Bedford Forrest or to John Morgan's fabled raiders. General William S. Rosecrans ("Old Rosy") replaced Buell, and when Rosecrans successfully defended the city, Johnson took the credit.

Soon Johnson and Rosecrans were at odds, partly over jurisdiction: who controlled state operations, the railroads, or confiscated goods, the military governor or the military commander? The lines weren't clearly drawn. To mollify an irritated Johnson, Secretary of War Stanton gave him, as military governor, authority over the completion of the Nashville and Northwestern Railroad and over public buildings and property. Johnson was also in charge of dispersing abandoned lands and plantations, which meant he had to provide for the welfare and employment of former slaves. Lincoln, recognizing an enormous opportunity for propaganda, pressed Johnson to raise black troops. As the President explained, imagine Andrew Johnson, a slaveholder from a slave state, arming black men: "The bare sight of fifty thousand armed, and drilled black soldiers upon the banks of the Mississippi, would end the rebellion at once," Lincoln told him.

But conservative Tennessee Unionists were fighting to save the Union not to abolish slavery. At the beginning of the war, Johnson had been one of them. "Damn the negroes," he'd reportedly said. "I am fighting these traitorous aristocrats, their masters!" Certainly Johnson had never questioned the morality of the so-called "peculiar institution." Quite the reverse: he insisted that slavery provided far better conditions for black men and women than they would enjoy in Africa and certainly enjoyed better conditions than the

Northern wage slave, who had to grind out a pittance in a factory. To Johnson, free blacks were much worse off than Southern slaves. As governor of Tennessee in peacetime, he'd sanctioned the American Colonization Society's attempt to export freed slaves to Liberia, and now, as Tennessee's military governor, he'd be happy to shove them right out of his state.

Johnson and other prominent Unionists managed to get Tennessee exempted from the Emancipation Proclamation, but of late Johnson's proslavery rhetoric had cooled. The only way to destroy the Confederacy and save the Union, Johnson came to believe, was to accept emancipation. "If you persist in forcing the issue of slavery against the Government," he had shouted in 1862 during a Fourth of July rally, "I say in the face of Heaven, 'Give me my Government, and let the negroes go!'"

Johnson's policy had little to do with any change of heart, for as one of his devoted private secretaries later commented, Johnson "sometimes exhibited a morbid distress and feeling against the negroes." Rather, he feared the proslavery Unionists who were organizing against him. With another rung on the political ladder to climb, Andrew Johnson, no fool, realized that his political future lay with the Lincoln administration—and with the Unionists of the North, even if he was a Democrat and they were Republicans. (Louis Wigfall had been right when he accused Johnson of pandering to the North.) And Lincoln, who had taken Johnson's measure, knew how to manage him. "In my opinion the country now needs no special thing so much as some man of your ability, and position, to go to this work," Lincoln sweet-talked him, referring to the "work" of emancipation.

By the summer of 1863, Johnson supported immediate, unconditional emancipation. His reasoning was consistent with his hatred of the aristocrat: emancipation would liberate the *white* man from the tyranny of the plutocrat slaveholder. He did not for a minute believe "that the negro race is equal to the Anglo-Saxon—not at all."

A recruiting agent for black troops, Major George Stearns, was

sent to Nashville. Formerly one of the so-called secret six abolitionists who'd funded John Brown's Harper's Ferry raid, Stearns was appalled by what he found there: black men grabbed off the street and
pressed into service; if they resisted, they were shot. On his way
home from church, one such black man, Armstead Lewis, had
been marched to a recruitment camp where he was left out in the
cold with other black men, none of them given coats or blankets,
none of them allowed to light fires, all of them surrounded by
guards. "The colored men here are treated like brutes," an aghast
Stearns reported to Stanton.

Johnson was furious when he learned of the Stearns report. As
military governor, he, Andrew Johnson, should have sole jurisdiction over the recruitment of black soldiers, not some pie-eyed philanthropist with airy notions.

Seen in retrospect, Johnson's anger forecast his conduct in the
future, for his racial animus had never wavered, and it would never
change.

GENERAL CARL SCHURZ reminisced that in 1863, when he'd
called on Military Governor Johnson at the Nashville State House,
he was told that the governor had suddenly taken ill. A few days
later, when Johnson did meet with Schurz, he deflected all questions about his health in a way that made Schurz suspicious. Charles
Dana also remembered Military Governor Johnson in Nashville.
As Stanton's assistant secretary of war, Dana had been sent to investigate rumors about General Grant's drinking. Dana went to Johnson's office, where Johnson offered him a whiskey. Dana took a
glass but noticed that Johnson mixed his own drink with water.
"The theoretical, philosophical drinker pours out a little whiskey
and puts in almost no water at all—drinks it pretty nearly pure—"
Dana said, "but when a man gets to taking a good deal of water in
his whiskey, it shows he is in the habit of drinking a good deal."

This too is recollection. So was the story of a Tennessee acquaintance who later called on Johnson in the White House. Learning

he was ill, she claimed that she immediately understood him to be "either drunk or recovering from the effects of deep drinking." Charles Sumner remembered that when Johnson arrived in Washington for his inauguration as Vice President, he brought with him two bulbous bottles that held from three to ten gallons of liquor, which he freely distributed. A soldier staying on the same floor as Johnson at the Kirkwood House counted twenty-six glasses of whiskey go into Johnson's room.

Most of these stories—and countless others—were offered in a spirit of rancor, and many of the slanders appear to be without foundation. More believable is the point of view of those who said that in Tennessee everyone drank, and Johnson never concealed the fact that he did too, although never to excess. "The Governor had 'his infirmities,'" a companion explained, "but was 'all right,' on the whole." As another old-timer put it, "he never got too drunk to disremember his friends." Johnson's private secretary said Johnson did not take wine with his meals, "he never drank a cocktail in his life, never was in a barroom, and did not care for champagne. He did take two or three or four glasses of Robertson County whiskey some days," the secretary added. "And some days less, and some days and weeks no liquor at all." The secretary concluded that "Johnson would have been termed a strictly temperate man." And Treasury Secretary Hugh McCulloch observed that while Johnson might be intemperate in his speeches, he was never uncontrolled in his drinking. That's what Abraham Lincoln had reportedly said too. "I have known Andy a great many years, and he ain't no drunkard." A drinker, yes; a drunkard, no.

But at his inauguration as Vice President, Andrew Johnson was definitely smashed: "Drunk as a fool & made a fool of himself," a witness said. The Blair family bundled the mortified man off to their estate in Silver Spring, Maryland, where he could recover from whatever it was that he needed to recover from—malaria or typhoid, Frank Blair, Jr., publicly stated. Privately, they noted "our friend will get out [of] all this if—these things are the result of illness—but if it is followed up—why he is lost—& of this he had been made fully aware." Shortly after Johnson took the oath of office as President, he broke down again, and Montgomery Blair offered cover while admitting, "I regret the President's illness very much & still more the whiskey as to the cause of it."

If Johnson could control his drinking, his two eldest sons could not. Charles, the eldest, an affable young man remembered as kind and loveable, went on such a wild bender during the Democratic convention in Charleston in 1860 that his younger brother Robert had to hustle him quickly out of town. Three years later, when Charles was thirty-three, he fatally fell or was thrown from his horse. The word was that he'd been drunk. By then, Robert too had a problem. In 1859, at the age of twenty-four, Robert Johnson had successfully run for the Tennessee state legislature, and during the war, he raised a regiment. But he had a reputation for inebriation, and though drinking in the army usually passed unnoticed, General Rosecrans warned Andrew Johnson that his son's alcohol consumption had "become a subject of remark everywhere."

In the spring of 1863, Robert did fight admirably against an Alabama cavalry of about two thousand men and apparently took fifty prisoners, but the following fall, his father, disgusted by more reports of Robert's drinking, made him resign his commission. "I have said and now repeat that I feared you would be dismissed from the Army unless you reformed and took Command of your Regiment and give Some evidence of determination to Serve the country as a sober upright and honorable man," Johnson told his son. Robert said he'd do better: "*The intoxicating bowl goes to my lips no more,*" the young man promised. But a pattern had been set in motion: Robert would swear off liquor, his parents would believe him, then he'd backslide. In the spring of 1865, he wasn't even sober enough to understand that President Lincoln had been shot.

Once in the White House, Johnson appointed his handsome young son as his private secretary, and Robert loved the job. Men and women were always offering him all manner of reward for access to the President, so much so that soon gossips were talking about prostitutes hanging about Robert's office in broad daylight—

even alleging that Robert procured them for his father as well. Johnson tried to arrange a long sea voyage for his son, to no avail. Secretary of the Navy Gideon Welles, that staunch and cantankerous Johnson ally, fretted about Robert's continuing unreliability and finally threw up his hands. The young man was incorrigible. The Johnsons sent their son to what passed for treatment programs, also to no avail.

About a year after Andrew Johnson exited the White House, Robert Johnson purchased a bottle of laudanum from the local Greeneville pharmacy and swallowed its entire contents. He was thirty-five.

IN 1864, REPUBLICANS across the political spectrum understood that to win the war and abolish slavery they needed to re-elect Abraham Lincoln. Even though several had toyed—and some had more than toyed—with nominating a different candidate, Republicans did not want to risk losing the election by splitting the party. Radicals acknowledged they needed to entice disgruntled conservatives. And since Vice President Hannibal Hamlin brought nothing new to the ticket, they'd have to replace him.

Andrew Johnson, the military governor of Tennessee, a Southerner, a Democrat, seemed too good to be true. Yes, Johnson had owned slaves; yes, he had never cared a fig about abolition. That made his Unionist credentials impeccable, his propaganda value indisputable. Even Charles Sumner had doffed his hat, hailing Johnson as the very "faithful among the faithless."

It's been said Lincoln refused to tip the scales against Hamlin. John Nicolay and John Hay, Lincoln's secretaries, claimed Lincoln kept his distance—because that's what Lincoln told them. Journalist Noah Brooks, who also knew Lincoln, recalled that he'd been studiously silent on the matter of his running mate until after the Republican convention, when he said, "Andy Johnson, I think, is a good man."

Other accounts of how Johnson came to be Vice President similarly suggest that Lincoln stayed impartial. But these accounts don't seem credible. Why would a sitting President, a gifted political tactician rightly concerned he might not be re-elected, a man who deeply felt the deaths by war of so many men, and who devoted himself to abolishing slavery, why would this President leave the selection of a running mate to others—unless of course he knew that his vaunted impartiality served to camouflage his handiwork.

A more plausible point of view is that Lincoln worked diligently, but covertly; he did not wish to appear disloyal to Hamlin. Yet whether Lincoln pulled strings or stayed genuinely impartial, he didn't protect Hamlin. Reportedly, he asked journalist John Forney to help nominate Johnson, and presumably he said much the same to Republican lawyer and convention delegate Abram Dittenhoefer, who claimed he knew "from the President's own lips," that Lincoln preferred Johnson. Johnson's private secretary claimed Johnson was privy to these secret machinations. "I know it to be a fact that Mr. Lincoln desired the nomination of Johnson for Vice President," the secretary asserted, "and that [William G. 'Parson'] Brownlow and [Horace] Maynard went to Baltimore at request of Lincoln and Johnson to promote the nomination."

Parson Brownlow and Horace Maynard were Tennessee Unionists who'd been among Johnson's most vocal enemies, but they'd recently worked closely with him to quash the rebellion in Tennessee. And they did speak persuasively at the Baltimore convention on Johnson's behalf. "I have battled against Andrew Johnson perseveringly, systematically and terribly, for a quarter of a century," Parson Brownlow said. "[Now] we are hand-in-hand fighting the same battle for the preservation of the Union. We will fight for each other against the common foe. He is now at the head of our new State Government; and I take pleasure in saying that he is the right man in the right place."

There were others who worked for Johnson because they assumed they were doing the President's bidding, whether they were or not, and because they had their own motives. Lincoln's secretary of state, William Seward, and Seward's friend Thurlow Weed, along with Henry Raymond, editor of *The New York Times*, both known as "Seward men," wanted to prevent New York War Democrat Daniel Dickinson from getting the vice-presidential nomination. If Dickinson was on the ticket, and Lincoln won, Seward would have to resign from the cabinet: two men from New York could not traditionally occupy such powerful positions in the administration at the same time. So Seward men turned into Johnson men—and Seward remained a Johnson man, which continued to suit his purposes.

At the convention, Andrew Johnson won the most votes on the first ballot (200, as compared to Hamlin's 150 and Dickinson's 108), but they weren't enough. Pennsylvania threw its votes to him, and Kentucky too, and then the stampede began, giving Johnson 494 votes, and Hamlin 17, Dickinson 9. The nomination was made unanimous, and Andrew Johnson of Tennessee was announced the vice-presidential candidate.

"Can't you find a candidate for Vice-President in the United States," Thaddeus Stevens griped, "without going down to one of those damned rebel provinces to pick one up?"

Manton Marble, editor of the Democratic newspaper the *New York World*, wasn't happy either, though for completely different reasons. "The age of statesmen is gone," Marble wailed. "The age of rail-splitters and tailors, of buffoons, boors and fanatics has succeeded. God save the Republic!"

IN NASHVILLE, CANNONS boomed out the good news. Vice-presidential nominee Andrew Johnson addressed a jubilant crowd in front of the St. Cloud Hotel. "Let the war for the Union go on," he shouted, "and the Stars and Stripes be bathed, if need be, in a nation's blood, till law be restored, and freedom firmly established."

But he wanted nothing to do with negro equality. Work, yes: the freed people might work—and "make something for themselves"—if they could. He said it again: he wanted nothing to do with equality. As for slavery and those rebels who accused him of helping to abolish it, he reminded the crowd that he had warned everyone that slavery would be better protected inside the Union than out of it. And it wasn't Lincoln who'd freed the slaves. And certainly *he* didn't free the slaves. The South freed the slaves. The decision to *secede* had freed them.

A huge torchlight parade of black men and women then landed at the steps of the Capitol, where Johnson again spoke out. "Looking over this vast crowd of colored people," he boomed, "and reflecting through what a storm of persecution and obloquy they are compelled to pass, I am almost induced to wish that, as in the days of old, a Moses might arise who should lead them safely to their promised land of freedom and happiness."

A reporter on the scene heard shouting. "We want no Moses but you!"

"Humble and unworthy as I am," Johnson shouted back, "if no other better shall be found, I will indeed be your Moses, and lead you through the Red Sea of war and bondage, to a fairer future of liberty and peace."

Although Johnson did not specify the exact whereabouts of this fairer future, several of his supporters advised Moses to locate fair Canaan somewhere beyond the Rio Grande—near Texas perhaps, but at the least far, very, very far away.

The South Victorious

"Peace if possible. Justice at any rate."

—WENDELL PHILLIPS

In the summer of 1865, a few miles north of Decatur, Alabama, a paroled Confederate soldier lured a former slave into the woods. The man was said to have gotten too "saucy" when he learned he was free, so the ex-soldier shot him three times in the head and hurled his body into a river. In Mobile, white men and their dogs guarded the roadways, and they crisscrossed waterways by boat in search of black men and women who'd left plantations where they'd once worked. If captured, they could be shot or hanged. "The white people tell them that they were free during the war," a white man said, "but the war is now over, and they must go to work again as before." Andrew Johnson had been President fewer than four months.

Near Hilton Head, South Carolina, a former Treasury agent named Albert Browne heard of the young black boy who'd been ambushed by a pardoned Confederate soldier who shot him fifty-seven times, mostly in the face and head. "What most men mean to-day by the 'president's plan of reconstruction' is the pardon of every rebel for the crime of rebellion, and the utter refusal to pardon a single black loyalist for the 'crime' of being black," Thomas Wentworth Higginson tersely observed.

A black woman, pregnant and too sick to stay at her spinning wheel, was stripped naked, gagged, kicked, and whipped by her white employer for not spinning more. Traveling south in the summer of 1865, Clara Barton saw that the lashes had cut so deep into the woman's back she could barely put on a dress. This was said to have been an isolated incident—deplorable, yes, but isolated.

Black men and women in Andersonville, Georgia, were told that because Abraham Lincoln was dead, they were no longer free. Mary Stewart, a former slave, was working for Thomas Day in Tangipahoa, Louisiana. When Day's son told her "he was going to kill the damned free niggers," he wasn't exaggerating. He then grabbed her, cut her several times with his pocket knife, and dragged her into his mother's house. Lucky for Mary Stewart, Day's mother put a stop to it and Stewart ran away. This too was supposed to have been an isolated incident.

In Twiggs County, Georgia, a white man fired at a black man strolling down the street—"apparently for the fun of the thing," said a person who witnessed the killing. This was an isolated incident, the witness said. "These negro-shooters and their accomplices were no doubt a small minority of the people," he claimed. The "better class" of white men and women, he also noted, didn't "deem it prudent" to assist in the arrest, never mind the trial, of the murderers. "The idea of a *nigger* having the power of bringing a *white* man before a tribunal!" a member of this better class exclaimed. "The Southern people a'n't going to stand that."

In Norfolk, Virginia, a black soldier was hanged near the black children's school so that the children could see his body when they looked out the classroom window. When federal troops were removed from Attala County, Mississippi, two black men and two white Union-sympathizers were murdered. In Nashville, Tennessee, where Johnson had been military governor, a Union man told a federal soldier that "if you take away the military from Tennessee, the buzzards can't eat up the niggers as fast as we'll kill 'em." Similarly, in Columbia, South Carolina, Major-General Adelbert Ames, future governor of Mississippi, said that if military left the area, the black population would be at serious risk. "They will be in a much worse condition than when slaves—for then they were worth from five to ten hundred dollars and were objects of care—now they are not worth the ground in which they are buried."

Journalist Whitelaw Reid, traveling through the South for a year right after the war, discounted as hyperbolic most of the tales he'd heard of shootings and whippings. Regardless, he relayed the story of a physician near Greenville, Mississippi, who threatened to shoot his employee, a black man, when the man didn't perform some small task. The employee ran, and the doctor did shoot him, dead. The doctor's wife had tried to stop her husband so he shot her too. This was also said to be an isolated incident.

One local paper accused Northerners of "seizing upon isolated instances of violence and crime in the Southern States—especially if the negro is in any way a victim—and commenting upon them to the prejudice of the returning loyalty and sense of justice of the Southern people." But Reid began to wonder. "People had not got over regarding negroes as something other than human," he decided.

There had been an epidemic of such apparently isolated incidents since Andrew Johnson took the oath of office, but Johnson declared he didn't believe the "*sensation* letter-writers and editors, who were endeavoring to create the impression that there exists in the South disaffection and dissatisfaction."

"The 'situation' is not decidedly smooth, yet, all things considered it is much better than could be expected," William Holden, North Carolina's provisional governor, accounted for the murders. "There are malcontents, radicals, & not good men who are engaged in misrepresenting facts & fermenting strife for certain purposes." Holden warned Johnson about a "Conflict of races" if the "old order of things" wasn't quickly restored, or if federal troops weren't removed from the South.

Everyone agreed about one thing: the situation was serious.

GRASS HAD SPROUTED up between the broken paving stones, and almost everywhere you looked, there were burned-out fields, trackless railroads, and trees that had been blown apart. In Charleston, South Carolina, white men and women, gaunt and worn, drifted aimlessly along the splintered wharves. Although the cannons had not destroyed the stately homes near the harbor, their windows had been smashed, their floors had buckled, and the walls lurched at ridiculous angles, while wagons rolled into a city already overflowing with refugees, black and white, desperate for jobs and shelter and food. According to Whitelaw Reid, residents of the city were fast becoming as vituperative and treasonous as they had been before the war.

In Richmond, the police stopped black men and women as they walked to market or to church, demanding they show the pass recently issued by Provost Marshal General Patrick. If they didn't have a pass, he ordered that they be arrested, and soon about 250 people were detained. Workers too were frequently seized, the police claiming that their passes must be counterfeit. One such man was Albert Brooks, a former slave who owned a livery stable that employed several black men. The police demanded Brooks shell out over $1,100 if he wanted to get out of jail.

In June of 1865, a delegation of seven black residents of Richmond arrived at the White House to protest the treatment of the black population. Richmond's mayor, Joseph Mayo, was an unrepentant Confederate, the delegation told President Johnson, and "our old masters have become our enemies, who seek not only to oppress our people but to thwart the designs of the Federal Government." Journalist Thomas Morris Chester, also black, read the petition aloud. "When we saw the glorious old flag again streaming over the capitol," it concluded, "we thought the power of these wicked men was at an end." President Johnson listened, received the accompanying affidavits, promised to look into the complaint, and told the men to be patient. He forwarded the petition to the head of the Freedmen's Bureau while a writer for the Richmond *Commercial Bulletin* scoffed at the grumblers, who'd poked "their woolly heads inside of the executive doors."

Later that month, the President also received a petition signed by almost fifteen hundred black people from South Carolina, asking that they be allowed to vote to protect themselves against the "unjust legislation" threatening their safety and their freedom. Johnson was courteous but impassive.

At the same time he was pardoning former rebels or rebel sympathizers at an alarming rate of almost one hundred a day, and now these pardoned Confederates were beginning to hold state offices. Colonel J.P.H. Russ of Raleigh, appointed postmaster, said his position on the slavery question was clear: if he had the power, he'd re-enslave everyone now free. Alexander Stephens, the Vice President of the Confederacy, was expected to return to Congress in the fall. "The present pardoning process will restore and unite the South and reinstate the worst Rebels in power," said a leading Republican.

Throughout the country, black men and women were meeting in assemblies, town halls, small gatherings, freedmen's conventions, and churches to discuss their rights and their future. In Vicksburg, Mississippi, and in Natchez, Tennessee, blacks prepared petitions claiming their right to vote. In Nashville, the Reverend James D. Lynch, a free black man who would later serve as Mississippi's secretary of state, reminded folks that "when the nation stood trembling on the precipice, the black man came to the rescue." In New Orleans, the National Union Republican Club, composed of both black and white men, arranged a celebration of freedom for the Fourth of July, and then under the auspices of the Friends of Universal Suffrage, black and white together backed voting rights for all adult men; they sent the young lawyer Henry Clay Warmoth, a white Radical formerly from Illinois, to speak for them in Congress. Black men and women drafted resolutions that they hoped would receive a hearing. One such, by a group of black men who met at the Union Street Methodist Church in Petersburg, Virginia, claimed they were entitled to vote as "true and loyal citizens of the United States, who had contributed militarily to the Revolution and the recent war."

The black citizens of Alexandria, Virginia, delivered a petition to President Johnson asking that the federal government retain control over the Alexandria city government, lest they be deprived of their civil rights. Johnson politely referred the petition to the War Department. James Gloucester, a black clergyman in New York, told the new head of the Freedmen's Bureau, General Oliver Otis Howard, that the Bureau should be staffed with "intelligent, experienced, uneducated, upright colored men"—but it had not been; it was staffed with white men. Though he was temperamentally conservative, Howard listened carefully and then confidentially told his wife that, after talking frequently with the President, he was "quite apprehensive, that the freedmen's rights will not be cared for."

Branches of the National Equal Rights League were also springing up, particularly in the South. Founded in 1864 in upstate New York by Frederick Douglass, Henry Highland Garnet, and John Mercer Langston, the League was committed to securing full citizenship for blacks—and voting rights for black men who'd fought in an American war. Langston, a Virginia-born lawyer and the League's first president, had encountered Johnson in Tennessee, and saw the new President just days after Lincoln's assassination. On behalf of the League, Langston asked that Johnson continue the work begun by Lincoln: executing all laws that protected the rights and privileges of citizenship for black people. Johnson told Langston that as the friend of "colored fellow-citizens," he'd make sure slavery was fully abolished and black men enfranchised, Langston recalled. Johnson added that his own past history as a staunch Unionist and a protector of the Constitution guaranteed that his future conduct could be trusted, which in a way it could: when the League petitioned Congress to pass a constitutional amendment guaranteeing that every state government prohibit such discriminatory legislation as the black codes, Johnson was indifferent.

Having issued proclamations and a huge number of pardons, more and more with each passing day, Johnson was roundly praised

The lawyer John Mercer Langston, leader of the National Equal Rights League, later served as consul-general in Haiti. He was the first African American elected to Congress from Virginia; he was also the great-uncle of the twentieth-century poet Langston Hughes.

as evenhanded, unprejudiced, and magnanimous, particularly by the Democrats. Advertising themselves as broad enough to embrace all patriots, in its state by state conventions, Democrats began to welcome, or entice, Johnson back into the fold, many of them contending that he'd never left. Its press reminded readers that though the Democrats weren't instrumental in the election of Lincoln and Johnson, "it did not desert the former when the nation was in peril, and it will not be the less ready to support the latter with its counsels and its cooperation." Johnson "sailed before the wind," *The New York Herald* praised him. After meeting with Johnson in Washington, Democratic leader Samuel Tilden reassured another leader, Samuel Barlow, that the President would soon be withdrawing federal troops from the South.

Johnson supporters among the Democrats—and even some Republicans—were weary of what they called the "everlasting negro question." The more cautious and conservative Republicans, like the Democrats, balked not just at voting rights but at any kind of federal aid to freedpeople. "We are in danger of *too much* northern managing for the negro," the Reverend Henry Ward Beecher said. "The black man is just like the white in this—that he should be left, & obliged, to take care of himself & suffer & enjoy, according as he creates the means of either."

And conservative Republicans and Democrats assailed Radicals: Wendell Phillips was the king of lunatics, Thad Stevens a bully, and Charles Sumner an officious bore nattering ad nauseum about equality and suffrage. Democrats also liked to remind Radical Republicans about their hypocrisy: they would give black men the vote but exclude white women. White women were at least able to read and write, and while they couldn't vote, they didn't make a fuss about it.

Actually, they were making a fuss. Elizabeth Cady Stanton and the National Women's Loyal League had collected almost 400,000 signatures of people in favor of women's right to vote. But many Radical Republicans flinched, saying they did not want to confuse the issue: mixing up women in the call for the vote "would lose for the negro far more than we should gain for the woman." Elizabeth Cady Stanton would have none of it. "Do you believe the African race is composed entirely of males?" she briskly replied.

"As Abraham Lincoln said: 'One war at a time,'" Wendell Phillips answered her. "This hour belongs to the Negro." To Phillips and other Radical Republicans, and even some women, the war had been a just war, fought to abolish slavery. And there would be no justice until de facto slavery—the means by which Southerners and Northerners still treated the black population unfairly—had been eradicated. Only the vote could do that.

Elizabeth Cady Stanton didn't back down. "Is there not danger that he, once intrenched in all his inalienable rights, may be an added power to hold us at bay?" That is, if men and men only were allowed to vote, then all women, black and white, would still be subject to men. "The disfranchised all make the same demand," she told Phillips, "and the same logic and justice which secures suffrage for one class gives it to all."

It didn't matter. Phillips and a number of Radical Republicans failed to see that if the door closed against women, it would likely remain shut for a very long time—Stanton predicted as many as a hundred years. Though a firm supporter of women's rights for more than two decades, Phillips, who'd never before caved to political expediency, believed he had to omit them. On many other issues—abolition, workers' rights, justice for Native Americans—he would in the future fight hard. Still, for him, voting rights for black men was now essential, and it would have to come first even if he might admit, in a pinch, that voting rights for women would not come easily or soon.

BACK IN 1864, Wendell Phillips had called Abraham Lincoln a first-rate second-rate man. Worried that Lincoln wouldn't fight to enfranchise black men, he refused to support Lincoln's re-election, passionately believing that only the ballot guaranteed justice for all. "Give the negro a vote in his hand, and there is not a politician, from Abraham Lincoln to the laziest loafer in the lowest ward in this city, who would not do him honor," Phillips had cried. "From the possession of political rights, a man gets means to clutch equal opportunities of education, and a fair space to work. Give a man his vote, and you give him tools to work and arms to protect himself." But many of his friends in the anti-slavery movement, notably William Lloyd Garrison, seemed to think that with slavery abolished, their job was finished.

If anyone was utterly unlike Andrew Johnson, it was Wendell Phillips. Tall and lean, patrician and handsome, a *Mayflower* descendant and a graduate of the prestigious Boston Latin School, Wendell Phillips finished Harvard University when he was just sixteen (he was born in 1811) and then studied the law, also at Harvard. In 1835, when he was twenty-four, he saw a proslavery mob drag Garrison, a rope tied round his neck, through the crooked streets of Boston. From that moment on, Phillips said, "I never could have been anything but an abolitionist."

Two years later, at Faneuil Hall in Boston, Phillips spoke without notes, as he always would, to protest a proslavery mob's murder of abolitionist editor Elijah Parish Lovejoy in Illinois. The doors of Faneuil Hall had been closed to abolitionists or anyone condemning Lovejoy's murder, but Phillips defiantly strode to the lectern to call out those weak-kneed Bostonians in public office, particularly the attorney general, or anyone else who'd condoned the murder or looked the other way. Phillips' speech effectively ended his career in the law. Clients deserted him, friends dropped him, conservative Boston rejected him. "He knew the penalty of his course," a friend recalled. "He paid it cheerfully."

Married to Ann Greene, an invalid heiress who seldom left her room but whose radicalism was said to be even more intense than his, Phillips embarked on a public career as agitator, tirelessly traveling from city to city—he was famous by the 1850s—to campaign against slavery. Detractors christened him the great apostle of the abolitionist cranks, a badge he wore with pride. "The republic which sinks to sleep, trusting to constitutions and machinery, to politicians and statesmen, for the safety of its liberties, never will have any," Phillips declared. With a broad-brimmed, slightly battered gray hat pulled down over his disappearing hairline, he looked like an old botanist, an acquaintance said, and you couldn't really believe that a man "so simple, so affable, is the nettlesome speaker, and the one placed by everybody in the foremost ranks of American orators."

His method was conversational, explained abolitionist Thomas Wentworth Higginson. Phillips would begin a speech in a fairly low voice, as if he were confiding something to a good friend, and when he repeated what he'd said, which he frequently did, he began to raise his voice ever so slightly. "The effect was absolutely disarming," Higginson recalled. Phillips used no spread-eagle rhetoric, and he spoke without affectation. And though his many critics called him sarcastic, impudent, and violent, at least in his speeches, he had fans who called him "direct, simple, persuasive, and luminous." They loved the tenor of his voice, his point-blank candor, and his obvious sincerity.

Opposition roused him, and he relished it. Detractors often met him with raised fists. A man of courage, he couldn't have cared

Nationally renowned Wendell Phillips gave up the profession of law and his social standing to speak out on causes such as equal rights; the inscription on his calling card read, "Peace if possible. Justice at any rate." Phillips detested Andrew Johnson (who returned the favor) and considered most members of Congress cowards.

less—he'd been pelted with apples, eggs, and rocks. "Always aristocratic in aspect," Higginson remembered, "he was never more so
than when walking through the streets of his own Boston with a
howling mob about him." But to be safe, Phillips packed a gun—he
was a good shot—particularly during the secessionist crisis of 1860–
1861, for which he was blamed. He was blamed for many things: for
John Brown's raid, for example, in which he had no part. He seemed
to court blame. As the historian Richard Hofstadter once observed,
Phillips viewed himself as an inveterate agitator. The inscription on
his small white calling card read, "Peace if possible. Justice at any
rate. W. P."

Men and women flocked to hear him, particularly during the
summer of 1865, when he insisted that Johnson's policies were betraying Republicans, Unionists, and blacks, and he declared the
President "a force to be resisted, not one to be counted on our side."
That fall, he went further. Bostonians packed the gorgeous Music
Hall on Winter Street to hear Phillips proclaim "The South Victorious."

The South victorious? How was that possible? Phillips suavely
answered: What principle had the South surrendered? Certainly
not state sovereignty. "The same oligarchy that broke up the Union
condescends to reenter it, with the same steps, with the same usage,
under the flag of the same principle," he sang out. Former Confederates are taking cover under Johnson's wing, Phillips continued,
and if Johnson isn't a traitor, he's definitely an enemy. Yes, sure,
slavery has been abolished, and black men and women can no longer be sold on the auction block. But were they free to set their own
price for their labor? Could they own property? Get married? Could
they choose to live where they wanted or travel freely? Could they
attend schools—and what schools? What about the ability to bear
witness or sit on a jury? Could they vote? In short, were they U.S.
citizens with all the rights of their neighbors? Didn't they possess
natural rights and shouldn't there be sufficient civil rights, never
mind political rights, legislated to protect them? "That is liberty."
Phillips was by now shouting. The audience cheered, and Phillips,

boarding trains from town to town, took his blazing speech on the road. The battle lines of peace were taking shape.

ANDREW JOHNSON WAS sure he knew Major-General Carl Schurz, so when Schurz returned from a fact-finding expedition to the Southern states, Johnson was equally sure Schurz had come to the conclusion about the South that Johnson wanted to hear.

Johnson had met General Schurz during the war when their objectives had been the same: to crush the rebellion. The Prussian émigré hated the very idea of disunion. Once in America, he had settled in Wisconsin, was admitted to the bar, and became the fluent anti-slavery advocate who, in 1860, as chair of the Wisconsin delegation to the Republican national convention, helped secure the German-American vote for Lincoln. Lincoln rewarded him with a consulship in Spain, and the pointy-bearded Schurz gracefully accepted. But he found the duties of a diplomat insipid, so after the war began, he returned to America, and commissioned as brigadier-general, he fought at Second Bull Run, Chancellorsville, and Gettysburg. He soon discovered, though, that his performance on the battlefield was not quite as indispensable as his performance with a pen.

Shattered by Lincoln's death, for a while Schurz, like so many others, retained his faith in Johnson. What Johnson saw in Schurz, beyond their shared Unionism, is more baffling. After Johnson decriminalized most of the former Confederates and began pardoning the rest, Schurz began to criticize the new President. "I fear that he has not that clearness of purpose and firmness of character he was supposed to have," Schurz told Charles Sumner. Southern delegations were crowding into Washington, "almost all governed by their old prejudices," Schurz reported, and these prejudiced delegations were influencing Johnson. Schurz was alarmed, informing Johnson that, strictly speaking, Johnson's North Carolina proclamation — his appointing a civil governor and ordering him to call a convention — was an unconstitutional usurpation of power.

It's not clear why Johnson sent Schurz to the South to offer his observations on conditions there. As one bystander remarked, Johnson was a man of moods, and his mood must have been just right when he and Schurz discussed the idea. In any case, the foreign-born Schurz could not run for President, and Johnson had no reason to fear him. He told Schurz to go, and that he'd heed his recommendations. Egotistically, Schurz believed him.

Almost certainly Schurz misunderstood his mission from the start—or misrepresented it—because he allowed Charles Sumner to arrange that his reports be printed in the *Boston Daily Advertiser*, without attribution, for a fee. That way, Schurz could pay for his trip, or so he later claimed. It was alleged, not without good reason, that he was happy to go South to furnish Radical Republicans with propaganda for their crusade to get black men the vote.

Despite whatever Johnson or Schurz thought the other man intended, or what either of them wanted or hoped the other might do, a collision was inevitable. It occurred when Mississippi Governor William Sharkey began organizing a state militia, composed of ex-rebels, to serve as the state police. General Henry Slocum, head of the Department of Mississippi, protested. The federal army was the state's enforcement agency; a state militia was not. Johnson initially agreed with General Slocum, but Sharkey heatedly explained to both men that the presence of black troops—some of these federal troops were black—posed a threat to the people (white); that all federal troops, or at least those posted in the South, should be white; that the Freedmen's Bureau was nothing but a curse that humiliated the (white) South; that there were rumors of an insurrection (black) brewing. The state therefore needed its own militia, Sharkey concluded.

Schurz was shaken. Who would put a fox in charge of the henhouse?

Sharkey may appear to be a Unionist, Schurz told Johnson, but he was surrounded by secessionists with whom Sharkey, a former slaveholder, seemed to agree. Imagine allowing the militia of a belligerent country to be reorganized right after that country had been defeated: impossible. And the Mississippi that Schurz visited was nothing like the one Sharkey liked to describe. Schurz found the black troops to be honest, reliable, and disciplined. Outrages weren't perpetrated by them—but *against* them. And the presence of federal troops, black or white, was absolutely necessary if law and order were to be maintained not just in Mississippi but in the whole of the South. "It is a stubborn fact that our truest friends are threatened and persecuted and that the negro is denied his freedom wherever the population has a chance to act upon its own impulses without being immediately checked," Schurz said. "The struggle against the results of the war is by no means at an end."

Johnson telegraphed Sharkey that if the new state convention were to draft a constitution that enfranchised literate blacks and those who owned property worth more than $250, "you would completely disarm the adversary and set an example other states would follow," he suggested. Johnson assumed there were few literate blacks or property-owners and that his suggestion was therefore harmless. But smart: "As a consequence," Johnson continued, "the radicals, who are wild upon negro franchise will be completely foiled, in their attempts to keep the Southern States from renewing their relations to the Union."

Sharkey did nothing. And Johnson never followed up, in Mississippi or elsewhere.

Schurz was angry. "If the President persists in pursuing a false course," he told his wife, "he must not be surprised if, later, I bring into the field against him all the artillery I am assembling now. He will find the armament pretty heavy."

Schurz did launch an attack in a scathing forty-six-page report, followed by sixty pages of documentation, which he composed on his return to Washington. Men and women of questionable loyalty were taking the loyalty oath, Schurz wrote, and they were thereby legally capable of holding office despite their continued sympathy with the rebels. Take Mr. Rodgers in New Orleans, who as superintendent of schools during the war had rubbed out the initials "U.S." in the history books and replaced them with "C.S." (for Confederate States). By the fall of 1865, Rodgers had been appointed to his old job. Meanwhile, Yankees and Union soldiers were still considered enemies, and Southern Unionists lived in a state of fear should federal troops be recalled and the Freedmen's Bureau eliminated. Highwaymen ruled the roads, and cotton-, horse-, and cattle-stealing were rampant.

Treason was not odious in the South, Schurz concluded. "Men who are honorable in their dealings with their white neighbors, will cheat a Negro without feeling a single twinge of their honor. To kill a Negro, they do not deem murder; to debauch a Negro woman, they do not think fornication; to take the property away from a Negro, they do not consider robbery. The people boast that when they get freedmen's affairs in their own hands, to use their own expression, 'the niggers will catch hell.'"

Yet Schurz was not completely unsympathetic to Southern whites—whether those who lost their plantations or whose farms were heavily mortgaged, or widows with children left to fend for themselves. He was aware of the many destitute people who indirectly depended on these farms and plantations to keep their own businesses afloat. He was aware too that the returning Confederate soldier did not easily find employment, as did his counterpart in the North. He saw wrecked homesteads, blackened chimneys standing in empty fields, shoeless boys and girls, and entire communities ravenous and sulky. These people were understandably suspicious.

But large numbers of freedmen still worked on plantations and were not being paid; they were subject to unfair contracts, poor conditions, and physical violence. The white planters believed that a system of free labor could never succeed—one Georgia planter, to prove his case, said that his black employee had actually refused to submit to a whipping. Other freedmen and -women flocked to cities and seaports, where they were penniless, jobless, and reviled. "Black codes," as they were called, deprived them of the freedom to travel, to testify in court, to open a business, to carry arms, to hunt or fish without permission, and in one weird case to buy or sell goods without written consent. And murder? "During my two days sojourn at Atlanta, one negro was stabbed with fatal effect on the street, and three were poisoned, one of whom died," Schurz wrote. "While I was at Montgomery, one negro was cut across the throat evidently with intent to kill, and another was shot."

These were not isolated incidents.

Schurz's conclusions—the conclusions that most incensed Johnson—were unambiguous: "One reason why the Southern people are so slow in accommodating themselves to the new order of things is, that they confidently expect soon to be permitted to regulate matters according to their own notions." This was a slap at Johnson's policy. "Every concession made to them by the Government has been taken as an encouragement to persevere in this hope," Schurz continued. "Hence their anxiety to have their State governments restored at once, to have the troops withdrawn, and the Freedmen's Bureau abolished."

It was obvious to Schurz that the federal government would have to prevent the South from falling at once "into the chaos of a general collision between its different elements." But if the black man had a voice in government—if he had the right to vote—then he would find the "best permanent protection against oppressive class-legislation, as well as individual persecution."

"A voter is a man of influence," Schurz declared, "small as that influence may be in the single individual, it becomes larger when that individual belongs to a numerous class of voters who are ready to make common cause with him for the protection of his rights."

Johnson is said to have quipped that so far his only mistake as President was letting Schurz go South. He had hardened, and when pushed, he lost his temper. Again he proclaimed, this time to the governor of Missouri, that "this is a country for white men and, by God, as long as I am president it shall be a government for white men." Many Republicans professed shock yet some of them defended the President. "We think it likely he did say so," temporized *The Chicago Times*, which then lay the blame at the feet of Radical Republicans. "If he used the language attributed to him, it was undoubtedly in reply to fanaticism and impudence."

Charles Sumner arranged to print Schurz's report—over 100,000 copies were distributed—at around the same time that the balmy observations of General Ulysses S. Grant appeared. Assuming that Grant would support Johnson's policy, which he then did, in November the President hurriedly dispatched Grant to the South to offset the Schurz testimony. And since Grant, the general who had vanquished the South, had not tarnished his reputation with incautious or partisan speech—under the guidance of advisers, the general hardly spoke at all—he would be admired for his forbearance and, better yet, the public would believe him.

Grant did not disappoint. Or at least he did not disappoint the President. When he arrived in South Carolina, soldiers who eagerly awaited him discovered a "plain, unpretentious, farmer like–looking man. . . . One would scarcely pick him out of the crowd as the hero he is." But Grant was on a whirlwind trip and spent only one day in Raleigh, two in Charleston, and a day each in Savannah and Augusta. Generously entertained by gracious white Southerners, who doubtless swayed him, Grant presumably said that if suffrage were insisted upon as a condition of reconstruction, it would certainly lead to a "war of races."

Grant did advise Johnson against removing the military from the region, although he agreed that the presence of black troops was incendiary and demoralizing—to the local whites, that is. He suggested that only white troops be stationed there. The young French correspondent for the Paris *Temps*, Georges Clemenceau, called Grant's milquetoast report a prop in Johnson's theater of restoration.

Were Northern visitors to the South finding what they wanted to find and seeing only what they wanted to see? Grant's senior aide-de-camp, Cyrus Comstock, thought not, and in his diary recorded the bitterness that white Southerners bore black men and women. Seeing what he wanted to see was the charge leveled against Schurz, a charge Schurz had anticipated, vowing he'd never have taken the mission in the first place "had I not felt that whatever preconceived opinions I might carry with me to the south, I should be ready to abandon or modify, as my perception of facts and circumstances might command their abandonment or modification." But his worst fears seemed to have come true. And he confirmed the worst fears of Sumner and of Stevens and of Phillips and of all those others growing disenchanted, if not outright hostile, to the policies of Andrew Johnson.

MEN IN GOVERNMENT or near it—whether William Seward or Salmon Chase or Montgomery Blair or Andrew Johnson—may be motivated by ideals but are just as often driven by a love of power and are susceptible to personal aggrandizement. The same could be said for Carl Schurz who, toying with the idea of becoming a journalist, took a position as Washington correspondent for the *New-York Tribune*. (He did not stay at the post long; soon he relocated to Detroit and then St. Louis to edit newspapers there.) Even the seventy-two-year-old Thaddeus Stevens briefly wondered if he might leave the House of Representatives for the Senate, although his enemies would never let that happen. But the imposing, pedantic Charles Sumner seemed as free of mixed motives as anyone in government could be, and in any case his congressional seat was fairly secure.

Having tried to persuade Andrew Johnson of the wrongness of his position and the rightness of his own, Charles Sumner had lost patience. "He has all the narrowness and ignorance of a certain class of whites," Sumner complained, "who have always looked upon the colored race as out of the pale of humanity."

Many Republicans still hoped that Johnson could be persuaded to consider giving the black man the vote, despite the President's insistence that suffrage was a matter for the states to decide—and despite his dogged assertion that suffrage would bring on a war between the races. Yet though many moderate Republicans were convinced that black suffrage, and suffrage alone, could prevent rebels from returning to power, they counseled patience. "Some foolish men among us are all the while bristling up for fight and seem anxious to make a rupture with Johnson," Ohio Representative James

Garfield moderately said. "I think we should assume that he is with us, treat him kindly, without suspicion and go on in a firm, calmly considered course, leaving him to make the breach with the party if any is made. I doubt he would do it under such circumstances." Similarly, the mercurial publisher of the *New-York Tribune*, Horace Greeley, wrote to the speaker of the house, Schuyler Colfax, "I pray you to take care that we do nothing calculated to drive the President into the arms of our adversaries. Let us respect his convictions and thus impel him to respect ours."

Republicans were also aware that in October and November, three states (Connecticut, Minnesota, Wisconsin) had voted down a ballot that included a constitutional amendment allowing the enfranchisement of black men. Republicans in those states had largely backed suffrage, but Democrats had voted against it. "The Connecticut vote *is* a very heavy blow, and a very bad indication," the editor Charles Eliot Norton acknowledged. "Johnson will feel much relieved by it." Going forward then, Norton moderately advised not advocating "negro rights" so much as "the principles of American democracy."

"Negro suffrage is not the main point," Norton starchily continued, "but equal political rights & privileges." In Pennsylvania, the Republican convention hadn't even mentioned black suffrage. It was "premature and unpopular," Thaddeus Stevens sighed. In light of these recent votes—and Johnson's intransigence—Republicans would have to change their political strategy. They would have to play down black suffrage and push hard instead for civil rights: the rights of citizenship, such as equal protection under the law.

For the President's behavior continued to be worrisome—and it was not just his proclamations that troubled the Republicans. "Prest. Johnson is said to be sick—seriously so," remarked Henry J. Raymond of the Johnson-leaning *New York Times*, "while others speak mysteriously of his *habits*." The allusion to "habits" was obvious: the chief executive was drinking far too much.

Johnson remained indifferent to gossip and unresponsive to criticism. For Andrew Johnson relied on Andrew Johnson. He could defy and then outlast the Jefferson Davises and the Southern planters who scorned him. As the grouchy but loyal Navy Secretary Gideon Welles would comment, Andrew Johnson would never truckle to partisans, fanatics, Radicals, Republicans, office-seekers—or to blacks, whom Welles also dismissed. Johnson was a proud, vain, and insecure man who distrusted almost everyone, and his talent for pitting himself against almost everyone, his friend Welles went on to say, would pillory him and warp the course of the entire country for years and years to come.

CHAPTER SIX

Not a "White Man's Government"

"This is not a 'white man's Government.'
To say so is political blasphemy."

—THADDEUS STEVENS

December 1865

Edward McPherson, the balding clerk of the House of Representatives, banged his gavel and opened a new chapter of American history.

For almost eight months, Andrew Johnson had been running the government completely without Congress. The legislature had not been in session since Johnson took the oath of office, and so he'd been governing without its approval, approbation, or interference, as if he were king. That had to stop. On Monday, December 4, 1865, the Thirty-Ninth Congress, with its Republican majority, was convening at last.

In the corridors and the galleries, it might have been a normal day. People shook hands and greeted one another pleasantly, although everyone was anxious about what might happen when delegates from the former rebel states appeared. Would they sweep into the very Congress from which they had seceded, or would they be turned away, their entrance to the great halls blocked?

Because the Constitution allowed Congress to judge the qualifications of its own members, the House managers could refuse to seat anyone they wanted, and Radical Republicans certainly hoped to bar men like Alexander Stephens, who'd been the Vice President of the Confederacy. For according to the terms of the Amnesty Proclamation, their military rank or government position in the former Confederacy should have prevented them from taking office, yet a number of these men, having been pardoned by Andrew Johnson, now occupied high-ranking positions in the South. Of them, nine former Confederate army officers, seven former members of the Confederate Congress, and three members of the secession conventions of 1860–1861 had arrived in Washington, intending to enter Congress. Many Radicals thus openly worried that this "old oligarchy" of planters, secessionists, and white supremacists would again dominate the South, and the nation.

"Either keep them out of Congress," the newspaper editor Horatio Woodman pleaded, "or find a way to let the negroes vote,—and this practically and not theoretically or philanthropically."

The atmosphere was so tense that Secretary of State William Seward, usually imperturbable, begged the navy secretary to find him a Cuba-bound steamer so he could duck the whole thing.

Horace Maynard had received the necessary certificate of election to Congress from none other than Tennessee Governor Parson Brownlow, the same fire-eating Radical who'd once bellowed "we must keep Southern rebels out of Congress, who only seek to get in to do mischief." Horace Maynard was no rebel. In 1861 he'd worked hard to keep Tennessee in the Union, so much so that he tried to make East Tennessee a separate Union state; Andrew Johnson, when military governor there, appointed Maynard attorney general. Slim and tall with a long, skinny face, Maynard, though he actually disliked Johnson, had crucially promoted his nomination as Vice President in 1864. Of all men, Maynard seemed the Southern representative most likely to be seated.

But many moderate and even conservative Republicans, horrified by reports from the South, and especially by the black codes, were not eager to seat the Southern delegates any more than the

Radicals were. If representatives from the seceded states were immediately admitted to Congress without any guarantee of good faith other than the surrender of their armies—and without Congress or the states having secured full rights of citizenship for the recently emancipated blacks—the clock would be turned backward, with nothing left but "degradation, misery, & servitude, for the blacks," as Charles Eliot Norton observed with disdain.

McPherson cleared his throat and read the roll. He skipped the name of Horace Maynard. Maynard jumped up to speak, but McPherson refused to recognize him. Tennessee was not in the Union.

New York Democrat James Brooks also jumped up. "If Tennessee is not in the Union, and has not been in the Union, and is not a loyal State, and the people of Tennessee are aliens and foreigners to this Union," Brooks shouted, "then by what right does the President of the United States usurp his place in the White House?" If Tennessee was not in the Union, Brooks was saying, then Andrew Johnson must be an alien and a foreigner with no right to be President.

Thaddeus Stevens replied that any question about credentials could not be posed until the House had elected its new Speaker.

Stevens understood House rules and regulations better than anyone. As always, he had come to Congress prepared. He was seventy-three, he'd been ill, he could barely walk, and as Carl Schurz noted, "he looked very much aged," but having met with Republican party leaders before Congress convened, he'd garnered their support for what he planned to do. After Schuyler Colfax was elected Speaker, Stevens swiftly moved to suspend the rules, cutting off debate. Stevens then proposed the establishment of a Joint Congressional Committee on Reconstruction to be composed of fifteen members, nine from the House and six from the Senate. This Reconstruction Committee would be charged with investigating conditions in the former Confederacy—in particular, the many reported murders and assaults—and determining under what terms representatives from those states could be admitted to Congress.

The resolution easily passed, 129 to 35, and having also passed the Senate, the Joint Committee was promptly formed with Maine Senator William Pitt Fessenden, a moderate Republican who leaned toward the conventional, as its chair. Three Democrats sat on the Joint Committee—Henry Grider of Kentucky, Andrew Rogers of New Jersey, and Reverdy Johnson of Maryland—but Democrats were generally indignant, complaining that Stevens had cracked his whip—which he had, and successfully. They groused about whether the Joint Committee on Reconstruction would act responsibly and prevent a "perpetually recurring wrangle" over the readmission of Southern states. They were particularly angry at Republicans like Henry Raymond, the youthful founder of *The New York Times*, whom they had considered reliably on their side. Elected to the House of Representatives in 1864, and though supposed to be a Seward man, Raymond had evidently surrendered to Thad Stevens.

In his annual speech to Congress, which the esteemed historian George Bancroft had skillfully helped to write, Johnson tried to calm the battling antagonists. He failed. Rehashing the debate about secession that Lincoln had called academic, Johnson insisted again that the Constitution had forbade secession and therefore it hadn't happened. The Southern states had not seceded; they'd merely, he repeated, "placed themselves in a condition where their vitality was impaired, but not extinguished—their functions suspended, but not destroyed." These states could therefore assume their rightful place in a representative government.

Stevens thought Johnson's argument ridiculous. "Nobody, I believe, pretends that with their old constitutions and frames of government, they [the former rebel states] can be permitted to claim their old rights under the Constitution. They have torn their constitutional States into atoms," he explained. "Dead States cannot restore their own existence 'as it was.'" And only Congress could readmit them.

Then Stevens posed another problem: the three-fifths issue. Once the Thirteenth Amendment was part of the Constitution, those persons once counted as three-fifths a person were to be counted as full persons; that would increase the number of representatives allowed in the House from the Southern states once those states were readmitted to Congress. How was that fair, if non-white persons couldn't vote?

Stevens wasn't finished. Governor Perry of South Carolina and the other provisional governors appointed by Johnson—and reputedly Johnson himself—had proclaimed "this is a white man's government." That kind of declaration revolted Stevens. "What is implied by this?" he trenchantly asked. "That one race of men are to have the exclusive right forever to rule this nation, and to exercise all acts of sovereignty, which all other races and nations and colors are to be their subject, and have no voice in making the laws and choosing the rules by whom they are to be governed? Wherein does this differ from slavery except in degree?

"This is not a 'white man's Government,'" Stevens blasted them. "To say so is political blasphemy, for it violates the fundamental principles of our gospel of liberty. . . . Equal rights to all the privileges of the Government is innate in every immortal being, no matter what the shape or color of the tabernacle which it inhabits."

Whether he was loved or hated—and he was both—there was no one like Thaddeus Stevens. Born in Vermont during the administration of George Washington, in 1792, Stevens was another self-made man, very much like Lincoln or, for that matter, Andrew Johnson. And he too had been shaped by the loss of a father, a ne'er-do-well who abandoned his wife and four sons, and by extreme poverty. But unlike Johnson, Stevens came to regard poverty as "a blessing—for if there be any human sensation more ethereal and divine than all others, it is that which feelingly sympathizes with misfortune." His generosity was admired even by enemies, who considered his charity almost obsessive. Sometime in the 1830s, he heard of a widow about to lose her farm to foreclosure. Stevens went to the auction, bid, and won the farm. He paid the widow's debt and had the sheriff turn over the deed to the widow; then Stevens rode away.

With the strenuous help of his mother, Stevens had attended the

University of Vermont and then Dartmouth. "I was feeble and lame in youth, and as I could not work on the farm, she concluded to give me an education," he later said. "She worked day and night." In his will, he stipulated that the sexton of the cemetery where she was buried keep her grave green and plant roses on its four quarters every spring.

Eventually settling in Gettysburg, Pennsylvania, where he was admitted to the bar, Stevens was known as an inspired litigator with a quick tongue. (Once, when accused of leading a witness, Stevens retorted, "why, he looked so young and innocent, I felt it my duty to lead him.") Elected to the Pennsylvania legislature in 1831, he proudly defeated wealthy rivals who tried to destroy the free public school system, which he'd helped to establish. By then, though, he suffered from a disease that caused him to lose his hair, and ever after wore an ill-fitting, chestnut-colored wig. Despite this, and despite his decided limp, he stood six feet tall and was considered handsome in a stern sort of way; he was also considered something of a rake, although no indiscretions ever came to light.

Successful but seeking a wider field, Stevens had moved to Lancaster, Pennsylvania, amassed a great deal of real estate, and, though he had no head for business, acquired an ironworks; a former employee recalled that "Mr. Stevens used to call it his sinking fund, and only kept it running to give the people work." During the war, rebel troops went out of their way to destroy it. "I only wish you had been in your works," a former Confederate told him, "and had been subjected to a little fire yourself."

A friend recalled that Stevens had been an abolitionist long before abolitionists had a name. Elected in 1849 to the U.S. House of Representatives as a Whig, he fought tirelessly against slavery in the courts and on the streets, protecting and even freeing fugitives whenever he could and often at great risk to himself. In 1852 he defended the men charged with killing and wounding would-be captors of runaways, and for such apostasy, he briefly lost his seat in the House. When he was re-elected in 1858, as a Republican, he soon became chairman of the powerful Ways and Means Commit-

Thaddeus Stevens, leader of the House of Representatives, said reconstruction should revolutionize Southern institutions—and the country as a whole. Refusing to be buried in a cemetery that discriminated against blacks, he was branded a fanatic.

tee, which oversaw the difficult task of financing the war, and as its chair, he worked to make sure that former slaves were armed—and freed.

Considered the kind of ideologue whose bleak face, Lincoln once said, was always "set Zionward," Stevens was an unprejudiced, formidable, and visionary leader with a practical streak. He would make a deal, when necessary, because he always considered the big picture. A fighting man, he also wanted to get things done, and as he once said, he had to compromise at times, because "Congress is composed of men, and not angels." And though he'd believed Lincoln hadn't prosecuted the war fast enough or hard enough—and that he hadn't abolished slavery quickly enough—Stevens aggressively campaigned for Lincoln in 1864.

For he never lost his moral compass: justice for all and a fair shot at equal opportunity. Frequently disappointed, he was also an idealist, which accounted in part for his cynicism. "I lead them, yes," Stevens once said of his colleagues, "but they never follow me or do as I want until public opinion has sided with me." That wasn't quite true. A peerless and powerful legislator as well as tactician, he'd pushed military appropriations bills through the House during the war, and he helped pass unpopular laws, such as drafting men into the army, and the Habeas Corpus Suspension Act, which allowed citizens suspected of crimes to be detained indefinitely without trial.

Mark Twain was transfixed by Stevens. "Very deep eyes, sunken unshaven cheeks, thin lips, long mouth, & strong, long, large, sharp nose—whole face sunken & sharp—full of inequalities—" Twain jotted in his notebook. "Dark wavy hair Indian, club-footed,— Ablest man." This ablest man was a terror in debate. "Not seldom a single sentence sufficed to lay a daring antagonist sprawling on the ground amid the roaring laughter of the House, the luckless victim feeling as if he had heedlessly touched a heavily charged wire," Carl Schurz recollected. Stevens would rise by degrees, "as a telescope is pulled out," another observer dourly said. "And then, reaching to his full height, he would lecture the offender against party discipline, sweeping at him with his large, bony right hand, in uncouth gestures, as if he would clutch him and shake him."

Yet despite his cutting wit, Stevens could be charming. Raising one of his long legs and companionably placing his foot on Henry Raymond's nearby desk—"always the club foot, with characteristic cynicism," an observer remarked—Stevens might wave Raymond over, and the two very different men would chuckle together as if they agreed, which they mostly did not, about Andy Johnson. He'd never withdraw into conservatism: "all his life he held the outpost of thought," even Horace Maynard would salute him. Had Stevens been a poet, recalled another colleague, he'd have been worshipped as a seer.

For more than twenty years, until his death, the man known far and wide as the "Old Commoner" lived companionably with the widowed Lydia Hamilton Smith, a mixed-race woman, who was said either to be his housekeeper or his lover. Lydia Smith helped manage his home, his business, and his family, and together the two of them raised her sons and Stevens' adopted nephews. He built a brick house in Lancaster, which he deeded to Smith for $500, and in his will, he bequeathed his furniture to her as well as a lump sum to be paid each year for the rest of her life. With the inheritance, she purchased Stevens' house and made certain his grave was tended.

By December 4, 1865, Stevens' health was poor. He had to be carried into the Capitol by two young officers of the House, whom he was said to address with a twinkle. "Thank you, my good fellows," he chuckled. "What shall I do when you are dead and gone?"

THADDEUS STEVENS MAY have been an idealist, and he may have been a crusader—but he wasn't a Puritan or a perfectionist, which is how Charles Sumner was regarded. Like Stevens, Sumner was principled and sincere, but he was also doctrinaire and arrogant, and he had something of the pompous schoolmaster about him. He larded his prolix speeches, some of which lasted for four or five hours, with citations from the Greeks and the Romans, and containing none of Stevens' pith, these orations also had none of Wendell Phillips' high voltage. But he shared with Stevens and Phillips a conviction about the rightness of his views, whether on abolition or civil and political rights for all (with the exception, presently, of political rights for women). Though often sanctimonious, Charles Sumner was definitely a knight ready to break his lance.

He inspired respect, not love. "I hold him to have been the purest and most sincere man of his party," said Confederate General Richard Taylor, President Zachary Taylor's son and someone who demonized most Radicals. Even so, Sumner could make himself friendly when he wanted—"but he either does all the talking himself and goes off into long disquisitions," said a secretary, "or he simply draws out the other person and lets him do the talking, so it is a monologue on one side or the other." Perhaps ruefully, he once confided to Julia Ward Howe that "I have outlived the interest in individuals." Yet as Lydia Maria Child explained to a friend, "never in this, or any other country, have I known of a public man, who did treat eternal principles of right so invariably, so steadfastly, and so fearlessly as Charles Sumner. If he don't get all *he* claims, he enables *us to get* more than we should."

A graduate of Harvard and Harvard Law, Sumner preferred poetry and politics to the legal profession, and in 1851, at the age of forty, he joined the Free-Soil party, a coalition of Massachusetts Democrats and Whigs who opposed the extension of slavery into the territories. Elected to the U.S. Senate, he fought this battle fiercely. But he often misjudged the effect of his jeremiads. In 1856, for example, when he insulted his colleague Andrew Butler, claiming the genteel senator from South Carolina worshipped a harlot named slavery, Butler's nephew, Congressman Preston Brooks, avenged his uncle's honor by whacking Sumner senseless with a gutta-percha cane while several colleagues egged him on. It took Sumner more than three years to recover, but Sumner became even keener, if that was possible, on the subject of justice and equality.

Imposing, he stood over six feet tall, although lately his waist had thickened and the flesh of his face had started to sag. Yet nothing seemed out of place with him. He arranged his luxuriant dark hair with deliberate carelessness, and while Thaddeus Stevens was indifferent to clothes and allowed his wig to sit at a weird angle atop his head, Sumner grandly marched forth in a chestnut-brown coat, lavender or brightly checked pants, and shoes with white gaiters. At times there was something almost childlike about him. "If one told Charles Sumner that the moon was made of green cheese," a friend chuckled, "he would controvert the fact in all sincerity, and give good reason why it could not be so."

Stately and impassioned, if long-winded, Senator Charles Sumner of Massachusetts was brutally beaten on the Senate floor in
1856 after denouncing slavery and his Southern colleagues. Opposing Johnson and his policies, during the Grant administration he continued the battle for civil rights legislation.

Since he was thought to be a confirmed bachelor, it came as
something of a surprise when, at the age of fifty-five, he married the
widowed Alice Mason Hooper. Her beauty later the subject of a
portrait by John Singer Sargent, Alice Hooper was sociable, wealthy,
and almost thirty years his junior. She was no match for a man so set
in his ways, and vice versa. Soon Democratic Representative James
Brooks (no relation to Preston Brooks) in his paper, the *New York
Express*, was publicizing gossip about an affair between Mrs. Sumner and a Prussian diplomat. Sumner's enemies began calling him

"The Great Impotent." The couple almost immediately separated and later divorced.

After the war ended, Sumner renewed his battle for equal rights. "Liberty has been won," he insisted. "The battle for Equality is still pending." Disturbed that Andrew Johnson had allowed Southern states to ignore black suffrage when they called for new state conventions, he met with Johnson at the White House before Congress convened. The two men danced around each other for over two hours, and Sumner noticed with revulsion when he picked up his silk hat from the floor and prepared to leave that Johnson had used it as a spittoon. "Ignorant, pig-headed and perverse," Sumner himself nearly spat. And when in December Sumner read the President's annual message, in which Johnson again left the question of black rights to the individual states, he with contempt called the speech a "whitewashing message" and compared it to Franklin Pierce's defense of proslavery guerillas before the war. Conservative Republican Senator James Doolittle, a devoted Johnson man, demanded that Sumner retract. Sumner waved him away.

Though he had badly wanted to chair the new Joint Committee on Reconstruction, he wasn't even asked to sit on it. Undeterred, he continued to present bill after bill to Congress to protect the freedmen, including one that gave them deeds to land on the South Carolina Sea Islands that they'd been farming. And then he threw down the gauntlet to Andrew Johnson with this warning: "If you are not ready to be the Moses of an oppressed people, do not become its Pharaoh."

Sumner was gearing up.

THE THIRTEENTH AMENDMENT abolishing slavery was part of the U.S. Constitution at the end of 1865 when twenty-seven out of thirty-six states ratified it. Secretary of State William Seward had counted all Southern states, even though they had not yet been admitted to Congress. And so he too, with Andrew Johnson, considered reconstruction basically unnecessary and black voting rights a moot question as far as the federal government was concerned.

"What's the use to give us our freedom," a former slave wanted to know, "if we can't stay where we were raised, and own our houses where we were born, and our little pieces of ground?"

Although the Freedmen's Bureau had been organized without specific instructions about how or even whether to redistribute land confiscated from the rebels, its mandate had overlapped with General Sherman's Special Field Order No. 15, which allowed freedmen to settle on abandoned coastal property from Charleston to Jacksonville. Sherman had presumably wished to help black families, even if his reasons were not entirely altruistic; the army had over 80,000 black refugees to house and feed, and the sooner these people could take care of themselves, the better. Hence Field Order No. 15: every black family might obtain as many as "forty acres of land and a mule."

Those forty acres and that mule furnished Thaddeus Stevens with an opening, for he'd already been hatching a radical plan to redistribute the wealth of the South. Divvy up the confiscated property and give it to the families of former slaves and thus effectively overturn the propertied class system that so long had ruled the region.

There was, of course, a catch. Special Field Order No. 15 didn't stipulate that black families actually owned the land they were allotted. While some freedmen might claim a moral right to the land they'd cultivated for generations, and which they were now homesteading, it wasn't clear that they had a legal right to it. So the legal and moral questions were tricky: Did the land still actually belong to the white planters who'd abandoned it, or should these planters be considered traitors and forfeit any rights to that land? Or were they to be full-fledged citizens of the Union once again, as Johnson wanted to argue, as soon as they were pardoned?

In South Carolina there was a rumor that Governor Perry was allowing confiscated property to be furtively transferred to former rebels just to keep it out of the hands of the Bureau or to prevent any of it from being used as schools, hospitals, or orphan asylums. And recently pardoned planters were actively lobbying Johnson to give them back any land seized by the federal government. Johnson, sympathetic, ordered the one-armed General Oliver Otis Howard, the head of the Freedmen's Bureau, to return to the ex-rebels territory confiscated by the Treasury Department during the war that had not yet been sold to a third party. There were some 450,000 acres at stake, and freedmen had been resettled on much of it.

Nicknamed the "Christian General" because during the war he'd liked to hand out religious material, General Howard, though an anti-slavery man, was not a Radical, not an abolitionist, and not a peacetime fighter. Still, he considered this disputed land exempt from the President's injunction to return the land to planters, and in July of 1865 he issued what became known as Circular 13, urging Bureau commissioners to leave alone the forty-acre tracts already occupied by freedmen. Circular 13 also carved out additional forty-acre tracts from the confiscated and abandoned lands to be sold or leased to freedmen for a three-year period, and at the end of that period, they had an option to purchase the land at its 1860 appraised value.

The planters protested. Since they'd been pardoned, they argued, they should be able to reclaim their property—particularly if it was being used by the Bureau or was being occupied by freedmen. In New Orleans, for instance, Pierre Soulé, who'd received a special pardon, wanted his mansion back. A minister to Spain under President Buchanan and a former U.S. senator from Louisiana, Soulé thought he deserved it, even if he had served as a buccaneering member of Confederate General Beauregard's staff and, after Appomattox, helped relocate Confederate veterans to Mexico, where they could resume life as it had been, or even organize another rebellion.

Soulé's mansion had been converted early in the war into a "Colored Orphans Home" for the children of freedpeople and black soldiers. Louise De Mortier, a noted free woman of color, who had been a sought-after public speaker, was ably running the orphanage, often raising money by giving concerts locally (she sang) or traveling north to do so. Since the property was being put to good use, the Freedmen's Bureau initially refused the Soulé request, but the eastern district court ordered the property to be seized and sold. "Shouldn't we resist in this?" Assistant Commissioner General Absalom Baird asked General Howard. The property was initially sold to Thomas Conway, assistant commissioner of the Bureau in Louisiana, so that the orphanage could be continued, but the sale was not allowed to be completed. Instead, Johnson issued a special pardon to Soulé, who eventually took possession of the mansion. The Louisiana legislature ludicrously proposed to apprentice out the displaced orphans, at no pay; if they ran away, they were to be arrested and handed back to their employer. This would be child labor—or slavery by another name.

Although the President had been a child laborer himself, he was insensitive to the issue. He'd instructed General Howard to revoke Circular 13 and return all confiscated lands to their original owners, who needed only to show proof of ownership and a pardon. General Howard tried to hedge, but the appointee in charge of recovering confiscated property, William Henry Trescot, a former slave-owner and planter in South Carolina, accused him of exciting and aggravating the antagonism between the races by dispossessing the white population. General Howard obeyed Johnson's directive, knowing that Bureau commissioners who didn't agree would be sacked. Thomas Conway was removed. "Could a just government drive out these loyal men who have been firm and loyal in her cause in all her darkest days?" General Rufus Saxton complained to General Howard. A former abolitionist who'd been the leader of the first federally authorized black troops during the war, Saxton, as assistant commissioner of the Bureau in South Carolina, had helped the freed slaves open their own bank, start their own schools, and cultivate the confiscated land given them. They lost the land; he lost his post.

As William Trescot later admitted, land ownership was political power. That's exactly what Thaddeus Stevens had incisively argued—and why he wanted to redistribute the land. Four million former slaves had been freed, Stevens had said, "without a hut to shelter them or a cent in their pockets. . . . If we do not furnish them with homesteads, and hedge them around with protective laws; if we leave them to the legislation of their late masters, we had better left them in bondage.

"If we fail in this great duty now, when we have the power," Stevens' voice rang with urgency, "we shall deserve and receive the execration of history and of all future ages."

CHAPTER SEVEN

Reconciliation

On New Year's Day 1866, for the first time since Abraham Lincoln's death, President Andrew Johnson opened the doors of the White House to the public.

It had been a leaden morning of sleet, and a slimy drizzle so streaked the windowpanes that the threadbare carpets in the public rooms were wrapped in linen to protect them from the muck. The White House, which had not yet been refurbished, was shabby and gray. But the soiled sofas and scuffed chairs had been removed, and gilded vases loaded with lilies and camellias had been placed on lacquered tables. The chandeliers twinkled. Members of the cabinet—Secretary Stanton had come early—and the Supreme Court were already removing their coats. Stanton was smiling, and the regal Chief Justice Salmon Chase, whose likeness could be seen engraved on every dollar bill, entered the rooms, his beautiful daughter Kate, looking somewhat pale, on his arm. Foreign ministers in elaborate dress, epaulets on their shoulders and medals pinned to their chests, had been driven in the mud to the White House, accompanied by their wives or their sisters, and congressmen, more conservatively attired, were accompanied by theirs.

It was already a large gathering when, at half past eleven, Lieutenant General Ulysses S. Grant and his entire staff strode into the mansion. Then at noon about four thousand citizens began trekking through the East Room. A police detail of at least forty men, wearing starched new uniforms and white gloves, waited nearby. No one was taking chances. The Marine Band in red regalia struck up overtures from *Tannhäuser* and *William Tell* as the crowd passed, two by two, toward the Blue Room as if heading to Noah's ark, where the President gripped outstretched palms for a quick, hard shake. He wore his ivory-colored gloves.

Smartly dressed in a black frock coat and a satin vest with a stand-up collar, Johnson offered words of polite greeting despite being exhausted and bored. His daughters, Mrs. Patterson and Mrs. Stover, stood by his side, the first time they'd been seen in public. Martha Patterson, the wife of Tennessee Senator David T. Patterson, had braided her dark hair, which she'd pulled back from her face, and put on a dress of heavy black silk trimmed with black lace. A careful woman, she was managing expectations and soon was widely praised for remarking that "we are plain people from the mountains of Tennessee, called here for a short time by a national calamity. I trust too much will not be expected of us." Johnson's other daughter, the statuesque Mary Stover, took the same tack. She'd chosen dark colors, high-necked and funereal, since she was still mourning her deceased husband, a colonel in the Union army, who had died of cold and starvation during the war. Johnson's invalid wife remained upstairs—no one was surprised to learn she was indisposed—although Johnson's son Robert, working now as secretary to his father, was said to be busy in his office. Or, less kindly, gossips said he was ill, meaning he was drunk and had passed out somewhere.

Several Southerners, pressing for pardons, approached the President. He told them to call tomorrow, and when lobbyists tried to corner him, he coldly turned his back.

The eldest child of Andrew Johnson, Martha Johnson
Patterson successfully assumed the role as presidential
White House hostess; she also received praise for tending
the dairy cows that grazed on the White House lawn.

After the general reception concluded, the black men and
women of Washington were permitted to enter the Executive Mansion. Very few did.

Overall, the reception was a success despite the lingering melan-
choly of those who felt the presence of the gangly Lincoln, who had
not so long ago walked through these rooms. "He would have enjoyed the day," Gideon Welles sadly noted, "which was so much in
contrast with all those he had experienced during his presidency."

The weekly Washington receptions—the "season"—had officially begun. Socialites were serving ice cream on silver trays and
brandy punch for the gentlemen in a city that was no longer an
armed camp. Almost every evening there was a ball or a dinner or a

weekly event, like the Wednesday evenings at the home of Speaker of the House Schuyler Colfax, affably nicknamed "Smiler" for his perpetual grin. On Saturdays, the towering Chief Justice Salmon Chase received callers, and the presidential daughters held their receptions on Tuesdays. Often the Marine Band played at Secretary Stanton's, and the man of iron seemed momentarily to relax. The Marquis de Montholon, the French minister to the United States, threw a party that lasted until sunrise, at which time he served breakfast. "Washington seemed to have gone wild," noted one of the hostesses. Journalists mingled with jurors, the diplomatic corps with seedy lobbyists, and members of the cabinet talked, if briefly, with the clerks who worked with the Freedmen's Bureau and slept in attic rooms.

The gas lamps in the brothels glowed until late, the gambling halls were full. Yet sentries still guarded the homes of cabinet members, and on the streets everything seemed for sale. Confederate General Richard Taylor said shady brokers dashed in and out of the White House "for the transactions of all business," he drily noted. Government hospitals were closing, and in the hospitals that remained, the poet Walt Whitman saw "cases of the worst and most incurable wounds, and obstinate illness, and of poor fellows who have no homes to go to." They weren't attending the brilliant receptions.

"The spectacle of sudden loss and sudden elevation to wealth and prominence was equally demoralizing," Johnson's bodyguard observed. When Josephine Griffing, a volunteer agent at the Freedmen's Bureau, complained that men and women lived in poverty all over the District, she was fired. "You will see how our cause has been made to suffer from the proslavery spirit, which has power in the Freedmen's Bureau," she confided to a friend, "and this is not strange when we see that the men who fill too many of these offices were six years ago wedded to the Institution of Slavery."

THE RESTAURANTEUR GEORGE Thomas Downing, a longtime abolitionist and advocate of civil rights, would tenderly clasp

Charles Sumner's dying hand, but that was in the future. In the past, Downing had been owner of a hotel in Newport, Rhode Island, and now he managed the members' dining room in the House of Representatives, where he picked up political tips and chatter. He was heading a delegation from the national convention of the Colored Men's Equal Rights League come to speak to President Johnson.

With Downing were several other notable black activists: Frederick Douglass, one of the most famous and certainly one of the most eloquent men in America, and Douglass' son Major Lewis Douglass of the fabled black regiment, the Massachusetts 54th, during the war; wealthy Chicago tailor John Jones; William E. Matthews of Maryland; John F. Cook of the District; A. J. Raynor of South Carolina; Joseph E. Oats of Florida; A. W. Ross of Mississippi; and lawyer and veteran William Whipper of Pennsylvania. They'd come to speak to the President about the vote.

"We respectfully submit that rendering anything less than this will be rendering to us less than our just due," George Downing politely informed Johnson.

Johnson's answer was predictable: the federal government should not impose black voting rights on "the people" of any state. Downing must have smiled to himself, for he quickly replied that in South Carolina, say, most of "the people" were black. Johnson ignored him.

Frederick Douglass approached. Born a slave in Maryland to parents he never knew, Frederick Augustus Washington Bailey had escaped from bondage to remake himself as Frederick Douglass, and in 1845, after the publication of his *Narrative of the Life of Frederick Douglass*, he leaped onto the public stage. The bestselling chronicle of his life in bondage and his escape from it, told with unsurpassed verbal dexterity, was an international sensation that ironically exposed Douglass to the threat of recapture as a slave. But as a brilliant speaker on behalf of abolition and then the editor of his own newspaper, *The North Star* (later renamed *Frederick Doug-*

lass' Paper), Douglass had persuasively prodded many politicians to action, including Abraham Lincoln, whom he met at the White House in 1863.

Douglass would depict Lincoln as "tardy, cold, dull, and indifferent," at least when viewed from the vantage point of a genuine abolitionist—but, Douglass sharply added, when judged next to fellow officeholders, Lincoln was "swift, zealous, radical, and determined." Johnson was an entirely different man. "Full of pomp and swaggering vanity," Douglass later characterized Johnson, and he well remembered the first time they saw each other. It was in 1864, inauguration day, when Lincoln tapped Johnson on the shoulder and pointed Douglass out. In an instant Douglass spotted the look of aversion that flashed over Johnson's face. Noticing that Douglass had seen it, Johnson hastily recovered himself and tried to appear friendly, "but it was too late," Douglass noted with disdain. "Whatever Andrew Johnson may be," Douglass confided to a companion, "he certainly is no friend to our race."

Douglass explained that the delegation was calling on the President as a matter of respect—but, as men who'd served in the military or were subject to the draft, he and his fellow delegates were also presenting their claim for the privilege of the vote, which was owed them.

Johnson didn't listen well, and when nervous, as he evidently was, he repeated himself or rambled. He intended to be the black man's Moses, he said. The two races, black and white, were natural enemies, he continued, and if "turned loose upon the other"—that is, if "thrown together at the ballot-box with this enmity and hate existing between them"—there'd be a race war. Working himself up, Johnson crossly added that he'd risked life and property in the war, and he certainly didn't like, as he put it, "to be arraigned by some who can get up handsomely rounded periods and deal in rhetoric, and talk about abstract ideas of liberty, who never periled life, liberty or property." Johnson referred to Douglass' reputation as a speaker but seemed not to know Douglass had been enslaved—

that he certainly had periled life and liberty—and he probably hadn't read Douglass' *Narrative*. But Johnson despised what seemed to him to be sophisticated rhetoric in others—especially blacks.

He proudly claimed, as he often did, that he had never sold any of his slaves, as if this information might impress the delegation as much as it apparently impressed him.

Downing and Douglass and the others in the delegation silently listened to the President go on. They must have been stunned, but Douglass was unruffled. "We did not come here expecting to argue this question with your Excellency," he said, "but simply to state what were our views and wishes in the premises."

Visibly flustered, Johnson suggested black people leave the South. Douglass calmly observed that even if black men and women should want to leave it, which they didn't, they'd be immediately arrested since they weren't allowed to move around. But the interview had for all intents and purposes ended, and detecting the President's irritation, the delegation thanked the chief executive and exited the room.

Johnson by then was furious. "Those d—d sons of b-s thought they had me in a trap," he reportedly raged. "I know that d-d Douglass; he's just like any nigger, & he would sooner cut a white man's throat than not."

When the delegation walked out of the White House, a messenger from the House of Representatives invited them to meet with a few congressmen in the House anteroom, and then they published a public reply to Johnson, taking care to note that his idea about deporting four million former slaves—"for no other cause than having been freed"—was not an act of justice or of peace. "Peace is not to be secured by degrading one race and exalting another," Douglass said, "but by maintaining a state of equal justice between all classes."

Embarrassed, Johnson sympathizers tried to make Johnson sound reasonable: the President had merely said he couldn't grant voting rights to the former slave "after the demoralizing influence of one hundred years of bondage." Regardless, the President's arrogance and his prejudice struck many people as reprehensible. Learning of the President's response to the black delegation, Adam Gurowski, the garrulous Polish count who seemed to appear everywhere in Washington, exclaimed that he was actually "ashamed of belonging to the white race!"

SENATOR LYMAN TRUMBULL was an intelligent and prudent man considered by colleagues as one of the most exceptional lawyers in the country, even if some of them found him cold, humorless, and pinched. The acerbic Gideon Welles called Trumbull "freaky and opinionated, though able and generally sensible." A former Democrat and judge, Trumbull early in his career had been sent to the U.S. Senate by the Illinois legislature, but he did protest against slavery's extension into the territories, and he joined the Republicans, although he was no real friend to black men or women. "We, the Republicans, are the white man's party," he had emphatically said before the war. He didn't support the right of black men to vote, but he did believe in civil rights for all. The great natural truth, Trumbull declared, is "that all men are created equal."

During the war, he found common cause with the Radical Republicans because he too thought Lincoln wasn't waging the war vigorously enough, and as chairman of the Senate Judiciary Committee, Trumbull had helped write the Thirteenth Amendment. After the war, he was a peacemaking moderate who didn't want to sever ties to Johnson. Certainly he didn't want to play into the hands of Democrats and Southern-sympathizing Copperheads. Instead, like many a moderate, he counseled compromise, and in that spirit, or so he thought, and with gold spectacles perched on a dry face beginning to wrinkle, he worked on two related bills, the Freedmen's Bureau Bill and the Civil Rights Bill, which he introduced in the Senate after it reconvened in early January 1866.

Trumbull prepared the Freedmen's Bureau Bill after conferring with General Howard, the head of the Bureau. The bill extended the life and reach of the Bureau—and also authorized its leasing of those forty-acre tracts of unoccupied land to the freedmen for a three-year period, much as General Howard had done in his circular. The Freedmen's Bureau Bill also validated the land titles already conferred under Sherman's Special Field Order.

The secretary of war supported the bill. "Pass it," said Stanton, "& I will have it executed, so help me God."

Thaddeus Stevens thought well of the bill but wanted more. If the freedpeople or refugees could not afford to rent or buy their land after the allotted period, they'd be turned away, and this struck Stevens as cruel, so in his updated version of the legislation, he proposed that all forfeited and public lands be reserved for freedmen and refugees. He also wanted the Bureau to provide them with public education. But his amendment was defeated. Conservatives such as Delaware Democrat Willard Saulsbury opposed it, histrionically conjuring an imaginary Senate gallery teeming with hundreds of indolent freedmen paid by the Treasury Department to come to Washington and "doing nothing to support themselves"— while the white people of the country were taxed to pay for them.

Trumbull answered with incontrovertible logic, declaring that the pernicious legislative and judicial system had been spawned by slavery and devised in its interest solely "for the purpose of degrading the colored race." It had to be dismantled, once and for all. Trumbull thus also proposed that citizenship be conferred on all native-born persons regardless of race or color (with the exception of Native Americans unless they were "domesticated," paid taxes, and resided in "civilized society," not their own tribes). No one else, then, could be deprived of the rights of citizenship based on race, color, or prior condition of involuntary servitude. That is, black codes would be illegal; blacks would be able to rent and own property, make and enforce contracts, and appear in courts as plaintiffs or witnesses.

Taken together, the Freedmen's Bureau Bill and the Civil Rights Bill could bridge the widening and rancorous conflict between Johnson and Congress. Trumbull sent President Johnson copies of both bills.

Johnson was silent.

The House and Senate passed the Freedmen's Bureau Bill; in the House, only one Republican voted against it.

Carl Schurz fully expected that Johnson would sign it. So did Lyman Trumbull. White House clerks knew better. Johnson despised the Radical Republicans so deeply that he'd veto any bill that he thought they might have put their hands on. And in the end, he did veto both the Freedmen's Bureau Bill and the Civil Rights Bill.

WHEN ANDREW JOHNSON vetoed the Freedmen's Bureau Bill on February 19, 1866, there was no mistaking his position, no rationalizing, no pretending he or it would change.

Trumbull was puzzled. "I thought in advocating it," he said of the bill, "that I was acting in harmony with the views of the President."

Not at all. Johnson listed his objections, one by one. He claimed the Freedmen's Bill would authorize a military court system in the South, where there already was a civil one. He said it cost too much; the Freedmen's Bureau was just a patronage scheme for blacks, after all; and besides, the freedmen would earn respectability and prosperity only through their "own merits and exertions." He ignored the statistics: that the Bureau had educated almost a million people and had effectively worked with black activists, evangelicals, and Northern aid societies to wipe out illiteracy. He ignored the letters and pleas from Southerners, white and black, who said the Bureau protected the freedmen, or tried to protect them, from unfair labor contracts, violence, local guerilla organizations, and the destruction of their schools. Johnson agreed that the freedmen should be protected by civil authorities—state authorities. Each state could take care of itself.

Johnson also said the bill was unconstitutional because the eleven former rebel states had not yet been seated by Congress. They belonged in Congress. After all, he repeated, they'd never left the Union. As a result, Johnson said that he, as President, would reject all legislation concerning the freedmen until representatives from these former rebel states were admitted to Congress.

That last statement seemed to be his major point. He wanted to force Congress to do his bidding—and in fact he was denying the legitimacy of a Congress that refused to embrace, with virtually no questions asked, the representatives of the former Confederacy. With this point made clear, the President flung the bill right back in the face of the legislature, whose authority he seemed completely willing and happy to undercut.

Maine Senator William Pitt Fessenden, no Radical, noted with tart displeasure that if Johnson could "veto one bill upon that ground"—that Congress, as presently constituted, was basically illegitimate—"he will and must, for the sake of consistency, veto every other bill we pass on that subject."

"The President has sold us out—and we may as well look the matter square in the face now as at any time in the future," a former Union intelligence officer groaned. In South Carolina, a Freedmen's Bureau agent conceded that the President obviously "has gone all over to the South." In Cleveland, the *Leader* said that "the news of the Veto Message has awakened through the North a feeling of indignation in every loyal breast, only equaled by the joy manifested by every Copperhead."

Conservatives and Democrats were overjoyed. "The South and the Government are in the same boat one more time, thank the gods!" the Montgomery (Alabama) *Ledger* exulted, and in Kentucky, Johnson was praised as courageous and independent. Former Attorney General Jeremiah Black told Johnson that his veto message had gladdened the hearts of millions, and in New York City, at the large hall of the Cooper Institute, the city's best-known conservative politicians, bankers, and lawyers—men like Henry Raymond of *The New York Times*, Hamilton Fish (later Grant's secretary of state), journalist Parke Godwin and William Cullen Bryant of the *Evening Post*, and Congressman Edwin D. Morgan—praised the President's policy as hastening reconciliation, peace, goodwill, and business. Secretary of State Seward applauded Johnson from a platform wrapped gaily in red, white, and blue bunting. Behind Seward loomed giant pictures of the President and Generals Ulysses Grant and William Sherman. It was a triptych of heroes—although the *Chicago Tribune* parodied the meeting as a bunch of Rip van Winkles come to sing, "Oh dear, we are all fagged out, and cannot battle for Right any longer."

A smiling Seward brushed aside all insults. By marginalizing Radicals like Thaddeus Stevens and Charles Sumner—casting their positions as obstructionist and extreme—Seward believed he and Johnson could lure conservative and perhaps moderate Republicans into a new Union party. He and Andrew Johnson would be at the helm of this party, and the country would inevitably follow them, wherever.

TOWARD THE END of the Lincoln administration, William Pitt Fessenden had replaced Salmon Chase as treasury secretary, and then Hugh McCulloch, sleek and mild and blond, had in turn replaced Fessenden just the month before Lincoln's death. McCulloch would remember his job as "laborious and thankless," but he served Johnson loyally and advised him carefully, particularly on the financial issues about which Johnson was said to lack both understanding and interest. And McCulloch consistently praised Johnson as a man of integrity thoroughly devoted to the country; he'd admired his brave stand against secession back in 1860, and he completely shared the President's conviction that suffrage should be a matter for the states to decide. When it came to extemporaneous speaking, though, McCulloch did not trust the President's judgment.

Johnson wanted to address a throng of boisterous fans in celebration of Washington's birthday, but McCulloch gingerly warned the President that, if he must, then he should stick to pleasantries. Johnson assured his secretary that he merely planned to greet the well-wishers, but the fact was that he could never resist a crowd. And it was a pretty large crowd, singing and chanting, that had marched to the White House from a rally at Grover's Theater. Arriving at the portico, they yelled out for the President to come and say a few words, and Johnson happily, gratefully, complied. But he proceeded to unleash such a startling chain of venomous epithets and head-turning images—about decapitation and crucifixion—that many people, then and later, had to assume Andy Johnson was completely drunk.

He hadn't been drinking; he was seething. By his lights, he, the President, had been traduced, humiliated, and insulted. Congress had refused to seat Southern delegates in defiance of his stated preference that they do so. Men like George Downing had dared to argue with him. The Radicals were insatiable and insolent. Hadn't Charles Sumner called him Pharaoh? It was his life that had been endangered during the war, not the lives of the freedpeople. Didn't Thad Stevens say that if a British king ignored Parliament the way Johnson ignored Congress, it would've cost him his head? This posse of maniacs and revolutionists was conspiring to overthrow the government and boot him out of his job, to topple everything sacred and then to nail him to the cross. These traitors were none other than Charles Sumner, Thaddeus Stevens, and Wendell Phillips.

Johnson worked himself up to a pitch, and whatever veneer of composure he had adopted cracked wide open. Mixing self-pity with pride, he balefully described his origins, his diligent life as a tailor, his fixed devotion to the Constitution, and the fact that he was cut from the same patriotic cloth as the noble George Washington. Whatever the charms of the White House, he raved on, they held no charm for him. He cared for neither food nor clothing; he was just a simple man, without frill or ambition, who wished only to do his duty by his country. And lest anyone forget, he'd been willing to sacrifice everything for the Union. "Who has suffered more by the rebellion than I have?" Johnson burst out. "If my blood is to be shed because I vindicate the Union and insist on the preservation of the Government in its original purity, let it be shed out," he cried. "The blood that now warms and animates my existence shall be poured out as the last libation as a tribute to the union to the States."

Dumbfounded by Johnson's tirade, George Templeton Strong began to think the unthinkable: impeachment. Strong almost groaned, "Imagine it!!!!!" Johnson seemed unfit for office. William Lloyd Garrison too wondered if Johnson wasn't guilty of an impeachable offence, like the usurpation of power, "in undertaking to reconstruct states for peremptory admission into the Congress of the United States"—and in attacking "some of its most estimable and distinguished members as assassins who are conspiring to take his life."

Edwin Stanton decided not to resign as war secretary, which he'd said he'd been considering: he could not abandon the military, especially now that Johnson was seemingly unhinged. If the President wanted him gone, let the President fire him. But it was with something like relief that Senator William Pitt Fessenden heard of Johnson's tirade. "The long agony is over," Fessenden concluded. "He has broken the faith, betrayed his trust, and must sink from detestation into contempt."

RELINQUISH ALL BITTERNESS and spleen, the President suggested, although he himself did just the opposite. Forgive white Southerners their trespasses. For though Johnson's tirade stupefied even his admirers, it tapped into deeply held beliefs about mercy and redemption, and if the rhetoric seemed empty, it effectively replaced political issues with foggy but familiar injunctions to forgive and forget. And that offered solace to those tired of war, tired of fighting, and tired of problems with no easy solutions.

The institution of slavery had been abolished, its sinfulness washed clean, and those who did not forgive were themselves with sin, like the vindictive and vengeful Thaddeus Stevens, a man without mercy or magnanimity. We are one people, united in sympathy, the Reverend Henry Ward Beecher preached. As for the South, "their mistakes, their evil cause, belonged to the system under which they were reared, but their military skill and heroic bravery belong to the nation."

"My enemy is dead, a man as divine as myself is dead," Walt Whitman reminded his readers in a recent poem aptly called "Reconciliation." Whitman's friend the essayist John Burroughs praised the poem's commitment to peace, benevolence, and a kindly compassion.

Burroughs had met Walt Whitman in the rubber supply store of Allen, Clapp & Company, located between 10th and 11th Streets in Washington. The poet was large, muscular, his beard shaggy, his shirt collar open, his soul large. "I was struck with the look of him

The poet Walt Whitman once said, "Life is seen more richly in Washington than at any other one point on this continent." Living there during the Johnson administration, he composed the three essays about American politics and culture later published as *Democratic Vistas*.

as he sat there in the gas light," Burroughs said. Whitman extended a warm hand, and the two men became friends for a lifetime.

Burroughs learned that Whitman lived in a room with just a bed and a table and a chair, that he ate not much more than bread and tea, and that he ambled "looking old and young, both at the same time." Whitman continued to deliver tobacco and sweet crackers to the homeless Southern boys down with fever and the Union soldiers still recuperating, if they could recuperate, in the district hospitals. A Democrat before the war, Whitman had no fondness for what he called the "scum" of politics: rabid partisanship. To him, both Johnson and the Radicals were ferocious, divided, and divisive. He was seeking reconciliation, the kind that rockets transcendentally above the petty concerns of petty people.

This too was the desire of novelist Herman Melville, for whom it was also time to forgive. Melville had sprung into vogue almost overnight twenty years earlier when his titillating maritime novel *Typee*, about his escapades as a young sailor in the South Seas, became a bestseller. He then published a number of similar books until 1851, when he produced the strange, brooding masterpiece, *Moby-Dick*, which few read and fewer understood, a book about obsession, madness, and revenge—and an interracial friendship of symbolic power. He was also writing stories—notably "Benito Cereno," a complex tale of a slave revolt—and in the summer of 1866 produced *Battle-Pieces and Aspects of War*, a small, red-covered volume of unconventional poems. Confounding the public once again, Melville's poetry was a combination of Emerson, Browning, and Mother Goose, said one reviewer, who winced at the irregular rhymes, jarring metaphors, and jagged verse. Oddest of all, though, was the prose "Supplement" at the volume's end.

In the "Supplement," hardly read even today, Melville said he wanted what every other "sensible American" wanted: reconciliation. Of course, as he also noted, "nothing has been urged here in the foolish hope of conciliating those men—few in number, we trust—who have resolved never to be reconciled to the Union." But since Northerners were the victors in the war, they had an obligation to remember that Southern women who scatter flowers on the graves of their husbands, sons, and fathers are "as sacred in the eye of Heaven as are those who go with similar offerings of tender grief and love into the cemeteries of our Northern martyrs."

What's more, former Southerners—even secessionists—should be readmitted into Congress because they represent the people. But as George Downing had pointed out to Andrew Johnson, this "people" did not include blacks.

As for the blacks, Melville had a plan: "paternal guardianship" might be offered the former slaves, although, he warned, any concern for them "should not be allowed to exclude kindliness to communities who stand nearer to us in nature." We need to be kind to former slaveholders too. "In our natural solicitude to confirm the benefit of liberty to the blacks," Melville reminded the reader, "let us forbear from measures of dubious constitutional rightfulness toward our white countrymen—measures of a nature to provoke, among other of the last evils, exterminating hatred of race toward race."

Nervous about insurrections, nervous about constitutionality, nervous about irritating the South, and eager to conciliate, Melville sounded a bit like Andrew Johnson. "Benevolent desires, after passing a certain point," the novelist added, "can not undertake their own fulfillment without incurring the risk of evils beyond those sought to be remedied."

Conservative reviewers praised Melville's political "Supplement." "So far from spoiling the symmetry of the book, this supplement completes it, and converts it into what is better than a good book—into a good and patriotic action," *The New York Herald*'s critic declared, quoting the supplement at length in the paper. At *The New York Times*, Henry Raymond also admired Melville's disapproval of Radicals, who would probably pitch the book out the window. Radicals *were* in fact willing to toss *Battle-pieces* into the trash. To them, Melville had a smiling, Panglossian view of civil rights. "'Something,' says this happy optimist, 'may well be left to the graduated care of future legislature and of Heaven,'" Radical editor Theodore Tilton wrote in *The Independent*. "To which we have only to reply that 'something' was left eighty years ago to the graduated care of future legislation and of Heaven; and that something turned out to be a gigantic war, from which we escaped by the skin of our teeth."

Yet Melville and Whitman weren't alone. "Everybody is heartily tired of discussing [the Negro's] rights," grumbled *The Nation*. Melville and Whitman were giving voice to those whites bewildered or oblivious or just uncaring and who didn't want to turn back the clock so much as bury the past and move on.

CHAPTER EIGHT

Civil Rights

T here was no reason, none at all, to assume that the Civil Rights Bill was objectionable or that it would provoke much controversy, or that it would prevent the healing of the nation. Or that Johnson would veto it. The bill said nothing about a black man's right to vote—or a white woman's, for that matter. It contained no controversial language. Its intent was reconciliation and peace. James Gordon Bennett, a Democrat, called the bill sensible. It merely granted citizenship to all persons born in the United States and not subject to any foreign power (though excluding Indians who lived in tribes), and it allowed these people, as citizens, to make contracts, to testify in court, and to move, to marry, or to own property. No punishment meted out to a black man or woman could differ from that inflicted on a white person for the same offense.

"The *thing itself* is desirable," Henry Ward Beecher informed President Johnson. "Aside from that, I am persuaded that it would go far *to harmonize the feelings* of men who should never have differed, or permitted a difference." Ohio governor Jacob D. Cox, another Johnson ally, told the President that if he wasn't sure about the bill's constitutionality—Cox wasn't either—at least the bill *was* popular, and it would unite Republicans. Sign it, Cox advised. "It will be well *to sustain a point* in order to meet the popular spirit and impulse rather than to make a strict construction of duty the other way." Even Wendell Phillips, who insisted citizenship was meaningless without the right to vote, conceded the bill was at least half a loaf, which meant it was better than nothing at all.

Not a man to take risks, Lyman Trumbull had showed a copy of the Civil Rights Bill to President Johnson. Johnson didn't say he objected, and in March, the bill sailed through both Houses. Seward suggested Johnson sign it but said that if he didn't, Johnson should definitely "find a way to intimate that you are not opposed to the policy of the bill but only to its detailed provisions." If Johnson were to veto the bill, he continued, he'd thereby "make the support of the veto easier for our friends in Congress."

The President paced back and forth. He clearly did not want to sign. "Sir, I am right," he burst out to his secretary, though it's not clear what he was right about. "I know I am right, and I am damned if I do not adhere to it."

ANDREW JOHNSON'S POLITICAL instincts were failing him. Whatever combination of talent and skill and cheek and sheer bravery that had taken him from obscurity to the U.S. Senate, and from the Senate to the vice presidency, no longer sufficed. If the winning combination had been demagoguery and orneriness, with a touch of malice, that combination too no longer worked so well. Johnson had no gift for oratory or singing phrases like Lincoln's "better angels of our nature." He possessed little humor, less wit, and not much reputation for unassailable kindness. And if the backwoods Lincoln or the rugged Jackson had challenged the old myth of the President as a well-born, noble patriarch, staid like General George Washington, Johnson further undermined it with intransigence, prejudice, and a whiff of strong whiskey.

On March 27, 1866, Johnson vetoed the Civil Rights Bill.

"Fraught with evil," he labeled it. The bill placed too much power in the hands of the federal government. It deprived individual states of the ability to make or enforce their own laws—such as black codes, presumably. It operated "in favor of the colored and against the white race." Johnson said immigrants had more of a right to citizenship than black people did. And most repugnant of all, the bill had been passed by what Johnson called a "rump" Congress—that is, a Congress that had not yet seated representatives from the eleven former Confederate states.

Johnson's veto electrified the nation. It stupefied Senator John Sherman, who'd assured audiences that the President would never throw over loyal voters. In fact, as Sherman told his brother the general, the bill was "so clearly right that I was prepared for the very general acquiescence in its provisions." Representative Henry Dawes, also a moderate, was distraught: "I am forced to the conclusion that the President is lost to us, depriving every friend he has of the least ground upon which to stand and defend him." William Cullen Bryant was baffled. "The President probably did not know what he was doing when he returned it to Congress," he guessed. The Republican Congress was livid. "It [Congress] grows firmer every day, knowing that it stands for the Right," House Speaker Schuyler Colfax declared.

Astonished and offended, Lyman Trumbull frostily reminded the President why those eleven Southern states had not been seated: recall, they had rebelled against the federal government, and their representatives were "fresh from the rebel congress or rebel armies, men who could not take the requisite oath to entitle them to admission to seats" since they couldn't swear they'd never borne arms against the United States.

Trumbull proceeded to refute the President's argument at every turn. The rights of citizenship did not confer political privileges, as in the case of white women and children, who were American citizens but couldn't vote. Foreigners were already protected by the rights enumerated in the bill. And since the President had weirdly

Illinois Republican Senator Lyman Trumbull, chair of the Judiciary Committee, wrote the Freedmen's Bureau and Civil Rights Bills, and was astonished when President Johnson vetoed them.

alluded to marriages between blacks and whites in his veto message, Trumbull inquired why he had mentioned marriage at all — except, he specifically added, as "an argument to excite prejudice — the argument of a demagogue and a politician."

Johnson didn't seem to notice. On his own, he proclaimed that the war was over (except in remote parts of Texas, where fighting continued), and even though the Joint Committee on Reconstruction was continuing its work, collecting information about conditions in the South and interviewing witnesses.

In early April, blacks and whites crowded into the Capitol to learn what Congress would do, and when the House and the Senate overrode the President's veto on April 9, the Civil Rights Act, major legislation passed over a presidential veto.

True, the Senate had unseated the Democrat John Stockton of New Jersey to make sure Republicans had the two-thirds vote necessary to override Johnson, charging that the New Jersey legislature had elected Stockton illegally; the case had been debated for some time, and Stockton had even at one point voted for himself. But the packed gallery applauded and cheered passage of the Civil Rights Bill, and the perceptive journalist Mary Clemmer Ames reported that "even Charles Sumner, the grim Greek, hat in hand, unbent his brows and condescended to look delighted."

"The people have made too many sacrifices to give up the fruits of victory at his bidding," Indiana Representative Godlove Orth wrote a friend. "If the rebels under the misguided and mischievous policy of the Prest. could obtain control of the Govt. all will be lost. But they will not succeed." Not only had Johnson alienated moderate Republicans like Orth, he was again unifying the entire Republican party against him. "He is fool enough or wicked enough, I don't know which, to furnish them with material fuel for the flame," Dawes complained, "depriving every friend he has of the least ground upon which to stand and defend him." To Republicans, Johnson had cold-shouldered or showed contempt for Congress, usurping its prerogatives to indulge the very foes he'd said he despised, the Southern foes of the Union. "What a pity he had not stuck to making trousers," one woman joked without humor, "and been a good rebel, like the rest of Tennessee." James Russell Lowell dismissed Johnson as a stump speaker "with a plebeian tone of mind," and the essayist Edwin Whipple said Johnson listened only to news that justified what he already thought—and anyway the man didn't understand the Constitution he professed to love so much.

At the same time, the conservative press in Memphis hailed the President as the savior he claimed himself to be, a forgiving and merciful man who didn't give an inch, particularly not to Radical Republicans.

THE PROTECTIONS OFFERED in the Civil Rights Act, now a rule of law, meant nothing in Memphis. On a warm spring morning, April 30, 1866, three weeks after Congress overrode the President's veto, three black soldiers in blue uniforms were walking down Causey Street in South Memphis when they bumped into four white policemen headed the other way. The two groups exchanged some heated words, which was no surprise since they didn't much like each other, and black men wearing Union blue particularly irritated Southern white police officers. Eyewitnesses later admitted they couldn't hear exactly what was said. Nor would it be clear what happened next. When the soldiers moved aside to let the policemen pass, apparently one of the police shoved one of the black soldiers, who tripped and fell. The policeman then stumbled on top of the soldier.

The police officers drew their weapons. One of them struck a soldier so hard with the butt of his gun that the gun broke. Another soldier grabbed a stick and whacked the policeman, while a different police officer hit one of the soldiers with a brick.

A skirmish like this was not unusual, and it would probably have gone unnoticed if there hadn't been a bigger brawl the next day.

A party of black soldiers, noisily celebrating their discharge from the Union army, was toasting Abraham Lincoln, much to the annoyance of a few white police nearby. "Your old father, Abe Lincoln, is dead and damned," a policeman with red whiskers yelled at the soldiers. The police soon arrested two of the soldiers for disorderly conduct. While the police were marching them off to jail, a different band of black soldiers indignantly followed, firing their pistols in the air. Assuming the shots had been meant for them, the police fired back. In the confusion, one police officer was killed, though it was later discovered he'd shot himself with his own gun.

Most of the other black soldiers had already returned to Fort Pickering, their base. But rumors had already begun spreading through Memphis that black soldiers were rioting and shooting anyone and anything in sight. Enraged and armed, white mobs of fire-fighters, shopkeepers, and police took to the streets on the lookout for black offenders or, for that matter, any black person, male, female, or child.

"Boys, I want you to go ahead and kill the last damned one of the nigger race, and burn up the cradle, God damn them," John C. Creighton, a judge in the recorder's court, shouted from atop his horse. "They are very free indeed, but, God damn them, we will kill and drive the last one out of the city."

John Prendergast, a white grocer, grabbed his guns, and with one in each hand, joined the gang in the streets. Impatient for action, he aimed at the back of a man's head and after he pulled the trigger realized he had killed a white neighbor, Henry Dunn. "I have shot one of our men," Prendergast wailed. "I thought it was a damned yellow nigger." To make things right, he then shot Lew Robinson, a black man, and proceeded to beat Robinson with his pistol.

Austin Cotton, a black carpenter, was walking home from work. "Halt, you damned nigger, or we will knock you on the head," someone yelled. Cotton took off, but a couple of men caught him and pounded him with their guns. Jackson Goodell, a black drayman, had gone to the store to buy cornmeal for his wife. Two men knocked him down and punched him fifteen or so times before they shot him and, not quite satisfied, shot him again. Seven white men, two of whom were police, burst into the home of a washerwoman, Frances Thompson. She was living in a small place with sixteen-year-old Lucy Smith, who helped out with chores. The men demanded supper. Thompson nervously lit a fire and served some biscuits and coffee, but when the men saw pictures of Union officers in the house and a quilt of red, white, and blue cloth, four of them raped her. The others raped Lucy Smith, who had tried to escape through the window.

Around dusk, the constable Bill O'Hearn, riding a pony, arrived on Mulberry Street where two policemen held a black soldier.

"Gentlemen," O'Hearn said, "let me shoot that fellow." He took aim and fired into the soldier's neck.

That same night several white men broke into the home of a pregnant Lucy Tibbs and raped her. Nearby, when Jane Sneed's daughter Rachael ran into the house next door to hers to rescue her neighbor, the men who'd set fire to the place warned Rachael that they'd shoot her if she came out. She did. Her clothes were on fire, and the men shot her while she burned.

"Colored men, women & children were shot in open day light [*sic*] as if they were mad-dogs—& when night came on then began scenes which were more inhuman & diabolical," noted Yankee missionary Reverend Ewing Tade. Barbers were gunned down at their chairs, laborers at the wharves, hackmen in their hacks. Men, women, children were pistol-whipped, clubbed, knifed. Mary Black's house went up in flames, as did Lucy Hunt's. A blacksmith shop was torched and so was Caldwell Hall, where public meetings were held. At night, flames lit the sky, and on the streets of Memphis lay the fly-covered corpses that relatives were afraid to retrieve.

A cheer went up for "Andy Johnson" and a "white man's government."

The tall, clubfooted, inexorable Thaddeus Stevens demanded that the House of Representatives investigate the Memphis melee, and the committee learned that by the next day, May 2, 1866, few black men or women would venture out into the streets. Understandably: as early as seven in the morning, John Callahan was shooting any black person who happened along, and there were widespread reports about a black insurrection—the old and feared idea that had haunted white communities before the war. Businesses did not open. By ten o'clock, white policemen and citizens, many of them still drunk from the night before, were riding into South Memphis. They shot Fayette Dickerson, a veteran of the 15th Colored Infantry. They invaded Harriet Armour's home and asked if her husband was a soldier. When she said yes, the men raped her.

Memphis Sheriff Patrick Winters asked General Stoneman, commanding officer of the Department of Tennessee, to send in federal troops, but the general said he couldn't spare men to quell a mere civil disturbance. He had too much government property to defend.

Black men and women had rushed for protection to the offices of the Freedmen's Bureau. General Benjamin Runkle, in charge, said he had all he could do just to protect the office. But Runkle decided to speak to General Stoneman personally. Stoneman finally took action, after a fashion, a day later, on May 3, when almost forty-eight insane and savage hours had gone by. Claiming, as he already had, that he had too few troops and must in any case guard government property—and that his white soldiers didn't much like blacks either—he ordered the black soldiers at Fort Pickering to stay inside, and he ordered his white troops to restore order to sections of South Memphis.

In all, forty-six black people were killed in the Memphis riot; at least five black women were raped, and fifty-three people wounded. Two white men were dead, one of them the policeman who shot himself.

When U.S. Representative Elihu Washburne, as part of the congressional investigating committee, arrived in Memphis in late May, he saw the brick Baptist Church on Main Street, the oldest black church in the city, in ashes; so too the black church on Poplar Street and the Lincoln Chapel, where all that remained were just one Bible, the mainspring of a clock, and a fragment of the melodeon. More than seventy homes and schools and every black church had been torched. Ninety-three robberies had been recorded—likely there had been more. Washburne told his colleague Thaddeus Stevens that General Stoneman admitted, with some remorse, that "it was no negro riot, for the negroes had nothing to do but to be butchered."

"The civil-rights bill," Washburne added, "is treated as a dead letter."

Illinois Representative Elihu Washburne was a savvy patron
of Ulysses S. Grant both during Grant's military career and
during his for bid the presidency.

General Stoneman may have been slow to act but there was
blame enough to go around. The city's respectable white folk—
lawyers and doctors and newspaper publishers and former
secessionists—said it was a terrible event that would never have
happened if only they, the former secessionists, had been allowed to
hold political office. The spiteful Republican party of Lincoln and
the abolitionists had prevented former secessionists, those Confederates who had left the Union, from entering the government. After
all, they said, they wanted only the best for their former slaves.

No, others replied; the fuse had been lit by the Irish police because the Irish feared that free blacks would steal away their jobs.
Still others blamed a Memphis press that branded black people as
barbarians, and called the Freedmen's Bureau a bunch of "negro-

worshippers." This same press then crowed, with satisfaction, that the black man and his Union friends had just received a good first lesson in civil rights.

Many also pointed a finger at President Andrew Johnson. Johnson's magnanimous policy toward former rebels, his willingness to forgive and embrace them and to welcome them back into the Union, reassured them that white supremacy was true and right and to be defended to the hilt, if not with legislation then with torches, bricks, and guns.

CHAPTER NINE

Mutual Concessions, Mutual Hostilities

"I will take all I can get in the cause of humanity and leave it to be
perfected by better men in better times."

— THADDEUS STEVENS

"Our difficulties here are not over," Senator Sherman of Ohio
told his brother, the general. "Johnson is suspicious of every
one." Clerks in various government positions heard that
they'd be fired if they didn't support the President. "If Andrew Johnson turns out everybody who despises his recent course," an observer remarked, "he will have naught left to fill the offices."

Jane Grey Swisshelm was sacked from the quartermaster's office
mainly because, since 1865, she'd also been publishing a newspaper, *The Reconstructionist*, critical of the administration—and
staffed by women without regard to color, giving it twice the circulation of any Washington newspaper, Swisshelm had joked early on.

A divorcée and single mother, a longtime publisher in Pennsylvania and Minnesota advocating women's rights, a freelancer for
Greeley's *Tribune*, and a nurse during the war as well as a clerk in
the War Department, where she and Stanton became friends,
Swisshelm was small in stature and described by those who hated
her as having a face like a hatchet. They hated her because she was
intentionally provocative. She'd rented two floors of a building on

Tenth Street between N and O Streets, and declared in the prospectus of *The Reconstructionist* that "liberty is in danger of betrayal." And liberty's leading betrayer was Andrew Johnson: "His ambition was and is, to be the hero of Southern chivalry, to restore to slaveholders their lost dominion over their slaves, and to do this he will risk all." Swisshelm dubbed Johnson's veto of the Freedmen's Bureau Bill "the Sumter guns of this second era of the war" and accused Johnson of murdering Lincoln yet again by killing the peace—and the freedmen.

Johnson asked why the government should employ a traitor like Swisshelm.

But Swisshelm lost more than her job. Her printing press was doused in coal oil and set on fire. Arriving in the nick of time, a servant put out the fire before the entire house went up in flames. Puddles of oil were discovered near the press. "An enemy so reckless is not one to be defied," Swisshelm said and closed down the paper.

Thirty years earlier, the burning of a printing press had sparked national outrage—and galvanized abolitionists—but in 1866 the fire that shut down a newspaper went unheeded, and its editor was ridiculed as a female scourge.

FLAMBOYANT DURING THE war, partial to bright white hats and soft velvet shirts, General George Armstrong Custer reported to the Joint Committee on Reconstruction that in Texas Union men were being murdered for no crime other than being Union men, and when he'd left that state the previous winter, the number of murders had been increasing. Ditto the number of freedmen killed.

Madison Newby, a free black from Surrey County, Virginia, said that groups of about fifteen white men would ride up to the homes of black people at night and beat those who lived there. The Committee on Reconstruction listened to story after hair-raising story of unrepentant Southerners who didn't consider the oath of allegiance binding, of wanton brutality, of ruthless night-riders and of cold-blooded murder. The Committee also listened to stories about black soldiers who arrested white men and treated them harshly, just as they'd been treated for longer than some of them could remember, their antagonism a form of resistance. A black soldier had killed a white man in late December, and several black soldiers murdered a white shopkeeper the same month. For there were Bureau agents sympathetic to slavery, or as Northern journalist John Trowbridge noted, agents who, intending to do right, were nonetheless seduced "by the dinners to which they were invited by white planters with favors to ask."

Were any of the stories true? If some were exaggerated, the sheer preponderance of the testimony, delivered in public and in private correspondence, suggests that the conditions in the South may have been even worse than described. "Quite a number of negroes have been shot lately who have been over near the main land to fish or hunt," Daniel Richards, a tax commissioner in Fernandina, Florida, told Elihu Washburne. According to a former army surgeon, former secessionists now invested with state authority said they'd "accomplish by law and Legislation what they failed to accomplish by Arms in the war. We have no peace."

IT WAS CLEAR to Congress that something had to be done. Johnson's veto of the Civil Rights Bill suggested that basic freedoms needed constitutional protection. As James Garfield put it, the war had been fought to break the chains of bondage, but it would have been fought in vain if the injustices sustaining bondage weren't abolished as well. And since laws like the Civil Rights Act could be repealed when political tides changed, as they surely would, a constitutional amendment would be less vulnerable. That had been the reasoning behind the Thirteenth Amendment, which abolished slavery.

But the unintended consequence of the Thirteenth Amendment directly affected Congress, as Congress well knew, since every black person counted as a whole person, not three-fifths of one. As a result, about a million and a half people were added to the census of the former slave-holding states. The South, as a bloc, would have more than twenty more congressional seats and electoral votes. And so Northern Republicans continued to worry that if blacks were denied the vote, a South of former rebels would surely rise again, join with Northern Democrats, and control the legislature just as they had before the war, endangering the rights of black men and women.

Moderate Republicans still believed that there should be some qualifications attached to the right to vote, such as literacy or property ownership. But if black voters had to be qualified, shouldn't the same qualification apply to whites? And, at the very least, shouldn't loyalty to the Union be a qualification for a voter, black or white? "To those who say they [blacks] are unfit for the franchise, I reply they are more fit than secessionists," the late Henry Winter Davis, a Radical, had insisted. Yet there was another, serious question to be considered: could you federally mandate suffrage in just one part of the country? Shouldn't the states determine their own voting regulations, as they always had? Most Northern states didn't allow black men to vote, and Connecticut had recently refused to pass a suffrage amendment.

The Joint Committee on Reconstruction suggested a new constitutional amendment stipulating that if males over twenty-one were prevented from voting because of their race or color, the state's overall representation would be reduced by the total number of persons excluded. This would hurt the South, where the black population was significantly greater than in the North.

Charles Sumner tried to kill the new proposed amendment. He said there should be no denial of rights, civil *or* political, on account of race or color, in *any* state, period. All persons were equal before the law. Attacking the amendment, Sumner helped ensure its initial defeat, for many Republicans were all too eager to jettison the whole suffrage question, and Democrats opposed any reduction in Southern representation.

Sumner's position infuriated Thaddeus Stevens. The amendment was "slaughtered by a puerile and pedantic criticism," Stevens later exclaimed in exasperation, "by the united forces of self-righteous Republicans and unrighteous Copperheads." William Pitt Fessenden thought Sumner an ass. "The only ground of his opposition was mortified vanity," Fessenden declared. "Sumner is not only a fool but a malignant fool," Charles Eliot Norton fumed. "Sumner receives as little support as the President. Nobody but Longfellow approves his course; & in politics Longfellow is a mere sweet simple child."

Concerned that protracted Republican bickering might convince people that Congress had no plan, no direction, and no backbone, Representative Elihu Washburne sadly complained to his wife that "our friends are all split up among themselves." Norton urged the editor of The Nation to speak out. Congress must act.

But Lydia Maria Child felt there were good reasons to kill this new amendment. "If the South have to choose to diminish her representation for the sake of maintaining her pride of caste," Child said, "she would keep the blacks forever in *civil* bondage, if the proposed amendment to the Constitution were carried. Moreover," she gloomily added, "such an amendment would act as a temptation to *get rid* of the blacks, by expatriation, starvation, or slaughter." The Radical Republican Thomas Durant, formerly attorney general in Louisiana under General Nathaniel Banks, watched in dismay. Johnson's generous pardoning policy had allowed these ex-rebels to sit on local court benches, to serve in law enforcement, and to run for local office; they had little motivation to go to Washington if forced to give blacks the vote. Former Confederates sashayed into office, and as Durant wryly noted, "the oligarchy doesn't care for a representative in Congress if you allow them permanent control of the state."

Congressional debates dragged on until June. A newly proposed Fourteenth Amendment, revised and revised again, did confer citizenship—but not the right to vote—on all people born or naturalized in the United States. It also guaranteed these citizens equal protection and due process under the law.

Furthermore, its second section decreed that representatives would be apportioned according to a state's population unless the state denied the vote to male citizens over the age of twenty-one. In this case, the state's representation would be reduced in proportion to the number of men excluded.

The amendment did not therefore mandate suffrage. Rather, those states (Southern states, it was assumed) that denied black men the vote were penalized by having their representation in Congress reduced. In addition, anyone who'd engaged in rebellion against the Constitution was disqualified from holding state or federal or military office, although Congress could vote to remove that restriction.

In the fourth section, the federal government forgave the Confederate debt, and the fifth section allowed Congress to pass laws to enforce the amendment.

In its final form, the Fourteenth Amendment was what historian Eric McKitrick called an "odd contraption" that fully satisfied no one. A farrago of political jockeying, political compromise, and nagging anxiety about the future of a country where all people are created equal, it ignored the question of what to do with confiscated land, and certainly it sidestepped the issue of black suffrage, although it did open the door to a black vote, or so many Republicans wanted to believe. The amendment also implicitly addressed the question of a Union that still excluded eleven states, though it saw the question through a glass darkly. It wasn't clear, for instance, if the Southern states would be readmitted to Congress if they ratified the amendment. As it happened, only Tennessee ratified it right away, and Tennessee was allowed into the Union, the first of the eleven states to be so admitted.

Wendell Phillips hated the Fourteenth Amendment, saying it was a "fatal and total surrender," as he told Thad Stevens. Susan B. Anthony and Elizabeth Cady Stanton hated it too. They'd strongly protested the introduction of the word "male" into the amendment, which revealed the longstanding bias against a woman's right to vote—and against women. But hammered together by congressional leaders with clashing visions for the future, this ground-breaking legislation, changing our concept of citizenship, was passed in a spirit of hopefulness. "We were each compelled to surrender some of our individual preferences in order to secure anything, and by doing so became unexpectedly harmonious," Iowa Senator James Grimes told his wife.

Exhausted, Charles Sumner went along, and Thaddeus Stevens, yielding temporarily on suffrage, declared it was no sacrifice of principle to admit you can't undo the past at one sitting. "I would not for a moment inculcate the idea of surrendering a principle vital to justice," Stevens explained with passion. "But if full justice could not be obtained at once, I would not refuse to do what is possible." That is, if the states would not yet ratify an amendment giving black men the right to vote, so be it. "I shall not be driven by clamor or denunciation to throw away a great good because it is not perfect," Stevens declared. "I will take all I can get in the cause of humanity and leave it to be perfected by better men in better times.

"Men in pursuit of justice," Stevens concluded, "must never despair."

Thaddeus Stevens spoke again, this time elegiacally. "In my youth, in my manhood, in my old age, I had fondly dreamed that when any fortunate chance should have broken up for a while the foundation of our institutions, and released us from our obligations the most tyrannical that ever man imposed in the name of freedom, that the intelligent, pure and just men of the Republic, true to their professions and their consciences, would have so remodeled all our institutions as to have freed them from every vestige of human oppression, of inequality or rights, of the recognized degradation of the poor, and the superior caste of the rich.

"This bright dream has vanished," he concluded. Our institutions are not yet devoid of human oppression or inequality, he went on to say. And yes, we might have done better if we had the cooperation of President Johnson. But we don't. The President would have the former Confederacy remain a slave empire under a different name. We cannot allow that or forgive that. So we must not delay, we must not give up, we must take and do what we can: "Mutual concession," Thaddeus Stevens added, "is our only resort, or mutual hostilities."

LEGISLATION IN WASHINGTON didn't stop the murders—and definitely not in New Orleans that summer. New Orleans, where, as Thomas Durant had said, ex-Confederates had taken control of government.

The Louisiana state government was chock-full of former secessionists, and Confederate veterans made up two-thirds of the police force; some still liked to wear their gray uniforms. New Orleans' mayor, John T. Monroe, was himself a proud Confederate—jailed during the war as a traitor and elected mayor before he'd even been pardoned. And the state governor, James Madison Wells, was a conservative Unionist who forced Unionists out of office to reinstate former rebels, and at President Johnson's urging revamped the Freedmen's Bureau and installed there a Johnson lackey, General Joseph Fullerton. Governor Wells and Fullerton proceeded to give land back to former planters and discouraged poor rural blacks from coming to the city, arresting them on trumped-up charges and then jailing them indefinitely.

Then, strangely enough, Governor Wells supported a call for a state constitutional convention intending to remodel the state's 1864 Unionist constitution and to include, this time, amendments guaranteeing black suffrage. A number of state legislators and office-holders, particularly the wealthiest and most prominent ex-rebels, had wanted Governor Wells gone. The legislature offered to nominate him for the U.S. Senate and pack him off to Washington, but Wells refused. "The Governor has become fully convinced that the late returned Rebs are not to be trusted with power in their hands," an observer noted.

The governor therefore supported the call for a convention to shore up the Radical Republicans and strengthen his own position by doing so. "He intended to beat the rebels and keep them from power," Henry Warmoth wrote in his diary, "even if in so doing he destroyed the state government and produced anarchy for twenty years." Wells thus took up the Radicals' appeal for a new state constitutional convention. After all, he reasoned, during the 1864 convention two years ago, many of the state's parishes hadn't been represented. And since a loophole in the constitution allowed the convention to be reconvened if its president issued a call for one, the convention would be legal, at least technically. When the convention's original president refused, Governor Wells appointed Judge Rufus K. Howell as president pro tem. He also issued writs of election for new delegates who advocated black suffrage.

The whole thing seemed extraordinary, particularly to New Orleans Democrats. *The New Orleans Crescent* declared that "it is our general belief, fixed and unalterable, that this country was discovered by white men, peopled by white men, defended by white men, and owned by white men, and it is our settled purpose that none but white men shall participate in its government." These white men would stop, by force if need be, any convention bent on ousting them, especially the one slated to meet on Monday at the redbrick Mechanics Institute.

The Friday before the state convention, about 1,500 people, black and white, rallied at the steps of City Hall in support. There were speeches, but not the rabble-rousing kind reported in the press, at least according to one journalist, who didn't find anything he heard that night any more extreme than the speeches he'd heard at any other political rally. But the conservative papers said the rally augured revolution, and that a dentist, Anthony Dostie, a Radical Republican from the North, was telling the crowd to drench the streets in blood.

The next day, Saturday, Mayor Monroe called a private meeting at which he told General Absalom Baird, in temporary command of Louisiana, that there was to be an illegal assembly on Monday that might disturb the peace, never mind subvert the present government. General Baird more or less brushed him off, saying that if the convention wasn't legal, as Monroe claimed, the mayor should think of it as a bit of "harmless pleasantry." According to Henry Warmoth, on that same Saturday, Mayor Monroe gave the police orders to kill every member of the convention, especially its leaders.

Albert Voorhies and Andrew Herron, state lieutenant governor and state attorney general, contacted President Johnson: the convention, they said, was illegal, and they planned to arrest its delegates, and they wanted to make sure the military wouldn't meddle. Johnson's reply was just what they'd hoped: the "military will be expected to sustain, not obstruct or interfere with, the proceedings of the courts," he reassured them. The President then contacted Governor Wells: what was going on, he wanted to know, and by what authority was this illegal convention to be held? Wells dodged. So on Monday, July 30, the day of the convention, President Johnson told Andrew Herron to "call on Genl. Sheridan, or whoever may be in command for sufficient force to sustain the civil authority in suppressing all illegal or unlawful assemblies who usurp or assume to exorcise [sic] any power or authority without having obtained the consent of the people of the State."

That day, by noon, about twenty-five delegates arrived at the Mechanics Institute, but since there was no quorum, a recess was called so the sergeant-at-arms could round up absentees. Outside the Institute, a crowd of mostly black men and women had been waiting around for hours when a procession of black Union army veterans, accompanied by fife and drum, came marching from the French Quarter to Dryades Street. They waved the Stars and Stripes, and the crowd cheered, or some of them did, for there were a number of white men standing by, apparently as many as a thousand, who began to hoot and hiss.

Information about what exactly happened that day is contradictory. There was a scuffle. One journalist reported he saw "several negroes lying dead" on the sidewalk. Someone had fired a shot— perhaps it had been the police. No one knew, but the police had brought pistols with them; nightsticks wouldn't do.

The drums of the marchers stopped pounding, the fife fell silent. More shots. In minutes, a white mob, white handkerchiefs knotted round their necks and their hats facing backward so they could recognize one another, fired at the black marchers. After the marchers fell, the mob shot at their corpses. The firefighters showed up, and they too attacked the marchers.

"I'll shoot down every damned son of a bitch in the building," a member of the mob yelled as many of the black men from the procession, seeking refuge, ran toward it. "We'll go and tear down the Institute, and we'll get a cannon." The police stationed in front of the Mechanics Institute blasted out the windows, and together, the mob, the police, and the firefighters pushed inside. The delegates grabbed whatever they could to defend themselves. "It seemed ridiculous to me that men should with chairs, battings, and piece of railings contend against an armed force, regularly organized," recalled a delegate. Another of them dropped to the floor so that the bullets might pass over him. Others scrambled to the second story. The police followed, and though a few protected the delegates they recognized, soon the walls were splattered with blood, which congealed on the floorboards. A couple of delegates jumped out of windows onto the broken glass below. They were shot when they landed. The mob grabbed another delegate. "Hang him," they cried.

Waving a handkerchief that he'd tied on to one of the little flags in the room, the Reverend Dr. Horton tried to surrender. "Stop firing," he shouted. "We are noncombatants; if you want to arrest us, make any arrest you please, we are not prepared to defend ourselves."

"God damn you," replied one of the mob. "Not one of you will escape from here alive." The reverend was hit in the arm, one of his fingers was broken, his skull crushed by a brick. Dr. Dostie was shot, and his body was tossed into a cart of corpses. An officer grabbed Dostie's hat and flapped it in the air. "Let Dostie's skin be forthwith stripped and sold to Barnum," the *Mobile Daily Tribune* taunted, "the proceeds to go to the Freedmen's Bureau and negro newspapers."

From his law office on nearby Carondelet Street, Thomas Durant saw former Governor Michael Hahn dragged along the street by the police while rioters from behind stabbed him until his back and bare head dripped with blood. Hahn screamed for the police to kill him and get it over with. Though a Radical, Durant had thought the convention illegitimate and harmful, but he became a target anyway. Hurriedly he left his office, slipped into a nearby alley, and fled New Orleans that night, never to return. Armed rioters ransacked his home.

The Mechanics Institute was empty. Any men in the procession still alive had scattered. Others lay wounded or dead. But the violence had not stopped. Some men (all blacks) were executed point-blank while kneeling and praying for their lives; others were kicked, cudgeled, and stabbed after they were already dead, sometimes by persons elegantly dressed. A white citizen stopped to kick the body of a black man shot near a millinery shop. A gray-haired man, walking at a distance from the Institute, was shot through the head when a policeman riding in a buggy took aim from his carriage. Another policeman boarded a streetcar on Canal Street and fired his gun at a boy and then dragged him onto the street, where he beat him to a pulp—"pounded to a jelly," said an eyewitness. One of the delegates darted away from a policeman and crawled on all fours before he was arrested by a less violent officer. He heard someone shout, "Kill the Yankee nigger."

"I have seen death on the battlefield," declared former Vice President Hannibal Hamlin's son, who happened to be in New Orleans that day, "but time will erase the effects of that, the wholesale slaughter and the little regard paid to human life I witnessed here on the 30 of July I shall never forget." Within three hours, over one hundred men and women lay dead or dying and as many as three hundred were wounded, perhaps more.

"It was a dark day for the city," Warmoth said.

"It is Memphis" all over again, a reporter cried in horror. It wasn't, though. Deadly, yes; spontaneous, not at all. The thing had been planned.

———

This huge painting (8 by 12 feet) was part of artist Thomas Nast's "Grand Cari-caturama," a humorous moving panorama of American history. Nast regularly depicted Andrew Johnson as "King Andy," and here shows him smiling while black men and women are being slaughtered in the background.

GENERAL PHILIP SHERIDAN was the commanding officer in the Gulf instructed to keep an eye on the Texas-Mexico border. On July 30, he'd been doing just that, but when he returned to New Orleans the next day, he discovered that in his absence nothing short of a sadistic massacre had occurred. "No milder word is fitting," he said.

"The more information I obtain of the affair of the 30th in this city the more revolting it becomes," Sheridan told General Grant.

Federal troops didn't arrive on the scene until the riot was pretty much over. General Baird said he hadn't known military action had been required. "Not to know that was to be an idiot," an eyewitness scoffed. Actually, though, two days before the massacre, an evidently nervous Baird had wired Secretary of War Edwin Stanton asking for instructions. He'd been informed that the convention would be unlawful and that city authorities intended to break it up by arresting the delegates. "I have been given no orders on the subject," Baird said, "but have warned the parties that I could not countenance or permit such action without instructions to that effect from the President."

Stanton did not answer, nor did he turn Baird's request for instructions over to the President, as Baird had suggested he do.

Edwin Stanton, the secretary of war, did not answer.

The only man to reply to Baird's request for instructions was Lieutenant Governor Voorhies, who said that while no arrests should be made, General Baird should place troops on Dryades Street, outside the Mechanics Institute, about an hour before the convention. But Voorhies may have misled Baird about when that hour would be. Whatever the case, whatever General Baird was told, or whether he was hoodwinked or negligent, Stanton's silence is peculiar. It is inconceivable that he hoped for or even anticipated the agonizing bloodshed, but he had definitely withheld from President Johnson any information about possible trouble. Perhaps Stanton feared that if he told Johnson, the President would somehow prevent the convention from occurring. Perhaps he didn't want to defy Johnson openly, which he would have to do if he ordered Baird immediately to New Orleans. Perhaps he hoped that the convention, if successful, would discredit Johnson, and if unsuccessful—or if it turned ugly—that too would discredit the President. Certainly Stanton had been upset when Johnson leaked the results of a cabinet meeting during which all members of the cabinet, including Stanton himself, said they opposed the Fourteenth Amendment. Certainly he was sickened by the nonstop violence in the South and the slow dismantling of the Freedmen's Bureau.

Democrats believed that the war secretary kept mum to feather his own nest. "Stanton avoids the responsibility of checking the riots and therefore appears to side with the radicals and will be found in league with them," a critic declared. "If Johnson comes out all right, Stanton will assume the credit. If wrong, he will get the credit from Radicals."

Perhaps, perhaps, perhaps: with motives so mixed, Stanton may not have known himself why he suppressed Baird's telegram and did nothing. "That he had a political objective in mind seems highly probable," Stanton's sympathetic biographers admitted, though a less approving one called the withholding of Baird's telegram "political passive-aggression." Certainly Gideon Welles thought Stanton complicit somehow in what he believed was a plot to overthrow the Louisiana government. In a cabinet meeting after the massacre, Stanton "manifested marked sympathy with the rioters," Welles haughtily wrote in his diary. According to him, Stanton had stormily referred to Mayor Monroe and Louisiana's attorney general "as pardoned Rebels who had instigated the murder of the people in the streets."

Whether Stanton felt responsible for the massacre, in whole or in part, he did deplore it. Whether he was partly to blame is another matter. The only ascertainable fact is that after he learned of the slaughter, Edwin Stanton told Senator Charles Sumner that Johnson and his horrendous Southern policy were at fault.

The next year, Andrew Johnson would remove Stanton from office. The wonder is that he didn't do it sooner.

Andy's Swing
Around the Circle

In 1864, the Republican party, needing votes from War Democrats, had temporarily changed its name to the National Union
party, and it was under this banner that Abraham Lincoln had
been elected President. Two years later, the National Union party
was moribund—though not to Andrew Johnson.

"The mere fact of the north and the south meeting again in fra-
ternal relations will be a great object lesson," he exuberantly
claimed, "and go far towards allaying sectional strife and promoting
concord between these sections." More to the point, Johnson
thought a revived National Union party, consisting of sympathetic
Democrats as well as conservative or moderate Republicans, could
block reconstruction, crush the Radical Republicans in the fall
elections, and put Southerners back into Congress on his theory
that they had never left the Union. Johnson would then secure the
White House in 1868, not as a Vice President who'd become an
accidental leader but as the nationally elected chief executive.

A National Union convention, a sort of rally for this new party,
was to occur in Philadelphia on August 14, 1866. A month earlier,

Thurlow Weed, William Seward's powerful political ally, had called on Henry Raymond to ask if he would speak at the convention. When Raymond hesitated, Seward pressured the publisher, who was also a U.S. representative. Raymond seemed hesitant though he'd written in his paper, *The New York Times*, that he supported the convention; but, as chairman of the regular Republican National Committee, Raymond was responsible for preserving that party, and since he wanted to stay its chairman, he worried what might happen if former rebels with "purposes hostile" captured the National Union convention—or, worse, if the Democrats took control of it. He'd have to resign from the Republican party, he explained to William Seward. Seward shrewdly replied that if men like Raymond refused to participate in a convention intended only to strengthen the Republic, then they were responsible for it falling into the wrong hands. Go see the President, Seward advised.

Raymond approached Johnson, who met him in the White House library, where Johnson assured him that he didn't wish to restore the Democrats to power, just to bring former War Democrats into the fold in order to rout the Radical Republicans. Johnson said he wanted only to make the Union whole again, and the best way to accomplish this was to find representatives willing to welcome Southerners to Congress. Raymond capitulated.

In Congress, all Republicans except Raymond slammed the National Union convention as a conspiracy to destroy the Republican party. Outside of Congress, Republicans were similarly skeptical. As General Benjamin Butler told Johnson, "It encourages those against whom every Union soldier has fought for four years, to hope that they may seize the Government of the Country by means of political movements, which in their unholy attempt by arms they have so signally failed to do." The more moderate Republican William Evarts, later one of Johnson's attorneys at the impeachment trial, made the same point. The only result of such a convention, Evarts observed, would be "the transfer of the political power in the country from the party which carried the war to the party which opposed it." A National Union convention risked putting former Peace Democrats, who'd opposed the war, in the driver's seat; it spelled disaster at the polls; and it had to be a Democratic confidence game— a ruse to get conservative Republicans to bolt their party or undercut it.

Evarts wasn't wrong. Democrats intended, as one of them actually said, "to rupture the Republican Party, to form a strong Democratic Party in the convention, and without committing the Democratic Party to any policy, to secure the convention for their purposes."

There was another reason Johnson backed a National Union convention. Any plan to admit Southern representatives to Congress would quash the Fourteenth Amendment. And since this was plainly Johnson's objective, when he asked his cabinet to endorse the National Union convention, three cabinet members actually decided they must resign. Grabbing his hat, Postmaster General William Dennison walked out of a cabinet meeting. Interior Secretary James Harlan also left, and Attorney General James Speed said he wouldn't participate in any attempt to block the Fourteenth Amendment or damage the Republican party; he too had to go. Gideon Welles brusquely asked Stanton to "show your colors." Stanton, though he condemned the convention, did not resign. "He holds on like grim death," an unfriendly paper reported.

But Republican defections were the least of the convention's problems. As diarist George Templeton Strong curtly noted, the National Union convention consisted of "Rebels and Copperheads mostly." Nathan Bedford Forrest, the Confederate general infamous for the slaughter of black troops at Fort Pillow, was nominated a vice president of the convention. Peace Democrat Clement Laird Vallandigham, who'd been banished from Ohio during the war for sedition, wanted a seat at the National party table. So did another Peace Democrat, Fernando Wood of New York. Excluded from the proceedings, they had caused a commotion, and though Wood withdrew, Vallandigham insisted that his letter of protest be read aloud. And despite a turnout of about seven thousand—and the symbolic pageantry of Union general Darius Couch, from Massachusetts, a big man, entering on the arm of South Carolina Governor James Orr, a small one—the whole thing fizzled. The roof leaked, the flowers wilted, and the damp feathers of the huge stuffed eagle behind the podium glumly stuck together.

"As matters now look," the lawyer Edwards Pierrepont predicted, "Andrew Johnson will not be the candidate of any party." Again, the man in the White House, with his transparent attempt to head a new party, had managed to alienate both Republicans—for trying to divide the party—and Democrats still indignant that he hadn't sacked Edwin Stanton.

JUST AFTER THE debacle of the National Union convention, during the last week of August 1866, Johnson went on the road to drum up support for what he liked to call "My Policy," or his effort to get a white supremacist South into Congress as quickly as possible. More to the point, though, he was eager to slam, widely and loudly, the Fourteenth Amendment.

The pretext for the trip was the laying of the cornerstone in Chicago for a monument to fellow War Democrat Stephen Douglas. Although Johnson hadn't voted for Douglas for President in 1860, Douglas had notoriously argued against anything that smacked of emancipation or civil rights for black people, and now, as Charles Eliot Norton bitingly observed, "there could hardly be a fitter man, however, than Andrew Johnson to dedicate the monument to Douglass [sic]."

The trip quickly degenerated into a Barnum-like carnival of unabashed self-promotion. Dubbed "Andy's Swing Around the Circle," it was roundly mocked as "the event of the season," The Nation snickered, "if not the age." Johnson had intended otherwise, of course, firstly by surrounding himself with able deputies. But Treasury Secretary Hugh McCulloch had begged off, and so had Edwin Stanton. New to his post, Interior Secretary Orville Hickman Browning said he had too much to do, and the recently appointed Attorney General Henry Stanbery, Speed's replacement, pleaded poor health. That left William Seward and Gideon Welles and the

Postmaster General Alexander Randall. Johnson also dragooned two celebrated war heroes, Admiral David Farragut and General Ulysses S. Grant, along with a retinue of several other generals, including General George Armstrong Custer, who would join them later. Rounding out the party was the Republican Senator from Wisconsin, James Doolittle (who also joined later), the young Mexican minister Matías Romero, members of Johnson's family (though not his wife), his staff, a caterer, and the press.

The presidential party departed Washington on a presidential train provided by the Baltimore & Ohio Railroad and outfitted with private berths, cushioned seats, and luxurious curtains. It would run on a special timetable with the track cleared for its passage. No expense was spared: the party ate from engraved plates of red, white, blue, and gold prepared for the occasion. The dining car was loaded with a seemingly unlimited supply of wines, liquor, and cigars, and the menus typically included terrapin, canvasback ducks, prairie chicken, and champagne, which according to one member of the group, "were far more plentiful than bread and butter or cold water."

The Baltimore and Philadelphia city councils declined to host official receptions, and in Philadelphia the mayor had left town. Still, well-wishers greeted the presidential entourage. In New York City, Johnson relished the noisy cheers he heard as he traveled from the Battery to City Hall and then to a gala banquet for 250 men at the elegant Delmonico's restaurant, where the doors were draped in flags and banners, and throngs of bystanders lined the street for a glimpse of the stocky President treated to a dinner that cost $11,000, said the adversarial press.

Johnson must have felt as though he had come home, what with the screaming crowds, fluttering streamers, and the wooden stages hastily knocked together in city after city. From New York City by riverboat, the group continued to upstate New York and west, from Albany to Buffalo, stopping along the way in such small places as Seward's hometown of Auburn. But the trip didn't go very well. James Doolittle had warned Johnson not to speak extemporaneously, which was going to be hard for him to resist, and Thurlow

Weed, who greeted Johnson in Albany, reminded him that men were like flies; you catch more with honey than with vinegar. Johnson turned a deaf ear. As one historian explained, Johnson had an "itch for speechmaking," and even in prepared remarks, which could last an hour, he couldn't resist letting loose about his enemies. Those come to hear him also noticed how often he used the personal pronoun or referred to himself, and how often he called reconstruction "My Policy," emphasizing the "my."

In Springfield, Illinois, home of Lincoln, the houses were shut, the streets deserted, and the flags unfurled over the headquarters of the Grand Army of the Republic, which welcomed only Grant and Farragut. Abraham Lincoln's son Robert pleaded a previous engagement. When Johnson addressed crowds, he heard hisses and hecklers, particularly when he spoke from the balcony of his hotel in Cleveland. "Three cheers for Congress," someone yelled. And when Johnson angrily yelled back, "Where is the man or the woman who can place his finger upon one act of mine deviated from any pledge of mine in violation of the Constitution?" more than one person replied, "New Orleans."

New Orleans had become a refrain, an epithet, a reminder of the violence produced by a "My Policy" of pardoning former rebels and ushering them into power.

"Why don't you hang Jeff Davis?" someone hollered. Captured more than a year earlier, the president of the Confederacy was imprisoned at Fort Monroe; no one yet knew whether to put him on trial for treason in a civilian court in Virginia, where he had been indicted—and where he would likely not be convicted. People jeered. Someone else in the crowd shouted out to Johnson, "Don't get mad."

"I will tell you who is mad," Johnson snapped. "'Whom the Gods want to destroy they first make mad.' Did your Congress order any of them to be tried?" It wasn't quite clear what or whom he meant, except for Jefferson Davis.

The boisterous crowd would have none of it. The hecklers baited the President. "Three cheers for Congress," they again cried.

Johnson went on, this time referring to the assassination attempt on William Seward. "If I were disposed to play the orator and deal in declamation, even tonight, I would imitate one of the ancient tragedies, and would take Mr. Seward, bring him before you, and point to the hacks and scars upon his person. I would exhibit the bloody garments, saturated with gore from his gaping wounds. Then I would ask you who is the traitor?" Again, it wasn't clear whom or what he meant.

But the President did have fans, for someone screamed, "Thad Stevens!"

"Why don't you hang Thad Stevens and Wendell Phillips?" Johnson yelled back. Some people cheered.

But something had gone very wrong. Later, when Senator Doolittle reminded Johnson about the dignity of his office, Johnson snorted, "I don't care about my dignity."

"The President was fortunate if he escaped insult, wherever the train stopped," Sylvanus Cadwallader reminisced. Cadwallader was traveling with the presidential party as the correspondent for *The New York Herald*, which defended Johnson although it wouldn't much longer. "Grant and Farragut were continually called for, and Johnson's name jeered and hooted at whenever mentioned," Cadwallader recalled. "At one point a lively scene was witnessed, when Mr. Johnson undertook to speak: There was a determination to drown his voice, by cries of: 'Grant-Grant.' The President roared out: 'Why this interruption? Gen. Grant is not against me—I am not against him. He is not a candidate, I am not a candidate, there are no candidates here,'" Cadwallader said. "At Lockport Mr. Seward undertook to speak, but was howled down by the cry: 'We don't want to hear you or Johnson. We shall only cheer for Grant and Farragut. You others are bad men.'"

The morning after the Cleveland speech, Johnson looked ill, Postmaster Randall seemed unwell, Señor Romero rattled on about mosquitoes, and Johnson's son-in-law Senator David Patterson was miserable.

St. Louis was no better. The presidential procession entered the

Calm and almost bullish during the war, General Ulysses
S. Grant was considered its greatest hero; but when
Johnson attempted to subvert Congressional reconstruction, Grant vigorously sought to protect the freedmen
and loyal whites in the South.

Lindell Hotel and, after walking through the parlor, went out to the
balcony over the main entrance, where thousands of spectators
stood below, waiting for a glimpse of Johnson, but more especially
of General Grant. That night, at a ceremonial banquet at the Southern Hotel, Johnson appeared on the portico, where he addressed an
eager crowd. With his characteristic opening—I am not here to
make a speech—he speedily returned to the subject of New Orleans, accusing "this radical Congress" of instigating the riot there
by encouraging the city's black population to arm.

Someone called Johnson a traitor.

"I have been traduced and abused," he shot back, his voice trem-
ulous with self-pity. "I have been traduced, I have been slandered, I
have been called Judas Iscariot," he shouted. And just because he

exercised his veto power over the Freedmen's Bureau Bill or Civil Rights, his enemies said he ought to be impeached. The sympathetic members of the crowd cried out, "Never."

"Yes, yes!" he answered, and then speaking of himself in the third person, cried, "They are ready to impeach him."

"Let them try it," his supporters answered back.

But he was incoherent. "There was a Judas once," Johnson babbled, "one of the twelve apostles. Oh, yes! And these apostles had a Christ, and he could not have had a Judas unless he had twelve apostles.

"If I have played the Judas, who has been my Christ that I have played Judas with?"

It was bewildering. Again, he yelled, "Why don't you hang Thad Stevens and Wendell Phillips?

"I call upon you here tonight as freemen to favor the emancipation of the white man as well as the colored man," Johnson fired up the crowd. One reporter noted in muted horror, "The President continued in this strain at great length." "Who ever heard of such a Presidential Ass?" an officer of Olivet College asked. The headline in the Republican *Chicago Tribune* groaned, "The Ravings of a Besotted and Debauched Demagogue."

In Indianapolis, rowdy spectators booed and clamored so noisily for Johnson to shut up that he couldn't speak. He withdrew into the hotel. General Custer heard the popping of gunfire. General Grant appeared on the hotel balcony to calm the crowd, to no avail. A local man was killed, others were wounded, and it was said there had been an attempt to assassinate Johnson. Gideon Welles, slightly paranoid, thought that the whole thing had been planned—Radicals conspiring with rogues to disrespect the President.

Even if that were true, Johnson had no one but himself to blame. The publisher James Bennett had reminded him that the press in an instant could telegraph Johnson's speeches to the entire nation, that reporters would scurry back to their hotels and transcribe their notes to cable stories as fast as possible. Every word of Johnson's, every hasty wisecrack and intemperate outburst, would flash on the front page of papers throughout the country. And they did.

In Johnstown, Pennsylvania, another horrible disaster occurred when the wooden platform that covered an old, dry canal collapsed under the weight of almost two thousand spectators. Hundreds of men, women, and children plunged twenty feet into the bottom of the canal, where they lay atop one another in the midst of splintered planks and rubbish. At least six people were killed and about three hundred, including dozens of children, were severely hurt.

As Johnson headed back to Washington, the Baltimore city council decided that the President had perverted the object of his visit—in fact, the object of his entire tour—by embarking on an electioneering campaign completely inconsistent with Union principles. Moderate Republicans began to distance themselves. Henry Ward Beecher insisted he was no longer a "Johnson man," although he had agreed with some of the President's policies. Beecher believed the Southern states should be welcomed back into the Union, albeit one at a time, and he claimed this would have been possible— except that as far as he was concerned, the inflexible President was preventing it. Johnson was a man who stood in his own way, and it was not even clear which way, except backward, he wanted to go.

It was an astute observation. "Proud and sensitive, firm to obstinacy, resolute to fierceness, intelligent in his own sphere (which is narrow)," Beecher declared, "he often mistakes the intensity of his own convictions for strength of evidence." As for Johnson's recent speeches, on what planet would they be considered conciliatory?

"The 'so-called' President whom it is evident the Gods wish to destroy has been doing the cause of freedom good service every day," Frederick Law Olmsted agreed. "Every card he has played has been against him."

Henry Raymond of The New York Times finally abandoned the President. "What a muddle we are in politically!" he exclaimed. "Was there ever such a madman in so high a place as Johnson?" Senator John Sherman told his brother that the President had "sunk the Presidential office to the level of a grog-house." Some moderates were even less kind: they said Johnson might be cunning and skillful, but he was basically a hazy-headed demagogue who should resign his office so it might be said that "nothing in his official life ever became him like his leaving of it." James Russell Lowell remarked that if the President's rallies weren't so pathetic, they'd be funny. Johnson was turning himself into a buffoon. William Cullen Bryant said the President's behavior was not only indiscreet but stupid. Essayist Edwin Whipple compared Johnson to Charles Dickens' Uriah Heep, what with his ostentatious humility and addiction to the personal pronoun. "If he left Washington the ninth part of a man," John Greenleaf Whittier remarked, "what a pitiful decimal fraction he brings back."

Thaddeus Stevens called the road show a traveling circus. Former Congressman Isaac Arnold, a strong Lincoln supporter, resigned from his position in the government Post Office Department. "How can you, Mr. President, occupy the Executive Mansion as the successor of Lincoln," he directly berated Johnson, "how could you visit his grave with the bloody outrages of Memphis and New Orleans unpunished?" Carl Schurz was contemptuous. "If there is any man that ought to hang," he said, "it is Andrew Johnson."

Democrats too soured on the President. "Does Seward mean to kill him off by this tour," one of them asked, "and are we to stand by (& see him kill us off too?)" Others speculated that Seward was playing a double game, letting the President destroy himself so people would flock to *him*. Publisher James Gordon Bennett had had enough. Johnson had been too lenient with the South; the rebels were implacable; and Johnson should sever ties with Seward, who was leading the President right into a Dismal Swamp. The best way to restore the Southern states to Congress, Bennett continued, was to adopt the Fourteenth Amendment. William Phillips, an editor at Bennett's *Herald*, told Johnson that if he'd stop fighting against the Fourteenth Amendment, the *Herald* would go easy on him. Concentrate on foreign and fiscal affairs, Phillips advised, and tariff and monetary issues, or on the French occupation of Mexico.

Actually it was Seward who'd brought Matías Romero on the President's tour to pacify critics of what had appeared to be Johnson's lackadaisical Mexican policy. When Napoleon III's puppet, Emperor Maximilian of Austria, displaced Mexican president Benito Juárez, Seward had resisted Grant and others who wanted to intervene militarily, and lately it seemed that his diplomacy was paying off; France was going to gradually withdraw its troops from Mexico. But Romero was a protégé of Juárez, the leader of the liberal Mexican government in exile, and he was hoping for more support from the administration. Not for long: the usually tireless Romero said he was too tired to continue on the trip. Aghast at Johnson's speeches, he privately remarked that he had no intention "to mix myself in the domestic business of this people."

By the middle of September, Admiral Farragut and General Grant were also distancing themselves from Johnson and "My Policy," claiming they had joined the presidential entourage because they'd been instructed to do so. In fact, Grant had briefly left the tour, apparently so upset by Johnson's behavior that he'd gone on a bender. According to Sylvanus Cadwallader, in Buffalo, after waiters passed through the cars, plying everyone with food and drink, the general got so drunk he had to lie down on a pile of empty sacks in the baggage car. Until he'd recovered enough from his "indisposition" that they could steer him into a carriage, Grant was shielded by Cadwallader and Grant's friend John Rawlins, who kept away all callers. But Grant returned to the tour just before the President landed in Cincinnati. There, he loyally stood up for Johnson, though equivocally: "The President of the United States is my superior officer, and I am under his command," he said. Of course Grant had supported the President's lenient policy toward the South, and his own hasty report on conditions there, back in 1865, could have been written by Johnson himself. Grant had also argued for dropping all charges against Robert E. Lee unless he violated his parole, which Lee had not. But now he stood beside a President whose tirades offended him. In Buffalo he'd presumably told a friend, "I wouldn't have started if I had expected any thing of the kind." And he confided to his wife that he considered Johnson "a National dis-grace."

With crowds calling for him, not the President, or hailing Gen-eral Grant as their next chief executive, the relationship between Grant and Johnson cooled. Seward again stepped into the breach, shrewdly affirming Grant's support of the President's policy. By doing so, Seward cost Grant the confidence of many Republicans. "If the public get an idea that Grant is with the President it will do us great injury," one of them had complained to Grant's friend Rep-resentative Elihu Washburne. Said another, "the Genl. may say that he will take no part in the political issues, but the people think he is taking part now by traveling with Johnson on his electioneer-ing trip." Letters of exasperation and gossip about Grant landed on Washburne's desk: it was Seward who'd gotten Grant drunk in Buf-falo to help get Johnson re-elected. Keep Grant quiet, Washburne was advised from one side; make Grant talk, Washburne was urged from another: "his reticence had led some of our friends to doubt him, and all the Democrats claim him as their own."

Other backers reported in relief that Johnson's behavior had cured some of Grant's most influential friends, like John Rawlins and Adam Badeau, of their good opinion of Johnson. And the thick-set general returned to Washington alone, not with the President. As Grant explained to Sheridan, Johnson seemed increasingly "vio-lent with the opposition he meets with, until now but few people who were loyal to the Government during the Rebellion seem to have any influence with him." And after New Orleans, Grant was making his position clear: the military must intervene when and if the civil authorities allowed the massacre of men and women, as it seemed too often to be doing.

Johnson, perceiving Grant as a rival, decided he must rid him-self of the popular general without exactly removing him from his prestigious post as general of the Army of the United States, a title revived the previous summer for the hero. Johnson would send Grant to Mexico to accompany Lewis D. Campbell, the new min-ister to the Juárez government. In an ill-defined advisory role, Grant was to pressure the French to withdraw their troops, which would presumably suit Grant, a supporter of Juárez and his government. The real objective of the mission wasn't the French or even Mexico; it was getting Grant out of Johnson's hair and pairing him with Campbell, who had a known drinking problem. With Grant gone and his reputation again damaged by drink, Johnson could appoint the more conservative William Tecumseh Sherman as interim general-in-chief.

Johnson overlooked one important detail—that Grant and Sherman had been friends for more than twenty-five years. And Sherman was no more a fool than Grant. "There is some plan to get Grant out of the way, & to get me here," Sherman told his wife, "but I will be a party to no such move." No need. Grant unequivocally declined the mission. The essentially diplomatic assignment was beyond the scope of his office, he said, and besides, he possessed neither the training nor a taste for it.

Irritated, Johnson instructed Secretary of State Seward to order Grant to Mexico, but on the recommendation of the cabinet, Johnson backed off, suggesting instead that Seward "request" that Grant go. Grant again declined, saying it was expedient for him to stay in Washington. Growing angry himself, Grant said he was not subject to orders from the secretary of state: he was an officer in the military, and this was a *civilian* posting. "No power on earth can compel me to it." Johnson apparently banged his fist on the table in a pique of anger, and Grant stormed out of the room.

The result was a grudging truce, and William Tecumseh Sherman accompanied the feckless Campbell to Mexico. "I cheerfully consented because it removes at once a crisis," Sherman told his brother John. "Both Grant and I desire to keep plainly and strictly to our duty in the Army, and not to be construed as partisans."

Grant apparently thought it had been Seward even more than Johnson who had devised the plot to sequester him in Mexico. "The influence of Mr. Seward over the President is complete," Matías Romero concurred. "One does not need to be with them for long to learn that Seward knows how to gain the confidence of Mr. Johnson to a high degree." Seward had tried to climb into the Lincoln White House by a back window, James Russell Lowell decided, and since the Republican party had ditched him in 1860, Seward felt no compunction about deserting it now.

"Poor Seward! What a miserable close to his career!" Charles Eliot Norton exclaimed. "What a loss to him, & to the country, that he did not die with Lincoln!"

CHAPTER ELEVEN

Resistance

One of the chief architects of Andrew Johnson's impeachment was Andrew Johnson. The man had a penchant for martyrdom. It allowed him to cling to his belief that he was cruelly beset, deeply unappreciated, wholly persecuted, and denied the respect he rightfully deserved. If his great destiny—his crucifixion—was to be fulfilled by impeachment, so be it. For his temperament allowed no other choice. He thus welcomed a struggle to the death, with the hero, himself, going down to defeat in a blaze of unforgettable glory.

Speculation about impeachment had been in the air for months. The preceding spring—before New Orleans, before the swing around the circle—the spellbinding orator Anna Dickinson had mesmerized audiences with her call to impeach Andrew Johnson. "Permit this government to be reestablished on the old foundations of falsehood & oppression—permit the white traitor to legislate for themselves, for us, & for the freedmen of the South, & this war will have been fought in vain, this treasure spent in vain, this perilous blood spilled & black lives sacrificed in vain," Dickinson cried.

Johnson had launched "that miserable abortion known all over as 'My Policy.' The man should be slain politically," she rousingly added, "so politically killed, that there would be no hope of his political future." Wendell Phillips too had said Johnson and Seward, who were working to smash the Republican party, did not care a jot about black suffrage, or whether black men and women were "sunk into eternal perdition."

Impeachment rhetoric was not limited to the Radicals. If a majority of Radical Republicans returned to Congress, Montgomery Blair cried, they'd run the President out of office and push Ben Wade, one of the worst of the Radical bunch, into the White House. They'd soak the streets with blood, Blair continued, "and a devastation, to which that of the South was nothing, would overwhelm the entire north." The outgoing minister to France, John Bigelow, heard that Johnson would be impeached as soon as Congress met. General James Steedman told Interior Secretary Browning that the country was on the brink of revolution; the only way to stop it was to "prepare"—he meant militarily. Browning went to Secretary of State William Seward and frantically said that the President's impeachment was on the horizon. Calm as ever, Seward was nonplussed.

Not so the fusty Gideon Welles. "I have sometimes been almost tempted to listen to the accusation of his enemies that he desired and courted impeachment," Welles would privately mutter.

Egging on the Republicans, Johnson railed at them, particularly at the Radicals who wanted to depose and destroy him. Over and over, he called Congress a body hanging on the verge of the government; he frustrated the laws of Congress; he branded its leaders as traitors. But Congressman George Boutwell, former governor of Massachusetts, disingenuously noted that Congress was not taking the bait: Never in public session nor in any of the Republican caucuses had the House of Representatives considered or proposed Johnson's impeachment; "the grounds of his fear," Boutwell continued, "are known only to himself."

His beard trimmed to a point, his sense of purpose just as pointed,

George Sewall Boutwell was the industrious son of poor Massachusetts farmers. He'd worked as county clerk, a teacher, a storekeeper,
and had studied in the office of a local attorney so that he could
practice law. He was also a crafty politician. When he was just
twenty-one, in 1839, he was elected as a Democrat to the local
school committee, and from there he went on to the Massachusetts
House of Representatives, never losing his taste for agriculture or
for educational issues. After he suffered a series of political losses, in
1851 a coalition of Free-Soilers and Democrats elected him Massachusetts governor. An opponent of slavery, he eventually joined
the Republicans, whose party he helped organize, for he supported

Massachusetts Representative George S. Boutwell, one of
the principal framers of the Thirteenth and Fourteenth Am-
dendments, strongly opposed Andrew Johnson's restoration
policies and served as one of the principles prosecuting
Johnson's impeachment.

equal voting rights and detested all cant about so-called "inferior races." He would enter President Grant's cabinet as treasury secretary, and much later, when eighty years old, in 1898, he again left his party—this time the Republicans—to protest American military aggression in the Philippines. Until his death, Boutwell served as president of the American Anti-Imperialist League.

Gideon Welles labeled Boutwell a Massachusetts fanatic who somehow had helped to plan the New Orleans debacle, for Welles knew that as soon as Johnson created the state government in North Carolina by proclamation in the spring of 1865, an appalled Boutwell had rushed to the White House. Johnson assured Boutwell that his proclamation was tentative—an experiment—which it was not. That interview was the first and last time Boutwell and the President talked together and from then on, Boutwell distrusted Johnson. "A conspiracy was on foot to put the government into the hands of rebels," Boutwell gathered, "and the president was a party to it."

That fall, Boutwell ripped into Johnson in an essay he published in the widely read *Atlantic Monthly* magazine. Johnson was a dictator, Boutwell said; he'd imposed his policies on the South, organizing provisional governments, inaugurating constitutional conventions, and booting out elected or appointed officers. Such autocratic actions were a usurpation of power—and as such were impeachable offenses. For Johnson and his cabinet were denying the legitimacy of the Congress by demeaning it as a "rump," and the President was capable of ordering the army to empty congressional halls. Paranoia made for good politics. Boutwell was not a paranoid man, but he understood political expediency.

And he had good reason to believe his own propaganda. Johnson continued to turn good men out of office, replacing them with lackeys or conservatives. Seward's office had falsely accused John Nicolay, the American consul in Paris and formerly Lincoln's secretary, of being lazy, corrupt, and unsympathetic to the President: more evidence of the President's morbid sensitivity, his need for absolute loyalty, and his wariness. In Augusta, Georgia, Johnson's Freedmen's Bureau appointee General Davis Tillson refused to permit blacks to leave flowers on the graves of the Union dead, and when the freedmen protested labor contracts, he cut their rations until they complied. "This tells well for the reconstructed, & still better for our own apostate officers," a disgusted officer remarked. Wendell Phillips direly predicted that "what New Orleans will be today, Washington will be in December: ruled by the President and his mob—unless the people prevent it."

The brashest call for impeachment came from Benjamin Franklin Butler, a former Democrat who'd voted for his friend Jefferson Davis over fifty times during the 1860 Democratic convention. In those days, Butler had held abolitionists in contempt, but after Fort Sumter Butler joined the war effort with such fervor that Lincoln asked General Winfield Scott to curb his pugnacious enthusiasm. A bona fide Radical Republican from then on, he did part company with many of them, particularly on currency reform. He favored greenbacks over so-called "hard" money (or specie) when he entered the House of Representatives in 1866, and in later years, Butler ran for President as a candidate for the short-lived Greenback party. He was a maverick, an opportunist, and a paradox in an age of paradox. Called by a contemporary the "best abused, best hated man in the House," Butler was accused of vindictiveness, of vaulting ambition, and of vulgarity—and managed to sweep all criticism away with the back of a hand.

Bald, stubby, and with hooded lids that made him look a bit like the thief he was often accused of being, Butler had been raised by his widowed mother, who ran one of the boardinghouses that lodged the mill girls of Lowell, Massachusetts. Rejected by West Point, he'd graduated from Colby College in Maine and then studied law. Tremendously successful at the bar, he was an aggressive, hardworking advocate who adored histrionics and a good fight—the wilder and woolier the better—and brazenly championed women, workers, and racial equality.

After being given command of a regiment of volunteers, Butler achieved a kind of notoriety in 1861 when three black field hands rowed across the James River to Fort Monroe, a Union-held post,

Keen and possibly corrupt, Massachusetts lawyer and politician General Benjamin F. Butler, formerly a Democrat, was the Radical Republican who, during the war, declared fugitive slaves free. Elected to Congress, he served as chief prosecuting representative during the impeachment trial, which he said he'd conduct as if he were trying to convict a horse thief.

and Butler, now a Union major-general, didn't return them to their rebel master. Declaring them "contrabands of war," he said that as such they were slaves no more. Butler's decision was thus an act of emancipation, and the idea of "contrabands" as people—not slaves—entered the Northern vocabulary. Though not an unalloyed abolitionist victory (a contraband was still a kind of property), it was such a radical idea that Jefferson Davis said anyone who captured Butler could hang him then and there.

In 1862, while Major-General Butler was military-governor of Union-occupied Louisiana, he ruled with a crooked, iron fist. Nicknamed "Spoons," Butler was said to have pilfered silver servingware, which he presumably stashed in a coffin. He was also called the "Beast," for he arrested the New Orleans mayor, none other than John Monroe, who would be mayor in 1866 during the riots, and he executed a man for pulling down the Stars and Stripes. And after the Crescent City's rebellious ladies presumably poured the contents of their chamber pots on the heads of Union soldiers, Butler issued an order that promised to treat all females who harassed his troops as common prostitutes. More troubling were allegations about shady trade in sugar and cotton, perhaps with his brother

Andrew. Years later, the historian Bruce Catton, who detested Butler, said that though no one ever proved Butler was dishonest, "there always seemed to be a dead rat behind the wainscoting somewhere." Or, as Henry Adams noted, "Butler is the only man who understands his countrymen and even he does not quite represent the dishonesty of our system."

There was no love lost between Generals Butler and Grant. Butler never won a major battle, and in the spring of 1864, he and his men, having been defeated near Richmond, retreated to a narrow neck of land between the James and Appomattox Rivers, where they were trapped. The retreat was a serious strategic blunder. The usually taciturn General Grant noted that Butler had sealed off his army "as if it had been a bottle, strong corked." Humiliated in public, Beast Butler was now known as "Bottled-Up Butler." Then, after Butler failed to destroy Fort Fisher near Wilmington, North Carolina, and withdrew his forces, Grant not only asked Lincoln to remove him from his command but to make certain he'd never receive another one.

Yet Butler retained his own devoted following. "He was no pretender and no hypocrite," said Assistant War Secretary Charles Dana. And there was a charming effrontery about him. When a boisterous group in front of New York City Hall greeted him with hisses and groans, Butler stood calmly on the platform, a gold toothpick in his mouth, until the crowd quieted down. As he began to speak, someone threw an apple, striking him on the forehead. Butler caught the apple, bowed to the man who'd thrown it, and in his studied way coolly bit into it. The crowd laughed, and Butler continued his speech.

Almost immediately after Johnson entered the White House, Radicals suggested that he replace Seward as secretary of state with Ben Butler. That was not going to happen, especially since Butler went on record saying black soldiers should, at the very least, be given the vote. Yet because he coveted a cabinet post, Butler was initially reluctant, as were many Radical Republicans, to criticize the President. Regardless, like Stevens, he had hoped to redistribute planter lands to black and white soldiers, and he wanted the leading Confederates to be punished, so when Johnson favored letting them back into Congress, Butler began to lose heart.

"A collision will come between Congress and the President," Butler predicted in the spring of 1866, "which if he is not a coward (and I think he is not) will result in revolution." Butler suggested a plan of reconstruction that allowed all male citizens over the age of twenty-one the right to vote. As for congressional representation, Butler suggested that it be determined by the number of qualified voters. His plan went nowhere.

In the fall of 1866, Butler ran for Congress from the Essex district of Massachusetts, where he owned some property—he didn't live there, but he didn't want to compete with his friend George Boutwell, who lived in Butler's home district. Such "squatting" struck detractors as another example of Butler's shiftiness. Ignoring the accusations, Butler successfully attracted excited crowds not just in Massachusetts but throughout the country by demanding that Johnson be impeached.

"We will not yield to usurpation," Butler shouted. Revisiting the New Orleans massacre, Butler charged Johnson with conspiring with Mayor John Monroe to foment the riot. He told audiences that Johnson had distorted General Sheridan's account of the riot in order to downplay it. He reminded them that neither the instigators of the massacre nor the murderers had been arrested. You just couldn't trust Andy Johnson. "The war did not end with the surrender of Lee," Butler declared. "The moral victory of every war depends upon the moral gain that is obtained after its close, by the indication and maintenance of the immutable principles of truth for which the contest was inaugurated and waged.

"Come back to the true principles of justice for all—equal rights for all men—away with the idea this is a white man's Government— it is God's government," Butler cried. "It is made for white men, black men, or gray men—all men, and all men with a perfect equality."

Audiences loved him, Massachusetts elected him, the President would come to rue him.

AS THE FALL elections approached, moderate Republicans were hopeful. "The massacre at New Orleans will open many eyes," said George William Curtis, the editor of *Harper's Weekly.* "If the elections are against us, we shall submit," declared Rutherford B. Hayes, who placed himself above the fray, and while he wouldn't dare consider impeachment, he didn't think Republicans should surrender to the President. "Don't let Andy Johnson deceive you," Hayes cautioned a friend. Frederick Law Olmsted considered himself a mild and rational man, but he'd lost his transcendental calm. "The events at New Orleans &c. & Mr. Johnson's exhibition of Southern White character have greatly strengthened and confirmed the conclusion that the risk of adopting Mr. Johnson's policy would be too great," Olmsted told Charles Eliot Norton. Resist Johnson and his plans.

Johnson was defied. The congressional elections in the fall of 1866 were a Republican landslide, with Republicans gaining more than a two-thirds veto-proof majority in both houses—173 to 53 in the House, and 43 to 9 in the Senate. Memphis and New Orleans had spoken. No new Johnson party had been formed. The "Swing Around the Circle" had shown the President to be vain, vulgar, and vindictive. The London *Spectator* called him blind and crazy. Tennessee Governor Brownlow said he was a dead dog. Caricaturist Thomas Nast mocked him. Humorist Petroleum Vesuvius Nasby satirized him. Frederick Douglass indicted him. Johnson's policy had failed. It was failing. It would continue to fail.

Impeachment was now necessary, Ben Butler cried: election results may vex Johnson, they may rile him, they may momentarily stop him, but they will never change him.

Part Two

IMPEACHMENT

Pasteboard tickets of admission, numbered, dated, and color-coded, were distributed in order to organize the crowds of people clamoring to attend the first-ever impeachment trial of a United States President.

CHAPTER TWELVE

Tenure of Office

January 7, 1867

now had fallen for three days in early January, the sky was leaden, and white powdery stuff drifted up the Capitol steps. Inside, the gallery in the House of Representatives teemed with observers, attentive and breathless, black and white, and they got what they'd come for.

A barrel-chested James Mitchell Ashley, his face pale, his hands trembling, rose from his seat in the House of Representatives and declared, "I do impeach Andrew Johnson, Vice President and sitting President of the United States, of high crimes and misdemeanors."

The spectators clapped and stamped, and when the din subsided, Ashley continued: "I charge him with a usurpation of power and violation of law.

In that he has corruptly used the appointing power;
In that he has corruptly used the pardoning power;
In that he has corruptly used the veto power;
In that he has corruptly disposed of public lands of the United States:

In that he has corruptly interfered in elections, and committed acts that, in contemplation of the Constitution, are high crimes and misdemeanors: Therefore,

Be it resolved, that the Committee on the Judiciary be, and they are hereby authorized to inquire into the official conduct of Andrew Johnson."

WHEN ASHLEY CALLED for the impeachment of Andrew Johnson, the President of the United States, he was acting rashly. Most Republicans didn't think an impeachment resolution should be brought to the House floor, not yet. A group of Republicans had met just before Ashley's announcement, Ashley among them, and though Thaddeus Stevens had strongly argued for impeachment, claiming that Johnson had single-handedly prevented any reconstruction of the Union, what with his pardons and his vetoes and his putting rebels back in office, many of his colleagues hedged. They said that if an impeachment resolution were to be brought forward at all, it should go to the Judiciary Committee before it reached the full House. In committee, they hoped, impeachment would die a quiet death.

Ashley had been impatient. But rather than vote Ashely's resolution completely down, the House authorized the Judiciary Committee, by a vote of 108 to 39, to investigate Ashley's charges.

Unsettled by the whole business, but not for long, William Seward too assumed the Judiciary Committee would bury the whole business. The committee certainly wouldn't recommend impeachment. The Jacobins might be restless, Seward said, but they weren't to be taken seriously. Besides, Ashley was far from a perfect vessel. "He constituted himself the chief impeacher," journalist Benjamin Perley Poore recalled with contempt, "and assumed a position that should have been held by a strong-nerved, deep-sighted, able man." Known by those who disliked him as an ambitious lightweight interested only in his own advancement, Ashley the vain peacock was said to promenade up and down the aisles of the House while taking sidelong looks at the ladies' gallery. Representative Elihu Washburne indicated he wouldn't touch an impeachment resolution with Ashley's fingerprints on it, and James Garfield backed off. "If we could succeed in an impeachment of the President it would be a blessing, probably, but it is perfectly evident that with the Senate constituted as it is, we cannot effect an impeachment," Garfield calculated. "Ashley and such like impracticable men, are determined to push the insane scheme of making the attempt and setting the country in a ferment." But Ashley said more than once that he had no use for that "rascally virtue, called discretion," and he long maintained he'd done right in calling for Johnson's impeachment. "I did it as a public duty," he later said, "without undertaking to count the cost to myself personally."

Historians haven't been kind. C. Vann Woodward dismissed Ashley as "a nut with an idée fixe," and Eric McKitrick called him "an occult mixture of superstition and lunacy." Yet though Congress had its share of mountebanks and cheats, Ashley had been quite serious about ending slavery, and as manager of the House floor, he'd been largely responsible for passing the Thirteenth Amendment. Washington reporter for *The Independent,* Mary Clemmer Ames, said Ashley was the most genial man in Congress and the kindest. Most men in government were churls; not Ashley. Frederick Douglass ranked him among the likes of Sumner, Stevens, and Benjamin Wade, all of them valiant white men determined to secure equal justice for all. Not only had Ashley fought against slavery and aided in the recruitment of black troops, after the war he rendered his best service to liberty and to the nation by actually attempting to impeach Andrew Johnson. "Yet it has happened to him, as it has happened to many other good men," Douglass reflected, "to have his best work in the world least appreciated and commended by the world." William H. Young, president of the Afro-American League of Tennessee, would similarly declare that neither he nor the freedpeople would forget what Ashley had done or stood for, despite the "chill and gloom of ingratitude" with which he was predictably remembered. Ashley's deeds, Young said, "shall be a precious legacy to our children's children."

So Ashley's resolution was referred to the Judiciary Committee. But though conservative and moderate Republicans thought that they could squelch impeachment by dumping it on the committee, impeachment was in the air. "Hardly a speech is made in either house which does not begin or end with it," an observer remarked. That was the point—or part of it: impeachment put the President on notice. "The Radicals are holding the threat in *terrorem* over the President merely to keep him in check," a friend of the Democratic leader Samuel Barlow reported from Washington. "They have at present no idea of prosecuting the matter."

Johnson was furious—"cross as a cinnamon bear" a journalist noticed—but took comfort in the Supreme Court's recent ex parte *Milligan* decision, which stipulated that a citizen could not be tried, convicted, or sentenced by a military tribunal if the state courts were operational. That meant that the Southern courts could do what they wanted, or as one Savannah native exclaimed, "It would be just as easy to get a jury in the State of New York to convict a person of manslaughter for shooting a mad dog, as to get a jury of Rebels to find a Rebel guilty upon a charge of killing a negro." Many Southerners—particularly blacks—had been depending on military courts to provide a fair hearing—or any hearing, for that matter. Take Georgia, where three hundred black men and women had been killed; only one percent of the perpetrators were punished. Even the middle-of-the road *New York Times* wondered if the Supreme Court hadn't thrown "the great weight of its influence onto the scale of those who assailed the Union."

Take too the infamous case of Dr. James L. Watson. When the carriage of William Medley, a man of color, collided with Dr. Watson's buggy, the wheels of the two vehicles had locked, breaking one of the spokes on the Watson carriage, which contained Dr. Watson's wife and daughter. Although no one was injured, and Watson's wheel was fixed for fifty cents, Watson regarded the traffic accident as an insult to him and his family. He tracked Medley down and beat him; Dr. Watson later testified that this was his right. Medley broke free from Watson and ran, but Watson ran after him, threatening to shoot unless Medley stopped, which Medley didn't do. Good as his word, Watson drew his pistol and fired twice.

Medley died a few hours later. Dr. Watson surrendered himself to the authorities, freely admitting his crime because to him the murder of a black man was not murder. Agreeing, the county examining court refused to indict. But General John Schofield, assistant commissioner of the Freedmen's Bureau in Virginia, ordered Watson rearrested and held over for trial by a military commission: not only would Watson be held responsible for his action, other white men or women would be made to understand that wanton acts of intimidation or violence would not be tolerated. The presiding judge of the Circuit Court of Virginia issued a writ of habeas corpus for Watson's release, but Schofield disregarded it. Then, at Andrew Johnson's behest, Attorney General Henry Stanbery claimed the Watson case fell under the jurisdiction of *Milligan*. The military commission was dissolved. Watson went free.

This notorious case was one among many. Augustus Higgs of the Freedmen's Bureau in Virginia reported that in Perryville, a young white man beat to death a black man who'd been standing on a street corner one evening. "This excels in brutality the Watson case," Higgs cried, "as the killing was done for sport."

"Anyone who hopes that the Sumners, the Stevenses, and the Phillipses, the noblest and finest men of the nation, will stand silently by and see their country fall into moral ruin without making strong efforts to prevent it, is hoping for the country's misfortune," the young French journalist Georges Clemenceau declared. Congress had no choice but to prevent Johnson from precipitating more acts of violence "tacitly encouraged by the approval of a population which long slave-holding has demoralized." That implied Republicans might be acting out of pure conviction, as Charles Sumner always seemed to do. But on the matter of impeachment itself, Sumner was cautious. "I say nothing," he explained, "as I should be one of his judges." So he hoped.

"WE ARE HAVING pretty serious times here, in Congress, &c—
I rather think they are going to impeach Johnson & bring him to
trial—it is a serious business—I cannot tell how it will turn out—only
I know both sides seem determined, & neither will give an inch,"
Walt Whitman wrote his mother. But people didn't really seem to
know what impeachment was. It might take the shape of an avalanche, as Mark Twain had said, or maybe a loud thunderclap—or
maybe the roof would cave in.

For Ashley's call was the first ever *presidential* impeachment.
The House of Representatives had voted to impeach only four
times, and the Senate had convicted only twice. In 1797, William
Blount, a senator from Tennessee, tried to persuade Creek and
Cherokee Indians to help Great Britain seize Spanish Florida and
Louisiana. Blount, charged with behavior inconsistent with his
public duty, was expelled from the Senate. In 1804, Judge John
Pickering, chief justice of the New Hampshire Supreme Court,
whom Washington then appointed federal district judge, was removed from the bench for showing up drunk. Though Pickering
was clearly unfit for office, the proceeding had a political odor since
Thomas Jefferson wanted Republican judges on the bench anyway.
That same year, Supreme Court Justice Samuel Chase was also impeached for using rude language—as well as for delivering an opinion on the law before he'd heard evidence. Here the proceedings
against Chase, a Federalist, were unambiguously political, for the
case hinged on whether "high crimes and misdemeanors" should
be interpreted broadly to include partisanship or interpreted more
narrowly—and require the violation of a specific law.

Justice Chase was not convicted because his accusers, divided
on the issue, couldn't reach a two-thirds majority.

A more recent impeachment case involved District Judge West
Humphreys of Tennessee, who became a Confederate judge without resigning his federal district judgeship. It was Andrew Johnson,
as military governor of Tennessee, who recommended Humphreys'
impeachment.

But what were sufficient grounds to impeach a sitting President of the United States? What were the right reasons to impugn him and challenge his leadership, disregard his stature, and ignore his electoral standing? Had Andrew Johnson abused the national trust? Had he perpetrated any overt act against Congress, or had he confined himself to wielding his authority, which was a matter of policy, not abuse? And how to distinguish between these things? That is, when Johnson recognized the formerly rebel legislatures of the South and vetoed all Northern bills, was it policy, or abuse?

Then there was debate about what should be considered constitutional. Did Johnson have the authority to appoint governors in the former Confederacy? Were these appointments constitutional? For that matter, did Congress act constitutionally when it created, passed, and sent out the Thirteenth Amendment, abolishing slavery, to the states in 1865 while the country was nominally at war? What about after the war? Every time Johnson vetoed a bill aiming to reconstruct the South he argued that the bill wasn't constitutional because the ex-rebel states weren't represented in Congress. "There is never a lack of legal texts any more than of religious texts, when men seek to stifle their consciences," Georges Clemenceau commented with more than a touch of acerbity.

To many observers, the moral verdict against Andrew Johnson had already been rendered. Johnson had endorsed rebels and rebel legislature, he'd fired competent people, he'd abused the pardoning privilege, he'd blocked or subverted the civil rights legislation, and he was obstructing ratification of the Fourteenth Amendment. Yet the question remained: had the President committed *illegal* acts and hence demonstrably impeachable ones?

"The long haired men and cadaverous females of New England think you are horrid," Johnson's secretary reported to him. "I had a conversation with an antique female last night, in the course of which she declared that she hoped you would be impeached. Said I 'Why should he be impeached—what has he done that he should be impeached?' 'Well,' replied she, 'he hasn't done anything yet, but I hope to God he will.'"

That woman's response, if typical, suggested that impeachment does require a criminal offense, a breaking of the law rather than an abuse of power, a subversion of Congress and hence a failure to execute the laws of the people. But, as some reasonably argued, shouldn't deplorable, bigoted, or reckless acts be considered impeachable, particularly if they weakened or flouted other branches of government? In that case, impeachment shouldn't be considered a legal issue at all.

There were questions too about procedure: would the President be required to leave office during an impeachment trial, or would he be tried as a sitting, functioning President? And would he stand before the bar; would he—or should he—speak in his own defense? Despite all these questions, all this debate, all this uncertainty, impeachment began to seem necessary—to be undertaken with reluctance and only as a last resort. Congressional Republicans knew this.

They also knew, or wanted to believe, that impeachment implied hope, the glimmering hope of a better time coming, a better government, a fairer and more just one. But that was far off. For now, impeachment did seem a calamity, the national roof tumbling down.

BECAUSE REPUBLICANS HAD clearly carried the fall elections, Frederick Douglass rejoiced in the *Atlantic Monthly* that the Congress had been vindicated; the President's sham reconstruction policy had been condemned; a new world order was at hand. "If with the negro was success in war, and without him failure," Douglass said, "so in peace it will be found that the nation must fall or flourish with the negro." And because of the Republican success in the elections, some of the President's allies advised him to patch up his quarrel with the Republicans. "The folly of continuing the present struggle, is only equaled by that of the gamester," a Southern lawyer said, "who after loosing [sic] heavily at the gaming table, continues to play to win back his losings."

If Johnson would only have bent a little on the matter of the

Fourteenth Amendment, he might have been able to work with Congress. "I think you will agree with me that it will be wiser not to stem an overwhelming current but rather to use it, and control it, as far as possible, for the welfare of the country," a journalist for *The Herald* likewise suggested. "Swallow even the constitutional amendment as a man would a nauseous dose of medicine to releive [sic] himself from a painful disease." Another Johnson friend suggested the President allow black men to vote with qualifications. "The tendency of all the great populations of the Earth, just now, is in the direction of general enfranchisement," he explained.

Concerned that Johnson might be listening to such suggestions— they'd heard unsettling rumors—Democratic power-brokers dispatched the former congressman Samuel Cox to Washington. "When I told him what you wanted to know,—whether he was going to modify his views as to the Amndt [Fourteenth Amendment], he got as ugly as the Devil," Cox reported to his friends. There was no reason to worry, because Johnson wasn't going to negotiate with anyone. And true enough, once Johnson made up his mind, he wasn't going to change it. He was simply unable. He took political decisions and strategy personally, dubbing his position "My Policy" so often that it was the butt of grim humor. To criticize or doubt his policy was to criticize or demean him.

Though a deep-dyed radical among the Radical Republicans, Senator Wade had suggested that a Southern state could get back into Congress by ratifying the Fourteenth Amendment, but President Johnson choked off compromise, telling a delegation of citizens from South Carolina never to trust a Radical. And when the Alabama legislature reconsidered its vote against the amendment, Johnson immediately let it be known there should be no wavering. The Fourteenth Amendment, with its guarantee of civil rights and citizenship for blacks, was unconstitutional, and it would "change the whole character of our Government," he cried.

The President's obstinacy—and commitment to white supremacy—began to wear even on the patience of friends. If he wasn't going to support an amendment that would allow the South, on ratification of it, to come back to Congress, he should keep his mouth shut. Do nothing rather than do harm, said Representative Henry Raymond of *The New York Times*. Raymond decided not to run for re-election — his association with Johnson assured his defeat. Johnson did not listen, and he didn't budge. Instead he hinted that he *might* have considered the Fourteenth Amendment if Radical Republicans weren't so radical.

When all Southern states except Tennessee rejected the Fourteenth Amendment, the usually sanguine James Garfield, representative from Ohio, was ferocious. "They have deliberated; they have acted; the last one of the sinful ten [states] has at last, with contempt and scorn, flung back into our teeth the magnanimous offer of a generous nation; and it is now our turn to act. They would not cooperate with us in rebuilding what they destroyed; we must remove the rubbish and rebuild from the bottom," he declared. "We must see to it that the frightful carnival of blood now raging in the South shall continue no longer."

General Grant, who supported the Fourteenth Amendment, had been watching the President in mute disgust. When Grant offered the cabinet a report about the desperate conditions that white and black Unionists faced in the South, Welles predictably belittled the report as "newspaper gossip" or "rumors" originating in "negro quarrels." But the violence was documented, and it was as real as New Orleans had been real. To General Phil Sheridan, Johnson's indifference to the bloodshed "made plain," Sheridan would recall, "that he was seeking to rehabilitate the seceded States under conditions differing not a whit from those existing before the rebellion; that is to say, without the slightest constitutional provision regarding the status of the emancipated slaves, and with no assurances for men who had remained loyal in the war."

What now, though? Should these Southern states oversee, then, their own reconstruction? Johnson continued to manipulate them, replacing Freedmen's Bureau officials with flunkies, sacking over a thousand postmasters, and discharging federal employees in the

Treasury office who didn't agree with him. "He is refractory and lavishes his official patronage on Copperheads of the worst and most 'septic' type," George Templeton Strong protested.

When a bill giving black men the vote in the District of Columbia landed on the President's desk, Johnson refused to sign it, saying the admission to the ballot box of a new class of voters—black men—would weaken, degrade, and finally destroy the government. Delaware Senator Willard Saulsbury, a Johnson supporter, said black men were morally unfit to vote and then staggered from the Capitol so drunk that an aide had to keep him from falling into the gutter. Radical Republicans seized on Saulsbury's folly, quickly pointing out that it was he who was morally unfit.

The Radicals and the more moderate Republicans decided they must act. Johnson had to be curtailed, particularly if he attempted to remove those who dared to disagree. Congress therefore drafted a bill requiring the President to secure the approval of the Senate before firing or suspending any federal officer, including members of the cabinet, who'd been confirmed by the Senate. This would become the contentious Tenure of Office Act—so contentious, in fact, that it was finally and fully repealed, but not until 1887.

As to be expected, the Tenure of Office Act initially (and subsequently) was controversial. Certainly in 1867 moderates and conservatives in Congress weren't altogether willing to come between a President and his closest advisers. So a compromise was suggested, and it did pass: cabinet members would be able to hold their office for and during the term of the President who appointed them, plus one month, subject to the advice and consent of the Senate.

The wording would prove ambiguous, and even Edwin Stanton doubted the validity of the Act. Johnson proceeded to veto it, and Congress overrode the veto.

Stanton had moved to curb Johnson in a different manner when he suggested to George Boutwell that he add a rider to the upcoming military appropriations bill. That rider required the President issue any and all orders through the general-in-chief, who happened to be Ulysses S. Grant. The general-in-chief could not be removed without Senate consent, and his headquarters would be in Washington.

Yet Johnson continued to receive letters from supporters, North and South, outraged by Congress and any talk of impeachment. "I blush for the honor of the American name," said a manufacturer in Cincinnati, "to think, that any one calling himself an American citizen, and having enjoyed high military office in the gift of his country, should so far forget the honor and respect due to the President of the United States." Another defender advised Johnson that should the President find himself on the eve of impeachment, "*Arrest the traitors.*"

John Bigelow, former ambassador to France, found the President looking peaked. William Seward, unapologetic Johnson booster, assured Bigelow that Johnson was healthy as an ox, even if the atmosphere in Washington was toxic. "They don't cut throats any longer here," Bigelow reported, "but the work they make of character is something only paralleled in the declining days of the Girondists." Representative Henry Dawes said much the same thing. "There are men in the House who consider themselves absolved from all obligations of decorum or respect to the man or his office because he has seen fit to disregard his own dignity," Dawes had told his wife. He had called on the President, which he felt obliged to do. The President seemed pleased to welcome visitors— "few of our side call on him," Dawes had observed—but the saturnine Johnson was unable to muster any small talk or initiate much conversation.

The principled Charles Sumner made no secret of his desire to see Johnson booted out of the White House. Thanks to the President, Senator Sumner said, "there was a war still being waged upon loyal Unionists, without any distinction of color, so that both white and black are sacrificed." But the Judiciary Committee wasn't making much headway on the question of whether Andrew Johnson should be impeached, or for what crime. For one thing, it seemed distracted by Johnson's peccadillos, according to testimony leaked to the public. There had long been rumors about dissolute behavior. "Johnson has resigned himself to drunkenness and now whoreing is added and prostitutes are seen emerging at late hours of the night," Judge William B. Napton of Missouri had noted with disdain.

More recently, the Judiciary Committee heard the sensational testimony of General Lafayette Baker. During the war, Baker was in charge of the Federal Detective Bureau. In its two-story brick headquarters on Pennsylvania Avenue, the agency had operated under the umbrella of Stanton's War Department, although Baker also ran a rogue group of spies that arrested rebels, counterfeiters, and other disloyalists, presumably without much regard for their constitutional rights. When Baker's position was eliminated, Stanton continued to pay him for various clandestine tasks, and after Lincoln was shot, Stanton sent Baker to track Booth and his conspirators, which he very successfully did.

Baker had also set up a sting operation to nab the notorious Washington pardon-broker Mrs. Lucy Cobb, the pretty black-eyed woman whom Baker and many other Washington insiders said had been intimate with the President. But though Democrats scoffed, saying Baker "never told the truth, even by accident," a caricature of Mrs. Cobb had been circulating through Congress showing Mrs. Cobb holding a baby whose face bore an uncanny likeness to Andrew Johnson's. That proved nothing, of course, except what everyone already knew—namely, that pardons were being bought and sold in the District, and that neither Mrs. Cobb nor General Baker was to be trusted.

When the Fortieth Congress convened, it authorized the Judiciary Committee to continue the investigation of Andrew Johnson's actions and indiscretions, although one member of the committee, Andrew J. Rogers, a Democrat, strongly protested that not a particle of evidence against Johnson had been found. Newly seated in the House, Ben Butler asked to be added to the committee. Ohio Representative John Bingham vehemently objected. A member of Congress almost steadily since 1854, Bingham prided himself on

Ohio Representative John A. Bingham had prosecuted the alleged conspirators to assassinate Lincoln and helped draft the Fourteenth Amendment. Though reluctant at first to impeach Andrew Johnson, when Bingham "puts his hand on the wheel," a journalist noted, "he never looks back."

his integrity and thoroughly disliked Butler, whose integrity was a matter of dispute. Still, the perpetually peevish Gideon Welles distrusted Bingham, calling him a "shrewd, sinuous, tricky lawyer" — not unlike Butler himself, but with far more subtlety, if far less talent.

Angular and slightly stooped, the grimly sober John Bingham buttoned his coat tightly at his waist, and while usually a nervous, long-winded man sometimes called a gasbag, he could be eloquent. "When he puts his hand on the wheel," said journalist Emily Briggs, "he never looks back." Previously an anti-slavery Whig, Bingham was instrumental in the drafting of the Fourteenth Amendment and believed the former rebel states should be admitted to Congress if they ratified the amendment—but he also believed that these same states had to allow the vote to all men, without distinction to race. At the same time, he was pleased the amendment didn't mandate black suffrage nationwide.

Bingham taunted Butler, first by making fun of the general's military failures. "I did all I could, the best I could," Butler serenely replied. "But the only victim of the gentleman's prowess that I know of was an innocent woman hung upon the scaffold, one Mrs. Surratt." The reference to Surratt, in whose boardinghouse the conspirators had met, was a pointed jab. As assistant judge-advocate during the trial of the Lincoln assassination conspirators, John Bingham had been partly blamed for her conviction and execution. Butler argued that Surratt didn't necessarily know that Booth intended to assassinate Lincoln when his kidnapping plan fell through, and if she didn't know, she shouldn't have been found guilty of conspiracy. Butler's argument hit its mark—that is, John Bingham—especially since it was generally believed that Surratt had been victim of a rush to judgment.

Poor Bingham, Emily Briggs wryly observed. "He can comfort himself with the idea that there is one the less of the so-called gentler sex to perpetrate mischief."

Butler also knew that after Lincoln's assassination, Surratt's son John, another alleged conspirator, had successfully sneaked out of Washington. A recognized courier for the Confederacy, presumably working out of the tavern his mother owned in Maryland, he'd been stuffing secret messages in his boot to carry to Richmond until at least 1864, when his mother rented out the tavern and moved to Washington, where she ran her boardinghouse on H Street. There, John Surratt had shared a room with his former classmate, a small, handsome, weak man named Louis Weichmann, who would end up testifying against Mrs. Surratt.

Doubtless, John Surratt was valuable to another friend, John Wilkes Booth, who drafted Surratt into his knuckle-brained plot to abduct Lincoln. "I was led on by a sincere desire to assist the South in gaining her independence," John Surratt would proudly say. "I had no hesitation in taking part in anything honorable that might tend toward the accomplishment of that object."

When Surratt fled Washington, he'd escaped first to Canada and then to Rome, where he enlisted in the Papal guard under a pseudonym. But an acquaintance from Maryland, Henri Beaumont de Ste Marie, recognized him and informed Rufus King, the U.S. minister, adding that Surratt had confessed his complicity in the assassination plot—and had named such coconspirators as the Confederate secretary of state Judah Benjamin.

The U.S. government dragged its feet. Eventually it was the Vatican's secretary of foreign affairs, Cardinal Giacomo Antonelli, who ordered Surratt's arrest. But either with uncanny luck or the assistance of the Papal guard, or both, Surratt managed yet another escape, landing eventually in Egypt, where he was arrested and this time extradited.

Back in Washington, Surratt was indicted for complicity in the assassination of Abraham Lincoln and was to be tried by a criminal, not a military, court. For four months he awaited trial in conditions that permitted him to wander freely around his section of the jail, except at night, and he received plenty of reading material and choice delicacies to eat.

George Boutwell had been asking why the government had not acted sooner to arrest Surratt. What did the President know? Was the President implicated in the conspiracy to kill Lincoln, and was he covering it up? James Ashley, ruining an already spotty reputation, traveled throughout the country trying to scrounge up information on Johnson's role in the Lincoln assassination. He met a number of times with convicted perjurer Charles A. Dunham in Dunham's jail cell—Dunham assured Ashley he could produce letters between Booth and Andrew Johnson, which he never did, and said he also had damning information about John Surratt. William Seward joked that pretty soon he too would likely be "tried with Surratt for conniving at the attempt upon *his* own life."

Dunham never delivered anything, but later he alleged that Ashley had urged him to manufacture evidence. The brouhaha served only to damage Ashley's reputation even further and, not coincidentally, to pour cold water over impeachment. Walt Whitman remarked that "there is much talk about impeachment—but I think it is very doubtful if there is any impeachment." Emily Briggs said impeachment had "growled and thundered in the political horizon, but for some unaccountable but wise reason it has all subsided." And as Henry Dawes noted, "if nothing is done to give it new life it will die of too much nursing."

Dawes was partly right, but Butler was not going to let the matter drop. Joining with Ashley and George Boutwell—"a baleful trio of buzzards as ever perched in the House," a renowned historian mocked them—Butler persisted. What had happened to the diary of John Wilkes Booth, and why were eighteen pages missing? Testifying before the Judiciary Committee, Stanton remembered the diary coming to the War Department with the pages already torn out. Had Andrew Johnson ordered those missing pages to be cut in order to conceal his own hand in Lincoln's assassination?

When the Judiciary Committee began investigating his finances, Andrew Johnson exploded. "I have had a son killed, a son-in-law die during the last battle at Nashville, another son has thrown himself away, a second son-in-law is in no better condition, I think I have had sorrow enough without having my bank account examined by a Committee of Congress."

He presented an impenetrable, stubborn front; he looked neither tired nor disconcerted nor ill; he walked with a decided step, smiled a bit, dressed well, and conscientiously combed his mouse-gray hair.

The Judiciary Committee trudged forward. It interviewed General Rufus Saxton, who had been fired from the Freedmen's Bureau in South Carolina; it received reports about land and property returned to former Confederates. It interviewed men who had been pardoned by the President and men who had been sacked. It interviewed Thomas Conway, fired from the Freedmen's Bureau in

New Orleans, and General Fullerton, who replaced him. It heard testimony about the President's responsibility for the massacre in New Orleans, and it asked if Johnson had somehow given preference to former Confederates when the railroads seized during the war were sold, or if he'd been involved with an improper sale and seizure of cotton after the war. It asked if the President had obstructed passage of the Fourteenth Amendment or if he had used intimidation to block Colorado's admission as a state to the Union. And it returned to the matter of that Booth diary and those missing pages to discover whether Johnson had ripped them out. "The President's cook is daily expecting a summons from the impeachment committee for putting black pepper in the soup," sniped a Boston paper.

The committee had been told to keep its tedious process going, even when Congress took its spring recess — "to sit all summer on the impeachment eggs," as Emily Briggs put it. By now Thad Stevens had his doubts; yes, certainly Johnson deserved impeachment, but the country did not need the "fussy, unnecessary and absurd" actions of a committee that took any oral testimony whatsoever. "They should not have called a witness," Stevens declared, "but reported that Congress had quite sufficient ground for the impeachment, if they desired to take that political step, in the encroachments and usurpation of the President."

"Instead of investigating charges of impeachment against the President of the United States on specific allegations, charges extending to every crime and every folly which a wicked, bad man could be guilty of," Stevens later said, "the investigation entered upon with a malignity and feeling which could do no credit to so high a tribunal." That damaged the process and the outcome. "These innumerable eggs were thrown into the nest of his investigation, until it was more than full," Stevens lamented. "They thought to break the elephant's back, broad as it was, by piling upon it straws."

The country could and should — and in time would — bear witness that Andrew Johnson had failed to execute the law. He had used every means in his power to defeat or suppress it. He'd sought to arrogate to himself the power of Congress, and instead of taking the President to task for his official malfeasance, the committee, as far as Stevens was concerned, was "making a mere pretense of prosecuting impeachment."

On June 3, 1867, the Judiciary Committee hatched its eggs, voting five to four against a recommendation of impeachment although it decided to continue its investigation. It also lamely voted to censure Johnson, which was tantamount to a slap on the wrist. The revolutionary farce is over, the shameful crusade ended, Democrats crowed, and yet the publisher James Gordon Bennett said Congress should definitely reconvene for a special session in July to expel the President. Otherwise the war would have been fought in vain.

Walt Whitman took to his desk to celebrate the spirit of democracy, which was wider, deeper, and grander than the party politics of paltry men. "Amid whatever clouds, seductions, or heart-wearying postponements," the poet rejoiced, "we have never deserted, never despaired, never abandoned the Faith." Thaddeus Stevens had never abandoned the faith, but he was far more cynical than Whitman about craven politics and paltry men.

CHAPTER THIRTEEN

A Revolutionary Period

"The situation was approaching mutiny on one side,
or else treason on the other."

— ADAM BADEAU

Impeachment was an extreme measure—as yet, much too extreme—and impeachment would not settle the immediate question, already deferred far too long: how, when, and under what conditions could the so-called former Confederate states re-enter the Union? So in late February 1867, just before it adjourned, the Thirty-Ninth Congress of the United States again placed itself across the path of the President by passing a different measure, known as the Military (or First) Reconstruction Act.

The act placed ten formerly seceded states into five temporary military districts. (Tennessee was excepted since it had ratified the Fourteenth Amendment.) Each of these five districts might contain only one state, as was the case of the First Military District, which included Virginia; or they might cover several states, as was the case of the Third Military District, which included Georgia, Alabama, and Florida. Supervising each district was a military commander (none below the rank of brigadier-general) charged with keeping the peace, preventing insurrection, and punishing all agitators. This commander thus had the authority to remove civil officers, should the need arise, and although the civil courts would remain open, he could authorize a military tribunal, should he see fit.

The Reconstruction Act also outlined the qualifications for a state's readmission to Congress. The five military commanders were to oversee elections in the several states they superintended. Any adult male citizen, regardless of race or color, who had resided in his state for at least one year and had not previously been disqualified by felony or because of his participation in the rebellion was eligible to vote for delegates to the state's constitutional convention. These chosen delegates would then draft a new state constitution, to be ratified by the voters of that state, *again* regardless of his race or color; the new constitution was required to grant voting rights, in all future elections, to black men. Then, after ratification of the new constitution, the state could elect a governor and legislators to replace the governments Johnson had established.

If and when Congress approved the state's new constitution, that state's newly elected representatives and senators would be admitted into Congress—provided too that the state had ratified the Fourteenth Amendment, conferring citizenship on black men and women and guaranteeing their civil rights. Thus, the power structure of the South was forever to change, or so exclaimed House Speaker Schuyler Colfax with pride: the Military Reconstruction Act guaranteed that "new wine could not be put in old bottles."

But as John Sherman explained to his brother, the act left the actual machinery of voting to the individual states. That is, a state could allow former rebels to vote, should it so choose. The only real objection the Southern states might have to the Military Reconstruction Act would be the granting of suffrage to black men, Senator Sherman added. But they could get around that: the states could impose qualifications on voters—say, by mandating that a citizen had to own property in order to vote, or by introducing "poll taxes," which forced an otherwise eligible voter to pay a fee at the polls. In this way a state government could keep black men, who owned little property, or poor people, black or white, from exercising their right to vote.

Wendell Phillips predicted that the states would turn away its black voters. And he was amazed that Congress had actually allowed President Johnson to appoint the five military commanders in the first place. That's like putting a "lunatic" in charge of a "lunatic asylum," Phillips joked without mirth. Further, the act did not mandate the disbanding of the state governments; it did not address the matter of land redistribution or programs for black education. But to most Republicans, particularly moderates, the Reconstruction Act had been a workable compromise cobbled together in the last days of the Thirty-Ninth Congress to reorganize the South without stepping on too many toes. To these Republicans, the Reconstruction Act was a giant leap forward in improving the condition of black and white loyalists in the South by endowing them with real political power.

White Southerners and Democrats perceived the Reconstruction Act quite differently. To them, it created martial law in the South: unheard of. "We are still warred upon with a ruthlessness and fierceness which filled us at once with amazement and despair," Judge Absalom Chappell complained to the head of the Democratic National Committee. And when the bill had first landed on Johnson's desk, Democratic leader Francis Blair, Sr., warned the President that the "furious dogs" and "Revolutionists" of Congress had passed it in order to intimidate him, since the threat of impeachment was hanging over his head. But Johnson was already fuming. The "military despotism" bill, as he called it, "gives universal suffrage to the ignorant blacks, thus overriding the provision that each state shall determine who shall be entitled to its suffrage." The military commanders were to wield arbitrary power over a "beaten, helpless, well nigh hopeless country," he continued. And even more categorical when talking in private to his secretary, he said he'd rather "sever my right arm from my body" than sign the Military Reconstruction Act.

If Johnson had signed, he could have demonstrated a willingness to cooperate with conservative and moderate Republicans. If he had signed, he could have undermined opposition, tamped down hostility, effected some rapprochement, enhanced his prestige, and won more popular support. He could have strengthened his presidential hand. Told again and again that by signing the bill, even under protest, he would prevent more extreme measures from landing on his desk: with just his signature, Johnson could knock the wind right out of Radical Republican sails and avoid his own impeachment.

Journalist Charles Nordhoff called on Johnson at the White House to tell the President that his friends at the Democratic *Evening Post* had defended his policy until circumstances—the atrocities in the South, to say nothing of Johnson's tirades—made its defense utterly impossible. Everyone wanted reconstruction, Nordhoff continued, and since Johnson's policy was dead beyond resurrection, "it was the duty of all who wished good to the country, to unite together in some practicable scheme." Johnson would not listen. The white people of the South were poor, quiet, unoffending, and harmless, he replied, and didn't deserve "to be trodden under foot 'to protect niggers.'"

Nordhoff said that this kind of bias served only to frustrate "sensible Republicans" and encourage men like Thad Stevens. Johnson did not understand. He said he'd read about the rape of a twelve-year-old girl in New York, and no one made a fuss. "If it happened in the South, and the girl was black," he added with contempt, "what an outcry there would have been."

"For starters, the criminal had been promptly arrested and sorely punished," Nordhoff replied.

"It's all damned prejudice," the President snarled back. Nordhoff decided that the prejudice belonged to Johnson, who wanted to protect the old guard in the South—those who, as Johnson emphasized, "must in the nature of things rule."

Nordhoff left the White House dazed. The President is cunning but mulish, he muttered, "with only one idea, & that is bitter opposition to universal suffrage." Johnson listened only to men who told him what he wanted to hear, men like reactionary Fernando Wood. "Whatever else you lose," Wood had advised, "preserve your

manhood." Or, as Charlotte Cushman commented, "the southerners pat the President on the back, hobnob with him & keep him
vetoing everything that is presented to him."

"The President was raining vetoes, which rolled off Congress
like water off a duck's back," noted John Bigelow. But when the
President vetoed the Reconstruction Bill, Bigelow was equally astonished at the utter contempt with which any communication or
message of the President was treated. "He is of no account," Senator
Nye of Nevada said with a shrug. "We pay no attention any more
[sic] to what he says."

Congress again overrode Johnson's veto. "He is a nullity & will
be treated as such," Charles Sumner said.

BUOYED BY THE Republican success in the fall of 1866, the
Thirty-Ninth Congress had authorized the Fortieth Congress to be
called to order immediately at noon on March 4, 1867, right after
the Thirty-Ninth adjourned. "Radicalism desires a perpetual session to override the Executive," Gideon Welles declared. "We are
living in a revolutionary period."

Crowds of men and women were again pulsing through the
Capitol's passageways and corridors to catch a glimpse of new representatives, like the brash General Ben Butler and the outspoken
General John Logan of Illinois, both Radicals, or the two Democrats from New York, Fernando Wood and John Morrissey, the latter a broken-nosed prizefighter who owned a string of gambling
houses. Schuyler Colfax was promptly elected House Speaker
again, and Benjamin Wade was named president pro tempore of
the Senate. Radical Republicans considered Wade's election as
Senate leader a triumph. But so did conservative Republicans and
Democrats: since there was no sitting Vice President, as president
pro tem of the Senate, Benjamin Wade was next in line for the
White House. If Johnson were impeached, then the idea of a Radical like Wade in the Executive Mansion would terrify—or could be
made to terrify—the country. Andrew Johnson would be saved.

TREASURY SECRETARY HUGH McCulloch had suggested that Johnson appoint post haste the five military commanders mandated by the Reconstruction Act to demonstrate his goodwill. "The President got very angry and swore vehemently," Interior Secretary Orville Browning confided to his diary, "and said they might impeach and be d-m-d he was tired of being threatened—that he would not be influenced by any such considerations, but would go forward in the conscientious discharge of his duty without reference to Congress, and meet all the consequences."

Johnson did appoint the military commanders quickly, choosing the men that Grant presumably recommended: Philip Sheridan and Daniel Sickles as well as John Schofield, George Thomas, and Edward Ord were posted to the five newly created districts. "The slime of the serpent is over them all," complained Gideon Welles, who, hating Edwin Stanton, believed he too had influenced the President, particularly in his selection of Sickles and Sheridan.

Adjourning for the recess in late spring, many members of the Fortieth Congress left the Capitol relieved that reconstruction in the South could and would at last proceed without the President. For at the end of March, they had passed a Second Reconstruction Act to fix what had been missing in the first: the actual supervision of elections. The new bill authorized the military to register eligible voters, black and white, and to schedule elections as well as convene conventions, since intransigent white Southerners had been reluctant to do so. Then, thanks to the rider that George Boutwell had included with the Military Appropriations Bill, the five military commanders would now report to and receive orders from General Grant as general-in-chief, not from the President. The rider also specified that General Grant could not be dismissed without the consent of the Senate.

And equally pleased that impeachment was sputtering into nonsense, congressional Republicans also believed they'd sufficiently hamstrung Johnson, whose job was simply to execute their laws.

Charles Sumner, however, was uneasy. "Our President is a bad man," Senator Sumner reminded colleagues. "Search history and I am sure that you will find no ruler who, during the same short space of time, had done so much mischief to his country." Chiding those fellow congressmen who were eager to go home, Sumner begged them to reconvene in early July. "Witness Memphis. Witness New Orleans," he cried. Do not wait for months and months and months to return to Washington, he pleaded, while Johnson had a free hand.

Sumner was right to worry. Johnson did try to circumvent the Reconstruction Acts, which he continued to brand "military despotism" legislation, and he instructed Attorney General Stanbery to issue an opinion about how best to get around it. Stanbery obliged. His conservative credentials impeccable, Henry Stanbery was the former law partner of Thomas Ewing and a friend of Interior Secretary Orville Browning but, as an Ohio jurist once said, intending a compliment, Henry Stanbery didn't possess any "marked characteristics."

Per Johnson's instructions, Stanbery announced in early June that no military commander had the right to remove any civil officeholder. And since the military possessed neither the education nor the training for the delicate task of interpreting the law, the military was entitled to exercise only a very limited authority in the districts. The civil governments of the South must stand; their state governments alone could enforce the Civil Rights Act—not ignorant military commanders, as Stanbery alluded to the district generals, deliberately insulting them. Stanbery also claimed that former rebels should be able to vote even if they'd participated in or aided the rebellion.

"Mr. Stanbery cuts the heart out of the military bill," a startled Horace Greeley protested. Senator Fessenden was amazed. "It is quite astonishing that he and his advisers could not see the necessity of letting well enough alone."

If impeachment seemed to pit an increasingly embittered President against an increasingly estranged Congress, each of them intractable, and defiantly proclaiming that they fought only for the good of the nation, Andrew Johnson's clash with the military was as

Aggressive and diminutive, Major-General Philip Sheridan took command of Louisiana and Texas after the war, and after removing the perpetrators of the New Orleans massacre and the governors of Louisiana and Texas, he registered thousands of black voters; President Johnson then relieved him of his command.

stark and significant. And it was just as responsible for the impeachment trial that would occur in the last year of his presidency. General Philip Sheridan, commander of the Fifth Military District (Louisiana, Texas), promptly ignored Stanbery's opinion, which he labeled "a broad macadamized road for perjury and fraud to travel on." Widely known as "Little Phil" because he measured five foot six, Sheridan was also called the "Field Marshal of the Radicals" although he'd never been a Radical Republican—until, that is, he found himself military commander of Louisiana and Texas. "Game was scarce down that way then, and some gentlemen amused themselves by shooting negroes," Sheridan would grimly recall. "I stopped this sport and they loved me not." Sheridan made sure that half the police force consisted of former Union soldiers, and when the Texas Governor James Throckmorton, a former Confederate officer, told Sheridan to take his army to the frontier to fight Comanche and leave him alone, Sheridan replied that "there are more causalities from outrages perpetrated upon Union men and freedmen in the interior of the state than occur from Indian depredations on the frontier." He then yanked Throckmorton from office.

In fact, the New Orleans massacre had already sickened Sheridan, and in the spring of 1867, bolstered by the Reconstruction Acts—and with his signature flair for the dramatic—he kicked out of office the men he held criminally responsible for it, such as Mayor John Monroe. Sheridan also sacked Louisiana Governor James Madison Wells. As he explained to General Grant, "we have gotten rid of an unprincipled Governor and the set of disreputable tricksters which he had about him," and *The New Orleans Times* reported that "All's well that ends Wells." Even Johnson's friend General James Steedman advised the President not to reinstate such sleazy characters—although, Steedman added, Sheridan's real intention had been to embarrass Johnson.

General Grant and War Secretary Edwin Stanton had both approved Sheridan's actions, and if Johnson tried to remove Sheridan as a result of them, Grant said every loyal man and woman in the country would rise up in protest. "Philip has a strong hold on the hearts of the people," a New Orleans conservative agreed, "and it would hardly be policy for Johnson to attempt it." The radical *Independent* was blunter. "The people would throw a thousand Andy Johnsons into the sea sooner than permit one Phil Sheridan to walk the plank."

Having determined that it would reconvene if there was a quorum and a necessity—that is, if Johnson proved disruptive—Congress did reconvene. Complaining about the sticky July heat, its members swiftly passed a Third Reconstruction Act to obstruct the President's course by giving to the general of the army—namely, General Ulysses S. Grant—complete authority over the execution of congressional reconstruction; it also gave full authority to the district commanders, should they choose to fire civil officers; and it allocated over a million and a half dollars to defray expenses. In addition, the House voted its thanks to General Sheridan as well as to the other military commanders in the districts.

The President of course promptly vetoed the Third Reconstruction Act, and Congress just as promptly overturned his veto.

IT REMAINED A summer of discontent, with talk about real reconstruction come at last—or about military despotism, and the so-called military occupation of the South. Plus, with the assassination plot against Abraham Lincoln again in the news, the wounds of war were made fresh once more. "You hear nothing but the newsboys singing out the 'trial of John H. Surratt,'" said a Washington resident in August. For fifty-two days, a carnival of witnesses had paraded through the courtroom to testify for or against the Southern-sympathizer; but to beat the charge, Surratt's lawyers had merely to show he couldn't have been in Washington on the day of the assassination. That is, John Surratt had been indicted for assassination—not conspiracy, as his mother had been—and he was being tried in a civilian court, not a military one, also as his mother had been.

Anticipating a drawn-out deliberation, the jurors lugged big suitcases into the jury room as well as a large supply of food, while John Surratt waited, fanning himself with a huge palm leaf. He didn't have long to wait, for the jury admitted that it too, like much of the country, was divided. Surratt went free. But those convinced of his guilt regarded the trial as a political maneuver designed to generate sympathy with the secessionist South—and with Andrew Johnson. "Some of them probably could see no harm in killing a Union President," General Grant's aide Orville Babcock bitterly remarked. "All loyal people here are disgusted with the result—all the Rebs highly pleased." It was said jurors had been intimidated, a few had received death threats, and the man who'd found Surratt in Rome told Walt Whitman he was afraid he'd be murdered.

Journalist Emily Briggs saw photographs of Lee shamelessly displayed about town, and one bookstore conspicuously placed a picture of him right next to one of General Grant. She wouldn't have been more surprised, she said, if the shopkeeper put Booth alongside Lincoln. "The cool way in which the beaten side demanded constant conciliation from the victor was getting to be a joke," Charlotte Cushman observed. "Then the southerner will come back into all their former glory with undimmed luster after four years of traitorism."

Mark Twain in Washington observed much the same thing. "Church congregations are organized, not on religious but on political bases," he remarked, "and the Creed begins, 'I believe in Abraham Lincoln, the Martyr-President of the United States,' or 'I believe in Jefferson Davis, the founder of the Confederate States of America.'" In fact, Jefferson Davis, detained at Fort Monroe for two years, was now in civilian custody too, awaiting an indictment for treason by the federal grand jury in Virginia district court. Though Chief Justice Salmon Chase was to preside as district judge in a trial, if one was to occur, Chase was reluctant to spoil his chances at another presidential bid, which a not-guilty verdict in a Southern court would surely do. "The idea that we cannot get the Chief Justice of the United States to try the head of a rebellion of four years standing—and that we cannot get a jury at the Capitol to find a crime in a combination of treason and the foulest of murders, does not add much strength to the Republic," General Grant's aide-de-camp lamented. "I hope we shall see better men and better days."

But many Northerners also wanted to move on. A group of them that included the publisher Horace Greeley, the railroad and shipping baron Cornelius Vanderbilt, and the radical abolitionist Gerrit Smith together raised $100,000 for Davis' bail. When he walked out onto a Richmond street at last, he and his wife, Varina, were greeted with screams of joy. He'd have to return when the court reconvened, but for now the Davises were headed to Canada, where, as it happened, John Surratt had initially taken refuge after Lincoln was shot.

YET EVERYONE WANTED to rub elbows with General Ulysses S. Grant, the hero of Appomattox. If he walked into the House of Representatives, his perpetual cigar clenched in his teeth, the young pages rushed to his side to ask for an autograph. At his lovely four-story brick home at 205 I Street, NW, the general and his wife hosted grand parties that were the talk of the town, with men attired in their formal best, women in colored velvets, and Mrs. Grant in a décolleté short-sleeved gown of green silk. His popularity was wide and resounding. But no one was completely sure how he saw his future.

"I am not a candidate for any office," he had stated as early as 1863. Likely he believed what he'd said: that he'd never run for office. Yet he was slowly entering the political arena, particularly since in his own quiet way he'd begun pushing against Southern governors and editors who refused to support the Reconstruction Acts or who actively encouraged disloyalty and the breaking of the law. The exact nature of Grant's party affiliation, however, was unclear. He welcomed conservatives like Gideon Welles, moderates like Lyman Trumbull, and Southerners like former vice president of the Confederacy Alexander Stephens to his receptions. Andrew Johnson and his two daughters might appear, but when Thaddeus Stevens showed up one night, Gideon Welles suspected Radicals of trying to "appropriate" the general.

For everyone wanted him, everyone wondered what he had to say. He certainly had made his disgust known after the Memphis mayhem, which stamped, he said, "lasting disgrace upon the civil authorities." Then there was the President's awful "Swing Around the Circle," which Grant had loathed. But his presence by Johnson's side had chilled many a Republican heart. Representative Elihu Washburne, Grant's political mentor, was deluged with questions: What is the general doing? What is he thinking? "Many of our friends are afraid that Grant will fall into and give countenance to the Johnson-Copperhead Party," a prominent Indiana Republican nervously confided to Washburne. "If the public get an idea that Grant is with the President it will do us great injury. How can it be counteracted?" Regardless, Grant did not commit himself, at least not yet. "He is the only eminent man in America," a British visitor observed, "who knows how to hold his tongue: this makes the newspaper speculation still more vague, as he stands committed to nothing."

Committed to nothing? Anxiety mushroomed. "If Grant will throw himself away by following Johnson it will be merely the worse *for him*," Horace White of the *Chicago Tribune* angrily warned Washburne. Was Grant a Democrat in disguise? "His reticence had led some of our friends to doubt him, and all the democrats claim him as their own," the surveyor general of New Mexico morosely observed.

After Johnson tried to push Grant out of Washington by dispatching him to Mexico, Grant pushed back. He would protect his generals, white Unionists, and the freedmen. "Send me a list of authenticated cases of Murder, and other violence, but upon Freedmen, northern or other Union men, refugees etc.," Grant had instructed General Howard. His intention was clear: to show Congress that the courts, as he said, in the unreconstructed South "afford no security to life or property of the classes here referred to, and to recommend that Martial Law be declared over such districts as do not afford the proper protection."

"The General is getting more and more Radical," one of his aides conjectured. Still, Grant seemed indifferent to politics, or he pretended he was. He slyly told John Bigelow that his main complaint against Washington was that it lacked a long half mile on which he could ride his horses fast. Perhaps he enjoyed the speculation. Forty-five years old and applauded everywhere as the man who had saved the nation, Grant had traveled far: from his hometown of Georgetown, Ohio, to West Point, where his father had sent his reluctant son, who, though a fine horseman, graduated only twenty-first in a class of thirty-nine. After the Mexican War, he'd been posted in the Pacific Northwest where, overcome by loneliness, he was said to drink. And drink. Then, after he resigned from the army, he floundered and failed; he failed to support his adored wife and four children, he aptly named his home "Hardscrabble," and as if anticipating the famous O. Henry story, one year he sold his watch to buy Christmas presents.

The war changed that. Heading a volunteer regiment, Captain Grant was soon promoted, and the unkempt, solemn, and unprepossessing soldier with a reputation for drunkenness had captured Forts Henry and Donelson in Tennessee. He earned the sobriquet "Unconditional Surrender" Grant, and Lincoln again promoted him, this time to major-general. "I can't spare this man," Lincoln had reportedly said. "He fights."

Squarely built, with a closely cropped beard, light hair, and steely eyes, Grant was a marvel of sangfroid although he was something of a loner, isolated except when he was with his beloved family or his friend General William Tecumseh Sherman. Seemingly imperturbable, according to Charles Francis Adams, Jr., Grant "might pass well enough for a dumpy and slouchy little subaltern." But he was also called a butcher who needlessly sacrificed his men, particularly during the terrible slaughter of the Wilderness campaign in the spring of 1864—two days of fighting and 18,000 Union casualties that an unsympathetic Grant biographer called "a nightmare of humanity," ranking it with the worst disasters in the whole history of warfare. Yet Grant seemed unflappable. And contradictory: he was a kind man said to hate the sight of blood so much he could not stand rare meat. "It is difficult to comprehend the qualities of a man who could be moved by a narrative of individual suffering," George Boutwell recalled, "and who yet could sleep while surrounded by the horrors of the battles of the Wilderness." Walt Whitman, who admired him, praised Grant as an "acceptor of things." Herman Melville characterized him as man in whom "meekness and grimness meet."

After the war, when Grant, as the nation's hero, was wined and dined and serenaded by brass bands wherever he went, he didn't respond with enthusiasm. And he was notoriously hard to read. He was regarded as sodden, sullen, and impassive, and it would be said that the "U. S." in his initials stood for "Unbelievably Stupid." He was regarded as a man of judgment, tact, and shrewdness. Henry Adams, who disliked him, recalled that even Grant's acolytes "could never measure his character or be sure he would act. They follow a mental process in his thought. They were not sure that he did think." In Washington when Charles Sumner's private secretary saw the general driving his horses at full tilt on a Sunday, he said that if not for photographs—and the ever-present cigar—he'd have thought him just an ordinary-looking hooligan. Grant also possessed the sort of deadpan humor frequently mistaken for inanity. "I know of only two tunes," he presumably said. "One is Yankee Doodle and the other isn't."

Such wit disconcerted the humorless President Johnson. Johnson had apparently asked Grant not to run for President, and though Grant said he was definitely not a candidate, he mischievously added, "but suppose the people insist on making me one, what can I do? And besides, Mrs. Grant has been recently looking at the White House, and she thinks she can run that establishment quite as well as it is run now. And you know, Mr. President, that these women will do pretty much as they please. And Mrs. Grant would decidedly object to my giving any such promise." Johnson didn't know if Grant was pulling his leg.

Was the General really eyeing Johnson's job? Radical Republicans wrung their hands when he seemed noncommittal. So did Democrats. His background did not reveal much, for he had initially fought the war to preserve the Union, not to emancipate slaves, and he was known to have voted in 1856 for President James Buchanan. However, Grant was seeing more and more clearly that there could be no real reconstruction without first allowing black men to vote. Without federal troops, in places like Austin, Texas, Grant told Charles Nordhoff, a federal officer wouldn't dare wear his uniform on the streets. "The General is getting more and more Radical," surmised an aide.

The general wished to follow the law—the reconstruction laws, in which he happened to believe. And he readily assisted the district commanders in executing them. "Enforce your own construction of the Military Bill until ordered to do otherwise," he had instructed General Pope in June. Then after the Third Military Reconstruction Act was passed in July, Grant promised his generals, as he had promised Sheridan, that he would shield them from executive interference. The military would oversee voter registration in the various districts and expunge civil officials, as Sheridan had done, should they need to do so. It was Johnson who was defying the laws of Congress, and in turn, the army was defying him. "The situation was approaching mutiny on one side, or else treason on the other," said Grant's aide Adam Badeau.

Grant had the backing of Secretary of War Edwin Stanton, who had formally stated that he would obey the Reconstruction Acts passed by Congress, and he would protect Grant and the army. For when Johnson had brought Attorney General Stanbery's opinion on the Reconstruction Acts to the cabinet, the cabinet agreed to its provisions—all cabinet members except Edwin Stanton, who denounced Stanbery's evisceration of the legislation. Speaking of himself in the third person, Stanton said that "he had already given the opinion that military authority was established over the rebel states, and the power rested in the commanding generals who should interpret the law for themselves, and therefore, that no instructions should be given them but to follow the Acts of Congress." General Grant would comment that Stanton "used his position in the Cabinet like a picket holding his position on the line."

But as far as the very conservative Gideon Welles was concerned, Stanton had shown his untrustworthy hand at last.

Together, Ulysses S. Grant and Edwin Stanton controlled the military, which Congress had empowered to curb—if not completely undercut—Johnson's policy in the South, a policy that had been undermining white Union loyalists, allowing the murder of black men and women, and reviving state militias; it was a policy that, as they saw it, effectively restored the antebellum aristocracy.

By August, Johnson was again livid. The time had come. Congress was still in recess. He would get rid of General Philip Sheridan—and while at it, he would get rid of Edwin Stanton. Don't do it, General Grant strongly advised: Sheridan is universally beloved, and as for Stanton, he is a cabinet member protected by the Tenure of Office Act, which was passed in order to shield him. "I know I am right in this matter," Grant said.

Treasury Secretary Hugh McCulloch also pleaded with Johnson to ignore Sheridan. Even Gideon Welles advised the President to leave General Sheridan alone. The clever Welles had learned how to influence Andrew Johnson—how to goad the President—he pretended to console, reminding Johnson that Congress had nibbled away at his power until there was nothing left: no authority, no force, no dignity. Johnson had been misled by designing men like William Seward in order to retain other even more designing men, like Edwin Stanton, whose perfidiousness—and power—was far greater than that of a perverse subordinate like Little Phil Sheridan. Leave Sheridan in place, Welles again advised; and leave Grant alone: Grant was nothing more than a simpleton who could be controlled—if only Edwin Stanton were cashiered.

To defang the Military Reconstruction Acts and restore the South to its rightful place, to readmit those unoffending Southerners into the marble halls of Congress, the disloyal Secretary of War Edwin Stanton had to go.

CHAPTER FOURTEEN

The Rubicon Is Crossed

On the morning of August 5, 1868, Andrew Johnson composed the stiff formal note that he sent over to Secretary Stanton's office. "Public considerations of a high character constrain me to say, that your resignation of Secretary of War will be accepted," the President wrote to Stanton, who wasted no time replying. "Public considerations of a high character," Stanton replied with bite, "constrain me not to resign the office of Secretary of War before the next meeting of Congress." As far as Stanton was concerned, the Tenure of Office Act stipulated that Johnson could not fire him without the Senate's approval. To do so was to break the law.

Stanton's refusal to resign seemed to please Johnson. Johnson was banking on a public outcry about a man staying where he was not wanted—and when he'd been asked to resign by the President himself. So for the next few days, Johnson decided to leave Stanton "hanging on the sharp hooks of uncertainty," as he gloated.

Johnson then informed Grant that he intended only to *suspend* Stanton, so as not to violate directly the Tenure of Office Act.

He also intended to appoint Grant as secretary of war ad interim. After all, Congress was in recess, and Grant's appointment would be only temporary, until Congress returned and approved the selection of a new war secretary, presumably Grant. So, Johnson asserted, he was acting within the legal limits of the Tenure of Office Act. Johnson also believed that Congress would applaud General Grant's nomination, and he counted on Grant's popularity—and his acquiescence—to smooth over possible difficulties.

Johnson also hoped to drive a wedge between Stanton and Grant, two men who, despite their different dispositions, had been working well together to execute the Military Reconstruction Acts and support the five district commanders. With Grant heading the War Department, Johnson surmised, Edwin Stanton would come to distrust the general.

Grant had warned Johnson that suspending Secretary Stanton would be impolitic to say the least, and that the people who wanted Stanton out of office were precisely the same ones who'd opposed the war—mainly, the Peace Democrats. Johnson did not quite understand. No one could say that *he*, Andrew Johnson, had opposed the war, he responded furiously—and again, those "public considerations of high character" were at stake.

But on a scorching Sunday, August 11, Grant accepted the appointment as interim war secretary, and with satisfaction, Johnson went to church.

The next day, Monday, August 12, 1867, Andrew Johnson, good as his word, suspended Edwin Stanton. Colonel Moore, the President's secretary, found Stanton in his office and, embarrassed, handed Stanton the President's latest letter. Stanton read it, folded it in half, and said he'd answer in writing.

In his reply, Stanton informed the President that Johnson had no legal right to remove him without cause—but since "the General commanding the Armies of the United States has been appointed Secretary of War *ad interim*," Stanton forcefully added—and since the general had accepted the appointment—"I have no alternative but to submit, under protest, to superior force." Weary and worn though he was, Edwin Stanton was boiling with anger.

When the President received Stanton's note, he nodded to Colonel Moore. "The turning point has at last come," Johnson remarked with some satisfaction. "The Rubicon is crossed."

"HE IS A madman," Carl Schurz said of Andrew Johnson. Johnson assumed that, as a longtime and deft political marksman, he had fatally damaged Grant's political future. By accepting a cabinet position—and of all cabinet posts, Secretary Stanton's as secretary of war—Grant would appear to be in Johnson's pocket. The Radical Republicans would abandon him.

Radical Republicans didn't really trust General Grant anyway. When Grant's friends claimed that he'd conferred with Stanton before he accepted the office, and that Stanton had consented, the reliably radical gadfly Wendell Phillips said he didn't believe it for a minute. As far as Phillips was concerned, by accepting the position, Grant had stabbed Stanton in the back.

The editor of the *Chicago Tribune*, a Grant ally, said the general should have refused the job "even at the risk of Johnson appointing Surratt secretary of war." But Grant claimed he took Stanton's post because, as he told his wife, "it's most important that someone should be there who cannot be used." Grant desired above all to sustain the army, to execute the law, and to protect the freedmen. Such men deceive themselves with their good intentions, Carl Schurz scoffed. "Grant, in my opinion, made a bad mistake in accepting the secretary-ship of war and thereby rendering easier the removal of Stanton. . . . He has allowed himself to be imposed upon and placed in a false position. Everything depends on how he is going to get out of it."

What *had* Grant been thinking, and how *would* he get out of it? "Make Grant speak out & take sides, or crush him back into his tent to smoke there," Wendell Phillips pressed the managing editor of the *New-York Tribune.* "The time is fast approaching," the diplomat John Lothrop Motley acknowledged, "when Ulysses must cease to do the 'dumb, inarticulate man of genius' business."

That time came sooner than Grant may have anticipated. On August 17, the President acted again. He dismissed General Sheridan from his command of the Fifth Military District. He ignored Grant's trenchant plea that Sheridan's removal would be understood as a slap at both Congress and reconstruction laws generally. "The unreconstructed element in the South, those who did all they could to break up this government by arms," Grant told Johnson, will regard the dismissal of General Sheridan "as a triumph."

Johnson responded by saying Grant's point of view was so offensive it deserved no reply, although he couldn't keep from answering. He said Sheridan was obnoxious and tyrannical, and by getting him out of Louisiana and Texas, he was making sure the laws of the land were fully implemented—that is, he continued, he was protecting the Constitution, which upheld state sovereignty. As he explained, Sheridan's "sole purpose seemed to be to secure negro supremacy and degrade the whites."

Grant fired back. "I urge—earnestly urge, urge in the name of a patriotic people who have sacrificed Hundreds of thousands of loyal lives, and Thousands of Millions of treasure to preserve the integrity and union of this Country that this order be not insisted upon," Grant wrote the President. He then took another step and, removing his sphinxlike mask, Grant released his letter to Johnson to the press.

"Every word is golden," the *Army and Navy Journal* praised the general's riposte. "These are truths that Mr. Johnson would have done well to heed."

SECRETARY OF WAR Edwin Stanton had been suspended. General Philip Sheridan had been removed. Next came General Daniel Sickles, commander of the Second Military District, the Carolinas.

These generals would be replaced with men willing to prevent blacks from voting, running for office, serving on juries, or riding in the front of a streetcar. Johnson also wanted to fire General Oliver Otis Howard, head of the Freedmen's Bureau, whom he detested. Mild and acquiescent, General Howard had not explicitly defied Johnson, certainly not as Stanton or Sheridan had, but the "malignant guillotine of Mr. Johnson," as one observer noted, was being cheerfully "whetted" for Howard's head.

Johnson calculated that he could replace General Howard with a black man and thereby placate moderate Republicans while foiling the Radicals. For Johnson assumed that many Bureau officers would quit their jobs rather than take orders from a black superior, which would be all to the good, to Johnson's way of thinking. He floated the name of Frederick Douglass. Douglass immediately said he wouldn't place himself "under any obligation to keep the peace with Andrew Johnson." Radicals took heart. "The greatest black man in the nation," the editor Theodore Tilton declared, "did not consent to become the tool of the meanest white."

When John Mercer Langston also refused the position, Johnson offered it to black activist Robert Purvis, an early member of the American Anti-Slavery Society. Purvis consulted Wendell Phillips, who said Johnson had no real intention of appointing a black person to lead the Bureau, and even if he did, it would be just another bait-and-switch game, the same one he'd tried to play with the War Department: with an enormously popular Grant controlling the War Department, Johnson wanted to distract the public from the fact that the far less popular Stanton had been suspended.

Not Douglass nor Langston nor Purvis would become Johnson's pawn.

And Grant? His supporters swiftly came to the general's defense with the excuse Grant had given his wife: he'd taken the position to prevent Johnson from mischief. "What mischief has he prevented?" Wendell Phillips wanted to know. "Texas is in anarchy, Tennessee full of assassins, Kentucky becomes once more the dark and bloody ground." Besides, why did Grant always need so much defending, rationalizing, and justifying? Why did his motives and actions always require explanation? "Butler does not need any explanation. Nobody explains Sumner," Phillips shouted. "I should like to see a man undertake to explain Stevens."

Irate and determined, Phillips was again traveling cross-country to depict Congress as spineless, Grant as weak, Johnson as dangerous. And he wasn't the only one speaking out. The sporadically radical Horace Greeley was declaring that "all that is fishy and mercenary in the Republican ranks combines with everything copperhead to escort Grant as the man destined to curb and restore conservatives to power." The admirers of Chief Justice Salmon Chase were likewise energized, raising money in the South while spreading rumors that Grant was a drunken philanderer. And Ben Butler presumably put detectives on Grant to find out if the stories about his boozing sprees were true.

Still, Grant's popularity soared. His name was on the lips of *The New York Herald*, at one extreme, and the Quaker poet John Greenleaf Whittier, longtime abolitionist, at the other. "Grant is true," Whittier swore. Buoyed by tides of money from New York merchants and a political machine already taking shape, with men like Elihu Washburne at the helm, Grant clubs were springing up nationwide. With the general leaning in their direction, moderates were hoping to quash Thaddeus Stevens and his radical dreams about universal suffrage, land redistribution, and the disenfranchising of former Confederates.

And by selectively communicating in his tight-lipped way, Grant was blocking the President. During cabinet meetings, he affirmed his devotion to the law, which was to say to Congress, and when Gideon Welles nastily asked if Grant didn't consider the Reconstruction Acts "palpably unconstitutional," Grant quietly replied with a piercing question of his own: who "is to decide whether the law is unconstitutional?" Annoyed, Interior Secretary Browning decided that this arrogant general was delivering "crude opinions upon all subjects, and especially upon legal questions."

Accusing Grant of being "tampered with, and I believe seduced by the Radical conspirators," Welles advised Johnson to make Grant state what he would do if the President were impeached. What if Congress ordered Johnson to leave his office? What if Congress arrested the President? Would Grant and the military defend him? Would Grant obey the orders of the President? Welles' paranoia was real, palpable, contagious. As was Johnson's.

With an air of harried intensity, Johnson walked over to the War Department in the brick building on Seventeenth Street to confront Grant. Grant evidently indicated that he would obey the President, and also indicated, or so Johnson understood him to say, that he'd give the secretaryship back to Johnson should the Senate try to reinstate Stanton.

Just to make sure, Johnson summoned General William Tecumseh Sherman to Washington to sound him out. Johnson considered Sherman an ally, particularly because Thomas Ewing, Sherman's

The irascible General William Tecumseh Sherman, who famously declared that "war is hell"—and just as famously loathed politicians—after the war advocated a generous peace that appeared to restore the South to its former status, just without slavery.

father-in-law, was an unofficial adviser to the President. Sympathetic to Johnson to an extent—and still miffed at Stanton for having publicly denounced his peace agreement at the end of the war—Sherman promised to do what he could. His opinion of Washington had not changed, though. Understanding politics and political power as well as the next person, Sherman knew his hotheaded self well enough to stay away from them. "If forced to choose between the penitentiary and the White House for four years," he'd again declared, "I would say the penitentiary, thank you."

Johnson peppered Sherman with questions: What would happen if Congress proceeded with impeachment? Would General Grant obey the President, or would he take his marching orders from the Radical mob in Congress? Though at one time considered unruly, if not mad, General Sherman was calm, conciliatory, and clear. Congress would not impeach the President; Grant would act to prevent any and all violence; Grant would obey the orders of the President. As for himself, Sherman would not take any position that superseded Grant's authority and particularly not the secretary of war's job.

But Sherman could not soothe Republicans, especially once Johnson had removed Sheridan and Sickles. The editor-in-chief of the *Boston Daily Advertiser* wondered if the President were cracked—or pickled. "I am afraid his doings will make us all favor impeachment," he grumbled. Was it true that the President planned to arrest members of Congress and spark another civil war? "People say that Johnson's more intimate pals talk as if he contemplated a coup d'état—a purging of Congress after the manner of Cromwell," the diarist George Templeton Strong reported. Everyone was jittery. "It is not impossible that he [Johnson] is preparing to resist the impeachment with force," Carl Schurz speculated. Rumors shot through the nation. An armed insurrection was near at hand, spearheaded by the President or by Congress, depending on whom you asked.

Sherman too had heard the rumors, though he was more dismissive. "There have been so many idle threats that both parties are scared," he conceded. "The President would be wrong to attempt violence against Congress or Congress against the President."

Yet with Stanton suspended and Sheridan and Sickles removed from their districts, the House Judiciary Committee, which had continued to listen to impeachment testimony, decided to vote yet again on the question when Congress returned in the fall. To everyone's surprise, one of its members, New York Representative John C. Churchill, a judge from upstate, changed his vote, declaring that Johnson was obstructing the laws of Congress rather than executing them. It was immediately alleged that Churchill had been bribed, although nothing was proved. On November 24, 1867, in a 5 to 4 vote, the committee recommended the impeachment of President Andrew Johnson.

Next stop, then, the Judiciary Committee recommendation would go to the full House.

CHAPTER FIFTEEN

The President's Message

"Ours is a funny Government in some respects," Mark Twain noted with demonstrable distaste. Twain was not just referring to racial prejudice, congressional dithering, or the President's precipitous and autocratic actions. He was pointing to another significant force behind all political jockeying: money. For it was Twain who would coin the phrase "the Gilded Age," and though it came to denote the theft and greed associated with Grant's administration, government scams and frauds had been longstanding.

With the end of the Civil War, the line separating the federal government and the unbridled business community had grown progressively blurrier. There were taxes being pocketed and government railroad subsidies grabbed and big business demanding public assistance. Swindling government agents and traders in the West were bilking Native Americans. And the spoils system had spawned a great deal of graft—to the victor, or bosses in power, went the booty. A host of racketeering syndicates, or so-called "rings," had sprouted up: "Indian Rings, Patent Rings, Stationery Rings and Railroad Rings," journalist John Russell Young drily noted.

Then there was the currency. During the war, the government had issued paper money, or "greenbacks"—legal tender printed with tough-to-counterfeit green ink—to pay for the war, stimulate the economy, and maintain confidence in the Union. This paper currency was not backed by gold or silver, so after the war, many wanted greenbacks taken out of circulation. Yet those favoring a return to hard currency, or specie, cut across overlapping political lines: Radical Republicans on issues of civil rights were often in favor of hard imperishable money over greenbacks. Radical Republican Charles Sumner was a hard-money man who wanted the gold standard restored, as did such moderate Republicans as James Garfield, John Sherman, Lyman Trumbull, and William Pitt Fessenden. So too did rich Democrats. But Radical Republicans like Benjamin Wade were dead set against hard money, as were Radicals Ben Butler and Thaddeus Stevens, who favored greenbacks despite the risk of inflation, arguing that paper money benefitted farmers and workers for whom flat wages had caused particular suffering or who had borrowed heavily. Thaddeus Stevens said he had to fight with Republicans of his own party who wanted a tight economic policy, which was Johnson's.

And there was the huge war debt, approximately $2.3 billion just before Appomattox. For not only had the federal government printed money during the war, it had borrowed, and now many of the war bonds were coming due. How were the lenders to be paid? In greenbacks or gold? "Public credit should be 'like Caesar's wife: above suspicion,'" said Republican Senator Henry W. Corbett of Oregon. Hadn't people purchased those bonds with the assumption they'd be repaid in coin? Then again, who exactly were these bondholders? Were they the patriotic members of the general public, mechanics and farmers, clerks and shopkeepers, or were they an aristocracy of speculators? Hadn't many of them purchased bonds with greenbacks, which made repayment in specie a windfall for them?

If the war against slavery had united Republicans who otherwise differed, especially on fiscal matters, those differences threatened to splinter the same party or cost them votes in the coming fall 1867 elections. Treasury Secretary Hugh McCulloch's monetary policy—slowly taking greenbacks out of circulation—had damaged the Republican party, especially in the West. "The Secretary's 'contraction' system, at the time when the industrial interests of the country are not able to bear the increased pressure it entails, is regarded with high disfavor by all engaged in commerce and manufactures," Mark Twain flatly observed.

Democrats faced their own schisms. Breaking ranks with the hard-money kingpins of the Northeast, many Democrats wanted the national debt paid in greenbacks. Most vocal among them was George Hunt Pendleton, the former Virginia gentleman who'd run for Vice President on George McClellan's 1864 ticket. Though Pendleton had once denounced paper money as inflationary, he declared that treasury bonds should be redeemed in greenbacks so that Yankee bondholders and banks would no longer be paid interest in specie. Arguing for greenbacks and swearing that his plan was financially stable, Pendleton said he wasn't suggesting that an infinite supply of greenbacks be circulated, just enough to pay off the national debt. That is, if the $338 million dollar principle of the so-called 5–20 bonds—U.S. Treasury bonds that would mature in twenty years but could be redeemed in five—were paid in greenbacks, not specie, then the Treasury would save $18 million in gold.

Of course there were problems with "Pendleton's Ohio Idea," and they were partly concealed in a fog of numbers and a bunch of unanswered questions about taxes, customs revenue, wages, and inflation. And several prominent rich Democrats, including Montgomery Blair and Samuel Barlow, distanced themselves from Pendleton. Manton Marble considered the Pendleton idea not just inflationary but morally dubious. "Greenbacks are a debt," he complained; "nothing is paid by mere promises to pay."

Whatever their internal rifts, in the fall of 1867 Democrats had concocted a winning brew, compounded of anger over Republican monetary policy—and racial prejudice. Republicans in Congress recognized the brew's potency, and soon after the House reconvened in the fall, it forbade Treasury Secretary McCulloch from taking more greenbacks out of circulation. Four states—Connecticut, New Jersey, New York, and Kansas—had voted Democratic in the fall elections, and governorships in three states—Connecticut, California, and Pennsylvania—went to Democrats. Although Rutherford B. Hayes, a Republican, was narrowly elected governor in Ohio, the state decisively rejected black suffrage, as did Minnesota and Kansas. "A great many of our party here are mean enough to want it in the south & not in the North," admitted a Westerner. "We went in on principle," Senator Benjamin Wade said, "and got whipped." Thaddeus Stevens unhappily predicted that "the Republicans once beaten into a minority by the force of negro prejudice will never again obtain the majority, & the nation will become despotism."

"The negro question has shown them the hand writing on the wall," Thomas Ewing cheerfully informed the President, and conservatives crowed that "any party with an abolition head and a nigger tail will soon find itself with nothing left but the head and the tail." Yet regardless of the Democratic victories, Johnson knew that he couldn't safely rely on Democrats any more than on Republicans. "Andrew Johnson is certainly the best-hated man this side of the Atlantic," George Templeton Strong remarked.

Grant supporters, however, were highly pleased with the results of the state elections. Voters were evidently drifting away from Radical Republicans, and Grant could thus step into the breach and save Republicans from their more fanatical selves. As Thomas Ewing observed with pleasure, "no extreme Radical will be Johnson's successor." Chief Justice Salmon Chase, who wanted to be President, could be written off as an extremist, and the Ohio legislature, now controlled by Democrats, would not return Benjamin Wade to the Senate. So from the office of The New York Times, Henry Raymond excitedly counseled the general just to keep his mouth shut: "Say nothing, write nothing & do nothing which shall enable any faction of any party to claim you."

Ditto impeachment: say nothing and by all means do nothing.

"Johnson is as useful to us as the devil is to orthodox theology," Horace Greeley noted. "We can't afford to get rid of him till we have elected our President." Most Republicans didn't want to make a martyr out of him, especially since Democrats might urge him to counterattack, which would result in a risky confrontation between the executive and the legislature. Besides, Johnson had only about fifteen months left in office, not a very long political life. There was no need to impeach him—unless of course the man grew reckless, as Charles Eliot Norton sneered, given "a man of his temper."

As for letting Johnson remain in office until the next election and hoping he wouldn't do anything calamitous, Wendell Phillips was scornful: "With a cabinet composed of his own adherents, all enemies to the nation and its loyal inhabitants; with a treasury full of money, and a large 'secret service fund' at his disposal; with military officers in command at the South sympathizing with his views; a general of the army so hedged round with military etiquette, and timid in mental force, as to refuse to assume the responsibility of enacting what may ultimately be the last resort—revolution; with a large Southern population seething with rebellion, hordes of secret societies there, only waiting for the signal to spring to arms—what can't the President do in all this time?"

House Republican John Bingham didn't listen to Wendell Phillips. He and his colleague Elihu Washburne both wanted General Grant elected President, impeachment off the table, the party united, and Radical Republicans run out of town. They assumed that if the House passed articles of impeachment, Grant would be lost, for they believed that the impeachers wanted to put the radical Senator Benjamin Wade in the White House, and they weren't entirely wrong.

"I BELIEVE THE Prince of Darkness could start a branch of hell in the District of Columbia (if he has not already done it)," Mark Twain tartly observed. Washington was a den of criminality and caprice, especially in the hallowed halls of Congress, where preen-

Born Samuel Clemens, Mark Twain had been a riverboat pilot, speculator, reporter, lecturer, and humorist before briefly landing in Washington, where he wrote about political duplicity for several newspapers, saying, "I believe the Prince of Darkness could start a branch of hell in the District of Columbia (if he has not already done it)."

ing members read newspapers at their desks or dashed off letters and hemmed and hawed over their allegiances. "As politics go, so goes the weather," Twain continued. "Today it is a Democrat, tomorrow a Radical, the next day neither one thing nor the other. . . . Some people like Washington weather. I don't. Some people admire mixed weather. I prefer to take mine 'straight.'"

Mark Twain had arrived in Washington, acerbic pen in hand, in November of 1867 as the Washington correspondent for several newspapers, including the *New-York Tribune* and *The Herald*. He wasn't particularly known as a political correspondent but rather as a lecturer and comic author who tickled audiences with a hilarious tale about a frog or stories about his travels in the Sandwich Islands and the Holy Land. "Back from the Holy Land, and he looks it," Nevada Senator William Stewart remembered the youngish man (Twain was thirty-two) with the thicket of auburn hair whom he had met in a mining camp. Twain had showed up on his doorstep wearing a rumpled suit. "I thought he had been hanged or elected to Congress," Stewart said.

Briefly employed part-time as Senator Stewart's clerk, Twain was as keen a political commentator as Washington had. And since he already distrusted cant, pretense, and candy-box mawkishness—as well as racial violence—he didn't much like the place. When a black man bumped into a white man in the street, "the negro apologized," Twain reported, "but the white man would not be appeased, and grew abusive, and finally stabbed the negro in the heart." Fecklessness in the Capitol also repelled him. In Congress he sat through several sessions and jotted down notes about empty-headed whipper-snappers and which of the representatives was ugliest—the tubular Ben Butler, whose head looked like a blister.

On December 3, Twain, in Congress again, watched as the President's secretary carried a bulky parcel into the Senate chamber and handed it to the clerk. The clerk extracted a small pamphlet from it and announced that the President's annual "Message" had arrived. The journalist John Forney, as secretary of the Senate, read the document aloud. The senators, each of whom had a copy, followed along in more or less dignified silence until Forney finished. Then there was pandemonium.

A masterpiece of vitriol and venom, the President's message was the handiwork of Jeremiah Black, the superb constitutional lawyer who'd recently argued in the celebrated *Milligan* case that civil courts, not military tribunals, should hear civil complaints. Black, who'd once called abolition a "devil's dance," was reputed to be sour, sardonic, mean-spirited, and pitiless. Even those who admired him said he never forgot an injury. Johnson often consulted with

Black on domestic affairs, and Black darted in and out of the White House so often that he set the jealous Gideon Welles again to complaining.

Doubtless inspired by the routing of Radical Republicans in the recent elections, Johnson delivered a defiant, polarizing, blinkered document that conservatives like Thomas Ewing hailed as magnificent. For in it he again asserted that the states formerly in rebellion were part of the Union, that they had never in fact left it, and that the late war had been fought only to preserve the Constitution. What's more, without the Southern states, Johnson exclaimed, the Union did not exist.

Nothing new there. But Johnson also played with the word "slavery," using it not to refer to the formerly enslaved black population but to white state governments that Congress presumed to hold in thrall, state governments, as Johnson prophesized, that would be subjected to a "negro domination" far worse than the "military despotism under which they are now suffering." Johnson declared that the recent Reconstruction Acts of Congress needed to be repealed, for they unconstitutionally sanctioned the vengeance being wreaked upon all (white) classes, sects, parties, and communities. And although the Reconstruction Acts were only provisional measures, Johnson continued, they effectively "enslaved" the states.

Think of the implications of those acts, Johnson added: black people permitted to "rule the white race, make and administer State laws, elect Presidents and members of Congress, and shape to a greater or lesser extent the future destiny of the whole country. Would such a trust and power be safe in such hands?" Andrew Johnson answered his own question. "Negros have shown less capacity for government than any other race of people," he announced. If left "to their own devices, they have shown a constant tendency to relapse into barbarism." He begged Congress to stop, stop, stop the (radical) attempt to "Africanize the half of our country."

It was an astounding broadside. "There was one thing that the white South feared more than negro dishonesty, ignorance, and incompetency," W.E.B. DuBois later remarked with pith, "and that was Negro honesty, knowledge, and efficiency."

Then, remarkably, Johnson said he had decided against using the armed forces to resist Congress, for he didn't want to trigger another civil war. That the use of force would be illegal or insurrectionary was not his point, or his concern. Rather, his bellicose conviction was that if he did decide to resist Congress, he would be acting as he'd always acted, merely to uphold the Constitution. The Constitution was, once again, the curtain behind which Johnson hid, not very successfully, his prejudice, his arrogance, and his authoritarianism.

"The President's Message is making a howl among the Republicans," Twain reported. Moorfield Storey, Sumner's young secretary, was horrified by the President's message. "Incendiary in its suggestions, illogical in argument, low and narrow in its tone, it completely shows to my mind the unfitness of the signer, for I will not call him author," Storey said, calling the whole document an "abominable appeal to prejudice."

"If anything could warrant impeachment," Storey burst out, "it seems as if that document might." He wasn't the only person stupefied by the President's insolence and bigotry. "One thing is very sure: the message has weakened the President," Mark Twain noted. "Impeachment was dead, day before yesterday. It would rise up and make a strong fight to-day if it were pushed with energy and tact. But it won't be done."

To Twain, as to others, it wouldn't be done because Congress was a bunch of moral jellyfish.

AN EXCEPTION WAS Massachusetts Representative George Boutwell. For two days after the President had delivered his spiteful message, Boutwell defended the Judiciary Committee's new resolution in favor of Johnson's impeachment. The House of Representatives was crammed with eager onlookers instructed not to applaud or cheer. But if the people in the galleries were riveted on the proceedings, about two-thirds of the representatives weren't paying attention. They wanted to ignore what they knew was coming.

George Boutwell stood, his hands trembling but his argument steady. By the term "high crimes and misdemeanors," the Constitution did not only mean an actual violation of federal law. Rather, a civil officer, even a President, might be removed from office if, for example, he violated a civil law in one state that was not applicable in another. "Practically it would be found impossible to anticipate by *specific* legislation *all* cases of misconduct which will occur in the career of criminal men," Boutwell argued. Since that would be unreasonable, the Founders used the term "high crimes and misdemeanors" precisely and in accordance with the rule of reason, which lay at the foundation of English common law.

Boutwell then cited such opinions as those offered by Alexander Hamilton in the *Federalist Papers*, no. 65, where Hamilton said that impeachment should result from the misconduct of public men or abuse of the public trust. That is, impeachment did not depend solely on an indictable offense per se. "At the present moment," Boutwell explained, "we have no law which declares that it shall be a high crime or misdemeanor for the President to decline to recognize the Congress of the United States, and yet should he deny its lawful and constitutional existence and authority, and thus virtually dissolve the Government, would the House and Senate be impotent and unable to proceed by process of impeachment to secure his removal from office?"

It was a good question.

Should Johnson remain in office, the consequences would be disastrous, Boutwell went on. Johnson commanded the army and the navy. Deploying them, he could prevent black men from voting. And why assume he would do otherwise? A man of courage and tenacity in pursuit of a bad cause, Andrew Johnson had single-handedly restored the rebellious states to the Union, had appointed Southern governors, disbursed funds to them, suspended the loyalty oath, and had effectively returned ex-Confederates to offices, all in defiance of Congress. He had vetoed all Reconstruction Acts, campaigned against the Fourteenth Amendment, restored land to planters and confiscated railways to rebel owners. He had declared that black men in the South had no right to vote whatsoever. In other words, Andrew Johnson had usurped the function and the will of Congress. "If you are satisfied these tributary offenses were committed as the means of enabling him to accomplish this great crime," Boutwell asked, "will you hesitate to try and convict him upon those charges of which he is manifestly guilty?"

There was nothing inflammatory about Boutwell's speech, nothing incendiary about his manner. If impeachment was voted down, Boutwell said, he would abide by that decision. But he implored the members of the House to follow their consciences, as he was doing, and thus to impeach President Andrew Johnson.

The chair of the Judiciary Committee was Iowa Representative James F. Wilson. Not yet forty years old, this boyish man who'd started life as an apprentice to a harness-maker wore a scraggly goatee that seemed to magnify his pudgy face. He'd been considered more or less Radical when he'd supported the Thirteenth Amendment to abolish slavery and later when he'd defended the enfranchising of black men in the District of Columbia. But since Wilson had continued to vote against recommending Johnson's impeachment, and since he'd written the committee's minority report, it was fitting that he answer Boutwell. Wilson was concise. He refuted the legal precedents, cogent as they were, by arguing that impeachment depended on an indictable offense, not a "bundle of generalities."

Wilson's legal argument carried less weight than his deft response to Boutwell's call to conscience. The Republican House of Representatives may very well follow its Republican conscience, as Boutwell had suggested, but a House stocked with Democrats might step to a different but just as conscience-stricken drummer. Did Mr. Boutwell really intend to plant a government on the "shifting fortunes of political parties," Wilson asked.

Refusing to impeach Johnson did not imply that he, Wilson, endorsed the President or his policies. "I am not here to defend the

President," he declared, "for I believe him to be the worst of the Presidents." He would not, however, impugn Andrew Johnson's motives, which he believed patriotic.

Yet if Johnson's motives were patriotic but his actions wicked, shouldn't he be held accountable for those actions? And who could really know his motives anyway? Or, even if you could, did his motives offer comfort or compensation, never mind freedom, to the people who'd been injured by those actions? But with his argument, Wilson had held out to Republicans, particularly moderates, a thin reed of good intentions, should they choose to seize it to justify their refusal to impeach. They could believe that their own motives were pure, their condemnation of Johnson undiminished. And they could collectively share the blame that Wilson said they all deserved for the terrible mistake they'd made when they nominated Andrew Johnson to be Lincoln's running mate. That blunder was, he said, "a political crime."

Wilson's strategic mea culpa achieved its intended result. Far better to fall on one's own sword than to spear a President and, by so doing, possibly damage the presidential office. With men like the very capable Ohio Representatives John Bingham and James Garfield pulling levers behind the curtain, and James Wilson speaking in front of it, the House of Representatives voted against the impeachment resolution, 108 to 57.

"The impeachment 'question' is killed," one of Grant's fans rejoiced. Another noted with relief, "the country is tired of Butler & the blacks."

VINDICATED, JOHNSON LET loose, just as Wendell Phillips had predicted. He dismissed another of the five military commanders, General John Pope, who supervised the Third Military District (Alabama, Florida, Georgia). "I fear there will be sad calamities here unless this fiendish & malignant spirit is quelled," General Pope informed General Grant. "It is a misnomer to call this question in the South a political question—It is *War* pure & simple." Pope had witnessed the rush of black voters to the polls—89,000 of them in Alabama, a larger number than white voters, and in Georgia as many as 95,000, which was almost the same turnout as white voters. But when General Pope said black men should be allowed to serve on juries, Johnson removed him from the district.

"Shall the Union men & Freedmen, be the slaves of the old negro aristocracy or not?" General Pope wondered in despair.

Johnson also dismissed the commander of the Fourth Military District (Arkansas and Mississippi), General Edward O.C. Ord, who, though no radical, admitted that "the black population have a gloomy prospect before them."

And on December 12, Johnson sent to the Senate a fairly long paper outlining why he had suspended Edwin Stanton as Secretary of War. Stanton was a double-dealer. Look at his slippery handling of the Tenure of Office Act, which Stanton himself had deemed unconstitutional; the scoundrel now hid behind the very law he'd criticized and refused to resign. Or take the fact that Stanton had told the Judiciary Committee he'd never doubted the President's authority to reorganize Southern state governments and then had reneged. And he'd withheld from the President the telegram that General Absalom Baird had sent about a possible riot in New Orleans in the summer of 1866, begging for instructions on how to handle it if there was one, so that it was Stanton who'd been responsible for that riot, not the President. Johnson did admit that he might not have helped Baird even if he had known, but he would have liked to have had the choice.

There was absolutely no cause for regret, none at all, about the suspension of the disloyal Edwin Stanton, Johnson went on, and especially not while the administration's true hero—the true Republican hero—was the interim war secretary, none other than General Ulysses S. Grant. Grant was already reducing government expenditure, already fattening Treasury coffers, and already saving lives and careers—principally, that is, or so it seemed to the President, the career of Andrew Johnson.

CHAPTER SIXTEEN

A Blundering,
Roaring Lear

A ndrew Johnson, acting as one of the chief architects of his own impeachment, was tangling with Ulysses S. Grant and precipitating a crisis that he didn't know how to resolve or, more to the point, that he didn't want to fix.

Stony-faced, Grant avoided talking about the upcoming presidential election, even to his friend William Tecumseh Sherman, who with sensitivity had advised Grant not to tell him what he, Grant, did not yet want to reveal, especially since Sherman wouldn't approve. Sherman, who hated politics and hated Washington, was there only to draft a report on the "Articles of War" for Congress and, as a member of the Peace Commission, to map out treaties between the white settlers homesteading along new railroad lines and the various Indian tribes affected by them. To Sherman, both parties were responsible for the resulting violence—though the Indians had the worse end of the bargain, if you could call the history of broken treaties a bargain, as he wryly remarked. Still, Sherman preferred the West to the capital.

While Sherman was in town, the President frequently summoned him to the White House, seeking his advice, only to ignore it. This was especially true during the second week of January, 1868, when the President and the popular General Grant were at odds. The issue was Johnson's suspension of Edwin Stanton as war secretary, a matter that the Senate Committee on Military Affairs was then discussing. When news leaked that the committee would soon vote on whether Stanton should be reinstated, Grant suddenly realized that if Stanton's position was upheld, Grant, as interim war secretary, would find himself in violation of the Tenure of Office Act. He would have no business staying in the War Department—and could be sentenced to five years in prison and fined $10,000.

So on Saturday, January 11, Grant told the President in person that if the committee voted to reinstate Stanton, then he, Grant, would have to step down. Johnson offered to pay the fine and serve the jail term, which in any case he assumed wouldn't be imposed, but if Grant wished to resign, he should do so quickly so the President could immediately appoint someone else to the post. According to Johnson, Grant said he didn't know what he'd do—but indicated, again according to Johnson, that if he decided to resign, he would submit his resignation before the Senate committee voted. When Grant left the Executive Mansion, Johnson expected to talk with him again Monday morning.

Grant remembered the Saturday meeting differently. Denying that he'd promised Johnson anything, he alleged that the President knew full well that he considered the Tenure of Office Act binding unless and until the proper legal tribunal set it aside. Grant also claimed he told Johnson that if Stanton was reinstated, Grant's duties as interim secretary of war ceased then and there. And he'd never promised to continue the conversation on Monday.

No one really knows what happened between the two men that Saturday. And strict truth was not really the issue. The issue was the growing friction between the plainspoken General Grant—that is, when he did speak—and the prickly Andrew Johnson. The issue was the conflict between a bona fide war hero and a Republican apostate; between a popular presidential aspirant and a sitting President nursing his own aspirations. The issue was the execution of the reconstruction laws — or their undoing.

Anticipating trouble, Grant consulted with Sherman over the weekend. They decided Sherman should tell Johnson that if the President were to replace Stanton with a moderate Republican, Grant could step aside. No one would object to Ohio's outgoing governor General Jacob Dolson Cox, a tolerably popular Republican opposed to universal suffrage: he was perfect for the secretary of war job. Maryland Senator Reverdy Johnson, a Democrat, thought so too. So did Thomas Ewing, Sherman's father-in-law, who also urged the President to nominate Cox. Cox would immediately be confirmed, Ewing explained. "No direct vote will be taken on Stanton. Indirectly this will sanction his removal." Case closed.

Johnson did not nominate Cox. He did nothing. And Monday morning, Grant didn't go back to the Executive Mansion to meet with the President. Instead, at about eleven, Sherman went to see Johnson to lobby for Cox's nomination, but Johnson ignored him. Sherman suspected that Johnson might have a Copperhead in mind for the post. "Well I have done my duty, and if Stanton is white-washed and thrust back in the office it is not my business," Sherman wrote his wife. "I want to befriend Mr. Johnson, but I cannot give my consent or assistance to having in the Cabinet a man who may decide that the war was wrong or unnecessary."

That evening, at eight o'clock, the full Senate overruled the President's suspension of Edwin Stanton as war secretary in a 35 to 6 vote. Stanton was to stay. Even moderates had voted to sustain him.

Johnson was probably surprised, but the perspicacious Sherman wasn't — Republicans had voted to save their own — but he did wonder why Stanton would wish to return to a position where he wasn't wanted, at least not by the President. "But he & the President both are strong stubborn willful men that would embroil the world rather than yield their point," Sherman decided. He was right — Stanton and Johnson were stubborn. And so was Grant.

That same Monday night, while heading to a reception at the

White House, Grant and his wife were about to climb into their waiting carriage when a messenger delivered news of Stanton's reinstatement. Grant silently read the note, boarded the carriage, and rode on to the reception. Later he confessed that he'd been uncomfortable when the President, affably greeting him, warmly clasped his hand. Evidently Johnson hadn't yet heard about the Senate's vote on Stanton, and Grant didn't mention it.

Early the next morning, Tuesday, Grant walked over to the War Department, bolted one of the doors of his office on the inside, locked another on the outside, and handed the keys over to the adjutant, General Edward Townsend, to give to Stanton. "I am to be found over at my office at army headquarters," Grant explained. "I was served with a copy of the Senate resolution last evening." He dispatched an official memorandum to the President informing him that he'd vacated the office.

Grant hadn't resigned as interim war secretary before the Senate vote so that Johnson could choose someone else. Instead, he had handed the keys of the kingdom to Stanton, who wasted no time picking up those keys. Johnson was livid. "This was not the first time Grant had deceived him," the President's secretary confided to his diary. Grant had to realize Johnson would be furious.

Stanton was cheerful. Asthmatic and stressed but buoyed up by the Senate, he told well-wishers that he'd come back to protect those without protection. Convinced that his presence in the War Department helped prevent Johnson from aiding former Confederates, he certainly wasn't going to resign, and there had been no reason to assume he would. Moderates and Radicals both congratulated him on the vindication: Lyman Trumbull, Thad Stevens, Shelby Cullom, James Wilson, Ignatius Donnelly, Henry Dawes, Robert Schenck, and Horace Maynard. They told him not to resign. "Don't give up the Ship! Keep on, and 500,000 Blues will sustain you," wrote General W. G. Mark.

"Johnson is now a full-blown rebel," Senator Charles Sumner said, "except that he does not risk his neck by overt acts."

By now, though, Stanton had grown leery of Grant, for he'd

learned that Grant and Sherman would have thrown him over for Jacob Cox. That's why, it was said, he had hurried back to his office with what seemed to Grant like undue haste. Grant thought Stanton should have taken at least two days before returning to the War Department. By not waiting, he had compromised Grant, making it seem as though the two of them had been in cahoots. Johnson had already heard rumors to that effect.

Everyone was guarded, jumpy, looking over his shoulder, making accusations. It was, all knew, an explosive situation, one that could permanently cost Stanton his job, Grant the presidency, Johnson his head. At the White House, the President angrily demanded that Grant attend the scheduled weekly cabinet meeting, and when Grant appeared, Johnson could barely control himself. "Why did you give up the keys to Mr. Stanton and leave the Department?" the President badgered the general. "That, you know, was not our understanding." Grant said that he had not fully examined the Tenure of Office Act when he first accepted the interim post. And he insisted that he had never promised to tell the President if he decided to resign. Johnson disagreed. Hadn't Grant said that he'd continue the discussion on Monday?

Grant presumably conceded, adding that he'd been busy with General Sherman and other matters. Other matters? A feeble excuse.

Interior Secretary Browning reminded Grant that he'd said he would stay until the courts ruled on the Tenure of Office Act. Gideon Welles, who recounted the conversation in his diary, said that Grant then skulked out of the meeting, shamefaced and miserable. Treasury Secretary Hugh McCulloch thought Grant had been hitting the bottle. If he had, Grant retained enough composure to refuse being called "Mr. Secretary."

Sherman and Grant met with the President yet again on Wednesday, January 15, the day after the cabinet meeting. In more control of the situation, Johnson greeted the two generals pleasantly. Grant was clutching a copy of the *National Intelligencer*, the administration newspaper, which had essentially called him a liar, claiming that he hadn't kept his Monday appointment with the President because he'd been secretly cooking up a plan with Edwin Stanton. Grant indignantly insisted he had not colluded with Stanton. Johnson coolly said he hadn't read the article.

Sherman listened in silence. Johnson and Grant seemed eventually to accept each other's explanations of what had transpired at their last meeting, but without any real rapprochement in the works, Sherman threw up his hands. "I have done my best to cut the Gordian Knot, but have failed & shall do no more," he said. "The whole matter is resolved into a war between parties, and neither care or seem to care for the service or the Country." Yet three days later, on January 18, the President again summoned General Sherman to the White House. "I thought by his disregarding my advice on Sunday, he had a plan of action of his own," Sherman complained, "but from his conversation of today, I find he has none but wants me to do it for him."

Sherman did not want to be involved. "I'm afraid that acting as go-between for three persons," he told Grant, "I may share the usual fate of meddlers, at last, and get kicks from all."

FOR THE REST of January, a transfixed country read Grant's and Johnson's two very different accounts of their discussion about Stanton's job. The two most prominent men in the country, each politically motivated, were publicly quarreling over issues that could change the course of the entire nation. Newspapers printed gossip about Grant's drinking and Johnson's hurling a chair. Overall, though, it seemed the President had been injudicious. Why hadn't he taken Sherman's advice and nominated Jacob Cox, who would have been accepted by the Senate? And he had proposed nominating Sherman as war secretary even though Sherman had no use for politics or Washington.

But Sherman did sympathize to an extent with the President. "I feel for Mr. Johnson," Sherman told his wife, "but must say for his experience he has made some fatal mistakes. He should have taken care to have in his interest at least the half of one branch of Congress." For Johnson was not a man of even modest ability, "or a good administrator," Sherman added. "He deals in generalities but when he comes to apply principles to fact, he is lost."

As for Grant, Sherman also noted that he was more "uneasy than usual, at the criticism on his [Grant's] mode of getting out of the War Dept." To exonerate himself and make his position clear, Grant addressed Johnson in a publicly circulated letter, insisting that he hadn't promised to call on the President on Monday, January 12, or at any definite time, and that he assumed the President knew that. Johnson replied, also in public. If Grant had not wanted to be party to the controversy with the President, never mind Congress or Stanton, he was to return the office to him before the Senate acted so that the President could designate his successor. But Grant had vacated the office without giving Johnson notice of his intention.

Neither man budged. Both were obstinate, both careful, and both of them wanted to control the public's perception. Johnson asked cabinet members to confirm his version of events, and as usual, they did, except for William Seward, who acknowledged that Grant's saying he'd give the President advance notice of his intentions had been "indirect and circumstantial, though I did not understand it to be an evasive one."

Secretary of State Seward was himself a canny man, secretive, intelligent, and adept at playing both ends. But he genuinely liked Andrew Johnson and told his friend the actress Charlotte Cushman that Johnson was "a true firm honest affectionate man—perhaps the truest man he has almost ever known." Plus, and this was no small consideration, Johnson continued to allow the expansionist secretary of state free rein in foreign affairs. The French had left Mexico, as promised, which was a Seward victory, and more recently, Seward had been negotiating the purchase of Alaska and trying to buy the Danish West Indies, British Columbia, or, according to one hostile newspaper, "the whole hemisphere from the glaciers of Greenland to the volcanoes of Tierra del Fuego."

But Seward was Stanton's friend too. Together, they had served

Lincoln, and together they had waged war. Yet it seemed to many that after Lincoln's assassination and the attempt on his own life, Seward was no longer the staunch anti-slavery fighter who'd coined such prophetic phrases as "the irreconcilable conflict." Or as Wendell Phillips would remark, "Seward lost his brains." But Seward hadn't really changed. The heart of a conservative had always beat underneath his smooth exterior. And if Seward disagreed with Stanton about Johnson's Reconstruction policy, he was not eager to undermine the President.

Seward had advised Johnson to leave Stanton alone—to leave him in the War Department. When Johnson didn't heed his advice and suspended Stanton, Seward offered the President his resignation as secretary of state, which Johnson refused, as Seward knew he would.

Resignation was an empty gesture designed for public approval. Seward didn't want to resign, and he was sure Johnson wanted him close by. And Seward too had an eye on the upcoming presidential election; there was nothing for him outside of Washington. His wife had died, and so had his daughter. "A man is of no count here who does not represent a power behind him," Seward told John Bigelow. He had to bolster his position but not alienate Grant, who was edging closer and closer to the nomination; Seward knew he'd fare better with a Grant administration than with the radical Benjamin Wade in the White House.

With Johnson and Grant engaged in a public spat, some Republicans previously skeptical about Grant's loyalty to the party rushed to his side. Radical Republicans kept their distance. Horace Greeley, that seasonal Radical, distrusted Grant; Ben Butler was downright hostile; Chief Justice Salmon Chase wanted the White House for himself. And Democrats thought Grant nothing more than the puppet of Edwin Stanton, "who has corrupted the mind of Grant," said Frank Blair, Jr., "and whispered to him the project of absolute and permanent power." Conservative Senator James Doolittle, friendly with the Democrats, reminded the *New York World*'s Manton Marble that the cigar-chewing Grant had come out against black suffrage in 1865—and again the next year—because it would spark a war between the races. Now look at him: he was "in favor of negro supremacy."

Marble hesitated, reminding Doolittle that General Grant could be the candidate of either party—Republican or Democrat, no one was yet sure—and "then we shall know what his opinions on the most momentous issues of our time, have then come to be, before nominating or voting." Marble didn't have to wait very long. Johnson ordered General Grant not to recognize Stanton's authority as war secretary and forbade Grant from following any orders to the army that Stanton might issue. The formerly imperturbable Grant refused.

The news was stunning. The President of the United States had not only impugned the character of the country's biggest war hero but was asking him to break the law: to disobey the Tenure of Office Act, which protected Stanton's position as war secretary. The Senate had not approved Stanton's suspension, as the act had stipulated it should, and Stanton had stayed put.

With icy condescension, Grant formally addressed the President on February 3, again in a public way. "Where my honor as a soldier and integrity as a man have been so violently assailed, pardon me for saying that I can but regard this whole matter, from the beginning to the end, as an attempt to involve me in the resistance of law, for which you hesitated to assume the responsibility in orders, and thus to destroy my character before the country," Grant wrote. "I am in a measure confirmed in this conclusion, by your recent orders directing me to disobey orders from the secretary of war—my *superior* and your subordinate—without having countermanded his authority to issue the orders I am to disobey."

Newspaper editors gleefully covered the dramatic and in many ways extraordinary dispute. "In a question of veracity between a soldier whose honor is as untarnished as the sun, and a President who has betrayed every friend, and broken every promise," Horace Greeley's *New-York Tribune* exulted, "the country will not hesitate." Johnson's cabinet predictably rallied round the President: Attorney

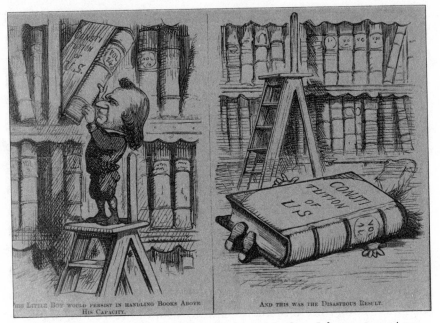

THIS LITTLE BOY WOULD PERSIST IN HANDLING BOOKS ABOVE HIS CAPACITY.

AND THIS WAS THE DISASTROUS RESULT.

Attributed to Thomas Nast, the cartoon depicts Andrew Johnson removing a
book too large for him to handle; it's the "Constitution of U.S.,"
which then knocks him over, crushing him.

General Henry Stanbery was appalled at the tone of Grant's most
recent letter, Browning dismissed it as "disreputable," and the irrepressible Welles declared that Grant "has great ambition, and is a
most remorseless man."

Congress was a different story. Walt Whitman told his mother
that the Republicans "seem thoroughly waked up & full of fight."
"Congress is on its mettle," Mark Twain reported, "—Stanton, the
President, Treasury frauds, reconstruction. . . . Even Wendell Phillips ought to be satisfied now."

The public quarrel breathed momentary life into a moribund
impeachment attempt, or at least into Thaddeus Stevens who,
clearly unwell, had to support himself by holding on to the table
when he stood. His voice fairly strong, he asked the Committee on
Reconstruction—he was its chair—to take control of impeachment
proceedings by opening its own investigation. Johnson's recommendation to Grant that he disobey the Tenure of Office law con-

stituted a conspiracy to obstruct justice, Stevens insisted. And Johnson had actually instructed Grant to disregard Secretary Stanton's orders.

After a long session, Stevens' resolution went to a subcommittee, but it never moved out of the committee to the larger House. Doing what he could—which wasn't much—he demanded that the yeas and nays be recorded for the nation. Only he, George Boutwell, and John Franklin Farnsworth of Illinois voted in the affirmative on impeachment. The other six men on the subcommittee voted against.

"Died: In this city, Feb. 13, at his lodgings in the chamber of the House Reconstruction Committee, our beloved brother, IMPEACHMENT," Mark Twain composed the obituary. "The malady of the deceased was general debility." But Twain congratulated Thaddeus Stevens. "Hon. Thad. Stevens, the bravest old ironclad in the Capitol, fought hard for impeachment, even when he saw that it could not succeed." And to its face, the old ironclad had called Congress a pack of damned cowards—"the finest word," Twain said, "that any congressional topic has produced this session."

CONVINCED THAT GRANT and his friends had blocked the impeachment movement, Thaddeus Stevens chatted with a group of reporters who, after the recent vote, had rushed to his modest redbrick house on South B Street near Capitol Hill. Stevens told them the quarrel between Johnson and Grant didn't matter, and he didn't care if Johnson and Grant settled it with fists in his backyard—even though, he chuckled, he wouldn't want his backyard dirtied by the likes of them. More seriously, he exclaimed, "What the devil do I care about the question of veracity as they call it, between Johnson and Grant? That's nothing to do with the law. Both of them may call each other liars if they want to, perhaps they both do lie a little, or let us say, equivocate, though the President certainly has the weight of evidence on his side. But Johnson being right or Grant being wrong, it makes no difference." To Stevens, the issue was the law.

Impeachment was about respect for and obedience to the law.

"The Senate had confirmed the Tenure of Office law. What right had a President to deny, defy, or seek to disobey that law?" Stevens demanded. "If this direct attempt of the President to violate a law made by the Congress of the United States doesn't render him liable to be impeached, what does?"

Yet Stevens said he would drop impeachment: "There is no sense making ourselves ridiculous before the country."

A SWAGGERING ANDREW Johnson granted an interview to the twenty-six-year-old conservative journalist Joseph B. McCullagh, known familiarly as Mack, the Associated Press reporter for *The Cincinnati Commercial*. The men talked for over an hour, with Johnson wondering aloud if he didn't have a right to dispute congressional legislation. After all, he wasn't supposed to follow Congress blindly, was he, and how else could he test a law? He was floating what would become a major part of his story: that he'd wanted Grant to sit tight in the war secretary's chair until the Supreme Court decided on the constitutionality of the Tenure of Office Act. He could easily imagine the Supreme Court striking down the Reconstruction Acts.

Not only had the Court's *Milligan* decision about keeping civil courts open dealt a blow to Radical Republicans, but, more recently, William H. McCardle, the editor of the *Vicksburg Daily Times*, was challenging them. A former soldier in the Confederate army, McCardle had been arrested by General Ord of the Fourth Military District (Mississippi, Arkansas) for a set of blistering editorials that undermined military commanders and implicitly incited ex-rebels to violence. McCardle wanted to bring his case before a civil, not a military, tribunal to protect himself from Ord. And since under the Judiciary Act amended in early 1867 and known as the Habeas Corpus Act of 1867, federal courts had the power to issue

writs of habeas corpus "in all cases where any person may be restrained of his or her liberty in violation of the Constitution,"
McCardle could go to a federal judge to bring his case before the
Supreme Court, which he did. Interestingly, his attorney was Jeremiah Black, who likely helped write the President's recent and belligerent message to Congress.

Since five of the Supreme Court judges were said to consider
the Reconstruction Acts unconstitutional, the McCardle case, as
argued by Black, would test them—and they would likely be tossed
out by the conservative-leaning court. Or so Black and Johnson
hoped. Black was arguing that the exercise of military law, in the
form of military courts, was unconstitutional because civil courts
were open. "If McCardle gains his case," Mark Twain nervously
predicted, "negro suffrage and the Reconstruction Acts will be dis-
sipated into thin air for the present."

But the Supreme Court postponed the McCardle case, and in a
hasty, if not altogether slick parliamentary maneuver, Congress ret-
roactively denied the Supreme Court jurisdiction over the case by
repealing the Habeas Corpus Act of 1867 under which McCardle
had made his appeal. The reconstruction laws were not tested, not
yet. Still, it is not at all certain that when Andrew Johnson suspended Stanton he was really thinking about the Supreme Court.
That seemed to come later, when Johnson needed to defend his
action—a defense probably concocted by Jeremiah Black.

For the moment, though, Johnson was cocky: as for impeachment, Congress wouldn't dare. McCullagh wasn't so sure. "Well,"
the President serenely replied to the journalist, "let them go ahead.
When they bring in the charges, I'll try and answer them, that's all."
And he laughed.

McCullagh was startled. Would the President really allow him
to print the entire interview—and that the President was laughing?
Perhaps he'd like something off the record? Not at all, Johnson happily answered, not at all.

ANDREW JOHNSON NOMINATED William Tecumseh Sherman
as General of the U.S. Army in command of the new military Division of the Atlantic. There were no military reasons for this new
division, which included the District of Columbia, Maryland, Delaware, Virginia, and West Virginia, and there were no military reasons for the rank. Johnson had not consulted with the army
beforehand. His sole aim was to humiliate General Grant.

Johnson was foolish to assume that Sherman would be willing to
resettle in Washington, where his division would be headquartered,
or that he would accept a position in rank equal to that of his friend.
Sherman wearily told Johnson that the battle-tested Grant, the
often-slandered Grant, the Grant who'd seen his soldiers slit the
gullets of starving mules to satisfy their own hunger, this Grant now,
today, had never been more upset. "If this political atmosphere can
destroy the equanimity of one so guarded and prudent as he is,"
Sherman explained, "what will be the result with one so careless
and outspoken as I am? Therefore, with my consent, Washington
never."

Sherman had lost patience with Johnson. "I suppose that because I gave him full credit for his first efforts to reconstruct the
South on principles nearer right than have since been attempted,
that I will go with him to the death, but I am not bound to do it,"
Sherman complained to his father-in-law. "He is like a General
fighting without an army—he is like Lear, roaring at the wild storm,
bareheaded and helpless. And now he wants me to go with him into
the wilderness."

Johnson acted as if surprised by Sherman's refusal to accept the
newly created command. And maybe he was. Maybe he had not
listened. Maybe he could not listen. Whatever the case—and it's
hard to know—the misunderstanding between the President and
another celebrated general again electrified the nation, sparking a
new set of speculations about Johnson's motives. Clearly he wanted
to checkmate Grant by offering Sherman a position that implicitly
vied with Grant's and that would bring Sherman to Washington—
perhaps to the war office. Sherman would have none of it.

With Sherman's name spread all over the papers, rumors again flew through Washington. The President's foes claimed that, fearing impeachment, Johnson intended to resist Congress by military force, with Sherman marshaling troops near the Capitol. Sherman too suspected something of the sort, telling his brother that "the President would make use of me to beget violence, a condition of things that ought not to exist now."

"Almost every positive affirmative step of his for the last two years has done harm not only to the country, but to himself and his party, if he have any party," George Templeton Strong confided to his diary. "'Andrew's Adventures in Blunderland' would be a good title for a political squib."

A blundering, roaring Lear. Enraged, Johnson felt he had only one option: to return to the source of the problem, to pluck it out, root and branch, once and for all. To him, that source was Edwin Stanton, secretary of war, in league with the military, with Grant, with all those who had defied or tried to undermine him. If getting rid of Stanton meant he would have to lock horns with Congress, so be it. He said his self-respect demanded it: "If the people did not entertain sufficient respect for their Chief Magistrate, enough to sustain him in such a measure," Johnson asserted, "then he ought to resign.

"I have ever battled for the right of the people and their liberties and I am now endeavoring to defend them from arbitrary power." He could not grasp that more and more people thought that he, Andrew Johnson, the Accidental President, was the one wielding power arbitrarily.

Andrew Johnson was not a statesman. He was man with a fear of losing ground, with a need to be recognized, with an obsession to be right, and when seeking revenge on enemies—or perceived enemies—he had to humiliate, harass, and hound them. Heedless of consequences, he baited Congress and bullied men, believing his enemies were enemies of the people. It was a convenient illusion.

Those closest to him were unsure of what he might do next.

When another conservative journalist, Jerome Stillson, met with Johnson in the White House in the middle of February, the President paced up and down, vowing to smash his foes.

"Mr. President," Stillson prodded him. "I'm hanged if I can see why either Grant or Stanton are to remain where they are much longer."

Johnson stopped. "That's just it, Mr. Stillson," the President replied. "There never was a clearer case of insubordination in military history."

"When is the devil to pay?" Stillson, a Democrat, prodded.

Johnson hesitated. It was impossible, he explained, "for outside people to know how hampered and forced to deliberation and self-control the President is." But he hinted he might have something up his sleeve. "I am not unwilling, as I have told you time and again, to talk plainly to you and afford you any confidence that I am able to," Johnson said. "But as it is, I can only give you a *general* idea of what is going on. My intentions ought to be pretty apparent to you. But I will neither mislead you nor anybody by making direct statements of what I am *myself* undecided upon, at last as to means."

Johnson would say nothing more, and he would not take anyone into his confidence.

On Friday, February 21, 1868, the day before Washington's birthday, a day that dawned bright and clear, President Andrew Johnson entered his office early in the morning and promptly wrote out the directive firing Edwin Stanton.

CHAPTER SEVENTEEN

Striking at a King

"When you strike at a king, you must kill him."

— RALPH WALDO EMERSON

Edwin Stanton was to be replaced by a bumbling desk officer, the sixty-three-year-old Adjutant General Lorenzo Thomas, a man widely recognized as vain, weak, and completely incapable of performing any public service credible to the country. Or as the Democrats put it, Lorenzo Thomas was a horse's ass.

Everyone knew he was completely different from Edwin Stanton. Stanton was respected for his organizational brilliance, his indefatigable energy, and his unflagging loyalty. Not so Thomas, who was loyal mainly to his desk, his epaulets, and his alcohol. According to John Hay, if Lorenzo Thomas spoke favorably of any public issue, he'd do so only if the country had already leaned that way. "He was a straw which shows whither the wind is blowing," Hay had said. The wind was blowing from Johnson's White House.

Thomas was uneasy, but Johnson assured him he wouldn't be breaking the law to accept the position without the Senate appointing him. Thomas' appointment was only as interim war secretary, until there was a permanent appointment. As such, his position was lawful and constitutional—not to worry, the President repeated.

General Thomas went to Stanton's office, where he handed Stanton a sheaf of papers. Stanton sat down on his office sofa to read them. "Do you wish me to vacate at once, or am I to be permitted to stay long enough to remove my property?" Stanton asked, glancing up. Thomas said Stanton could take the weekend. It was Friday. Saturday was a holiday, Washington's birthday. Thomas reported back to the President. Irritated that Stanton hadn't packed up his desk right away, Johnson ordered Thomas to return to the War Department to take charge the very next day, Saturday.

In the meantime, Stanton had sent for General Grant, for it was important to know where he stood. Grant was behind him. He would not order the army to remove Stanton by force. "I want some little time for reflection," Stanton then told Lorenzo Thomas. "I don't know whether I shall obey your orders or resist them." He also informed the House of Representatives that he'd been sacked.

Hearing the news, the excited representatives huddled in groups. Barely able to walk, Thaddeus Stevens limped from one to another, asking over and over, "Didn't I tell you so? What good did your moderation do you? If you don't kill the beast, it will kill you."

Shaking himself as if from a stupor, John Bingham said with revulsion that the President had opened a can of worms—the impeachment—that he'd thought he'd nailed firmly shut. And for what? Why act so recklessly? Why appoint someone without the Senate's consent? What kind of coup d'état was this?

John Covode of Pennsylvania introduced a formal resolution of impeachment. When James Pike of Maine shouted, "Stand up, impeachers!" almost every Republican jumped to his feet.

In the Senate, Roscoe Conkling was delivering a long-winded speech when the President's private secretary arrived a little before two o'clock with several sealed messages. Conkling was told to sit. The senators gathered around two Radical Republicans, Zachariah Chandler and Benjamin Wade, who opened the envelopes, which reported that the President had fired Stanton.

Johnson had actually fired Secretary of War Edwin Stanton.

The Senate went into immediate executive session. Charles

Sumner sent Stanton a telegram from the Senate floor. "Stick!" was all it said. Several other senators ran over to the War Department to encourage Stanton not to leave his post until the Senate decided what to do. "Resist force by force," one senator cried. In high spirits, Stanton agreed that if the Senate deemed Johnson's action illegal, he would definitely stay put in his office and, if he must, sleep there.

Stanton "stuck." His office under siege, he took his meals at his desk and slept on his sofa. The first night, General John Logan set up a cot in the war office, and a battalion of infantry was stationed on each side of the building in case there was trouble. There was none. Later that night, the Senate declared Stanton's removal unconstitutional, and Stanton, edgy but energetic, asked David K. Cartter, the chief justice of the District's Supreme Court, to come by. A former Ohio Democrat, an early Republican, and a staunch Lincoln supporter, Cartter helped Stanton draw up a complaint that charged Thomas with violating the Tenure of Office law. It was after midnight.

That same night, General Thomas went to a masquerade ball where he had much too much to drink. Early the next morning, the morning of Washington's birthday, he was stumbling around the street, boasting that he would remove Stanton by force, if need be, and that he'd call on General Grant to authorize that force, and if Stanton bolted the door, he'd break it down. It was before nine o'clock that General Thomas, half-drunk, was arrested for violating the Tenure of Office Act.

After being released on $5,000 bail, Thomas went straight to the White House, where Johnson told him he should have taken immediate possession of the War Department the day before. Hungover, Thomas hurried back to Stanton's office and, as Johnson had told him to do, demanded that the secretary's keys be turned over to him right away. Bleakly amused, Stanton refused. Thomas began to whine. He'd been arrested that morning before he'd even had time to eat breakfast or have a drink.

Stanton tousled Thomas' thick white hair, wrapped an arm around his shoulders, and asked an adjutant to fetch him a bottle so that he could offer Thomas a stiff shot of whiskey. The two men clinked their glasses and drank. Stanton reminded Thomas about the report on national cemeteries he'd asked him to prepare. Yes, yes, the general genially replied, he would work on it that very night. The wind had changed direction again.

General Townsend asked Stanton if he'd tricked Thomas into conceding that Stanton was still in charge. With a look of mock astonishment, Stanton asked how Townsend could ever think such a thing.

"When you strike at a king," Ralph Waldo Emerson had once said, "you must kill him."

THE NIGHT THAT he fired Stanton, the President had attended a state dinner for the diplomatic corps. Former ambassador John Bigelow noticed that Johnson seemed weary and distracted. After dinner, though, he chatted for a half an hour with a journalist, smiling all the while. Perhaps Johnson had unwittingly wandered into Blunderland, but he was doing exactly what he said he would do all along—prudently, he thought, and without heat, unafraid of impeachment or, for that matter, of Congress. "I know they are capable of doing anything," he declared. And if he had once delayed in the matter of firing Stanton, he had delayed only so that the country—"the people"—could witness for themselves the kind of man Stanton was, a man who did not resign when he knew he was not wanted, a bully, a conspirator, a backstairs intriguer.

Did the President expect Congress to impeach him?

"I don't know, indeed," Johnson bristled. "Nor do I care."

Georges Clemenceau was wiser. "The President called upon the lightning," he said, "and the lightning came."

CHAPTER EIGHTEEN

Impeachment

"Impeachment is peace."

— HORACE GREELEY

As early as seven o'clock on a bitterly cold Saturday morning, the snowy walkways were lined with people, black and white, waiting outside the White House. Newspaper boys yelled "Extra, extra" the way they had during the war, and at the Capitol, the metropolitan police had joined forces with the Capitol police, blue-uniformed and brass-buttoned, to guard every entrance. They stopped a reporter to check if he'd hidden nitroglycerine in the bundle of papers tucked under his arm.

"There are men in Washington who would blow up the Capitol fast enough," Mark Twain observed, "if they could achieve an illustrious name, like Booth, by doing it and be worshipped as Booth is worshipped."

Despite the fact that it was Washington's birthday, a holiday, the House of Representatives had decided to hold a special session, and when the doors of the building opened, men and women pushed into seats usually reserved for diplomats and reporters. "I recall nothing like it for size or eagerness since Mr. Lincoln's second inauguration," journalist Benjamin Perley Poore declared. "I suppose there were five or six thousand persons there who could not even get near the gallery doors; the corridors were completely packed for two or three hours."

In the early afternoon, Poore caught a glimpse of Thaddeus Stevens in one of the committee rooms. He was eating his lunch, which consisted of a few crackers, cheese, and a glass of water. He looked pasty, and news of his death would not have surprised anyone, but he assured Poore that he was "first rate, first rate." Mark Twain grabbed a seat in the reporters' gallery and was scribbling notes. Roll was called, and just before it was finished, several more representatives appeared. "Boutwell came in [sensation]; afterwards, at intervals, Bingham [sensation], Paine [sensation], several other committee men," Twain wrote, "and finally Thad. Stevens himself [super-extraordinary sensation!]."

Stevens leaned on the arm of a friend, and while barely able to walk down the center aisle, he gingerly lowered himself to his seat. Boutwell walked over to him and handed him something.

Twain continued to admire Stevens. "There was a soul in his sunken eyes, but otherwise he was a corpse that was ready for the shroud," Twain noted. "He held his precious impeachment papers in his hand, signed at last! In the eleventh hour his coveted triumph had come." The place fell silent. Stevens passed the papers over to Edward McPherson, clerk of the House, who began to read. Everyone knew what to expect. After Stanton's dismissal the day before, the matter of impeachment had been swiftly referred to the Committee on Reconstruction. If the committee recommended impeachment, the entire House would vote on Monday, and it would take just a simple majority of its members to impeach Andrew Johnson.

No one spoke, no one applauded, no one protested. The committee vote was announced. With only two members dissenting, it recommended the first impeachment of an American President. Twain saw a sudden brightness light up the faces around him.

Still, the recent cascade of events—the abrupt firing of Stanton,

Lincoln's postmaster general until 1864, Montgomery Blair, member
of a powerful Democratic family, was an important if unofficial adviser
to President Johnson, arguing for the speedy readmission of the Southern states to the Union. His brother Francis Blair, Jr., was a vice-
presidential candidate in 1868, on a white supremacist ticket.

the antics of Lorenzo Thomas, the Senate's declaration that Johnson had violated the law—had been stupefying. Moderates were
panicky, Democrats astonished, Radicals perplexed. James Doolittle begged Johnson to write a letter to Congress and explain himself. Johnson said he'd do nothing of the kind, but he privately
suggested that his secretary think about looking for another job.

What *was* Johnson doing? Edwards Pierrepont, the lawyer who
had prosecuted John Surratt, remarked that "Johnson acts like a
man who allows passion & spite to destroy his judgment." The Pres-

ident apparently hadn't consulted anyone before letting Stanton
go. Montgomery Blair, who had wanted Stanton axed for a very
long time—and Seward too—had been spotted going to the White
House pretty often, but close advisers like Attorney General Henry
Stanbery and other members of the cabinet had been left in the
dark. So too Jeremiah Black. When asked if he had advised Johnson
to rid himself of Stanton, Black had excitedly replied, "The papers
talk about me as the President's chief adviser. That's all humbug; he
sends for me sometimes, but he rarely follows my advice; if he did
he wouldn't make such a damned fool of himself so often."

On the same Friday that Johnson had sacked Secretary Stanton,
executive members of the Democratic National Committee were
gathering in Washington for their annual meeting. The coincidence was striking, if it *was* a coincidence and not just Johnson's
hamfisted attempt to rally Democrats to his side. If it was, it flopped.
On Saturday, the mood was dreary at the elegant White House banquet for well-heeled members of the committee. Only a fraction of
them actually showed up, and all of them were uncomfortably
aware that Congress was preparing to charge the banquet's host, the
President, with high crimes and misdemeanors. August Belmont,
head of the committee, suavely disavowed Johnson through his
newspaper mouthpiece, *The World*: Democrats would not comment on a personal tiff between the President and Mr. Stanton.
After all, Mr. Stanton should have been removed from the war office long ago; now it hardly mattered. Besides, Johnson was a Republican, not a Democrat, and he had done very little for Democrats.
"He aims now, when too late to get Democratic aid," Pierrepont
scoffed. "He will be dropped by all."

It seemed true. *The Herald*'s James Bennett repeated that the
President was not a Democrat, he hadn't been elected by Democrats, and in this recent brouhaha he neither consulted with nor
confided in them. Best that the Democratic party did not identify
itself with him in the firing of the secretary of war. Other Democrats expressed their feelings more bluntly. They refused "to tie
themselves to a corpse."

Johnson seemed oblivious. He was surprised that Democrats were miffed because he hadn't confided in them. "He swore that his course ought to have been plain enough," Jerome Stillson told Samuel Barlow. And Johnson believed himself shrewd. Assuming that the appointment would burnish his own reputation, he sent to the Senate the name of Major-General George H. Thomas (not Lorenzo Thomas) to be appointed lieutenant-general by brevet. But the war hero familiarly known as the "Rock of Chickamauga" politely asked the Senate not to confirm him, insisting he had done nothing in peacetime to deserve it. Closer to the truth was that he didn't want to involve himself in the Washington mess, and he didn't want himself linked to the President.

Johnson also thought it shrewd to appoint Thomas Ewing as interim war secretary. "Too late, Mr. President," Horace Greeley sneered. "The question before the country now is the violation of law." The Senate didn't bother to consider Ewing's nomination. "Johnson is like a blind man reaching out in every direction for something to take hold of," a Missouri Democrat noted, "but he finds only vacancy."

Nationwide, people waited impatiently for news and heard terrifying talk about an invasion of troops from Maryland—or about another civil war. Certainly Stanton's dismissal had been a defiant salvo against Congress, well aimed, presumptuous, deadly. Many people recalled how alarmed they'd been right before secession and then their anxiety after Lincoln's death. Mass meetings were held throughout the country, and congressmen were pelted with telegrams and letters. "Nearly the entire loyal sentiment of the North is now with Congress & they look to the removal of Johnson as the only way to peace & quiet," said Edwards Pierrepont. "The truest portion of the Republican Party in Delaware depends on the conviction and removal of Andrew Johnson from his accidental position," a former member of the legislature told Thaddeus Stevens. From the South, a white Alabama man implored Benjamin Butler that "as American citizens, we ask you to hurry up impeachment."

In California, the black journalist Philip Alexander Bell announced that "Andrew Johnson deserves impeachment." Representative William Kelley, Pennsylvania Radical, was passionate on the House floor. "The bloody and untilled fields of the ten unreconstructed States, the unsheeted ghosts of the two thousand murdered negroes in Texas cry for the punishment of Andrew Johnson." Conservative Virginia Governor Francis Pierpont had already admitted the President "ought to be removed." General John Logan ecstatically told Wendell Phillips, "I think we have 'caught the rat.'"

"Sound the tocsin," Mark Twain exclaimed. "I don't know what a tocsin is, but I want it sounded all the same!"

But there were naysayers too. A self-proclaimed Union man from Baltimore wrote Senator William Pitt Fessenden that "as President Johnson only has a short time to serve, don't set such a bad precedent as turning him out because of a mere difference of opinion." And Fessenden, cautious to the bone, had doubts about impeachment. "Either I am very stupid, or my friends are acting like fools, and hurrying us to destruction," he complained. Charles Eliot Norton deplored the "indecent eagerness" of the impeachment vote. "There was something truly shocking in the manner in which men charged forth, and tried to get themselves on the record as original impeachers," Norton complained to the editor of The Nation, who agreed.

IN THE FUTURE, after the political tides had changed, many of these men would loudly denounce impeachment, which they recalled as hysteria, and many an impeacher would regret his enthusiasm. But in early 1868, the nation faced questions that the unsettled, fragile peace had not fully answered: what were the duties of the executive, the legislature, and the judiciary toward the people it represented—more specifically, to those people not yet represented by the ballot, the four million formerly enslaved individuals whose representation hung in the balance? Who was responsible for them, or were they, because they were now free, responsible for themselves, as Johnson and others argued?

If, in 1868, impeachment seemed risky, if it was unprecedented and frightening, it also promised a better, fairer future: prospects seemed good for real and lasting change. The black editor of Augusta's *Loyal Georgian* said it would be "not a blunder, but a crime" not to impeach Andrew Johnson. "If you do not crush Johnson," Senator Fessenden was warned, "he is determined evidently to crush the Congress & annul the work of Reconstruction." And a Georgian (white) declared that "the removal of Andrew Johnson would be a lifting from the Southern people a greater load than any under which they have ever suffered. We are like men struggling with a fiend—our steps are watched, our words noted, our lives threatened, our labor plundered, our best men slandered, our great improvements retarded, our friends kept away, our brethren driven off."

And if, after the war, Republicans were split over other issues, like fiscal policy, Johnson had managed once again to unify them—to bring them together on this contentious issue of impeachment, of all things. Johnson's rashness riled even the loyal Gideon Welles. "By a final hasty move, without preparation," Welles complained, "he took a step that consolidated the Radicals of every stripe."

Most Republicans had been disinclined to impeach, preferring instead to tie Johnson's hands and wait until the next election. But Johnson had pushed them too far. "We have tolerated a Rebel in the White House long enough, & all expect you will permit it no longer," a Washburne constituent wrote to him. Reconstruction was at stake. The law was at stake. Johnson had shaken "a scarlet cloak or a red rag" at the Radicals, Thomas Ewing admitted, that "neither wild bulls, nor cock turkeys" could ignore.

Ewing was correct. No Republican could ignore the chief executive's direct assault on the legislative branch of government. When Illinois representative Shelby Cullom asked Lyman Trumbull what he should do, Trumbull surprised him by saying, vote for impeachment. Senator John Sherman too supported the impeachment resolution. In the House, Elihu Washburne, fanning the Grant flame, had opposed impeachment, believing it would hurt Grant's chance for the nomination. Now he was for it. The more conservative Henry Dawes had deplored the idea of impeachment; no longer. James Wilson no longer muzzled impeachment, and conservative Michigan Representative Austin Blair announced that "I have been among those who have hesitated long before resorting to this measure." No longer.

AS SCHEDULED, THE debate in the House began Monday morning, February 24. It was snowing heavily, and the chamber was dark. Several senators walked over to the House to listen. Representative John Bingham, who had been opposed to impeachment from the start, rose from his seat. "I stand here," he said, "filled with a conviction as strong as knowledge that the President of the United States has deliberately, defiantly, and criminally violated the Constitution, his oath of office, and the laws of the country."

Then the lid blew off. Washburne burst into a radical denunciation of Johnson. Look at the Navy Department and its profligacy; look at Treasury and its frauds; look at the Interior Department with its absurd Indian contracts and land jobbing; look at the Post Office and State, stuffed with traitors. Representative after representative spoke, Republicans for impeachment, arguing, like Sydney Clarke of Kansas, that "Andrew Johnson, in my judgement [sic], is guilty as inciter and provoker of the nameless crimes which have been inflicted upon the freedmen of the South; the two thousand murders known to have been committed in the State of Texas alone; and of the thousands of similar atrocities which have afflicted the loyal citizens, white and colored, throughout the rebel States."

Ben Butler said that by violating the Tenure of Office law, Johnson was obviously guilty of a "high misdemeanor." And yet what about the shameless pardon brokerage? What about consorting with traitors and murderers in New Orleans? What about his removal of military personnel from their commands in the South? What about his attempt to draw the army of the United States into

conspiracy so as to get possession of the military? What about usurpation, lawlessness, and tyranny? What about his contempt for
Congress? These too were crimes.

The House Democrats answered, somewhat lamely, that Republicans wanted to discard the President in order to increase their
power in Congress. This was their party line, and it rang true, particularly to future critics who tarred Radical Republicans as power-
hungry ideologues. Radicals were ambitious for power, of course,
and they wanted Republicans to remain in Congress — not only for
the sake of power, though there was that, but to protect their victory
over slavery, an insidious, damaging, embarrassing national crime,
and to eradicate its effects as best they could.

When arguing more substantively, Johnson allies stressed the
President's recent justification for firing Stanton: the President was
just testing the constitutionality of the Tenure of Office Act, which
he said impinged on his constitutional prerogatives. Noting that the
law applied only to cabinet members who'd been appointed by sitting Presidents, they said that since Stanton had been appointed by
President Lincoln, the Tenure of Office Act, even if it was constitutional, which it wasn't, didn't apply to Stanton.

Was this a legal quibble? Possibly; it remained to be seen. Stanton meanwhile had taken steps to foil Johnson. He dropped the
charge against Lorenzo Thomas for violating the Tenure of Office
Act, thus preventing Thomas from appealing the case to the Supreme Court, which would consider the law's constitutionality, as
the President now insisted he'd intended to have happen all along.
In reply, Republicans argued that an ordinary citizen — but not the
President — might challenge a law by disobeying it. No one is above
the law. And they reasoned that since Johnson had obeyed the Tenure of Office Act when he first suspended Stanton, he had accepted
Congress's right to approve or disapprove his actions — only later
had he defied the Senate's decision, with a retrospective justification about testing the act's constitutionality. "The President has
openly and clearly violated the law," Representative Austin Blair
bitterly explained. "He has thrown down the gauntlet to Congress,

and says to us as plainly as words can speak it: 'Try this issue now betwixt me and you; either you go to the wall or I do.'"

To those who argued that the President of the United States *could* legitimately test the constitutionality of the law, the legally minded James Wilson said that once he took the oath of office, the President merged "his individuality into that official creature which binds itself by an oath as an executive officer to do that which, as a mere individual, he may not believe to be just, right or constitutional. Such an acceptance removes him from the sphere of the right of private judgement [*sic*] to the plane of the public officer," Wilson continued, "and binds him to observe the law, his judgment as an individual to the contrary notwithstanding."

Johnson had to obey the law, and if he disagreed, he should resign. It was that simple.

Just before five o'clock that afternoon, under the gaslights, Thaddeus Stevens hobbled to the front of the Speaker's podium, bracing himself against the marble desk. His voice was hoarse. The room fell silent. But the effort to say what he wanted to say was too much for him. He handed his speech to McPherson.

"The framers of our Constitution did not rely for safety upon the avenging dagger of a Brutus, but provided peaceful remedies which should prevent that necessity," McPherson read. Their peaceful remedy was impeachment, whose whole and only punishment was removal from office.

The long debate was over, the roll finally called. The impeachment resolution passed, 126 to 47. All the Republicans in the chamber had voted to impeach Andrew Johnson, the seventeenth President of the United States.

It was then that Mark Twain wrote, with certain satisfaction, that "out of the midst of political gloom, impeachment, that dead corpse, rose up and walked forth again!"

CONGRESSIONAL REPUBLICANS RECEIVED bagsful of mail congratulating them on a deed long overdue, and in several cities,

the Union Leagues fired fifty-gun salutes. "The man who was inaugurated in drunkenness, who has ever since been a living disgrace
to his name, to his position, and to his country, now will go to 'his
own place' in history, in the company of Benedict Arnold and Jeff
Davis," the editor of *The Independent* rejoiced. In Maine, the House
of Representatives passed a resolution endorsing impeachment,
and in New York the governor put New York City under martial law
in case of trouble. Horace Greeley proclaimed that "impeachment

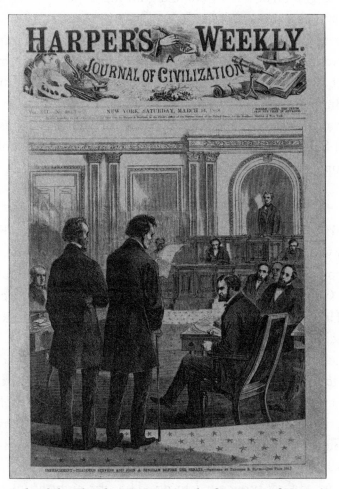

A sketch by Theodore R. Davis on the front page of *Harper's
Weekly* (March 14, 1868) portrays Representative Thaddeus
Stevens and John Bingham at the bar of the Senate, come to
announce the House decision to impeach Andrew Johnson.

is peace." According to him, the wealthiest and most conservative voters favored impeachment. New York diarist George Templeton Strong disagreed; he believed Democratic millionaires would be happy to finance a ragtag militia to prevent it. Greeley clarified. "Some of our people may rant and swear, and gnash their teeth; but we shall have no war—no disturbance—no arresting the wheels of Government—not the shimmer of the bayonet, nor the click of the trigger—" he predicted. "There is something grand to us in this spectacle of a great nation changing an incompetent ruler by the gentle and easy process of law."

Impeachment was indeed a spectacle of sorts: a nation impeaching a President, its President, for the first time and without fanfare, bayonet, or trumpet. The ailing Thaddeus Stevens and the angular John Bingham, one man an avowed Radical, one man far more conservative, walked together, arm in arm, down the main aisle of a hushed Senate chamber. And then the House of Representatives rolled up its sleeves.

THE HOUSE OF Representatives was to identify the specific articles for which the President was to be tried. Speaker Schuyler Colfax appointed George Boutwell, Thaddeus Stevens, General John Logan, George Julian, Hamilton Ward, and two of the more conservative House members, John Bingham and James Wilson, to write the specific charges against Andrew Johnson.

To secure Bingham's and Wilson's votes, the House had been forced to focus on Johnson's violation of the Tenure of Office Act, an indictable offense, and not, as Stevens would have preferred, the President's abuse of power. Ill and weak though he may have been, Stevens worried that "the committee are likely to present no articles having any real vigor in them." And he believed that was exactly what they proceeded to do. The first eight articles dealt mainly with Stanton's dismissal, including the allegation that Johnson had conspired with Lorenzo Thomas to prevent the secretary of war from occupying his office. The ninth article concerned the

President's alleged suggestion that General William H. Emory, military commander of the District, disobey the Military Appropriations Act and take orders from Johnson instead of Grant, even though Emory had declined to do that. Whether or not Johnson's suggestion was an indictable offense, the ninth article also suggested a broader interpretation of the requirements for an impeachment conviction.

These articles, even the ninth, didn't satisfy Thaddeus Stevens, who didn't want impeachment defined in such crabbed terms. An impeachable offense need not be an indictable one, like pocketing the spoons. This was the Radical Republican position earlier articulated by George Boutwell, and now again by Wendell Phillips. Addressing an auditorium filled to the brim in Cincinnati, Phillips explained that "my wish to impeach him tonight is not technical, but because the man, by either his conscience or perverseness had set himself up systematically to save the South from the verdict of the war, and the necessity of the epoch in which we live. Every single act since the summer of 1865 points to that." Phillips recounted Johnson's transgressions: Johnson had restored the property of unrepentant Southern ex-rebels; he'd lined their pockets; he'd placed as governors men unable or unwilling to take the oath of office, men who encouraged "violations of unappeased hatred of the malignant white race to wreak itself unheeded on the Union whites, and on the black race."

"I do not care whether Johnson has stepped on a statute or not," Phillips raised his voice. "Impeachment is the refuge of the common sense of the nation, which in the moment of difficulty says to the magistrate, you ought to have known by your common sense, and your moral sense, that this has unfitted you for your office." Cheers.

Afraid the committee would ignore the common sense—not to mention the moral sense—of the nation if it defined impeachment too narrowly, Thaddeus Stevens, with Ben Butler's assistance, composed a tenth impeachment article that accused Johnson of disgracing the presidential office, particularly when he delivered the vituperative speeches that demeaned Congress or when he berated and threatened Wendell Phillips, Charles Sumner, and himself.

Intrigued, the young French journalist Georges Clemenceau decided to read Johnson's speeches again. And when he did, he had to admit that Butler was right. They were rather insulting.

Inexorable, almost compulsively so, Stevens was still not satisfied, so he lobbied for an eleventh impeachment article, which he wrote with the far more moderate James Wilson, no longer quite so moderate. This eleventh article ranged from Johnson's abuse of Congress—his insistence that Congress had no authority if Southern states were not represented—to his obstruction of such laws as the Military Reconstruction Acts. A comprehensive, catchall indictment, it was a kitchen-sink, deep and wide enough to give senators a chance to fish out and vote for at least one of the charges. It also summarized Johnson's presidency as including conspiracy, usurpation, and the obstruction of justice.

Then came the election of the group of men from the House who would prosecute the case against Johnson. Called managers, they included familiar names, such as Stevens himself, Bingham, Wilson, and Boutwell. In addition there were General John Logan, Thomas Williams of Pennsylvania, and Beast Ben Butler—the latter, it was said, because, as journalist Whitelaw Reid acknowledged, Butler was "one of the greatest criminal lawyers in the country and Johnson one of the greatest criminals."

Bingham flew into a rage when it was suggested Butler chair the committee. "I'll be damned if I serve under Butler, a man who denounced me to the country as a murderer," Bingham exploded, pounding his fist on the desk. Boutwell tried to calm him, but Bingham held his ground. To prevent a quarrel that might go public—which it did anyway—Boutwell diplomatically stepped aside, even though he was next in line to chair the committee. Bingham could be chair. Brash Ben Butler might be respected, he might be effective, and sometimes he was admired, but more often he was despised. And yet though Butler was not the chair of the committee, he would lead the charge.

CHAPTER NINETEEN

The High Court of Impeachment

March 1868

Over six feet tall, his head large and his features strong, Chief Justice Salmon Portland Chase, dressed in his long black silk robe, strode purposefully to the head of the Senate chamber. The president pro tempore of the Senate, Benjamin Wade, surrendered his chair to the regal chief justice.

"Senators," Chief Justice Chase gravely declared, "in obedience to notice, I have appeared to join with you in forming a Court of Impeachment for the trial of the President of the United States."

Henry Adams would call Chief Justice Salmon Chase nothing if not dramatic, and Thursday, March 5, was a dramatic day. Senior Associate Justice Nelson of the Supreme Court administered an oath of office to Chase, who swore he would serve impartially as judge during the trial of Andrew Johnson, President, and that he would faithfully administer the Constitution and the laws.

Beyond this, though, no one knew what to do. The Constitution offered no procedural guidelines to instruct the chief justice how to preside over an impeachment trial—or even how to organize the Senate. In fact, the Senate couldn't force Chase to serve as presiding officer, so if he refused to step up, there might be no trial at all. He was in an excellent position to bargain.

Chase had already seized the moment by writing to the Senate, saying that in case of a tie, he wanted to be able to cast a vote. (Since he was not a member of the Senate, technically he should not be allowed to vote.) He wished to rule on the admissibility of evidence — subject to the vote of the Senate — and on the reliability of witnesses. These stipulations afforded him leverage over the Senate, which he then argued should be organized as a court of law during impeachment proceedings. For if the Senate operated as a court during those proceedings and not as a legislative body, the chief justice was in control of it; he was President of the High Court of Impeachment.

Radical Republicans were incensed by what they perceived as judicial interference. They believed Chase intended to embarrass the Senate or, more chillingly, derail the impeachment process. "Chf. Ju. Chase to many showed his teeth and will give us all the trouble he can," General Logan complained after Chase announced his conditions. It was known that Chase considered the impeachment resolution absurd and Johnson within his rights when he dismissed Edwin Stanton. Chase's friends defended him. The chief justice was merely following the law, they said.

It's hard to know precisely where he stood: Salmon Chase was a peculiar amalgam of humility, vanity, and voracious ambition. Intelligent and skillful, he had contributed in no small way to the development of the Republican party, and he was known as a strenuous advocate of equal rights who fought against all the proslavery measures of the 1850s with considerable gusto. He was also humorless, distant, and self-righteous. Frederick Douglass distrusted Chase as a cold, greedy man who would sacrifice abolition, equality, and principle for power. The poet Walt Whitman called him a "bad egg."

Although he had during his abolitionist lifetime fiercely supported universal suffrage, Chase just as fiercely opposed what he called arbitrary military governments and military trials for civilians in peacetime. This was evident in his 1866 *Ex parte Milligan* decision. There, he declared that in a state where the civil courts were functioning, even if habeas corpus had been suspended, a resident citizen could not be tried, convicted, or sentenced by a military tribunal. Chase also believed that former Confederate military and political personnel should be able to vote.

That he had drifted away from his earlier radicalism was clear. This made him attractive to moderate Republicans and, he hoped, to the Democratic party, which had been his party when he was younger. He might also boast of his conservative credentials on the currency. As secretary of the treasury under Lincoln, Chase had reluctantly approved the circulation of greenbacks, but only as a wartime measure. After the war, he wanted the government to return to an economic policy that included the retirement of paper money. Maybe the Democrats would thus forgive his passion for universal suffrage, and if so, in 1868, Salmon Chase could hang up the gavel and enter the White House at last.

His wish to be President was an open secret, for despite his il-

Formerly Lincoln's treasury secretary, Salmon P. Chase was appointed chief justice of the United States Supreme Court and thus presided over Johnson's impeachment trial, which he opposed. Perennially in pursuit of the presidency for himself, Chase made no secret of his views, although he prided himself on his fairness.

lustrious career—governor of Ohio, senator, presidential contender, treasury secretary, and chief justice—or perhaps because of that illustrious career, Chase still feverishly sought the presidency, firmly believing that he was far more qualified than any bullet-headed general, particularly Ulysses S. Grant. "He feels, I believe, very confident that he will be the Republican candidate," Moorfield Storey noted.

Radical Republicans were thus suspicious of Chase. "I foresee, the Democrats are now for him for President and the foolish ambitious man seems 'well pleased,'" General Logan remarked, "but any that is fool enough to go back to the democratic party after leaving it, certainly does not understand their mode of doing business."

And Grant's people were concerned, having discovered that several national banks were contributing $300,000 to the Chase campaign and that Chase's son-in-law, William Sprague, had offered to raise $500,000. Whether true or not, a Grant supporter told Washburne, Chase had plenty of money at his disposal. But Chase was courting the equally wary Democrats. "The Radicals denounce him, but he has not broken with them, and he is not prepared to do so," the conservative legal scholar George Ticknor Curtis confided to Democratic party tycoon Samuel Barlow. "In fact, he does not know what to do." Increasingly, he did know that it was in his interest to buck the impeachers.

Gossips claimed Chase had gone to Johnson and told the President outright that there wasn't enough evidence for a conviction. True or not, Andrew Johnson and his two daughters had been invited to the chief justice's Wednesday reception on March 4, just the day before Chase was sworn to impartiality at the trial. Johnson and his daughters at the Chase party: what kind of impartiality was that? Chase petulantly justified the invitation. "I remembered his loyalty at the outset of the war and his patriotism throughout the war," Chase said of Johnson. He had never offended the President, he added, and the President had merely paid him the compliment of his attendance; that was all.

His campaign to organize the Senate as a legal court was largely successful. That meant Chase might cast a vote in case of tie, decide legal disputes, and determine the admissibility of evidence. If the managers appealed a point of law decided by the chief justice, only a senator—not the managers, who were representatives—could appeal the decision. One-fifth of the members present could overturn his ruling on evidence and incidental questions. When Charles Sumner and Missouri Senator Charles Drake tried to strip Chase of some of his power, their motion was defeated. The Senate did decide, though, that any one individual senator could call for a vote on the chief justice's rulings.

Basically, Chase had won a significant victory. The trial of the President conducted mostly as if it were a legal proceeding slanted the definition of impeachable offense toward a breach of law and away from questions of fitness, folly, or the autocratic abuse of power. The tide was already turning.

ALL SENATORS WERE to take the same oath that had been administered to Chief Justice Chase, but Indiana Democrat Thomas Hendricks objected to Benjamin Wade's swearing-in. As president pro tempore of the Senate, Wade would enter the White House if Johnson was convicted; Hendricks argued that Wade should therefore not be allowed to vote: the conflict of interest was obvious.

As a U.S. Senator from Ohio, Wade did have the right to vote—if, that is, the Senate tried impeachment as a legislative body and not as a high court. But the real issue for many was the idea of a President Benjamin Wade. "Three months of Ben Wade are worse than two years of A. J.," Charles Eliot Norton cried. James Garfield noted that his colleagues were panicky. "'Conviction means a transfer to the Presidency of Mr. Wade,'" he reported them as saying, "'a man of violent passions, extreme opinions and narrow views; a man who has never studied or thought thoroughly or carefully on any subject except slavery, a grossly profane coarse nature who is surrounded by the worst and most violent elements in the Republican party.'" After quoting his colleagues, Garfield disingenuously added, "now these sentiments are in many respects unjust to Wade,—of course you will understand they are not mine."

Muscular and stocky, Benjamin Wade was a steam engine, Emily Briggs declared, "built for use instead of ornament." Unlike Charles Sumner, who favored plaids and purples, Wade dressed plainly, always in a black broadcloth suit with an old-fashioned standing collar. He never wore jewelry, not even a ring. He trafficked in absolutes, and he didn't let go. Noah Brooks said that Wade possessed "a certain bulldog obduracy truly masterful." Certainly his support of such scandalous issues as women's suffrage, equal justice under the law, and paper currency rubbed a number of people the wrong way. He didn't care. When he brought Congress a bill allowing women the right to their own wages and property, Wade vehemently exclaimed, "I did not do it because they are women, but because it is right." In 1867, he'd signed a petition recommending Mrs. Frances Lord Bond for a consulate—because, he said, she was qualified.

"That vicious old agrarian, Ben Wade, of Ohio, tells you what is coming," conservative Southerners despaired: "The ballot for the women and free farms for the free negroes."

Born in the Connecticut valley, Wade and his family had moved to Ohio, where in his youth he'd worked as a farmhand, a teacher, and a laborer with spade and wheelbarrow on the Erie Canal before studying law with a local attorney and entering briefly into a partnership with the evangelical abolitionist Joshua Giddings. In 1851, as a former state senator and judge of the third judicial district, Wade was sent to the U.S. Senate by a coalition of Whigs and Free-Soilers the same year as Charles Sumner. Both men were contentious opponents of slavery. But Wade wasn't a windbag. With a brace of pistols in his desk, and a squirrel gun nearby, he put Southern fire-eaters on notice. "If he is a good friend," said a contemporary, "he is also a good hater." Wade never backed down.

In 1861, when he was sixty-one, he unsuccessfully tried to join the Union army, and consoled himself by chairing the Committee on the Conduct of War. He openly criticized Lincoln for prosecuting what he called a "rose-water war," and in 1864 actually tried to topple the President because Lincoln seemed too soft on reconstruction. Wade worried that slavery by another name would never be abolished if ex-rebels, no matter what kind of loyalty oath they swore, were allowed to hold office. Anyone who held a position of authority in the Confederacy or who had shouldered a rifle should be forbidden to serve as a delegate to the state constitutional conventions or even to vote for the delegates who did.

Wade's early plan for reconstruction didn't initially give black men the vote, but that soon changed. And he thought that the plantations of slaveholders should be broken up and distributed. Karl Marx, who called Andrew Johnson "a dirty tool of the slaveholders," admiringly quoted from Wade's public statement that "after the abolition of slavery, a radical change of relations of capital and of property in land is next upon the order of the day." Far less pleased, conservative Americans called Ben Wade a mixture of "Machiavelli, Munchausen, and Miss Nancy."

Wade, then, in the Executive Mansion? Not a chance. Andrew

Ohio Senator Benjamin Wade was the Radical Republican who, as president pro tempore of the Senate during the latter part of the Johnson administration, was next in line for the presidency should Johnson be impeached. (Johnson had no Vice President.)

Johnson may be impeached, but conviction seemed fairly remote. Wade was too frightening.

But Wade also had defenders. For one thing, whether friend or foe, no one had ever doubted his honesty. "He is therefore the kind of a man the country needs in this crisis, when the Treasury is being robbed by corrupt rings, who are protected by the administration," Whitelaw Reid declared. Yet for the most part, conservative Republicans and Democrats feared that Wade stood "cheek by jowl" with Wendell Phillips "on negro suffrage and Southern negro supremacy." He communicated with John Brown's ghost, they said, and mockingly imagined a Wade cabinet with Susan B. Anthony as secretary of the interior, and Frederick Douglass and George Downing as ministers to Haiti and Liberia. In fact, Johnson's friend, the journalist Joseph McCullagh, told the President that the impeachment trial would be more about blocking Wade than about banishing Johnson.

Johnson was incredulous. "[Johnson] thought every republican senator hated him," McCullagh said, "worse than he hated anybody else."

Ohio Senator John Sherman maintained that his state was entitled to *two* senators, namely himself and Wade, during the impeachment trial. Johnson's son-in-law, Senator David Patterson, represented Tennessee, and wasn't he also representing Andrew Johnson? Wasn't that a conflict of interest? Senator Sherman wanted to know. Democrat Reverdy Johnson countered that although the trial would take place in the Senate chamber, the Senate would be a court of impeachment, not a legislative body, so Wade should not be able to vote.

Charles Sumner informed Reverdy Johnson that the Constitution granted the power to try impeachments to the Senate, pure and simple; and whether you called the Senate a court or a tribunal or a senate, it was still the Senate, and Wade should vote. Others chimed in that any objections to Wade's vote should come from the President's defense team, not from the senators themselves.

On and on the debate raged, foreshadowing what was to come,

but on Friday, March 6, for reasons unknown, or because a deal had been made, Thomas Hendricks withdrew his objection, and Benjamin Wade took the oath with the other senators.

This was a victory for Radical Republicans and for Wade, it seemed. The Senate still conceived of itself as a legislative body with two representatives from every state. But at the same time, according to Salmon Chase, the Senate was reconstituted as a judicial court of impeachment, whatever that was. It was confusing. Yet moderate Republicans were sure of one thing: they didn't want an old-time abolitionist and inflationary rabble-rouser to emerge as top dog.

"THEY SAY THE city is full of rebels, who have been coming here for a week past," Moorfield Storey told his sister, "and they also say that nothing of the kind is true." Johnson would resign; he should resign; he could not get a fair trial. He would not resign. He would get in his own way. "Give Andy enough rope and he will hang himself *and* his friends," Democrats joked. He should be convicted for not having booted Stanton out years ago. Others predicted the Senate would drop the prosecution. "The Hon. Mr. Wiseacre thinks he [the President] has not committed a 'misdemeanor;' and the Hon. Mr. Somebody Else thinks it won't do to have Ben Wade President in a few weeks; and the Hon. Mr. Lord-Knows-Who is afraid it will have a bad effect on politics if we meddle with him; and the rich and ignorant classes of State and Wall Streets fear a rise in gold," said one reporter.

On Saturday, March 7, a petulant, pugnacious President received a summons to appear before the Senate. He said he would make some reply, sometime, maybe soon. Composed, he welcomed martyrdom. Or he would bring his case to the people. As for his enemies, he swore he'd show "these damned scoundrels, what fate is in store for them."

CHAPTER TWENTY

All the President's Men

There had been enough men to set impeachment in motion, but there were still plenty who, although they disliked Andrew Johnson, disliked impeachment more. And so Johnson was able to assemble a dazzling team of lawyers to defend him.

Benjamin Robbins Curtis had been a star. Esteemed for his keen and often unassailable arguments and highly recommended by Daniel Webster, Curtis was only forty-two in 1851 when Millard Fillmore appointed him to the Supreme Court. Just six years later, Curtis became even more well known as one of the two judges who had passionately dissented from Chief Justice Roger Taney's majority opinion in the notorious case of the formerly enslaved Dred Scott. Taney had claimed that Dred Scott possessed no rights a white man was bound to respect, stating that black people were not and could not be citizens. Refuting him, Curtis skillfully argued that five states had already given blacks citizenship and that their living on free soil made them free; he also said, in a final maneuver, that the court couldn't really argue the case if it ruled that Scott had no standing before it.

Convinced that the chief justice had contaminated the Constitution by subordinating it to politics, Curtis then indiscreetly released his dissent to the press before the majority opinion was published. Though he denied having done this, it was too late. Scandalized and offended, Taney accused Curtis of intentionally inflaming public opinion, which of course he had. Curtis resigned from the bench that same year, claiming he couldn't maintain his family in Washington or properly educate his children on the salary of a Supreme Court judge—in 1851, it was $4,500 ($135,000 today)—and he hated living in boardinghouses. President Buchanan was glad to see him go.

Yet though he'd willingly alienated Roger Taney, Curtis remained a conservative interpreter of the Constitution. What he hated was politics. And abolitionists. Though he'd dissented in Dred Scott, he'd defended the draconian Fugitive Slave Act, which allowed Southern slaveholders to travel North, nab runaways, and drag them back into slavery—assisted, if need be, by the full force of the federal government. Later he'd supported Johnson's policies. And he'd always detested radicals like Charles Sumner, whom he called "a person of no practical power, or ability, a declaimer, and rather sophomorically at that." He dismissed the rest of the Radical Republicans as demagogues.

A Boston Brahmin educated at Harvard and Harvard Law, Curtis was a chunky man whose hairline had receded to such an extent that his forehead dominated his upper face, not unlike Daniel Webster—or Andrew Johnson, for that matter. He spoke in a low, muffled voice. He claimed to belong to no party (patently untrue) and in 1864 voted for War Democrat George McClellan over Abraham Lincoln. After the war, he insisted that the former Confederate states had never left the Union and that their immediate restoration, in the terms Johnson had first proposed, was right and just. He despaired of the recent reconstruction laws passed by Congress and though the unmistakably boorish Andrew Johnson was not his cup of tea, Curtis did come to respect the President, or so he tried to convince himself. "He is a man of few ideas," Curtis said of Johnson, "but they are right and true, and he could suffer death sooner than yield up or violate one of them. He is honest, right-minded, and narrow-minded," Curtis concluded. "He has no tact, and even lacks discretion and forecast. But he is as firm as a rock."

Curtis contended, or his friends would contend, that he defended President Johnson from motives purely patriotic: "that in the intense excitement of party feeling the Senate might be hurried on to an act not only of injustice to an individual, but unconstitutional, and perilous to the country." No doubt this was true; but the statement that his "services at the trial were wholly gratuitous—that for all the labor and expense bestowed upon the case he neither asked nor received remuneration" was simply false. Each of Johnson's defense lawyers was paid a fee of $2,025 and then an extra $100 through funds quietly managed by Secretary of State Seward, Attorney General Henry Stanbery, and lawyer William Maxwell Evarts, whom Seward had brought on board. They apparently concealed the financial arrangement, even from the touchy Johnson, who had said more than once he wouldn't stoop to bribery or financial hanky-panky to secure acquittal. "How would I feel after I bought it?" Johnson exclaimed. "How would I feel if my conscience told me I owed my acquittal to bribery? I will do nothing of the kind." Johnson's secretary, Colonel Moore, consequently arranged for William Seward and the others to handle money matters "with extreme caution," Moore declared. "If the President would suspect his purpose, he would stop it."

Also arguing for Johnson was William Maxwell Evarts, a diminutive man with mushroom-colored skin. Grandson of Roger Sherman, who had signed both the Declaration of Independence and the U.S. Constitution, Evarts was one of the most distinguished lawyers in the country, famous for a "wit, diamond-pointed" that "cut into a legal problem, as one would cut into a pineapple—laying aside deftly the skin and the rind and getting at once at the pulp and juice of the controversy, and then sugaring it with a clear style." As Henry Adams said, Evarts was "confident in times of doubt, steady

Noted New York lawyer and raconteur William Maxwell Evarts, whom Henry Adams called "an economist of morals," ably defended Andrew Johnson at his impeachment trial, delivering a closing argument that lasted four days.

in times of disaster, cool and quiet at all times, and unshaken under any pressure."

Unlike Curtis, Evarts enjoyed politics, and he aspired to higher office—in particular, the one on the Supreme Court that Curtis had abandoned. Previously assistant district attorney for the Southern District of New York under Zachary Taylor, Evarts had been somewhat troubled by the policies of Franklin Pierce and the passage of the Kansas-Nebraska Act, even though he too at one time defended the Fugitive Slave Law. He helped establish the Republican party, he chaired the New York delegation to its national convention in 1860, and though he'd initially wanted his friend Seward to win the White House, at the convention he moved that the nomination of Lincoln be unanimous.

When Lincoln appointed Seward in his cabinet as secretary of state, Evarts hoped to take Seward's place as senator from New York, but that didn't happen. Nor was he nominated to replace Chief Justice Roger Taney in 1864; Lincoln instead chose Salmon Chase. But the suave Evarts took disappointment in stride and was eventually rewarded when Johnson nominated him as attorney general, when Rutherford B. Hayes appointed him secretary of state, and finally when he became U.S. senator from New York.

Evarts was known as a moderate. "He undoubtedly represents the old statesmen of the North, Adams, and Webster and Hamilton," a Missouri judge observed. "If he belongs to the Radical party, he is certainly vastly different from most of his party." The moderates wanted to defeat impeachment, believing that Republican success—and Grant's—depended on it. So early in 1868, Seward advised Johnson to telegraph Evarts, promising him a post if he signed on to Johnson's team. Evarts, like Curtis, considered Andrew Johnson somewhat vulgar, and later claimed that Johnson the man was of little consequence; he sought only to defend the office of the President. "I pride myself on my success in doing not the things I like to do," he also said, "but the things I don't like to do." When ribbed about working to defend Johnson on the sabbath, Evarts tellingly replied, " 'Yes,' said Mr. Evarts, 'but you know what the Bible says we may do in case an ox or an ass falleth into a pit.' "

Despite his considerable legal prowess, Evarts was, to Gideon Welles, a "cold, calculating, selfish man," and even Seward found him detached and devious. Charles Sumner, who was fond of him, thought he should never have defended Johnson, and Sumner's secretary Moorfield Storey was bewildered. "I wonder why Mr. Evarts takes the case," Storey said. Henry Adams would baptize Evarts, without irony, "an economist of morals." After the trial, Johnson nominated Evarts to be attorney general and Evarts, economizing those morals, readily accepted.

Evarts, however, was not the first choice to head the defense team. Jeremiah Black was. "Jeremiah S. Black in defense of Andrew Johnson against the Republican party," a Democratic lawyer later observed, "would have been an ever-living treat to students of the pathology of party politics." Black became a problem early on. Assuming that Johnson couldn't get a fair trial in the Senate, the crafty Black urged the President to resign so that the Democrats in 1868 could nominate him as their standard-bearer, a martyred hero trampled down by the likes of Beast Butler and the Radical Senator Wade.

But Johnson was a scrapper who would never consider backing down, and William Seward hated the idea of Johnson resigning, which would leave him out in the cold. Besides, Seward didn't want Johnson to headline the Democratic ticket. Contriving to oust Black, Seward quietly undertook a smear campaign against him. Black had been representing an American client who claimed rights to the lucrative guano (a rich fertilizer) in the small, uninhabited island of Alta Vela, near Haiti and just south of Santo Domingo (Dominican Republic). When government officials from Santo Domingo claimed ownership of Alta Vela, they expelled Black's client, destroyed the plant, and sold the rights to the guano to an American company in which Seward's friend Thurlow Weed had a financial interest. Furious, Black petitioned the federal government to investigate. Nothing happened. Black then asked Secretary of State Seward to dispatch an armed navy vessel to protect, which is to say repossess, the island. Seward refused. Black asked Johnson to intervene. He too refused.

The Alta Vela matter neatly furnished Seward with ammunition against Black. Black's son and law partner had presumably solicited a letter from four of the impeachment managers (Butler, Stevens, Bingham, Logan) in support of the Alta Vela claim, which was also signed by Representatives James Garfield and James G. Blaine. The letter seemed to suggest that Black would throw the trial and sell out Johnson for their help with Alta Vela. At the same time, Butler's former aide-de-camp was accused of circulating the letter in order to discredit Black. Whatever the truth behind the letter, the situation was complicated and ugly and left Black no choice but to resign from Johnson's defense team.

Black blamed Seward. "Mr. Seward's little finger it appears is thicker than the loins of the law," Black complained to the President. Thaddeus Stevens too thought Seward had manipulated the whole affair. Seward was helping his pal, the political boss Thurlow Weed—and promising Johnson that Weed would come through with money and political clout. Black was out by March 19.

Ohio War Democrat William Slocum Groesbeck replaced Black. A commanding presence, partly because of his height and partly because of his wealth, this Cincinnati lawyer and politician little known outside of Ohio joined Curtis, Evarts, and Attorney General Henry Stanbery, who'd resigned from the cabinet in order to serve on the team. Johnson liked Groesbeck and had once toyed with the idea of replacing Treasury Secretary Hugh McCulloch, whom he had begun to distrust, with the Cincinnati lawyer.

Thomas A.R. Nelson of East Tennessee rounded out the group. An articulate politician from Johnson's district whom Johnson trusted, Nelson had been a Unionist like Johnson and had courageously campaigned with him against secession. To his constituents in East Tennessee, Nelson was a champion until the Confederates captured and imprisoned him in Richmond. To win his freedom, he vowed to keep his Unionist feelings to himself, and he did so until federal troops occupied Tennessee. Then he changed sides again. But though a Unionist, he'd always opposed the Emancipation Proclamation, he supported McClellan over Lincoln in 1864, and he wholly endorsed Andrew Johnson's policies of reconstruction.

"Of these men," Emily Briggs quipped, "Stanbery is the tallest; Evarts the smallest; Nelson the grayest, Curtis the fattest, and Groesbeck the Adonis."

And all of them were committed to winning the trial of the century in a century that had already seen the trial of the century: that of the Lincoln assassination conspirators. But the impeachment trial was different. The impeachment trial was about the President himself, not about his murderers—even though Johnson believed the impeachers wanted to murder his presidency, and even though the impeachers believed Johnson had been conniving to murder the idea of a more perfect Union for which they'd fought. And so Andrew Johnson represented the painful division in the nation between the impeachers, grown larger and more visionary, and those who wanted to stop them: "To the one he is a vile, provoking obstruction," *The New York Herald* rightly noted, "to the other, a constitutional lighthouse, sending forth beacon rays warning of the rocks and shoals and quicksands that environ the ship of state."

The Trial, First Rounds

"The world moves, and we move with it."

— BENJAMIN BUTLER

Outside the Capitol, a cordon of police stretched along the building, and soldiers walked back and forth to protect it from the swarms of people who'd gathered there on Friday, March 13, 1868. The weather was gloomy and overcast, but people had come by railway car, by carriage, by plain cab, and on foot, clenching precious pasteboard tickets of admission, numbered, dated, and color-coded—red for one day, blue for the next, green for another. Members of Congress had been limited to four tickets per senator, two per each representative, and two for the chief justice, members of the Supreme Court, and the cabinet. Other people, not included in official rosters, scrambled to find or buy one on the sly. Only eight hundred tickets to the impeachment trial had been printed, and they were known as the hottest item in town.

The ticket-holders slowly entered the sloping galleries overlooking the Senate chamber at ten that morning and took seats in one of the eight tiers of benches. There was Salmon Chase's daughter, Kate Chase Sprague, the epitome of style, who wore fawn-colored

Both men and women gather at the impeachment trial,
as depicted by W.S.L. Lewett.

silk, Etruscan earrings, and bangles of frosted gold. She had an appetite for the White House even larger than that of her insatiable
father, and already she was thought to be campaigning for Johnson's acquittal on her father's presidential behalf.

More subdued was Benjamin Wade's wife in a black cloth dress,
although she'd placed a brown rose in her hair. Brash Ben Butler's
dark-eyed, sharp-minded daughter Blanche sat as near her father as
she could and exchanged glances with the soldier Adelbert Ames,
whom she would soon marry. The notorious former Confederate
spy Belle Boyd settled herself in the galleries; so did the sculptress
Vinnie Ream, a fidgety young woman with chestnut ringlets that
spilled down her shoulders, and Ottilie Assing, the German-Jewish
journalist and intimate friend of Frederick Douglass. There were
no black men or women in those galleries that day. They seemed
not to have received any tickets.

With opera glasses, the women and men in the galleries peered
at the scene below. On a raised platform at the head of the chamber
stood a massive desk and carved chair that was reserved for the pres-

ident of the Senate. To the right and the left of this desk, two long walnut tables had been placed, one for the managers and the other for the President's defense team. On each table there were piles of blank paper, rows of pens and inkstands, silver ice-pitchers on silver trays, and an assortment of water glasses. About one hundred cane-bottomed oak chairs and a few small sofas sat behind these tables, reserved for members of the cabinet, the House, and the judiciary. Behind them was the large semicircle of rosewood desks that the senators occupied.

The acoustics were poor, but at one o'clock, Benjamin Wade, as president pro tempore of the Senate, soundly banged his ivory gavel on the desk. He then rose and left his seat on the platform, and Chief Justice Salmon Chase gravely swept into the chamber and took his place at the head of the room, as presiding judge. He too sharply rapped the Senate to attention, calling the High Court of Impeachment into being.

The impeachment managers slowly filed into the chamber. Boutwell looked like one of the Salem witch trial's hanging judges, said a critic, but all eyes were turned on Thaddeus Stevens, who'd been carried into the room and carefully placed in his chair, where he half reclined. Despite his conspicuous pallor, "he looked strong enough to live as long as a hemlock," a journalist remarked, "which never dies until its sap is dead."

In a booming voice, the sergeant-at-arms summoned Andrew Johnson, President of the United States, to appear. He called three times for Johnson, just as the circular shape of Ben Butler was seen scrambling into the chamber. People laughed uncertainly. Many confessed they'd been imagining an Andrew Johnson shackled in chains, but since Johnson had not been compelled to show up, he did not and would not for the duration of the trial. His lawyers had begged him not to speak, even though he wanted to present his own case. But they couldn't trust what he might say when excited.

The side door opened, and three of the President's defense team solemnly entered the chamber: Stanbery, Curtis, and Nelson were the lawyers designated to reply to the summons. They arranged themselves at the table. Slightly stooped, Stanbery placed his head in his hand, and Curtis briefly chatted with the smooth-faced Nelson. They seemed to have no friends but one another.

Stanbery rose to his feet and asked that the defense be granted a continuance of forty days to prepare their answer to the eleven articles of impeachment. "Forty days—" Butler hollered, "as long as it took God to destroy the world by a flood!" Butler understood that any postponement of the trial could be fatal for a conviction, but the President's defense team argued that the entire proceeding deserved cautious, meticulous attention. After the Senate debated the request, all Republicans eventually agreed that the President had already had more than enough time to prepare. Forty days were cut to ten.

Then there was the debate about the trial date. Ben Butler, speaking on behalf of the managers, robustly pushed for a speedy trial, which, he said, would be more than possible in this, the day of the railroad and the telegraph. "The world moves," Butler cried out, "and we move with it." Besides, the Congress, the people, and the public safety all deserve a speedy trial and verdict. While the trial drags on, the work of government will stop. Defense disagreed. Should a trial of such extraordinary significance, a trial without precedent, proceed with locomotive speed, as if this were the trial of a petty criminal?

The President's lawyers lost that argument. The trial would begin right after they presented the President's response to the articles of impeachment, and the managers filed their reply.

At the White House, Andrew Johnson waited. Sometimes he walked out by himself up and down Seventeenth Street without being recognized. Thomas Ewing, Jr., contemptuously baptized him Sir Forcible Feeble. "I think Johnson was born in the month of March—which you know, 'goes in like a lion and comes out like a lamb,'" he scoffed. Democrats had continued to peel away from Johnson, saying he had only himself to blame—he should have urged the South to ratify the Fourteenth Amendment, for if it had, the eleven Southern states would've been seated in Congress, and this impeachment trial would never have happened. Or he should be convicted for not having removed Stanton sooner. "Johnson makes a muddle of everything," Samuel Barlow said.

Johnson seemed a man without a country. "A little while longer," Georges Clemenceau predicted, "he will be politically dead, like Pierce, Buchanan, and Fillmore." Johnson decided he should take his case to his beloved people in another swing around the states. Someone prudently counseled him to stay home.

Charles Dickens, recently in Washington on his second American tour, took a different measure of the American President. "He is a man with a remarkable face, indicating courage, watchfulness, and certainly strength of purpose," Dickens observed. "Figure, rather stoutish for an American; a trifle under the middle size; hands clasped in front of him; manner, suppressed, guarded, anxious." Johnson dressed to perfection. Not a crease anywhere— a man not to be trifled with. "A man (I should say) who must be killed to get out of the way."

GENERAL WINFIELD SCOTT Hancock had arrived in Washington. Arrogant and self-righteous, Hancock was a romantically handsome figure who had been pleased when General George McClellan conferred on him the nickname, "Hancock the Superb." Hancock had repulsed Pickett's charge from behind Cemetery Ridge at Gettysburg and represented the "*beau ideal* of a soldier, blue-eyed, fair-haired Saxon," said another enamored soldier, "strong, well-proportioned and manly, broad-chested, full and compact."

Hancock too believed himself superb, but so did other people, especially Democrats, for more recently he'd undone the work of General Phil Sheridan, whom Johnson had removed from the Fifth Military District. Johnson sent Hancock to replace him, as he alleged, because the general "had not been mixed up in political affairs."

Not quite true. Hancock's wife, a Southerner, had been thrilled with her husband's new posting. When Hancock battled the rebels, she said she'd battled with him, but in New Orleans, they were very happy together—"fighting the Radicals." Hancock was an unapologetic white supremacist committed to states' rights—which to him meant the rights of a white state. In Louisiana and Texas he lost no time revoking Sheridan's orders, disbanding military courts, and in New Orleans ejecting black city councilmen from office. In Texas, the murder rate immediately skyrocketed, with as many as fifty-four a month being reported (in a population of 700,000). Jeremiah Black and other conservative Democrats took admiring notice, and Johnson, hoping to humiliate Grant, asked Congress to offer Hancock some sort of official recognition or appreciation. Congress essentially laughed off the request.

Grant, who'd known Hancock ever since their days at West Point, was growing disillusioned with his superb colleague, and would later characterize him as corruptible and vain—and as a duplicitous political conniver. When Grant countermanded General Hancock's orders in New Orleans and reinstated several of the officials Hancock had ousted, Hancock bitterly decided he had to resign his command of the Fifth Military District, where, as he archly said, it was neither useful nor agreeable for him to serve.

Hancock was just the man Johnson had been looking for. He despised Radicals, spurned congressional reconstruction, and he believed Grant had humiliated him. Johnson beckoned him to Washington. Once there, he paraded himself around the city, snubbing General Grant when the two men met on the street. Hancock formally touched his hat and kept walking, but he'd thought Grant had been insulting. It was a small political world compounded of policy, partisanship, and principle—as well as self-righteousness, delicate feelings, and slights, both real and imagined. So Hancock rode over to the White House, where he was frequently spotted holding court in the East Room.

By the end of March, as the impeachment trial was moving forward, Johnson appointed General Hancock to the newly created Division of the Atlantic, the division he had created to move Sherman closer to Washington. Unlike Sherman, Hancock did not re-fuse, even though the legality of the division was never really determined. Still, the idea of Hancock, commander of the Division of the Atlantic, headquartered in Washington, inspired a new round of rumors: in the case of his conviction, Johnson intended to fo-ment a rebellion, with Hancock leading the assault.

If Johnson harbored a fantasy of revenge, bolstered by military might—and he likely did—he was not really a man to do more than bluster. His appointment of Hancock and Hancock's acceptance were political maneuvers, not acts of violence. Yet they did strike fear in the hearts of the weak-kneed or paranoid—and Johnson's recklessness disturbed his defense team. As for the rumors, cooler heads said they should be ignored. "I cannot believe there is really any danger of armed resistance to impeachment, the force which Johnson could command is so small, and the suicidal folly of such a course so evident," Moorfield Storey wisely observed. "Still," he added, as if with a shake of the head, "Johnson is an exception to all rules."

A MASSEUSE RUBBED Henry Stanbery down every morning, as if preparing him for the ring. "Do not lose a moment's sleep, Mr. President," Stanbery gaily told Johnson, "but be hopeful."

On March 23, when the court of impeachment reconvened, William Evarts laid out before the Senate the President's long reply, speaking in businesslike fashion and taking turns with Benjamin Curtis to read the document aloud. It took two hours to present their case.

Presumably, the spectators were familiar with the broad outlines of the impeachment articles. The first one was simple enough: Johnson had violated the Tenure of Office Act by sacking Secretary of War Stanton. The second article charged Johnson with violating that law by appointing Lorenzo Thomas interim replacement of Stanton. The third article of impeachment was more complicated.

It accused the President of violating the Constitution by appointing Thomas because the position (Stanton's) was not vacant.

The fourth impeachment article alleged that there had been a conspiracy between Johnson and Thomas, and perhaps others, to hinder and prevent Edwin Stanton from holding his office, in violation of the Constitution. The fifth article alleged much the same thing, except that it charged that the conspiracy of Johnson and Thomas defied the Tenure of Office Act. And the sixth article of impeachment accused President Johnson and Lorenzo Thomas of using force to seize the war office.

Thus far, the articles dealt with specific legal infractions. Similarly, the seventh article of impeachment charged President Johnson and Lorenzo Thomas of conspiring, with intent, to seize the war office and violate the Tenure of Office Act. The eighth article was somewhat different in that it alleged the President had disregarded the Tenure of Office Act by issuing orders to General Thomas to seize the property of the war office even though the Senate was in session, which was, again, a breach of the Tenure of Office Act, since there was no vacancy in the Department of War.

The technical differences among these accusations had annoyed Thaddeus Stevens. And the ninth article continued to displease him: it accused President Johnson of intending to encourage General William Emory, commander of the Washington area, to ignore orders issued through General Grant in favor of those that might be issued by President Johnson himself. To define impeachment in terms of breach of office, Thaddeus Stevens and Ben Butler along with the more conservative James Wilson had stitched together the tenth and then the eleventh articles. The tenth impeachment article accused the President of intending to set aside the authority and powers of Congress as well as bring it into disgrace, contempt, and ridicule. It cited Johnson's hysterical speeches, particularly the ones made during his "Swing Around the Circle." And the eleventh impeachment article, the omnibus one, baldly accused the President of contravening and denying the authority of Congress, particularly when Johnson said Congress did not represent all the states. Similarly, Johnson had denied Congress' power to amend the Constitution, never mind remove the war secretary. And this eleventh article cited the President's attempt to hinder the execution of Reconstruction Acts passed by the legislature. Taken together, the tenth and eleventh articles accused Johnson of betraying the public trust—not just stepping on a statute.

Whether or not the spectators had memorized all eleven impeachment articles, or whether they could distinguish among them, they understood the basic character of the case. And the President's defenders began their argument by outlining it. To begin with, Johnson had planted himself firmly on the Constitution, which conferred on him the ability to appoint or remove all executive officers "for cause to be judged by the President alone."

Secondly, the President did not admit the constitutionality of the Tenure of Office Act, which he said that in any event he had not violated. He maintained that the law conflicted with the Constitution of the United States in that it interfered with his authority as chief executive. He had, though, initially obeyed that law while investigating whether it applied to Stanton—then he had discovered that it did not. Edwin Stanton had been appointed as secretary of war by President Lincoln, and presumably the act provided that cabinet members were subject to it for the term of the President who appointed them, plus one month.

Further, his lawyers said, Johnson had not entered into any conspiracy with any general, neither General Thomas nor General Emory. "No threat or threat of force was used," the lawyers also claimed on Johnson's behalf. "His sole intent was to vindicate his authority as President of the United States, and by peaceful means to bring the question of the right of the said Stanton to continue to hold the said office of Secretary of War to a final decision before the Supreme Court." As for the tenth article of impeachment, which accused the President of disrespecting Congress, his lawyers contended that Johnson merely claimed his right to speak as he chose, "within and according to his right and privilege as an American citizen and his right and duty as President of the United States." They also demanded proof of "the actual speech" that Johnson had presumably delivered. For Johnson had only insisted that the eleven Southern states excluded from Congress be represented there.

Finally, regarding article eleven, the catchall article of impeachment, Johnson's lawyers cleverly declared that there were no specific charges listed, and that at no time, whether on February 21, 1868, when he dismissed Stanton, "or at any other day or time, commit, or . . . was guilty of, a high misdemeanor in office."

Curtis was largely inaudible and Evarts unemotional. Members of the gallery began to yawn and dream of lunch. Sumner glanced for a moment through the newspaper. The managers listened closely, and occasionally John Bingham and General Logan grabbed a pen to jot a few notes. Only Logan supplied a few sparks. When Johnson's defense again asked for a further delay of thirty days, Logan exploded. "We, as the managers on the part of the House and the country, consider the President a criminal, but not an ordinary one," he shouted. "Ordinary criminals are either arrested and put under bonds or imprisoned, that no further violation of law may be committed by them during the pendency of their trial." Not so the President. He might endanger the people. We need a speedy trial.

The request for more delay was denied, and the trial was set to begin in earnest on March 30, the very next week.

The Trial

Not until Monday, March 30 did the curtain truly rise on the impeachment trial. Yet there would be three more long weeks of sparring to come, both the managers and the defense testy, and all the players performing their parts, whether those players were reporters or generals or the sometimes rapt, sometimes bored audience sitting before a carefully set stage: those long tables at which the prosecution and the defense conferred, the cane-bottom chairs and sofas spread over the red carpet, and the police guards, wearing bright blue, stationed at every entrance. Both the public and performers knew the stakes were high, far higher than any they'd witnessed in any theater except the theater of war. Yet the protagonist, the chief executive, would not be speaking his lines aloud, not on this stage anyway. It was like *Hamlet* played without the Hamlet.

The skylight was dull on rainy days, and on those days the number of spectators thinned. Generally, though, they crowded the hallways, gripping their tickets of admission. These spectators were mostly government people or their relatives—known as the aristocracy of the democracy, come from near at hand and far away: the wives and daughters of diplomats from several foreign embassies wore vivid spring colors, yellow and lavender and green. There were the actress Fannie Kemble and the orator Anna Dickinson, who had come to Washington to deliver a public indictment of the President; and at various times such well-known writers as Harriet Prescott or Ann Stephens appeared, seated together although they didn't agree about Johnson's guilt. Below them, on the sofas, were notables like General Carl Schurz, who had just arrived from Germany, his face thin as a blade, and the full-blooded Seneca Iroquois General Ely Parker from General Grant's staff. They arrayed themselves near the center of the chamber, where the senators performed in the court of inquiry.

Each day Thaddeus Stevens was carried in his chair through the rotunda into the Senate chamber at twenty past noon, and Chief Justice Chase, black silk robe rustling, followed shortly afterward. The sergeant-at-arms announced the rest of the managers and the defense team. They all took their seats at their respective tables, on which the Senate pages had arranged those silver pitchers and piles of paper and pens. Then came members of the House, who ceremoniously walked over the red carpet to their seats.

Chief Justice Chase called the Senate to order with his gavel. Ben Butler rose to his feet. The sharp debater and crack criminal lawyer known far and wide for his courtroom tactics—though not for his honesty—and the man who had clamored longest for the President's impeachment, Butler had been selected to deliver the managers' opening argument.

The room was like a vaulted tomb, said journalist Emily Edson Briggs, who peered from the gallery with her opera glasses. Everyone knew that to prepare, Butler had secluded himself for over a week, with very little sleep: only nine hours over three days. He later recalled that when he had to make his opening argument, he came as close as he ever had to running away.

Wearing a new swallowtail coat, Butler addressed the Senate for nearly three hours, with only one break for refreshments, which the crowd, though listening attentively, really needed. He provided very few rhetorical flourishes. When he spoke of the violence in New Orleans, for instance, he said that only silence did justice to the horror of it. Rather, he cogently presented the prosecution's argument against President Johnson and, more to the point, he outlined for the court and thus for the public a definition of impeachable offenses, starting with a definition of an impeachable misdemeanor.

An impeachable misdemeanor might be an act that subverted the principles of government, such as one that violated the Constitution or that flouted an official oath or duty or law; it could be an act that abused or usurped power. Claiming that the Senate was "bound by no law, either statute or common, which may limit your constitutional prerogative," Butler then argued that during the impeachment trial, the Senate, acting as a court, was a law unto itself, bound only by principles of equity and justice where the law of the people was supreme. And since an impeachment trial took place in the Senate, not a judicial court, it was not subject to a judicial court's restrictions regarding conviction—namely, certainty beyond a reasonable doubt. In an impeachment trial, the managers need only offer a preponderance of evidence to prove guilt.

Butler then listed legal precedents to bolster his argument before enumerating each specific article of impeachment, one by one. He concluded by declaring that the House of Representatives had done its duty in impeaching President Andrew Johnson. The safeguarding of liberty now lay in the Senate's hands. "I speak," Butler finished, "therefore not the language of exaggeration but the words of truth and soberness, that the future of political welfare and the liberties of all men hang trembling on the decision of the hour."

By avoiding the sidewinders and flamboyant accusations for which he was known, Butler did disappoint some spectators with a speech that they considered dry and dull. The partisan press predictably dissected Butler's overture. Conservatives and Democrats criticized him for drowning his audience in a sea of irrelevant precedents. Republicans generally praised Butler as comprehensive and formidable, but Charles Sumner's secretary Moorfield Storey was one of the dissatisfied ones. "He might have made a stronger argument on the point of the proviso in the Tenure-of-Office Bill," Storey grumbled, "and on the absurdity of the President's claim to dispense with the laws of Congress on the ground of their unconstitutionality."

But Butler had been effective enough, and while he spoke, defense attorney Curtis occasionally whispered to Stanbery, and Evarts sat with his head dipped down, catching every word. Nelson and Groesbeck scribbled quickly, as if trying to record Butler's every accusatory jab.

ON THE SECOND day of the trial, March 31, the room felt steamy not just because the chamber was badly ventilated, which it was, or the crowds were dense, which they were, but because the patience of all parties had already become strained.

For one thing, the managers and the chief justice faced off about Chase's role as presiding judge. The issue again came up when the managers called as a witness Walter Burleigh, a delegate from the Dakota Territory and a friend of General Lorenzo Thomas. Stanbery immediately objected; Burleigh's testimony wasn't relevant, Stanbery said, because he would be testifying about a conversation with General Thomas, and General Thomas was not on trial. Even more to the point, any references that Burleigh might make to the President were at best secondhand.

Mildly amused, Butler asked how the defense could object if it didn't know what Burleigh was going to say. Justice Chase interrupted, declaring that the testimony was admissible. Senator Charles D. Drake of Missouri, a Radical, objected from the floor. ("He was a man of small stature," Carl Schurz remembered Drake, "but he planted his feet upon the ground with a demonstrative firmness.") Did Chase really have the authority to decide whether evidence should be admissible or not? Drake asked. Justice Chase said he did. Drake disagreed and asked the Senate to vote, but Maine Senator William Pitt Fessenden said Drake was out of order—

a claim that may have indicated to anyone watching that Fessenden was becoming less and less eager to be identified with the impeachers.

Chase held his ground: the chief justice should decide questions of evidence, although the Senate could vote to refute him. Butler replied that if Chase had his way, the hands of the *managers* were tied. "The managers may propose a question to the Senate, and the Chief Justice decides it," Butler explained, "and [the managers] then cannot get the question we propose before the Senate unless through the courtesy of some senator." That is, the managers would have to hope some senator would intervene on their behalf and make a motion for them, since they couldn't make one themselves.

Although Butler liked to hear himself talk, his argument made sense. The precedents both in England and in the United States suggested that the presiding officer, even when a member of the deciding body, had no more rights than anyone else. And if he was not a member of the body, as Chase was not since he wasn't a senator, he could merely submit the question to the larger body, not decide it. John Bingham agreed with Butler; the Senate had sole authority over the impeachment trial.

Sumner's young and eager secretary Moorfield Storey, who attended the trial every day, was astonished that just when the Senate was deciding to discuss the issue further, "Mr. Chase made a little *coup d'état*," Storey said. "As soon as the vote was handed him to read he said, 'On the question the ayes are twenty-five, and the nays are twenty-five. The Chief Justice Votes "Aye," and the question is decided in the affirmative,' and immediately left the Chair and the Chamber, so that it was physically impossible to make any objection to his course."

"The secret of the matter is that some of the Republicans, Wilson, Edmunds, etc., were afraid that if they were to decide against Chase," Storey explained to his father, "he would get mad, think himself deprived of his constitutional rights, and decline to preside, thus making a very awkward complication, and they thought it better to yield on a point of no practical importance than to jeopardize the whole proceeding. In this I think they were weak and cowardly," Storey concluded, "nor do I believe that Chase would make such a fool of himself."

Storey was likely right. No fool, Chase would not quit the trial, which promised to be good for his presidential prospects. For Salmon Chase was an honorable man who believed himself to be the soul of impartiality when it suited him, and to a certain extent, he was impartial. Yet he was also a man who continued to covet— or need—power, power, and more power. As the supreme arbiter of impeachment, that power would be his, no matter what. By supervising the trial to please the Democrats, he might be able to secure their nomination for President, so he could be more impartial than usual when necessary.

Several senators prodded Charles Sumner to propose a resolution to prevent Chief Justice Chase from deciding on the admissibility of evidence. Sumner too believed that under the Constitution, Chase had no right to make those decisions precisely because he was not an elected official. Though Storey warned Sumner that the resolution would be defeated, Sumner was insistent. But Storey was right. The resolution lost by six votes. Fessenden had voted against Sumner, as did James Grimes of Iowa, Kansas Senator Ross, and Missouri's John Henderson. They were wobbly impeachers.

That night, on the way home on the streetcar, Sumner asked Vermont Senator George Edmunds why he had voted against the resolution since he'd agreed with it. Edmunds replied, "Mr. Chase was already very angry." Edmunds didn't want to provoke the chief justice any further. "So you see how constitutional questions are decided," Moorfield Storey noted in disgust.

THE DEBATE ON Chase's role in the trial had lasted three wearying hours, and now Stanbery and Evarts were regularly interrupting Butler's interrogation about whether Burleigh had heard General Thomas say he'd break down the doors of the war office. The question was leading, the conversations were not admissible evidence.

Moorfield Storey fumed. "The defense fight every bit of testimony to which they can possibly object, and yesterday their cross-examination was absurdly minute," he said. "It was as absurd as any of the caricatures given in novels, and its only point apparently was to make a joke of the testimony and so destroy its force."

On the fourth day of the trial, Thursday, April 2, a ferocious thunderstorm threw so much dust on the chamber skylight that the gas lamps had to be lit. General William H. Emory, military commander of the District of Columbia, took the stand.

The managers wanted to focus on the ninth impeachment article, which alleged the President had suggested Emory disobey the Military Appropriations Act and take orders from the President instead of from General Grant. Emory had refused to do so.

Again the testimony bogged down. The defense and the managers wrestled with one another until just before five o'clock, when tired Democrats called for an adjournment. Republicans wanted to plow ahead, or at least Charles Sumner did. The vote on adjournment was taken. It was a tie. Chase broke the tie. Adjourn—and delay.

Spectators had come to the trial expecting broad strokes and swashbuckling argument; broad strokes made for broad drama: heroes and villains and soaring rhetoric about the meaning of the presidency, democracy, nationhood, or the direction that the country ought to take after the recent war and the eradication, if there be eradication, of slavery. But the testimony was mired in finicky detail, and by the sixth day of the trial—Saturday, April 4—the number of spectators had dwindled even more. Occasionally Butler pretended to drop his papers on the floor to wake people up. But fewer and fewer of them heard testimony about President Johnson's tirades against Congress during the celebrated "Swing Around the Circle." Even fewer heard another lengthy back-and-forth between the lawyers, about whether the stenographer James Sheridan or James Clephane or Johnson's secretary Colonel Moore had copied the President's speeches accurately. What was the nature of the stenographer's abbreviations? Had the stenographer made slight changes or revisions to the text? Fewer still heard about whether stenographic shorthand was trustworthy and about whether the speech, as copied, was the very same speech that appeared in the newspapers, especially since the original stenographic notes were missing, if they in fact were missing. And, in any case, it was asked, was a reporter's testimony even admissible?

It seemed as though the lawyers were counting the number of angels on the head of a pin—and then demanding to know if the pin was real.

Butler questioned William Hudson, a reporter for the *Cleveland Leader*.

Mr. Manager Butler: You have been asked, Mr. Hudson, about the crowd and about the manner in which you took the speech; were there considerable interruptions?

A. There were.

Q. Were there considerable pauses by the President from step to step in his speech?

A. There were; and necessary pauses.

Q. Why "necessary"?

A. Because of the interruptions of the crowd.

Q. Was the crowd a noisy one?

A. It was.

Q. Were they bandying back and forth epithets with the President?

Mr. Evarts. We object to that. The question is, What was said? Sir.

Manager Butler. I do not adopt that question. I will repeat my question, Whether epithets were thrown back and forward between the President and the crowd?

Mr. Evarts and Mr. Curtis. We object to the question. The proper question is, What was said?

Mr. Manager Butler. That is your question.

Mr. Evarts. The question, as put, is leading and assuming a state of facts. It is asking if they bandied epithets. Nobody knows what "bandying" is or what "epithets" are.

Mr. Manager Butler (to the witness). Do you know what "bandying" means, Mr. Witness? Do you not know the meaning of the word?

Mr. Curtis. I suppose our objection is first to be disposed of, Mr.
Chief Justice?

Mr. Manager Butler. I wanted to see whether, in the first place, I
had got an intelligible English word. However, I withdraw the
question. [A pause.] My proposition is this, sir: it is not to give
language—

Mr. Evarts. There is no objection if you have withdrawn your question.

Mr. Manager Butler. I have not. I have only withdrawn the question
as to the meaning of a word which one of the counsel for the
President did not understand.

Butler was tart and amusing. William Evarts was not amused.

Absent spectators also missed the recitation of President Johnson's speeches—deemed admissible—the ones where he'd called
Congress tyrannical or said Thad Stevens and Charles Sumner
should be hanged or that the Freedmen's Bureau was a form of
slavery because it cost white people millions of dollars. They missed
hearing Johnson's speech about his own valiant heroism and how
he'd fought first against traitors in the South—and then the traitors
in the North.

But Butler returned to the central issue: the violation of the Tenure of Office Act, producing a letter from President Johnson to
Treasury Secretary Hugh McCulloch, dated the previous August 14, saying that the President had suspended Stanton, per the
Tenure of Office Act—which demonstrated that Johnson was at
that time willing to follow the law, not test its constitutionality.

Butler was satisfied, but he could not rest. He knew he had not
yet clinched the case.

IN 1868, THE public's attention span was not any better than it
would be in later years. Assuming this, the defense intended to slow
the progress of the trial. The House of Representatives had im-

peached President Johnson in February. It was April, and the President's men still insisted they be granted several more days to prepare.

In fact it wasn't until Thursday, April 9 that Benjamin Curtis began to defend the President. In a polished and dispassionate opening speech, Curtis maintained that the basic—indeed, the only—issue was the Tenure of Office Act, which did not in fact apply to Secretary of War Edwin Stanton because he had been appointed by Abraham Lincoln, not by Andrew Johnson. Curtis clarified: the Tenure of Office Act stipulated that the cabinet members "shall hold their offices respectively for and during the term of the President by whom they may have been appointed and for one month thereafter, subject to removal by and with the advice and consent of the Senate."

To Curtis, who interpreted the language of the law very closely, Stanton was serving out the remainder of Abraham Lincoln's term. Johnson's decision to replace the secretary of war was thus legal: "The necessary conclusion, that the tenure-of-office of a Secretary here described is a tenure during the term of service of the President by whom he was appointed; that it was not the intention of Congress to compel a President of the United States to continue in office a Secretary not appointed by himself." Since Andrew Johnson had not appointed Stanton, he was under no obligation to keep him.

Serious people might thus seriously disagree about the construction of the Tenure of Office Act.

Curtis also argued that Johnson was obliged to protect the Constitution, and the only way to protect it, in this case, would be to violate the Tenure of Office Act and put it before a court, which would test its constitutionality.

It was perplexing. Technically, Johnson could not break a law that did not apply to him, so if he appeared to break the law, it was only to test its legality.

People were understandably puzzled. "I cannot see how Mr. Curtis can reconcile his two lines of defense," Georges Clemenceau remarked. "The President either did or did not violate the Tenure of Office Bill. Mr. Curtis makes out that 1) he did not violate it, 2) he set out to violate it and did violate, but that in doing so he acted with the best intentions in the world. I leave to someone more clever than I the task of finding some connection between these two propositions."

The next day, April 10, as rain continued to pound on the skylight, Curtis resumed his circuitous defense for another two hours, droning on in a monotone.

As for the charge of conspiracy, Curtis insisted that Johnson had not plotted with General Lorenzo Thomas to violate the Constitution—and in any case Johnson had never appointed Thomas to any office. Rather, Johnson had made General Thomas an ad interim—temporary—war secretary in case a vacancy *might* occur. And the President's issuance of that appointment, and Thomas' accepting it, did not constitute any breach of the law, the Constitution, or any conspiracy.

The claim that President Johnson had intended to seize by force or through intimidation any property of the U.S. government, like the War Department, was utter nonsense, Curtis went on. True, the President had called General Emory to the White House, but he'd done so only to obtain routine information about military activities.

Curtis subsequently turned to the tenth article of impeachment, which focused on the President's contentious speeches. Johnson had every right to say what he thought—namely, that the Southern states should be represented in Congress.

Overall, then, Curtis asserted that there were no grounds for impeachment: certainly no treason, no bribery, no conspiracy to commit either treason or bribery, and as for "high crimes and misdemeanors," Curtis rhetorically wondered, "against what law? There can be no crime, there can be no misdemeanor, without a law, written or unwritten, express or implied. There must be some law, otherwise there is no crime."

Benjamin Wade played with his thumbs.

"My interpretation" Curtis persisted, "is that the language of 'high crimes and misdemeanors' means 'offences against the laws of the United States.'" To Curtis, the President had broken no law, as alleged in the first eight articles of impeachment; and as far as the tenth article was concerned, the Constitution guaranteed free speech. And there was no need, Curtis concluded, even to address the omnibus eleventh article of impeachment and Johnson's supposed obstruction of Congress and its laws. Curtis claimed he'd demolished it when he'd dissected the other ten.

Many listeners were predictably pleased; others, predictably disappointed. Curtis seemed to contradict himself, or at least his argument seemed inconsistent. Critics analyzed his argument: that Stanton had not been removed because he had not vacated the office, and Johnson had not broken the law in any case because Stanton had been appointed by Lincoln. So Johnson could not have intended to violate the Tenure of Office Act. Critics also pointed out that Curtis said the office had in fact been vacated so Lorenzo Thomas could temporarily occupy it while the President tested the constitutionality of a law that didn't pertain to him—and that Johnson had earlier complied with. Curtis had left this out.

Again, it was a puzzlement.

THERE IS A story about how Ben Butler and William Evarts found themselves guests at the same dinner party. When Butler good-humoredly said he wouldn't mind switching sides with Evarts in the trial, Evarts pleasantly replied that he didn't doubt it—and, as far as he was concerned, he wouldn't mind sitting on Butler's side of the fence.

Their banter notwithstanding, the two lawyers and their teams would in a sense change places in terms of tactics, for each of them did not follow the map that they—the impeachers and the defenders—had initially sketched for themselves. The impeachers were supposed to argue sweepingly, nobly, and idealistically. They were spokesmen for a rejuvenated nation recovering from the tragedies of war. They were supposed to conjure the more perfect

Union that Andrew Johnson had been set on destroying since he had chosen the crooked, not the straight, path for the present and the future, as Wendell Phillips had once said. They were supposed to keep before the Senate and hence the public the fact that the President had imperiled the peace of the country; that he had committed great crimes against the people, all the people, by allowing unreconstructed Southerners back into office; and that he had betrayed the country and the principles on which it was founded.

The President's defenders, on the other hand, were to hew to the letter of the law or what they conceived the letter of the law to be, as Curtis had done. They were to reduce the President's crimes to a series of legal loopholes stemming from the basic issue of whether he'd violated the Tenure of Office Act. They were to niggle and nitpick. Yet as the trial continued, impeachers and defenders seemed to be trading places, as when Butler argued technicalities about whether Andrew Johnson had broken a law, and what rules of evidence for breaking a law should include. Or when John Bingham, in a convoluted argument, claimed that whether he prosecuted a beggar or a President, the same rules of evidence applied. That meant he could establish "intent"—Johnson's intention to violate the law—by proving that Johnson broke the law and therefore had intended to do so.

And it was defense attorney Evarts who painted with the broad brush that Butler had not used. Evarts' subject was duty: at stake were the duties of the President of the United States, his role as leader, and as a corollary, the significance of the presidential office. Johnson had acted in the public interest for the public service, and he had acted faithfully, with the intelligent and conscientious opinion of those in public service. But more—and here Evarts smoothly addressed the Senate at large: "Now, senators; reflect you are taking part in a solemn transaction which is to effect, in your unfavorable judgment, a removal of the Chief Magistrate of the nation for some offence that he has committed against the public welfare with bad motives and for an improper purpose; and we offer to show you that upon consultations and deliberations and advice from those wholly unconnected with any matters of personal controversy and any matters of political controversy, and occupying solely the position of duty and responsibility in the military service of the country, he acted and desired to accomplish this change." The change was the removal of Stanton.

If we question the President's actions, Evarts further implied, we are questioning the very integrity of the office, not just the officer who serves it. And so we cannot try that officer as if this were a police court. Butler was prosecuting the case as if Andrew Johnson were a horse thief, not the President of the United States. This was not the trial of a horse thief; this was the impeachment trial of a President, a chief executive, and commander in chief—and to remove him would threaten to weaken the nature of the executive branch of government.

Instead of replying to this line of attack—that we must above all protect the office of the President—the prosecuting managers too often reduced the great legislative act of impeachment to complicated minutiae. And the President's defenders began to argue for government stability and presidential authority, the rock-solid foundation that the country deserved.

THE DEBATES OVER what evidence was admissible continued through Saturday, April 11, when Butler caught General Lorenzo Thomas, the hapless interim war secretary, in a web of contradictions. It wasn't long before the befuddled General Thomas started to appear ridiculous. He was clearly confused, indiscreet, and a braggart. Flustered, he seemed to suggest Johnson actually had recommended that he use force to remove Stanton from his office. The more Butler grilled Thomas, the more Thomas collapsed. "As he left the stand," Whitelaw Reid noted, "one could not repress a feeling of pity."

A more significant battle was waged when the defense called General Sherman later that afternoon. General Sherman and his father-in-law, Thomas Ewing, had been seated together for several days, with General Sherman attracting a good deal of attention: here was the celebrity war hero who had famously snubbed Secretary of War Stanton during the Grand Review back in the spring of 1865 when he'd refused to shake Stanton's hand. The secretary, Sherman believed, had slandered him because of the truce he'd negotiated with Confederate Joe Johnston.

Men and women in the galleries raised their opera glasses to catch a glimpse of the straight-arrow general loaded down with a large sheaf of notes and papers. "The high forehead and eagle eyes; the thin, quivering nostril, and square manly shoulders; the muscles of wire-drawn steel," Emily Briggs observed, "like an exquisite stringed instrument, he must be kept up to concert pitch." Sherman was wearing his full dress uniform, albeit in shabby-genteel fashion, as was his style. The cloth on his elbows and knees was scuffed, as if he had just been riding his horse.

General Sherman was at first permitted to answer very few questions, for the managers and the defense were again squabbling about whether Sherman's account of a conversation with the President should be admitted as evidence. Why take Sherman's word for what was said? Did the President actually ask Sherman to be interim war secretary in order to place a "tool" in the War Department (which surely Sherman was not), as Butler was insinuating? The debate went on for an hour and a half before the question was put to the Senate, which voted Sherman's conversation with Johnson inadmissible. The inconsistencies were glaring. The Senate had voted to admit General Thomas' testimony but not General Sherman's.

The interrogation continued, the squat Butler leaping up again and again to object. Stanbery asked Sherman if the President intended to place the Tenure of Office Act before the Supreme Court when he appointed Sherman interim war secretary. Objection: leading the witness. Stanbery reframed the question. Butler jumped up again. "I submit that that is contrary to all rule. When a leading question has been put, it cannot be withdrawn and put in another

form." Stanbery was visibly annoyed. The Senate agreed with Butler and voted to exclude the question.

A frustrated Charles Sumner, opposing Butler, voted to admit
Sherman's testimony and soon Sumner was proposing that all evidence be admitted to avoid these long, needless lectures. The Senate tabled the motion. Senator Doolittle asked that the court
adjourn. "No! No!" others shouted.

Evarts was unflappable. Dueling was his forte. But not until
Monday, April 13, after more wrangling, was the question finally
put to Sherman about the President's offering him the position of
interim war secretary. "He did not state to me then that his purpose
was to bring it to the courts directly," Sherman replied, "but for the
purpose of having the office administered properly in the interest of
the army and of the whole country."

Sherman's answer surprised the defense. Johnson was not thinking about the constitutionality of the Tenure of Office Act; he
merely wanted to get rid of Stanton. "It is one of the curious revenges of history," the *Cincinnati Daily Gazette* observed, "that this
man, who refused to speak to Secretary Stanton on the day of the
grand review, should be here now to give evidence touching his
refusal to aid in getting Stanton out of office."

Sherman continued. "I made this point," Sherman explained.
"'Suppose Mr. Stanton do not yield?' He answered, 'Oh! he will
make no objection; you present the order, and he will retire.' I expressed my doubt, and he remarked, 'I know him better than you
do; he is cowardly.'"

Yet if Sherman bore Stanton no love, he bore Johnson none either. Johnson was incompetent. He did not know how to govern.
He had mismanaged the Stanton affair. And the bickering of both
sides disgusted Sherman. He prided himself on bearing an erect
posture in all things, which is why he lugged those notes and day-
books into the Senate chamber. He delivered a blow to the President's defense when he claimed Johnson had wanted to oust
Stanton, not test the Tenure Act's constitutionality, but he delivered

a blow to the prosecution too. After more haggling between the lawyers, Democratic Senator Reverdy Johnson directly asked Sherman to differentiate between an initial interview with the President and a second one. During the second interview, Sherman said, the President did in fact talk about the constitutionality of the Tenure of Office Act. "It was the constitutionality of that bill which he seemed desirous of testing and which, he said, if it could be brought before the Supreme Court would not stand half an hour," Sherman clarified. He was now assisting the President's defense.

Having at first failed to elicit the testimony he desired from Sherman, Henry Stanbery was upset. And Butler's doggedness took his breath away, according to Moorfield Storey. "The bland impudence with which Butler stares at him when he rises to reply seems to excite him as much as a red cloth does a turkey cock." His temper in tatters, Stanbery did not show up at the Capitol the next day. Evarts said Stanbery had caught a cold and would soon be back, but seasoned reporters guessed that he'd cracked under the pressure of Butler's badgering. Except to make his closing argument, Stanbery never did return to the trial, though he continued to pursue the President's policies long after Johnson left office. In 1871 he would join with Reverdy Johnson in South Carolina to defend the Ku Klux Klan against charges of conspiracy.

Momentarily deterred because Stanbery had been their leader, the defense team retained its composure by unspooling reams of documentary evidence and pages and pages of precedents, pages and pages of them, to prove that President Johnson had exercised his right to remove officials even though the instances cited had all occurred before the Tenure of Office Act had been passed. Delay, delay, delay. Irritated, Ben Butler objected when Curtis and Evarts wanted to adjourn again to allow Stanbery to recover. "Far be it from me not to desire to be courteous, and not to desire that we should have our absent and sick friend here to take part with us," Butler said. "But the interests of the people are greater than the interests of any one individual.

"We have been here in the Senate," Butler explained more specifically, "for thirty-three working days, twenty-one of them given over to delays—and four early adjournments, all to accommodate the defense. The government was practically shut down. Nothing can be done, and the whole country waits upon us and our action."

And then Butler could no longer keep his emotions under wrap. "While we are waiting for the Attorney General to get well, numbers of our fellow-citizens are being murdered day by day," he fairly shouted. "There is not a man here who does not know that the moment justice is done on this great criminal, the murders will cease.

"While we are being courteous, the true Union men of the south are being murdered, and on our heads and on our skirts is this blood if we remain any longer idle."

Let the trial go on, he begged. He was speaking with considerable warmth, he said, because "I feel warmly." Every day he received in the mail some account of a murder, an atrocity, an assassination, often the handiwork of a secret organization called the Ku Klux Klan, which also threatened him and his colleagues daily. "I want these things to stop."

Patronizingly, Evarts dismissed Butler's speech as a harangue. Butler had wasted as many as twenty minutes blathering about a mythical Ku Klux Klan. Senator Simon Cameron of Pennsylvania took offense; Butler held firm. For he steadfastly believed both in what he was doing and in how he was doing it.

ANOTHER DRENCHING RAIN kept almost everyone indoors that day, April 16, the same day the black community in the District of Columbia celebrated Emancipation Day, commemorating the act Lincoln had signed on April 16, 1862, to end slavery in the capital. It was no accident that on that day Butler continued to wave what was known as the "bloody shirt," a colloquial shorthand for the rabble-rousing claim that since the war the killing hadn't stopped. Either side could wave that shirt, though the Republicans mostly did it, and Butler certainly knew how to wage a politics of blood and fear.

That did not diminish very real concern about the mysterious organization, recently founded, called Ku Klux: "an organization which is thoroughly loyal to the Federal constitution," declared the *Richmond Examiner*, "but which does not permit the people of the South to become the victims of negro rule." Spreading from Johnson's home state of Tennessee throughout the South, already the Klan was said to have five thousand members in Alabama alone. Targeting black men and women and their white Republican friends, Klansmen visited them in the middle of the night, yanked them out of bed, and whipped them with beech sapling switches before they rode off. Masked and hooded, Klansmen pounded through the streets, come to redress, they said, injustices that had been inflicted on the rebels. They met at the city cemeteries, claiming they rose straight from hell, for the handwriting was on the wall, they said, and the devil is out of the den. "Death's angels are always on the lookout," they said. "Unholy Blacks, Cursed of God, take warning and fly."

In Tennessee, they dragged black people out into the fields and made them promise never again to vote Republican. Klansmen burned a courthouse in Eutaw, Alabama, and in Jackson, Mississippi, they executed a prominent white lawyer. In Georgia, they placed placards around various towns threatening to punish "evil politicians, renegades, scalawags and wrong-doers." In Columbus, Georgia, the Radical Republican Colonel George Ashburn (white) was murdered at his boardinghouse just after midnight by a group of masked men who seemed, in spite of the masks, nattily dressed. Ashburn had been shot in the eyes and the mouth and his body twelve times. Soon it was said there was at least one murder a day in Tennessee. A report from Knoxville counted 70,000 Klansmen, but no one knew for sure how many there were. Charles Sumner called the atrocities "an orgy of blood."

George T. Downing was one of the delegates who along with Frederick Douglass had called on Johnson in 1866—and who'd recently sent oyster soup over to the War Department to fortify Stanton, still barricaded there. Downing received a warning. "Remember

Civil rights activist and wealthy restauranteur George T. Downing headed the delegation, along with Frederick Douglass, that met with Andrew Johnson in 1866 to urge Johnson to grant black men the vote.

Lincoln," it read. "Stick to your oysters and let politics alone." The bootblack at Willard's Hotel received a similar threat. Ben Butler opened a letter on which death's heads and coffins had been scrawled. Thaddeus Stevens received a note saying he'd eaten the bread of wickedness and drunk the wine of violence and he'd soon reap the whirlwind. Benjamin Wade was told he'd be assassinated for sure if he became President. Wade replied he'd lived too long to be afraid.

Charles Sumner received more than one death threat. "The Ku Klux Klan send letters every day," said his secretary, "fitted with gallows, coffins, skulls, daggers, and corpses, announcing to Charles that the avenger is on his track, and that he will be awakened at midnight only to find his room filled with masked figures, and to meet his doom at their hands."

Reports about this terrorist organization, whose name was as mysterious as its members—perhaps it referred to the sound that a cocked rifle made, several writers guessed—had been flooding the national press ever since the impeachment had begun. Conservatives, Democrats, Copperheads together dismissed stories about the Klan as a joke, a fairy tale, a Republican bogey contrived to "frighten old ladies in their tea-cups." Republicans countered that the Ku Klux Klan had come to the assistance of President Johnson—in particular, to prevent black men from voting in the South. Presumably the organization had been initially conceived in New York and then implemented first in Pulaski, Tennessee, by well-known Tennessee bigots like Nathan Bedford Forrest, the notorious Confederate General of Fort Pillow infamy.

To retain President Johnson in office was to give license to this secret organization, with its robed and masked men galloping at night, avenging the dead Confederacy and claiming to redeem it by sowing terror in the name of the government they cherished, a government for and by white men. That was the nub of the argument made by that dumpy, brash, and impassioned impeacher Benjamin Butler, who for the moment dropped all mention of technicalities.

GIDEON WELLES, THE glowering secretary of the navy, appeared in the Senate, bearded and growly and eager to talk. He'd been prepared by Stanbery, with a series of written questions about the cabinet's response to the Tenure of Office Act: What had each secretary said about it? What had each said about those cabinet members appointed by Lincoln? Did you or any other cabinet member know if President Johnson had proposed to bring the Tenure of Office Act before the Supreme Court?

Ben Butler popped up. Why should discussions that took place in the cabinet about the Tenure of Office Act be relevant, he objected. Why should cabinet members shield the President?

"Senators," Butler turned to the chamber, "you passed this Tenure-of-Office act. That might have been done by inadvertence,"

Secretary of the navy under President Lincoln and a former Democrat, Gideon Welles had successfully enlarged the navy, and was a Johnson supporter who recorded in his invaluable if waspish diary the goings-on of the cabinet, both during the war and after.

he conceded, and quickly added that "the President then presented it to you for your revision, and you passed it again notwithstanding his constitutional argument upon it. The President then removed Mr. Stanton, and presented its unconstitutionality again, and presented also the question whether Mr. Stanton was within it, and you, after solemn deliberation and argument, again decided that Mr. Stanton was within its provisions so as to be protected by it, and that the law was constitutional. Then he removed Mr. Stanton on the 21st of February, and presented the same question to you again; and again, after solemn argument, you decided that Mr. Stanton was within its provisions and that the law was constitutional. Now

they offer to show the discussions of the cabinet upon its constitutionality to overrule the quadruple opinion solemnly expressed by
the Senate upon these very questions—four times upon the constitutionality of the law, and twice upon its constitutionality and upon
the fact that Mr. Stanton was within it."

The Senate sided with Butler. Welles' testimony about the cabinet's discussion was deemed irrelevant, and although other members of the cabinet were ready to take the stand, there was no point.
The President's defenders said the cabinet had been muzzled.

But Butler was the man of the hour, the man who called witnesses, examined them, explained their testimony. Butler was the
acute take-no-prisoners prosecutor rebutting with aplomb the President's brilliant lawyers. Ready at all times with a joust, a jibe, a
precedent, the man was cool, cheeky, and vain. Even Republicans
who condescended to this stubby man with the pink pate, raised in
a Lowell boardinghouse, were impressed. "Genl. Butler swallows
and eclipses the other managers," William Evarts admitted, "and
without him they would have made but a poor figure."

Evarts dismissed Gideon Welles. By April 18, both the prosecution and the defense had rested their case.

THE SPECTATORS WERE restless, the American public was restless, and everyone was tired. "Stick to the point, gentlemen," Emily
Briggs cried in frustration. Legal casuistry had dwarfed the real
meaning of impeachment and its implications, all of which, again,
had to do with responsibility: the responsibilities of a President, his
responsibility to his office—and to the maintenance of its dignity;
the responsibilities of Congress and its relation to public order
when the relationship to the executive had broken down. And,
again, there was the tacit issue too of what might be owed the four
million recently enslaved people still deprived of political power.

The Senate changed its mind as often as the weather, said an
exasperated Mark Twain, who left Washington for good.

On balance, the President seemed irresponsible, and his errors of judgment included a deliberate violation of law. For it seemed to the impeachers, and much of the public, that when he fired Stanton, Johnson did not then intend to bring the Tenure of Office Act to the courts. The courts were an afterthought. Plus, no court case could be made, in fact, while Stanton remained in office. And Stanton did remain in office. Then Sherman's testimony had been damaging, for when the President offered Sherman the position of war secretary, he had not mentioned the courts, saying he had to get rid of Stanton for the good of the country, not to test the law. And Johnson seemed to think Stanton would comply and leave the war office.

As Moorfield Storey explained to his father, Johnson's intention seemed to be to eject Stanton—"first by resignation, then under the Tenure-of-Office Bill, then in violation of it." The violation included Johnson's appointment of an interim war secretary—whom the Senate did not confirm. For when Stanton refused to leave his office, Johnson did not go to the courts. He simply replaced him with Lorenzo Thomas, whom he invited to the cabinet as war secretary.

Although the President's son-in-law, Tennessee Senator David Patterson, who'd been residing in the White House, was now looking for a new place to live, William Evarts was supremely confident. Johnson would not be convicted. A friend warned Evarts not to count his chickens before they hatched, but Evarts believed that a good number of Republicans would prefer the status quo—and electing General Grant—to throwing Johnson out of office and putting in Benjamin Wade. Evarts was also quite aware of certain goings-on behind the scenes.

The Beginning of the End

"None are above the law; that no man lives for
himself alone, 'but each for all.'"

— JOHN BINGHAM

Both the impeachers and the defenders of the President expressed confidence and then doubt and then confidence again about the outcome of the trial. And they traded insults, propaganda, and innuendo. The President's defenders belittled the peripatetic politicians in mangy suits who'd come from the South to Washington, squeezed themselves into cheap hotels, and hysterically declared that if the President wasn't removed, a make-believe organization called Ku Klux Klan would devour all blacks. "The Dems pooh-pooh the KKK outrages just as they did the Black Ruffian outrages in Kansas," said Schuyler Colfax, referring to the proslavery murders of the late 1850s. Impeachers insisted that if Andrew Johnson was acquitted, white Unionists and every black man and woman in the South was in mortal danger.

Less histrionically, inside the Senate the President's lawyers intended to prolong the trial as long as possible and to pick off Republican senators who would side with them. With fifty-four men in the Senate, the impeachers needed a two-thirds majority—thirty-six votes, in other words—to convict the President. Only nineteen were needed for acquittal.

All nine Democratic senators would vote in a bloc for acquittal, and three very conservative Republicans could be counted on as voting in the Democratic column. That meant only seven more Republicans were needed to exonerate President Johnson.

Although Wendell Phillips assumed that prudent politicians like Representatives Elihu Washburne and John Bingham would never have voted for impeachment if they couldn't count on the thirty-six votes necessary for conviction, Phillips worried that more delays would allow Johnson's henchmen to chip away at the resolve of several Republicans. "Delays are dangerous," Moorfield Storey agreed. Charles Sumner proposed that the proceedings begin at ten in the morning instead of noon and continue until six in the evening. The Senate voted against the motion, although in early April, Senators did consent to convene at eleven.

That vote once again demonstrated to Senate-watchers that not all Republicans were of the same mind. James Grimes, the burly Senator from Iowa known for his droopy mustache and mutton-chops, had been an energetic foe of slavery, but his disposition toward most Radicals and his intimate friendship with William Pitt Fessenden left him unsure that the decision to impeach had been wise. Although he had backed congressional reconstruction ever since it was first proposed, impeachment seemed to Grimes the revolutionary design of anarchists. He also shared his friend Fessenden's contempt for Charles Sumner.

Grimes didn't much like Andrew Johnson either, and he did hope to curb the President's recklessness. "What Republican will dare run the risk of being made responsible for AJ's d—d brutal, hard-headed acts," journalist Benjamin Perley Poore had wanted to know. "Acquit him, and he would act like a mad elephant who had had a fight with his keepers, and had conquered." Grimes understandably worried that if conservative senators voted to acquit Johnson, the President might then encourage rebels to undermine reconstruction even more than they'd already done. There had to be another way, and Grimes thought he'd found one.

As chair of the Senate Naval Affairs Committee, Grimes had become good friends with Gustavus Fox, former assistant secretary of the navy, and he suggested to Fox, then in Washington, that if the President would promise to appoint "a man [as] Secy of War in whom the country had confidence, it would help him." Fox told Gideon Welles what Grimes had suggested, which is where the possible nomination of General John Schofield as war secretary entered the picture. As war secretary, Schofield might prevent the President from acting rashly. He was no Stanton, to be sure, and he

Chair of the Joint Committee on Reconstruction, William Pitt Fessenden of Maine had briefly been Lincoln's treasury secretary before returning to the Senate. Increasingly disgusted by President Johnson, he tried to head off the radical measures of Charles Sumner, whom he disliked.

wouldn't have been the first choice of either Johnson or the Radical Republicans—or perhaps of many moderates—but impeachment had changed everything. Though a middling general, Schofield could be trusted, and wavering senators might be inclined to acquit the President if they didn't have to agonize about the consequences. These wavering senators, Edwin Stanton had heard, were Lyman Trumbull, Jim Grimes, and William Pitt Fessenden.

Grimes evidently conferred with Fessenden about the plan to nominate Schofield, and the two of them contacted William Evarts. On the morning of April 21, the day before closing arguments were to begin, Evarts sent a note requesting that Schofield meet him at the bustling Willard's Hotel, where Evarts had taken rooms. Evarts told Schofield that he wished to discuss the safety of the country, the preservation of the Constitution, and Andrew Johnson. "A majority of Republicans in both houses of Congress and throughout the country now regret the commencement of the impeachment proceedings, since they find how slight is the evidence of guilty intent," Evarts said. "But now the serious question is, how to get out of the scrape? A judgment of guilty and removal of the President would be ruinous to the party, and cause the political death of every senator who voted for it as soon as the country has time to reflect upon the facts and appreciate the frivolous character of the charges upon which the removal must be based. The precedent of the impeachment and removal of the President for political reasons would be exceedingly dangerous to the government and the Constitution; in short, the emergency is one of great national peril."

National peril: how could Schofield refuse? And if he saved the nation, he could pave the way to Grant's election. Schofield said that before he consented, he had to confer with General Grant. Evarts reluctantly agreed.

That evening after dinner, Schofield and Grant talked about Evarts' proposition without naming Evarts as its author. Certain that Johnson would be convicted and that Benjamin Wade, as the new President, would be hard-pressed to assemble a new cabinet quickly,

Grant told Schofield that he had no objection to him as war secretary.

Schofield returned to Willard's about eight o'clock, and when he and Evarts talked, Evarts said that although he wasn't at liberty to provide the name of "prominent Senators" who now regretted impeachment, he did say that he feared for the life of the Republican party. As war secretary, Schofield could preserve it, thus ensuring Grant's election while restraining Johnson if Johnson remained in office. Schofield went back to Grant, who said that under the circumstances, Schofield had no choice but to accept.

Johnson, who had gone along with the plan, withdrew his earlier nomination of Thomas Ewing as war secretary, which the Senate had ignored, and nominated John McAllister Schofield on Friday, April 24, two days after the closing arguments had started. But the appointment made to allay the fears of such moderates as Grimes, Fessenden, and Trumbull suddenly alarmed General Grant. Johnson would be acquitted, and there would be no way to stop him. As if waking to the shenanigans—and the dangers of Johnson staying in the White House—Grant dashed off a confidential note to Schofield: Schofield should renege.

It was too late.

"HOW DULL WASHINGTON would be without the Impeachment Trial," a spectator sarcastically remarked. "It quite takes the place of morning receptions." The days dragged on. The Senate had decided to hear anyone on the defense or prosecution teams who wished to speak in closing. General John Logan submitted his speech in writing, and Benjamin Curtis would soon hurry back to Boston, but the others wanted an opportunity, one last opportunity, to talk for or against conviction.

George Boutwell was the first manager to address the Senate on behalf of conviction. Conviction of the President would guarantee the safety of the nation, no small thing, precisely because the President had not faithfully executed his constitutional obligation to execute the law. Rather, Johnson had seized, or had attempted to seize, a government office.

As for the argument that the President had consulted his cabinet about the Tenure of Office Act, Boutwell said that Johnson had consulted his cabinet the way Hamlet consulted Polonius — to hear what he wanted to hear. Boutwell then offered a forensic analysis of the President's power to remove or fill vacancies, of the Tenure of Office Act, of its applicability to Stanton, and of the President's alleged violation of his oath of office when he dismissed Stanton. Johnson's alleged purpose to test the law in the courts was simply a pretext. If Johnson had wanted to test the law, he could have instituted proceedings earlier with what is called a *quo warranto* against Stanton — that writ, challenging Stanton's right to hold on to his office, would have immediately referred the matter to a court. Johnson had not done this.

Boutwell bored the listeners, who were again hoping for fire and brimstone, and not finishing his speech before adjournment, the next day he offered a specific chronology of events, lest anyone had forgotten: Johnson's appointment of Grant as interim war secretary; Johnson's sacking of Stanton; Johnson's appointment of Lorenzo Thomas as interim war secretary; Johnson's nomination of Thomas Ewing as secretary of war. Boutwell proceeded to discuss the impeachment articles, one by one. He cited instances when federal judges had been impeached and demonstrated how they might be relevant to the presidential impeachment. And for those listeners growing impatient, he ended his oration with a rambling set of images: "Travelers and astronomers inform us that in the southern heavens, near the southern cross, there is a vast space which the uneducated call the hole in the sky, where the eye of man, with the aid of the powers of the telescope, has been unable to discover nebulae, or asteroid, or comet, or planet, or star, or sun," Boutwell declaimed.

"If this earth were capable of the sentiments of justice and virtue," Boutwell continued, summoning all his strength, "it would heave and throw, with the energy of the elemental forces of nature, and project this enemy of two races of men into that vast region, there forever to exist in a solitude eternal as life."

William Evarts turned to Benjamin Curtis. "I'll put Boutwell into that hole in the sky so that he'll never get out of it again," he murmured.

Then and later Boutwell's summation was widely mocked, but if it offered skeptics a good laugh, it also revealed the extent of the man's despair—and the depth of his conviction that Andrew Johnson was a very guilty man.

"WHO IS ANDREW Johnson?" shouted the member of the President's defense team from Tennessee who, up to this point, had not opened his mouth. Thomas Nelson rose to his feet and, according to Emily Briggs, this old-timey semi-rebel defending Johnson mistook the Senate for a congregation of Tennessee sinners. Preacher Nelson cajoled, censured, and unwittingly entertained. Over and over he bellowed, "Who is Andrew Johnson?" and over and over, he answered his own question with somersaulting adjectives: undismayed, unfaltering, unsubdued, unbent, unbroken, unawed, unterrified.

Several members of Congress softly tiptoed out of the chamber.

And with a rhetorical gambit that virtually conceded the case, Nelson asked, "Suppose he committed an error; suppose he is wrong; suppose Congress is right." Co-counsel William Groesbeck was offended. Nelson was assuming the President might actually have broken the law.

Nelson swiftly returned to his tumble of obsequious compliments. "In the name of all that is sacred, can anyone say he is a traitor to his principles, or a traitor to the party that elected him?" Nelson roared. No: the managers were the revolutionists, dangerous to the country, dangerous to liberty, and dangerous to the government that they would gladly overthrow. They were the very men who'd excluded the Southern states from the Union.

Nelson was saying exactly what the President wanted him to say and probably what Johnson had instructed him to say, particularly about the President's bravery and sterling character. This oratorical encomium continued the next day, Friday the 24th, when Nelson enumerated, as George Boutwell had done, the articles of impeachment, and concluded that nothing the President had done or said could rightly be considered a high crime or misdemeanor.

The galleries were almost empty. By the time Thomas Nelson finished, the managers and even the defense had slipped out, leaving only Butler and Benjamin Curtis behind. It was widely thought that Nelson had damaged the President's case. But the next day, Saturday, the President's able lawyer William S. Groesbeck hoarsely characterized Johnson as a conciliator, a reconciler, a kind and forgiving man whom the Senate could embrace. And with that description of Johnson, in a relatively short speech Groesbeck systematically refuted the argument that a crime could be committed without motive—and that, of course, Johnson's motive was pure.

Groesbeck also restated the now familiar argument that the Tenure of Office law, a law of doubtful construction, did not apply to Stanton, who had been appointed by Lincoln, or at the very least could easily be construed that way. But even if the law did apply to Mr. Stanton, was Johnson's removal of Stanton a criminal act?

Groesbeck cleverly argued that it was not—that, in fact, Johnson acted reasonably and with the purest motives when he questioned the constitutionality of a law that was in any case open to more than one interpretation. He argued that even if the President did not possess the power to remove Stanton, as many of the managers had claimed, there were established constitutional opinions concluding that he did. As Groesbeck pointed out, referring to the creation of executive departments in 1789, Congress had discussed whether the President could remove department heads, and the result of that debate was inconclusive.

"Is the Senate prepared to drag the President in here and convict him of crimes because he believed, as the Supreme Court believed, as thirty-eight of the thirty-nine Congresses believed? That is the question." The answer was evident. "In the condition of Andrew Johnson you can find no criminality in what he did," Groesbeck asserted. Johnson did not use force; he did not conspire. What did he do? "He tried to pluck a thorn out of his very heart." He had to act the way he did to test a law that Johnson's own cabinet thought dubious—although the Senate in its wisdom had refused to hear testimony from all the members of that cabinet. Thus if the President had authority to fire Stanton and appoint Thomas, which Groesbeck said the President believed he had, then eight of the nine articles of impeachment immediately fall by the wayside.

A few of the managers congratulated Groesbeck on his speech.

HIS CHEEKS SO hollow that his bones seemed to be poking through the skin, Thaddeus Stevens faced the Senate and the galleries, spurred on by the trial. With some trouble, he read his prepared remarks and the people in the galleries had to lean forward in their seats, cupping their ears. In minutes, his voice completely gave out. He handed his speech to Ben Butler to read aloud. And yet, despite the pallor and rasping whisper, there was still something rugged about Thad Stevens, something that despite his obvious frailty still inspired both adulation and contempt, detractors labeling him a malignancy fueled by spite and admirers hailing him as the principled and unfailing avatar of justice.

His intention was to discuss only the eleventh omnibus article, which he had urged Butler to write, and he easily demolished Groesbeck's argument for the President's defense, noting that theoretical debates about whether a President could remove an executive officer were moot after Congress had passed the Tenure of Office Act. For Stevens did not doubt that Johnson had broken the law. After all, in his correspondence with Grant, Johnson had admitted that he'd wanted Stanton out of office. As for pretending that Johnson wanted to test the Tenure of Office Act, what is that, asked Stevens, except a tacit admission of malfeasance? What if Andrew Johnson, when he swore his oath of office, had said, "Stop; I have a

further oath. I do solemnly swear that I will not allow the act entitled 'An act regulating the tenure of certain civil offices,' just passed
by Congress over the presidential veto, to be executed; but I will
prevent its execution by virtue of my own constitutional oath."

Besides, where in the Constitution does it say that the President
is "to search out defective laws that stand recorded upon the statutes
so that he can advise their infraction," Stevens trenchantly wondered. If the President did not want to execute the laws of Congress,
he should have resigned.

The real issue was reconstruction, Stevens went on to explain. It
had always been. For Johnson had encouraged defunct rebellious
states to live as unjustly as before and as unwilling to create a free
and fair country. In fact, he had actually directed these same states
to oppose all laws intended to remake the nation free and fair forever.

He may have been ill, but Thaddeus Stevens remained Thaddeus Stevens.

SPECTATORS STILL HOPING for the rocket's red glare, especially
from the mordant Thaddeus Stevens, were again disappointed. But
at least Stevens had been brief. "This trial has developed in the
most remarkable manner the insane love of speaking among public
men," James Garfield complained. "Here we have been wading
knee deep in words, words, words, for a whole week."

The prosecutor Thomas Williams followed Thaddeus Stevens,
and though his argument for conviction seemed a bit threadbare,
Williams passionately confronted Thomas Nelson, asking not who
Andrew Johnson *was*, but who Johnson *is*. What has he done since
becoming President? He did not convene Congress after Lincoln's
assassination but rather set up, by himself, state governments in the
former Confederacy. He laid out qualifications for their voters. He
determined the conditions for their admission into the Union. He
created government offices and packed them with former rebels
legally banned from public service. He usurped Senate privileges

by appointing government officers during its recess and then refusing to nominate them formally, so as to bypass Senate confirmation. He stripped the Freedmen's Bureau of its endowment and restored to the rebels the land they'd forfeited. He insulted Congress by saying reconstruction belonged to him alone and that Congress had no legislative right or duty to interfere. He arraigned Congress as revolutionary and treasonous. He abused his veto power and tried to persuade the states formerly in rebellion from accepting the Fourteenth Amendment, and he winked at—if not encouraged—the murder of loyal citizens by Confederate mobs, particularly but not exclusively in New Orleans. He had soaked the streets with the blood of our citizens.

That is the real Andrew Johnson, said Thomas Williams. Andrew Johnson was the man who had effectively "reopened the war, inaugurated anarchy, turned loose once more the incarnate devil of baffled treason and unappeasable hate, whom, as we fondly thought, our victories had overthrown." And if these crimes weren't enough, Andrew Johnson had unlawfully attempted to remove the rightful secretary of war and replace him with his own flunky.

Given this, given that Andrew Johnson had demeaned himself, given that he did not respect the laws or those men who made them—that he in fact encouraged disobedience to them and that he with all his might had opposed the restoration of peace by arrogating power to himself—the republic was no longer safe with Johnson at the helm. And since we care about the nation's safety and the rights of its citizen, Williams insisted, Andrew Johnson must be convicted.

For the nation is too great, Williams concluded, ever to be affected by the loss of one man—even if that man is a very great President, like President Lincoln. And if you're tempted by Mr. Nelson's plea for mercy, consider the men and women to whom no mercy was shown, people piled into carts like swine during the bloodbath that was Memphis, during the holocaust in New Orleans, during the violence and murder and assassination still occurring daily in the South.

IF THOMAS WILLIAMS blew hot, William Evarts blew cold. At half past two in the afternoon of April 28, Evarts rose to speak as if he were the guest of honor at a legal banquet.

Representing himself as an objective authority, above the fray of a very frayed politics, he declared that he was not a Tennessee partisan, like Nelson, or even a presidential sympathizer. Rather, he had come to the defense table merely to defend the Constitution.

Holding notes that he drew out of one of the dozen envelopes he carried—though he seldom referred to them—Evarts talked interminably, or indefatigably, according to one's point of view, as if he could secure acquittal merely by the length of his argument. It lasted fourteen hours stretched out over four days.

Evarts did at times divert his listeners, especially when he mercilessly punctured Boutwell's bloated astronomical metaphor. "Indeed, upon my soul, I believe he is aware of an astronomical fact which many professors of that science are wholly ignorant of," Evarts said. "Mr. Manager Boutwell, more ambitious, had discovered an untenanted and unappropriated region in the skies, reserved, he would have us think, in the final councils of the Almighty, as the place of punishment for convicted and deposed American Presidents."

Chief Justice Chase seemed to snicker.

Evarts skewered Boutwell several minutes longer before launching into his central defense, and much as if he were lecturing a classroom of students, he painstakingly explained the responsibilities of the Senate during peacetime, as if no one knew them, and the gravity of an impeachment proceeding. He wondered aloud if the three branches of government could stay separate, distinct, and balanced when provocative words like "traitor" and "rebel"—a lexicon inappropriate to peacetime—were so casually tossed around after the war. Political slogans overpower reason. "Cardinal Wolsey said that in political times," Evarts reminded his listeners, "you could get a jury that would bring in a verdict that Abel killed Cain."

The war had debased public discourse, but the issue was not language, or at least not language alone, even though the language in the Tenure of Office Act was ambiguous, and this was an important fact. For while Evarts believed the Tenure of Office Act was unconstitutional, he said its language was so unclear that the Senate couldn't possibly hold the President guilty for violating it. Didn't the President have the right to interpret the Tenure of Office Act, Evarts rhetorically asked. And besides, if the law was unconstitutional, as Evarts believed, then no one could violate it; unconstitutional law is not binding to the President or anyone else. The President, like any citizen, had the right to test the constitutionality of a law, and he was not endangering public safety by doing so.

Evarts was in his element: political, literary, and idiomatic discourse deftly interwoven. At every turn, he swapped logical argument for down-home anecdote and braided them together with lines from the Bible or the poet William Cowper or Daniel Webster. And he analyzed the speech of others—that is, of the President. The President had spoken intemperately, he admitted, but his unfortunate statements had occurred during impromptu speeches, when he'd become irritated. Compare this with the diatribes of congressmen. "Let him who is without sin cast the first stone," Evarts cried with mock solemnity.

The galleries, bored much of the time, snapped to attention. Evarts quoted from the Honorable Charles Sumner's diatribe against the President, whom Sumner had labeled "an enemy of the people." He noted that Ben Butler had once accused John Bingham of spilling the blood of Mary Surratt—and that Bingham had called his newfound friend Ben Butler "a man who lives in a bottle, and is fed with a spoon." (Laughter.) Evarts said he didn't know what Bingham meant (more laughter), but he did know that name-calling was standard practice in the House. And do not forget, Evarts calmly observed, that these gentlemen, Benjamin Butler and John Bingham, had indulged in such behavior during a discussion of "charity." (Laughter again.) "Charity vaunteth not itself, is not puffed up." (Even more laughter.)

Bingham forced a smile. Butler, head in hand, sat poker-faced.

But Evarts was deadly serious when he said that the Senate was bound to observe rules of law. The court of impeachment was not a law unto itself, as Butler had claimed. It was a court, and as a court, if it did not proceed as an altar of justice, it would become an altar of sacrifice. But sacrifice the President? For what crime? Had Johnson surrendered a fleet? Abandoned a fort? Betrayed the country to a foreign state? Fleeced the government? No, President Johnson had removed a member of his cabinet, and he had appointed an interim replacement.

Although the managers claimed Johnson had violated a 1795 statute that limited an interim term to six months, Evarts accused the Senate of not having considered that law, back in 1863, when it honored Lincoln's request to grant the President the authority to make interim appointments. So the President had violated nothing. And had the President conspired with anyone? No, of course not. Nor was there any preparation or meditation of force, any application of it, any threat or expectation of it.

In conclusion, on Friday, May 1, Evarts offered a last plea, this time with emotion:

> And this brings me very properly to consider, as I shall very briefly, in what attitude the President stands before you when the discussion of vicious politics or of repugnant politics, whichever may be right or wrong, is removed from the case. I do not hesitate to say that if you separate your feelings and your conduct, his feelings and his conduct, from the aggravations of politics as they have been bred since his elevation to the Presidency, under the peculiar circumstances which placed him there, and your views in their severity, governed, undoubtedly, by the grave juncture of the affairs of the country, are reduced to the ordinary standard and style of estimate that should prevail between the departments of this government, I do not hesitate to say that upon the impeachment investigations and upon the impeachment evidence you leave the general standing of the President unimpaired in his conduct and

character as a man or as a magistrate. Agree that his policy has thwarted and opposed your policy, and agree that yours is the rightful policy; nevertheless within the Constitution and within his right, and within his principles as belonging to him and known and understood when he was elevated to the office, I apprehend that no reasonable man can find it in his heart to say that evil has been proved against him.

The strategy was brilliant: to rouse emotion in his audience by playing on Republican ambivalence, Evarts provided moderates and even radical-leaning Republicans a way out of their dilemma, which was in effect to respect and preserve the office of the presidency even though they disapproved of Johnson for his crudeness, his bias, his obstructionism, and his disdain for a legally reconstructed nation.

Evarts thus manipulated fellow Republicans, speaking for those who, like himself, thought Johnson a boor who had actually harmed the peace but who also believed that his conviction would destroy the party. He manipulated fellow Republicans who feigned contempt for politics and political rhetoric, knowing that their contempt was theater, artfully staged. He even manipulated those Republicans who believed Johnson wanted to reinstate slavery by another name, for he implicitly asked them to remember who Johnson was: a man without learning, never having enjoyed a day's schooling, always devoted to the state and to its citizens, always a public servant, always struggling against aristocratic influences, always faithful to the common people, and while he was no theorist or fancy philosopher, he had been forged in that furnace of Tennessee politics and firmly and forcefully adhered to the Constitution — yes, perhaps more than the Declaration of Independence, for sure — but he loved the country as much as they did.

Exploiting the Senate's fear of rocking the boat and its equally real commitment to the Union and its perpetuation, Evarts was ready to rest. "Can we summon now resources enough of civil prudence and of restraint of passion to carry us through this trial," he asked, "so that whatever result may follow, in whatever form, the people may feel that the Constitution has received no wound!"

Mary Clemmer Ames reported that Evarts' labyrinthine sentences so exasperated listeners that in the galleries men and women spread their lunch on tissue paper and chatted as they nibbled their sandwiches. "It seems inert," George Templeton Strong conceded, "as an ounce of Epsom salts dissolved in ninety gallons of dishwater." William Lloyd Garrison remarked that Evarts' speech seemed to begin and to end without any real point—if, that is, you could say it ever ended. "Fourteen mortal hours," he complained. And Evarts' mockery of the managers made Moorfield Storey cringe. "He contrived in a gentlemanly way to say things more uncalled for and in worse taste than anyone else during the trial, if we make a possible exception in favor of General Butler," Storey noted.

Wendell Phillips loathed the slick Evarts too much even to endure his speech, though he probably did read it; he wouldn't give Evarts the satisfaction of saying so—or having to comment on it. "No rule of the profession obliged him to take the President's case," Phillips also noted with bite. "His doing so will, rightfully, do more to intensify and deepen the popular belief that lawyers have no consciences." In this, he echoed the sentiment of other Radicals who believed, wrongly as it turned out, that Evarts had dug the grave of his own reputation.

Yet Radicals admitted that Evarts had performed well even if he hadn't grappled with the central questions, like the removal of Stanton, which he seemed to consider trivial. Groesbeck had done a better job of this.

But Secretary of State William Seward was greatly relieved. The day after Evarts began his speech, Seward visited him at Willard's Hotel. "Ah, Mr. Evarts," Seward reportedly said, "the country is safe."

"MR. STANBERY IS to speak on the trial, & I may go in & hear him a few minutes," Walt Whitman told his mother. "But I guess I shall spend my half-holiday mostly in jaunting around in the open air." Whitman wasn't the only one to prefer open air. Stanbery was a yawn.

Having pulled himself out of his sickbed, he insisted that if the President was convicted, "the strong arms of the people" would then raise him up, "and we shall live to see him redeemed, and to hear the majestic voice of the people, 'Well done, faithful servant; you shall have your reward!'" After the opening fanfare, Stanbery seemed as drained as his listeners. "Most men prefer to be deceived, cheated, anything rather than to be bored," one spectator carped.

And now the prosecution faced the difficult task of summarizing their case. John Bingham of Ohio, reluctant impeacher but the man who'd helped craft the Fourteenth Amendment—and the man who vigorously opposed impeachment when it first reared its head—was chosen to deliver the managers' finale. Earnest, serious, and although a man with his hand on the brake, whatever Bingham undertook, said an observer, "must be carried out to the bitter end."

On May 4, Bingham attracted the throngs of spectators that Stanbery had driven from the galleries. Neatly dressed in a new coat, Bingham no longer looked as if he needed a shave, though he seemed hunched over from the weight of the past weeks. He had come to the impeachment trial neither as a partisan nor as a man with a chip on his shoulder, he said, but as a full-throated patriot who would refuse to stoop to trifles—like the long debate about whether for the purposes of impeachment the Senate was a court. He could dispense with the argument simply by quoting the Constitution, which stated, "the Senate shall have the sole power to try all impeachments." That's what Butler meant when he said the Senate was not a court: the Senate is the Senate, and as the Senate, it possessed the power to convict or acquit the President.

Bingham brushed away the verbose cobwebs, as he called them, that Evarts had spun. He condemned the President for taking the law into his own hands. "In spite of the technicalities, in spite of the lawyer's tricks, in spite of the futile pleas that have been interposed here in the President's defense," he said, "that is the issue." The

President is not a king, and he cannot claim to disregard the Constitution and its provisions. He cannot set aside the law or defy it. And if he were to set aside such a law as the Tenure of Office Act, then he could set aside every other act of Congress. That places Congress and the Constitution and the people at the mercy of executive pleasure. Even the President's defender and former Supreme Court justice Benjamin Curtis had agreed with him. Bingham quoted from Curtis' pamphlet, "Executive Power," published in 1862, where he stated that if the President disobeys the laws of his own country, he is a usurper of power.

Bingham then dismissed other justifications for the President's action that the defense had argued. The Tenure of Office Act of 1867 had effectively repealed the Act of 1789, so there was no point discussing it. And in the final analysis, the President's duty was to execute the law; it was not for him to make the law, or to interpret the Constitution for himself, or to arrogate to himself the means of testing any law's constitutionality. In any case, the supposition that Johnson was trying to test the law's constitutionality was at best a convenient, insincere afterthought.

Bingham also assailed the entire defense team as hired guns, and he aimed some of his most pointed criticism at Evarts, a man with more Latin than law, more bombast than logic, and more intellectual pyrotechnics than either law or logic—and who aimed to prove that the best way "a man may make his speech immortal is to make it eternal." Laughter.

Most of the listeners fell on every word, though not everyone. New York Democrat John Van Pruyn noisily opened his newspaper. When Chief Justice Chase sent one of the Senate pages over to Pruyn to tell him to lower the paper, which was covering his face, Pruyn stalked out of the chamber. Some said Bingham's style was so tangled it took a machete to cut through it. Bingham was articulate but unoriginal. He was prolix. He was dogmatic and wordy. Benjamin Wade said he now believed Demosthenes and Cicero to be the greatest mischief-makers ever to have lived.

Several Republican senators had not shown up for Bingham's

closing argument. That was a bad sign. Had they already decided how they would vote? Nervous whispers, nothing said aloud, canards and accusations whipped through the Capitol, the newspapers, the nation.

Yet Bingham had brought tears to the eyes of many who did hear him, and his own eyes seemed shiny and damp. "I ask you to consider that we stand this day pleading for the violated majesty of the law, by the graves of a half million of martyred hero-patriots who made death beautiful by the sacrifice of themselves for their country, the Constitution, and the laws, and who, by their sublime example, have taught us that all must obey the law," Bingham resoundingly concluded; "that none are above the law; that no man lives for himself alone, 'but each for all'; that some must die that the state may live; that the citizen is at best but for to-day, while the Commonwealth is for all time; and that position, however high, patronage, however powerful, cannot be permitted to shelter crime to the peril of the republic."

The galleries burst into applause, men and women stood up, boisterous, shouting, clapping, waving. Frowning, the chief justice vainly rapped his gavel and called for order. He too was standing, robes fluttering. Burly James Grimes barked that the galleries should be instantly cleared and reporters and diplomats expelled too. Spectators applauded louder. They hissed and stamped. Reporters and members of the diplomatic corps were indignant. Senator Simon Cameron objected to Grimes' motion, but Senator Lyman Trumbull, gold spectacles glimmering, said the guards should immediately arrest all disorderly persons.

Bingham looked up and smiled with weary patience as the galleries were emptied. Asked how he felt, he sighed, "I don't know. God knows I have tried to do my duty; it is in the hands of the Senate now. The great work of my life is done."

Chief Justice Chase announced that arguments on both sides of the great question of impeachment were closed. The beginning of the end was at hand.

Part Three

VERDICT

Senate roll call and vote, the eleventh article of impeachment of President Andrew Johnson, May 16, 1868.

Cankered and Crude

"Our American politics are in an unusually
effervescent condition."

— WALT WHITMAN

"Society, in these States, is canker'd, crude, superstitious, and rotten," Walt Whitman wrote.

The poet strolled over to the Capitol to hear some of the closing speeches on impeachment. "Our American politics," Whitman told another friend, "are in an unusually effervescent condition." Recently the poet had been annoyed by Thomas Carlyle's apocalyptic "Shooting Niagara: And After?" a pamphlet that denounced democratic America as a "swarmery" in which braying, fire-breathing Radicals and their deliriously stupid agitations—first over slavery, then over equality—led to the frightening horror of voting rights for the masses. As if in direct reply, Whitman sketched out an essay in response. Though he'd encountered shameless politicians jockeying for power, partisans who cared only for party and thieves who bought their offices with money instead of merit, he forced himself to stay hopeful. "While the piled embroidered shoddy gaud and fraud spreads to the superficial eye," Whitman declared, "the hidden warp and weft are genuine, and will wear forever."

Whitman's somewhat cluttered syntax suggests that he was actually very worried. And Whitman wasn't alone. It seemed the fate of the entire country would soon be decided—though not until Tuesday, May 12, six long days after John Bingham's closing argument, six long days during which anything could happen. If a senator was glimpsed dining at Willard's or at Welcker's popular restaurant on Fifteenth Street people began to speculate, although no one knew anything for sure. Men kept lists of the senators in their pockets, and they checked and rechecked their tallies when they thought they knew which way a senator tended. Everyone knew the arithmetic: fifty-four senators, so it would take nineteen votes to acquit, thirty-six to convict.

Predictions changed from hour to hour. Someone heard the President was going to leave office right before the vote, and it was said that General Grant had bet Secretary Stanton a box of cigars that Johnson would resign. Schuyler Colfax seemed certain of Republican success. Senators James Henderson of Missouri and Edmund G. Ross of Kansas would certainly vote guilty—Ross had volunteered that information to Charles Sumner, who was rather surprised at the confidence, not having solicited it. Ross had never walked over to Sumner's desk before. And Ross' brother said he wished he were as sure of going to heaven as he was of Edmund's vote to convict the President.

Then again, Senator Fessenden, sitting at a card table, showed his hand to Colfax's sister one night, suggesting that he'd vote to acquit. "After this impeachment trial is over," Fessenden said, "I shall be one of the most unpopular men in the country." Fessenden, it was later said, had never recovered from not having been appointed president pro tempore of the Senate instead of Benjamin Wade. Had he been, he'd have been next in line for Johnson's job and might have voted differently.

Before the vote was taken, the Senate went into secret executive session during which each of the senators was allotted fifteen minutes to give his estimation of the case. Inside, the heat and thick tobacco smoke were suffocating. Outside, reporters were trawling for clues and representatives from the House gathered in the cloak-rooms and lobbies. Clusters of men and women loitered nearby, some of the men laying bets and hoping to buttonhole whatever senator might stray outside the chamber. "Is there anything new?" they asked. "How is Fowler? Is he sure for conviction?" "I hear he is silent as an infant oyster."

After the session recessed, it became known that John Sherman had spoken against the validity of the first article of impeachment. The impeachers were rattled. Sherman had said that Stanton's current position as secretary of war was not protected by the Tenure of Office Act, a point he had made when the Senate first discussed it. He did add that he believed the President had violated the law when he appointed General Thomas interim secretary. It seemed, then, that Sherman would vote to convict on the second and third articles of impeachment, which dealt directly with the appointment of General Thomas, and the eleventh, or omnibus, article of impeach-ment, which accused Johnson of repudiating the Thirty-Ninth Congress and its reconstruction legislation.

As for James Grimes, having secured the appointment of General Schofield as war secretary, Grimes said Johnson was within his rights when he fired Stanton, for Stanton held his office at the plea-sure of the President. Grimes also dismissed the conspiracy charges against Johnson—that the President had conspired either with General Thomas or with General Emory—and so he wouldn't vote to convict on any of the articles of impeachment. Senator Trumbull could not be depended on either. "Moral debauchery under a de-cent exterior," one disappointed impeacher described Trumbull. "I have believed from the first that Trumbull would go back on us when it comes to a vote," a friend told Elihu Washburne.

With Fessenden, Grimes, and Trumbull set to vote against con-viction, the President needed only four more Republican votes for acquittal. The two West Virginia Senators, Peter Van Winkle and Waitman Willey, along with New Jersey Senator Frederick Freling-huysen, Tennessee's Joseph Fowler, and William Sprague of Rhode Island might be available. The wealthy Sprague was suspected of being influenced by his wife, Kate Chase Sprague, who desperately wanted her father, the chief justice, to win the presidency. Johnson's acquittal would help Chief Justice Chase seem less radical. Then again, Sprague wanted to be respected as his own man, especially since he faced re-election, so no one knew for sure what he'd do.

Peter Van Winkle's deep-dyed conservatism troubled many Radicals. Bald, portly, and with a fluff of white whiskers on each cheek, the wealthy former lawyer had been a strong Unionist during the war. Though no supporter of the Civil Rights Act, the Fourteenth Amendment, or universal suffrage—he'd opposed them adamantly—Van Winkle had supported the Reconstruction Act of 1867, mainly because he despised former Confederates and did not want them in power. Still, Van Winkle often voted with the Democrats, particularly since he believed that a burgeoning federal authority was encroaching on state sovereignty. When Charles Sumner wanted Congress to establish cholera hospitals to combat the epidemic of 1866, Van Winkle had fought him on the basis of state's rights. Yet Van Winkle did suggest he might vote for conviction on a couple of articles.

Suggestions about who would vote what were hearsay. Everything was hearsay. "This impeachment worries a fellow to death," journalist Benjamin Perley Poore said, "and there is no other news."

There was some information on Joseph Smith Fowler. A stalwart Tennessee Unionist, born in Ohio, Fowler had served during the war as Tennessee state comptroller under the military governorship of Andrew Johnson, and he'd successfully argued for Johnson being Vice President on Lincoln's 1864 presidential ticket. Elected to the Senate in 1865, the baby-faced Fowler was able to take his seat in Washington only after Tennessee ratified the Fourteenth Amendment, which allowed the state to rejoin the Union. Since then, he'd spoken against Johnson's policies as too lenient, and had clearly declared after Johnson removed Stanton that the President had committed high treason. So far, so good.

Tennessee Radicals placed Fowler in their column, though just to make sure, a few days before the vote, a delegation from Tennessee called on him. It seemed he might actually desert the Radicals, for every day when the court of impeachment convened, Fowler left his chair to sit with two of the Democrats. And though in private Fowler had said he'd vote to convict, the journalist John Russell Young had heard that when Fowler's wife was mortally ill, Johnson's allies—particularly Johnson's widowed daughter, Mary Stover— had helped nurse her. Fowler was grateful; it was rumored he and Johnson's daughter were engaged.

Senator John Henderson of Missouri also seemed to waffle. Tall and good-looking with curly dark hair and a bushy beard, Henderson had been a Democrat, then a Republican and friend of Lincoln. He spoke out against the first ten articles and afterward dined with Chief Justice Chase and Democrat Reverdy Johnson, both vehement anti-impeachers. Gideon Welles assumed that Mary Foote, a sturdy Democrat, had influenced Henderson, her fiancé, to vote for acquittal.

On the same morning the vote was to be taken, Senator Henderson had told a delegation of Missouri House Republicans that he *could* vote for the President's conviction on the eleventh, or omnibus, article. And though both Henderson and the Missouri delegation would soon dispute the account of what happened during their meeting, Henderson seemed also to promise that if he couldn't vote for Johnson's conviction, he'd resign his seat so that Missouri's radical governor could replace him with someone who would.

Horrified at hearing this, General James Craig rushed to Henderson's rooms. President of the Hannibal & St. Joseph Railroad and a transparent Johnson supporter, Craig had been authorized to offer Henderson anything he wanted—carte blanche—if he would vote for acquittal. "He was the man to do it," said a man who knew Craig, "since Craig was responsible for his [Henderson's] election." Craig also added that if Henderson was "turned out of the Republican Church" because he voted to acquit, the Democrats would gladly welcome him in theirs.

After Craig left, Henderson said that he would stay in office and acquit Andrew Johnson. According to Henderson, Johnson had promised to nominate new men to the cabinet—all Republicans—and would abide by congressional reconstruction. Fretting, the Missouri delegation quickly telegraphed Henderson: "Can your friends hope that you will vote for the eleventh article?"

"I am sworn to do impartial justice according to the law and the evidence," Henderson loftily replied, "and I will try to do it like an honest man."

"Fessenden, Trumbull, Grimes, Henderson have expressed themselves for acquittal," a Cincinnati lawyer in Washington cheerfully told Washington McLean, the Democratic publisher of the *Cincinnati Enquirer.*

"Everything has gone to hell," Elihu Washburne exclaimed. For the first time in ten years, President Johnson and his two daughters went to the theater.

ON THE MORNING the vote was to be taken, the morning of Tuesday, May 12, the crowds again gathered at the Capitol, and when the doors opened, they poured into the corridors and halls. Policemen in blue broadcloth uniforms guarded every entrance, and with polished clubs in their white-gloved hands and revolvers in their belts, they made the people in the galleries feel like criminals.

Thaddeus Stevens was carried in early. John Logan, Ben Butler, and George Boutwell milled among the representatives. When Moorfield Storey asked Boutwell what he thought, Boutwell replied, "Well, I don't give up yet." Trumbull and Fessenden sullenly sat side by side, and Grimes, eyes fixed on the floor, avoided the Radicals, who refused to come near him. Henry Stanbery had returned to the Senate for the first time since his own speech and wordlessly tucked himself into the defense table.

The chaplain concluded the morning prayer. Senator Chandler announced that Michigan Senator Jacob Howard was too ill to enter the chamber, even on a cot, which he had very much hoped to do. Unanimously, the Senate voted to adjourn until Saturday.

Four more days of waiting: in all, ten long days would pass between John Bingham's final argument for the prosecution and any decisive vote on the conviction of the President of the United States, who needed seven Republicans, only seven, to unite with Democrats and acquit him.

Impeachers were now pessimistic. Had the vote been taken as planned that Tuesday, they said, "we might have carried it."

THE NEXT DAY, Wednesday, May 13, President Johnson also received a telegram. "Henderson matter all right," it read. "So says Evarts." Montgomery Blair, walking straight out of the White House, calculated that the President had enough votes to save him. Postmaster General Alexander Randall said he was sure the President would be acquitted. Treasury Secretary Hugh McCulloch was equally sanguine—Grimes, Fessenden, Trumbull, Van Winkle were in the bag. Gideon Welles wondered what McCulloch knew and how he knew it.

HUMORIST DAVID ROSS Locke was much more popular than President Andrew Johnson. Familiarly known as Petroleum V. Nasby, the cracker-barrel philosopher, he satirized Johnson without mercy. "I desire to glide into history ez a marter (with a halo round my head)," Nasby's Johnson shouted. "I shel not pervent the people from testifying their devoshen to me and bearin witness to my many virchoos. I hev already received tenders uv percessions ez terrible ez armies with banners. . . . In the South, ef the confederits I hev pardoned will all turn out the percessions will be miles in length, and eve thy do not the Ku-Klux will be on hand."

IF IMPEACHMENT FAILED, what would happen to the South? Wouldn't Johnson possess unshackled power, particularly over the military commanders stationed there? Apprehensive, both Radical and conservative Republicans pushed to admit the newly reconstructed Southern states into the Union. The House of Representatives quickly passed a bill restoring South Carolina, North Carolina, Georgia, Louisiana, and Alabama, provided they never revoked the black man's right to vote. The bill proposing the readmission of Arkansas had already been sent to the Senate. To expedite its passage, Radicals chucked their earlier demands about voting restrictions on former rebels and about legislation guaranteeing education of the former slaves.

After all, these reconstructed Southern states, if they had Republican senators, would surely vote for conviction, provided they could take their place in the Union soon enough. But they did not come back in time.

THE AMERICAN ANTI-SLAVERY Society celebrated its thirty-fifth anniversary on Wednesday, May 13, at Steinway Hall in New York City. His optimism undimmed, his language robust, Wendell Phillips rallied the crowd. "Every great question in American history has involved race," he told the throngs of cheering people, "and no matter if Presidents betray us, or Senators fail their duty, we will one day see the flag floating from the lakes to the coast, from sea to sea, and it will represent impartial justice to all races and people."

Elizabeth Cady Stanton also spoke that evening. To her fell the unpleasant task of reminding the audience that women too needed the vote. Only with women voting would there be a safe, secure, and lasting reconstruction.

ON WEDNESDAY, MAY 13, Edwin Stanton, still barricaded in the war office, sent a note in cipher to John Russell Young. "Those who are well advised think the success of the impeachment certain," he said. "I have no reason for a different opinion as matters now stand."

But a backlash against impeachment was growing. The Republican party had been the nation's first powerful, national anti-slavery party, a motley group compounded of old Whigs, Free-Soilers, former Democrats, conservatives, Radicals, greenbackers, xenophobes, Eastern financiers, and western humorists. With the war over and slavery abolished, the bonds holding them together were starting to frazzle. Conservative Republicans rebuked Ohio Representative Robert Schenk, chairman of the powerful Ways and Means Committee, for begging the public to write their senators about the "great danger to the peace of the country and the Republican cause if impeachment fails."

EVERYONE KNEW THAT Chief Justice Salmon Chase wanted to be President. And Chase didn't hide his contempt for General Grant—a small man, Chase sneered, among small men. Chase had been spotted at dinner with Fessenden, Grimes, and Trumbull early in the week, and Senators Henderson and Fowler at different times had ridden in the chief justice's carriage.

Presumably Chase had told all of them they could be leaders of a breakaway party—or with him they could start a new party, sprung out of Republican ruins. On Wednesday, May 13, Peter Van Winkle, Trumbull, and Waitman Willey all met at Chase's house to talk about the new movement.

"It is treachery for personal ends and deserves the contempt of all good men," said James Garfield, who'd heard about the movement.

Although it didn't form at the time, this was the nub of what would become known as the Liberal Republicans, former reformers and abolitionists who railed against the federal intervention in the South and opposed the reconstruction laws they'd once passed.

ON THURSDAY, MAY 14, at about half past nine o'clock in the evening, Kansas Senator Samuel Pomeroy called on Peter Van Winkle in his rooms at the National Hotel, a watering hole for conservative

Republicans, Democrats, and Copperheads. The junior senator from Kansas, Edmund Ross, was there along with Lyman Trumbull, John Henderson, and Waitman Willey.

Willey, a former slaveholder, was something of a cipher. He had opposed the repeal of the Fugitive Slave Act back in 1864. He'd opposed establishing the Freedmen's Bureau in 1865, and he'd voted against its extension in 1866. But he had supported the Civil Rights Bill and the Fourteenth Amendment and the right of black men to vote in the District of Columbia. He'd also supported the Tenure of Office Act. One of his biographers, frustrated by Willey's fickleness, accused him of sacrificing conservatism "at the altar of political ambition."

These men were in Van Winkle's room to talk about the impeachment vote. Henderson told Pomeroy that the eleventh omnibus article would be defeated by four votes. Not at all, replied Pomeroy. We will convict on the eleventh by one vote. Willey was pledged to vote for conviction on the eleventh article.

Edmund Ross said he'd vote to convict on all the articles except perhaps the eighth—about seizing the property of the war office—but Ross wanted the whole thing postponed as long as possible, as if putting it off would make it go away. Trumbull also favored postponement because he wasn't sure there were enough votes to acquit on the eleventh article. Postponement gave presidential lobbyists more time.

Henderson said he figured there could be a postponement of the vote—and an acquittal of the President—if Johnson reorganized his cabinet, which he'd been told the President would.

Pomeroy scoffed. "Who will take a place in the cabinet now?"

"Reverdy Johnson," Henderson knowingly answered. "And Mr. Hooper would, Mr. Evarts would." Hooper would be treasury secretary; Evarts, secretary of state.

After the meeting, Henderson slammed the Missouri delegation in the press, saying it had tried to coerce him. The Missouri delegation publicly refuted him. "Without any suggestion or requirement from us, you offered to resign your position as Senator from Mis-

Edmund G. Ross of Kansas, once known as an abolitionist, arrived in Washington to finish the term of the Senator Jim Lane. Once there, he boarded with the Ream family, where he seemed enthralled by the sculptress Vinnie Ream.

souri, if we would request you to do so. This we did not wish to do," the delegation declared. "We did not desire you to vote against your conscience, but if you believed the President guilty as charged in the eleventh article, and would vote so, this was all we desired."

Accusations like these, pitching back and forth, did not look good for the impeachers.

TRUMBULL STAYED AT the National Hotel with Peter Van Winkle until midnight. The next morning, the day before the vote, Van Winkle said he had changed his mind and would vote to acquit the President.

DURING THE IMPEACHMENT trial, when the Senate was debating such issues as the admissibility of evidence, Senator Benjamin Wade was silent, and he didn't vote. Voting wouldn't look right. President pro tempore of the Senate, Wade knew that if Johnson was convicted, he'd be President, since there was no Vice President. But he might have to cast a vote for conviction if the vote was close. That probably meant that he'd have to decline the vice-presidential nomination at the upcoming Republican convention. It would be the honorable thing to do.

SOCIETY IS CANKER'D, crude, superstitious, and rotten, as Whitman said. The state of Kansas was no exception.

A newspaper editor formerly known as an abolitionist, Edmund Gibson Ross was a political nobody who didn't look a person in the face, dressed in black, and walked with a slouch. He'd been sent to the Senate in 1866 to finish the term after Senator Jim Lane put a loaded gun in his mouth and pulled the trigger. No one quite knew why Lane had committed suicide, though it was rumored he had lost the support of his constituency when he supported Johnson's veto of the Civil Rights Bill. More likely, financial chicanery was about to be exposed.

Edmund Ross did not in any way distinguish himself in the Senate. A clerk in the House of Representatives regarded him as a lily-livered and malleable man who "may be artfully operated on without his own apprehension of the fact." Shortly after Johnson was impeached, the *National Anti-Slavery* sourly commented that "Mr. Ross is suffering from the effects of bad associations." One of those bad associations was the conservative Thomas Ewing, Jr., under whose command Ross had served during the war. Another was Perry Fuller, who let Ross know it would be to his advantage — Ross' seat in the Senate — if Johnson was to stay in the White House.

For Ross, like the other Kansas senator, Samuel Pomeroy, had acquired his seat with the assistance of the shady Indian trader Perry Fuller, an adept backroom politician with a reputation for fleecing the Sac, Fox, and Chippewa tribes before the war and after it, for brokering unfair deals with the various tribes for huge payoffs to himself. An active member of the Democratic National Committee, Fuller was also on familiar terms with General Sherman and with the Ewings. Besides, Ross needed money, and he didn't want to lose the patronage he already enjoyed. He wouldn't have that if Ben Wade became President.

Samuel Pomeroy was also an operator, although with a different pedigree. A longtime abolitionist and women's rights advocate, he'd arrived in Kansas from Massachusetts in 1854 as agent of the Emigrant Aid Company. Once a U.S. senator, he conveniently failed to acknowledge conflicts of interest, for he was also president of the Atchison, Topeka & Santa Fe Railway with a yen for lucrative railroad contracts. But unlike Ross, he would presumably benefit if fellow Radical Benjamin Wade went to the White House.

Trying to frame Pomeroy, Andrew Johnson's allies claimed that he took money for his vote, and with his reputation for dishonesty, Pomeroy could be discredited even if he hadn't taken a bribe, at least not this time. Nothing was ever proved against him, though Mark Twain and Charles Dudley Warner would later caricature Pomeroy in their aptly titled novel, *The Gilded Age*, lampooning him as the chubby, smarmy Senator Abner Dilworthy, a money-grubber who reads his Bible upside down.

EDMUND ROSS RECEIVED a telegram. "Kansas has heard the evidence, and demands the conviction of the President," it read. "Every loyal man says impeach the President for his crimes. There is no division here and we hope there will be none in Washington. Signed D. R. Anthony and a thousand others of our best and truest men." Daniel Anthony, a publisher, was the younger brother of Susan B. Anthony.

"STANTON IS A brick," Francis Lieber said. There were people who thought Edwin Stanton would make a good President—he was by far the fittest of them all—but he would not run. He would not even consider it. He was beginning to make plans to return to Ohio, or so one of Johnson's spies reported. Spies were everywhere, and Stanton may have planted the story himself. He'd been funneling information through John Russell Young to the *New-York Tribune*.

But the last weeks had taken their toll. Stanton's nerves were shot. He'd been holed up in the War Department too long. He began sneaking out in the evening from time to time to eat dinner with his family, and while his son kept watch over affairs in Washington, he and his wife secretly traveled to Baltimore for a rest. His chest was tight, his breathing labored.

ON FRIDAY, MAY 15, the day before the vote, several senators who previously said they'd vote for conviction now said they were voting to acquit the President. Impeachment was a dead duck, said the Democratic press. But since putting General Grant in the White House was a Republican priority, many Republicans sighed in relief. Conviction would mean that Senator Wade, next in line as President, might actually be Grant's running mate, and with such a red-hot Radical anywhere near the Executive Mansion, the Republicans might lose in November. Acquit—and they could win.

"What in the name of all that's honest is the matter with our party," a friend asked Thaddeus Stevens. Radical Republicans believed Grant would win even if Johnson was convicted, and conviction was necessary for the sake of the black population, the South, the nation, the future.

The Radical Republican press also condemned Fessenden, Trumbull, Grimes, and Henderson for their upcoming vote: "History will record that Andrew Johnson was convicted by the country, though it will be compelled to relate how he escaped the consequences of his crimes through the weakness of dishonored Senators." For the Radical Republicans, it was not the longevity of the party that was at stake. At stake was the soul of the country.

Point-Blank Lying

"There has been more point-blank lying done in Washington
during the past week, than ever before in the same
space of time, and that is saying a great deal."

— The New York Times

The African Methodist Episcopal Church, originally the Free African Methodist Society, was founded by Richard Allen, born a slave in Philadelphia. Having managed to buy his own freedom, Allen became a teamster, a chimney sweep, a shoemaker, and a charismatic abolitionist preacher influenced by American Methodism. In 1816, he joined together sixteen representatives from Bethel African Church in Philadelphia and African Churches in Baltimore, Wilmington, and Attleboro, Pennsylvania, and by 1868, there were over 70,000 members of the African Methodist Episcopal Church nationwide. At its annual conference, held in Washington that spring, it declared Friday the fifteenth a day of fasting, and it offered up a prayer that the Senate pass a guilty verdict, in the interest of all humanity, to bring peace to the nation.

Several of the conference delegates later called on Thaddeus Stevens at his unobtrusive redbrick home. He thanked them for their kind compliments, which he said he didn't deserve, and he promised, should he live, that he would make every effort to be worthy of them. He also apologized for the injustice and the many grievances inflicted upon them by the white men and women who dared to call themselves Christians.

The Democratic press called the conference "Methodistical darkydom," where "hog and hominy are at a discount and chicken stealing is left off for less sacred churches."

SLOWLY RECOVERING, MICHIGAN Senator Howard pulled himself up in his bed. He would get to the Senate if he had to be carried on a stretcher. New York Senator Roscoe Conkling was also ill but just as determined.

Senator James Grimes suffered a paralytic stroke said to be caused by stress. "His temperament is more excitable and delicate than one would suppose, and I think the struggle has affected him," Fessenden observed.

ON FRIDAY, MAY 15, the night before the vote, at least half the Republican senators met for three hours at Pomeroy's house. With the Radical editor Theodore Tilton, who had arrived in Washington from New York, they calculated how they thought the vote would go. They regarded Willey now doubtful on conviction but Ross certain on the eleventh article: Pomeroy had the information from Ross' own mouth. Earlier that night, when Ross had dinner with Pomeroy and his family, he said he'd vote to convict the President on the eleventh article, the strongest, although he still hoped for a postponement, probably so that he wouldn't have to do anything at all.

Democratic Senator Reverdy Johnson had been spreading rumors that the eleventh would fail by two votes, but the Republicans at the Pomeroy meeting decided the eleventh impeachment article was close to a lock. The senators should vote on it first.

ROSS RECALLED THE dinner conversation at Pomeroy's differently. He insisted that he and Pomeroy had not discussed the vote, except perhaps while he waited on the Pomeroy porch for a street-car. That's when he said he hoped for a postponement; otherwise, he hadn't committed himself one way or the other about his vote.

"There has been more point-blank lying done in Washington during the past week," said a correspondent for *The New York Times*, "than ever before in the same space of time, and that is saying a great deal."

That same evening, Perry Fuller called on Ross at the Capitol Hill boardinghouse, 325 North B Street, where Ross had rooms on the second floor. Fuller knew the house well, for it was the home of his in-laws, the Reams. Perry Fuller and Mary Ream had married in 1865, four years after Robert Ream, head of the household, had brought his family to Washington from Wisconsin, where he had been a clerk in the surveyor general's office. In addition to the daughter Mary, the Reams had a son, who had enlisted in the Confederate army, and another daughter, Vinnie, whose exact age was never clear. She was born in 1845 or 1847 or 1850, depending on who asked.

In days to come, Benjamin Butler would receive an anonymous tip. "If the impeachment managers could make Vinnie Ream tell the truth, they could find just what is wanted to show what made Senator Ross vote not guilty."

Vinnie Ream probably knew more about the impeachment than many of the impeachers, although she kept remarkably mute: "The shrewdest politician of them all," Mark Twain had chuckled. For she had her career to consider. Thanks to the generosity of her father's friend, Missouri representative James Sidney Rollins, a former slaveholder though a Unionist, Ream had been employed as a clerk in Rollins' office, where she'd met many prominent politicians and studied with great success the art of persuasion. Rollins, evidently smitten, took Ream to the studio of the sculptor Clarke Mills, whose statue of Andrew Jackson, the largest equestrian statue ever produced at that time, loomed over Lafayette Park.

Glancing around the studio, Vinnie Ream exclaimed, "Why, I can do that." Mills was apparently charmed, and Ream became his apprentice. As Ream's sympathetic biographer notes, "Vinnie had a faculty for catching the fancy of older men."

Soon Ream was sculpting such Democrats as Indiana Representative Daniel Voorhees, a former Copperhead known as the "tall sycamore of the Wabash," and the brash Frank Blair, Jr. These men tilted as far away from the Republicans as possible, but notable Republicans, like Thaddeus Stevens, also sat for Ream. Or she worked from photographs, although that isn't crystal clear. She'd allegedly sculpted Abraham Lincoln during the war when Lincoln rather astonishingly consented to sit for her. Mary Todd Lincoln, who didn't remember Ream, firmly denied that the President would allow this "self-satisfied and rather presuming" young woman to model him in the White House while a war was raging.

A charming mythmaker, Vinnie Ream would tell the Danish critic George Brandes that she'd been asked to sculpt Lincoln because she'd been staying at the White House when he was assassinated. Brandes knew she was lying but, after all, she was a real "*American girl*," he rationalized, "for without rank or privilege she'd fought for what she had." And Vinnie Ream had sized up her prey, a male cabal of politicians who coveted a sculpted berth in history. After Lincoln's assassination, again with the assistance of Rollins, Ream competed for a $10,000 congressional commission to sculpt a marble, life-sized statue of the deceased President. Even though such noted sculptors as Mills had entered the competition, Ream confidently submitted her bust of Lincoln to Congress, as well as a petition signed by Generals Ulysses S. Grant and George Armstrong Custer, by more than half of the members of the House, by more than half of the senators—and by President Johnson. Interviewed about the commission, she didn't mention any of her meetings with Lincoln, an oversight she later attributed to nervousness.

Ream won the commission. As the journalist James Parton observed, "Five minutes' conversation with Miss Vinnie Ream explains this ridiculous behavior of Congress. She is one of those

Awarded a $10,000 commission to mold a life-sized marble
statue of Abraham Lincoln, Lavinia (Vinnie) Ream had never
made a statue in her life, but having lobbied Congressmen,
she successfully launched her career as a sculptor. "The
shrewdest politician of them all," Mark Twain called her.

graceful, animated, bright-eyed, picturesque, undaunted, twinkling
little women, who can make men say Yes to anything they ask." Five
feet tall, with a round open face framed by cascades of long, curly
auburn hair—she said she created the waves with a combination of
sugar and water—the pretty Ream ushered her many visitors to the
basement studio in the Capitol building that another besotted ad-
mirer, John H. Rice, chairman of the House Committee on Public
Buildings and Grounds, had managed to provide for her. Many
senators met there to talk politics.

And so, explaining that he hadn't brought his family to Washington because he couldn't afford it, Ross became a boarder on the second floor of the Ream house. He was also one of Vinnie Ream's most ardent admirers. He signed a petition to recommend that her father receive a diplomatic appointment to Italy, and he suggested to the lieutenant governor of Wisconsin that Vinnie Ream receive a commission to sculpt two former governors—at $10,000 each. (The Wisconsin legislature resoundingly rejected the proposition.) When Ream traveled to Madison to lobby on her own behalf, Ross looked after her studio.

His behavior raised eyebrows. "Ross though a man of family is at present infatuated to the extent of foolishness with Miss Vinnie Ream," Ben Butler had been told. He was also informed that Vinnie Ream, Perry Fuller's sister-in-law, had joined forces with Fuller "to advance the interests of the family." And Fuller owned Senator Ross, the anonymous author continued, having "bought his election and has since used him as an agent in pushing his frauds through the Indian Bureau and Quartermasters Department. He aspires to be Commissioner of Internal Revenue." That was all true.

Butler sent Ross a copy of the accusation. "I have suffered too much from ungenerous and secret slanders," Butler remarked, "not to desire in such matters 'to do as would be done by.'" That was likely true too. But Butler was also hinting that Ross should vote to convict Johnson.

Ross was jumpy. Fuller arranged for him to propose a deal to his friend Interior Secretary Orville Browning. Browning was an Ohio man and also a friend of the Ewings and Henry Stanbery. If President Johnson would approve the constitutions of South Carolina and Arkansas, and send them over to Congress, which so far he'd procrastinated doing, "it would exert a salutary influence upon the trial now pending," Browning confided to his diary, "and that he [Ross] and others would then vote against impeachment."

The deal was similar to the one Grimes had brought to the President: demonstrate your willingness to work with us, and we'll acquit you. In public, though, Ross continued to say he favored conviction, at least on the eleventh article, while vainly hoping the whole thing would just go away.

The night before that vote in the Senate—as late as eleven-thirty—Ross' former commander, Thomas Ewing, Jr., called on Ross at the Ream home for reasons unknown. As Ewing entered, Daniel Voorhees was leaving. Voorhees was a strong Johnson supporter. So was Vinnie Ream.

Ross repeated to Ewing that he planned to convict the President. "I stated to him in the course of the conversation that in my opinion the whole impeachment proceeding was purely partisan," Thomas Ewing, Jr., later said, "that the conduct of the trial had been flagrantly unfair, and that no conviction would be justifiable on any one of the articles."

Ross showed Ewing the telegram from Daniel Anthony. Ewing said Ross should answer immediately, and the two men walked to the telegraph office. "Gentlemen, I do not recognize your right to demand that I shall vote either for or against conviction," Ross haughtily replied. "I have taken an oath to do impartial justice according to the Constitution and Laws, and trust I shall have the courage and honesty to vote according to the dictates of my judgement [sic], and for the highest good of my country."

Anthony didn't let the matter drop. "Your telegram received," Anthony wrote back. "Your vote is dictated by Tom Ewing not by your oath. Your motives are Indian contracts and greenbacks. Kansas repudiates you as she does all her perjurers and skunks."

"A GREAT DEAL of anxiety is felt here," Ulysses S. Grant dolefully noted the night before the vote. "Impeachment is likely to fail."

THE DAY OF the vote arrived at last, overcast and murky. Edmund Ross ate breakfast at Perry Fuller's house on the corner of 12th and K Streets along with Thomas Hendricks, a strong Democrat and

Johnson supporter. Ross seemed unhappy, and when Fuller asked him what was wrong, he moodily replied, "I would rather have my right arm cut off, than to have this vote taken today."

That same morning, on the day of the vote, at the John Wesley African Methodist Episcopal Zion Church on Connecticut Avenue the Reverend Sampson Jones opened the convocation with a prayer for the removal of Andrew Johnson, the "demented Moses of Tennessee."

The Crowning Struggle

"It was the crowning struggle between
the Rebellion and the people."

—*New-York Tribune*

"President will be acquitted if a vote is had today. Tell my wife." This was the telegram sent by an Ohio lawyer, Charles Woolley, to George Pendleton, the Midwestern greenbacker hoping to be the next Democratic President. "We have beaten the Methodist Episcopal Church north, Hell, Butler, John Logan, [Radical journalist] George Wilkes and impeachment," Woolley merrily announced at eight in the morning on Saturday, May 16.

The folks streaming in and out of hotels, government offices, stores, and barrooms had no idea about the telegram. They had no idea about the vote on impeachment or what the outcome would be—an outcome Woolley seemed to know in advance.

Crowds again formed at the Capitol, where extra police were again on guard, polished clubs again in their white-gloved fists, revolvers in their holsters. Ushers steered the diplomats and visitors into the rotunda, men and women elbowing one another, reporters hovering nearby. "Through the glass doors of the ante-room we could see Senators stalking up and down, anxiously talking to each other," Moorfield Storey wrote to his sister.

Bony and drawn, William Pitt Fessenden walked into the chamber, hands stuffed into his pockets, his mouth slightly twitching. Head lowered, Lyman Trumbull sat at his desk, busily writing or pretending to write and affecting indifference. Peter Van Winkle shuffled papers. Joseph Fowler pulled on black kid gloves as though preparing for a funeral—"probably his own," a reporter whispered. John Henderson chatted with Edmund Ross, who for some reason was tearing paper into small pieces and tossing them onto the floor.

The chief justice strode to his post at the head of the chamber. Looking smallish in his frock coat, Ross returned to his seat, and Republican Senator Henry Wilson, who'd seen General Sickles chatting with Ross, walked over to Sickles, who whispered something to Wilson. The color drained from Wilson's face, noted the spectators in the gallery who'd been watching the little drama. "Mr. Ross is gone," they whispered.

Chief Justice Chase pounded the gavel. Oregon Senator George

House impeachment managers, seated, from left: Benjamin F. Butler, Thaddeus Stevens, Thomas Williams, John A. Bingham. Standing, from left: James F. Wilson, George S. Boutwell, John A. Logan. Photograph by Mathew Brady, 1868.

Williams proposed that the chief justice read the eleventh article of impeachment first. This was the catchall article that pushed beyond the technicalities of the Tenure of Office Act to Johnson's disregard of Congress, his denial of its authority, and his attempt to prevent its laws from being executed. It was the article assumed most likely to produce a guilty verdict. Fessenden immediately objected since James Grimes had not yet arrived. Reverdy Johnson said Grimes was in the building, and as if on cue, Grimes tottered into the chamber. His doctor had advised him to leave Washington but here he was, bolstered by two friends and leaning to one side, his features a mask of pain. He was eased into a large chair near the door.

The motion to hear and then vote on the eleventh article of impeachment passed. Benjamin Wade voted for the first time, even though the outcome directly concerned him. In a matter of minutes, he might move closer to the presidency.

Few people were completely sure how Willey, Fowler, or Ross would vote on the eleventh article. Ross went on tearing paper into little bits.

"Ross has been bought, so has Fowler," said a fellow claiming insider information. "Talk about their consciences? The idea is preposterous."

Rising from his seat, Chief Justice Chase said that he'd call out the name of each senator in alphabetical order and warned the galleries that persons making any disturbance whatsoever would be promptly evicted. He wanted no more outbursts like the one that occurred after Bingham's closing argument.

The clerk began to read the eleventh article out loud. No one was listening. Henderson walked over to Ross to confer one last time. The air was heavy. "The grass would be green, and the corn would grow, and men would be happy or miserable, whether Andrew Johnson should be acquitted or condemned," said a reporter. And yet something deeply significant hung in the balance.

"I felt the importance of this event to humanity," he added. "It was the crowning struggle between the Rebellion and the people."

"Mr. Senator Anthony, how say you?" Chief Justice Chase called on the Rhode Island senator. "Is the respondent, Andrew Johnson, President of the United States, guilty or not guilty of a high misdemeanor, as charged in this article?"

Henry Anthony jumped to his feet. His face was flushed. "Guilty," he said. The crowd murmured softly.

Senator Bayard? "Not guilty."

Senator Buckalew? "Not guilty." No sound of surprise from fellow Democrats.

Before the chief justice called out Simon Cameron's name, Cameron jumped up. "Guilty." Senators Cattell, Chandler, Cole, Conkling, Conness, Corbett, and Cragin also voted to convict. Davis, Dixon, and Doolittle voted to acquit. Still no surprises.

William Pitt Fessenden heard his name. He unfolded himself. "Not guilty," he declared, sounding defiant.

Joseph Fowler was next. His face the color of skimmed milk, the senator from Tennessee half rose from his seat and mumbled. "We do not hear the answer," Charles Sumner shouted out. Did Fowler say "guilty"?

"The Chair did not hear the Senator's answer," Chief Justice Chase repeated. Fowler was unsteady. "Not guilty," he gasped, and dropped back into his chair, sapped of strength.

Journalist Mary Clemmer Ames was contemptuous. What a hypocrite, she said. Not long ago, Fowler had furiously declared, "if we refuse to impeach Andrew Johnson from office the blood of loyal men slain in the South will rest upon our souls."

New Jersey's Frederick Frelinghuysen pronounced the President "guilty," and when his turn came, James Grimes awkwardly tried to stand. The chief justice said he might remain in his chair. "Not guilty."

"Not guilty," Senator Henderson voted after he heard his name. The Radicals had lost him after all.

The voting continued, with no more surprises, until Chief Justice Chase read out the name of Edmund Ross. Ross had promised to vote for conviction on the eleventh article, and so it still seemed, at this the eleventh hour, he would.

"Mr. Senator Ross, how say you: guilty or not guilty?"

Ross swept the tiny flakes of torn paper from his lap.

White-faced, he answered. "Not guilty."

The galley sighed in unison. The policemen did not stir. "It's all up," said a number of spectators. "He promised only last night to vote for the eleventh article," said others in disbelief. Hadn't Horace Walpole declared that every man has his price, Mary Clemmer Ames wondered.

The portly Van Winkle sealed the already sealed case with his "not guilty." President Andrew Johnson was acquitted on the eleventh impeachment article. Sure, the Senate had still to vote on the other ten articles, but the die was cast.

THE GALLERIES QUICKLY emptied. In a sweat, harried telegraph operators clacked out dispatches, as many as six wires within a couple of hours to just one newspaper:

On the eleventh article of impeachment:

For acquittal, 19.

For conviction, 35.

"Messrs. Fowler, Fessenden, Graves, Henderson, Van Winkle, Trumbull, and Ross voting not guilty." Just enough: seven Republicans, recusant Republicans as they were called. It was said the President's friends had another vote or even two in reserve, should they have needed them.

AT ONE-THIRTY IN the afternoon, Charles Woolley sent another telegram, this time directly to his wife. "Virtue has triumphed over vice," he exulted. "Our children will have a country when we are gone. Thank God."

"THE VALLEY OF the Shadow is passed safely," the *New York World* reporter Jerome Stillson wrote to Democrat kingmaker Samuel Barlow. "Butler, Greeley & their cohorts are ruined and what is of more consequence than all else beside, the country is spared the disgrace & the danger of a bad precedent which might have been followed by equally bad & unscrupulous men on our side, at another time, and in the end we should have become another Mexico."

COLONEL WILLIAM CROOK, President Johnson's bodyguard, had been seated in the galleries, and as soon as he heard Van Winkle declare "not guilty" on the eleventh article, he jumped to his feet, sprinted down the Capitol steps, and raced all the way down Pennsylvania Avenue to the White House. Johnson was in the library eating his lunch with Gideon Welles and two other men when Crook burst through the door. "Mr. President," Colonel Crook cried with joy, "you are acquitted." The President's eyes swelled with tears. Embarrassed, Crook looked away but Johnson quickly recovered himself and ordered whiskey up from the cellar for a toast. The men raised their glasses.

Colonel Crook then ran upstairs to tell Mrs. Johnson, who shakily rose from the rocking chair where she sat sewing. "I knew he would be acquitted," she declared. "I knew it."

MEN AND WOMEN spilled out of the Capitol, walking every which way, gesticulating and arguing or hanging their heads in shock. Pennsylvania Avenue was mobbed, and near the White House people paced up and down, hoping that Andy Johnson might show his face or wave a hand from the balcony. They were disappointed.

Edmund Ross rushed to the White House. "There goes the rascal to get his pay," Representative James Blaine was said to mutter.

Henry Stanbery and Thomas Nelson sped to the White House in a carriage. "Well, thank God, Mr. President, you are again free," Nelson exclaimed.

William Seward had been in his office, stretched out on his sofa, smoking and reading Jean-Jacques Rousseau. An assistant entered, nervously asking if there'd been any news about the eleventh article. Seward smiled and said conviction had failed by a single vote and then, recalled the assistant, "went on reading, as if the country had not just passed through a crisis of tremendous importance."

Assuming that the failure of the eleventh article spelled the collapse of impeachment, well-wishers were surging into the White House reception rooms. Hugh McCulloch congratulated the President, and Gideon Welles, without removing his black slouch hat, shook hands all around. Several congressmen came to pay their respects, and a few women, like the writer Harriet Prescott Spofford, joined them. The President talked amiably to a reporter. "I do not know that I am altogether out of the woods," he observed. "It strikes me, however, that their strongest blade has been put forward." Victory did not belong to him alone, he diplomatically added. The Constitution had triumphed.

The night of the vote, at least two dozen men thronged the White House, among them General Hancock and General Lorenzo Thomas. Serenaded by the Georgetown College band, they celebrated until after midnight, and President Johnson happily attended Secretary Seward's gala reception in his home near Lafayette Square where the lights were twinkling until morning.

"THE COUNTRY IS going to the devil," Thaddeus Stevens groaned right after the vote on the eleventh article.

Oregon Senator George Williams then called for a ten-day adjournment before the Senate voted on the other ten impeachment articles. Henderson moved to postpone until July 1, and Senator Ross, who continued to dream that the whole thing might evaporate if pushed far enough into the future, suggested that the final vote be put off until September. But it was scheduled for May 26, ten days away and just after the Republican national convention in Chicago. Radicals hoped that by then the rebellious senators among them would have again changed their minds and this time vote to convict

Andrew Johnson. If not, at least there would be the election of a new President, a different President and not an accidental one. For Republicans were pretty sure that General Ulysses S. Grant, heroically astride one of his fast horses, would be galloping straight into the White House.

The Cease of Majesty

The cease of majesty
Dies not alone; but, like a gulf, doth draw
What's near it with it. . . .

—*Hamlet*, III, 3

The country was far from the nation it hoped to become. Earnest men tossed around words like "justice" and "equality" and "suffrage" although women demanding the right to vote did not have the support of most of them, and Native Americans and Chinese went unmentioned in discussions about citizenship and political rights. "Anglo-Saxon justice cannot go quite to that length," Georges Clemenceau, still reporting on America for the Paris *Temps*, caustically observed. "It has difficulty enough in extending as far as the negro." Reconstruction remained undone.

Having returned to its legislative function, the Senate discussed whether to admit Arkansas back into the Union, now that it had fulfilled all the requirements: Arkansas would supply more Republicans to Congress, and that was important. Reconstruction had to be completed.

But much as he too wanted to admit Arkansas into the Union, Charles Sumner believed the Senate should conduct no business with the President until the impeachment trial had officially ended. And despite the vote earlier that day on the eleventh article, Sumner said it was not over. Ten articles of impeachment remained. Sumner had made this point before, but now, as if in tacit acknowledgment of what was to come, he added that even if the President were to be acquitted, Andrew Johnson would forever be a "blasted public functionary."

Sumner also noted with disdain that a number of senators continued to hobnob with the President and ask for perks and favors. Insulted and a bit thin-skinned, John Henderson yelled out that no one had a right to judge his conduct or that of his associates, especially since he despised the political course of Andrew Johnson as much as Sumner did. He'd voted against impeachment, he said, "according to the law and the evidence." Unruffled, even amused, Sumner politely reassured Henderson that he hadn't been referring to him or any one person, but not able to stop himself, he impishly added that while listening to the honorable senator, he couldn't help thinking of an old saying: "Who so excuses himself, accuses himself."

"HOW DOES IT happen that just enough & no more republican Senators are convinced of the president's innocence," Ben Butler wanted to know. "I think we shall be able to show where some of these men got their consciences and how much they are worth."

"The Democrats only smile when bribery is mentioned," Butler was told, "and make no defense of Ross, Van Winkle, Fowler, Henderson, & Trumbull." Men and women of all classes assumed "Ross & some others were bought up." There must have been payoffs, bribes, and bullying. Some of the allegations warranted a serious look, John Bingham said, and citing probable cause, he asked the House to appoint a subcommittee to investigate. John Chanler, the wealthy New York Democrat who'd called the reconstruction laws wicked and revolutionary, objected, saying the House had no power to put a senator on trial. Bingham explained that no one was talking about the trial of a U.S. senator. But since the Constitution had vested the House with the legal and proper impeachment of a President, the House could and should find out whether corruption had influenced the voting. Besides, Charles Eldridge, Democrat from Wisconsin, had already proposed an investigation into the Missouri delegation's apparent attempt to strong-arm Henderson.

Although the House did vote to authorize a committee to investigate corruption, composed of the impeachment managers, everyone knew it would be difficult, if not impossible, to find hard evidence. Sleaziness is hard to nail down.

EDMUND ROSS RECEIVED another telegram. "Probably the rope with which Judas hanged himself is lost, but the pistol with which Jim Lane shot himself is at your service."

IN CHARLESTON, SOUTH Carolina, at Courthouse Square, black men and women gathered to hear speeches denouncing the President's acquittal on the eleventh article, and in Memphis, about five hundred black men and women assembled at Greenlaw's Opera House and passed resolutions denouncing the vote.

WILLIAM PITT FESSENDEN briskly justified himself. "The people have not heard the evidence as we have heard it," he said. "They have not taken an oath to 'do impartial justice according to the Constitution and the laws.' I have taken that oath."

Sumner would have none of it. "The apologists are prone to remind the Senate that they are acting under the obligation of an oath," he scoffed. "It is a mistake to suppose that the Senate only has heard the evidence. *The people have heard it also, day by day, as it was delivered, and have carefully considered the case on its merits, properly dismissing all apologetic subtleties. It will be for them to review what has been done.*"

Privately, Sumner wrote Fessenden off as a sneak. "Had he

openly joined the enemy several years ago," Sumner said, "it would have been better for us."

"FOR MORE THAN two years he has set your laws at defiance; and when Congress, by a special enactment, strove to constrain him, he broke forth in rebellion against this constitutional authority," Charles Sumner condemned Andrew Johnson and justified his vote. "Perhaps you ask still for something more. Is it a long catalogue of crime, where violence and corruption alternate, while loyal men are sacrificed and the rebellion is lifted to its feet? That also is here."

GEORGE ALFRED TOWNSEND, correspondent for the *Chicago Tribune*, succinctly summarized why impeachment was failing. "1. Bad articles. 2. Lame Managers. 3. Doubtful consequences."

Had the managers mangled their case? Should they have emphasized the larger questions of usurpation, power, and responsibility—and the consequences that might follow Johnson's acquittal? After all, hadn't Johnson been guilty of bartering the peace and turning the country away from the values it presumably cherished and fought for?

"IF TWO AND two were four last February, in the mind of a Senator, we ask that they shall make four now," said old-time abolitionist Thomas Wentworth Higginson. To the Radicals, the acquittal of Andrew Johnson was utter folly and worse. Senators Fessenden of Maine, Trumbull of Illinois, Henderson of Missouri, and Grimes of Iowa—all of them, it was said, had "died of weakness, meanness, betrayal of their county, and violation of their oaths." They had been firm on the Tenure of Office Act and the firing of Stanton when it was easy to be firm.

Maybe a verdict of guilty would have let us think that Trumbull was intelligent, Fessenden was pure, and that Congress was immune to bribery or jobbing, Wendell Phillips said. But you just can't trust a politician. They're corruptible by nature. Phillips was not discouraged, and he would not disappear. The impeachment verdict means we must do more, he said, try harder, and finally carve with a sharp blade an amendment into the Constitution that guarantees citizenship for the black population of this country, guarantees the right to the ballot, to education, to land, and to equality, unassailable and tangible.

Without such an amendment, he concluded, the aristocratic rebel power will ride roughshod over black men and black women all over again—and in just ten years. If not sooner.

"IMPEACHMENT IS DEAD," *The Daily Memphis Avalanche* exclaimed with obvious joy. "Johnson is virtually acquitted. Radicalism has gone to——, and the country is safe." *The Baltimore Sun* reported that Johnson's acquittal on the eleventh impeachment article had been received nationwide "with cordial approbation by reflecting men of all parties. Especially is this the case among business men—mercantile, mechanical and others—who are anxious to see the country quieted and trade revived."

Conservative Republicans shooed away the claim that Chief Justice Chase had destroyed impeachment—or that Fessenden's pique, Grimes' animosity, and Trumbull's personal ambition had killed it; or that Wade's greenback radicalism had scuttled it; or that the duplicity of Fowler and Ross had ruined it; or that there had been bribery or fraud. Conservatives believed justice had prevailed. The rectitude of Fessenden, Grimes, and Trumbull had prevailed, ending a "side-splitting farce," as Republican Edwin Godkin wrote in *The Nation*.

Many conservative—and moderate—Republicans thought the impeachment trial should now pack up its tent and go home. "We are beaten and must take it quietly," Horace Greeley instructed

John Russell Young. If the issue had been as simple as Johnson's perversity, or even his incompetence, he should doubtless be convicted, but the impeachment of a President, a *President*, was no remedy for the underlying issue—although John Bigelow defined that issue somewhat oddly: that the Republicans' stupid choice of an incompetent man to run alongside Lincoln had caused all the problems. But since Johnson had only several months more in office, Bigelow then reasoned, Johnson could do nothing more than bring more shame to his already dishonored self.

Remove Johnson at your peril, Lyman Trumbull had argued. You'll make him a martyr and, even worse, from Trumbull's point of view, you'll so weaken the executive branch of government that the President of the United States will be nothing but a figurehead. And these Republicans also believed they were more likely to win the next presidential election if they showed themselves capable of uniting. No more internal bickering. "Democrats have voted together on every interlocutory question," George Templeton Strong warned, "and on the final decision, as a strictly partisan corps."

Trumbull, Fessenden, and Grimes said they supported Ulysses S. Grant, and that they'd differed with fellow Republicans on impeachment simply on the matter of Johnson's provable guilt. The prosecution had not made its case about Andrew Johnson. "His speeches and the general course of his administration have been as distasteful to me as to any one, and I should consider it the great calamity of the age if the disloyal element, so often encouraged by his measures, should gain political ascendency," Trumbull explained. "If the question was, is Andrew Johnson a fit person for President? I should answer, no; but it is not a party question, nor upon Andrew Johnson's deeds and acts, except so far as they are made to appear in the record, that I am to decide."

Wendell Phillips said he completely understood what men like Trumbull meant. "Putting aside such causes of the Senate's action as women, whiskey, cowardice, greenbacks, Free Masonry, Negrohate, offices for one's sixteen pine-tree cousins, a diseased Chief Justice, spite, dyspepsia and noodleism," Phillips scathingly noted,

"—it is evident, on the face of things, that while a very large majority of the people, and specially of the Republican party, wished its success, there was a very strong doubt among the party *leaders* whether such success would help the party."

A conviction would not help the Republican party—precisely because it would elevate Radical Senator Benjamin Wade.

Let Us Have Peace

Ulysses S. Grant may have detested Johnson, and he may have approved of impeachment, but Republicans working hard to make him the next President regarded impeachment as a radical conspiracy aimed at stopping the Grant juggernaut. Johnson's conviction would elevate Benjamin Wade, and Ben Wade as interim President could distribute patronage to Radical Republicans, cause inflation by circulating greenbacks, even promote legislation allowing black men—and maybe all women—to vote: incalculable damage that threatened to divide and possibly destroy the party.

"I think the failure of the impeachment is a good thing," John Hay declared with relief. "The Republicans lose nothing," he added. "The party organization seems much better and stronger since than before. . . . Weed and Raymond have wheeled into line for Grant, and all the stragglers are coming in."

The nomination of Grant the Silent as a full-throated Republican for President would conveniently and finally take the air out of the impeachment balloon, Hay predicted, a balloon that only those inconvenient Radicals continued to fly.

AFTER SATURDAY'S VOTE on the eleventh article of impeachment, several senators rushed to the Chicago convention to place Ulysses S. Grant securely on the ticket. On May 20, the one-legged General Daniel Sickles, with pride and poise, led a procession of Republicans into the newly built, five-story Crosby Opera House, and General Carl Schurz, now senator-elect from Missouri, temporarily chaired the convention. Eight thousand delegates had arrived, and on the convention's second day, General John Logan, fresh from the managers' table at the impeachment trial, nominated General Grant for the presidency.

A red, white, and blue pigeon flapped its wings, bursting out of the top gallery, and on the stage, as the curtain rose, Thomas Nast's gigantic painting of General Grant and the Goddess of Liberty starkly celebrated the new birth of freedom. Grant was nominated on the first ballot by all delegates present, including James J. Harris and P.B.S. Pinchback, the first black delegates ever to attend a presidential convention. Men tossed their hats into the air, and the band played "Hail to the Chief."

Johnson's acquittal on the eleventh impeachment article had effectively wrecked Benjamin Wade's chance to snag the vice-presidential nomination, but just to make sure, circulars suggested Wade's age essentially disqualified him—he was sixty-nine. And though Maine's Hannibal Hamlin, whom Lincoln had dropped from his ticket in 1864 in favor of Johnson, suddenly looked good, Smiler Schuyler Colfax, the affable man serving his third term as speaker of the House, became Grant's running mate on the fifth ballot. Smiler Schuyler had offended far fewer people than had Wade. Republicans collectively exhaled. The ticket could mean more to the country than any vote on impeachment, and Democrats could have Andrew Johnson to themselves.

As for the Republican platform, it was broad and it was bland. It contained promises to reduce taxes, to eliminate federal corruption, to pay the national debt but sidestepped the suffrage question. Voting rights of black men were to be sustained in the South by virtue of the Reconstruction Acts. Whether black men could vote in the North would be left to the individual states. Wendell Phillips commented that if Johnson had been convicted on the eleventh article of impeachment, maybe the Republican platform would have pledged itself to *something* rather than to empty *nothings.*

The platform also condemned Andrew Johnson. Reminding Republicans that Johnson had been impeached by the House of Representatives for high crimes and misdemeanors, it noted that thirty-five Republican senators had quite properly voted to convict him. But neither Johnson's conviction nor his acquittal should ultimately matter if the trial had been conducted fairly, which it had. It was therefore irrelevant how any particular senator voted. Why waste ammunition on one another when there was so much at stake in the coming election?

"We make platforms to get men into the party—not to drive them out," Indiana Governor Henry S. Lane cried. That's what John Greenleaf Whittier thought as well. The Quaker poet who had been pelted with stones and mud for his abolitionism, whose newspaper office had once been sacked and burned while a crowd yelled "hang Whittier," was singing a different tune. "Impeachment, I see, has failed," Whittier told Henry Raymond. "Well, it is unfortunate; but let us not lament over it, nor quarrel about it, more than we can help. Our business now is to elect Grant, & in his election impeachment is not an issue at all; and whoever goes for the Republican candidate, must be recognized as a Republican, whatever his views may have been."

BENJAMIN WADE TOOK defeat with grace and immediately congratulated Schuyler Colfax. Andrew Johnson, hearing of Grant's nomination, said he could easily beat Grant in November if only the Democrats would nominate him. But the Democrats didn't want anything to do with him. "The President is surrounded by a lot of fools, who, it is said, have persuaded him that he has some chance of securing the nomination," the journalist Jerome Stillson observed with derision. The Democratic lobbyist Sam Ward remarked, with some surprise, "I should think he had had enough of the White House pig sty!"

"I THINK THERE was buying and selling enough to save Johnson,—that is to acquit him on the impeachment," Jeremiah Black said. That's what the managers believed. They'd begun their corruption inquiry right away, interviewing such witnesses as Perry Fuller, Thomas Ewing, Jr., and the lawyer Charles Woolley. Woolley, about forty years old, stout, and silent, refused to explain what he had done with $10,000 given him by a deputy collector of internal revenue in New York named Sheridan Shook. Woolley had suspiciously withdrawn the money in $1,000 bills but refused to answer any question unrelated to impeachment.

All the witnesses blathered, evaded the subject, or feigned complete ignorance. Sheridan Shook too answered very few questions, or he replied nonsensically. For instance, midway through Shook's initial testimony, Ben Butler asked him, "Did you state in Mr. Woolley's rooms, in the presence of four persons, that if the Committee called you as a witness they would find you the greatest know-nothing they ever saw?"

A. I have no recollection of making any such statement as that.

Q. Did you, or did you not?

A. No, sir. If I did I must have been drunk or crazy, one or the other.

Then there was the wheeling and dealing around Chief Justice Chase. Perry Fuller had evidently told a special agent in the Kansas Post Office Department named James Legate that if impeachment failed, Salmon Chase would lead a third party to the White House, and money raised for Chase's presidential bid was really a fund for

THE SMELLING COMMITTEE.

The cartoon satirizes the prosecuting managers of the impeachment trial who tried to learn whether bribery or other chicanery influenced the vote. Pictured from left to right are John A. Logan, George S. Boutwell, Thomas Williams, Benjamin F. Butler, Thaddeus Stevens, and John A. Bingham. At the far right is Andrew Johnson, who says, "It's no use Gentlemen. Your old nag is dead and you can't ride it any more; my Woolley friend finished him."

the President's acquittal. A Chase "circle" was set up. "I think 'circle' was the word he used; it may have been 'ring,'" Legate testified.

Soon the euphemisms faded away, most witnesses allowing that they had heard talk of purchasing votes, though they couldn't recall whom they heard it from or what precisely might have been said.

"People here are afraid to write letters, and I must be a little cautious at present," Jerome Stillson complained to Samuel Barlow. "Spies are, *really*, everywhere."

But the prosecutorial zeal was backfiring. With the committee high-handedly seizing telegrams, even if by subpoena, and Ben Butler sniffing into the bank accounts of private citizens who happened to have withdrawn large sums, Democrats denounced the whole thing as a "smelling" committee. Republicans too were dubious. "Butler has ruined the cause: all his partisans are disgusted with him," Stillson observed with satisfaction.

Still, the managers were pretty sure that they were on the right track, although men in the know, like Thomas Ewing, Jr., assumed they'd never get anywhere. "The managers are pushing the investigation & profess to believe that Woolley's $20,000 went into Ross's pocket," Ewing boasted. "Logan says 'only one or two links are wanting.' That is, they can't tell who got it from Woolley or who paid it to Ross!"

Thurlow Weed shed some light, although he said a great deal more by what he didn't say. Tall, broad-shouldered, and cunning, Weed was a former New York assemblyman and powerful newspaper publisher who, at seventy years old, was still a crack political boss whose advice, influence, and friendship had been essential to William Seward—and to Andrew Johnson. Most recently, though, Weed too considered Johnson's sacking Stanton to be stupid. "I followed the President into the Ditch," Weed had complained. He also despised the whole impeachment business and harnessed the full weight of his paper, the *New-York Commercial Advertiser*, to stop it.

He told the committee that there had indeed been a group of men determined to acquit the President—a group that included Henry Smythe, the collector of customs in New York, an oily character accused of corruption in the Customs House and nearly thrown out of office; Weed's friend Sheridan Shook; former Congressman Samuel "Sunset" Cox; and Julia Ward Howe's jovial brother Sam Ward, the epicurean lobbyist with a taste for poetry, champagne, and backroom politics.

Everyone accused everyone.

What role had William Seward played? "Mr. Seward also looked at matters in a businesslike way," a friend acknowledged. It seemed that Seward, along with Postmaster Randall, had been in touch with Cornelius Wendell to arrange bribes. Wendell, a Washington printer who'd fattened his bank account by overcharging the government, told the committee he hadn't wanted any part of this plan and in turn pointed a finger at Seward's aide Erastus Webster, who'd apparently put together a purse of $165,000 to pay for acquittal votes. Most of the money had been raised by Postmaster Randall, Secretary McCulloch, and Henry Smythe at the Custom House. The conspirators used middlemen like Perry Fuller and James Legate, though it was also said that Fuller and Legate had pocketed most of the cash.

And then there was the matter of incriminating telegrams. Several hours before the vote on May 16, Woolley had telegraphed George Pendleton, "Andy all right."

The day before the final vote was taken, Ben Butler delivered a preliminary report of the committee's findings, and it did seem that the committee had amassed a great deal of circumstantial evidence suggesting that some senators had been bribed.

There was a great deal of smoke, in other words, but no fire.

WHEN CHARLES WOOLLEY refused to recognize the authority of the committee and did not appear, Butler recommended that the House arrest him for contempt and hold him in custody until he agreed to testify. Authorizing Woolley's arrest, the House placed him in the basement studio of the Capitol, the one occupied by Vinnie Ream, who was told she had to vacate right away.

A NUMBER OF Republicans believed the committee's findings might justify censure, a change of vote, or perhaps even a "tainted" verdict, if the recusant senators continued to vote against impeachment. Several of them silently entered the House, along with the President's son-in-law David Patterson, when Butler read the committee's report. Trumbull seated himself with the Democrats, as did Edmund Ross.

AND WHAT OF the vehement Edwin Stanton, whose firing had set all this in motion, the man Walt Whitman had called "wonderfully patriotic, courageous, far-seeing" and "the best sort of man"? What of Stanton and his future? He had already been warned about the verdict. "Mr. Evarts has been at my house this day," his friend Edwards Pierrepont confided the day before the vote was scheduled. "He assures me that he knows and that the President will surely be acquitted."

Stanton said he'd stay in the War Department until the other ten impeachment articles had been voted upon, and he waited alone there for the verdict on May 16, the windows in his office open to the warm spring air. The army telegraph had delivered the vote on the eleventh article; it was what he had expected, having already learned at least of the defection of Grimes, Trumbull, and Fessenden. He did not speak to reporters, and he locked the door to his office.

The nomination of Grant and Colfax had pleased him. He'd been standing by the telegraph in the War Department when the news arrived. Stanton rushed to Grant's office. "General," he said, "I have come to tell you that you have been nominated by the Republican party for President of the United States."

Grant said nothing beyond a simple thank-you, asked about the platform, and handed out a few cigars. A few days later, Grant released a formal acceptance letter that ended with the plea, soon to become a mantra, "Let us have peace."

IN NEW ORLEANS, a musical review called *The Impeachment Trial* became a local favorite.

THERE WAS TALK of another impeachment article, to be written by Thaddeus Stevens, health permitting, but Stevens was growing more feeble every day. And now with the presidential campaign of the enormously popular Grant under way, there was also talk of shutting down the trial as quickly and quietly as possible. No one really expected the seven recusants to change their votes. But if *this* impeachment failed, given all the favorable circumstances, all the breaches of law, all the usurpation, the staunchest Radicals felt that no American President would ever be successfully impeached and convicted, and there would alas be no limit to a President's power.

For think what Andrew Johnson had done: "From the date of his infamous speech of 22nd of February, down to the present time, he has openly and covertly worked toward the realization of an avowed object, with an earnestness and consistency worthy of a great cause," declared John Forney. "That cause, as he presents it, is the restoration of the late rebel States to their places in the Union as co-equal members thereof, *under their old constitutions and with their old bodies politic*. He has steadily pursued this policy regardless of the good of the country; regardless of the law of the land; reckless of his own reputation; through good report and through evil report; and justifying the means by the end, he has introduced the most fearful system of corruption and demoralization into any government known in modern history."

It wasn't just the rings, the corruption, and the abuse of power, Forney was insisting; Johnson had been steadily and scrupulously restoring a system of slavery, of inequality and indignity by other means. "Before any Senator who was elected as a Republican, who voted for the reconstruction laws, the civil rights bill, or the tenure-of-office bill, who believes in the doctrine of human rights against class privilege, who reveres the memory of the soldiers that fell; for the Union, who believes in progressive civilization and the dignity of labor," Forney was begging, "before any such Senator votes for Andrew Johnson's acquittal, we implore him to look ahead."

IT WAS SAID the trial would live as long as history itself, that it was the wonder of the world. Yet it soon disappeared into history's thick annals, and if it was a wonder of the world, it was an ephemeral one, a spectacle that gathered only the dust of time and, later, obloquy. If the public thought the trial would be showy, shiny, and prosecuted with speed, they were wrong. The showiest person was the equivocal Ben Butler, an opportunist, an operator, a tireless and dogged prosecutor hated by many but after all considered, as Benjamin Perley Poore said, "the life, soul, body, boots and breeches of impeachment."

And trials are slow, ponderous, and in this case, far too serious for speed. Despite partisan bickering, name-calling, and ugliness, the issues were serious and worthy of a serious debate. What constituted an impeachable offense? Had the trial been a judicial hearing or a political event? And what would the results, either of acquittal or conviction, come to mean? For the issues were, many also felt, a matter of life and death, not just of human beings but of the nation itself, for the country had to ask why the recent war had been fought, if the rebels had won after all, and what the consequences to one nation, presumably indivisible, were likely to be.

ONCE AGAIN MEN and women in bright colors streamed into the Capitol. British novelist Anthony Trollope deposited himself in a front-row seat, and Kate Chase Sprague, dressed in a violet dress with a springlike sheen, peered down at her presidential father. They had come to witness the very last act.

Several senators wanted to adjourn until the end of June to give the investigating committee time to collect more evidence about possible corruption. The motion was defeated. No one—not the spectators nor the senators nor most of the public—believed that in the end the allegations could be proved.

So the fifty-four U.S. senators sitting in the court for the impeachment trial of Andrew Johnson, on this day, May 26, 1868, took up the second impeachment article and then the third. The second article accused Johnson of intending to violate the Constitution and the Tenure of Office Act by issuing and delivering to General Lorenzo Thomas a letter of authority as interim secretary of war on February 21, 1868. The third article accused Johnson of violating the Constitution by appointing General Thomas as interim war secretary on the same date.

The roll was called. The result was the same as it had been ten days earlier: thirty-five senators voted "guilty," and nineteen men voted to acquit. Ross flushed pink.

It was a little before two o'clock in the afternoon. The President had been acquitted of high crimes and misdemeanors on both articles.

The Senate, sitting as a court of impeachment, adjourned sine die, without setting a future date to reconvene.

It was over.

Part Four

DENOUEMENT

The United States Capitol, with the Washington monument in the background,
at the time of Ulysses S. Grant's inauguration, 1869.

Human Rights

"The day is coming when the black man will vote,
and he will be the balance of power."

—HENRY JEROME BROWN

At midnight on August 11, eleven weeks after the acquittal of Andrew Johnson, the seventy-six-year-old Thaddeus Stevens quietly died. By his side were his companion Lydia Smith, his nephews, and two sisters of charity, Loretta O'Reilly and Genevieve Ewers. Earlier that same day, of all the many people knocking at his door, only Reverend Mr. Hall and the Reverend Mr. Reed, two black clergymen, had been admitted. Stevens whispered thank you as he pressed each of the ministers' hands.

For months, the old lion, though ailing, had kept going almost by sheer force of will, he so fervently wanted to see the impeachment trial to conclusion. And while disappointed but not surprised by the outcome, he submitted new impeachment resolutions to Congress that, as he expected, went nowhere. "My sands are nearly run, and I can only see with the eye of faith," he acknowledged while gesturing toward Speaker Colfax, now the Republican nominee for Vice President. "But you, sir, are promised length of days and a brilliant career. If you and your compeers can fling away ambition and realize that every human being, however lowly born or degraded by fortune, is your equal, that every inalienable right which belongs to you belongs also to him, truth and righteousness will spread over the land."

Earlier, a reporter had walked over to his house on South B Street, fronted by linden trees, where Stevens lived with Lydia Smith. Stevens was reclining on his bed, vest and jacket off, in a low-roofed room decorated only with a photograph of Lincoln and a bust of Stevens sculpted by Vinnie Ream. Stevens was talkative. "I am very sick indeed," he ruefully told the reporter, but with characteristic generosity added, "come to me any time [sic] whenever you are in difficulty or doubt, and I will do all I can for you."

He still showed up for work. "They'll miss me at the Council board, and before the game is up, they'll own that I was not very far wrong," he wryly told journalist John Forney. Many associates did say just that—Stevens wasn't far wrong. "No single mind has done more to shape this era," Wendell Phillips declared, and when Stevens died, Georges Clemenceau exclaimed that "the nation has lost in him a great citizen." Enemies like Fernando Wood of New York, the notorious anti-war Democrat, saluted Old Thad. "That he has left an impress on the page of our history none can dispute," Wood conceded. "That he was a thoroughly honest, as well as a truly great man, all will admit."

He was also feared. "The death of Thaddeus Stevens is an emancipation for the Republican Party," James Blaine reportedly exulted. And in the future, Stevens would frequently be remembered as autocratic, relentless, almost demonic. "Of course he was hated," the writer known as Grace Greenwood said, "as every great, wholesome, courageous nature is hated—as every proud, honest, absolute character is hated—by the weak, the cowardly, and the false."

A company of black Zouaves from Massachusetts requested the privilege of standing watch over Stevens' body when it lay in state under the great dome in the Capitol rotunda. And that's where Thad Stevens belonged: he was the essential man of Congress, of the Capitol, of Washington and the nation. When the doors to the east side of the Capitol opened, a crush of citizens approached the rosewood coffin that sat before a life-sized statue of Abraham Lincoln. The Zouaves hoisted the little black children from St. Aloysen's Orphanage so that they could take a last look at Mr. Stevens, and more than 15,000 people, black and white, mechanics and farmers, soldiers, homemakers and clerks and clergy, as well as congressmen, both Republicans and Democrats, friends and foes, passed through that rotunda. The outpouring of sorrow reminded many of the day they wept for Lincoln.

"In time," a reporter mourned, "we shall come to recognize the wisdom of his views."

Congress had recently adjourned, but during the funeral ceremony, the massive head of Senator Charles Sumner, who stood a little to the right of the bier, could be seen from afar, and Senator Trumbull, gold spectacles gleaming, was seated nearby. "In the last few years, in shaping the destinies of our Government, he has had more to do than any one man," the Reverend Dr. Emery described Thaddeus Stevens. The cause that he pleaded most eloquently was the cause of all mankind—"hence there is a vacancy. Who among our peers can fill it?"

After the service, mourners followed the hearse, which was pulled by four white horses and accompanied by 125 men from an organization sponsoring the election of General Grant. At the Baltimore & Ohio Railroad depot, a special train waited to convey Stevens to his home in Lancaster, Pennsylvania, where over 10,000 people, some say 20,000, lined the streets in anticipation of his return. As the train chugged to its destination, bells tolled throughout the nation, pealing loudly.

EDMUND ROSS WENT on the defensive, and vindication was soon the occupation—or preoccupation—of his life. "I have borne in silence, until now, assaults on my character and motives as a member of the court, such as few, if any of my associates have endured," he grumbled the day after the final impeachment vote. Two months later, he again spoke on his own behalf. "I do not deny that it has been my intention to support a portion of the articles of impeachment," he said, somewhat pretentiously, "nor that I have given numbers of those who approached me on that subject to understand that such was my intention." But didn't men change their minds? he wanted to know. Hadn't John Bingham, once an opponent of impeachment, changed his mind?

Ross conveniently overlooked the fact that Bingham's change of mind came after Johnson violated the Tenure of Office Act, not before. That was of no concern to Ross, who claimed he'd been singled out and badmouthed because he was a relatively new and powerless member of Congress, patriotic and honest but pursued by the unscrupulous retailer of smut and scandal—Benjamin Butler—while Ross, in his "humble way," as he put it, had been working hard for Grant's nomination and didn't want to see it spoiled by an interim President.

Ross also conveniently forgot that he'd capitalized on Johnson's acquittal. Less than two weeks after the final vote, Ross proposed that Johnson appoint a friend of his as Southern superintendent of Indian affairs. He said he hated to bother the President since it meant removing one of Johnson's men, but, he deliberately added, "in consequence of my action on the Impeachment, that I feel constrained to ask." After Johnson consented, Ross returned to the President, this time requesting that Johnson support a treaty ensuring that eight million acres belonging to the Osage Indians be sold to the Leavenworth, Lawrence & Galveston Railroad at a pittance of its worth. The President complied. That wasn't enough. Ross requested that the President appoint Perry Fuller as commissioner of the Internal Revenue. Johnson again agreed, and when the Senate rejected the appointment, Johnson named Fuller as interim collector of customs in New Orleans. Even that was not enough. Early in July, Ross requested that Johnson appoint Ross' brother as a special mail agent in Florida. That wasn't enough either. Ross asked Johnson to appoint a friend of his as agent for the Pottawatomie Indians, another as agent for the Kiowa and Comanche Indians, and a third as surveyor general in Kansas. "I am aware that I am asking a good deal of you," Ross again explained, "but I feel constrained to do so by the persistent efforts that are being made for my destruction."

Ross was not the only one demanding or receiving post-impeachment favors. Johnson had attended the wedding of John Henderson and Mary Foote, whose father was then nominated as U.S. commissioner of patents. Johnson named the corrupt customs house collector Henry Smythe minister to Austria, although Smythe had been put under temporary arrest and criminal prosecution. Cornelius Wendell, the printer who'd allegedly arranged an acquittal slush fund, was appointed government director on the Union Pacific Railroad board. And Perry Fuller made Vinnie Ream's father superintendent of warehouses in New Orleans, although within months Fuller was arrested for a scheme to defraud the government of tax revenue. Edmund Ross guaranteed the bond for Fuller's release.

Like many conservatives, Ross defended himself by noisily blasting the Radical Republicans. Impeachment had sprung full-blown from "the malevolence of Stevens, the ambition of Butler, the theories of Boutwell, & the folly of an unthinking crowd of party followers," the lawyer John Codman Ropes reassured William Pitt Fessenden. Ross joined the ranks of those Republicans who considered themselves moderates, not conservatives. Believing themselves merely judicious, they claimed it was "the duty of Congress to make the best of Mr. Johnson." To celebrate their own judiciousness, they planned a public dinner in Boston to toast Fessenden for what they called his courage, his conscience, and his conviction. The invitation list included Massachusetts Governor Alexander H. Bullock and more than seventy other politicians, industrialists, Brahmins, Harvard trustees, and leading men of the area: Charles Francis Adams, Jr., Francis Parkman, jurist Lemuel Shaw, industrialist Amos Lawrence, John Murray Forbes, Richard Henry Dana, Jr., James Russell Lowell, and editor Samuel Bowles: men of probity, prudence, and profound self-regard—an intellectual and often financial elect who regarded blacks and white Southerners with condescension and assumed that they knew best what served the country and their class.

Sumner regarded the Fessenden dinner as a slap in the face. Conservative Republicans certainly wanted to kick Sumner out of the Senate, although several moderates, like Sumner's friend Edward Atkinson, pointlessly assured Sumner that they intended no insult. As it happened, Fessenden declined the dinner invitation, taking the high ground. "I offer no excuse nor apology, and ask no vindication; nor do I consider myself entitled to any special credit for courage or conscientiousness," he replied to the New England elite. He said he paid no heed to petty squabbles with unorthodox men—by which, he meant Charles Sumner. Privately, Fessenden said he regretted Edwin Stanton's firing and didn't much care for Andrew Johnson, but that he'd been absolutely right to vote as he had.

To Republicans like Fessenden, the defeat of impeachment ensured the restoration of a laissez-faire government guided by the invisible hand of the best men—not by women, black people, or anyone regarded as a nut. Or by Andrew Johnson. "I think we have a better chance now than we had any right to expect so soon for reforming the party & freeing it from the burden of the sins of the extremists who have tried to usurp the leadership," Charles Eliot Norton rejoiced. "Butler is sinking himself so low that he will hardly be able to hold his head above the mire into which he plunged with native alacrity. The other original impeachers will share his fate." The impeachment verdict also protected the party, particularly important before a presidential election. As young Republican writer William Dean Howells, whose Radicalism lay in the future, conceded, while it had been "a serio-comic necessity . . . the impeachment of Presidents is hardly an 'issue' to inspire enthusiasm in their election."

In Appleton, Wisconsin, a twenty-gun salute announced President Johnson's acquittal, and an extra round was fired to honor Chief Justice Chase. Keen as ever to occupy the Executive Mansion, Chase was arduously trying to convince Democrats that he'd never really left the fold, repeating that he too loathed military despotism in the form of military governments, or commissions for the trial of civilians in peacetime. Where he differed from Democrats was on the question of slavery, though he claimed that he'd never said that Congress should interfere with slavery in the states where it existed. He did affirm that the Thirteenth Amendment abolishing slavery "requires, in my judgment, the assurance of the right of suffrage to those whom the Constitution has made freemen & citizens."

Making obvious his bid for the nomination by saying he did not seek it—a standard ploy—Chase did set terms on suffrage. For while conservative Republicans skated around it, Chase faced the issue head-on. "I have long been a believer in the justice & wisdom of securing to all citizens [except women] the right of suffrage," Chase explained to *New York World* editor Manton Marble. "It is the best guarantee of the stability of institutions & the prosperity of communities." He could change his party but not his principle. If nominated by Democrats, it was rumored, Chase would insist on putting the right of black men to vote into the Democratic party platform—although he probably knew that would never happen. Still, Chase pointed out that his views were well known to Democrats. Democrats had elected him to the Senate in 1849, and with a party or without one, he would now work as hard as he could to end bitterness and reunite the country, whether in or out of office.

The vagaries of American politics would thus allow Chase, the former Radical, to court Democrats, while Ulysses S. Grant, the former moderate, was the darling of the Radicals, or at least most of them.

Suffrage continued to stick in the craw of the country. "The one great duty before us is the reconstruction of the Southern States upon the basis of equal rights for every race and color," William Dean Howells affirmed. Moderates wanted to keep suffrage a Southern issue, something Republicans could legislate in the former rebel states while leaving the others alone. The Reconstruction

Act of 1867 had demanded that the Southern states hold new constitutional conventions with delegates elected by both black and white men, and it stipulated that their constitutions include the right of black men to vote. The state constitutions of the North, though, were not regulated in this way. They could do what they wanted.

Alabama, Arkansas, Florida, Georgia, Louisiana, and the two Carolinas did fulfill the conditions mandated for readmission to the Union, particularly since a fourth Reconstruction Act, passed on March 11, 1868, over Johnson's veto, required that a simple majority of the votes cast—rather than the registered number of voters—would be necessary to ratify the new state constitutions. This would prevent what had happened in Alabama, where there were 95,000 registered black voters and 75,000 registered white voters. But only a small fraction of the registered white voters actually showed up at the polls, and though there were 70,182 votes in favor of the new state constitution—and only 1,005 against it—the overall number of voters participating in the referendum didn't come anywhere near the requisite majority of those registered.

Charles Sumner and other Radical Republicans had argued that black male suffrage was a constitutional issue, and though many of them agreed in principle, they were uneasy about the coming presidential contest. They didn't want to promise what they couldn't deliver, and mostly they didn't want to alienate the conservative and moderate wings of the party. Blacks would vote Republican anyway, they assumed, and they needed their votes in the South. So the Republican platform wound up distinguishing between suffrage for blacks in the South, which they believed necessary, and suffrage for blacks in the North, which they thought wasn't.

And conservative Republicans decided that they'd simply done enough. Southern blacks were free. The rest of their lives was up to them. In the North, "the man of African descent is as secure as his white neighbor in the possession of the rights to life, liberty and the pursuit of happiness," Harvard professor Sherman Adams Hill claimed. "And, however just may be the prejudice of race, which causes his disfranchisement here and there, he has slight cause to complain, so long as the blessings and privileges of a good government are his." Edwin Godkin, editor of *The Nation* and at the forefront of the coming Liberal Republicans, insisted that "people are more concerned about the kind of government in which the black man is to share than about the precise mode or time in which he is to share it"—as if to say, we're tired of this discussion. Back off; let us have peace.

The issue of suffrage would of course not disappear, neither for blacks nor for women. Yet Frederick Douglass considered black suffrage over women's voting "certainly more urgent, because it is life and death to the long-enslaved people of this country," as he said. "While the Negro is mobbed, beaten, shot, stabbed, hanged, burnt, and is the target of all that is malignant in the North, and all that is murderous in the South, his claims may be preferred by me."

"The epoch turns on the negro," Wendell Phillips declared, still able to stir large audiences. "It is not my fanaticism; it is not my prejudice; it is not a fatal conceit. Justice to him saves the nation, ends the strife, and gives us peace; injustice to him prolongs the war. You can't help it. You may shut yours eyes to it, and say you don't want to hear about it; but the thunders of a thousand cannons will ring it into your ears, and into the ears of your children."

"The day is coming when the black man will vote, and he will be the balance of power," said black leader Henry Jerome Brown at a convention of black Republicans in Baltimore. "He will then stand by well-tried and true friends." But Republican James Doolittle argued that the races were distinct—and blacks inferior. In a fury, Irish-born Republican Senator John Conness of California confronted Doolittle. "He rises here and gives us dissertations on the inequality of men, the impossibility of the negro being the equal of the Caucasian," Conness roared. "The distinction was not made by their Maker. We are not told that there are dividing places in Heaven for classes and castes and colors." Doolittle chalked up

Conness' anger to Johnson's acquittal; Radical Benjamin Wade wouldn't be President, so Conness had lost his pew in Wade's hypothetical cabinet.

But Charles Sumner spoke up, as Sumner always had. *"There can be no State Rights against Human Rights."*

ON FEBRUARY 25, 1869, the House of Representatives did pass legislation that would become the Fifteenth Amendment, guaranteeing that the right to vote not be denied or abridged by any state "on account of race, color, or previous condition of servitude." In the Senate, even Peter Van Winkle voted for it, as did Fessenden and Trumbull. Edmund Ross, James Grimes, and John Henderson were absent, though Henderson had introduced the resolution. Sumner abstained: true to himself, he contended that the amendment didn't go far enough—it did not prevent the states from disqualifying voters on the basis, say, of not owning property; it said nothing about the right of a black man to hold office; it said nothing about how the amendment would be enforced.

WHILE THE COMMITTEE investigating the impeachment conviction subpoenaed witnesses, the House of Representatives was meeting in night sessions that Henry Dawes ridiculed as discussing "one of the most important questions that absorb the public mind in this momentous crisis—none other than whether Vinnie Ream, who is supposed to have unduly influenced Ross, shall longer occupy rooms in the Capitol." She'd had to move out of her studio so it could serve as a prison for Charles Woolley, but conservatives accused Ben Butler of spitefully targeting her.

Butler didn't care. "I am sure we ought all to do what we can to save the country and to be refrained by no false notions of delicacy from doing our duty," he declared. Ignoring the fusillade of abuse hurled against his military service, his success as a criminal lawyer, his character, and even his chubby face, Butler dispatched detectives who for six weeks ransacked telegraph offices, rummaged wastebaskets, and rifled desk drawers looking for proof of bribery while he and members of the committee interviewed witnesses or, in some cases, Butler interrogated them alone. Joseph Fowler called Butler a grand inquisitor feeding on the barroom gossip whispered against senators of integrity like himself.

Because Butler couldn't firmly establish that the seven senators who'd voted for acquittal had been bought—not even Ross or Henderson—Butler himself was blamed for the President's acquittal. He'd bungled the prosecution and then the investigation. He'd focused on Woolley instead of the real culprits, men like Seward or Weed. He'd presumably salted away thirty-six volumes of incriminating telegrams he could use to strong-arm colleagues when he needed something from them in the future. It was also said he'd offered Cornelius Wendell $100,000 for information, but since he didn't want the bribe made public, he'd suppressed evidence. "Bosh!" Butler laughed.

Thaddeus Stevens had noted with regret that anyone could be bought, even the most intelligent and well educated. Wendell Phillips too was convinced that the "money-kings" had paid for Johnson's acquittal. Deciding to launch his own investigation, biographer and journalist James Parton headed to Washington, and by the time he published his results in *The Atlantic Monthly* the next year, Parton had been convinced that "the greatest triumph of the Washington lobby was the Johnson lobby." There was actually more than one lobby, Parton observed, naming them: "The Johnson lobby proper, who wanted to get or keep places and chances under the President; the Chase lobby, who wished to place the President under such obligations that he would drop General Hancock and take up Mr. Chase for the succession; the Pendleton lobby, whose aim was to secure the same advantage for Mr. Pendleton; the whiskey lobby, who wanted another year of impunity; and a 'conservative' lobby, who had a very lively sense of what would happen if Mr. Wade should change his quarters to the White House."

Parton's sources said they knew which senator pocketed exactly how much; which senator had grabbed Indian contracts; and which senator had received railroad shares more valuable than either cash or contracts. These sources knew of nighttime assignations, of customhouses that had raised huge sums and of distillers that had done the same and that, if it had been needed, these two sources had more than a million dollars stashed away. They knew who had lost at cards the night before the final vote, and who changed his vote as a result. The sources went unnamed.

Butler's investigation didn't distress most Democrats, and his failure to find hard proof of bribery amused them. "If he could jump Jim Crow into Tammany he would do it tomorrow," Sam Ward derisively observed, meaning he'd put a black man in Tammany Hall if he could. To them, Butler's apparent fixation on black people would get him nowhere. "Dissolve your committee and drop your investigation which can do no good—" Ward advised— and repay the President for the price of his acquittal ($25,000).

Sam Ward knew more than he let on. "I am proudest of the part I took in defeating the impeachment of Andrew Johnson than of any of my grand and lofty tumbling," Ward would exclaim years later. "I contributed my money & effort & we won & saved the country from being Mexicanized."

THE STORY OF bribery, whatever story there was, remained so incomplete and elusive that William A. Dunning, a Columbia University academic, contacted Manton Marble in 1906, long after Johnson and Seward and Butler and Sam Ward had all died, to see what he could learn.

Dunning was well on his way to becoming the influential scholar whose "Dunning school" of historians asserted that reconstruction had been a tragic failure: the so-called "carpetbaggers"—a derogatory term for Northerners come to teach, invest, or to farm—had invaded the South merely to plunder and then profit from its white misery. Freedmen and -women had been nothing more than inferior beings easily manipulated; and the Ku Klux Klan was a patriotic guild that repaired the dignity of white folk. Andrew Johnson had been maligned and mistreated.

Marble and Dunning generally shared the same bias, except that Marble didn't care much for Andrew Johnson. Regardless, Dunning hoped Marble would deliver the goods about Johnson's acquittal. Marble obliged—up to a point. Drafting a garbled letter that he didn't ultimately send—but that he saved—he admitted that Democratic leaders did in fact foil what he called "the seizure" of the federal government. Marble named the financier August Belmont, head of the Democratic National Committee; Dean Richmond, a railroad powerbroker and Democratic loyalist; the prosperous lawyer Samuel Tilden; and New York's wartime governor Horatio Seymour. (Horatio Seymour and Samuel Tilden would be the Democratic nominees for President in 1868 and 1876.) Marble also said Republicans seemed not to know that the collector of the New York Custom House, Henry Smythe, was a cousin by marriage of Democratic boss Samuel Barlow, and that Barlow had arranged his appointment, which meant Smythe had access to a great deal of money. Marble was hinting, then, that Barlow had used that access to buy votes for acquittal.

These men had been so well organized, discerning, and discreet that they were never exposed, even by 1906. But stopping the President's conviction hadn't been easy, Marble said; "The vote on impeachment tells how difficult was that prevention."

"There was no contemporary record of all this," Marble finished. And then he added one further detail: Andrew Johnson was hell-bent on revenge, should he have found the opportunity.

"MR. JOHNSON, LIKE Medea, stands absolutely alone," Georges Clemenceau noted. "He is his own sole remaining friend. Unhappily, he does not suffice."

Johnson deeply wanted the Democrats to endorse him for President. "Why should they not take me up?" he plaintively asked. "They profess to accept my measures; they say I have stood by the

Constitution and made a noble struggle. It is true I am asked why don't I join the Democratic party. Why don't they join me?"

The reason was that he'd been disloyal.

Not only had he trafficked with Republicans to become Lincoln's Vice President, when he entered the White House he kept the odious Stanton and the shifty Seward in the cabinet. "Tis not in the power of mortal man to save him unless he will give up Seward & Stanton which he is determined apparently not to do," Montgomery Blair had noted with disdain. And that harebrained Philadelphia convention of his, that feeble stab at a third party, offended old-time Democrats, who saw themselves being undermined. Washington McLean, the powerful publisher of the *Cincinnati Enquirer*, wanted nothing more to do with Andrew Johnson; neither did Barlow or Democratic National Committee chair August Belmont.

Johnson was bewildered. As he saw it, he'd scored a victory over the impeachers, he and his policies had prevailed, and yet he might lose the contest he most wanted to win: election to the White House on his own merits—he'd been the Accidental President, a mere custodian, thanks to the bullet of an assassin. But he was not dead yet. He issued another general proclamation of amnesty, his third, slated for publication on the Fourth of July and timed to coincide with the Democratic party's national convention, which would open on July 7. Unconditionally pardoning every person who, directly or indirectly, participated in "the late insurrection," Johnson declared that unless they were under indictment, they were no longer guilty, and their property, unless already divested and "except as to slaves," would be restored.

At the Democratic national convention, Thomas A.R. Nelson loyally nominated Johnson, and with some Southern support, Johnson did manage to place second on the first two ballots. Democrats graciously thanked the President for his service, and on the twenty-second ballot nominated the dark horse from upstate New York, Governor Horatio Seymour, the man who in 1863 had supported the murderous draft rioters, the man who in 1864 had supported

McClellan against Lincoln, and the man who had supported a peace agreement with the South. A smooth-faced and soulless person, at least according to diarist George Templeton Strong, Seymour had said he didn't care a fig for the presidency, and startled by the nomination, he reportedly wept on hearing of it—whether out of joy or fear, no one knew.

Insiders claimed Seymour had been the choice of the New York Democrats all along, and they were the ones who controlled the convention. But Charles Dana of the New York *Sun* regretfully noted that Chase was the man who would have saved the party, renewed it, strengthened it. Seymour's nomination was party politics as usual. "Does anybody want a revised and corrected edition of Andrew Johnson in the presidential chair for the next four years?" Frederick Douglass scoffed.

Seymour's running mate, General Francis (Frank) P. Blair, Jr., was actually more like Johnson than Seymour: a boozy zealot whose gift for intemperate white supremacist speech rivaled the President's. Frank Blair said a Democratic administration would declare all Reconstruction Acts unconstitutional because Republicans had replaced the white man "with a host of ignorant negroes, who are supported in idleness with the public money, and combined together to strip the white race of their birthright." Unstoppable and ugly, Blair also claimed that Republicans of the North had placed the white South under the heel of a "semi-barbarous race of blacks who are polygamist and destined to subject white women to their unbridled lust." Republicans nimbly replied, "Seymour was opposed to the late war; Blair is in favor of the next one." And as Georges Clemenceau observed, Horatio Seymour and Frank Blair represented "those who have forgotten nothing and learned nothing."

With their election slogan "The Union, the Constitution, and the Laws," even Sam Ward, who proudly called himself Copperhead-light, was miserable. "A terrible platform," he groaned. Andrew Johnson calmly digested news of Seymour's nomination but, enraged, threatened not to endorse the ticket, although in the end he did.

By fall, Democrats realized they were in trouble. "Substitute Chase for Seymour and Thomas Ewing for Blair, we win," said one of them. Seward supposed that Johnson could now be nominated and promptly traveled to New York to sound out the Democratic committee; it was too late. The Democrats stuck to Seymour.

Ulysses S. Grant won the presidency by a sizeable electoral margin — 214 electoral votes from 26 states for Grant versus 80 electoral votes from 8 states for Seymour. But Grant received only 52 percent of the popular vote. White men had overwhelmingly voted for Seymour. It was the 500,000 votes of black men in the South that carried the election for Grant — the votes of black men, that is, who had not been prevented, at gunpoint, from voting.

THAT INTIMIDATION AND murder accompanied black men to the polls was beyond dispute. A black man named Larry White in Jacksonville said he saw so many men stabbed, knocked down, and beaten up on voting day that he tore up his ballot. If he wanted to live, he later said, he'd better not cast it.

That the Ku Klux Klan directed much of the violence was also beyond dispute. In 1868, their numbers reached 40,000 in Tennessee alone, where, traveling by night in their masks, they whipped, hanged, or opened fire on Republicans and, in particular, any black man or woman for whom the Klan, said the governor, "seems to have a peculiar and mortal hatred." Former Confederate General Nathan Bedford Forrest, leading the terrorist posse, bragged that more than 550,000 men all over the South had joined what he called a "protective, military, political organization."

In Macon, Georgia, for instance, a committee of white men protested the Reconstruction Acts, which they considered cruel and unjust. "In making this earnest protest against being placed, by force, under negro domination, we disavow all feeling of resentment toward that unfortunate race," the men declared. "As they are made the dupes of unscrupulous partisans and designing adventurers, we pity them; as they are ignorant, dependent, and helpless, it is our purpose to protect them in the enjoyment of all the rights of person and property to which their freedom entitles them." But the committee then concluded that the white men of Georgia should organize in order to protect themselves and their families against this "direful rule of negro supremacy."

That committee may well have been the Klan. The Klan burned one-third of the town of Lewisburgh, Arkansas, after gunning down a black man named George Washington and leaving him for dead. The justice of the peace, L. B. Umpsflet, said that unless he received federal protection, he was leaving Arkansas, and maybe the country. Congressman James M. Hinds was killed with a double-barreled shotgun, and in South Carolina Klansmen assassinated a black state representative. Mounted men shot the black state senator Benjamin F. Randolph as he waited on a railroad platform. Teachers, black and white, were seized, schoolhouses torched, printing presses smashed, assemblies raided, men lynched. The stories were bone-chilling. "The 'Klu Kluxe Klan' is in full blast here and have inaugurated their nefarious proceedings by visiting, on two occasions, families of Negroes in this place," Charles Cotton reported from Camden, Alabama. "On one occasion they went to a place where the Freedmen were, halting a meeting and one of the party deliberately shot a negro through the head."

There was nothing Secretary Edwin Stanton could do. Although friends and supporters had urged him to stay in the War Department, he said he'd resign if Johnson was acquitted, and just two hours after the final verdict, he made good on his promise and packed up his private papers, having already prepared a letter announcing his resignation. The White House received it in the middle of the afternoon, and in a matter of weeks, the House and Senate passed a resolution thanking Edwin Stanton for the purity and fidelity with which he had discharged his duties as secretary, both during the war and afterward. General John Schofield took over the office.

President Andrew Johnson forged ahead. He appointed generals he believed he could control to head the military districts in the

South. And in his fourth annual message to Congress, in December, he again denounced the legislative branch of government. The recent civil war had been fought to protect the Constitution, he said, and he'd fought to protect the Constitution, but Congress, by meddling with the peaceful progress of restoration, had placed the country in a state of terrible turmoil. He called for the annulment of all reconstruction legislation, which he deemed pernicious and failed. He scorned black suffrage in the South, which he called an "attempt to place the white population under the domination of persons of color."

Two weeks later, on Christmas Day, Johnson issued a Fourth Amnesty Proclamation, this time to pardon unconditionally and without reservation anyone, whether Robert E. Lee or Jefferson Davis, who'd participated either directly or indirectly in the recent rebellion, and to provide immunity from the charge of treason.

Mark Twain, unable to let the moment pass, wrote his own version of Andrew Johnson's last speech: "And when my term began to draw to a close, & I saw that but little time remained wherein to defeat justice, to further exasperate the people, & to complete my unique & unprecedented record, I fell to & gathered up the odds & ends, & made it perfect—swept it clean; for I pardoned Jeff Davis; I pardoned every creature that had ever lifted his hand against the hated flag of the Union I have swept the floors clean; my work is done."

Thaddeus Stevens neither laughed nor despaired. In one of his last speeches, fully aware of what Johnson had done—and what his congressional colleagues had left undone—he affirmed his faith in the government he'd loved, saying if it "never depart from the principles of the Declaration of Independence, especially from the inalienable rights of life, liberty, and its necessary concomitant— universal suffrage—she never can take a step backward, but will sail forward on a sea of glory." To him, impeachment had not completely succeeded; but neither had it completely failed.

CHAPTER THIRTY

Epilogue

"The whirligig of time has brought about its revenges."

— CHARLOTTE FORTEN

O n the day of Grant's inauguration, the mood on the street was hopeful, the impeachment trial largely forgotten. The clouds had been thick in the morning, the March air damp and chilly, and though the sun began to shine at noon, the gaslights in the White House were blazing. Andrew Johnson, his trunks packed, would soon vacate the mansion. Members of the diplomatic corps had gathered to say goodbye, and then the doors of the Executive Mansion opened to well-wishers come to shake Andrew Johnson's still-presidential hand.

Not even for the sake of appearances would there be a rapprochement between Johnson and Grant. Neither of these two proud men could forget or forgive. Grant hadn't attended Johnson's New Year's reception, and he hadn't allowed his children to join a White House birthday party to celebrate Johnson's sixtieth year, although Ben Butler had come to pay his respects. And when the committee planning Grant's inauguration invited Johnson to ride in a column parallel to the general's, it was clear that the President-elect did not wish to ride in the same carriage with Johnson, as was the custom.

Johnson wondered what he should do. Gideon Welles, who took the insult personally, told him not to inconvenience himself. After all, when President-elect Andrew Jackson had failed to call on John Quincy Adams, Adams chose not to attend Jackson's inauguration, and as for himself, Welles waspishly added, he had no intention of celebrating a double-dealing general. "Knowing these things," Johnson declared two days later, "shall we debase ourselves by going near him?"

At Johnson's farewell reception, the night before the inauguration, such a crush of visitors had arrived at the White House that at least a third of them had to be turned away. The police were forced to shut the doors, and outside the building, there was a racket of bucking horses and cursing drivers. Inside, it was so suffocatingly hot that it was hard to breathe, and there was pandemonium in the cloakrooms, women losing their wraps or their escorts. But President Johnson, at the entrance of the East Room in his striped trousers, smiled and welcomed visitors with a polite greeting as if he didn't have a care in the world. His daughter Martha Patterson again stood at his side, dressed much as she had dressed when the crowds first met her there three years earlier: a black velvet dress trimmed with bands of satin over which she had thrown a white lace shawl.

The next morning, Inauguration Day, General John Schofield, as secretary of war, arrived at the cabinet room early. Johnson was already at his desk, reading and signing bills. He had asked Congress to forward them to the White House, having decided not to go to the Capitol on the last morning of the session, as was customary, to sign them there. William Evarts entered the room and, assuming that the cabinet and the President would soon be leaving for the inauguration, didn't bother to remove his overcoat. Browning and McCulloch, already there, were itching to go. Head bowed, Johnson went on signing. Browning said nothing, and neither did Schofield. Seward appeared, puffing on his cigar. "Ought we not to start immediately?" he asked. The President merely said the cabinet should finish its work.

A gunner had been posted in front of the White House and waited to fire the shot signaling that the President had left the building. Yet there was no sign of Johnson. Grant, who'd evidently changed his mind about riding with him, ordered his polished carriage to stop at the Executive Mansion. Johnson still didn't appear. Someone said he was too busy, and Grant's carriage rolled away.

When Chief Justice Chase administered the oath of office to Ulysses S. Grant on the East Portico, President Andrew Johnson was nowhere to be seen.

Johnson had retained his self-respect, or so he believed. But like the impeachment verdict, this victory was a Pyrrhic one, if it was a victory at all. "No one will lament the passing of this administration," Georges Clemenceau observed. The public seemed to agree. "No President has had grander opportunities than Andrew Johnson; no one has failed so lamentably," a Democratic paper noted. "He defied the people he said he loved and succeeded in destroying only himself."

Johnson released a farewell address that typically broadcast his grievances about being misunderstood, abused, and unfairly criticized. "I have nothing to regret," he concluded.

A LITTLE AFTER noon, Johnson finally emerged from the White House, and before he closed the door of his carriage, he inhaled deeply. Leaning over to Secretary Welles, he said, "I fancy I can already smell the fresh mountain air of Tennessee."

BUT ANDREW JOHNSON would not go gentle into that good night. "Depend on it," journalist William Robinson said, "we shall see Andy on the stump again." And they did. In March of 1875, after a near-fatal bout of cholera and though he'd been defeated in two congressional races, Andrew Johnson triumphantly returned to the U.S. Senate, much the same man: headstrong and quarrelsome, fulminating against reconstruction, black people, and President Grant.

"Thank God for the vindication," Johnson crowed. He looked surprisingly well. His hair had grayed slightly, and his pasty face was more slack, but his bearing was erect. Andrew Johnson, U.S. Senator from Tennessee, settled himself on the Democratic side of the aisle, where he'd been before the war.

Doubtless, he noticed the changes in Congress he'd worked hard to prevent. The first black member of the Senate had been Hiram Rhodes Revels, who'd occupied the seat previously held by Jefferson Davis, and Blanche K. Bruce, born a slave in Virginia, was currently the new senator from Mississippi. Pinckney Pinchback of New Orleans had been the first black governor of Louisiana, and he was waiting to be sworn in as senator.

In the House of Representatives, John Menard of Louisiana, the first black man ever elected to Congress, arrived in Washington in January 1869, and though Democrats successfully challenged his election, he addressed the House, the first black man ever to do so. As a friend noted, "the ice is now broken." Joseph Rainey of South Carolina, born a slave, then became the first black congressman. South Carolina's at-large representative had been Reverend Richard H. Cain, another black man, who would be re-elected in 1876. South Carolina also sent Robert De Large to the House, as well as the renowned Robert Brown Elliott, who alleged that former Confederates, now considered respectable, were cheering on the Klan. From Georgia came Jefferson Long, the only black congressman from Georgia throughout the nineteenth century; from Alabama, Benjamin Turner; from Florida, Josiah T. Walls, teacher and lawyer, also born a slave. "The whirligig of time has brought about its revenges," black schoolteacher Charlotte Forten had said.

Time had wrought other changes too, for the old stagers had been leaving the stage. Benjamin Wade had already failed to win re-election to the Senate, and in 1869, the fifty-five-year-old Edwin Stanton, his health ruined by the long siege in the War Depart-

ment, breathed his last—just after President Grant, in a gesture of
gratitude and mercy, appointed him to the Supreme Court. Fessenden, Grimes, and Van Winkle had all died within two years after
they voted to acquit Johnson, and a weakened William Seward
caught a fatal cold in the fall of 1872. Chief Justice Salmon Chase
died after a stroke in the spring of 1873, and Charles Sumner suffered a massive heart attack the next March.

The eloquent Robert Brown Elliott was selected to deliver a
funeral oration for Sumner, who'd been pushing for a new civil
rights bill, which would prohibit racial discrimination in schools,
churches, hotels, burial grounds, and also in jury selection. Just before his death, Sumner had begged Representative George Frisbie
Hoar to get the legislation passed. It did, thanks in no small part to
Ben Butler's tenacity, though it passed without the clause mandating integrated schools. President Grant signed the bill into law in
1875, the year Johnson returned to Washington.

Still associated with patronage politics and chicanery of all kinds,
Ben Butler had continued to fight for Radical issues: that federal
bonds be paid with greenbacks, that women have the vote, that
working days be shortened to eight hours. And the scent of corruption followed him wherever he went. After losing and regaining his
seat in the House of Representatives, in 1879 Butler was elected
governor of Massachusetts, much to the horror of the Brahmins. For
the liberal wing of the Republican party had been pecking away at
the foundations of Radical Reconstruction. Free traders, civil service crusaders, and for the most part advocates of hard money, they
included Congressman James Ashley, the man who had first introduced articles of impeachment against President Johnson, as well
as journalists Whitelaw Reid and Murat Halstead of *The Cincinnati
Commercial.* Even old Democrat William Cullen Bryant of the
New York Evening Post signed up, and the Republican weathercock
Horace Greeley. "What the South wants now is not military commanders, and carpet-bag Congressmen, and stump orators, and col-
lectors of internal revenue, but missionaries," Greeley's *Tribune*
declared.

Before drifting to the Democrats, Lyman Trumbull joined this Liberal conclave of these so-called missionaries, and so had former Radicals and once blunt Johnson-haters like Anna Dickinson, who in front of a large audience wondered why, if the war had in fact ended, the government insisted on its military occupation of the South. The war was over; freedmen were citizens. "Before the law they stand on a level with the whitest man here. [Applause] That being the case there is no need and there should be no excuse for special legislation for any special class of people, since there is none such in the Republic. [Applause, again.]" The time had come to clasp hands, embrace amnesty, to welcome former Confederates in the body politic.

"Liberal Republicanism is nothing but Ku-Klux-Klanism disguised," Wendell Phillips exclaimed. After his election to the Georgia House of Representatives, Henry McNeal Turner, a black preacher and politician, was hounded by the Klan, denied his legislative seat, his church torched. "We meet the relics of slavery in the railroad cars, in the churches, and everywhere, but above all, we meet them when we come up for civil and political rights," Turner declared. Until President Grant more or less broke up the Klan, it had continued to rampage through the South, targeting black voters, office-seekers, teachers, anybody speaking out or learning how to read and write. But new groups, like White Liners, emerged, often with ties to the Democratic party. On Easter Sunday, 1873, a white paramilitary group killed more than eighty black men in Grant Parish, Louisiana, where black men controlled the local government. The men accused of the murders went free. Congressman Robert Brown Elliott went so far as to accuse New York's Tammany Hall of funneling money to the South to keep up the violence and get the Democrats back into power.

Linking the increased number of crimes against black men and women to the war against various Indian tribes in the West, Wendell Phillips insisted over and over that "the great poison of the age is race hatred." Still considered crazy or foolish or both, Phillips had not slid backward. The struggle for equality was far from over.

"When I see that Capitol at Washington, with its pillared halls crowded with black and white, Indian and Saxon, Christian, Pagan and Jew, looking up with the same gratitude to the same banner, and uttering the same shibboleth of nationality in a hundred tongues," Phillips said, "I shall feel that the American Anti-Slavery Society has done its work, and that the epoch is ended." It had not ended, not yet, not by a long shot.

"We turned around, and instead of looking fearlessly and relentlessly in the face of the great problem, we went to work and called up our magnanimity," Phillips again took to the stump. "We forgot the war record. You would have thought we had been out on a picnic." And magnanimity, what is it? Phillips asked, when the magnanimous Yankee claims that "New Orleans is an idle tale, and Memphis is a romance, and there never was any such man as Forrest."

But Phillips' audience was increasingly consumed by getting and spending. "Wendell Phillips and William Lloyd Garrison are not exactly extinct forces in American politics," *The New York Times* patronized. "They represent ideas in regard to the South which the majority of the Republican party have outgrown."

The winds cooling whatever ardor there may have been for a Phillips or a Garrison were blowing in Johnson's direction. "I am only trying to carry out the measures Mr. Lincoln would have done had he lived," Johnson had told his bodyguard. In coming years, that would become scripture: Johnson had been simply trying to execute Lincoln's policy of malice toward none when he was viciously thwarted by the implacable Furies known as the Radicals.

Those who insisted Johnson was only following Lincoln's lead conveniently forgot that Lincoln had said, just days before being shot, that since slavery had caused the war, this terrible war would be waged "until all the wealth piled by the bondsman's two hundred and fifty years of unrequited toil shall be sunk, and until every drop of blood drawn with the lash shall be paid by another drawn with the sword, as was said three thousand years ago, so still it must be said 'the judgments of the Lord are true and righteous altogether.'" Lincoln had not blinked. Despite his penchant for kindness and mercy, there was no reason to suppose he would have betrayed a people that he'd fought hard to free.

Like Lincoln, those who understood that slavery had caused the war also understood how it was slavery that lay behind Johnson's impeachment. And thus not to eliminate the monstrous power of slavery or its aftereffects, and not to prevent its recurrence in any form, Charles Sumner declared, "leaves the country prey to one of the most hateful tyrannies of history."

To forget, then, that it was slavery, pernicious slavery, that lay behind the impeachment of Andrew Johnson is to ignore Lincoln's response to secession, to the war, and hence to slavery itself. "If slavery is not wrong," Lincoln had said, "nothing is wrong."

To forget the reasons why Andrew Johnson was impeached, to denude or belittle them, ignores how a divided, culpable nation had destroyed so many lives, and how it then came near to destroying itself. If those reasons are forgotten, the impeachment of Andrew Johnson seems unreasonable or ludicrous. It was neither.

The impeachment and trial of Andrew Johnson represented yet another attempt to preserve the Union and free the slaves, which, to the impeachers, were the self-same thing: to preserve the Union meant creating a more perfect one, liberated at last from the noxious and lingering effects of an appalling institution that treated human beings as property.

THAT SLAVERY AND its effects lay at the heart of Johnson's impeachment does not suggest that the verdict was wholly unjust or the trial improperly conducted. Certainly, and despite the various and reasonable reservations about the chief justice's behavior and motivations, thirty-five men of good faith voted to convict Johnson — and some men of good faith had voted to acquit him.

A strong and sound case had been made by both sides, despite the sniping and the grandstanding, and despite the legal pyrotechnics. Underlying questions about the meaning of impeachment had been deftly argued, and they were not finally settled, nor could they be. Even now, those questions are not settled: was impeachment to be understood as a judicial matter, where the Senate decided if an actual law or statute had been broken; or was impeachment designed to punish malfeasance in office, "where there was no actual crime committed," as Thaddeus Stevens had reasoned. And Charles Sumner had made a good point: in the matter of Andrew Johnson, or perhaps impeachment generally, the violation of a law and malfeasance in office were not unconnected. "As well separate the Siamese twins," he explained, "as separate the offences now charged from that succession of antecedent crimes with which they are linked."

Nor was one specific issue, brilliantly examined from both points of view, immaterial: that is, whether a President, and not an ordinary citizen, might test the constitutionality of a law by violating it, whether or not you argued that Andrew Johnson had indeed violated a law or whether that law had been ambiguously worded.

That the impeachment of a President is a court of last resort, solemnly undertaken, was amply and ably demonstrated. Congress had been reluctant to impeach Johnson, but many impeachers believed that, after a war that separated the Union, the fate of the country was at risk. Yet they were forced to wait until no one could wait any longer. Certainly not all the impeachers were without their failings, but many did firmly and forcefully maintain that impeachment implied a commitment to—and responsibility for—a just nation.

WELCOMING HIM BACK, a large bouquet of flowers had been placed on Andrew Johnson's polished desk in the Senate. Faulting President Grant and the scandals associated with his administration, *The Nation* gushed that Johnson's comeback augured a new age of personal integrity. Thurlow Weed, too, eagerly praised Johnson in order to damn Grant. The country could rejoice: Johnson was an honest man, and these were dishonest times. As for Johnson's impeachment: it had been triggered by a delusion.

Even some of the impeachers were now voicing regret. With hindsight—and growing conservatism—several former Radicals repudiated their vote. Congressman George Julian, who had fought slavery for thirty years, said the impeachment had been cooked up by partisans in a reckless moment, though Julian did concede that the Civil War had understandably unnerved the country. Congressman James G. Blaine likewise recalled that at the time of the verdict, the "cool-headed" Republicans regarded it as a "fortunate exit from an indefensible position."

Blaine complimented himself as a man in possession of a very cool head. It was true, he said, that Johnson had been guilty of trying to obstruct passage of the Fourteenth Amendment; of ignoring the rights and safety of the formerly enslaved; of a willingness to return the reins of power to the formerly rebellious; and of insisting that the black man be denied the vote but counted in determining the number of representatives to send to the House. It was true that Johnson bore responsibility for the slaughters at Memphis and New Orleans. "Could the President have been legally and constitutionally impeached for these offenses," Blaine continued, "he should not have been allowed to hold his office for an hour beyond the time required for a fair trial." That is, though the list of Johnson's transgressions was long, Johnson had been tried on the technicality known as Tenure of Office Act, which would be repealed in 1887.

His acquittal had therefore been correct, he claimed, and Blaine's own vote a function of frenzied politics and bad times.

MANY OF THE men in Congress who'd voted to impeach Andrew Johnson back in 1868 offered to shake Johnson's large hand, although privately they said they were glad he possessed far less power these days. Several colleagues asked him to keep his mouth shut. They may have known he intended to settle old scores, and they should have known the man could never resist an audience. In Washington less than a month, Johnson delivered a harangue on the Senate floor. Patting himself on the back as the lonely

Constitution-crusader, he blasted Grant as the military despot tram-
pling on the liberties of the nation.

Sneering innuendos won him few friends. Here was Andrew
Johnson, it was said, a village alderman who rose up to be one of the
greatest criminals of the age.

In the galleries sat Frederick Douglass and also Phoebe Couz-
ins, who was soon to be the country's first female lawyer. They symbolized the present and the future. Johnson was the past come alive
again. It was ominous.

When he finished speaking, the galleries emptied, largely in disgust. Andrew Johnson had not discovered the better angels of his
nature.

IMPEACHMENT HAD EVIDENTLY been designed to remedy peculiar situations for which there were no remedies. The impeachment of a sitting President was uncharted territory. Given the
somewhat ambiguous instructions in the Constitution, it is largely
uncharted to this very day. It was successfully used to threaten Richard Nixon, who resigned from office to escape impeachment, and it
was waged with partisan fury against William Jefferson Clinton. But
the walls did not come tumbling down. For the framers of the Constitution considered that if impeachment removed the President
from office, the office of the President—the presidency itself—
would remain intact. That was their aim.

In 1868, the situation was far more serious, the consequences
more far-reaching, than those of Richard Nixon's bungled burglary
or of Clinton's peccadillos. The country had been broken apart,
men and women lay dead. And yet the nation lurched toward a renewed sense of itself, ready with the opportunity, for the first time,
of fulfilling its promise of a free and fair republic in which the blessings of liberty and justice were secured for everyone. Reasonably
and with passion, the impeachers had argued that the Constitution
allowed the removal of a President precisely to protect and
preserve—and perfect—this republic. They had been undertaking

this work, despite Andrew Johnson, for three years, waging impeachment as a threat, and moving ahead with the reconstruction legislation he hated.

But in 1868, there was the matter of both the law and the man, this President, this Andrew Johnson, who had proved even to his supporters—there were always fewer and fewer—that he was incompetent, inadequate, unfit for office, and a menace to the welfare of the people, all the people, he had sworn to serve. The impeachers believed that with Andrew Johnson, a man who was not an adroit leader, not a supple thinker, and not a humanitarian but a man who'd repeatedly vetoed postwar legislation, imperiled the lives of at least four million people, sought to inflame racial tensions, render black citizens defenseless, and restore civic power to slaveholders, who'd insulted Congress as well as individuals, and who had coarsened public discourse—that with this man, this President who would and did break the law, no future worth the many hopeful lives lost on the battlefield, in the cities and the countryside, would ever be possible.

It was therefore preferable—necessary—to impeach Andrew Johnson, hopefully to convict and remove him from office, and then to bear the consequences.

DURING THE CONGRESSIONAL recess, just four months after he'd returned to Washington, Andrew Johnson died of a stroke while visiting one of his daughters. Buried in Greeneville, Tennessee, at his request, he was wrapped in the American flag, his head placed on a copy of the U.S. Constitution.

In retrospect, a modern biographer generously eulogized him as a child of his time who failed to grow with it. True, he never grew into the presidency but rather clung to opinions benighted at best, and his legacy was that of white supremacy and spite. Yet under his watch, the Thirteenth Amendment had been ratified, and in spite of his obvious displeasure and the obstructionist campaign he'd mounted against them, the Fourteenth and the Fifteenth Amendments would soon help complete the structure the impeachers had envisioned: a house not divided but inhabited by equals, free and fair.

True too that Andrew Johnson had been saved largely through the generosity of his enemies who, though they did not care for him, allowed him to serve out his term. Yet, with that, the impeachers had done the best they could—and their best was far better than that of Andrew Johnson. As for the impeachment itself: it had proceeded in an orderly, even elegant fashion despite its being a somewhat improvised affair and despite the corruption or bribery and self-interest that gnawed at its edge or threatened its execution. The arguments it had inspired were cogent, lucid, and genuine, and were initiated by the very process that tested, renewed, and again sustained the government, this time without a war.

And so impeachment had not fully succeeded, as Thaddeus Stevens had ruefully admitted. But unless forgotten, it had not entirely failed. It demonstrated that the American President was not a king, that all actions have consequences, and that the national government, conceived in hope, with its checks and balances, could maintain itself without waging war, even right after one. And that the national government could struggle to free itself from all vestiges of human oppression. It had not succeeded, but it had worked. The impeachers had reduced the seventeenth President to a shadow— a shadow President; that is, a President who did not cast a long shadow, although his regressive policies would. The impeachers had warned the country about these policies as best they could, and offered to us, clearly and without apology, a cautionary tale. And they provided hope. For in an essential way, impeachment had accomplished what it had set out to do. It spoke beautifully and with farsighted imagination of the road not yet taken, but that could exist: the path toward a free country, a just country, a country and a people willing to learn from the past, not erase or repeat it, and create the fair future of which men and women still dream.

Acknowledgments

I'm often reminded of Huck Finn's remark at the end of his adventures, when he exclaims, "what a trouble it was to make a book." True enough; but the trouble is mightily lessened by the friends and strangers who so graciously help along the way. I'd like to thank a few of them.

Thanks to the National Endowment for the Humanities Public Scholars Grant in 2016–2017, whose generous award assisted the research and writing of this book. And similarly, for their cordial cooperation, I'm enormously grateful to the following people as well as to the collections they so ably represent: the staff at the Abraham Lincoln Presidential Library; Caroline Moseley, at the Bowdoin College Library, George J. Mitchell Department of Special Collections & Archives; Jennifer J. Betts, University Archivist at the John Hay Library, Brown University; the staff at the Buffalo History Museum; at the Chicago History Museum and the University of Chicago Library; at the Samuel J. May Anti-Slavery Collection, Special Collections, Cornell University Library; at Columbia University, Butler Library, Rare Book and Manuscripts; at the Connecticut Historical Society; Jay Satterfield, Special Collections Librarian, Rauner Special Collections Library, Dartmouth College; Megan O'Connell at Duke University's Rubenstein Rare Book & Manuscript Library; Kaitlyn Pettengill, Program Associate and Researcher at the Historical Society of Pennsylvania; the staff at Houghton Library, Harvard University; at the Huntington Library, Arts Galleries, and Botanical Gardens, Library Division; Bethany Fiechter, Rare Books and Manuscripts Supervisor at Indiana State Library; the staff at the Kansas State Historical Society; Sally R. Polhemus, McClung Historical Collection Archivist, at the Knox County Public Library, East Tennessee History Center; Rebecca Williams at the Wilson Library, the University of North Carolina at Chapel Hill; the staff at the Southern Historical Collection, University of North Carolina at Chapel Hill; at the Library of Congress, Manuscript Division; at Louisiana State University's Hill Memorial Library; at the Maine Historical Society and at the Massachusetts Historical Society; at the National Archives and Records Administration; at the New-York Historical Society Museum and Library; at the New York Public Library, Brooke Russell Astor Reading Room for Rare Books and Manuscripts; at the Hesburgh Library, University of Notre Dame; at Princeton University Library Special Collections; at the Ohio History Connection; at the University of Rochester, Rush Rhees Library, Department of Rare Books & Special Collections; Nan J. Card, Curator of Manuscripts, at the Rutherford B. Hayes Presidential Center; Karen Kukil, Associate Curator at the Sophia Smith Collection, Smith College; the staff at the South Carolinian Collection, University of South Carolina; Cara Dellatte, Archivist, at the Staten Island Museum, History Archives and Library; Nicole C. Dittrich, Reading Room Supervisor at the Syracuse University Library, Special Collections Research Center; Tom Kanon, at the Tennessee State Library and Archives; Annette LeClair, Director of Collection and Technical Services at Union College; the staff at Vassar College Library, Archives and Special Collections; at the University of Virginia Library; at the Western Reserve Historical Society; at Wichita State University's Special Collections and University Archives; Lee Grady at the Wisconsin Historical Society; and the staff at Archives and Manuscripts, Sterling Memorial Library, Yale University.

I am also grateful for the conscientiousness of two research assistants, Patrick Callihan, again a model of diligence, and the intelligent and thorough Victoria Beale. In addition, I'm grateful to my colleague Luis Jaramillo, Director of the MFA Program in Writing at The New School University, for sending his student Kristy Chambers my way; Kristy's imaginative rendition of several nineteenth-century buildings and advertisements was a delight. And while working on this book, I was consistently cheered by the camaraderie of longtime, talented colleagues both at the New School and at Columbia University's School of the Arts. I am also grateful to the dedicated students I have taught at both places. Then, special thanks go to my friend, the author Philip Lopate, former head of nonfiction at Columbia, and to the present head of nonfiction, Leslie S. Jamison; and at the New School, along with Luis Jaramillo, I am also indebted to Honor Moore and to the indefatigable Lori Lynn Turner.

Thanks too to Arlo Haskell, Executive Director of the Key West Literary Seminar, who cordially invited me to speak about the background of the impeachment trial during its 2017 session, "Revealing Power: The Literature of Politics," and to participate in a conversation with the incomparable Robert A. Caro, aptly entitled "Rhythm Matters. Mood Matters. Everything Matters: On Writing History." No one is better versed in these issues, or better deploys them, than this remarkable writer.

Once again, too, I am happily in Robert Gottlieb's debt. A man as munificent in friendship as he is in editorial wizardry, he read my manuscript with the virtuosity and dazzling intelligence for which he is justly known, and his amazing generosity included his calling me from Paris to answer last minute, frantic questions about structure. Other remarkable readers of this book on whom I've imposed include the extraordinary David Ebershoff, whose company—and superb novels—have sustained me for many years. So has the friendship of the excellent writer Christopher Bram, who again provided indispensable notes; and the exceptional Sean Wilentz, for whom history is a living thing, and who once more scrupulously read my manuscript;

I'm again the indebted beneficiary of such a keen, probing historical imagination. And of course I could not have written this book without relying on the deep research and penetrating insights of so many predecessors, the accomplished historians, biographers, novelists, or critics on whose work I've relied for these many years and whose work I outline in the notes.

For the letters they've written on my behalf, I'm grateful to Annette Gordon-Reed, Wendy Lesser, and Robert K. Massie, as well as other friends, old and new, and colleagues not already mentioned, I owe them much more than a simple acknowledgment for their sympathetic patience, their support and advice—and their willingness to put up with my reclusiveness: David Alexander, Alida Becker, Ina Caro, Robert A. Caro, Ron Chernow, Fernanda Eberstadt, Benita Eisler, Gary Giddins, Wendy Gimbel, Judith Ginsberg, Brad Gooch, George Gross, Molly Haskell, Peter Heinegg, Rosemarie Heinegg, Virginia Jonas, Joe Lelyveld, Doug Liebhafsky, the late J. D. McClatchy, Tom Mallon, Michael Massing, Daphne Merkin, Benjamin Moser, Jed Perl, Deborah Rosenthal, Max Rudin, Helen Schulman, Ileene Smith, Domna Stanton, Annalyn Swan, Benjamin Taylor, Michele Underwood, Paul Underwood, Robert Weil, and Bob Wilson.

Then, a special thanks to my friend of many, many years, the peerless Richard Howard, poet, translator, essayist, teacher, and man for whom the word "friend" is too narrow. I will always remember his advice, more than thirty years ago, which has kept me aloft in dark times.

And I'd like to thank another person without peer, my remarkable agent Lynn Nesbit. For two decades now, I've now had the distinct privilege of working with a woman justly regarded as independent, perspicacious, wise, and fearless. She is those things and more: a person unrivalled in loyalty, candor, thoughtfulness, energy, and hard work. I'm proud to be the recipient of her priceless knowledge, proud to know her, proud to call her, too, friend.

The editor extraordinaire of this book is another legend; the reputation of Kate Medina, not just at Random House but in the larger world of publishing, is stellar. I can see why: She has been unfailingly professional and passionate, both at the same time; she is resourceful, good-humored, and sharp. With polish, efficiency, and patience, she read and reread my manuscript, and with her meticulous editing and perceptive advice, made suggestions about shape and form that vastly improved the book—and that taught me a great deal. I am grateful for her understanding, her enthusiasm, and, plainly speaking, her unflagging commitment to publishing. Then, she surrounds herself with an incredible "team." Her terrific assistant editor, Erica Gonzalez, has been a godsend: Reassuringly proficient, she is also a person of grace and skill, whether we're talking about pictures or captions or flap copy. Earlier, Anna Pitoniak, former senior editor, read the manuscript at Kate's behest, and I benefitted from her comments. Many thanks, too, to Benjamin Dreyer, executive managing editor and copy chief, for kindly answering questions early and late; to the meticulous, generous, and gimlet-eyed reader par excellence, the executive production editor Dennis Ambrose; to the freelance proofreader Liz Carbonell; to Toby Ernst, associate director, subsidiary rights, and Karen Fink, executive publicist. I also extend thanks to those who designed the book's interiors and jacket.

These many years, while I worked on this book, my mother, now ninety-seven years old at this writing, has lost her ability to read but nonetheless remains excited about all new projects. And she's remained, too, a woman of rare resourcefulness, imagination, and will; caring for her has not been easy, but I've been able to share this, like so much of my life, with my brilliant and beloved husband, the composer Michael Dellaira. Again, he read and edited every single page of this book—an astonishing number of times—intent on every word, every sound, every rhythm, every concept. I talked with him, debated with him, listened to him, learned from him, and laughed with him. I dedicate this book to him, always.

BRENDA WINEAPPLE
New York City, 2019

Appendix A

Tenure of Office Act

[Note: The Tenure of Office Act was fully repealed in 1887 as unconstitutional.]

SECTION 1. Every person holding any civil office to which he has been appointed by and with the advice and consent of the Senate, and every person who shall hereafter be appointed to any such office, and shall become duly qualified to act therein, is, and shall be entitled to hold such office until a successor shall have been in like manner appointed and duly qualified, except as herein otherwise provided: *Provided*, That the Secretaries of State, of the Treasury, of War, of the Navy, and of the Interior, the Postmaster-General, and the Attorney General, shall hold their offices respectively for and during the term of the President by whom they may have been appointed and for one month thereafter, subject to removal by and with the advice and consent of the Senate.

SECTION 2. And be it further enacted, That when any officer appointed as aforesaid, excepting judges of the United States courts, shall, during a recess of the Senate, be shown, by evidence satisfactory to the President, to be guilty of misconduct in office, or crime, or for any reason shall become incapable or legally disqualified to perform its duties, in such case, and in no other, the President may suspend such officer and designate some suitable person to perform temporarily the duties of such office until the next meeting of the Senate, and until the case shall be acted upon by the Senate, and such person so designated shall take the oaths and give the bonds required by law to be taken and given by the person duly appointed to fill such office; and in such case it shall be the duty of the President, within twenty days after the first day of such next meeting of the Senate, to report to the Senate such suspension, with the evidence and reasons for his action in the case, and the name of the person so designated to perform the duties of such office. And if the Senate shall concur in such suspension and advise and consent to the removal of such officer, they shall so certify to the President, who may thereupon remove such officer; and, by and with the advice and consent of the Senates, appoint another person to such office. But if the Senate shall refuse to concur in such suspension, such officer so suspended shall forthwith resume the functions of his office, and the powers of the person so performing its duties in his stead shall cease, and the official salary and emoluments of such officer shall, during such suspension, belong to the person so performing the duties thereof, and not to the officer so suspended: *Provided*, however, That the President, in case he shall become satisfied that such suspension was made on insufficient grounds, shall be authorized, at any time before reporting such suspension to the Senate as above provided, to revoke such suspension and reinstate such officer in the performance of the duties of his office.

SECTION 3. And be it further enacted, That the President shall have power to fill all vacancies which may happen during the recess of the Senate, by reason of death or resignation, by granting commissions which shall expire at the end of their next session thereafter. And if no appointment, by and with the advice and consent of the Senate, shall be made to such office so vacant or temporarily filled as aforesaid during such next session of the Senate, such office shall remain in abeyance, without any salary, fees, or emoluments attached thereto, until the same shall be filled by appointment thereto, by and with the advice and consent of the Senate; and during such time all the powers and duties belonging to such office shall be exercised by such other officer as may by law exercise such powers and duties in case of a vacancy in such office.

SECTION 4. And be it further enacted, That nothing in this act contained shall be construed to extend the term of any office the duration of which is limited by law.

SECTION 5. And be it further enacted, That if any person shall, contrary to the provisions of this act, accept any appointment to or employment in any office, or shall hold or exercise or attempt to hold or exercise, any such office or employment, he shall be deemed, and is hereby declared to be, guilty of a high misdemeanor, and, upon trial and conviction thereof, he shall be punished therefor by a fine not exceeding ten thousand dollars, or by imprisonment not exceeding five years, or both said punishments, in the discretion of the court.

SECTION 6. And be it further enacted, That every removal, appointment, or employment, made, had, or exercised, contrary to the provisions of this act, and the making, signing, sealing, countersigning, or issuing of any commission or letter of authority for or in respect to any such appointment or employment, shall be deemed, and are hereby declared to be, high misdemeanors and, upon trial and conviction thereof, every person guilty thereof shall be punished by a fine not exceeding ten thousand dollars, or by imprisonment not exceeding five years, or both said punishments, in the discretion of the court. *Provided*, That the President shall have power to make out and deliver, after the adjournment of the Senate, commissions for all officers whose appointment shall have been advised and consented to by the Senate.

SECTION 7. And be it further enacted, That it shall be the duty of the Secretary of the Senate, at the close of each session thereof, to deliver to the Secretary of the Treasury and to each of his assistants and to each of the auditors and to each of the comptrollers in the treasury, and to the treasurer, and to the register of the treasury, a full and complete list, duly certified, of all the persons who shall have been nominated to and rejected by the Senate during such session, and a like list of all the offices to which nominations shall have been made and not confirmed and filled at such session.

SECTION 8. And be it further enacted, That whenever the President shall, without the advice and consent of the Senate, designation authorize, or employ any person to perform the duties of any office, he shall forthwith notify the Secretary of the Treasury thereof; and it shall be the duty of the Secretary of the Treasury thereupon to communicate such notice to all the proper accounting and disbursing officers of his department.

SECTION 9. And be it further enacted, That no money shall be paid or received from the treasury, or paid or received from or retained out of any public moneys or funds of the United States, whether in the treasury not, to or by or for the benefit of any person appointed to or authorized to act in holding or exercising the duties or functions of any office contrary to the provisions of this act; nor shall any claim, account, voucher, order, certificate or warrant, or other instrument providing for or relating to such payment, receipt, or retention, be presented, passed, allowed, approved for, proved, certified, or paid by any officer of the United States, or by any such person exercising the functions or performing the duties of any office or place of trust under the United States, for or in respect of such office, or the exercising or performing the functions or duties thereof; any person who shall violate any of the provisions of this section shall be deemed guilty of a high misdemeanor, and, upon trial and conviction thereof, shall be punished therefor by a fine not exceeding ten thousand dollars, or by imprisonment not exceeding ten years, or both said punishments, in the discretion of the court.

Appendix B

Articles of Impeachment

ARTICLE 1. That said Andrew Johnson, President of the United States, on the 21st day of February, in the year of our Lord, 1868, at Washington, in the District of Columbia, unmindful of the high duties of his oath of office and of the requirements of the Constitution, that he should take care that the laws be faithfully executed, did unlawfully, in violation of the Constitution and laws of the United States, issue an order in writing for the removal of Edwin M. Stanton from the office of Secretary of the Department of War, said Edwin M. Stanton having been, therefor, duly appointed and commissioned by and with the advice and consent of the Senate of the United States as such Secretary; and said Andrew Johnson, President of the United States, on the 12th day of August, in the year of our Lord 1867, and during the recess of said Senate, having suspended by his order Edwin M. Stanton from said office, and within twenty days after the first day of the next meeting of said Senate, on the 12th day of December, in the year last aforesaid, having reported to said Senate such suspension, with the evidence and reasons for his action in the case, and the name of the person designated to perform the duties of such office temporarily, until the next meeting of the Senate, and said Senate therafterwards, on the 13th day of January, in the year of our Lord 1868, having duly considered the evidence and reasons reported by said Andrew Johnson for said suspension, did refuse to concur in said suspension; whereby and by force of the provisions of an act entitled "An act regulating the tenure of certain civil offices," passed March 2, 1867, said Edwin M. Stanton did forthwith resume the functions of his office, whereof the said Andrew Johnson had then and there notice, and the said Edwin M. Stanton, by reason of the premises, on said 21st day of February, was lawfully entitled to hold said office of Secretary for the Department of War, which said order for the removal of said Edwin M. Stanton is, in substance, as follows, that is to say:

Executive Mansion, Washington, D.C., Feb. 21, 1868.

Sir: By virtue of the power and authority vested in me, as President, by the Constitution and laws of the United States, you are hereby removed from the office of Secretary for the Department of War and your functions as such will terminate upon receipt of their communication. You will transfer to Brevet Major-General L. Thomas, Adjutant-General of the Army, who has this day been authorized and empowered to act as Secretary of War ad interim, all books, paper and other public property now in your custody and charge. Respectfully yours,

ANDREW JOHNSON.
To the Hon. E. M. Stanton, Secretary of War

Which order was unlawfully issued, and with intent then are there to violate the act entitled "An act regulating the tenure of certain civil offices," passed March 2, 1867, and contrary to the provisions of said act, and in violation thereof, and contrary to the provisions of the Constitution of the United States, and without the advice and consent of the Senate of the United States, the said Senate then and there being in session, to remove said E. M. Stanton from the office of Secretary for the Department of War, whereby said Andrew Johnson, President of the United States, did then and there commit, and was guilty of a high misdemeanor in office.

ARTICLE 2. That on the 21st day of February, in the year of our Lord 1868, at Washington, in the District of Columbia, said Andrew Johnson, President of the United States, unmindful of the high duties of his oath of office, and in violation of the Constitution of the United States, and contrary to the provisions of an act entitled "An act regulating the tenure of certain civil offices," passed March 2, 1867, without the advice and consent of the Senate, then and there being in session, and without authority of law, did appoint one L. Thomas to be Secretary of War ad interim, by issuing to said Lorenzo Thomas a letter of authority, in substance, as follows, that is to say:

Executive Mansion, Washington, D.C., Feb. 21, 1868.

Sir: The Hon. Edwin M. Stanton having been this day removed from office as Secretary of the Department of War, you are hereby authorized and empowered to act as Secretary of War ad interim, and will immediately enter upon the discharge of the duties pertaining to that office. Mr. Stanton has been instructed to transfer to you all the records, books, papers and other public property now in his custody and charge. Respectfully yours,

ANDREW JOHNSON.
To Brevet Major-General Lorenzo Thomas, Adjutant-General
United States Army, Washington, D.C.

Whereby said Andrew Johnson, President of the United States, did then and there commit, and was guilty of a high misdemeanor in office.

ARTICLE 3. That said Andrew Johnson, President of the United States, on the 21st day of February, in the year of our Lord one thousand eight hundred and sixty-eight, at Washington in the District of Columbia, did commit, and was guilty of a high misdemeanor in office, in this: That without authority of law, while the Senate of the United States was then and there in session, he did appoint one Lorenzo Thomas to be Secretary for the Department of War, ad interim, without the advice and consent of the Senate, and in violation of the Constitution of the United States, no vacancy having happened in said office of Secretary for the Department of War during the recess of the Senate, and no vacancy existing in said office at the time, and which said appointment so made by Andrew Johnson of said Lorenzo Thomas is in substance as follows, that is to say:

Executive Mansion, Washington, D.C., Feb. 21, 1868.

Sir: The Hon. E. M. Stanton having been this day removed from office as Secretary for the Department of War, you are hereby authorized and empowered to act as Secretary of War ad interim, and will immediately enter upon the discharge of the duties pertaining to that office. Mr. Stanton has been instructed to transfer to you all the records, books, papers and other public property now in his custody and charge. Respectfully yours,

ANDREW JOHNSON.

To Brevet Major-General L. Thomas, Adjutant-General
United States Army, Washington, D.C.

ARTICLE 4. That said Andrew Johnson, President of the United States, unmindful of the high duties of his office, and of his oath of office, in violation of the Constitution and laws of the United States, on the 21st day of February, in the year of our Lord 1868, at Washington, in the District of Columbia, did unlawfully conspire with one Lorenzo Thomas, and with other persons to the House of Representatives unknown, with intent, by intimidation and threats, to hinder and prevent Edwin M. Stanton, then and there, the Secretary for the Department of War, duly appointed under the laws of the United States, from holding said office of Secretary for the Department of War, contrary to and in violation of the Constitution of the United States, and of the provisions of an act entitled "An act to define and punish certain conspiracies," approved July 31, 1861, whereby said Andrew Johnson, President of the United States, did then and there commit and was guilty of high crime in office.

ARTICLE 5. That said Andrew Johnson, President of the United States, unmindful of the high duties of his office and of his oath of office, on the 21st of February, in the year of our Lord one thousand eight hundred and sixty-eight, and on divers other days and time in said year before the 28th day of said February, at Washington, in the District of Columbia, did unlawfully conspire with one Lorenzo Thomas, and with other persons in the House of Representatives unknown, by force to prevent and hinder the execution of an act entitled "An act regulating the tenure of certain civil offices," passed March 2, 1867, and in pursuance of said conspiracy, did attempt to prevent E. M. Stanton, then and there being Secretary for the Department of War, duly appointed and commissioned under the laws of the United States, from holding said office, whereby the said Andrew Johnson,

President of the United States, did then and there commit and was guilty of high misdemeanor in office.

ARTICLE 6. That Andrew Johnson, President of the United States, unmindful of the duties of his high office and of his oath of office, on the 21st day of February, in the year of our Lord 1868, at Washington, in the District of Columbia, did unlawfully conspire with one Lorenzo Thomas, by force to seize, take and possess the property of the United Sates at the War Department, contrary to the provisions of an act entitled "An act to define and punish certain conspiracies," approved July 31, 1861, and with intent to violate and disregard an act entitled "An act regulating the tenure of certain civil offices," passed March 2, 1867, whereby said Andrew Johnson, President of the United States, did then and there commit a high crime in office.

ARTICLE 7. That said Andrew Johnson, President of the United States, unmindful of the high duties of his office, and of his oath of office, on the 21st day of February, in the year of our Lord 1868, and on divers other days in said year, before the 28th day of said February, at Washington, in the District of Columbia, did unlawfully conspire with one Lorenzo Thomas to prevent and hinder the execution of an act of the United States, entitled "An act regulating the tenure of certain civil offices," passed March 2, 1867, and in pursuance of said conspiracy, did unlawfully attempt to prevent Edwin M. Stanton, then and there being Secretary for the Department of War, under the laws of the United States, from holding said office to which he had been duly appointed and commissioned, whereby said Andrew Johnson, President of the United States, did there and then commit and was guilty of a high misdemeanor in office.

ARTICLE 8. That said Andrew Johnson, President of the United States, unmindful of the high duties of his office, and of his oath of office, on the 21st day of February, in the year of our Lord, 1868, at Washington, in the District of Columbia, did unlawfully conspire with one Lorenzo Thomas, to seize, take and possess the property of the United States in the War Department, with intent to violate and disregard the act entitled "An act regulating the tenure of certain civil offices," passed March 2, 1867, whereby said Andrew Johnson, President of the United States, did then and there commit a high misdemeanor in office.

ARTICLE 9. That said Andrew Johnson, President of the United States, on the 22nd day of February, in the year of our Lord 1868, at Washington, in the District of Columbia, in disregard of the Constitution and the law of Congress duly enacted, as Commander-in-Chief, did bring before himself, then and there, William H. Emory, a Major-General by brevet in the Army of the United States, actually in command of the Department of Washington, and the military forces therefor, and did and there, as Commander-in-Chief, declare to, and instruct said Emory, that part of the law of the United States, passed March 2, 1867, entitled "An act for making appropriations for the support of the army for the year ending June 30, 1868, and for other purposes," especially the second section thereof, which provides, among other things, that all orders and instructions relating to military operations issued by the President and

Secretary of War, shall be issued through the General of the Army, and in case of his inability, through the next in rank was unconstitutional, and in contravention of the commission of Emory, and therefor not binding on him, as an officer in the Army of the United States, which said provisions of law had been therefore duly and legally promulgated by General Order for the government and direction of the Army of the United States, as the said Andrew Johnson then and there well knew, with intent thereby to induce said Emory, in his official capacity as Commander of the Department of Washington, to violate the provisions of said act, and to take and receive, act upon and obey such orders as he, the said Andrew Johnson, might make and give, and which should not be issued through the General of the Army of the United States, according to the provisions of said act, whereby said Andrew Johnson, President of the United States, did then and there commit, and was guilty of a high misdemeanor in office; and the House of Representatives, by protestation, saving to themselves the liberty of exhibition, at any time hereafter, any further articles of their accusation or impeachment against the said Andrew Johnson, President of the United States, and also or replying to his answers, which will make up the articles herein preferred against him, and of offering proof to the same and every part shall be exhibited by them as the case shall require, do demand that the said Andrew Johnson may be put to answer the high crimes and misdemeanors in office herein charged against him, and that such proceedings, examinations, trials and judgments may be thereupon had and given had and given as may be agreeable to law and justice.

ARTICLE 10. That said Andrew Johnson, President of the United States, unmindful of the high duties of his high office and the dignity and proprieties thereof, and of the harmony and courtesies which ought to exist and be maintained between the executive and legislative branches of the Government of the United States, designing and intending to set aside the rightful authorities and powers of Congress, did attempt to bring into disgrace, ridicule, hatred, contempt and reproach, the Congress of the United States, and the several branches thereof, to impair and destroy the regard and respect of all the good people of the United States for the Congress and the legislative power thereof, which all officers of the government ought inviolably to preserve and maintain, and to excite the odium and resentment of all good people of the United States against Congress and the laws by it duly and constitutionally enacted; and in pursuance of his said design and intent, openly and publicly and before divers assemblages of citizens of the United States, convened in divers parts thereof, to meet and receive said Andrew Johnson as the Chief Magistrate of the United States, did, on the eighteenth day of August, in the year of our Lord one thousand eight hundred and sixty-six, and on divers other days and times, as well before as afterwards, make and declare, with a loud voice, certain intemperate, inflammatory and scandalous harangues, and therein utter loud threats and bitter menaces, as well against Congress as the laws of the United States duly enacted thereby, amid the cries, jeers and laughter of the multitudes then assembled in hearing, which are set forth in the several specifications hereinafter written, in substance and effect, that is to say:

"Specification First. In this, that at Washington, in the District of Columbia, In the Executive Mansion, to a committee of citizens who called upon the President of the

United States, speaking of and concerning the Congress of the United States, heretofore, to wit: On the 18th day of August, in the year of our Lord, 1866, in a loud voice, declare in substance and effect, among other things, that is to say:

"So far as the Executive Department of the government is concerned, the effort has been made to restore the Union, to heal the breach, to pour oil into the wounds which were consequent upon the struggle, and, to speak in a common phrase, to prepare, as the learned and wise physician would, a plaster healing in character and co-extensive with the wound. We thought and we think that we had partially succeeded, but as the work progresses, as reconstruction seemed to be taking place, and the country was becoming reunited, we found a disturbing and moving element opposing it. In alluding to that element it shall go no further than your Convention, and the distinguished gentleman who has delivered the report of the proceedings, I shall make no reference that I do not believe, and the time and the occasion justify. We have witnessed in one department of the government every endeavor to prevent the restoration of peace, harmony and union. We have seen hanging upon the verge of the government, as it were, a body called or which assumes to be the Congress of the United States, while in fact it is a Congress of only part of the States. We have seen this Congress pretend to be for the Union, when its every step and act tended to perpetuate disunion and make a disruption of States inevitable. We have seen Congress gradually encroach, step by step, upon constitutional rights, and violate day after day, and month after month, fundamental principles of the government. We have seen a Congress that seemed to forget that there was a limit to the sphere and scope of legislation. We have seen a Congress in a minority assume to exercise power which, if allowed to be consummated, would result in despotism or monarchy itself."

"Specification Second. In this, that at Cleveland, in the State of Ohio, heretofore to wit: On the third day of September, in the year of our Lord, 1866, before a public assemblage of citizens and others, said Andrew Johnson, President of the United States, speaking of and concerning the Congress of the United States, did, in a loud voice, declare in substance and effect, among other things, that is to say:

"I will tell you what I did do? I called upon your Congress that is trying to break up the government. In conclusion, beside that Congress had taken much pains to poison the constituents against him, what has Congress done? Have they done anything to restore the union of the States? No. On the contrary, they had done everything to prevent it: and because he stood now where he did when the Rebellion commenced, he had been denounced as a traitor, Who had run greater risks or made greater sacrifices than himself? But Congress, factions and domineering, had undertaken to poison the minds of the American people."

"Specification Third. In this case, that at St. Louis, in the State of Missouri, heretofore to wit: On the 8th day of September, in the year of our Lord 1866, before a public assemblage of citizens and others, said Andrew Johnson, President of the United States, speaking of acts concerning the Congress of the United States, did, in a loud voice, declare in substance and effect, among other things, that is to say:

"Go on; perhaps if you had a word or two on the subject of New Orleans you might understand more about it than you do, and if you will go back and ascertain the cause of the riot at New Orleans, perhaps you will not be so prompt in calling out 'New Orleans.' If you will take up the riot of New Orleans and trace it back to its source and its immediate cause, you will find out who was responsible for the blood that was shed there. If you will take up the riot at New Orleans and trace it back to the Radical Congress, you will find that the riot at New Orleans was substantially planned. If you will take up the proceedings in their caucuses you will understand that they knew that a convention was to be called which was extinct by its powers having expired; that it was said that the intention was that a new government was to be organized, and on the organization of that government the intention was to enfranchise one portion of the population, called the colored population, and who had been emancipated, and at the same time disfranchise white men. When you design to talk about New Orleans you ought to understand what you are talking about. When you read the speeches that were made, and take up the facts on the Friday and Saturday before that convention sat, you will find that speeches were made incendiary in their character, exciting that portion of the population, the black population, to arm themselves and prepare for the shedding of blood. You will also find that convention did assemble in violation of law, and the intention of that convention was to supersede the organized authorities in the State of Louisiana, which had been organized by the government of the United States, and every man engaged in that rebellion, in the convention, with the intention of superseding and upturning the civil government which had been recognized by the Government of the United States, I say that he was a traitor to the Constitution of the United States, and hence you find that another rebellion was commenced, having its origin in the Radical Congress. So much for the New Orleans riot. And there was the cause and the origin of the blood that was shed, and every drop of blood that was shed is upon their skirts and they are responsible. I could test this thing a little closer, but will not do it here to-night. But when you talk about the causes and consequences that resulted from proceedings of that kind, perhaps, as I have been introduced here and you have provoked questions of this kind, though it does not provoke me, I will tell you a few wholesome things that have been done by this Radical Congress in connection with New Orleans and the extension of the elective franchise. I know that I have been traduced and abused. I know it has come in advance of me here, as elsewhere, that I have attempted to exercise an arbitrary power in resisting laws that were intended to be forced upon the government; that I had exercised that power; that I had abandoned the party that elected me, and that I was a traitor, because I exercised the veto power in attempting, and did arrest for a time, that which was called a "Freedmen's Bureau" bill. Yes, that I was a traitor. And I have been traduced; I have been slandered; I have been maligned; I have been called Judas Iscariot, and all that. Now, my countrymen, here to-night, it is very easy to indulge in epithets; it is easy to call a man a Judas, and cry out traitor, but when he is called upon to give arguments and facts he is very often found wanting. Judas Iscariot? Judas! There was a Judas, and he was one of the twelve Apostles. O, yes, the twelve Apostles had a Christ, and he never could have had a Judas unless he had twelve Apostles. If I have played the Judas who has been my Christ that I have played the Judas with? Was it Thad. Stevens? Was it Wendell Phillips? Was it Charles Sumner? They are the men that stop and compare themselves with the Savior, and everybody that differs with them in opinion, and tries to stay and arrest their diabolical and nefarious policy is to be denounced as a Judas. Well, let me say to you, if you will stand by me in this action, if you will stand by me in trying to give the people a fair chance, soldiers and citizens, to participate in these offices, God be willing, I will kick them out. I will kick them out just as fast as I can. Let me say to you, in concluding, that what I have said is what I intended to say; I was not provoked into this, and care not for their menaces, the taunts and the jeers. I care not for threats, I do not intend to be bullied by enemies, nor overawed by my friends. But, God willing, with your help, I will veto their measures whenever any of them come to me."

Which said utterances, declarations, threats and harangues, highly censurable in any, are peculiarly indecent and unbecoming in the Chief Magistrate of the United States, by means whereof the said Andrew Johnson has brought the high office of the President of the United States into contempt, ridicule and disgrace, to the great scandal of all good citizens, whereby said Andrew Johnson, President of the United States, did commit, and was then and there guilty of a high misdemeanor in office.

ARTICLE 11. That the said Andrew Johnson, President of the United States, unmindful of the high duties of his office and his oath of office, and in disregard of the Constitution and laws of the United States, did, heretofore, to wit: On the 18th day of August, 1866, at the city of Washington, and in the District of Columbia, by public speech, declare and affirm in substance, that the Thirty-ninth Congress of the United States was not a Congress of the United States authorized by the Constitution to exercise legislative power under the same, but on the contrary, was a Congress of only part of the States, thereby denying and intending to deny, that the legislation of said Congress was valid or obligatory upon him, the said Andrew Johnson, except in so far as he saw fit to approve the same, and also thereby denying the power of the said Thirty-ninth Congress to propose amendments to the Constitution of the United States. And in pursuance of said declaration, the said Andrew Johnson, President of the United States, afterwards, to wit: On the 21st day of February 1868, at the city of Washington, D.C., did, unlawfully and in disregard of the requirements of the Constitution that he should take care that the laws be faithfully executed, attempt to prevent the execution of an act entitled "An act regulating the tenure of certain civil office," passed March 2, 1867, by unlawfully devising and contriving and attempting to devise and contrive means by which he should prevent Edwin M. Stanton from forthwith resuming the functions of the office of Secretary for the Department of War, notwithstanding the refusal of the Senate to concur in the suspension theretofore made by the said Andrew Johnson of said Edwin M. Stanton from said office of Secretary for the Department of War; and also by further unlawfully devising and contriving, and attempting to devise and contrive means then and there to prevent the execution of an act entitled "An act making appropriations for the support of the army for the fiscal year ending June 30,1868, and for other purposes," approved March 20, 1867. And also to prevent the execution of an act entitled "An act to provide for the more efficient government of the Rebel States," passed March 2, 1867. Whereby the said Andrew Johnson, President of the United States, did then, to wit, on the 21st day of February, 1868, at the city of Washington, commit and was guilty of a high misdemeanor in office.

Appendix C

Dramatis Personae, Denouement

A Selection:

Although **James Ashley** lost his seat in Congress, President Grant appointed him territorial governor in Montana; but Grant soon dismissed him, and Ashley's already tattered reputation continued to deteriorate even though, three years before his death, the Afro-American League of Tennessee roundly praised him as a "consummate statesman, patriot, philanthropist and benefactor."

Serving in Congress until 1872, **John Bingham** had written the due process and equal citizenship clauses of the Fourteenth Amendment, and he insisted that the former Confederate states ratify it before being readmitted to Congress; but he was not a Radical Republican: Thaddeus Stevens said Bingham had no backbone. Under President Grant, he became the U.S. minister to Japan.

Montgomery Blair, regarding himself as unofficial adviser to President Johnson, had angled for a position in his cabinet to no avail. Retaining the ear of traditional Democrats, especially because his loudmouthed brother Frank was their vice-presidential nominee in 1868, Blair returned to the Democratic party, and in 1876 loudly insisted that fellow Democrat Samuel J. Tilden had been legally elected although the Electoral Commission ruled in favor of Rutherford B. Hayes.

George S. Boutwell long championed black voting rights and worked hard on the Fifteenth Amendment—just as hard as he'd fought to have Andrew Johnson impeached. President Grant installed Boutwell as treasury secretary, and Boutwell remained in politics, serving in the Hayes administration and then returning to Congress as a senator. In later life, as founding member and first president of the

American Anti-Imperialist League, he passionately opposed American intervention in the Philippines.

Emily Edson Briggs was the first president of the newly founded Woman's National Press Association and one of the first women admitted to the congressional press gallery—"a favor that is given at best grudgingly, and never unless the need is imperative," as she said. After she and her husband had settled in the District of Columbia in 1861, she wrote her spiky column in the *Washington Chronicle* and the *Philadelphia Press* for more than twenty years.

Benjamin F. Butler, the Massachusetts man with the squashed look and brilliant mind, remains a controversial figure, perpetually linked with corruption, though nothing was ever proved. A savvy politician capable of mending fences, Butler regarded Grant as a fool, but soon after Grant's election supported him. Butler also strongly backed the 1875 Civil Rights Bill, helped pass legislation to suppress the Ku Klux Klan, advocated women's suffrage, and despite his association with congressional scandals, was elected governor of Massachusetts on the Democratic ticket in 1882. The overseers at Harvard University refused to grant Beast Butler the honorary degree typically bestowed on the governor, and when Butler attended the commencement, the president of the alumni association resigned rather than shake his hand.

Salmon Portland Chase was a lifelong politician with a very high opinion of his own abilities, for by the time he took on the robes of chief justice, Chase had already been Ohio senator, governor, presidential contender, and Lincoln's treasury secretary. But he ruined his reputation, then and later, by currying favor with the Democrats in 1868, hoping desperately—some say pathetically—to be their choice for the upcoming presidential contest.

Georges Clemenceau had fled Napoleon III, arriving in New York City in 1865, where this versatile, radically minded French doctor anonymously covered the American political scene for Paris *Temps* and became one of the regulars at Pfaff's Beer Cellar, the Bohemian hangout frequented by Walt Whitman. Clemenceau returned to France in 1869 with his American wife. There, as a journalist, he defended Dreyfus; as a politician, he would twice become premier of France, and after the First World War, known as The Tiger, he insisted on full German disarmament when he negotiated the peace.

The African American activist, businessman, entrepreneur, and restauranteur **George Downing** was also keeper of the restaurant in the U.S. House of Representatives, where he efficiently used it to lobby for civil and political rights— and on behalf of jobs for black men. A graduate of Hamilton College, Downing with a group of twelve others had resisted the Fugitive Slave Law and though a determined Republican, he frequently criticized the party for using black men and women as mere "bagged black ducks." When Liberal Republicanism overtook the party, Downing joined the Democrats; his business prowess and restaurant empire had secured him financial as well as political independence.

Born into slavery, **Frederick Douglass** escaped in 1831, and for a time allied himself with William Lloyd Garrison's abolitionist movement, becoming such a powerful speaker, said William Wells Brown, that many white people stayed away from his lectures lest they be converted to abolitionism against their will. His memoir of his captivity, *The Narrative of the Life of Frederick Douglass, an American Slave*, rocketed Douglass to international acclaim; today it's a classic of American literature. Also an author, speaker, and untiring advocate for equal human rights, Douglass continued to call Johnson treacherous, unscrupulous, ambitious—and plausible.

A supremely confident member of Johnson's defense team, as his attorney general after the President's acquittal, **William Maxwell Evarts** was said to be the only man who could curb Johnson's worst tendencies. After Johnson's presidency, Grant sidelined Evarts because of his association with Johnson. Yet Evarts was instrumental as a member of the legal team who secured the presidency for Rutherford B. Hayes. Secretary of state under Hayes, Evarts later served as a one-term senator from New York. Henry Adams adored Evarts as a man-of-the-world who took pride in doing the things he did not like to do, although it seems that Evarts did precisely as he wished, with panache.

The sometimes prickly **William Pitt Fessenden** had gone back to the Senate just before Lincoln's assassination (Fessenden had served as Lincoln's treasury secretary after Salmon Chase); Lincoln considered Fessenden a Radical, which he decidedly was not. Since Lincoln had dropped Vice President Hannibal Hamlin, also of Maine, Fessenden had wanted to make sure he kept his seat in the upper House. Tall and slim, his face long and increasingly lined, Fessenden was reserved, he was spare, he was disciplined, he was something of a prude, and he disliked conflict although he despised Charles Sumner. Placing his eyeglasses on his head before he spoke, he was deft in parliamentary debate, practical, logical, precise, incorruptible, and reasonably, if not insufferably, convinced of his own rectitude—although one dubious acquaintance would call him a "crooked stick."

Walt Whitman greatly admired the "grandly noncommittal" **Ulysses S. Grant,** who continued after the war to realize the principles embodied in the Thirteenth, Fourteenth, and then Fifteenth Amendments. And despite the many scandals associated with his presidency, Grant presided over the passage of the Fifteenth Amendment, giving blacks the right to vote, and helped to crush the Ku Klux Klan.

Andrew Johnson stayed sensitive—thin-skinned, actually—and continued to seek advice from those he thought he could trust: practically no one. Said a former general in the Confederate army, Johnson was possessed with an obstinate, suspicious temper: "Like a badger, one had to dig him out of his hole." Firm and courageous as a Southern senator, representing Tennessee, and the Southerner who had valiantly stood by the Union when his colleagues seceded, Johnson was chosen by Lincoln as his running mate in 1864. The rest is history.

Eliza McCardle Johnson is one of the enigmatic presidential wives, having disappeared from public view after arriving at the White House in late summer 1865.

There, she tended her five grandchildren, who were the children of her two daughters (one widowed), who also lived in the Executive Mansion. But she left the supervision of state dinners and other public duties to her eldest child, Martha Patterson, presumably Johnson's favorite. Despite fragile health and her son Robert's suicide in 1869, Eliza McCardle Johnson outlived her husband by nearly six months.

Wendell Phillips was unabashedly the Wendell Phillips his admirers and detractors expected: relentless, farsighted, and slightly arrogant. Although Navy Secretary Gideon Welles couldn't stand Phillips, Welles had to admit his "extraordinary gift" for public speaking. Charismatic, Phillips always drew a crowd, whether his topic was slavery, impeachment, or later labor reform. By the time Rutherford Hayes entered the White House, Phillips was convinced that the weak-kneed, white Republicans had yet again sold out the ideals for which the war had been fought. Somehow, though, the optimistic Phillips, a man insensible to praise or censure, never lost his belief in himself—or the country he so loved.

Born in Wisconsin, **Vinnie Ream,** who began her career as a sculptor in Washington, D.C., and operated there as an informal lobbyist in the studio where she worked— which happened to be located in the Capitol Building—married the wealthy Lieutenant Richard Leveridge Hoxie of the Army Corps of Engineers in 1878. He urged her to abandon sculpture, and after the birth of a son in 1883, she began to suffer from a series of illnesses. An 1870 portrait of Ream by G.P.A. Healy hangs in the National Museum of American Art, Washington, D.C.

Formerly a Kansas journalist, during the war **Edmund G. Ross** served as captain in a Kansas regiment under the command of Thomas Ewing, Jr., and then returned to Topeka, where he edited the Topeka *Kansas Tribune* until the suicide of Senator James Lane created the vacancy that Ross was elected to fill. General Daniel Sickles would recall that fellow Radical Republicans asked him to sway Ross the night before the Senate voted in the impeachment trial. Presumably, Vinnie Ream distracted Sickles, preventing him from talking with Ross, until four in the morning. Ream and Ross denied the story. Later, Ross, as a Democrat, importuned President Cleveland to appoint him territorial governor of New Mexico. Charged with nepotism, he served four years and then tried to rehabilitate his reputation with a published defense of his vote in the impeachment trial.

Serving in the Lincoln and Johnson administrations, **William H. Seward** baffled many former admirers with his loyalty to Andrew Johnson. A crafty politician, he held his cards close to his chest; even his personal letters were composed so as not to give much away. Intelligent, cultured, witty, and an able raconteur, Seward kept his eye on the main chance, which was William Seward. Slight and slim, he was described by Henry Adams, who admired him, as having a "head like a wise macaw; a beaked nose; shaggy eyebrows; unorderly hair and clothes; hoarse voice; offhand manner; free talk; and perpetual cigar." Georges Clemenceau, less admiring, was certain he played a considerable part in the acquittal of Andrew Johnson—others called Seward a coward and a sneak; Mark Twain parodied the slippery secretary as saying, "I have always done my duty by my country when it seemed best. I was always the first to desert it when it lost its prestige. . . . I have been always ready & willing to embrace Christianity, infidelity, or paganism, according to which held the most trumps." A territorial expansionist, Secretary Seward oversaw the U.S. purchase of Alaska for $7.2 million during the waning days of the Johnson administration and intended also to acquire Hawaii.

A West Point graduate, wiry, short, with hair that seemed painted onto his head and a handlebar mustache, General **Philip Sheridan** had a well-deserved reputation for titanic daring, and he was beloved by his troops. "If a wounded man stumbled," recalled one of Grant's aides, "he called out to him: 'There's no harm done'; and the trooper went on with a bullet in his brain till he dropped dead on the field." As military governor in Texas and Louisiana after the war, Sheridan strenuously supported the enrollment of black voters—and met with such opposition he famously said, "If I owned both Hell and Texas, I'd rent out Texas and live in Hell." In 1884 he became commander in chief of the army, serving until his death, and though active in the creation of Yellowstone National Park, he was also known for ruthless campaigns against the Oklahoma Cheyenne and the Southern Plains Indians.

After the death of his father, a nine-year-old **William Tecumseh Sherman** (he'd been named after the Shawnee chief Tecumseh) was raised by Thomas Ewing, the first secretary of the interior, fourteenth treasury secretary, and U.S. senator from Ohio. Ewing helped secure Sherman admission to West Point, and Sherman married Ewing's daughter Ellen. In 1853, he resigned from the army and for a short time became a banker in San Francisco; that didn't go well. Appointed infantry colonel at first during the war, after Bull Run Sherman said that at least two thousand troops would be needed to win the war; he was called insane and temporarily relieved from duty. Reinstated, he headed the Georgia campaign in the notorious "march to the sea," for by then his friendship with Grant was crucial to winning the war. But Sherman opposed the Radical Republican blueprint for reconstruction, which Grant did not. Restless, ruthless, brilliant, fond of Dickens and Shakespeare, whom he often quoted, Sherman later waged war against Native Americans. With amoral clarity, he'd unhappily predicted that any sustained assault would be "a sort of predatory war for years"—which is what happened; Sherman ordered the army to strike Native Americans brutally and without hesitation.

Lincolnesque, at least in looks, **Henry Stanbery** was the law partner of Thomas Ewing and, like Ewing, adamantly opposed giving black men or women the vote. When Johnson renominated Stanbery as attorney general after the impeachment trial, the Senate refused to confirm him.

The abrasive **Edwin Stanton** was one of the big guns of the wartime administration, said Walt Whitman; you could rely on him. "He was touchy, testy, yet also wonderfully patriotic, courageous, far-seeing," the poet noted. After Grant's inauguration as President, Stanton said, more than anything, he had wanted a seat on the Supreme Court, and at the end of 1869, when one became vacant, he was swiftly confirmed by Congress. His health already shattered, he died just a few days later, at age fifty-five.

As the recognized leader of the House Republicans, **Thaddeus Stevens** always inspired hatred, devotion, contempt, fear, and affectionate respect; still does. Born into poverty, partly lame because of a congenital clubfoot, Stevens was a fighter; he had fought in Pennsylvania for free public education—and for a war to end slavery once and for all, which he hoped Lincoln would wage with ferocity. Known for his sarcasm, his masterful intelligence, and his generosity, he might annihilate a colleague on the House floor, it was said, and then take him to lunch. He had no use for Andrew Johnson.

Fresh out of Harvard Law School, **Moorfield Storey** went to work as Charles Sumner's private secretary, where the fairly conservative young man was soon radicalized. Back in Massachusetts in 1869, Storey passed the bar, and as a Liberal Republican, then a Democrat, supported the presidential bid of Grover Cleveland. Although he never held public office, he did briefly consider running for President on a third-party ticket; in later life, and always an activist, he became founding president of the NAACP (the National Association for the Advancement of Colored People) as well as a charter member and president of the American Anti-Imperialism League, which vigorously opposed American intervention in Cuba and the Philippines.

Called great and weak, philanthropic and selfish, venomous and sincere, **Charles Sumner** could be insulting, which is how Congressman Preston Brooks regarded Sumner's 1856 public excoriation of his cousin Andrew Butler as beholden to his mistress, the "harlot slavery." On the Senate floor, with colleagues standing by, Brooks proceeded to thrash Sumner within an inch of his life. Sumner left the Senate to recuperate for more than three years while Massachusetts kept the seat open. Returning to the Senate, Sumner continued to condemn slavery as barbaric, and after the war, like Stevens, he deplored what he saw as Johnson's betrayal of Republican ideals. He then supported Grant for President but when not nominated his secretary of state, as Grant's antagonist, he prevented passage of a treaty to annex Santo Domingo, which he considered to have been fraudulently negotiated. As a result, Sumner lost his position as chair of the Senate Foreign Relations Committee. All the while, though, Sumner continued the battle for civil and political rights for blacks, even after he joined the Liberal Republicans, mainly to prevent Grant's 1872 re-election.

Keen, sharp, reserved, and logical, **Lyman Trumbull** struck contemporaries as looking like a schoolmaster. After serving as a judge on the Illinois Supreme Court, Trumbull defeated Lincoln in 1854 for the Senate seat, although the two men admired each other and shared the similar aim, preventing the extension of slavery into the territories. Though he helped draft the Thirteenth Amendment, he called the Radical Republicans rash and ruthless. During Grant's administration, Trumbull became a Liberal Republican to protest government corruption. Urged to a run as the Liberal Republican candidate for President in 1872, Trumbull was passed over in favor of the once-powerful publisher Horace Greeley, even though Greeley was widely dismissed as an inept, half-cracked huckster. In 1876, Trumbull became a Democrat, but in 1894, allying himself with Populists, he and Clarence Darrow defended labor leader Eugene V. Debs for having participated in the Pullman railway strike.

Né Samuel Clemens of Missouri, **Mark Twain** had paddled the Mississippi until the Civil War; had fought very briefly on the side of the Confederacy during that war; had lived in Nevada and prospected in San Francisco; and worked as a lecturer, humorist, inventor, stand-up comic, and writer who hated cant: that same Mark Twain, author of such iconic books as *The Adventures of Huckleberry Finn*, was also an incisive, coruscating, and basically compassionate political journalist living in Washington in the months before the impeachment trial.

Considered the most honest man in the Senate but also the unsubtle conscience of the Republicans, **Benjamin Wade** was burly and belligerent, profane and tenacious, and not without his prejudices. During the first days of the Civil War, Wade attempted to block the Union retreat at Bull Run by grabbing his rifle, overturning his carriage, and threatening to shoot runaway soldiers. Though an elector for Rutherford B. Hayes in the disputed election of 1876, Wade considered Hayes' withdrawal of federal troops from the South a tragic and treacherous mistake.

Along with his two brothers, who had each been elected from different states, **Elihu Washburne** was a supporter of Lincoln—he'd written his campaign biography—and then managed Grant's presidential campaign. A cautious but energetic broad-shouldered man with bushy eyebrows, Washburne was appointed secretary of state by Grant, but he immediately resigned. Then, as minister to France, he stayed there during the Franco-Prussian War and the Commune. In 1880, he permanently and bitterly fell out with Grant over the presidential contest.

Familiarly known as the Old Man of the Sea, or Neptune, Secretary of the Navy **Gideon Welles** was a fusty, cranky man with a bushy beard who had been a Democrat, albeit an anti-slavery one, in the Connecticut House of Representatives. Rewarded by Lincoln with a cabinet post, during the Civil War Welles efficiently expanded and rebuilt the navy, and, increasingly embittered, believed he and the navy never received their due for their contribution to the Union victory. During both the Lincoln and Johnson administrations, Welles, a former journalist, faithfully kept a diary in which he transcribed the daily goings-on in the cabinet and government, generally with a waspish pen. For better and worse, the diary has become essential, if biased, source material.

An anti-slavery Democrat before the war, **Walt Whitman** traveled to Washington after the battle at Fredericksburg to find his brother. He stayed there but lost his job as a clerk when Interior Secretary James Harlan found in Whitman's desk a working copy of *Leaves of Grass*, which he called obscene. Whitman was then hired in the attorney general's office, and friends rallied round him with a campaign that famously turned him into the Good Gray Poet. Shaggy and massive, he was often seen swinging slowly down Washington's broad avenues, an old felt hat perched on his head, his collar unbuttoned. During the Johnson years, the poet wrote essays later collected as *Democratic Vistas*, and which had been inspired in part by the corruption of politicians—and what Whitman celebrated as the strong, vital, lasting, and forever sublime spirit of America.

Notes

People

The following abbreviations are used for frequently cited names:

AJ: Andrew Johnson
BB: Benjamin F. Butler
HCW: Henry Clay Warmoth
OOH: Oliver Otis Howard
USG: Ulysses S. Grant
WPF: William Pitt Fessenden
WTS: William Tecumseh Sherman

Archives, Libraries, Collections

For frequently cited libraries or manuscript depositories, the following abbreviations are used:

BRFA: Registers and Letters Received by the Commissioner of the Bureau of Refugees, Freemen, and Abandoned Lands, 1865–1872
Bowdoin: George J. Mitchell Department of Special Collections and Archives, Bowdoin College Library, Bowdoin College, Brunswick, Maine
Butler: Rare Book and Manuscripts Library, Butler Library, Columbia University, New York, New York
Cornell: Samuel J. May Anti-Slavery Collection, Special Collections, Cornell University Library Division of Rare Books and Manuscripts
LC: Library of Congress, Manuscripts Collections, Washington, D.C.

Hayes: Rutherford B. Hayes Presidential Center, Special Collections, Fremont, Ohio

Houghton: Houghton Library, Harvard University, Cambridge, Massachusetts

Huntington: Huntington Library, San Marino, California

KSHS: Kansas State Historical Society, Topeka, Kansas

NA: National Archives and Records Administration, Washington, D.C.

Notre Dame: Archives, Hesburgh Library, University of Notre Dame, Notre Dame, Indiana

NYHS: New York Historical Society Museum and Library, Manuscripts Department, New York, New York

NYPL: The New York Public Library, Manuscripts and Archives Division. Astor, Lenox and Tilden Foundations, New York, New York

SHA: Southern Historical Collection at University of North Carolina, Chapel Hill

SCA: South Caroliniana Collection, University of Southern Carolina, Columbia, South Carolina

Smith: Sophia Smith Collection, Smith College, Northampton, Massachusetts

Western Reserve: Western Reserve Historical Society, Cleveland, Ohio

WHS: Wisconsin Historical Society, Madison, Wisconsin

Yale: Archives and Manuscripts, Sterling Memorial Library, Yale University, New Haven, Connecticut

In addition to the archives gratefully credited above, I also gleaned significant material among the following papers:

Francis W. Bird papers bMS Am 1851; Edwin Lawrence Godkin Papers, bMS Am 1083, Charles Eliot Norton Papers, bMS 1066; Frederick Law Olmsted Papers, bMS 1088; Wendell Phillips Papers, bMS Am 1953, Charles Sumner Papers, bMS Am 1, Houghton Library, Harvard University.

Samuel L. M. Barlow Papers, MS BW 42, boxes 56–68, plus the Jerome Stillson Correspondence, HM 82487–82516, The Huntington Library, San Marino, California.

The Bigelow Family Papers, MSS 299 and John Bigelow Papers, MSS 301; Horace Greeley Papers, MSS 1231; Bryant-Godwin Papers, MSS 422, Henry J. Raymond Papers, MSS 2532; Gideon Welles Papers, MS 3275, in The Brooke Russell Astor Reading Room for Rare Books and Manuscripts, New York Public Library.

The following abbreviations are used for frequently cited books, reports, or articles:

CWL: *Collected Works of Lincoln,* ed. Roy Basler. New Brunswick: Rutgers University Press, 8 vols.

CG: *Congressional Globe: Debates and Proceedings, 1833–1873.* Washington, D.C.: Blair and Rives, 1834–1873.

"Impeachment Investigation": National Archives Files, 40th Congress, Various Papers, Files 40B–A1, C–A2, Boxes 1–12.

Impeachment Testimony: Impeachment Investigation: Testimony taken before the Judiciary Committee of the House of Representatives in the Investigation of Charges Against Andrew Johnson, 39th Cong., 2nd Session and 40th Congress, 1st Session. Washington, D.C.: Government Printing Office, 1867.

"Memphis Report": *Report of the Select Committee on the New Orleans Riots.* Washington, D.C.: Government Printing Office, 1867.

Moore: "Notes of Colonel W. G. Moore, Private Secretary to Andrew Johnson." ed. George L. St. Siousset. *American Historical Review*, Oct. 1913: 98–131.

OR: "War of the Rebellion" *Official Records of the Union and Confederate Armies.* Washington, D.C.: Government Printing Office, 1880–1901.

PAJ: *Papers of Andrew Johnson*, ed. Roy LeGraf, Ralph Haskins, and Paul Bergeron. 16 vols. Knoxville: University of Tennessee Press, 1967–2000.

PUSG: *Papers of Ulysses S. Grant*, ed. John Y. Simon. Carbondale: Southern Illinois University Press, 1974–2009, 31 vols. (Supplementary volume 32, ed. John F. Marszalek.)

"Raising of Money": "Raising of Money to Be Used in Impeachment," *Report to the Committees of the United States House of Representatives for the Fortieth Congress*, 75, CG 40: 2, July 3, 1868. Washington, D.C.: Government Printing Office, 1868.

Trial: *The Trial of Andrew Johnson, President of the United States, before the Senate of the United States, on Impeachment by the House of Representatives for High Crimes and Misdemeanors.* ed. Benjamin Perley Poore. 3 vols. Washington, D.C.: Government Printing Office, 1868.

PROLOGUE

xviii *"This is a country for white men"*: quoted in McKitrick, *Andrew Johnson and Reconstruction*, p. 184.

xviii "If we have not been sufficiently": CG 39: 1, Dec. 18, 1865, pp. 74–75.

xviii "'All men are created free and equal'": CG 39: 2, Jan. 15, 1867, p. 478.

xix "Peace had come": Josephson, *The Politicos*, p. 6.

xix It sounded like a death sentence: "Washington. Impeachment of Johnson at the Bar of the Senate," *Cincinnati Daily Gazette*, 02-26-1868, p. 3.

xix "And out of the midst": Mark Twain, "Mark Twain's Letter," *Chicago Republican*, March 1, 1868, p. 1.

xix "Andrew Johnson was the queerest man": Cullom, *Fifty Years of Public Service*, p. 143.

xx "The multitude of strangers were waiting for impeachment": "Mark Twain's Letter," *Chicago Republican*, March 1, 1868, p. 11.

xxi Still, the impeachment of a President: see C. M. Ellis, "The Causes for Which a President Can Be Impeached," *Atlantic Monthly* (Jan. 1867), p. 89. For a more modern point of view, written in the shadow of the possible Nixon impeachment, and one that argues against the Johnson impeachment, see Berger, *Impeachment*.

xxii "the negro is an animal": Andrews, *The South Since the War*, p. 87.

xxii "Can we depend on our President to exert his influence": F. A. Angell to BB, July 7, 1865, Butler, *Private and Official Correspondence*, vol. 5, p. 641.

xxiii "replanting the seeds of rebellion": quoted in Thaddeus Stevens, "Reconstruction," Sept. 6, 1865, in Stevens, *Selected Papers*, vol. 2, p. 22.

xxiii "It is our duty": quoted in Andrews, *The South Since the War*, p. 391.

xxiii Union General Philip Sheridan: Gen. Philip Sheridan to OOH, Aug. 3, 1865, Bowdoin.

xxiii In New Orleans: see Reid, *After the War: A Southern Tour*, p. 245.

xxiii "People had not got over regarding": Reid, *After the War*, pp. 420–22.

xxiv The whole episode left such a bitter aftertaste: see C. Vann Woodward, "The Other Impeachment," *The New York Times Magazine*, Aug. 11, 1974, p. 25.

xxiv The year before Woodward's pronouncement: see Michael Les Benedict, *The Impeachment and Trial of Andrew Johnson*.

xxv "political and legal train wreck": Stewart, *Impeached*, p. 315.

xxv "This is one of the last great battles with slavery": *Trial* III, pp. 247–48.

xxvii "unscathed cross upon": quoted in Stryker, *Andrew Johnson*, p. 822.

xxviii "The American people must be taught": AJ, "Reply to the Illinois Delegation," April 18, 1865, quoted in Moore, *Speeches of Andrew Johnson*, p. 470.

CHAPTER ONE: MARS

4 aggressive often insolent: see Flower, *Stanton*, p. 48.

4 "prone to despond": Dawes, "Recollections of Stanton under Lincoln," p. 164.

5 "Where is Mary?": Wolcott, *Edwin M. Stanton*, p. 100.

5 "I feel indifferent": Stanton to Salmon Chase, Nov. 30, 1846, LC; see also Thomas and Hyman, *Edwin Stanton*, pp. 40–41.

5 "as white and cold and motionless": *Inside Lincoln's White House: The Complete Civil War Diary of John Hay*, ed. Burlingame and Ettlinger, p. 37.

6 The good-looking District Attorney Key: Key was also the nephew of Chief Justice Roger Taney, the man who'd delivered the controversial Dred Scott decision.

6 "pantherlike pursuit of the evildoer": Hendrick, *Lincoln's War Cabinet*, p. 247.

6 "man of administrative scope": quoted in Burlingame, ed. *Lincoln's Journalist: John Hay's Anonymous Writings for the Press, 1862–1864*, p. 196; "make a tour of a smallpox hospital," quoted in Thayer, *John Hay*, vol. 1, p. 147.

7 During the war: See Howe, *Moorfield Storey*, p. 67.

7 "Stanton is a character such as Plutarch would have liked to describe": Francis Lieber to [Benson J. Losing?], Dec. 25, 1865, LC.

7 "Such hostility should": Blaine, *Twenty Years in Congress*, vol. 2, p. 60.

7 "My own personal knowledge": Black, "Mr. Black to Mr. Wilson," p. 261.

8 "run with the hare": Black, "Mr. Black to Mr. Wilson," p. 263.

8 Were there two different Stantons?: see DeWitt, *The Impeachment*, p. 242.

8 "Keep me alive": See Benjamin, "Recollections of Secretary Stanton," p. 760.

8 "in-betweenity": *Impeachment Testimony*, pp. 35, 403, 622.

8 "He seemed to regard": Benjamin, "Recollections of Secretary Stanton," p. 765.

9 "He was the bulwark of confidence": Albert E.H. Johnson, "Reminiscences of the Hon. Edwin M. Stanton, Secretary of War," p. 77; "In the dark hours": *Ibid.*, p. 92.

9, 10 "merry twinkle," "like a woman": Johnson, ed. "Sensitivity and Civil War: The Selected Diaries and Papers, 1858–1866, of Frances Adeline [Fanny] Seward," pp. 545, 869.

10 "mild as drawn butter,": quoted in Lowe, *Meade's Army, The Private Diaries of Theodore Lyman*, p. 345.

10 "giraffe,": See Piatt, *Memories of Men Who Saved the Union*, p. 59. Also note that Thomas and Hyman, *Edwin Stanton*, pp. 116–18, question Piatt's credibility.

10 "As soon as I can": Stanton to Charles A. Dana, Jan. 24, 1862, quoted in Flower, *Stanton*, p. 141.

10 "I consider him one of the heroic elements in our war,": Francis Lieber to [Benson J. Losing?] Dec. 25, 1865, LC.

10 "He was prone to be suspicious": Dawes, "Recollections of Stanton under Lincoln," p. 168.

11 "'God help me to do my duty,'": quoted in Flower, *Stanton*, p. 419.

11 "against which the breakers": quoted in Flower, *Stanton*, pp. 369–70.

11 "one of the great men of the Republic": quoted in Young, *Around the World with General Grant*, p. 334.

11 "It is not for you to say": Wilson, "Edwin M. Stanton," p. 243.

13 He oversaw Lincoln's burial attire: see Stahr, *Stanton: Lincoln's War Secretary*, p. 446.

14 "God will punish & forgive,": Willard Saxton diary, April 18, 1865, Yale.

14 "May God support": quoted in Trefousse, *Andrew Johnson*, p. 194.

14 "I was never so": Zachariah Chandler to Letitia Chandler, March 6, 1865, LC.

15 "clearly . . . that those who are good enough": "The President and the Rebel Chiefs," *Harper's Weekly*, p. 274.

15 "would prove a godsend": Julian, *Political Recollections*, p. 255.

15 "robbery is a crime": Julian, "George W. Julian's Journal," p. 335.

15 "So too was Ohio Senator Benjamin Wade,": Julian, *Political Recollections*, pp. 257, 255; see also Julian, "George W. Julian's Journal," p. 335.

15 "Thank God Stanton lives,": W. M. Dickson to Edwin Stanton, April 15, 1865, LC.

15 "The country cannot": George Bancroft to Edwin Stanton, April 26, 1865, LC.

15 "Stand your ground": J. K. Moorhead, inter alia., to Edwin Stanton, April 19, 1865, LC.

CHAPTER TWO: MAGNIFICENT INTENTIONS

16 "There is incompleteness": Willard Saxton diary, July 15, 1866, Yale.

17 some 40,000 freed blacks: see Litwack, *Been in the Storm So Long*, pp. 413–514.

17 "dead horses, dead dogs, cats, rats, rubbish, and refuse of all kind,": Larsen, ed., *Crusader and Feminist: The Letters of Jane Swisshelm*, p. 287.

17 "I have even heard its inhabitants tell stories of nightly pig-hunts in the streets,": Latham, *Black and White: A Journal of a Three Months' Tour in the United States*, p. 59.

18 "get back the political ascendancy dear to every Southern heart,": see Charlotte Cushman, notes on an unfinished ms., pp. 498, 532–33, nd, LC.

19 "the worst men of the South,": John Sherman to WTS, May 16, 1865, ed. Rachel Thorndike, *The Sherman Letters*, p. 251.

19 "inadmissible," "simple military view,": John Sherman to Edwin Stanton, April 27, 1865, LC.

19 "No one could be with him half an hour and doubt his greatness,": Badeau, *Military History of General Grant*, vol. 2, p. 19.

20 "He stood by me when I was crazy": Brockett, *Our Great Captains*, p. 175.

20 "Gossip of my having presidential aspirations": OR, part 47, section 3, May 28, 1865, p. 583.

20 "I will not accept if nominated . . . and will not serve if elected,": quoted in *Marszalek, Sherman: A Soldier's Passion for Order*, p. 493.

21 "we, the loyal people": April 11, 1865, CWL 8: 399–405. For the best summary

discussion of Lincoln's views, and his last cabinet meeting, see Foner, *The Fiery Trial: Abraham Lincoln and American Slavery*, pp. 290–336.

22 "This is a moment": Charles Sumner to Francis Lieber, [May] 14, [1864], Houghton.

22 "if the colored loyalists": Salmon Chase to Abraham Lincoln, April 11, 1865, *The Correspondence of Salmon P. Chase*, vol. 5, p. 15.

22 "the political power in the late insurrectionary State be intrusted exclusively": [George William Curtis], "The Main Question," *Harper's Weekly*, May 27, 1865, p. 322.

22 "Slavery is not abolished": quoted in "Anti-Slavery Society: Exciting Debate," *The New York Times*, May 11, 1865, p. 2.

23 Radical Republicans were not: see McKitrick, *Andrew Johnson and Reconstruction*, pp. 53–67.

23 "radical abolition": "The Prospects of the Administration and the South—the Negro Suffrage Question," *New York Herald*, June 30, 1865, p. 4.

24 Schuyler Colfax: See Hollister, *The Life of Schuyler Colfax*, p. 255; see also pp. 220–22.

24 providence had chosen him to: see for instance "President Johnson and the South Carolinians: An Interesting Conference," *Massachusetts Spy*, June 28, 1865, p. 3, where Johnson talks of his providential mission.

24 "dignified, urbane, and self-possessed": Strong, *The Diary of George Templeton Strong*, vol. 3, p. 591.

24 "I rejoice": see Lydia Maria Child, "Letter from L. M. Child," *The Liberator*, May 11, 1865, p. 4.

24 "Those occupying high official positions": "To New York City Merchants," May 22, 1865, *PAJ* 8: 104.

25 "We plebeians, the majority of the U.S.": Stephen M. Barbour to AJ, May 1, 1865, *PAJ* 8: 2.

25 "out Herod, Herod,": Daniel Dudley Avery to Dudley Avery, May 12, 1865, Avery Family Papers, serial J, part 5, reel 11, SHA.

25 "as colored men, we have entire confidence in President Johnson,": "Andrew Johnson President of the United States," *New Orleans Black Republican*, April 22, 1865, p. 1.

25 Hadn't Andrew Johnson: see "Moses of the Colored Men," Oct. 24, 1864, *PAJ* 7: 251.

25 "*in the question*": quoted in Stearns, *The Life and Public Service of George Luther Stearns*, p. 343.

25 "Sumner had too often taken": Donald, *Charles Sumner and the Rights of Man*, p. 224.

26 "He will break with them": Montgomery Blair to S.L.M. Barlow, May 13, 1865, Barlow papers, Huntington.

28 "It was a remarkable": Brooks, *Washington in Lincoln's Time*, p. 274.

CHAPTER THREE: THE ACCIDENTAL PRESIDENT

30 One newspaper: *New York Ledger*, quoted in "The Poisoning of Andrew Johnson on the Fourth of March," *The New York Times*, May 7, 1865, p. 1.

30 "We have an era of good feeling now": May 11, 1865, Strong, *The Diary*, vol. 3, p. 596.

30 "Johnson talks first rate": quoted in Marshall, ed. *Letters and Private Correspondence of Benjamin Butler*, p. 619.

30 "There is no guarantee": Stanley Matthews to Salmon Chase, April 19, 1865, *The Correspondence of Salmon P. Chase*, vol. 5, p. 28.

31 "carry its ballots": "From North Carolina Blacks," May 10, 1865, *PAJ* 8: 58.

31 "with freedom every thing they need is to come like manna from heaven": "Reply to Delegation of Black Ministers," May 11, 1865, *PAJ* 8: 62.

31 "In what new skin will the old snake come forth?": Frederick Douglass, "An Address Delivered in New York, New York," May 10, 1865, reprinted in *Frederick Douglass Papers*, vol. 4, pp. 80–85.

31 "aided by the Federal Government": see "Order Restoring Virginia," May 9, 1865, *PAJ* 8: 53.

31 "I see the President is precipitating": Thaddeus Stevens to Charles Sumner, May 10, 1865, Houghton.

31 "reconstruction is a very": Thaddeus Stevens to AJ, May 16, 1865, *PAJ* 8: 80.

32 "The Pierpont govt is nothing but a sham,": Charles Sumner to Wendell Phillips, May 11, 1865, Sumner, *Selected Letters of Charles Sumner*, vol. 2. p. 302.

33 "with all the powers necessary": see "Order Restoring North Carolina," May 29, 1865, *PAJ* 8: 136.

33 "Better, far better": see "Boston Anniversaries," *The New York Times*, June 1, 1865, p. 1, and *New-York Tribune*, June 2, 1865, p. 6.

33 "way to arrest the insane": Thaddeus Stevens to Charles Sumner, June 12, 1865, Houghton.

33 "I see our worthy": Thaddeus Stevens to William D. Kelley, *c*, vol. 2, p. 6.

33 "I am not well satisfied": Charles Eliot Norton to E. L. Godkin, June 15, 1865, Houghton.

34 "Nothing since Chancellorsville,": Charles Sumner to Gideon Welles, June 15, 1865, LC.

34 "a clime and country suited to you,": "Reply to Delegation of Black Ministers," May 11, 1865, *PAJ* 8: 46.

34 "Among all the leading Union men": Thaddeus Stevens to AJ, July 6, 1865, *PAJ* 8: 365.

34 "moral, political": Salmon Chase to Joseph W. Schuckers, June 25, 1865, *The Correspondence of Salmon P. Chase*, vol. 5, p. 55.

34 "These States have not gone out of": "Interview with John A. Logan," May 31, 1865, *PAJ* 8: 154.

35 "*vacated*," "by all local": Sumner, "Our Domestic Relations," p. 527.

35 "The theory that": CG 39: 1, Dec. 18, 1865, p. 73.

35 they be "held in a territorial": *Reconstruction: Speech of the Honorable Thaddeus Stevens*, Sept. 7, 1865 pp. 3–4.

35 Welles nonetheless considered: Gideon Welles, "Recollections of Andrew Johnson and His Cabinet," nd, NYPL. See also Carl Schurz, *The Reminiscences of Carl Schurz*, vol. 3, pp. 202–03.

37 "God damn you Seward": Van Deusen, *William Henry Seward*, p. 249.

37 But as historians have persuasively argued: see Cox, *Politics, Principle, and Prejudice*, p. 401 ff.

37 But hardline Democrats loathed: see for instance Montgomery Blair to S.M.L. Barlow, nd; April 28, 1865; June 14, 1865; July 21, 1865; August 3, 1865; Thomas Pratt to S.M.L. Barlow, August 18, 1865; and William Shipman to S.M.L. Barlow, August 21, 1865, all in Barlow papers, Huntington.

37 "Seward entered into him,": quoted in McCall, *Thaddeus Stevens*, p. 325.

38 Carl Schurz, the noted German refugee: see Schurz, *The Reminiscences of Carl Schurz*, vol. 3, pp. 202–03.

38 The radical *National Anti-Slavery Standard*: see *National Anti-Slavery Standard*, Oct. 28, 1865.

38 "we give them political power": Sumner, "Clemency and Common Sense," p. 760.

39 The dynastic Blair family: Francis Preston Blair Sr., the patriarch, had served in Andrew Jackson's cabinet and for many years published the renowned Democratic mouthpiece *The Globe*. The patriarch's son Francis P. Blair, Jr., or Frank, was a leading Missouri politician and Union general who opposed slavery but wanted slaves emancipated gradually—and then deported. Charles Francis Adams, descendent of a political clan that included two American Presidents, referred to them as a motley gang, with "one statesman, one politician, two jobbers, one intriguer, and two respectable old gentlemen": Quoted in Van Deusen, *William Henry Seward*, p. 274.

39 "there will be but few [Southerners] punished after all": Montgomery Blair to Samuel L. M. Barlow, May 13, 1865, Barlow papers, Huntington.

39 "there may be mischief done": Montgomery Blair to Samuel L. M. Barlow, June 14, 1865, Barlow papers, Huntington.

39 "Public events have shown": George T. Curtis to Manton Marble, July 19, 1865, LC.

40 "What chance at conservative ideas": George T. Curtis to Manton Marble, July 19, 1865, LC.

40 "Seward & Stanton are jubilant": Samuel Cox to Samuel L. M. Barlow, August 18, 1865, Barlow papers, Huntington.

40 "He is nominally a President of a republic": William D. Shipman to Samuel L. M. Barlow, August 26, 1865, Barlow papers, Huntington.

40 "Now while the President would doubtless appoint better men": William D. Shipman to Samuel L. M. Barlow, August 26, 1865, Barlow papers, Huntington.

CHAPTER FOUR: MOSES

41 "I am opposed to secession,": CG 36: 2, Dec. 18, 1860, p. 117.

41 "He that is unwilling": CG 36: 2, Dec. 18, 1860, p. 117.

41 "as the ship-wrecked mariner": CG 36: 2, Dec. 19, 1860, p. 141.

42 Mississippi Senator Jefferson Davis: see for instance "The State of the Nation," *New York Evening Post*, Dec. 21, 1860, p. 3. See also Winston, *Andrew Johnson*, p. 167.

42 "Hanging is too good": quoted in "Andrew Johnson," *Augusta [Georgia] Chronicle*, Feb. 14, 1861, p. 3.

42 Soon it was also rumored: see "The News," *New York Herald*, Feb. 8, 1861, p. 4, and Wigfall Wright, *A Southern Girl in '61*, p. 32.

43 "upstart, swelled-headed": "To the Freemen of the First District," Oct. 15, 1845, *PAJ* 1: 270.

43 "If Andrew Jackson": CG 36: 2, Feb. 6, 1861, p. 770.

43 "I care not whence the blows come": CG 36: 2, Feb. 6, 1861, p. 772.

44 "These two eyes of mine": CG 36: 2, March 2, 1861, p. 1350.

44 "Three cheers for Andy Johnson,": quoted in Temple, *Notable Men of Tennessee*, p. 398.

45 "He was free from": Lichtenstein, *Andrew Johnson as He Really Was*, pp. 14–15.

45 "family distinctions": AJ, "To the Freemen of the First District of Tennessee," October 15, 1845, *PAJ* 1: 270–71.

45 "by fatiguing their ingenuity,": CG 30: 1, June 5, 1848, p. 801.

45 "Because they had not sense": Turner, "Recollections of Andrew Johnson," p. 170.

45 *"The voice of the people"*: *PAJ* 2: 176.

45 He fiercely advocated homestead legislation: see, for instance, "The State of the Nation: The Virginia Election—Senator Seward's Opinion—Johnson's Onslaught," *New York Evening Post*, Feb. 6, 1861, p. 2.

46 "When a man has a home": Frank Moore, ed. "On the Homestead Bill, Speech Delivered in the Senate of the United States, May 20, 1858," in *Speeches of Andrew Johnson, President of the United States*, p. 33; see also pp. 36 and 62.

46 "Were I President of the United States": CG 36: 2, March 2, 1861, p. 1350.

46 A knot of men blocked his train at the Lynchburg, Virginia, station: see "Andrew Johnson in Lynchburg," *Alexandria Gazette*, April 23, 186, p. 3.

47 political equivalent: see "First Inaugural Address," Oct. 17, 1853, *PAJ* 2: 177.

48 "Though she sent me out penniless and friendless": "The President's Visit to Raleigh," *New-York Tribune*, June 4, 1867, p. 2.

48 "It would have satisfied my desire": see William H. Moore diary, July 8, 1868, LC.

48 Johnson said he could read it: see William H. Moore, diary, Jan. 10, 1867, and March 28, 1868, LC.

49 "road to distinction,": *The American Speaker*, p. iv.

49 In the spring of 1824: see Van der Zee, *Bound Over*, p. 354.

49 When Johnson returned: see Gordon-Reed, *Andrew Johnson*, p. 26.

49 Johnson was eighteen and Eliza a little over sixteen, and his worldly possessions: see "East Tennessee: A Visit to President Johnson's Old Home," *Chicago Tribune*, Aug. 29, 1865, p. 2.

49 "sparkling": Truman, "Anecdotes of Andrew Johnson," p. 85.

50 He spent long periods separated: For rumors about the separation, see *The Diary of Claude August Crommelin, A Young Dutchman Views Post-Civil War America*, ed. Augustus J. Veenendaal, Jr., p. 118.

50 "in the end": Margaret Gray Blanton to Milton Lomask, June 14, 1961, University of Tennessee-Knoxville Special Collections.

51 "We must hold out": AJ to Eliza Johnson, March 27, 1863, *PAJ* 6: 195.

51 When Johnson entered the White House: see Cowan, *Reminiscences of Andrew Johnson*, p. 7.

51 "far more content": Gerry, ed., *Through Five Administrations: Reminiscences of Colonel William H. Crook*, p. 87.

51 "He was naturally and inherently": Temple, *Notable Men of Tennessee*, p. 363.

51 In 1829, he was elected alderman: see Temple, *Notable Men of Tennessee*, p. 363: "Stevenson [the opponent] was no match in debate for his young antagonist. Johnson hacked and arraigned Stevens until his friend pitied him."

52 the tailor's profession: see Hunt, "The President's Defense: His Side of the Case, as Told by His Correspondence," p. 427.

52 Years later a rumor circulated: see Gordon-Reed, *Andrew Johnson*, pp. 38–39; see also *PAJ* 16: 761. Dolly's children were Liz, 1846–circa 1900; Florence; and William, 1858–1943.

52 Having successfully: See Turner, "Recollections of Andrew Johnson," p. 168.

53 "He was always a candidate for Something,": Emerson Etheredge to Oliver P. Temple, July 26, 1892, Temple Papers, Knoxville, Univ. of Tennessee.

53 Johnson served: On the paving of the streets see Trefousse, *Andrew Johnson*, p. 70.

53 Later, one of his favorite books: see "Andrew Johnson Collection," *Catalogue of Sale* (NY: Anderson Galleries, Inc., 1919), pp. 50–51.

53 "Party, to him, as to most politicians": Temple, *Notable Men of Tennessee*, p. 380.

53 "he is very vindictive and perverse": Quaife (ed.), *Diary of James Polk During His Presidency*, vol. 4, p. 264.

54 "plebeian origins": Craven, *Prison Life of Jefferson Davis*, p. 262.

54 "had no sense of humor,": Turner, "Recollections of Andrew Johnson," *Harper's*, p. 169.

54 "lacked the luster": Cowan, *Reminiscences of Andrew Johnson*, p. 6.

54 "Cato was a man who would not compromise": see Moore, Feb. 16, 1868, p. 87.

55 "from as mean a family": see Trefousse, *Andrew Johnson*, p. 52.

55 When vilified as an atheist: see Winston, *Andrew Johnson*, p. 65.

55 "faith": p. 215, CG: 1, July 27, 1861, p. 29.

55 "The passion of his life": Temple, *Notable Men of Tennessee*, p. 452.

55 A clairvoyant had whispered: See Trefousse, *Andrew Johnson*, pp. 123–24.

56 Johnson just raised his voice louder and kept talking: Temple, *East Tennessee*, pp. 185–86.

56 "My wife and children have been turned,": CG 37: 2, Jan. 31, 1862, p. 587.

57 "Let Andrew Johnson beware,": quoted in "A Pleasing Invitation," *New York Evening Post*, April 11, 1862, p. 3, quoting *Memphis Daily Appeal*, March 19, 1862, p. 1.

57 By spring, he was boasting: see *PAJ* 5: 445–46.

57 "I hardly ever got my hands": quoted in Beard, *Nashville: The Home of History Makers*, p. 63. See also Hardison, *In the Toils of War*, pp. 98–101, 116.

58 "The bare sight of fifty thousand": Abraham Lincoln to AJ, March 16, 1863, LC.

58 "Damn the negroes,": quoted in Palmer, *Personal Recollections*, p. 127.

59 free blacks: see CG 36: 1, Dec. 12, 1859, pp. 319–21.

59 "If you persist": AJ, Rally, July 4, 1862, *PAJ* 5: 536.

59 "sometimes exhibited a morbid": William G. Moore, diary, April 9, 1868, LC.

59 "In my opinion": Abraham Lincoln to AJ, March 26, 1863, *PAJ* 6: 194.

59 "that the negro race is equal to the Anglo-Saxon": Jan. 8, 1864, *PAJ* 6: 582.

60 On his way home from church: "Statement of Armstead Lewis," OR series 3, vol. 3, p. 841.

60 "colored men here are treated like brutes,": George Stearns to Edwin Stanton, Sept. 25, 1863, OR series 3, vol. 3, p. 840.

60 "The theoretical, philosophical": Dana, *Recollections*, p. 106.

61 "either drunk or recovering": Turner, "Recollections of Andrew Johnson," p. 175.

61 Charles Sumner remembered: see Annie Fields diary (November, 1865) quoted in *Memories of a Hostess: a Chronicle of Eminent Friendships*, ed. Howe, p. 312.

61 "The Governor had 'his infirmities'": quoted in Schurz, *Reminiscences*, p. 95.

61 "he never got too drunk": quoted in Winston, *Andrew Johnson*, p. 104.

61 "he never drank a cocktail": Truman, "Anecdotes of Andrew Johnson," p. 438.

61 "I have known Andy": quoted in McCulloch, *Men and Measures*, p. 373.

61 "Drunk as a fool": William Prime to Samuel L. M. Barlow, March 7, 1865, Barlow papers, Huntington.

61 The Blair family bundled: see David Hitchcock to Frank P. Blair, Jr., nd, LC.

62 "I regret the President's illness very much": Montgomery Blair to S.M.L. Barlow, Aug. 3, 1865, Barlow papers, Huntington.

62 The word was that he'd been drunk: see for example Bergeron, "Robert Johnson: The President's Troubled and Troubling Son," p. 1.

62 "I have said and now repeat": AJ to RJ, Nov. 21, 1863, *PAJ* 6: 485.

62 *"The intoxicating bowl goes to my lips no more,"*: RJ to AJ, Feb. 14, 1864, PAJ 6: 620.

62 Men and women: On prostitutes in the White House, see Norman B. Judd to Lyman Trumbull, Feb. 14, 1866, LC.

63 "faithful among the faithless": Charles Sumner, "Our Domestic Relations," p. 521.

63 John Nicolay and John Hay: also agreeing that Lincoln did not tip the scales is Fehrenbacher, "The Making of a Myth: Lincoln and the Vice Presidential Nomination in 1864," 273–90; see also Glonek, "Lincoln, Johnson, and the Baltimore Ticket," 255–71; and Hamlin, *The Life and Times of Hannibal Hamlin*, pp. 461–89, 591–615.

63 "Andy Johnson, I think, is a good man,": quoted in Brooks, "Two War-Time Conventions," p. 723.

64 Reportedly, he asked journalist John Forney: see Forney, *Anecdotes of Public Men*, vol. 1, p. 167 "from the President's own lips," Dittenhoefer, *How We Re-Elected Lincoln*, p. 89.

64 "I know it to be a fact that Mr. Lincoln": quoted in McClure, *Lincoln and Men of War Times*, p. 467.

64 "I have battled against Andrew Johnson": Johnson, ed. *Proceedings of the First Three Republican National Conventions, 1856, 1860, and 1864*, pp. 188–89.

65 "Seward men": see for instance, "The Presidency," *New York Herald*, June 9, 1864, p. 5.

65 "Can't you find a candidate": quoted in McClure, *Abraham Lincoln and Men of War Times*, p. 260.

65 "The age of statesmen is gone,": quoted in Waugh, *Reelecting Lincoln: The Battle for the 1864 Presidency*, p. 202.

65 "Let the war for the Union go on": quoted in Savage, *The Life and Public Services of Andrew Johnson, Seventeenth President*, p. 297.

65 "make something for themselves": see AJ, speech near Gallatin, July 19, 1864, *PAJ* 7: 41–42.

66 "Looking over this vast crowd . . . peace.": Oct. 24, 1864, *PAJ* 7: 251.

66 Johnson did not specify: for the location of Canaan, see James R. Doolittle to AJ, Sept. 9, 1865, WHS. Frank Blair, Jr., had made the same suggestion.

CHAPTER FIVE: THE SOUTH VICTORIOUS

67 A few miles north: see "Let Us Clearly Understand Each Other," *New-York Tribune*, June 30, 1865, p. 4.

67 "The white people tell": quoted in Schurz, *Report on the Condition of the South*, p. 21.

67 Near Hilton Head: see Albert G. Browne to Wendell Phillips, Sept. 17, 1865, Houghton.

67 "What most men mean": Thomas Wentworth Higginson, "Too Many Compliments," *The Independent* (Oct. 26, 1865), p. 4.

68 A black woman, pregnant: see *Report of the Joint Committee on Reconstruction,
    at the First Session, Thirty-ninth Congress,* Feb. 23, 1866, p. 105.
68 in Andersonville: see *Report of the Joint Committee on Reconstruction, at the
    First Session, Thirty-ninth Congress,* Feb. 23, 1866, p. 103.
68 "he was going to kill": August 20, 1865, BRFA, Microfilm M1027, roll 34.
68 "apparently for the fun of the thing,": Trowbridge, A *Picture of the Desolated
    States,* p. 468.
68 "These negro-shooters . . . stand that.": Trowbridge, A *Picture of the Desolated
    States,* p. 464.
68 A black soldier: Freedmen's Bureau, "Freedmen's Bureau Journal, 1865," Oct.
    13, 1865, Swem Library Digital Projects, http: //scrcdigital.swem.wm.edu/items/
    show/1264.
68 "if you take away the military: see *Report of the Joint Committee on Reconstruc-
    tion, at the First Session, Thirty-ninth Congress,* Feb. 5, 1866, p. 121.
69 "They will be in a much worse": Adelbert Ames to Martha and Jesse Ames, Sept.
    6, 1865, Smith.
69 "seizing upon isolated instances": "Injustice to the South," *Daily Clarion* (Me-
    ridian, Miss.), Aug. 23, 1865, p. 2.
69 "People had not got over regarding": Reid, *After the War,* pp. 420–22.
69 "*sensation* letter-writers": see n. 3, Sept. 11, 1865, *PAJ* 9: 68.
69 "The 'situation'": quoted in E. P. Brooks, "North Carolina: The Condition of
    Affairs," *New York Times,* Sept. 8, 1865, p. 1; "there are malcontent": William
    Holden to AJ, Aug. 26, 1865, *PAJ* 8: 660.
69 "Conflict of races": see James A. Seddon to AJ, June 22, 1865, *PAJ* 8: 272.
69 "old order of things" see Michael Cunningham to AJ, June 22, 1865, *PAJ* 8: 270.
70 In Richmond: For the account of what happened in Richmond, I have relied on
    "The Richmond Freedmen: Oppression of the Negress—An Outrageous
    Order—Blacks Imprisoned by Hundreds," *New-York Tribune* (June 15, 1865),
    p. 1, and "The Late Reign of Terror in Richmond: Letter From Rev. Dr. Pierson
    to Rev. Dr. Tyng. Statement of Albert Brooks," *The Independent* (July 13, 1865),
    p. 1.
70 "our old masters have become our enemies": "From Committee of Richmond
    Blacks," June 10, 1865, *PAJ* 8: 211; 213.
71 "their woolly heads": quoted in "The Richmond Negroes," *Detroit Free Press,*
    June 26, 1865, p. 1.
71 "unjust legislation,": "From South Carolina Black Citizens," June 29, 1865, *PAJ*
    8: 31.
71 Colonel J.P.H. Russ of Raleigh: quoted in "From North Carolina: The Pardon-
    ing Power—The State Convention," Aug. 2, 1865, *New-York Tribune,* p. 1.
71 "The present pardoning process will restore": Thomas Shankland to Thaddeus
    Stevens, Sept. 2, 1865, LC.
71 "when the nation stood trembling on the precipice, the black man came to the
    rescue.": quoted in Egerton, *The Wars of Reconstruction,* p. 189.
71 "true and loyal citizens of the United States": quoted in Hahn, *A Nation Under
    Our Feet,* p. 118.
72 "intelligent, experienced, uneducated, upright colored men": James N. Glouces-
    ter to OOH, June 1, 1865, Bowdoin; "quite apprehensive": OOH, Sept. 13,
    1865, Bowdoin.
72 "colored fellow-citizens,": Langston, *From the Virginia Plantation to the Na-
    tional Capitol,* p. 230.

72 Johnson added: see "Response to John Mercer Langston," April 18, 1865, *PAJ* 7: 585.

73 Advertising themselves as broad: see Samuel L. M. Barlow to Samuel Tilden, Aug. 25, 1865, NYPL.

73 "did not desert the former": "President Johnson—His Main Idea," *Detroit Free Press*, Aug. 31, 1865, p. 2. See also "The Democracy," *Albany Argus*, Aug. 26, 1865, p. 4, and "Great Meeting at the Capitol. The Democracy of Albany," *Albany Argus*, Oct. 6, 1865, p. 2.

73 "sailed before the wind": "The Prospects of the Administration and the South—The Negro Suffrage Question," *New York Herald*, June 30, 1865, p. 4.

74 "everlasting negro question.": "A New Crisis in Our National Affairs," *New York Herald*, Oct. 20, 1865, p. 4.

74 "We are in danger": Henry Ward Beecher to Edwin Stanton, May 3, 1865, Bowdoin.

74 White women were at least: see "Scenes and Thoughts in New York," *Springfield Republican*, Nov. 19, 1865, p. 2.

74 "would lose for the negro": see May 25, 1865, Stanton, *Elizabeth Cady Stanton as Revealed in Her Letters*, p. 105.

74 "As Abraham Lincoln said: 'One war at a time,'": Wendell Phillips, "Speech to Annual Meeting of the American Anti-Slavery Society," May 10, 1865, quoted in *The Liberator*, May 19, 1865, p. 78.

75 "Is there not danger . . . to all.": Dec. 26, 1865, Stanton, *Elizabeth Cady Stanton as Revealed in Her Letters*, p. 110.

75 "Give the negro a vote": "Speech of Wendell Phillips, Esq.," *The Liberator*, May 19, 1863, p. 87.

76 "I never could": quoted in Weld, *Memorial Services Upon the Seventy-fourth Birthday of Wendell Phillips*, p. 20.

76 "He knew the penalty of his course": George William Curtis, "The Eulogy," in *Memorial of Wendell Phillips*, p. 57.

76 "The republic which sinks": quoted in Hofstadter, *The American Political Tradition*, p. 139.

76 "so simple, so affable": Ernst Duvergier De Hauranne "Boston Portraits in French Setting: Passages from the last section of a serial, *Huit Mois en Amérique*," *Every Saturday*, Jan. 26, 1866, p. 85.

77 "The effect was absolutely disarming,": Higginson, *Wendell Phillips*, p. xi.

77 "direct, simple, persuasive": Smalley, *Anglo-American Memories*, p. 91.

77 Detractors: see "President Johnson and the Boston Fanatics, *New York Herald*, Aug. 24, 1865, p. 4.

78 "Always aristocratic in aspect,": Higginson, *Cheerful Yesterdays*, p. 242.

78 "Peace if": see Weld, *Memorial Services Upon the Seventy-fourth Birthday of Wendell Phillips*, frontispiece.

78 "a force to be resisted": see "Anti-Slavery Celebration at Framingham," *The National Anti-Slavery Standard*, July 14, 1865, p. 1.

78 "The same oligarchy that broke up the Union": and other quotations from this speech, see Wendell Phillips, "The South Victorious," *The National Anti-Slavery Standard*, Oct. 29, 1865, p. 13.

79 "I fear that he has not that clearness . . . prejudices,": Carl Schurz to Charles Sumner, June 5, 1865, Schurz, *The Speeches, Correspondence and Political Papers of Carl Schurz*, vol. 1, p. 259.

80 As one bystander remarked: see Whipple, "The President and Congress," p. 500.

81 "It is a stubborn fact": Carl Schurz to AJ, Sept. 4, 1865, in *Advice After Appomattox*, ed. Simpson, p. 122.

81 "you would completely disarm": AJ to William Sharkey, Aug. 15, 1865, *PAJ* 8: 637.

81 "If the President persists in pursuing": Carl Schurz to Margarethe Schurz, Sept. 2, 1865, in *The Intimate letters of Carl Schurz, 1841–1869*, ed. Shafer, p. 349; the subsequent paragraphs are derived from Wineapple, *Ecstatic Nation*, pp. 408–10.

82 "During my two days sojourn at Atlanta": Schurz, *The Speeches, Correspondence and Political Papers of Carl Schurz*, p. 317.

83 "One reason why the Southern people . . . protection of his rights.": see Schurz, *The Speeches, Correspondence and Political Papers of Carl Schurz* pp. 359–60; 366.

83 "this is a country": "From Washington," *Albany Argus*, Sept., 30, 1865, p. 2.

83 "We think it likely": quoted in "From Washington," *Albany Argus*, Sept. 30, 1865, p. 2.

84 "plain, unpretentious . . . he is.": Willard Saxton diary, Dec. 1, 1865, Yale.

84 "war of races": James Doolittle to Manton Marble, Dec. 21, 1867, LC.

84 The young French correspondent: see Clemenceau, *American Reconstruction*, ed. Baldensberger, p. 61.

85 "He has all the narrowness": Pierce, ed. *Memoirs and Letters of Charles Sumner*, vol. 4, p. 276.

85 Many Republicans still hoped: for Johnson's view, see "The Subjugation of the States in Negro domination would be worse . . ." *PAJ* 13: 286.

85 "Some foolish men": see James Garfield to Hinsdale, December 11, 1865, in *Garfield-Hinsdale Letters*, p. 76.

86 "I pray you to take care that we do": Horace Greeley to Schuyler Colfax, Dec. 11, 1865, NYPL.

86 "The Connecticut vote *is* a very heavy blow": Charles Eliot Norton to E. L. Godkin, Oct. 4, 1865, Houghton.

86 "premature and unpopular,": Thaddeus Stevens to John Hutchins, Aug. 27, 1865, *The Selected Papers of Thaddeus Stevens*, vol. 2, p. 11.

86 They would have to play down: see for instance Trefousse, *The Radical Republicans*, p. 362.

86 "Prest. Johnson is said": Henry J. Raymond to George Jones, Aug. 25, 1865, NYPL.

87 As the grouchy but loyal Navy Secretary: see Gideon Welles, "Recollections of Andrew Johnson and His Cabinet," nd, NYPL.

CHAPTER SIX: NOT A "WHITE MAN'S GOVERNMENT"

89 Of them, nine former Confederate army officers: for a statistical breakdown, see Carter, *When the War Was Over*, n. p. 109.

89 "Either keep them out of Congress": Horatio Woodman to Edwin Stanton, April 24, 1865, LC.

89 "we must keep Southern rebels out of Congress": W. G. Brownlow to Schuyler Colfax, Nov. 19, 1865, Hayes.

90 "degradation, misery, & servitude": Charles Eliot Norton to Edwin Godkin, Oct. 4, 1865, Houghton.

90 "If Tennessee is not in the Union": CG 39: 1, Dec. 4, 1865, p. 3.

90 "he looked very much aged": Schurz, *The Reminiscences of Carl Schurz*, vol. 3, p. 215.

91 "perpetually recurring wrangle": "Reconstruction Congress and the President, *New York Times*, Dec. 5, 1865, p. 4.

91 "placed themselves in a condition": "Message to Congress," Dec. 4, 1865, *PAJ* 9: 470–71.

91 "Nobody, I believe, pretends": CG 39: 1, Dec. 18, 1865, p. 73.

92 "This is not a 'white man's Government' . . . inhabits.": CG 39: 1, Dec. 18, 1865, p. 74.

92 "a blessing—for": see "On the School Law," April 11, 1835, in Stevens, *Papers*, vol. 1, p. 24.

92 Stevens went to the auction: see Brodie, *Thaddeus Stevens*, p. 51.

93 "I was feeble and lame": Harris, *A Review of the Political Conflict in America*, p. 12; see also Hood, "Thaddeus Stevens," in Harris, ed. *A Biographical History of Lancaster County, Pennsylvania*.

93 "why, he looked so young and innocent": quoted in Brodie, *Thaddeus Stevens*, p. 53.

93 "Mr. Stevens used to call it his sinking fund": "An Ironmaster," *Philadelphia Times*, July 14, 1895, p. 25.

93 "I only wish you had been in your works": from "Your Southern Friend! and So-called Rebel" to Thaddeus Stevens, May 1, 1866, LC.

93 A friend recalled: see *Memorial Addresses on the Life and Character of Thaddeus Stevens, Delivered in the House of Representatives, Dec. 17, 1868*, p. 8.

94 "set Zionward": quoted in Burlingame and Ettlinger, eds., *Inside Lincoln's White House*, p. 101.

94 "Congress is composed of men": *Memorial Addresses on the Life and Character of Thaddeus Stevens*, p. 24.

95 "I lead them, yes": quoted in "Thaddeus Stevens," *Sacramento Daily Union*, August 15, 1868, p. 4.

95 "Very deep eyes": Twain, *Mark Twain's Notebooks & Journals*, vol. 1, p. 492.

95 "Not seldom a single sentence": Schurz, *The Reminiscences of Carl Schurz*, vol. 3, p. 217.

95 "And then, reaching to his full height": Poore, *Perley's Reminiscences of Sixty Years*, vol. 2, p. 101.

95 "always the club foot": L. J. Jennings, "Mr. Raymond and Journalism," *Galaxy*, April 1870, p. 472.

95 "all his life he held": *Memorial Addresses on the Life and Character of Thaddeus Stevens*, p. 22.

96 "Thank you, my good fellows": see Schurz, *Reminiscences*, p. 214.

96 "I hold him to have been": Taylor, *Destruction and Reconstruction*, p. 330.

97 "but he either does all the talking himself": quoted in Howe, *Moorfield Storey*, p. 60.

97 "I have outlived": quoted in Julia Ward Howe, *Reminiscences*, p. 174.

97 "never in this, or any other country": Lydia Maria Child to [SBG] [1866], Samuel J. May Anti-Slavery Collection, Cornell University.

97 He arranged his luxuriant dark hair with deliberate carelessness, and while: "Thaddeus Stevens: On Sumner's dress," see Brooks, *Washington in Lincoln's Time*, p. 24.

97 "If one told Charles Sumner": quoted in Schurz, *Charles Sumner: An Essay by Carl Schurz*, p. 15; for Puritan idealist, see p. 25.

99 "The Great Impotent.": see Donald, *Charles Sumner and the Rights of Man*, p. 314.

99 "Liberty has been won": *The Works of Charles Sumner*, vol. 9, p. 427.

99   "Ignorant, pig-headed and perverse": quoted in Donald, *Charles Sumner and the Rights of Man*, p. 238.
99   "whitewashing message,": CG 39: 1, Dec. 19, 1865, 79.
99   "If you are not ready to be the Moses": CG 39, 1, Dec. 20, 1865, p. 95.
100 "What's the use to give us our freedom,": "The Feelings of the Southern Negroes," *The Nation*, Sept. 28, 1865, p. 393.
100 In South Carolina there was a rumor that: see Charles Howard to OOH, Nov. 16, 1865, Bowdoin.
102 "Shouldn't we resist": Dec. 3, 1865, *Testimony Taken Before the Judiciary Committee of the House of Representatives, Thirty-ninth and Fortieth Congress* (1867), p. 94.
102 General Howard tried to hedge: see William H. Trescot to OOH, Dec. 4, 1865, Bowdoin.
102 "Could a just government": Rufus Saxton to OOH, Aug. 22, 1865, vol. 9, BRFAL.
103 "without a hut to shelter them or a cent": CG 39: 1, Dec. 18, 1865, p. 74.

CHAPTER SEVEN: RECONCILIATION

104 On New Year's Day 1866: see D.W.B. [David W. Bartlett], "Washington Correspondence," *The Independent*, Jan. 4, 1866, p. 1.
105 "we are plain people": quoted in Ames, *Ten Years in Washington*, p. 245. See also *Evening Star* (Washington), January 1, 1866, p. 2, for one of the many chronicles of the New Year's Day White House celebration.
106 Very few did: "The Latest News by Telegraph. News from Washington," *The Daily Age* [Philadelphia, Pennsylvania], p. 1.
106 "He would have enjoyed the day," Jan. 1, 1866, Welles, *Diary*, vol. 2, p. 409.
106 Socialites: see Briggs, *The Olivia Letters*, p. 4.
107 "Washington": Ellet, *The Court Circles of the Republic*, p. 550.
107 "for the transactions,": Taylor, *Destruction and Reconstruction*, p. 325.
107 "cases of the worst and most incurable wounds": Whitman, *Memoranda During the War*, p. 54; 55.
107 "The spectacle of sudden loss": Gerry, ed., *Through Five Administrations*, p. 91.
107 "You will see how our cause": Josephine Griffing to Elizabeth Buffum Chace, Dec. 26, 1865, in Wyman and Wyman, *Elizabeth Buffum Chace*, p. 285.
109 "tardy, cold, dull, and indifferent . . . determined.": Philip Foner, ed., *Frederick Douglass: Selected Speeches and Writings*, p. 621.
109 "but it was too late": Douglass, "The Life and Times of Frederick Douglass," in *Autobiographies*, p. 802.
110 "Those d—d . . . throat than not.": quoted in Philip Ripley to Manton Marble, Feb. 8, [1866], Manton Marble Papers, LC.
110 "for no other cause": "President Johnson and the Black Delegation," *New York Herald*, Feb. 9, 1866, p. 4.
110 "Peace is not to be secured": "Presidential Declarations," *The Independent*, Feb. 15, 1866, p. 8.
110 "after the demoralizing": "Negros and Negro Agitators," *New York Herald*, Feb. 12, 1866, p. 4.
111 "ashamed of belonging to the white race!": quoted in D.W.B., "Washington Correspondence, *The Independent*, Feb 15, 1866, p. 1.
111 "freaky": Feb. 13, 1866, Welles, *Diary*, vol. 2, p. 435. See also Cullom, *Fifty Years of Public Service*, p. 42.
111 "We, the Republicans": quoted in Litwack, *North of Slavery*, p. 269.

111 "that all men are created equal.": CG 36: 1, Dec. 12, 1859, p. 102.

112 "Pass it": quoted in Willard Saxton diary, Feb. 10, 1866, Yale.

112 If the freedpeople or refugees could not afford to rent: see CG 39: 1, Feb. 5, 1866, p. 658.

112 "doing nothing to support themselves": CG 39: 1, Jan. 23, 1866, p. 361.

112 "for the purpose of degrading": CG 39: 1, Jan. 19, 1866, p. 322.

113 White House clerks: see Philip Ripley to Manton Marble, Feb. 8, [1866], Manton Marble papers, LC.

113 "I thought in advocating it": CG 39: 1, Feb. 20, 1866, p. 943.

114 "veto one bill upon that ground": CG 39: 1, Feb. 23, 1866, p. 986.

114 "The President has sold us out": John I. Davenport to Sidney Gay, Feb. 22, 1866, Butler.

114 "has gone all over to the South.": Willard Saxton, diary, Feb. 22, 1866, Yale.

114 "the news of the Veto Message": quoted in McKitrick, *Andrew Johnson and Reconstruction*, p. 290.

114 "The South and the Government are in the same boat": Reid, *After the War*, 575; see also "Veto of the Freedmen's Bureau Bill," *Daily Courier* [Louisville, KY] Feb. 21, 1866, p. 1.

115 "Oh dear, we are all fagged": "The Rip Van Winkles at Cooper Union," *Chicago Tribune*, Feb. 24, 1866, p. 2.

115 By marginalizing: see William Henry Trescot to James Orr, Feb. 28, 1866, SCA. See also Benjamin Rush to Andrew Johnson, Feb. 3, 1866, *PAJ* 10: 22, and John Cochrane to AJ, Feb. 4, 1866, *PAJ* 10: 27.

115 "laborious and thankless,": see McCulloch, *Men and Measures*, p. 193.

116 These traitors: see also Welles, *Diary*, vol. 2, Feb. 13, 1866, p. 432.

116 "If my blood": all quotations from the speech are from Feb. 1866, *PAJ* 10, p. 152ff.

117 "Imagine it!!!!!": Feb. 3, 1866, Strong, *Diary*, vol. 4, p. 72.

117 "in undertaking to reconstruct states": William Lloyd Garrison, "The Verdict of the People," *The Independent*, March 29, 1866, p. 1.

117 If the President: see John I. Davenport to Sydney Gay, Feb. 22, 1866, Butler.

117 "The long agony,": WPF to Elizabeth F. Warriner, Feb. 25, 1866, Bowdoin.

117 "their mistakes, their evil cause": *Norwood*, p. 540.

118 Whitman's friend the essayist: see Burroughs, "Whitman and His Drum-Taps," p. 611.

118 "I was struck": Barrus, ed. *The Life and Letters of John Burroughs*, vol. 1, pp. 96–97.

119 "looking old and young": Barrus, ed. *The Life and Letters of John Burroughs*, vol. 1, pp. 96–97.

120 "So far from spoiling the symmetry of the book": "Literary Notices," *New York Herald*, Sept. 3, 1866, p. 5.

120 At *The New York Times*: see "Battle Pieces and Aspects of the War," *New York Times*, Aug. 27, 1866, p. 2.

120 "'Something,' says this happy optimist": "Book Table," *The Independent*, Jan. 10, 1867, p. 2.

121 "Everybody is heartily tired of discussing [the Negro's] rights,": [E. l. Godkin] *The Nation*, July 6, 1865, p. 1.

CHAPTER EIGHT: CIVIL RIGHTS

122 "The *thing itself*": Henry Ward Beecher to AJ, March 17, 1866, *PAJ* 10: 264.

123 "It will be well": Jacob D. Cox to AJ, March 22, 1866, *PAJ* 10: 287.

123 Even Wendell Phillips: see "The Civil Rights Bill," *National Anti-Slavery Standard*, April 14, 1866, p. 2.

123 "find a way": quoted in Cox and Cox, *Politics, Principle, and Prejudice, 1865–1866*, p. 197.

123 "Sir, I am right": quoted in W. G. Moore, "Small Diary," [nd] 1866, LC.

124 "Fraught with evil": *PAJ* 10: 319 ff.

124 "so clearly right": John Sherman to WTS, April 23, 1866, *The Sherman Letters*, ed. Rachel Thorndike, p. 270.

124 "I am forced to the conclusion": Henry Dawes to Electa Dawes, March 31, 1866, LC.

124 "The President probably did not know": William Cullen Bryant to Fanny Godkin Bryant, April 17, 1866, *The Letters of William Cullen Bryant*, p. 89.

124 "It [Congress] grows firmer every day": Schuyler Colfax to Kline Shryock, April 7, 1866, Brown University.

124 "fresh from the rebel congress": see *CG* 39: 1, April 4, 1866, p. 1756.

125 "an argument to excite prejudice—": *CG* 39: 1, April 4, 1866, p. 1757.

126 "even Charles Sumner,": M.C.A. [Mary Clemmer Ames], "A Woman in Washington," *The Independent*, April 19, 1866, p. 1.

126 "The people have made too many": G. S. Orth to Stephen Neal, April 29, 1866, quoted in McKitrick, *Andrew Johnson and Reconstruction*, p. 325.

126 "He is fool enough or wicked enough": Henry Dawes to Electa Dawes, March 31, 1866, LC.

126 "What a pity he had not stuck to making trousers,": quoted in Lydia Maria Child to [my dear friend], April 1, 1866, Samuel J. May Anti-Slavery Collection, Cornell.

126 "with a plebeian tone of mind,": James Russell Lowell, "The President on the Stump," p. 531; E. P. Whipple, "The President and Congress," pp. 500–01.

126 the conservative press in Memphis: see *Memphis Daily Avalanche*, April 1, 1866, p. 1; see also; March 20, p. 2; March 28, 1866, p. 2; April 11, 1866, p. 2.

127 "Your old father, Abe Lincoln, is dead and damned": "The Memphis Riots," in *The Reports of the Committees of the House of Representatives 1865–1866*, vol. 3, p. 7; 182; subsequent references to this volume on the Memphis riot will appear as "Memphis Riots," *Report*, followed by the page number. Most of the accounts are taken from this report.

127 In the confusion, one police officer was killed: see "Memphis Riots," *Report*, p. 8.

128 "Boys, I want you to go ahead . . . city": "Memphis Riots," *Report*, p. 24.

128 John Prendergast: see "Memphis Riots," *Report*, pp. 308, 317, 343–44.

128 "I have shot": "Memphis Riots," *Report*, p. 8.

128 "Halt, you damned nigger,": "Memphis Riots," *Report*, p. 101.

128 The others raped: "Memphis Riots," *Report*, pp. 196–7.

129 "Gentlemen,": "Memphis Riots," *Report*, p. 199.

129 Her clothes were on fire: "Memphis Riots," *Report*, p. 15.

129 "Colored men, women": Reverend Ewing Tade, "The Memphis Race Riot and Its Aftermath, Report by a Northern Missionary," p. 66.

129 Barbers were gunned: see Brown, *The Negro in the American Rebellion*, p. 349–350.

129 A cheer went up: *Ibid.*, p. 350.

130 "it was no negro riot,": Elihu Washburne to Thaddeus Stevens, May 24, 1866, LC.

130 "The civil-rights bill is treated as a dead letter,": *Ibid.*
131 "negro-worshippers": for a summary view, see Carrière, "An Irresponsible Press: Memphis Newspaper and the 1866 Riot," pp. 2–15. See also "The Horrors of Memphis," *The Independent*, May 31, 1866, p. 2.

CHAPTER NINE: MUTUAL CONCESSIONS, MUTUAL HOSTILITIES

133 "Johnson is suspicious of every one,": John Sherman to WTS, March 20, 1866, LC.
133 "If Andrew Johnson": "Mrs. Swisshelm Guillotined," *Chicago Tribune*, March 2, 1866, p. 2.
133 Jane Grey Swisshelm was sacked: see also "Mrs. Swisshelm's New Paper," *Chicago Tribune*, Dec. 26, 1865, p. 1.
134 "liberty is in danger of betrayal.": "Prospectus," *The Reconstructionist*, February 10, 1866, p. 4.
134 "His ambition was and is": "Gone Back," *The Reconstructionist*, February 10, 1866, p. 1.
134 "Sumter guns": quoted in "Mrs. Swisshelm's Dismissal," *Chicago Tribune*, March 3, 1866, p. 2. See also Hoffert, *Jane Grey Swisshelm: An Unconventional Life*, p. 128, although she says that Swisshelm's satires and attacks "against Johnson began to verge on the hysterical."
134 "An enemy so reckless is not one to be defied,": "To the Editor of the NY Tribune," *New-York Tribune*, March 29, 1865, p. 10.
134 Thirty years earlier: as a female scourge, see "Mrs. Swisshelm in Trouble," *Detroit Free Press*, March 4, 1866, p. 2.
134 Flamboyant during the war: for General George Armstrong Custer testimony, see "Testimony of General George Armstrong Custer," March 10, 1866, *Report of the Committee on Reconstruction*, pp. 73–76.
134 Madison Newby: Testimony of Madison Newby, Feb. 3, 1866, *Report of the Committee on Reconstruction*, p. 55.
135 "by the dinners": Trowbridge, *A Picture of the Desolate South*, p. 181.
135 "Quite a number of negroes": David Roberts to Elihu Washburne, May 7, 1866, LC.
135 "accomplish by law and Legislation": and "we have no peace," Marion Roberts to Thaddeus Stevens, May 15, 1866, LC.
136 "To those who say they": Henry Winter Davis to unknown "Sir," May 27, 1865; published publically for the first time by the *Sacramento Daily Union*, April 13, 1866, and collected in Davis, *Speeches and Addresses*, p. 562.
136 This would hurt the South: As David Donald points out, despite Sumner's ringing rhetoric, Sumner had earlier suggested an amendment very much like the amendment he was trying to kill because it had been denounced in his home state of Massachusetts.
137 "slaughtered by a puerile and pedantic criticism": CG 39; 1, May 8, 1866, p. 2459.
137 "The only ground of his opposition": WPF to Lizabeth Fessenden Warriner, March 10, 1866, Bowdoin.
137 "Sumner is not only a fool but a malignant fool,": Charles Eliot Norton to E. L. Godkin, March 6, 1866, HU.
137 "Sumner receives": Charles Eliot Norton to E. L. Godkin, March 20, 1866, HU.
137 "our friends": Elihu Washburne to Adele Washburne,: March 11, 1866, LC.
137 Norton urged the editor: see *The Nation*, March 22, 1866, p. 358 ff.

137 "If the South have to choose": Lydia Maria Child to Sarah Shaw, [1866], Samuel B. May Anti-Slavery Collection, Cornell.

137 "the oligarchy doesn't care": Thomas J. Durant to HCW, Jan. 20, 1866, SHC.

138 "odd contraption,": McKitrick, *Andrew Johnson and Reconstruction*, p. 326. For the complicated origin of the Fourteenth Amendment, as well as its treatment by historians, see the superb overview by McKitrick, pp. 326–63; see also Eric Foner's classic *Reconstruction: America's Unfinished Revolution* and Garret Epps, *Democracy Reborn*, to name just a few of the salient sources.

138 "fatal and total surrender,": Wendell Phillips to Thaddeus Stevens, April 30, 1866, LC.

139 "We were each compelled to surrender": James Grimes to his wife, April 16, 1866, quoted in Salter, *The Life of James W. Grimes*, p. 292.

139 "I would not for a moment . . . despair.": CG 39: 1, May 8, 1866, p. 2459.

139 "In my youth . . . hostilities.": see CG 39: 1 June 13, 1866, p. 3148.

140 Governor Wells and Fullerton: see Thomas Durant to HCW, Jan. 13, 1866, SHC.

140 "The Governor has become": C. W. Stauffer to HCW, Feb. 6, 1866, SHC.

140 "He intended": Diary of HCW, March 28, 1866, SHC.

141 "it is our general belief": quoted in Joe Gray Taylor, "New Orleans and Reconstruction," p. 195. For the narration of the New Orleans riots, I have also drawn on Wineapple, *Ecstatic Nation*, pp. 412–44.

142 "harmless pleasantry,": see Absalom Baird to John T. Monroe, July 26, 1866, quoted in *Report of the Select Committee in the New Orleans Riots* (Washington: Government Printing Office, 1867), p. 56.

142 According to Henry Warmoth: Diary of Henry C. Warmoth, July 30, 1866, SHC.

142 "military will be expected": AJ to Albert Voorhies and Andrew S. Herron, quoted in McKitrick, *Andrew Johnson and Reconstruction*, pp. 423–24. For an overview of the New Orleans riot of 1866, see Reynolds, "The New Orleans Riot of 1866, Reconsidered," pp. 5–27, and Hogue, *Uncivil War: Five New Orleans Street Battles and the Rise and Fall of Radical Reconstruction*.

142 "call on Genl. Sheridan": AJ to Andrew Herron, July 30, 1866, PAJ 10: 760.

142 That day, by noon: see Wineapple, *Ecstatic Nation*, pp. 412–44, from which the following paragraphs have been taken.

142 "several negroes lying dead": *Report of the Select Committee in the New Orleans*, p. 16. Unless otherwise noted, all subsequent direct quotes about the riot have been taken from the *Report*, as is the summary of events.

143 "Let Dosties's skin be forthwith stripped and sold to Barnum": quoted in Egerton, *The Wars of Reconstruction*, p. 215.

144 Hurriedly he left his office: see Whitaker, *Sketches of Life and Character in Louisiana*, p. 24.

144 "I have seen death": quoted in the essential Rable, *But There Was No Peace: The Role of Violence in the Politics of Reconstruction*, p. 58.

144 "It was a dark day": Diary of HCW, July 31, 1866, SHC.

144 "It is Memphis": see for instance "Great Riot . . . The Fearful Scenes of Memphis Re-Enacted," *New York Times*, July 31, 1866, p. 1.

145 "No milder word is fitting": Sheridan, *Personal Memoirs*, vol. 2, p. 235.

145 "The more information I obtain": Philip Sheridan to USG, Aug. 2, 1866, PUSG 16: 289.

145 "Not to know that": "The New Orleans Horror," *Chicago Tribune*, August 8, 1866, p. 2.

145 "I have been given no orders": see *Report of the Select Committee on the New Orleans Riots*, p. 547.

146 "Stanton avoids the responsibility": Fitz-john Porter to Manton Marble, Aug. 3, 1866, LC.

146 "That he had a political objective": see Thomas and Hyman, *Stanton*, p. 445; "political passive aggression," Marvel, *Lincoln's Autocrat: The Life of Edwin Stanton*, p. 206. See also Hollandsworth, *An Absolute Massacre: The New Orleans Race Riot*, p. 71, and Riddleberger, *1866: The Critical Year Revisited*, pp. 191–94.

147 In a cabinet meeting after the massacre: Welles, *Diary*, vol. 2, Aug. 2, 1866, pp. 567–68, and Aug. 3, 1866, p. 560; see also "The President's Blunder," *New York Evening Post*, Aug. 6, 1866, p. 2.

CHAPTER TEN: ANDY'S SWING AROUND THE CIRCLE

148 "The mere fact of the north": Sylvanus Cadwallader, "Four Years with Grant," mss., Abraham Lincoln Presidential Library.

149 "purposes hostile": see Henry J. Raymond, "Extracts from the Journal of Henry J. Raymond," p. 275. My account of Raymond's hesitation is derived from the extracts.

149 "It encourages those against whom every Union": BB to AJ, Aug. 10, 1866, *PAJ* 11: 56.

149 "the transfer of the political power": William Evarts to John Dix, July 25, 1866, Butler.

150 "to rupture the Republican Party": Fitz-john Porter to Manton Marble, July 16, 1866, LC.

150 Interior Secretary James Harlan: see "From Washington," *Chicago Tribune*, July 15, 1866, p. 1.

150 "He holds on like grim death,": "Evening Dispatches," *Detroit Free Press*, July 13, 1866, p. 6.

150 "Rebels and Copperheads mostly": Aug. 14, 1866, Strong, *The Diary of George Templeton Strong*, vol. 4, p. 97.

151 The roof leaked: for an excellent overview of the convention, see Thomas Wagstaff, "The Arm-in-Arm Convention," pp. 101–19.

151 "As matters now look,": Edwards Pierrepont to John Bigelow, June 16, 1866, in Bigelow, *Retrospections*, vol. 3, p. 462.

151 "there could hardly be": Charles Eliot Norton to E. L. Godkin, August 30, 1866, Houghton.

151 "the event of the season": *The Nation*, Sept. 6, 1866.

152 "were far more plentiful than bread and butter or cold water.": Cadwallader, "Four Years with Grant," mss., Abraham Lincoln Presidential Library.

152 James Doolittle had warned Johnson: see James Doolittle to AJ, Aug. 28, 1866, *PAJ* 11: 153; Thurlow Weed, see Weed, *The Autobiography of Thurlow Weed*, p. 630.

153 "itch for speechmaking": see Rhodes, *A History of the United States*, vol. 6, p. 5.

153 "Why don't you hang": see, for example, "Mr. Johnson's Disgraceful Speech at Cleveland," *Chicago Tribune*, Sept. 6, 1866, p. 4.

154 "I don't care about my dignity": see for example, "The President's Tour: Extraordinary Scene at Cleveland, *New York Evening Post*, Sept. 4, 1866, p. 8; see also "Politicians and Journalists," *The Round Table*, Sept. 15, 1866, p. 100.

154 "The President was fortunate . . . bad men": Cadwallader, "Four Years with Grant," mss., Abraham Lincoln Presidential Library.

154 The morning after the Cleveland speech: see "The Tour," *New York Herald,* Sept. 5, 1866, p. 7.

155 "this radical Congress": "The President's Tour," *Washington Star,* Sept. 10, 1866, p. 1.

156 "Who ever heard of such a Presidential Ass?": quoted in McKitrick, *Andrew Johnson and Reconstruction,* p. 434.

156 The publisher James Bennett had reminded: see "President Johnson and Congress during the Past Year," *New York Herald,* Sept. 26, 1866, p. 8.

157 Moderate Republicans: see "America," *Saturday Review,* Sept. 15, 1868, p. 318.

157 "Proud and sensitive,": "Mr. Beecher's Second Letter," *The Independent,* Sept. 13, 1866, p. 1.

157 "The 'so-called' President": Frederick Law Olmsted to Charles Eliot Norton, Sept. 12, 1866, Houghton.

157 "What a muddle we are in politically!": Henry Raymond to E. P. Whipple, Oct. 11, 1866, NYPL.

157 "sunk the Presidential office": John Sherman to WTS, Oct. 26, 1866, in Thorndike, ed., *The Sherman Letters,* p. 278.

158 "nothing in his official life ever became him like his leaving of it,": "Let Mr. Johnson Resign," *The Round Table,* Sept. 22, 1866, p. 115.

158 "If he left Washington": Whittier, *The Letters of John Greenleaf Whittier,* vol. 3, p. 133.

158 "How can you, Mr. President": Isaac N. Arnold to AJ, Sept. 29, 1866, *PAJ* 11: 285.

158 "If there is any man": Reynolds, "The New Orleans Riot of 1866, Reconsidered," p. 15.

158 "Does Seward mean": William H. Hurlburt to Manton Marble, Sept. 2, 1866, LC.

158 Others speculated: see *The Boston Traveller,* clipping.

158 Johnson had been too lenient: see "President Johnson and the True Policy for His Administration," *New York Herald,* Sept. 14, 1866, p. 4; see also William B. Phillips to AJ, Sept. 16, 1866, *PAJ* 11: 227.

159 "to mix myself in the domestic business of this people.": Matías Romero of Ministro de Relaciones Exteriores, Sept. 2, 1866, in Romero, "The Mexican Minister Describes Andrew Johnson's 'Swing Around the Circle,'" ed. Thomas Schoonover, p. 157.

159 "indisposition,": Cadwallader, "Four Years with Grant," mss., Abraham Lincoln Presidential Library. See also Sept. 19, 1866, Welles, *Diary,* LC.

159 "The President of the United States is my superior officer, and I am under his command,": "The President's Tour: Grant and Farragut," *New-York Tribune,* Sept. 14, 1866, p. 5.

159 "I wouldn't have started if I had": Richardson, *Personal History of Ulysses S. Grant,* p. 528.

160 "a National disgrace": USG to Julia Grant, Sept. 6, 1866, *PUSG* 16: 308.

160 "If the public get an idea that Grant is with the President it will do us great injury,": William DeFrees to Elihu Washburne, Aug. 23, 1866, LC.

160 "the Genl. may say that he": Joseph Russell Jones to Elihu Washburne, Sept. 9, 1866, LC.

160 "his reticence": John A. Clark to Elihu Washburne, Oct. 11, 1866, LC.

160 "violent with the opposition he meets with": USG to Philip Sheridan, Oct. 12, 1866, quoted in Badeau, *Grant in Peace,* p. 51.

161 "There is some plan to get Grant out of the way": quoted in *PUSG* 16: 340.

161 Grant unequivocally declined: see Moore, "Notes of Colonel W. G. Moore," ed. St. George L. Syosset, p. 100.

161 "No power on earth can compel me to it": see Badeau, *Grant in Peace*, p. 54.

161 "I cheerfully consented": WTS to John Sherman, Oct. 31, 1866, in *The Sherman Letters*, ed. Thorndike, p. 280.

161 "The influence of Mr. Seward": Matías Romero of Ministro de Relaciones Exteriores, Sept. 2, 1866, in "The Mexican Minister Describes Andrew Johnson's 'Swing Around the Circle,'" ed. Thomas Schoonover, *Civil War History* (June 1973), p. 154.

162 Seward had tried to climb into the Lincoln": see Lowell, "The Seward-Johnson Reaction," p. 527.

162 "Poor Seward!": Charles Eliot Norton to E. L. Godkin, August 30, 1866 , Houghton.

CHAPTER ELEVEN: RESISTANCE

163 "Permit this government to be reestablished": Anna Dickinson, holograph speech, nd [early 1867?], LC.

164 "that miserable abortion": "'My Policy,' A Radical Analysis. Miss Anna E. Dickinson at the Academy," *Philadelphia Inquirer*, May 19, 1866, pp. 1, 8.

164 "sunk into eternal perdition,": "The Fanatics on the Rampage," *Daily (Albany) Argus*, May 10, 1866, p. 2.

164 "and a devastation": see "The President's Purpose Revolutionary Avowed," *The Wooster [Ohio] Republican*, Sept. 5, 1866, p. 1.

164 The outgoing minister to France: John Bigelow diary, Oct. 30, 1866, NYPL.

164 General James Steedman: see Browning, Nov. 1, 1866, *The Diary of Orville Hickman Browning*, vol. 2, pp. 109–10.

164 "I have sometimes been": Feb. 24, 1868, Welles, *Diary*, vol. 3, p. 291.

166 "inferior races": Boutwell, *Reminiscences*, vol. 1, p. 18.

166 "A conspiracy was on foot to put the government into the hands of rebels": quoted in Summers, *A Dangerous Stir*, p. 119.

166 Johnson was a dictator: see Boutwell, "The Usurpation," p. 509.

167 "This tells well": Diary of Rufus Saxton, Sunday, May 20, 1860, Yale.

167 "what New Orleans will be today": "The President's Riot at New Orleans," *National Anti-Slavery Standard*, Sept. 6, 1866, p. 2.

167 "best abused, best hated man in the House": Ellis, *The Sights and Secrets in the National Capital*, p. 163.

169 "there always seemed": Catton, *Terrible Swift Sword*, p. 359.

169 "Butler is the only man who understands": Henry Adams to Edward Atkinson, Feb. 1, 1869, Adams, *Selected Letters*, p. 103.

169 "as if it had been a bottle, strong corked": see Trefousse, *Ben Butler*, p. 183.

169 "He was no pretender and no hypocrite.": James Wilson, *The Life of Charles A. Dana*, p. 484.

169 The crowd laughed: see Macrae, *The Americans at Home*, pp. 163–164.

170 "A collision will come": BB to J. W. Shaffer, April 10, 1866, LC.

170 "We will not . . . The war did not end with the surrender of Lee": "Impeachment— Speech of Butler at the Brooklyn Academy of Music," *New-York Tribune*, Nov. 26, 1866, pp. 1, 8.

170 "Come back to the true principles": "Speech By General Butler," *The Wooster Republican*, Sept. 6, 1866, p. 2.

171 "The massacre at New Orleans will open many eyes,": George William Curtis to William M. Grosvenor, Aug 4, 1866, Butler.

171 "If the elections": Rutherford B. Hayes to Guy M. Bryan, Oct. 1, 1866, in *The Diary and Letters of Rutherford Birchard Hayes*, vol. 2, p. 33.

171 "The events at New Orleans &c. & Mr. Johnson's exhibition": Frederick Law Olmsted to Charles Eliot Norton, Sept. 12, 1866, Houghton.

CHAPTER TWELVE: TENURE OF OFFICE

175 "I charge him with a usurpation": CG 39: 2, Jan. 7, 1867, p. 320. See also, "Our Washington Correspondence," *Georgia Weekly Telegraph*, Jan. 21, 1867, p. 1.

176 he was acting rashly: see HVNB, "Letter from Washington," *Cincinnati Daily Gazette*, Jan. 8, 1867, p. 1.

176 The Judiciary Committee included James F. Wilson of Iowa (chair); George Boutwell of Massachusetts; Burton C. Cook of Illinois; William Lawrence of Ohio; Daniel Morris of New York; Francis Thomas of Maryland; Thomas Williams of Pennsylvania; Frederick E. Woodbridge of Vermont (all Republicans); and Andrew J. Rogers of New Jersey, a Democrat.

176 Unsettled by the whole business: on burying the impeachment, see Bigelow diary, Feb. 28, 1867, NYPL.

176 "and assumed a positon that should have been held": Poore, *Perley's Recollections of Sixty Years in the National Metropolis*, vol. 2, p. 202.

176 Known by those who disliked him: see "The Character of the Man Who Moves for the Impeachment of the President," [Columbus] *Crisis*, Jan. 23, 1867, p. 414.

177 "If we could succeed in an impeachment": JG to Burke Aaron Hinsdale, January 1, 1867, in *Life and Letters*, ed. Smith, vol. 1, p. 396.

177 "rascally virtue, called discretion," quoted in Arnett, *Souvenir of the Afro-American League*, p. 564.

177 "nut with an idée fixe": C. Vann Woodward, "The Other Impeachment," *New York Times Magazine*, Aug. 11, 1974, p. 28; "an occult mixture": McKitrick, *Andrew Johnson and Reconstruction*, p. 492.

177 Washington reporter for *The Independent*, Mary Clemmer Ames, said: see M.C.A., "A Woman in Washington," May 10, 1866, *The Independent*, p. 1.

177 "Yet it has happened to him": quoted in Arnett, ed. *Souvenir of the Afro-American League*, p. 7.

177 "chill and gloom . . . children": *Ibid.*, p. 883. See also Horowitz, *The Great Impeacher*, p. 169.

178 So Ashley's resolution: The Judiciary Committee was chaired by Representative James F. Wilson of Iowa, a moderate man and well-respected lawyer who'd been adamant about abolishing slavery but was not at all convinced about impeachment.

178 "Hardly a speech is made,": clipping from "The Corporal," *Philadelphia Press*, Jan. [indecipherable] 1867, Willard Saxton papers, Yale.

178 "The Radicals are holding the threat": John Nugent to Samuel L. M. Barlow, January 10, 1867, Barlow papers, Huntington.

178 "cross as a cinnamon bear": John Nugent to Samuel L. M. Barlow, January 10, 1867, Barlow papers, Huntington.

178 "It would be just as easy": quoted in "License to Murder," *New-York Tribune*, Dec. 24, 1866, p. 4.

178 "the great weight of its influence": "Trials by Military Commissions—The Supreme Court Decision," *New York Times*, Jan. 3, 1867, p. 4.

179 "This excels in brutality the Watson": A. F. Higgs to Elihu Wasbhurne, Dec. 27, 1866.

179 "Anyone who hopes": January 26, 1867, Clemenceau, *American Reconstruction*, pp. 83–84.

179 "I say nothing . . . as I should be one of his judges,": CS to Anna Cabot Lodge, Dec. 16, 1866, *Letters*, vol. 2, ed. Palmer, p. 386.

180 "We are having pretty serious times here,": WW to his mother, Jan. 15, 1867, in Whitman, *Correspondence*, vol. 1, ed. Miller, p. 307.

181 Had he perpetrated any overt act against Congress: see "The Impeachment of President Johnson," *Littell's Living Age*, Nov 17, 1866, pp. 440–41.

181 "There is never a lack of legal texts any more than of religious texts,": Clemenceau, *American Reconstruction*, Jan. 5, 1867, p. 75.

181 "The long haired men and cadaverous females": Benjamin Truman to AJ, Oct. 4, 1866, *PAJ* 11: p. 307.

182 shouldn't deplorable, bigoted, or reckless acts: see Berger: *Impeachment*, and also Roberts, "The Law of Impeachment in Stuart England: A Reply to Raoul Berger," p. 1419.

182 "If with the negro": Frederick Douglass, "Reconstruction," p. 765.

182 "The folly of continuing": Allen Pierse to AJ, Nov. 21, 1866, *PAJ* 11: 471.

183 "I think you will agree": William B. Phillips to AJ, Nov. 8, 1866, *PAJ* 11: 439.

183 "The tendency": Simeon M. Johnson to AJ, Nov. 18, 1866, *PAJ* 11: 469.

183 "When I told him": Samuel Cox to Manton Marble, nd [Monday], LC.

183 radical among the Radical: see for instance, "South Carolina: The President Advises the Southern States to Reject the Constitutions Amendment," *New York Times*, Dec. 27, 1866, p. 4; "The Reported Commissioner from South Carolina to Washington," *Augusta Chronicle*, Dec. 27, 1866, p. 3; "Colonel T. C. Weatherly," *Boston Advertiser*, Jan. 23, 1867, p. 2.

183 "change the whole character of our Government,": AJ to Lewis E. Parsons, Jan. 17, 1867, *PAJ* 11: 611.

184 "They have deliberated": CG 39: 2, Feb. 8, 1867, p. 1104.

184 "newspaper gossip," "rumors," "negro quarrels": Feb. 15, 1867, Welles, *Diary*, vol. 2, p. 42.

184 "made plain": Sheridan, *Personal Memoirs*, vol. 2, p. 242.

185 "He is refractory and lavishes": Nov. 26, 1866, Strong, *The Diary of George Templeton Strong*, vol. 4, p. 114.

185 Stanton had moved: see Boutwell, *Reminiscences*, vol. 2, p. 108.

186 "blush for the honor of the American name,": John Price to AJ, Oct. 6, 1866, *PAJ* 11: 319–20.

186 *"Arrest the traitors."*: Thomas Powell to AJ, Jan. 5, 1867, *PAJ* 11: 588.

186 "They don't cut throats any longer here,": Bigelow, *Retrospections*, vol. 4, March 6, 1867, p. 88.

186 "There are men in the House": Henry Dawes to Electa Dawes, Dec. 7, 1866, LC.

186 "few of our side call on him,": Henry Dawes to his daughter, Dec. 8, 1866, LC.

186 "there was a war still being waged": CG 39, 2, Jan. 18, 1867, p. 542.

187 "Johnson has resigned himself to drunkenness": March 14, 1867, in *The Union on Trial*, ed. Phillips and Jason Pendleton, p. 270.

187 "never told the truth, even by accident": *Testimony Taken Before the House Judiciary Committee*, p. 111. But soon there was a caricature: J. A. McKean to Elihu Washburne, May 30, 1866, LC.

187 Newly seated: The Committee now included Johnson C. Churchill of New York

(Republican) and Charles Eldridge of Wisconsin and Samuel S. Marshall of Illinois, who replaced Cook, Morris, and Rogers.

188 "shrewd, sinuous, tricky lawyer": Feb. 8, 1868, Welles, *Diary*, vol. 2, p. 274.

188 "When he puts his hand on the wheel": Briggs, *The Olivia Letters*, March 27, 1867, p. 36. On Bingham, see also Brooks, *Washington in Lincoln's Time*, p. 112; Nevins, *Hamilton Fish*.

188 Previously an anti-slavery Whig: see Magliocca, *American Founding Son*, p. 136.

189 "I did all I could, the best I could": *CG*, 40: 1, March 21, 1863, p. 263.

189 "He can comfort": Briggs, March 26, 1867, *The Olivia Letters*, p. 36.

190 "I was led on by a sincere desire": "A Remarkable Lecture! John Surratt Reveals His Story," *Washington Evening Star*, Dec. 7, 1870, quoted in Hatch, *John Surratt*, pp. 173–74.

190 Back in Washington: see January 25, 1867, and Feb. 19, 1867, Browning, *The Diary of Orville Hickman Browning*, vol. 2, pp. 126, 131.

190 George Boutwell: see *CG* 39, 2, Dec. 4, 1866, pp. 12–13.

190 "tried with Surratt for conniving at the attempt upon *his* own life,": Bigelow, *Retrospections of an Active Life*, vol. 4, March 6, 1867, p. 48.

191 "there is much talk about impeachment": WW to his mother, March 5, 1867, *Correspondence*, ed. Miller, p. 316; "growled and thundered": Briggs, March 27, 1867, *The Olivia Letters*, p. 34.

191 "if nothing is done to give it new life,": Henry Dawes to Electa Dawes, March 8, 1867, LC.

191 "I have had a son killed": Colonel W. G. Moore, March 1867, typescript of diary, LC, p. 33.

191 He presented: see M.C.A., "A Woman's Letter from Washington," *Independent*, May 9, 1867, p. 1.

192 "The President's cook": "Miscellaneous Paragraphs," quoted in the *Daily Albany Argus*, April 8, 1867, p. 2.

192 "to sit all summer": Briggs, March 27, 1867, *The Olivia Letters*, p. 34.

192 "fussy, unnecessary and absurd": "The Presidency: The Race for the Radical Nomination," *New York Herald*, July 8, 1867, p. 6.

192 "These innumerable eggs": "Speech on the Impeachment of the President," *Selected Papers of Thaddeus Stevens*, vol. 2, pp. 446–47.

193 "making a mere pretense of prosecuting impeachment,": quoted in DeWitt, *The Impeachment and Trial of Andrew Johnson*, p. 223.

193 The revolutionary farce is over, the shameful crusade ended: see "Cabinet Decision on the Powers of 787. Commanders—New Obstacles to Reconstruction," *New York Herald*, June 15, 1867, p. 6.

193 "Amid whatever clouds,": Walt Whitman, "Democracy," *Galaxy*, Dec. 1867, p. 930, 933. Whitman read Carlyle's essay the previous August and began composing his response then.

CHAPTER THIRTEEN: A REVOLUTIONARY PERIOD

195 "new wine could not be put in old bottles": *CG* 40: 1, March 4, 1867, p. 4.

195 The only real objection: see John Sherman to WTS, March 7, 1867, *The Sherman Letters*, ed. Thorndike, p. 289.

196 "lunatic": see "Reconstruction," *National Anti-Slavery Standard*, March 2, 1867, p. 2.

196 "We are still warred": Absalom Chappel to August Belmont, May 13, 1867, Butler, CU.

196 "furious dogs," "Revolutionists": see Francis P. Blair, Sr. to AJ, Feb. 24, 1867, *PAJ* 12: 59; see also Montgomery Blair to AJ, *PAJ* 12: 67.

196 "gives universal suffrage to the ignorant blacks": "Interview with Charles Halpine," Feb. 21, 1867, *PAJ* 12: 51.

196 "sever my right arm from my body,": Feb. 18, 1867, Colonel W. G. Moore diary, LC.

197 Told again and again: see for instance George P. Este to AJ, Feb. 27, 1867, *PAJ* 12: 70

197 "with only one idea": and summaries: see Charles Nordhoff to William C. Bryant, Feb. 27, 1867, NYPL.

197 "Whatever else you lose,": Fernando Wood to AJ, Feb. 21, 1867, *PAJ* 12: 52.

198 "the southerners pat the President on the back, hobnob with him & keep him vetoing everything that is presented to him,": Charlotte Cushman, notes, p. 532, LC.

198 "The President was raining vetoes": see Bigelow, *Retrospections*, vol. 4, p. 48; see also "The Reconstruction Veto," *Chicago Tribune*, March 4, 1867, p. 2.

198 "He is of no account": John Bigelow diary, March 2, 1867, NYPL.

198 "He is a nullity": John Bigelow diary, March 2, 1867, NYPL.

198 "Radicalism desires": Jan. 12, 1867, Welles, *Diary*, vol. 3, pp. 17–18.

199 "The President got very angry": Browning, *The Diary of Orville Hickman Browning*, vol. 2, p. 135.

199 "The slime of the serpent is over them all,": March 13, 1867, Welles, *Diary*, vol. 2, p. 65.

200 "Our President is a bad man": CG 40: 1, March 23, 1867, p. 307.

200 "military despotism,": see for instance May 21, 1867, Browning, *The Diary of Orville Hickman Browning*, vol. 2, p. 145.

200 "marked characteristics": Reed, ed. *The Bench and Bar of Ohio*, vol. 1, pp. 86–87.

200 Per Johnson's instructions, Stanbery announced: for Stanbery's opinion, see Stanbery, *Opinion of Attorney General Stanbery*.

200 "Mr. Stanbery cuts the heart out of the military bill": "Mr. Stanbery's Opinion," *New-York Tribune*, June 17, 1867, p. 4.

200 "It is quite astonishing": WPF to Edwin Morgan, June 27, 1867, New York State Library.

201 "a broad macadamized": see Philip Sheridan to Edwin Stanton, June 3, 1867, as quoted in Sheridan, *Memoirs*, vol. 2, pp. 266–67.

201 "Field Marshal of the Radicals": Bowers, *The Tragic Era*, p. 193

201 "Game was scarce down that way": quoted in Boyd, *Gallant Trooper*, p. 223.

202 "there are more casualties from outrages": quoted in Smallwood, inter alia., *Murder and Mayhem*, p. 43.

202 "All's well that ends Wells": see Hollandsworth, *An Absolute Massacre*, p. 152

202 Even Johnson's friend General James Steedman: see Steedman to AJ, June 1, 1867, *PAJ* 12: 348.

202 "Philip has a strong hold": Joseph Sumner to William Gorham Sumner, June 22, 1867, Yale.

202 "The people would throw": "The Progress of Reconstruction," *The Independent*, April 11, 1867, p. 4.

203 "You hear nothing": Mary H. Henderson from Mollie N. Cochran, Aug. 7, 1867, Chapel Hill, UNC.

203 "Some of them probably": Orville Babcock to Elihu Washburne, Aug. 13, 1867, LC.

204 Journalist Emily Briggs: summarized from Briggs, *The Olivia Letters*, p. 24.

204 "The cool way in which the beaten side": Charlotte Cushman, notes pp. 510, 533, LC.

204 "Church congregations": "Letter from Washington," April 16, 1867, *Alta California*, quoted in Fulton, *The Reconstruction of Mark Twain*, p. 122

204 "The idea that we cannot get . . . better days.": Orville Babcock to Elihu Washburne, Aug. 13, 1867, LC.

205 "appropriate,": see April 6, 1866, Welles, *Diary*, vol. 2, p. 477.

205 "lasting disgrace": USG to Stanton, July 7, 1866, *PUSG* 16: 234.

205 "Many of our friends . . . counteracted": [John] DeFrees to Elihu Washburne, Aug. 23, 1866, LC.

206 "He is the only eminent man in America": Latham, *Black and White*, pp. 63–64.

206 "If Grant will throw himself away": Horace White to Elihu Washburne, Sept. 16, 1866, LC.

206 "His reticence had led": John A. Clark to Elihu Washburne, Oct. 11, 1866, LC.

206 "Send me a list of authenticated": USG to OOH, Jan. 18, 1867, *PUSG* 17: 50.

206 "The General is getting more and more Radical,": March 1, 1867, Cyrus Comstock diary, LC.

207 "I can't spare this man": quoted in *Recollected Words of Abraham Lincoln*, ed. Fehrenbacher, p. 315.

207 "might pass well enough": quoted in *A Cycle of Adams Letters*, ed. Ford, vol. 2, pp. 133–34.

207 "a nightmare of humanity": McFeely, *Grant*, p. 165.

207 "It is difficult to comprehend": Boutwell, *The Lawyer, the Statesman, the Soldier*, p. 170.

207 an "acceptor of things": quoted in Traubel, *With Walt Whitman in Camden*, vol. 2, p. 539.

207 "meekness and grimness meet": Melville, "The Armies of the Wilderness," *Battle-Pieces*, p. 9.

208 In Washington when Charles Sumner's private secretary: see Moorfield Storey to his mother, Nov. 25, 1867, quoted in Howe, *Portrait of an Independent*, p. 43.

208 "I know of only two tunes": Childs, *Recollections of General Grant*, p. 40.

208 "but suppose the people": quoted in *Chicago Republican*, "Foreign News," Nov. 9, 1866, p. 2, and "General Grant and the Presidency," *New Hampshire Sentinel*, Nov. 15, 1867, p. 2.

208 Radical Republicans wrung their hands: see "The New Presidency," *The Independent*, May 30, 1866, p. 4.

208 Without federal troops: see USG to Charles Nordhoff, Feb. 21, 1867, NYPL.

208 "The General is getting more and more Radical,": March 1, 1867, Cyrus Comstock diary, LC.

209 "Enforce your own construction": USG to John Pope, June 28, 1867, *PUSG* 17: 192.

209 "The situation was approaching": Badeau, *Grant in Peace*, p. 72.

209 "he had already given the opinion": Cabinet meeting notes, June 20 1867, Stanton papers, LC.

209 "used his position in the Cabinet": Young, *Around the World with General Grant*, vol. 2, p. 358.

210 "I know I am right in this matter,": USG to AJ, Aug. 1, 1867, *PAJ* 12: 448.

CHAPTER FOURTEEN: THE RUBICON IS CROSSED

211 "Public considerations": for correspondence between AJ and Stanton, see Aug. 5, 1867, *PAJ* 12: 461.

211 "hanging on the sharp hooks of uncertainty": quoted in Trefousse, *Andrew Johnson*, p. 295.

212 "public considerations of high character,": see also Colonel W. G. Moore, Aug. 1, 1867, and Aug. 11, 1867, diary, LC.

212 "the General commanding the Armies": Edwin Stanton to AJ, Aug. 12, 1867, *PAJ* 12: 477.

213 "The turning point has at last come,": "Notes of Colonel W. G. Moore," ed. Sioussat, dated Aug. 12, 1867, p. 109.

213 "He is a madman,": Carl Schurz to his wife, Aug. 27, 1867, *Intimate Letters of Carl Schurz*, ed. Shafer, p. 391.

213 Grant's friends: see for instance, Wendell Phillips, "Johnson and Stanton," *National Anti-Slavery Standard*, Aug. 17, 1867, p. 1.

213 "even at the risk of": Horace White to Elihu Washburne, Aug. 13, 1867, LC.

213 "it's most important": quoted in Julia Grant, *The Personal Memoirs of Julia Dent Grant*, p. 165.

213 "Grant, in my opinion, made a bad mistake": Carl Schurz to his wife, Aug. 31, 1867, *Intimate Letters of Carl Schurz*, ed. Shafer, p. 392.

213 "Make Grant speak": Wendell Phillips to John Russell Young, Aug. 25, 1867, LC.

214 "The time is fast approaching,": John Lothrop Motley to Mary Motley, Aug. 14, 1867, in *The Correspondence of John Lothrop Motley*, p. 184.

214 "The unreconstructed element": USG to AJ, Aug. 17, 1867, *PUSG* 17: 278.

214 "sole purpose seemed": quoted in Aug. 22, 1867, *PAJ* 12: 505.

214 "I urge—earnestly urge": USG to AJ, Aug. 17, 1867, in *PUSG* 17: 277–8.

214 "Every word is golden,": "Grant Versus Johnson," *Army and Navy Journal*, Aug. 31, 1867, p. 1.

215 "malignant guillotine of Mr. Johnson,": J. Q. Thompson to OOH, Aug. 24, 1867, Bowdoin.

215 "under any obligation to keep the peace with Andrew Johnson.": Frederick Douglass to William Slade, July 29, 1867, LC.

215 "The greatest black man in the nation,": quoted in Quarles, *Frederick Douglass*, p. 239.

215 Purvis consulted: see "A Letter Addressed by Wendell Phillips to Robert Purvis," ed. Joseph Alfred Boromé, *The Journal of Negro History* (Oct. 1957), pp. 292–95.

215 "What mischief has he prevented?": Wendell Phillips, "Dunces," *National Anti-Slavery Standard*, Sep. 7, 1867, p. 1.

215 "Texas is in anarchy": Wendell Phillips, "Crime Not Statesmanship," *National Anti-Slavery Standard*, Aug. 31, 1867, p. 1.

216 "Butler does not need any explanation. Nobody explains Sumner,": Wendell Phillips, "The Surrender of Congress," newspaper clipping, LC.

216 "all that is fishy and mercenary": Horace Greeley to Zachariah Chandler, Aug. 25, 1867, LC.

216 The admirers of Chief Justice Salmon Chase: see for example, A. Watson to Elihu Washburne, Jan. 19, 1868, LC.

216 And Ben Butler presumably: see Orville Babcock to Elihu Washburne, Aug. 13, 1867, LC.

216 "Grant is true,": L. H. Caldwell to Elihu Washburne, Dec. 18, 1867, LC.

216 "palpably unconstitutional . . . ?": Aug. 13, 1867, Welles, *Diary*, vol. 3, p. 169.

216 "crude opinions upon all subjects, and especially upon legal questions": Browning, Aug. 15, 1867, *The Diary of Orville Hickman Browning*, p. 158.

216 "tampered with, and I believe seduced": Aug. 26, 1867, Welles, *Diary*, vol. 3, p. 185.

218 "If forced to choose between the penitentiary": WTS to Henry Halleck, Sept. 1864, quoted in O'Connell, *Fierce Patriot*, p. 322.

218 "I am afraid his doings": Peleg Chandler to Charles Sumner, Aug. 15, 1867, Houghton.

218 Was it true: see for instance, "Impeachment and the Rumors of Executive Resistance," *New York Times*, Oct. 1, 1867, p. 4; "The Public Situation," *The Independent*, Sept. 19, 1867, p. 4.

218 "People say that Johnson's more intimate pals": Sept. 13, 1867, Strong, *The Diary of George Templeton Strong*, vol. 4, p. 150.

218 "It is not impossible": Carl Schurz to his wife, Aug. 31, 1867, Schurz, *Intimate Letters*, ed. Shafer, p. 393.

218 "There have been so many idle threats that both parties are scared,": WTS to Ellen Sherman, Oct. 11, 1867, Notre Dame.

CHAPTER FIFTEEN: THE PRESIDENT'S MESSAGE

220 "Ours is a funny Government in some respects,": Mark Twain, "Public Stealing, Jan. 10, 1868," *Territorial Enterprise*, Jan. 30, 1868, quoted in Twain, *Mark Twain Newspaper Correspondent*.

220 "Indian Rings, Patent Rings, Stationery Rings and Railroad Rings,": John Russell Young to Elihu Washburne, Jan 5, 1869, LC.

221 Thaddeus Stevens said: the very best analysis of currency issues and their impact on Reconstruction and impeachment remains Benedict,: *The Right Way*, pp. 46; 389–99; 411–13.

221 "Public credit should be 'like Caesar's wife: above suspicion,'": CG 20: 2, March 11, 1868, p. 1810.

222 "The Secretary's 'contraction' system": Mark Twain, "Public Stealing, Jan. 10, 1868," *Territorial Enterprise*, Jan. 30, 1868, quoted in Twain, *Mark Twain Newspaper Correspondent*.

222 "Greenbacks are a debt": quoted in McJimsey, *Genteel Partisan*, p. 121.

223 "A great many of our party here": T. B. Shannon to Elihu Washburne, Oct. 13, 1867, LC.

223 "We went in on principle": Benjamin Wade to Zachariah Chandler, Oct. 19, 1867, LC.

223 "the Republicans once beaten into a minority": Thaddeus Stevens to F. A. Conkling, Jan. 6, 1868, LC.

223 "The negro question": Thomas Ewing to AJ, Oct. 10, 1867, PAJ 13: 164.

223 "any party with an abolition head": Ira Brown, "Pennsylvania and the Rights of the Negro," p. 51.

223 "Andrew Johnson is certainly the best-hated man this side of the Atlantic,": Strong, Sept. 13, 1867, *The Diary of George Templeton Strong*, vol. 4, p. 150.

223 "no extreme Radical": Thomas Ewing to Hugh Ewing, Oct. 16, 1867, LC.

223 "Say nothing, write nothing": Henry Raymond to USG, Oct. 1, 1867, PUSG 18: 331–32.

224 "Johnson is as useful to us as the devil is to orthodox theology,": Horace Greeley to John Russell Young, Dec. 4, 1867, LC.

224 "a man of his temper,": Charles Eliot Norton to E. L. Godkin, Oct. 13, 1867, Houghton.

224 "With a cabinet composed of his own adherents": Wendell Phillips, "Convention of Loyal Governors," *National Anti-Slavery Standard*, Sept. 14, 1867, p. 2.

224 "I believe the Prince of Darkness": Twain, "Impeachment, March 20, 1868," *Territorial Enterprise*, April 7, 1868, quoted in Twain, *Mark Twain Newspaper Correspondent*.

225 "As politics go, so goes the weather,": Twain, "Mark Twain's Letter from Washington, Dec. 4, 1867," *Territorial Enterprise*, Dec. 22, 1867, quoted in Twain, *Mark Twain Newspaper Correspondent*.

226 "the negro apologized": Twain, "Washington Crime," *Daily Alta California*, February 19, 1868, quoted in Twain, *Mark Twain Newspaper Correspondent*.

226 "devil's dance": Clayton, *Reminiscences of Jeremiah Sullivan Black*, p. 148.

227 "enslaved . . . Africanize the half of our country": all quotations from AJ, "Third Annual Message," Dec. 3, 1867, *PAJ* 13: 280–306.

228 "The President's Message," *Ibid.*

228 "Incendiary in its suggestions . . . might": Moorfield Storey to his father, Dec. 4, 1867, quoted in Howe, *Portrait of an Independent*, p. 47.

228 "One thing is very sure": Twain, "Mark Twain's Letter from Washington, Dec. 4, 1867," *Territorial Enterprise*, Dec. 22, 1867, quoted in Twain, *Mark Twain Newspaper Correspondent*.

229 "Practically it would be found impossible": Appendix to the *CG*, 40: 2, Dec. 5, 1867, p. 56. All subsequent quotations from the speech as recorded in *CG*, Appendix, 40: 2, Dec. 6, 1867, pp. 56–62.

230 "bundle of generalities": *CG*, Appendix, 40: 2, Dec. 6, 1867, p. 65. Quotations from the speech as recorded in *CG*, Appendix, 40: 2, Dec. 6, 1867, pp. 62–65.

230 "I am not here to defend the President": *CG*, Appendix, 40: 2, Dec. 6, 1867, p. 64.

231 "The impeachment 'question' is killed": George Fox to Elihu Washburne, Dec. 10, 1867, LC; "the country is tired of Butler & the blacks": R. N. Silent to Elihu Washburne, Dec. 13, 1867, LC.

231 "I fear there will be sad calamities . . . not": John Pope to USG, Dec. 31, 1867, *PUSG* 18: 95.

232 "the black population have a gloomy prospect before them": Edward O. C. Ord to USG, [nd] *PUSG* 18:6.

232 And on December 12, Johnson sent: see Dec. 12, 1868, *PAJ* 13: 328–41.

CHAPTER SIXTEEN: A BLUNDERING, ROARING LEAR

234 Johnson offered to pay: see Badeau, *Grant in Peace*, p. 110.

234 No one really knows: Chernow, *Grant*, p. 602.

235 "No direct vote will be taken on Stanton": Thomas Ewing, Sr., to AJ, [Jan. 12, 1868] *PAJ* 13: 465.

235 "Well I have done my duty": WTS to Ellen Sherman, Jan. 13, 1868, Notre Dame.

235 "But he & the President both": WTS to Ellen Sherman, Jan. 13, 1868, Notre Dame.

236 "I am to be found over at my office": Townsend, *Anecdotes of Civil War*, p. 124.

236 "This was not the first time Grant had deceived him,": see Moore, "Notes of Colonel W. G. Moore," p. 115.

236 Asthmatic and stressed: see "The Stanton Affair," *National Intelligencer*, Jan. 15, 1868, p. 2.

236 "Don't give up the Ship! Keep on, and 500,000 Blues will sustain you": General W. G. Mark to Edwin Stanton, Jan. 16, 1868, LC.

236 "Johnson is now a full-blown rebel,": Charles Sumner to John Bright, Jan. 18, 1868, quoted in Sumner, *Selected Letters*, p. 416.

237 Johnson had already heard rumors: see Colonel W. G. Moore, Jan. 14, 1868, small diary, LC.

237 "Why did you give up the keys to Mr. Stanton and leave the Department?": Jan. 14, 1867, Welles, *Diary*, vol. 3, p. 260.

237 Treasury Secretary Hugh McCulloch: see Colonel W. G. Moore, diary, Feb. 4, 1868, LC.

238 Grant indignantly: see WTS to USG, Jan. 18, 1868, LC.

238 "I have done my best to cut": WTS to Ellen Sherman, Jan. 15, 1868, Notre Dame.

238 "I thought by his disregarding": WTS to Ellen Sherman, Jan. 18, 1868, Notre Dame.

238 "I'm afraid,": WTS to USG, Jan. 18, 1868, LC.

238 "I feel for Mr. Johnson": WTS to Ellen Sherman, Jan. 23, 1868, Notre Dame.

239 "or a good administrator": WTS to Ellen Sherman, Jan. 28, 1868, Notre Dame.

239 more "uneasy than usual,": WTS to Ellen Sherman, Jan. 19, 1868, Notre Dame.

239 "indirect and circumstantial": William Seward to AJ, Feb. 6, 1868, *PAJ* 13: 533.

239 "a true firm honest affectionate man": Charlotte Cushman to Wayman Crow, July 11, 1868, LC.

239 "the whole hemisphere from the glaciers of Greenland to the volcanoes of Tierra del Fuego.": quoted in Stahr, *Seward*, p. 496.

240 "Seward lost his brains,": Wendell Phillips, "After Grant—What?" *Boston Advertiser*, Oct. 28, 1868, p. 1.

240 "A man is of no count here": quoted in Bigelow, *Retrospections*, vol. 4, p. 42.

240 "who has corrupted,": Francis P. Blair, Jr., to Francis P. Blair, Sr., Aug. 2, 1867, Princeton.

241 "in favor of negro supremacy,": James Doolittle to Manton Marble, Dec. 21, 1867, LC.

241 "then we shall know what his opinions": Manton Marble to James Doolittle, Dec. 29, 1867, WHS.

241 The President of the United States: for the written correspondence between Johnson and Grant, Jan. 25, 1868–January 30, 1868, see for instance *PUSG* 18: 113–22.

241 "Where my honor . . . disobey": USG to AJ, Feb. 3, 1868, *PUSG* 18: 126.

241 "In a question of veracity between a soldier": "The Situation," *New-York Tribune*, Jan. 17, 1868, p. 4. Even those papers partial to Johnson's interpretation of events, like Henry Raymond's *New York Times*, conceded that while the President had "the best of the case," General Grant was far more credible; and while the President had responded to Grant with dignity, he should never have been drawn into an ugly public spat in the first place. See *New York Times*, Feb. 15, 1868.

241 Johnson's cabinet: see "Notes of Colonel W. G. Moore," Feb. 4, 1868, p. 118.

242 "seem thoroughly waked up & full of fight.": Walt Whitman to his mother, Jan. 26, 1868, quoted in *Correspondence*, vol. 2, p. 14.

242 "Congress is on its mettle,": Twain, "The Political Stink Pots Opened," Jan. 11, 1868, *Territorial Enterprise*, February 18, 1868, quoted in *Mark Twain Newspaper Correspondent*.

243 The other six men: John Bingham, Beaman, Paine, Hubburd, Brooks, and Beach.

243 "Died: In this city, Feb. 13, at his lodgings in the chamber of the House": "Mark Twain's Letter," *Chicago Republican*, Feb. 19, 1868, p. 3.

243 "the finest word": Twain, "Letter from Washington," February 19, 1868, *Territorial Enterprise*, March 7, 1868, quoted in *Mark Twain Newspaper Correspondent*.

243 "What the devil do I care": see "Impeachment Dead," *New-York Tribune*, Feb. 14, p. 1.; see also "Washington; New York; Mr. Thaddeus Stevens; U. S. Grant; Mr. Bingham," *Boston Daily Advertiser*, Feb. 15, 1868, p. 2.

244 "The Senate had confirmed . . . what does?": see *Norwich Aurora*, Feb. 18, 1868; "Impeachment Dead," *New-York Tribune*, Feb. 14, p. 1.; see also "Washington; New York; Mr. Thaddeus; Stevens; U. S. Grant; Mr. Bingham," *Boston Daily Advertiser*, Feb. 15, 1868, p. 2; "Impeachment Proceedings," *Daily National Intelligencer*, Feb. 15, 1868, p. 2.

244 "There is no sense making ourselves ridiculous before the country": "Thad Forcibly Expresses Himself to Congressmen," *Boston Traveller*, Feb. 14, 1868, p. 2.

245 "If McCardle gains his case": "Mark Twain's Letter from Washington," Jan. 11, 1868, in *Territorial Enterprise*, February 18, 1868, quoted in *Mark Twain Newspaper Correspondent*.

245 "Well . . . let them go ahead.": "A Talk with Andrew Johnson," *Chicago Tribune*, Feb. 15, 1868, p. 2.

245 Not at all, Johnson happily answered, not at all: see Poore, "Washington News," *Harper's Monthly*, Jan. 1874, p. 234.

246 "If this political atmosphere": WTS to AJ, Jan. 31, 1868, quoted in Colonel W. G. Moore diary typescript, LC. p. 80–81.

246 "I suppose that because . . . wilderness": WTS to Thomas Ewing, Feb, 14, 1868, quoted in *Home Letters*, ed. Howe, p. 373.

247 "the President would make use": WTS to John Sherman, Feb. 14, 1868, quoted in *Sherman Letters*, ed. Thorndike, p. 305

247 "Almost every positive affirmative step": Jan. 18, 1868, Strong, *The Diary of George Templeton Strong*, vol. 4, p. 181.

247 "If the people did not entertain sufficient": "Notes of Colonel W. G. Moore," Feb. 19, 1868, p. 130.

247 "I have ever battled for the right": Colonel W. G. Moore, Feb. 22, 1868, diary, LC.

248 "Mr. President . . . means,": Jerome Stillson to Samuel L. M. Barlow, Feb. 12, 1868, Barlow papers, Huntington.

CHAPTER SEVENTEEN: STRIKING AT A KING

249 "He was a straw": quoted in Burlingame and Ettlinger, ed., *Inside Lincoln's White House*, p. 69.

250 "I want some little time": "Notes of Colonel W. G. Moore," Feb. 21, 1868, pp. 121–22.

250 "Didn't I tell you so": Feb. 28, 1868, quoted in Clemenceau, *American Reconstruction*, p. 153.

250 "Stand up, impeachers!": "The Political Crisis," *The Boston Daily Journal*, Feb. 22, 1868, p. 4.

251 "Stick!": Charles Sumner to Edwin Stanton, Feb. 21, 1868, LC.

251 "Resist force by force": John M. Thayer to Edwin Stanton, Feb. 21, 1868, LC.

251 he had too much: See *Trial* I, pp. 56, 74, 76.

252 With a look of mock astonishment: Townsend, *Anecdotes*, pp. 127–28.

252 "When you strike at a king": quoted in Holmes, *Emerson*, p. 74.

252 Former ambassador John Bigelow: Feb. 21, 1868, Bigelow, *Retrospections*, vol. 4, p. 154.

252 "I know they are capable . . . care": the remarks were widely reported. See for example, "The War Office Struggle," *Albany Evening Journal*, Feb. 22, 1868, p. 22; "Washington," *Cincinnati Daily Gazette*, Feb. 24, 1868, p. 3; "From Washington," Feb. 27, 1868, *Richmond Whig*, p. 2; "The President, Stanton, and Congress," *New Orleans Times-Picayune*, Feb. 26, 1868, p. 1.

252 "The President called upon the lightning,": February 28, 1868, in Clemenceau, *American Reconstruction*, p. 151.

CHAPTER EIGHTEEN: IMPEACHMENT

253 Newspaper boys: see "The Terrors of Congress," *New York Herald*, Feb. 25, 1868, p. 3.

253 "There are men in Washington": Mark Twain, "Letters from Washington," March 20, 1868, *Territorial Enterprise*, April 7, 1868, p. 1, quoted *in Mark Twain Newspaper Correspondent*.

253 "I recall nothing like it for size or eagerness": "The War Office Imbroglio," *Boston Daily Advertiser*, Feb. 24, 1868, p. 1.

254 "first rate, first rate": *Ibid.*

254 "There was a soul in": Twain, "Mark Twain's Letter from Washington: The Grand Coup D'État," Feb. 22, 1868," *Territorial Enterprise*, March 13, 1868, p. 1, quoted in *Mark Twain Newspaper Correspondent*.

255 James Doolittle begged: see Colonel W. G. Moore, diary, Feb. 24, 1868, LC.

255 "Johnson acts like a man": Edwards Pierrepont to John A. Dix, Feb. 25, 1868, Butler.

256 "The papers talk about me": "The President His Own Advisor," *Boston Daily Advertiser*, Feb. 26, 1868, p. 1.

256 After all, Mr. Stanton should have been removed: see "The President and His Cabinet," *New York World*, Feb. 26, 1868.

256 "He aims now": Edwards Pierrepont to John A. Dix, Feb. 25, 1868, Butler.

256 Best that the Democratic party: see "The Presidency," *New York Herald*, Feb. 23, 1868, p. 10.

256 "to tie themselves to a corpse": "The Crisis at Washington," *Chicago Tribune*, Feb. 25, 1868, p. 1.

257 "He swore that his course ought to have been plain enough,": Jerome Stillson to Samuel L. M. Barlow, Feb 25, 1868, Barlow papers, Huntington.

257 "Too late, Mr. President,": *New-York Tribune*, Feb. 24, 1868, p. 4.

257 "Johnson is like a blind man reaching out in every direction for something to take hold of,": quoted in Napton, *The Union on Trial*, p. 304.

257 "Nearly the entire loyal": Edwards Pierrepont to John Dix, Feb. 25, 1868, Butler.

257 "The truest portion of the Republican Party": J. G. Jackson to Thaddeus Stevens, March 2, 1868, LC.

257 "as American citizens,": Charles C. Cotton to BB, April 10, 1868, LC.

258 "Andrew Johnson deserves impeachment,": "The State of the Country, *The Elevator*, March 13, 1868, p. 2.

258 "The bloody and untilled fields of the ten unreconstructed States,": CG 40: 2, Feb. 22, 1868, p. 1348.

258 "ought to be removed," Francis Pierpont to William Willey": Sept. 11, 1867, quoted in Trefousse, *The Impeachment of a President*, p. 142.

258 "I think we have 'caught the rat' ": John Logan to Phillips March 4, 1868, Abraham Lincoln Presidential Library.

258 "Sound the tocsin,": Mark Twain, "Mark Twain's Letter, Feb. 24, 1868," *Chicago Republican*, March 1, 1868, p. 1.

258 "as President Johnson only has a short time to serve,": Daniel Miller to WPF, March 21, 1868, Western Reserve Historical Society.

258 "Either I am very stupid": WPF to Elizabeth Warriner, Feb. 22, 1868, Bowdoin.

258 "indecent eagerness . . . impeachers": Charles Eliot Norton to E. L. Godkin, March 1, 1868, Houghton.

259 "not a blunder, but a crime,": *Augusta Loyal Georgian*, February 15, 1868, quoted in Egerton, *The Wars of Reconstruction*, p. 232.

259 "If you do not crush Johnson": John C. Binney to WPF, Feb. 21, 1868, Western Reserve Historical Society.

259 "the removal of Andrew Johnson": quoted in "Effect of Impeachment at the South, *Charleston Free Press*, April 5, 1867, p. 1.

259 "By a final hasty move": March 14, 1868, Welles, *Diary*, vol. 3, p. 315.

259 "We have tolerated a Rebel": [A. W. Luce] to Elihu Washburne, Feb. 24, 1868, LC.

259 "scarlet cloak or a red rag": Thomas Ewing to Hugh Ewing, Feb. 26, 1868, LC.

259 Senator John Sherman: "The forcible removal of a man in office, claiming to be in lawfully," Sherman told his brother, "is like the forcible ejection of a tenant when his right of possession is in dispute. It is a trespass, an assault, a riot, or a crime.": see John Sherman to WTS, Feb. 23, 1868, quoted in Sherman, *Recollections of Forty Years*, vol. 1, p. 422.

260 "I have been among those who have hesitated": CG 40: 2, Feb. 22, 1868, p. 1337.

260 "I stand here,": quoted in Magliocca, *American Founding Son*, p. 143. See also CG 40: 2, Feb. 22, 1868, p. 1340.

260 "Andrew Johnson, in my judgement": CG 40: 2, Feb. 24, 1868, p. 1390.

260 Ben Butler: see CG 40: 2, Feb. 24, 1868, p. 1393.

261 The House Democrats: see CG 40: 2, Feb. 24, 1868, p. 1397.

261 "The President has openly and clearly": CG 40: 2, Feb. 22, 1868, p. 1368.

262 "his individuality into that official": CG 40: 2, Feb. 24, 1868, p. 1347.

262 "The framers of our Constitution did not rely": CG 40: 2, Feb. 24, 1868, pp. 1399–1400.

262 "out of the midst": Mark Twain, "Mark Twain's Letter," *Chicago Republican*, March 1, 1868, p. 1.

263 "The man who was inaugurated in drunkeness": HCB, The "Irrepressible Conflict" in Washington, *The Independent*, Feb. 27, 1868, p. 4.

263 "impeachment is peace . . . process of law": "Impeachment Is Peace," *New-York Tribune*, Feb. 26, 1868, p. 4.

264 "the committee are likely to present": Thaddeus Stevens to BB, Feb. 28, 1868, Butler papers, LC.

265 "I do not care . . . unfitted you for your office,": "Impeachment: Lecture by Wendell Phillips" *Cincinnati Daily Gazette*, March 3, 1868, p. 2.

266 "one of the greatest criminal lawyers in the country and Johnson one of the greatest criminals,": "Washington," *Cincinnati Daily Gazette*, March 2, 1868, p. 3.

266 "I'll be damned if I serve under Butler,": "Washington," *New York Herald*, March 3, 1868, p. 3.

CHAPTER NINETEEN: THE HIGH COURT OF IMPEACHMENT

267 "Senators,": see *The Great Impeachment and Trial of Andrew Johnson*, p. 23.

268 "Chf. Ju. Chase to many": John A. Logan to Wendell Phillips, March 4, 1868, Abraham Lincoln Presidential Library.

268 Chase considered: see Chase's remark in Hunt, "The Impeachment of Andrew Johnson," p. 429.

268 Frederick Douglass distrusted: see Frederick Douglass, "Salmon P. Chase," *National Anti-Slavery Standard*, July 18, 1868, p. 3.

268 "bad egg": Traubel, *With Walt Whitman in Camden*, vol. 5, p. 287.

270 "He feels, I believe": Moorfield Storey to his mother, Jan. 8, 1868, in Howe, *Portrait of an Independent*, p. 52.

270 "I foresee": John A. Logan to Wendell Phillips, March 4, 1868, Abraham Lincoln Presidential Library.

270 Whether true or not: see D. Richards to Elihu Washburne, Jan. 14, 1868, LC.

270 "The Radicals denounce him": George T. Curtis to Samuel Barlow, March 4, 1868, Barlow papers, Huntington.

270 Increasingly, he did know: see "The Chief Justice seems inclined to throw what influence he has against the impeachment": Moorfield Storey to father, March 17, 1868, quoted in Howe, *Portrait of an Independent*, p. 78.

270 "I remembered his loyalty at the outset of the war": Salmon Chase to J. E. Snodgrass, March 16, 1868, quoted in Warden, *An Account*, p. 682.

271 Basically, Chase had won: a good overview of the role Chase played in the trial is Kathleen Perdue, "Salmon P. Chase and the Impeachment Trial of Andrew Johnson," pp. 75–92.

271 "Three months": Charles Eliot Norton to E. L. Godkin, March 1, 1868, Houghton.

271 "'Conviction means a transfer": James Garfield to Harry Rhodes, May 7, 1868, quoted in Garfield, *Life and Letters*, vol. 1, p. 425.

272 "built for use instead of ornament.": Briggs, *The Olivia Letters*, p. 67.

272 Unlike Charles Sumner: see Eckloff, *Memoirs of a Senate Page*, p. 130.

272 "a certain bulldog obduracy truly masterful": Brooks, *Washington in Lincoln's Time*, p. 26.

272 "I did not do it because they are women": Briggs, *The Olivia Letters*, p. 67.

272 "That vicious": "Conservatives in Charlottesville," *New York Herald*, June 21, 1867, p. 1.

272 "If he is a good friend": Ellis, *The Sights and Secrets in the National Capital*, p. 124.

273 "rose-water war": CG, 37: 2, Jan. 21, 1862, p. 511.

273 "after the abolition of slavery": see Marx, *Capital*, vol. 1, p. xx.

273 "Machiavelli, Munchausen, and Miss Nancy": see for instance Trefousse, *Benjamin Franklin Wade*, pp. 288–90. See also DuBois, *Black Reconstruction in America*, pp. 201–03.

274 "He is therefore the kind of a man": "Senator Wade," *Cincinnati Daily Gazette*, April 14, 1868, p. 2.

274 "cheek by jowl": "The Hon. 'Ben Wade' as president pro tem of the United States," *New York Herald*, March 10, 1878, p. 6.

274 "thought every republican senator hated him,": quoted in J. B. McCullagh, "The Great Impeachment," *The Atlanta Constitution*, Aug. 7, 1875, p. 2.

275 "They say the city is full of rebels": Moorfield Storey to his sister, March 10, 1868, quoted in Howe, *Portrait of an Independent*, pp. 77–78.

275 "Give Andy enough rope and he will hang himself *and* his friends": see also "Notes at the Capitol," *National Intelligencer*, March 2, 1868, p. 2.

275 "The Hon. Mr. Wiseacre": June 17, 1867, quoted in Robinson, *Warrington*, p. 315.

275 Composed: see for instance J. B. McCullagh, "The Great Impeachment," *The Atlanta Constitution*, Aug. 7, 1875, p. 2.

275 "these damned scoundrels," *Ibid.*

CHAPTER TWENTY: ALL THE PRESIDENT'S MEN

277 Curtis resigned: see Winthrop, Jr., *A Memoir of Robert C. Winthrop*, p. 198.

277 "a person of no practical power, or ability, a declaimer, and rather sophomorically at that,": Benjamin R. Curtis to George Ticknor, Feb. 29, 1852, LC, quoted in Leach, "Benjamin R. Curtis: Judicial Misfit," p. 516.

277 "He is a man of few ideas": Benjamin R. Curtis to George Ticknor, April 19, 1868, quoted in Curtis, *A Memoir of Benjamin Robbins Curtis*, vol. 1, p. 417.

278 "that in the intense excitement": Robbins, *A Memoir of Benjamin Robbins Curtis*, p. 15.

278 "services at the trial were wholly gratuitous": *Ibid.*

278 Each of Johnson's defense lawyers: see "Henry Stanbery in account for defense of president in impeachment case," May 15, 1868, Evarts papers, LC.

278 "How would I feel after I bought it?": Colonel William Moore diary typescript, Feb. 29, 1868, typescript, p. 104, LC.

278 "with extreme caution": Colonel William Moore diary, March 18, 1868, LC.

278 "wit, diamond-pointed,": quoted in Evarts, *Arguments and Speeches of William Maxwell Evarts*, vol. 1, p. xxi; "cut into a legal problem": quoted in Barrows, *William M. Evarts*, p. 48.

278 "confident in times of doubt": Henry Adams to Charles Francis Adams, Jr., July 17, 1863, quoted in Henry Adams, *Selected Letters*, p. 58.

280 "He undoubtedly represents": Napton, *The Union on Trial*, p. 315.

280 The moderates wanted to defeat impeachment: see for instance Charles Eliot Norton to E. L. Godkin, March 7, 1868, Houghton.

280 Evarts, like Curtis, considered Andrew Johnson: see "Thoughts and Facts," *The Philadelphia Press*, May 5, 1868, p. 4.

280 "I pride myself on my success": Adams, *The Education of Henry Adams*, p. 33.

280 "'Yes,' said Mr. Evarts": Moorfield Storey to his sister, April 6, 1868, in Howe, *Portrait of an Independent*, p. 91.

280 "cold, calculating, selfish man": March 9, 1868, Welles, *Diary*, vol. 3, p. 307.

280 "I wonder why Mr. Evarts takes the case,": Moorfield Storey to his father, March 17, 1868, in Howe, *Portrait of an Independent*, p. 78.

280 "an economist of morals,": Adams, *The Education of Henry Adams*, p. 141.

280 After the trial: for other friends who were shocked Evarts defended Johnson, see the eminent jurist Ebenezer R. Hoar to William Evarts, July 18, 1868, quoted in Dyer, *The Public Career of William Maxwell Evarts*, p. 102: "Every criminal deserves the right to the aid of counsel on his trial, and if defended, to be ably defended. It is the right even of the thief and the counterfeiter," Hoar told Evarts. "But when, after the acquittal, the grateful client invites his counsel to go into partnership with him, some other considerations seem to apply."

280 "Jeremiah S. Black in defense": see DeWitt, *The Impeachment and Trial of Andrew Johnson*, p. 400.

281 Black became a problem: on Jeremiah Black and Johnson: see Brigance, "Jeremiah Black and Andrew Johnson," p. 209.

281 Assuming that Johnson couldn't: see "News from Washington," *Philadelphia Inquirer*, March 2, 1868, p. 1.

281 The Alta Vela matter: for the several versions of the story, see for instance "Mr. Johnson and His Counsel," *Philadelphia Inquirer*, March 20, 1868, p. 1; "Judge Black, Secretary Seward, and His Excellence," *New-York Tribune*, March 28, 1868, p. 1. "Jere. Black Missing—A Guano Island and a Very Curious Case," *New York Herald*, March 28, 1868, p. 3; for the direct quote, see [Emily Edson Briggs], "The Impeachment Trail: Scenes in the Senate," *Philadelphia Inquirer*, March 25, 1868, p. 3. Also see the comprehensive Brigance, "Jeremiah Black and Andrew Johnson," pp. 205–18.

282 "Mr. Seward's little finger": Jeremiah Black to AJ, March 19, 1868, *PAJ*: 13, p. 658.

282 "Stanbery is the tallest": [Emily Edson Briggs], "The Impeachment Trial: Scenes in the Senate," *Philadelphia Inquirer*, March 25, 1868, p. 3.

283 "To the one": "Washington Gossip: Impeachment of the President—How Washington Feels About It," *New York Herald*, March 21, 1868, p. 3.

CHAPTER TWENTY-ONE: THE TRIAL, FIRST ROUNDS

284 Salmon Chase's daughter, Kate: "From Another Correspondent," *Philadelphia Inquirer*, March 14, 1868, p. 1. For other descriptions, see also, for instance, Briggs, *The Olivia Letters*, pp. 50–62.

285 She had an appetite: see "Washington Gossip," *Cincinnati Daily Gazette*, March 19, 1868, p. 1.

286 To the right: see [Emily Edson Briggs], "The Impeachment Trial," *Philadelphia Inquirer*, March 16, 1868, p. 1.

286 About one hundred cane-bottomed: see, among other newspaper descriptions, "From Another Correspondent," *Philadelphia Inquirer*, March 14, 1868, p. 1.

286 "he looked strong enough to live as long as a hemlock,": "Impeachment! First Day of the Trial," *The Crisis* (Ohio), p. 61. See also for comment on Boutwell.

287 They seemed to have no friends: see "Washington," *New York Herald*, March 14, 1868, p. 3.

287 "Forty days—": *Trial* 1, p. 27.

287 "The world moves,": "The Impeachment Trial," *Baltimore Sun*, March 14, 1868, p. 1.

287 Sir Forcible Feeble: Thomas Ewing, Jr., to Hugh Ewing, March 8, 1868, LC.

287 Democrats had continued to peel: see "The President Alarmed," *Boston Daily Journal*, March 16, 1868, p 2 ; see also "President Becoming Discouraged," *Cincinnati Daily Gazette*, March 16, 1868, p. 3, and "Washington Gossip," *New York Herald*, March 20, 1868, p. 2.

288 "Johnson makes a muddle of everything": Samuel L. M. Barlow to Jerome Stillson, Feb. 28, 1868, Barlow papers, Huntington.

288 "A little while longer": Feb. 28, 1868, Clemenceau, *American Reconstruction*, p. 158.

288 "He is a man with a remarkable": Forster, *The Life of Charles Dickens*, vol. 2, p. 378.

288 "a man not to be trifled with": quoted in Dolby, *Charles Dickens*, p. 237.

288 "Hancock the Superb": see for instance, Porter, *Campaigning with Grant*, p. 58, and Jordan, *Winfield Scott Hancock*, p. 4.

288 "*beau ideal*": quoted in McFeely, *Grant*, p. 184.

288 "had not been mixed up in political affairs,": August 24, 1867, Colonel Moore diary typescript, p. 48.

289 "fighting the Radicals.": quoted in "Our Washington Correspondence," *The National Anti-Slavery Standard*, March 28, 1868, p. 2.

289 an unapologetic white supremacist: on Hancock's career, see Hancock, *Reminiscences of Winfield Scott Hancock*, p. 135; see also Jordan, *Winfield Scott Hancock*, p. 204.

289 Hancock formally touched: see Jordan, *Winfield Scott Hancock*, p. 213.

289 So Hancock rode: [Emily Edson Briggs], "The President's Levee," *Philadelphia Press*, March 25, 1868, p. 4.

290 "I cannot believe there is really any danger,": Moorfield Storey to his sister, March 28, 1868, in Howe, *Portrait of an Independent*, p. 85.

290 "Do not lose a moment's sleep": quoted in "Notes of Colonel W. G. Moore," March 16, 1868, p. 124.

292 "for cause to be judged by the President alone,": see *Trial* I, pp. 3, 42, 44, 46, 49, 50, 52.

293 Curtis was largely inaudible: see "Impeachment," *Republican Banner*, March 28, 1868, p. 1.

293 "We, as the managers": *Trial* 1, p. 71.

CHAPTER TWENTY-TWO: THE TRIAL

295 The room was like a vaulted tomb: see [Emily Edson Briggs], March 31, 1868, "Letter from Olivia," *Philadelphia Press*, p. 4.

295 for over a week: see Butler, *Butler's Book*, p. 928.

296 "bound by no law": *Trial* I, p. 90.

296 "I speak": *Trial* I, p. 122; see also "The Impeachment; The Opening of the Trial," *Cincinnati Daily Gazette*, March 31, 1868, p. 1. See also "The Impeachment Trial," *New-York Tribune*, March 31, 1868, pp. 1–2, 5.

297 "He might have made a stronger argument": Moorfield Storey to his father, April 2, 1868, in Howe, *Portrait of an Independent*, p. 90.

297 Burleigh's testimony: the controversy is documented in *Trial* I, pp. 175–85.

297 "He was a man of small stature": *The Reminiscences of Carl Schurz*, p. 294.

298 "The managers may propose a question": *Trial* I, p. 177.

298 "Mr. Chase made a little *coup d'état*": Moorfield Storey to his father, April 2, 1868, in Howe, *Portrait of an Independent*, p. 89.

299 "Mr. Chase was already very angry . . . decided,": Moorfield Storey to his father, April 2, 1868, in Howe, *Portrait of an Independent*, p. 90.

299 The question was leading: see *Trial* I, pp. 216–17.

300 "The defense fight every": Moorfield Storey to his father, April 2, 1868, in Howe, *Portrait of an Independent*, p. 90.

301 "*Mr. Manager Butler:* You have been asked, Mr. Hudson": *Trial* I, pp. 310–11.

303 "hold their offices respectively for and during the term": *Trial* I, p. 39.

303 "The necessary conclusion": *Trial* I, p. 40.

303 "I cannot see how Mr. Curtis": April 10, 1868, quoted in Clemenceau, *American Reconstruction*, p. 175.

304 "high crimes and misdemeanors . . . against what law?": *Trial* I, p. 409.

305 When Butler good-humoredly said: see April 6, 1868, Howe, *Portrait of an Independent*, p. 91.

306 "Now, senators; reflect": *Trial* I, pp. 504–05.

307 "As he left the stand": Agate, "The Impeachment Trial," *Cincinnati Daily Gazette*, April 14, 1868, p. 2.

308 "The high forehead and eagle eyes": Emily Edson Briggs, "Impeachment: April 14, 1868," in *The Olivia Letters*, p. 63.

308 "I submit that that is contrary to all rule": "The Crisis of the Impeachment Trial," *Cincinnati Daily Gazette*, April 15, 1868, p. 1.

309 "No! No!": *Trial* I, p. 489.

309 "He did not state to me then": *Trial* I, p. 521.

309 "It is one of the curious revenges": "The Crisis of the Impeachment Trial," *Cincinnati Daily Gazette*, April 15, 1868, p. 1.

309 "I made this point,": *Trial* I, p. 529.

310 "It was the constitutionality of that bill": *Trial* I, p. 529.

310 "The bland impudence": Moorfield Storey to his sister, April 12, 1868, in Howe, *Portrait of an Independent*, p. 93.

310 "Far be it from me . . . individual,": *Trial* 1, p. 628.

310 "We have been here in the Senate . . . cease": *Trial* I, p. 629.

311 "I feel warmly . . . stop": *Trial* I, p. 629.

311 Another drenching rain kept: On April 16, 1862, Lincoln signed into law the Compensation Emancipation Act to end slavery in the capital. In 1866, the black population there began celebrating April 16 as Emancipation Day.

312 "an organization which is": quoted in "An American Secret Society," *The Manchester Guardian*, April, 23, 1868, p. 6.

312 "Death's angels": "The Ku Klux Klan in Washington," *New York Herald*, April 13, 1868, p. 3.

312 "an orgy of blood": *Trial* 3, p. 281.

312 George T. Downing: "The Ku Klux Klan in Washington," *New York Herald*, April 13, 1868, p. 3; Downing released information about the threat to the *National Anti-Slavery Standard*, April 18, 1868, which published it in its entirety.

313 Thaddeus Stevens received a note: see "KKK" to Thaddeus Stevens, May 4, 1868, LC.

313 Benjamin Wade: see "Washington," *New York Herald*, April 4, 1868, p. 3.

313 "The Ku Klux Klan send letters every day": Moorfield Storey to Helen Appleton, April 20, 1868, in Howe, *Portrait of an Independent*, p. 98.

314 "frighten old ladies": see "Agony Coming to an End," *New York Herald*, April 24, 1868, p. 7, and also "The Maelstrom of Radical Ruin," *New York Herald*, April 19, 1868, p. 6.

314 Republicans countered: see "Washington," *New-York Tribune*, April 21, 1868, p. 4.

314 He'd been prepared by Stanbery: Gideon Welles to Henry Stanbery, April nd, 1868, Abraham Lincoln Presidential Library.

314 "Senators . . . within it": *Trial* I, p. 698.

316 Ready at all times with a joust: "Glimpses of the Great Trial," *Boston Advertiser*, April 4, 1868, p. 1.

316 "Genl. Butler swallows": William Evarts to Edwards Pierrepont, April 16, 1868, Yale.

316 "Stick to the point, gentlemen": Briggs, "Impeachment: April 14, 1868," in *The Olivia Letters*, p. 63.

317 "first by resignation, then under the Tenure-of-Office": Moorfield Storey to his father, April 19, 1868, in Howe, *Portrait of an Independent*, p. 9.

317 the President's son-in-law: "The Agony Coming to an End," *New York Herald*, April 24, 1868, p. 7.

317 A friend warned him: see William Evarts to Edwards Pierrepont, April 21, 1868, Yale.

CHAPTER TWENTY-THREE: THE BEGINNING OF THE END

318 The President's defenders belittled: see "Agony Coming to an End," *New York Herald*, April 24, 1868, p. 7, and "The Maelstrom of Radical Ruin," *New York Herald*, April 19, 1868, p. 6.

318 "The Dems pooh-pooh": Schuyler Colfax to John Russell Young, April 16, 1868, LC.

319 All nine Democratic: The three conservative Republicans were James Dixon of Connecticut, James Doolittle of Wisconsin, and Daniel Norton of Minnesota.

319 "Delays are dangerous": Moorfield Storey to Helen Appleton, May 17, 1868, in Howe, *Portrait of an Independent*, p. 107.

319 Although he had backed: He shared this point of view with Gideon Welles as well as conservatives like James Doolittle; see Salter, *The Life of James Grimes*, pp. 328–62.

319 "What Republican will dare run the risk": Benjamin Perley Poore to William W. Clapp, April 24, 1868, LC.

320 "a man [as] Secy of War": Gustavus Fox, diary entry, April 5, 1868, NYHS.

320 Fox told Gideon Welles: see April 25, 1868, Welles, *Diary*, vol. 3, p. 339.

321 These wavering senators: see John Russell Young to Edwin Stanton, May 6, 1868, LC.

321 "A majority of Republicans": Schofield, *Forty-six Years in the Army*, p. 415.

322 "How dull Washington would be without the Impeachment Trial": quoted in "A Woman's Letter from Washington," *The Independent*, May 14, 1868, p. 1.

322 Conviction of the President: see "no right to entrain any motive contrary to his constitutional obligation to execute the laws": *Trial* II, p. 74.

323 Boutwell then offered a forensic analysis: see "It is not specially the right of any person to so test the laws, and the effort is particularly offensive in the Chief Magistrate of the country to attempt by any process to annul, set aside or defeat the laws which by his oath he is bound to execute": *Trial* II, p. 95.

323 "Travelers and astronomers inform": *Trial* II, pp. 116–17.

324 "I'll put Boutwell": Moorfield Storey to his mother, April 24, 1868, in Howe, *Portrait of an Independent*, p. 100.

324 "Who is Andrew Johnson?": *Trial* II, p. 117; see also April 23, 1868, Briggs, *The Olivia Letters*, p. 72.

324 "Suppose he committed an error": *Trial* II, p. 124.

324 "In the name of all that is sacred": *Trial* II, p. 125.

324 Nelson was saying: see "Washington Letter," *The Independent*, April 30, 1868, p. 1.

325 The galleries were almost empty: see for instance, "Impeachment," *New York Times*, April 25, 1868, p. 1.

325 He argued that even if the President did not possess the power: see *Trial* II, pp. 204–06.

325 "Is the Senate prepared to drag . . . what he did": *Trial* II, p. 206.

326 "He tried to pluck a thorn out of his very heart": *Trial* II, p. 215.

326 "Stop; I have a further oath": *Trial* II, p. 226.

327 "to search out defective laws": *Trial* II, p. 229.

327 "This trial has developed": James Garfield to Harry Rhodes, April 28, 1868, quoted in *Life and Letters*, vol. 1, p. 424.

328 "reopened the war, inaugurated anarchy": *Trial* II, p. 234.

328 And since we care about the nation's safety: see *Trial* II, p. 260.

328 And if you're tempted: see *Trial* II, p. 262.

329 "Indeed, upon my soul": *Trial* II, p. 297.

329 "Cardinal Wolsey said": *Trial* II, p. 332.

330 "Let him who is without sin cast the first stone,": *Trial* II, p. 327.

330 "a man who lives in a bottle . . . puffed up,": *Trial* II, p. 329.

331 Bingham forced a smile: see "The Impeachment Trial," *Philadelphia Press*, May 1, 1868, p. 8; see also Poore, vol. 2, *Reminiscences*. p. 235.

331 Although the managers claimed Johnson had violated a 1795: As for the issue of an interim appointment: In 1863 Lincoln had asked that the President be allowed to make interim appointments to the cabinet in the event of death, resignation, sickness, or something vague called "absence from the seat of government." See *Trial* II, p. 334.

331 "And this brings me very properly . . . against him": *Trial* II, pp. 355–56.

332 "Can we summon now . . . no wound!": *Trial* II, pp. 357–58.

333 "It seems inert": May 2, 1868, Strong, *The Diary of George Templeton Strong*, vol. 3, p. 205.

333 "Fourteen mortal hours": "The Week," *The Nation*, May 7, 1868, p. 361.

333 "He contrived": Moorfield Storey to his father, May 3, 1868, quoted in Howe, *Portrait of an Independent*, p. 103.

333 "No rule of the profession obliged him to take the President's case,": see Wendell Phillips, "Impeachment," *National Anti-Slavery Standard*, May 16, 1868, p. 2; see also Grand Assize," *Zion Herald*, May 7, 1868, p. 225.

333 "Ah, Mr. Evarts,": quoted in Lewis, *Great American Lawyers*, vol. 7, *op. cit.*, p. 233.

334 "the strong arms of the people": *Trial* II, p. 388.

334 "Most men prefer to be deceived": "Long Stories," *The Round Table*, May 9, 1868, p. 292.

334 "must be carried out to the bitter end": Briggs, March 27, 1867, *The Olivia Letters*, p. 36.

334 "the Senate shall have the sole power to try all impeachments": *Trial* II, p. 393.

334 "In spite of the technicalities": *Trial* II, p. 392.

335 "a man may make his speech": *Trial* II, p. 394.

335 Chief Justice Chase sent one of the Senate pages: see "News from Washington," *Philadelphia Inquirer*, May 5, 1868, p. 1.

335 Some said Bingham's style: see "The Week," *The Nation*, May 7, 1868, p. 361.

335 Benjamin Wade said: see "Warrington upon the Situation in the State and National Capitols," *Springfield Republican*, May 9, 1868, p. 4; see also "Mr. Bingham's Summing Up," *Cincinnati Daily Gazette*, May 11, 1868, p. 1.

336 "I ask you to consider that we stand this day": *Trial* II, p. 468; see also M.C.A. "A Woman's Letters from Washington," *The Independent*, May 14, 1868, p. 4.

336 "I don't know": quoted in Briggs, May 7, 1868, *The Olivia Letters*, p. 81.

CHAPTER TWENTY-FOUR: CANKERED AND CRUDE

339 "Society, in these States": Whitman, *Poetry and Prose*, ed. Justin Kaplan, p. 937.

339 "Our American politics,": Walt Whitman to Moncure Conway, Feb. 17, 1868, Butler.

339 "While the piled": "Amid whatever clouds," Walt Whitman, "Democracy," pp. 930, 933. Whitman read Carlyle's essay the previous August and began composing his response then.

340 Someone heard the President: "Washington," *Chicago Republican*, May 12, 1868, p. 1.

340 Schuyler Colfax seemed certain: see Schuyler Colfax to John Russell Young, April 8, 1868, and April 16, 1868, LC, as well as J. R. Briggs to Young, April 17, 1868, for the suspicions discussed in this paragraph.

340 Henderson of Missouri and Edmund G. Ross of Kansas: see "Washington Gossip," quoted in the *Lowell Daily Citizen*, May 8, 1868, p. 2; Ross had volunteered: BB [for the committee], "Raising of Money," p. 30.

340 "After this impeachment trial is over": quoted in J.R. Briggs to Godard, April 17, 1868, LC.

341 "Is there anything new?": quoted in "The Impeachment Trial," *New-York Tribune*, May 13, 1868, p. 1.

341 "Moral debauchery under a decent exterior,": J. R. Briggs to Godard, April 17, 1868, in John Russell Young papers, LC.

341 "I have believed from the first": N. Kilgore to Elihu Washburne, May 7, 1868, LC.

342 Though no supporter: for a sympathetic but instructive view of Van Winkle, see Peter Strum, "Senator Peter G. Van Winkle and the Johnson Impeachment Trial," *West Virginia History* (1999), pp 25–43.

342 When Charles Sumner: see *Ibid.*, p. 32.

342 "This impeachment worries a fellow to death,": Benjamin Perley Poore to William W. Clapp, April 24, 1868, LC.

343 And though in private Fowler had said: see John Russell Young to Schuyler Colfax, April 16, 1868, LC.

343 Gideon Welles assumed: see May 7, 1868, in Welles, *Diary*, vol. 3, p. 349.

343 And though both Henderson and the Missouri delegation: see CG 40: 2, May 16, 1868, p. 2503. The issue of Henderson, the Missouri delegation, and his vote became a matter of some dispute.

343 President of the Hannibal & St. Joseph Railroad: Craig had also been appointed by Johnson as Collector of Internal Revenue for the St. Joseph, Missouri, district.

343 "He was the man to do it,": "Testimony of Alfred Lacey," May 19, 1868, "Impeachment Investigation," NA; see also BB, [for the committee], "Raising of Money," p. 16.

343 "turned out of the Republican Church,": "Testimony of Alfred Lacey," May 19, 1868, "Impeachment Investigation," NA.

343 After Craig left,: "Testimony of Joseph W. McClurg," May 16, 1868, "Impeachment Investigation," NA.

344 "Can your friends": these telegram exchanges are often quoted; see *Ibid*, p. 140 ff, but also *Daily Missouri Republican*, May 14, 1868, or Henderson, "Emancipation and Impeachment," p. 208.

344 "Fessenden, Trumbull, Grimes, Henderson have expressed themselves for acquittal,": Charles Woolley to Washington McLean, May 12, 1868, quoted in BB, [for the committee], "Raising of Money," p. 47.

344 "Everything has gone to hell,": quoted in "Washington," *Cincinnati Daily Enquirer*, May 12, 1868, p. 3.

344 Policemen in blue broadcloth uniforms: see M.C.A., "A Woman's Letter from Washington," *The Independent*, May 28, 1868, p. 1.

344 "Well, I don't give up yet,": Moorfield Storey to Susan Storey, May 14, 1868, quoted in Howe, *Portrait of an Independent*, p. 105.

345 "we might have carried it.": Moorfield Storey to Helen Appleton, May 17, 1868, quoted in Howe, *Portrait of an Independent*, p. 107.

345 "Henderson matter all right,": see "Testimony of Alfred Lacy, "Impeachment Investigation," NA; [for the committee], "Raising of Money," p. 17.

345 Montgomery Blair . . . save him.": quoted in D.W.B. [David W. Bartlett], "Washington Letter," *The Independent*, May 21, 1868, p. 1.

345 Gideon Welles wondered what McCulloch knew: see May 5, 1868, and May 9, 1868, Welles, *Diary*, vol. 3, pp. 346, 350.

345 "I desire to glide into history ez a marter": quoted in "Nasby," *Chicago Republican*, May 13, 1868, p. 2.

346 "Every great question": see "The Anniversaries," *New York Evangelist*, May 21, 1878, p. 2.

346 "Those who are well advised think the success of the impeachment certain": Edwin Stanton to John Russell Young, May 13, 1868, LC.

347 "great danger to the peace of the country": quoted in "The Senators from West Virginia," *National Intelligencer*, May 16, 1868, p. 2.

347 Chase had been spotted at dinner: see "Impeachments Speculations," *Boston Journal*, May 16, 1868, p. 1.

347 "It is treachery": James Garfield to Harry Rhodes, May 20, 1868, in Smith, *Life and Letters of James Abram Garfield*, p. 426.

347 On Thursday, May 14: see "Note on the Impeachment Trial," *New York Evening Post*, May 16, 1868, p. 4; see also Charles Woolley to Washington McLean, "Testimony of Charles Woolley," May 14, 1868, NA.

348 "at the altar of political ambition,": R. W. Bayless, "Peter G. Van Winkle and Waitman Willey," p. 79.

348 "Who will take a place in the cabinet now?": see "Testimony of Samuel Pomeroy," May 18, 1868, "Impeachment Investigation," NA.

348 After the meeting: see "Impeachment," *Boston Advertiser*, May 16, 1868, p. 1; see also "Washington: Vote to Be Taken Today," *Cincinnati Daily Gazette*, May 16, 1868, p. 3.

348 "Without any suggestion or requirement from us, you offered to resign your position,": "Washington: Vote to Be Taken Today," *Cincinnati Daily Gazette*, May 16, 1868, p. 3.

349 The next morning: see for example, "Washington," *Chicago Republican*, May 16, 1868, p. 5.

350 "may be artfully,": J. R. Briggs to John Russell Young, April 17, 1868, LC.

350 "Mr. Ross is suffering from the effects of bad associations,": *National Anti-Slavery Standard*, March 14, 1868.

351 "Kansas has heard the evidence, and demands the conviction of the President": The telegrams were widely published, and the first two are located in the Ross/Ream collection, LC. See also, for instance, "Impeachment," *Chicago Republican*, May 16, 1868, p. 1, and Plummer, "Profile in Courage?" p. 39.

352 "Stanton is a brick,": Francis Lieber to Thayer, March 2, 1868, quoted in Perry, ed. *The Life and Letters of Francis Lieber*, p. 381.

352 He was beginning to make plans: William Moore, diary, April 25, 1868, LC.

352 "What in the name of all that's honest is the matter with our party,": to [Jared Shock] to Thaddeus Stevens, May 14, 1868, LC; see also George Hicks to Elihu Washburne, May 15, 1868, LC.

352 Radical Republicans: see Warrington [William S. Robinson] "Warrington Upon Events at Washington," *Springfield Republican*, May 16, 1868, p. 5: "They have been growling and swearing at radicalism for years. Not a measure of congressional reform have they supported without the kick of admonition from their constituents and the war itself would have been continued until this time, or have ended in the triumph of the rebellion, if they had not been taken by the collar, dragged up to a standing position, and then shored up by radical men on each side."

352 "History will record that Andrew Johnson": quoted in "Senatorial Recreancy," *Cincinnati Daily Gazette*, May 16, 1868, p. 2.

CHAPTER TWENTY-FIVE: POINT-BLANK LYING

354 Several of the conference delegates: see "The Hon. Thaddeus Stevens to the Negroes," *New-York Tribune*, May 14, 1868, p. 1.

355 "Methodistical darkydom,": see "Impeachment," *New York Herald*, May 16, 1868, p. 3.

355 "His temperament is more excitable": see WPF to John Murray Forbes, June 21, 1868, in Forbes, ed. *Letters and Recollections of John Murray Forbes*, vol. 2, p. 110.

356 "There has been more point-blank lying": "Washington," *New York Times*, May 16, 1868, p. 1.

356 "If the impeachment managers": "Justice" to BB, May 20, 1868, LC.

356 "The shrewdest politician of them all,": Mark Twain, "Vinnie Ream," *Chicago Republican*, Feb. 19, 1868, p. 3.

357 "Why, I can do that": the quote was repeated as early as 1869, if not earlier. See "Miss Vinnie Ream," *American Phrenological Journal* (September, 1869), p. 339; see also Vinnie Ream Hoxie, "The Story of My Lincoln Statue," *La Follette's Weekly Magazine*, Feb. 13, 1909, p. 10.

357 "Vinnie had a faculty for catching the fancy of older men,": Cooper, *Vinnie Ream*, p. 3.

357 "self-satisfied and rather presuming": Mary Todd Lincoln to Charles Sumner, Sept. 10, 1867, quoted in Turner and Turner, *Life and Letters of Mary Todd Lincoln*, p. 387.

357 "*American girl*,": see George Brandes, *Recollections*, p. 323.

357 "Five minutes' conversation with Miss Vinnie Ream": Parton, *Topics of the Times*, p. 76.

359 He signed: Petition, May 14, 1867, LC.

359 "Ross though a man of family . . . interests of the family,": C. C. Warner to BB, April 5, 1868, Vinnie Ream Hoxie file, WHS.

359 "bought his election . . . Internal Revenue,": C. C. Warner to BB, April 5, 1868, Vinnie Ream Hoxie file, WHS.

359 "I have suffered too much . . . 'done by,'": copy of letter from C. C. Warner to BB, April 15, 1868, Vinnie Ream Hoxie file, WHS, and note from BB on the letter. BB notes that the original is at Ross's disposal, should he wish to see it.

359 "it would exert a salutary influence": May 4, 1868, *The Diary of Orville Hickman Browning*, vol. 2, p. 195.

360 So was Vinnie Ream: see pencil notes from interview with Fiske Mills, [June 11–20] but dated May 19, 1868, Butler papers, LC.

360 "I stated to him in the course of the conversation": "Testimony of Thomas Ewing, Jr.," "Impeachment Investigation," NA.

360 "Gentlemen, I do not recognize your right to demand . . . perjurers and skunks": The telegrams were widely published, and the first two are located in the Ross/ Ream collection, LC. See also, for instance, "Impeachment," *Chicago Republican*, May 16, 1868, p. 1, and Plummer, "Profile in Courage?" p. 39.

360 "Impeachment is likely to fail,": USG to Charles W. Ford, May 15, 1868, in *PUSG*: 18, p. 257.

361 "I would rather have my right arm cut off": "Testimony of Perry Fuller," May 18, 1868, "Impeachment Investigation," NA.

361 "demented Moses of Tennessee.": "Impeachment," *New York Herald*, May 16, 1868, p. 3.

CHAPTER TWENTY-SIX: THE CROWNING STRUGGLE

362 "President will . . . We have beaten the Methodist Episcopal Church north": see "Testimony of Charles Woolley," May 20, 1868, and June 11, 1868, NA; see also "Raising of Money," p. 48.

362 Ushers steered: "Impeachment!" *New York Times*, May 17, 1868, p. 1, and M.C.A. [Mary Clemmer Ames], "A Woman's Letter from Washington," *The Independent*, June 4, 1868, p. 1.

362 "Through the glass doors of the ante-room": Moorfield Storey to Susan Storey, May 14, 1868, quoted in Storey, *Portrait of an Independent*, pp. 106–07.

363 "probably his own": "The Impeachment," *Albany Evening Journal*, May 17, 1868, p. 2.

363 John Henderson chatted: see M.C.A., "A Woman's Letter from Washington," *The Independent*, May 28, 1868, p. 1.

363 "Mr. Ross is gone,": quoted in "New from Washington," *Philadelphia Inquirer*, May 18, 1868, p. 1.

364 "Ross has been bought, so has Fowler,": quoted in "Washington Reminiscence of the Impeachment Trial," *Boston Daily Journal*, May 18, 1868, p. 4.

364 "The grass would be green": "The Impeachment," *New-York Tribune*, May 17, 1868, quoted in *Albany Evening Journal*, May 18, 1868, p. 2.

365 "We do not hear the answer,": "A Scene in the Impeachment Court," *The Anamosa* [Iowa] *Eureka*, May 28, 1868.

365 "The Chair did not hear the Senator's answer,": see also, in addition to above, Durham, "How Say You, Senator Fowler?" pp. 39–57.

365 "if we refuse to impeach Andrew Johnson": see M.C.A., "A Woman's Letter from Washington," *The Independent*, May 28, 1868, p. 1.

366 "It's all up,": This and the rest of the paragraph from M.C.A., "A Woman's Letter from Washington," *The Independent*, May 28, 1868, p. 1.

366 "Messrs. Fowler,": "From Washington: The Test Vote," *Commercial Advertiser*, May 16, 1868, p. 3.

366 It was said: see "The Impeachment Trial," *Chicago Republican*, May 17, 1868, p. 1, or "Impeachment: The Vote," *Boston Advertiser*, May 18, 1868, p. 1.

366 "Virtue has triumphed over vice,": "Testimony of Charles Woolley," June 11, 1868, "Impeachment Investigation," NA.

366 "The valley of the Shadow is passed safely,": Jerome Stillson to S.M.L. Barlow, May 16, 1868, Barlow-Stillson correspondence, Huntington.

367 "Mr. President,": Crook, "Andrew Johnson in the White House, second paper,"
     p. 870.
367 Colonel Crook then ran upstairs: see Stryker, *Andrew Johnson*, pp. 723–24.
367 "There goes the rascal to get his pay,": quoted in Bumgardner, *Edmund G. Ross*,
     p. 86
367 "Well, thank God, Mr. President": as the information in this paragraph: see "Im-
     peachment! The Scene in the Senate," *Cleveland Plain Dealer*, May 18, 1868,
     p. 2.
368 "went on reading": Samuel J. Barrows and Isabel C. Barrows, "Personal Reminis-
     cences of William H. Seward," p. 389.
368 "I do not know": quoted in "Impeachment! The Scene in the Senate," *Cleveland
     Plain Dealer*, May 18, 1868, p. 2.
368 "The country is going to the devil,": quoted in Crook, *Through Five Administra-
     tions*, p. 133.

CHAPTER TWENTY-SEVEN: THE CEASE OF MAJESTY

370 "Anglo-Saxon justice": Jan. 19, 1867, Clemenceau, *American Reconstruction*,
     p. 80.
371 "blasted public functionary,": CG 40: 2, May 16, 1868, p. 2493.
371 "Who so excuses himself, accuses himself,": CG 40: 2, May 16, 1868, p. 2495.
371 "How does it happen that just enough": BB to John Russell Young, May 16,
     1868, LC.
371 "The Democrats only smile . . . bought up": "White House Report" [no name]
     to Benjamin Butler, May 16, 1868, LC.
371 But since the Constitution: see CG 40: 2, May 16, 1868, p. 2503.
372 "Probably the rope with which Judas hanged himself is lost": quoted in Ruddy,
     Edmund G. Ross, p. 154.
372 "The people have not heard": *Trial* III, p. 31.
372 "It is a mistake to suppose that": *Trial* III, p. 280.
372 "Had he openly joined the enemy": Charles Sumner to Francis Lieber, May 2,
     1868, quoted in Sumner, *Selected Letters*, vol. 2, p. 424.
373 "For more than two years": *Trial* III, pp. 279–80.
373 "1. Bad articles": "The Great Failure," *Chicago Tribune*, May 17, 1868, p. 1.
373 "If two and two were four": "Address of Col. T.W.H.," *National Anti-Slavery
     Standard*, May 30, 1868.
373 "died": quoted in *Philadelphia Press*, May 26, 1868, p. 2.
374 "Impeachment is dead,": "Impeachment. Exciting Scenes Saturday at Washing-
     ton," *Memphis Avalanche*, May 19, 1868, p. 1.
374 "with cordial approbation by reflecting men of all parties": "The President's Ac-
     quittal," *Baltimore Sun*, May 19, 1868, p. 1.
374 Conservative Republicans: see "Who Killed Cock Robin?" *New York Herald*,
     May 17, 1868, p. 6.
374 "side-splitting farce,": "The Week," *The Nation*, May 21, 1868, p. 401.
374 "We are beaten and must take it quietly,": Horace Greeley to John Russell Young,
     May 17, 1868, LC.
375 that the Republicans' stupid choice: These were John Bigelow's arguments in
     very long letter protesting a guilty verdict, printed in the *New York Evening Post*,
     May 4, 1868, and quoted in Bigelow, *Retrospections*, vol. 4, pp. 170–75.
375 "Democrats have voted together": May 16, 1868, quoted in Strong, *The Diary of
     George Templeton Strong*, vol. 4, p. 209.

375 "His speeches and the general course of his administration": *Trial* III, p. 328.

375 "Putting aside such causes of the Senate's action": Wendell Phillips, "Impeachment," *National Anti-Slavery Standard,* June 6, 1868.

CHAPTER TWENTY-EIGHT: LET US HAVE PEACE

377 "I think the failure of the impeachment": John Hay to John Bigelow, July 14, 1868, quoted in Bigelow, *Retrospections,* vol. 4, p. 196.

378 The ticket could mean: see "The Fate of Impeachment," *Boston Daily Journal,* May 23, 1868, p. 4.

379 "We make platforms": "About the Anti-Impeachers," *Cincinnati Daily Gazette,* May 21, 1868, p. 3.

379 "Impeachment, I see, has failed,": John Greenleaf Whitter to Henry Raymond, May 1868, NYPL.

379 Wade took defeat: see "Impeachment," *Boston Advertiser,* May 22, 1868, p. 1; see also "The President Thinks He Could Beat Grant If Nominated," *Boston Journal,* May 22, 1868, p. 2.

380 "The President is surrounded": Jerome B. Stillson to S.L.M. Barlow, June 30, 1868, Barlow papers, Huntington.

380 "I should think he had had enough": Samuel Ward to S.L.M. Barlow, June 17, 1868, Barlow papers, Huntington.

380 "I think there was buying and selling": Jeremiah Black to Howell Cobb, April 1868, quoted in "The Correspondence of Robert Toombs, Alexander Stephens, and Howell Cobb," p. 694.

380 "Did you state in Mr. Woolley's rooms,": "Testimony of Sheridan Shook," May 23, 1868, "Impeachment Investigation," NA.

381 "I think 'circle' was the word he used; it may have been 'ring,'": "Testimony of James F. Legate," May 23, 1868, "Impeachment Investigation," NA.

381 "People here are afraid to write letters": Jerome Stillson to S.M.L. Barlow, May 22, 1868, Barlow papers, Huntington.

381 "smelling" committee: see for example "Investigations of the Impeachment Managers," *New York Herald,* May 21, 1868, p. 7.

382 "Butler has ruined the cause": Jerome Stillson to S.M.L. Barlow, May 22, 1868, Barlow papers, Huntington.

382 "The managers are pushing the investigation & profess to believe": Thomas Ewing, Jr., to Thomas Ewing, June 3, 1868, LC.

382 "I followed the President into the Ditch,": quoted in Van Deusen, *Thurlow Weed,* p. 326.

382 He told the committee: for a description of the men involved, see Gath [George Alfred Townsend], "From Washington: The Sequel of Impeachment," *Chicago Tribune,* May 28, 1868, p. 2.

382 "Mr. Seward also looked at matters": "The Impeachment Trial: Here's Richness for You!" *Cincinnati Daily Gazette,* Dec. 25, 1869, p. 3.

383 The conspirators: see "The Impeachment Trial," *Cincinnati Daily Gazette,* Dec. 25, 1869, p. 3; see also "Letter from Washington, *Cincinnati Daily Gazette,* Oct. 18, 1869, p 1; "Letter from Washington: The Secret History of Impeachment," Dec. 20, 1869, *Cincinnati Daily Gazette,* p. 5; "The National Capital," April 4, 1869, *Cincinnati Daily Gazette,* p. 1. Henry Van Ness Boynton was responsible for most of this investigative journalism and likely used sources similar to those used by James Parton.

383 "tainted,": see "The Tainted Verdict," *New-York Tribune*, May 27, 1868, p. 4.

383 "wonderfully patriotic, courageous, far-seeing,": Traubel, *Walt Whitman in Camden*, vol. 3, p. 58.

384 "Mr. Evarts has been": Edwards Pierrepont to Edwin Stanton, May 9, 1868, LC.

384 "General": quoted in Badeau, *Grant in Peace*, p. 144.

384 "Let us have peace,": USG to Joseph Hawley, May 29, 1868, *PUSG* 18: 264.

385 "From the date of his infamous speech of 22nd of February, down to the present time, . . . ahead.": "Look Ahead!" *Daily Morning Chronicle*, May 26, 1868, p. 2.

386 "the life, soul, body, boots and breeches of impeachment,": Benjamin Perley Poore to William W. Clapp, May 27, 1868, LC.

387 The result: Those voting guilty included Fessenden, Fowler, Grimes, Henderson, Ross, Trumbull and Van Winkle.

CHAPTER TWENTY-NINE: HUMAN RIGHTS

391 By his side: O'Reilly and Ewers were from the Providence Hospital, which, thanks to Stevens, had been granted congressional funds. Recently, it's been argued that the two nuns were not black, as has been supposed, but white: see Sister Anthony Scally, "Two Nuns and Old Thad Stevens," pp. 66–73.

391 "My sands are nearly run": CG 40: 2, July 7, 1868, p. 3791.

392 "I am very sick indeed,": "Death of Thaddeus Stevens," *New-York Tribune*, August 13, 1868, p. 1.

392 "They'll miss me at the Council board": "Death of Thaddeus Stevens," *Louisville Daily Journal*, August 13, 1868, p. 1.

392 "the nation has lost in him a great citizen,": Clemenceau, *American Reconstruction*, p. 224.

392 "That he has left an impress on the page of our history none can dispute,": quoted in "Thaddeus Stevens: What Democrats Say of Him," *Cincinnati Daily Gazette*, Dec. 22, 1868, p. 1.

392 "The death of Thaddeus Stevens": quoted in Hoar, *The Autobiography of Seventy Years*, vol. 1, p. 239.

392 "Of course he was hated": Grace Greenwood, "Thaddeus Stevens," *The Independent*, Aug. 27, 1868, p. 1.

393 "In time . . . we shall come to recognize the wisdom of his views.": "Death of Thaddeus Stevens," *New-York Tribune*, Aug. 13, 1868, p. 1.

393 "In the last few years": quoted in "Funeral of Thaddeus Stevens," *Philadelphia Press*, Aug. 22, 1868, p. 1.

393 "I do not deny that it has been my intention": CG 40: 2, May 27, 1868, p. 2599.

394 "humble way,": CG 40: 2, July 27, 1868, p. 4514.

394 "in consequence of my action,": see Edmund Ross to AJ, June 6, 1868, *PAJ* 14: 177; for the treaty request see Edmund Ross to AJ, June 13, 1868, *PAJ* 14: 215–16.

395 "I am aware that I am asking a good deal of you": Edmund Ross to AJ, July 10, 1868, *PAJ* 14: 347; for the other requests see Ross to AJ, June 23, 1868, PAJ: 14: 258; Ross to AJ, July 1, 1868, *PAJ* 14: 295.

395 "the malevolence of Stevens, the ambition of Butler": John C. Ropes to unknown [mistakenly identified as Fessenden] May 25, 1868, NYHS.

395 "the duty of Congress to make the best of Mr. Johnson,": Edward Atkins to Charles Sumner, June 22, 1868, Houghton.

396 "I offer no excuse": quoted, along with the summation, in Fessenden, *The Life and Public Services of William Pitt Fessenden*, vol. 2, pp. 230–37.

396 "I think we have a better chance now than we had any right to expect": Charles Norton to E. L. Godkin, May 30, 1868, Harvard.

396 "a serio-comic necessity,": Howells, "The Next President," p. 629.

396 In Appleton, Wisconsin: see G. M. Robinson to James Doolittle, June 4, 1868, WHS.

397 "I have long been a believer": Salmon Chase to Manton Marble, marked private & confidential, May 30, 1868, LC.

397 "The one great duty": Howells, "The Next President," pp. 630–31.

398 "the man of African descent": Hill, "The Chicago Convention," p. 175.

399 "people are more concerned about the kind of government": see "Editorial," "The Remaining Work of the Republican Party," *The Nation*, Jan. 28, 1869, pp. 64–65.

399 "certainly more urgent, because it is life and death": see Frederick Douglass to Josephine Sophie White Griffing, Sept. 27, 1868, quoted in Douglass, *Selected Speeches and Writings*, ed. Philip S. Foner, p. 600.

399 "The epoch turns on the negro": Wendell Phillips, "After Grant—What?" *Boston Advertiser*, Oct. 28, 1868, p. 1.

399 "The day is coming when the black man will vote": quoted in H. J. Brown: Political Activist," Maryland State Archives, Maryland Historical Trust, Baltimore Heritage Research Collaborative.

399 "He rises here and gives us dissertations": CG 40: 2, June 6, 1868, p. 2902.

400 *"There can be no State Rights against Human Rights,"*: CG 40: 2, June 10, 1868, p. 3025.

400 "one of the most important questions that absorb": Henry Dawes to Electa Dawes, May 29, 1868, LC.

400 "I am sure we ought all to do what we can to save the country": draft of BB to L. B. Halsey on letter from Halsey, May 15, 1868, LC.

401 Joseph Fowler: see CG 40: 2, July 27, 1868, pp. 4512–13.

401 "Bosh!": quoted in "The Impeachment Case," Dec. 18, 1869, *Cincinnati Daily Gazette*, p. 2.

401 "money-kings,": see "Grant and Colfax, *National Anti-Slavery Standard*, May 30, 1868.

401 "the greatest triumph of the Washington lobby was the Johnson lobby": Parton, "The 'Strikers' of the Washington Lobby," p. 229.

401 "The Johnson lobby proper": Parton, "The 'Strikers' of the Washington Lobby," pp. 229–30.

402 "If he could jump Jim Crow into Tammany he would do it tomorrow,": Samuel Ward to Samuel L.M. Barlow, June 19, 1868, Barlow papers, Huntington.

402 "Dissolve your committee and drop your investigation": Samuel Ward to BB, June 14, 1868, LC.

402 "I contributed my money": Samuel Ward to unknown correspondent [nd], NYPL.

403 Marble also said Republicans seemed not to know that the collector of the New York Custom House, Henry Smythe: Smythe had been appointed Collector: see Montgomery Blair/Samuel L. M. Barlow correspondence, 1866, and March 21–27, 1867, Huntington, for some the machinations behind Smythe's nomination, which Barlow wanted kept secret, and also their concern over Smythe's corruption.

403 "The vote on impeachment tells how difficult": Manton Marble to William A. Dunning, draft, nd [1906], LC.

403 "There was no contemporary record of all this,": *Ibid.*

403 "Mr. Johnson, like Medea, stands absolutely alone": March 20, 1868, Clemenceau, *American Reconstruction*, p. 169.

403 "Why should they not take me up?": Moore, Large Diary, July 3, 1868, LC.

404 "Tis not in the power of mortal man to save him": March 23, 1867, Montgomery Blair to S.L.M. Barlow, Barlow papers, Huntington.

404 Washington McLean: see for instance, Washington McLean to S.M.L. Barlow, Oct. 11, 1867, Barlow papers, Huntington.

404 "the late insurrection": "Third Amnesty Proclamation," July 4, 1868, *PAJ:* 14: 317–18.

405 "Does anybody want a revised": Frederick Douglass, "Hornito Seymour's Letter of Acceptance," *The Independent*, August 20, 1868, p. 1.

405 "with a host of ignorant negroes": Frank Blair's letter of acceptance of the nomination for vice-president, July 13, 1868, quoted in *Appleton's American Annual Cyclopedia*, 1868, vol. 8 (New York: D. Appleton and Company, 1869), p. 752.

405 "semi-barbarous race of blacks who are polygamist and destined to subject white women to their unbridled lust": quoted in Foner, *Reconstruction*, p. 340.

405 "Seymour was opposed to the late war": quoted in Barreyre, *Gold and Freedom*, p. 175.

405 "those who have forgotten": June 12, 1868, Clemenceau, *American Reconstruction*, p. 197.

405 "A terrible platform,": Samuel Ward to Samuel M. L. Barlow, July 21, 1868, Barlow papers, Huntington.

406 "Substitute Chase for Seymour and Thomas Ewing for Blair, we win,": R. M. Johnson to S.M.L. Barlow, Oct. 15, 1868, Barlow papers, Huntington.

406 Seward supposed that Johnson could now be nominated: see Clemenceau, *American Reconstruction*, Oct. 21, 1868, p. 255.

406 It was the 500,000 votes: Before the election, hundreds of blacks were killed in in Louisiana and Georgia alone, with many other men and women simply disappearing, their fates unknown. See OOH, *The Autobiography of Oliver Otis Howard*, vol. 2, pp. 380–82.

406 A black man named Larry White: *Reports of the Special Committee of the House of Representatives*, 1871–72, p. 309.

406 "seems to have a peculiar and mortal hatred.": William Wisener, et al. to AJ, Sept. 11, 1868, *PAJ* 15: 47.

406 "protective, military, political organization,": quoted in August 28, 1868, from *Cincinnati Commercial* quoted in *Reports of the Special Committee of the House of Representatives*, 1871–1872, p. 32.

406 "In making this earnest protest against being placed": "Georgia," *Appleton's American Annual Cyclopedia*, 1868, vol. 8, pp. 309–10.

407 The justice of the peace, L. B. Umpsflet: see *Reports of the Special Committee of the House of Representatives*, 1871–1872, pp. 326–27.

407 "The 'Klu Kluxe Klan' is in full blast here": Charles C. Cotton to BB, April 10, 1868, LC.

408 "attempt to place the white population under the domination of persons of color.": December 9, 1868, *PAJ* 15: 282.

408 "And when my term began": 8–10 March 1869, in *Mark Twain's Letters*, vol. 3, pp. 459–60.

408 "never depart": CG 40: 2, July 7, 1868, p. 3790.

CHAPTER THIRTY: EPILOGUE

410 Johnson wondered what: see Jan. 2, 1869, Welles, *Diary*, vol. 3, p. 498.

410 "Knowing these things . . . shall we debase ourselves by going near him?": Jan. 5, 1869, Welles, *Diary*, vol. 3, p. 498; see also Feb. 20, 1869, p. 532.

410 At Johnson's farewell reception: for this paragraph, see "The President's Levee," *Washington Intelligencer*, March 3, 1869, p. 2.

410 Evarts entered the room: see March 2, 1869, Welles, *Diary*, vol. 3, p. 538.

410 "Ought we not to start immediately?": March 2, 1869, Welles, *Diary*, vol. 3, p. 541.

411 A gunner had been posted: *New York Herald*, March 3, 1869, p. 3.

411 "No one will lament the passing of this administration": Clemenceau, *American Reconstruction*, p. 277.

411 "No President has had grander opportunities than Andrew Johnson": "Walk Alone," *Albany Evening Journal*, March 3, 1869, p. 2.

411 "I have nothing to regret": "Farewell Address," March 4, 1869, *PAJ* 15: 515.

411 "I fancy I can already smell the fresh mountain air of Tennessee": "From Washington," *Albany Argus*, March 5, 1869, p. 1. See also "The Last—Positively the Last," *Chicago Republican*, March 3, 1869, p. 1.

411 "Depend on it": quoted in Robinson, *"Warrington" Pen-Portraits*, p. 321.

412 "the ice is now broken": A.B.B., "A Reminiscence: J. W. Menard," *Washington [Pennsylvania] Reporter*, May 26, 1869, p. 6.

412 "The whirligig of time has brought about its revenges": Charlotte Forten, "Life in the Sea-Islands," p. 587.

413 "What the South wants": "Civilization at the South," *New-York Tribune*, March 23, 1872, p. 4.

414 "Before the law": Quoted in Fahs and Waugh, eds., *The Memory of the Civil War in American Culture*, p. 171.

414 "Liberal Republicanism is nothing": quoted in McPherson, "Grant or Greeley? The Abolitionist Dilemma in the Election of 1872," p. 59.

414 "We meet the relics of slavery in the railroad cars, in the churches, and everywhere, but above all, we meet them when we come up for civil and political rights": Speech of H. M. Turner, *National Anti-Slavery Standard*, June 5, 1869.

414 "the great poison": quoted in Mardock, *The Reformers and the American Indian*, p. 39.

415 "When I see that Capitol at Washington, with its pillared halls": "Closing Speech of Wendell Phillips," *National Anti-Slavery Standard*, May 29, 1869.

415 "We turned around . . . Forrest.": Wendell Phillips, "After Grant—What?" *Boston Advertiser*, Oct. 28, 1868, p. 1.

415 "Wendell Phillips and William Lloyd Garrison": "Editorial," *New York Times*, June 1, 1876, p. 6.

415 "I am only trying to carry out the measures Mr. Lincoln would have done had he lived": Crook, *Through Five Administrations*, p. 138.

416 "leaves the country prey": *Trial* III, p. 247. This is also Moorfield Storey's argument; see Moorfield Storey to his father, May 17, 1868, in Howe, *Portrait of an Independent*, p. 111.

416 "If slavery is not wrong,": Abraham Lincoln to Albert G. Hodges, April 4, 1864, quoted in *Lincoln: Speeches and Writings*, vol. 2, p. 585.

417 "where there was no actual crime committed": see CG 40: 2, Feb. 24, 1868, p. 1399; see also CG 40: 2, July 7, 1878, p. 3787.

417 "As well separate the Siamese twins . . . as separate the offences now charged from that succession of antecedent crimes with which they are linked,": *Trial* III, p. 260.

417 The country could rejoice: see "Thurlow Weed on Andrew Johnson," *New-York Tribune*, January 30, 1875, p. 6.

418 "Could the President have been legally and constitutionally impeached for these offenses,": Blaine, *Twenty Years in Congress*, vol. 2, p. 377.

419 Here was Andrew Johnson: see "The Senate," *Chicago Tribune*, March 23, 1875, p. 5.

420 In retrospect, a modern biographer: see Trefousse, *Andrew Johnson*, p. 379. See also this volume, p. 377, for details of the burial.

Selected Bibliography

Adams, Charles Francis, inter alia. *A Cycle of Adams Letters*, ed. Chauncey Worthington Ford. 2 vols. Boston: Houghton Mifflin, 1920.

Adams, Henry. *The Education of Henry Adams*. New York: Library of America, 2010.

——. *Selected Letters*, ed. Ernest Samuels. Cambridge, MA: Harvard University Press, 1992.

Ames, Mary Clemmer. *Ten Years in Washington*. Hartford, CT: A.D. Worthington & Co., 1873.

Andrews, Sidney. *The South since the War, as Shown by Fourteen Weeks of Travel in Georgia and the Carolinas*. Boston: Ticknor and Fields, 1866.

Arnett, Benjamin, ed. *Souvenir of the Afro-American League of Tennessee to Hon. James M. Ashley of Ohio*. Philadelphia: A.M.E. Church Publishing House, 1894.

Badeau, Adam. *Grant in Peace: From Appomattox to Mount Gregor*. Hartford, CT: S. S. Scranton & Co., 1887.

——. *A Military History of General Grant*. 2 vols. Bedford, MA: Applewood Books, 1881.

Barreyre, Nicolas. *Gold and Freedom: The Political Economy of Reconstruction*. Charlottesville: University of Virginia Press, 2015.

Barrow, Chester. *William Maxwell Evarts*. Chapel Hill: University of North Carolina Press, 1941.

Barrows, Samuel J. and Isabel C. Barrows. "Personal Reminiscences of William H. Seward." *Atlantic Monthly*. March 1889: 379–97.

Bayless, R.W. "Peter G. Van Winkle and Waitman Willey in the Impeachment Trial of Andrew Johnson." *West Virginia History*. January 1952: 75–89.

Beard, William E. *Nashville: The Home of History Makers*. Nashville: Civitan Club, 1929.

Beecher, Henry Ward. *Norwood: or, Village Life in New England*. New York: Charles Scribner & Co., 1868.

Benedict, Michael Les. *A Compromise of Principle*. New York: W. W. Norton, 1974.

——. "From Our Archives: A New Look at the Impeachment of Andrew Johnson." *Political Science Quarterly*, Autumn 1998: 493–511.

——. *The Impeachment and Trial of Andrew Johnson*. New York: W. W. Norton, 1973.

——. *Preserving the Constitution: Essays on Politics and the Constitution in the Reconstruction Era*. New York: Fordham University Press, 2006.

——. *The Right Way: Congressional Republicans and Reconstruction, 1863–1869*. Rice University, 1971. Unpublished dissertation.

Benjamin, Charles F. "Recollections of Secretary Stanton." *Century Magazine*. March 1887: 758–68.

Berger, Raoul. *Impeachment: The Constitutional Problems*. Cambridge: Harvard University Press, 1973.

Bergeron, Paul. "Robert Johnson: The President's Troubled and Troubling Son." *The Journal of East Tennessee History*. 2001: 1–22.

Bigelow, John. *Retrospections of an Active Life*. 4 vols. Garden City, NY: Doubleday, 1913.

Black, Jeremiah S. "Mr. Black to Mr. Wilson," *Galaxy*, February 1871: 257–76.

Blaine, James Gillespie. *Twenty Years of Congress*. 2 vols. Norwich, CT: Henry Bill Publishing Company, 1884.

Blight, David W. *Frederick Douglass' Civil War: Keeping Faith in Jubilee*. Baton Rouge: Louisiana State University Press, 1989.

——. *Race and Reunion: The Civil War in American History*. Cambridge: Belknap Press of Harvard University Press, 2002.

Boulard, Garry. *The Swing Around the Circle*. Bloomington: iUniverse, 2008.

Boutwell, George S. *The Lawyer, The Statesman, The Soldier*. NY: Appleton & Co., 1887.

——. *Reminiscences of Sixty Years in Public Affairs*. 2 vols. New York: McClure, Phillips & Co., 1902.

——. "The Usurpation." *Atlantic Monthly*. October 1866: 506–13.

Bowen, David Warren. *Andrew Johnson and the Negro*. Knoxville: University of Tennessee Press, 1989.

Bowers, Claude. *The Tragic Era*. Boston: Houghton Mifflin Co., 1927.

Boyd, James P. *Gallant Trooper*. Philadelphia: Franklin News Company, 1888.

Brandes, George. *Recollections of My Childhood and Youth*. London: William Heinemann, 1906.

Brigance, William Norwood. "Jeremiah Black and Andrew Johnson." *The Mississippi Valley Historical Review*. September 1932: 205–18.

Briggs, Emily Edson. *The Olivia Letters, Being Some History of Washington City for Forty Years as Told by the Letters of a Newspaper Correspondent*. New York: The Neale Publishing Company, 1906.

Brockett, Linus Pierpont. *Our Great Captains. Grant, Sherman, Thomas, Sheridan, and Farragut*. New York: C.B. Richardson, 1865.

Brooks, Noah. "Two War-Time Conventions." *Century Magazine*, March 1895: 723–37.

———. *Washington In Lincoln's Time*. New York: The Century Company, 1895.

Brodie, Fawn. *Thaddeus Stevens: Scourge of the South*. New York: W. W. Norton, 1966.

Brogue, Allan G. *The Earnest Men: Republicans of the Civil War Senate*. Ithaca: Cornell University Press, 1981.

Brown, Ira. "Pennsylvania and the Rights of the Negro, 1865–1867." *Pennsylvania History*. January 1961: 3–61.

Brown, William Wells. *The Negro in the American Rebellion: His Heroism and His Fidelity*. Boston: Lee & Shepard, 1867.

Browning, Orville Hickman. *The Diary of Orville Hickman Browning*, ed. Theodore Calvin Pease. 2 vols. Springfield: Illinois State Historical Library, 1925.

Bryant, William Cullen. *The Letters of William Cullen Bryant*, ed. Thomas G. Voss. 5 vols. New York: Fordham University Press, 1992.

Bumgardner, Edward. *The Life of Edmund G. Ross: The Man Whose Vote Saved a President*. Kansas City, MO: Fielding Turner Press, 1949.

Burlingame, Michael. *Lincoln's Journalist: John Hay's Anonymous Writings for the Press, 1862–1864*. Carbondale: Southern Illinois University Press, 2006.

Burlingame, Michael, and John R. Turner Ettlinger, eds. *Inside Lincoln's White House: The Complete Civil War Diary of John Hay*. Carbondale: University of Illinois Press, 1997.

Burroughs, John. *The Life and Letters of John Burroughs*, ed. Clara Barrus. 2 vols. Boston: Houghton Mifflin, 1925.

———. "Whitman and his Drum-Taps." *Galaxy*. Nov. 1866: 606–16.

Butler, Benjamin F. *Butler's Book: The Autobiography and Personal Reminiscences of Benjamin F. Butler*. 2 vols. Boston: A. M. Thayer & Co., 1892.

———. *Private and Official Correspondence of General Benjamin F. Butler*. 5 vols. Norwood, MA: Plimpton Press, 1917.

Carrière, Marius. "An Irresponsible Press: Memphis Newspaper and the 1866 Riot." *Tennessee Historical Quarterly*. Spring 2001: 2–15.

Carter, Dan T. *When the War Was Over*. Baton Rouge: Louisiana State University Press, 1985.

Catton, Bruce. *Terrible Swift Sword*. New York: Doubleday, 1963.

Chase, Salmon. P. *The Salmon P. Chase Papers*, ed. John Niven. 5 vols. Kent, Ohio: Kent State University Press, 1998.

Chernow, Ron. *Grant*. New York: Penguin, 2017.

Chester, Thomas Morris. *Black Civil War Correspondent: His Dispatches from the Virginia Front*, ed. R.J.M. Blackett. New York: Da Capo, 1989.

Child, Lydia Maria. "Letter from L. M. Child." *The Liberator*. May 11, 1865.

Childs, George W. *Recollections of General Grant*. Philadelphia, Collins Publishing, 1890.

Clayton, Mary Black. *Reminiscences of Jeremiah Sullivan Black*. St. Louis: Christian Publishing Co. 1887.

Clemenceau, Georges. *American Reconstruction*, ed. Fernand Baldensberger, trans., Margaret MacVeigh. New York: Dial Press, 1928.

Cooper, Edward S. *Vinnie Ream: An American Sculptor*. Chicago: Academy Publishers, 2009.

Cowan, Frank. *Andrew Johnson, President of the United States: Reminiscences of His Private Life and Character by One of His Secretaries.* Greenesburg: The Oliver Publishing House, 1894.

Cox, LaWanda and John Henry Cox, *Politics, Principle, and Prejudice, 1865–1866.* New York: Free Press, 1963.

Craven, John J. *Prison Life of Jefferson Davis.* New York: George Dillingham Co., 1866.

Crook, William S. *Through Five Administrations,* ed. Margarita Spalding Gerry. New York: Harper & Brothers, 1910.

Cullom, Shelby Moore. *Fifty Years of Public Service.* Chicago: A. G. McClurg, 1911.

Curtis, Benjamin. *A Memoir of Benjamin Robbins Curtis,* ed. George Ticknor. 2 vols. Boston: Little, Brown, 1879.

Curtis, George William, inter alia. *A Memorial of Wendell Phillips.* Boston: Rockwell & Churchill, 1884.

Dana, Charles Anderson. *Recollections of the Civil War.* New York: D. Appleton and Company, 1902.

Dawes, Henry L. "Edwin M. Stanton." *Atlantic Monthly.* February 1870: 234–46.

——. "Recollections of Stanton under Lincoln." *Atlantic Monthly,* February 1894: 162–69.

Davis, Henry Winter. *Speeches and Addresses.* New York: Harper & Bros., 1867.

DeWitt, David Miller. *The Impeachment and Trial of Andrew Johnson, Seventeenth President of the United States.* New York: Macmillan, 1903.

Dittenhoefer, Abram J. *How We Re-Elected Lincoln,* ed. Kathleen Hall Jamieson. Philadelphia: University of Pennsylvania Press, 2005.

Dolby, George. *Charles Dickens as I Knew Him: The Story of the Reading Tours.* New York: Charles Scribner, 1910.

Donald, David Herbert. *Charles Sumner and the Rights of Man.* New York: Alfred A. Knopf, 1970.

Douglass, Frederick. *Autobiographies.* New York: Library of America, 1994.

——. *The Frederick Douglass Papers: Series One, Speeches, Debates, and Interviews,* ed. J. Blassingame & J. McKivigan. New Haven: Yale University Press, 1979.

——. "Reconstruction," *Atlantic Monthly.* December 1866: 761–64.

Downs, Gregory. *After Appomattox: Military Occupation and the Ends of War.* Cambridge: Harvard University Press, 2015.

Dray, Philip. *Capitol Men: The Epic Story of Reconstruction Through the Lives of the First Black Congressmen.* Boston: Houghton Mifflin, 2008.

Dubois, W.E.B. *Black Reconstruction.* New York: Harcourt Brace, 1935.

Durham, Walter T. "How Say You, Senator Fowler?" *Tennessee Historical Quarterly,* Spring 1983: 39–57.

Dyer, Brainard. *The Public Career of William Maxwell Evarts.* Berkeley: University of California Press, 1933.

Eckloff, Christian. *Memoirs of a Senate Page,* ed. Percival Melbourne. New York: Broadway Publishing, 1909.

Egerton, Douglas R. *The Wars of Reconstruction.* New York: Bloomsbury, 2014.

Ellet, Mrs. E. F. [Elizabeth Fries]. *The Court Circles of the Republic, or the Beauties and Celebrities of the Nation.* Hartford, CT: Hartford Publishing Company, 1870.

Ellis, C. M. "The Causes for Which a President Can Be Impeached." *Atlantic Monthly*. January 1867: 88–92.

Ellis, John. *The Sights and Secrets in the National Capital*. Chicago: Jones, Junkin & Co., 1869.

Epps, Garret. *Democracy Reborn: The Fourteenth Amendment and the Fight for Civil Rights in Post Civil-War America*. New York: Henry Holt, 2006.

Evarts, William M. *Arguments and Speeches of William Maxwell Evarts*, ed. Sherman Evarts. 3 vols. New York: Macmillan, 1913.

Fahs, Alice and Joan Waugh, eds. *The Memory of the Civil War in American Culture*. Chapel Hill: University of North Carolina Press, 2004.

Fehrenbacher, Don. "The Making of a Myth: Lincoln and the Vice Presidential Nomination in 1864." *Civil War History*. December 1995: 273–90.

Fessenden, Francis. *The Life and Public Services of William Pitt Fessenden*. 2 vols. Boston: Houghton Mifflin, 1907.

Flower, Frank. *Stanton: The Autocrat of Rebellion, Emancipation, and Reconstruction*. New York: The Saalfield Publishing Company, 1905.

Franklin, John Hope. *Reconstruction: After the Civil War*. Chicago: University of Chicago Press, 1961.

Foner, Eric. *The Fiery Trial: Abraham Lincoln and American Slavery*. New York: W. W. Norton, 2010.

———. *Reconstruction: America's Unfinished Revolution, 1863–1877*. New York: HarperCollins, 1988.

Foner, Philip, ed. *Frederick Douglass: Selected Speeches and Writings*. Chicago: Lawrence Hill Books, 1999.

Foner, Philip. *History of Black Americans*. 3 vols. Westport, CT: Greenwood Press, 1975.

Forbes, Sarah, ed. See *Letters and Recollections of John Murray Forbes*. 2 vols. Boston, Houghton Mifflin & Co., 1899.

Forney, John W. *Anecdotes of Public Men*. 2 vols. New York: Harper and Brothers, 1873.

Forten, Charlotte. "Life in the Sea-Islands." *Atlantic Monthly*. May 1864: 587–96.

Forster, John. *The Life of Charles Dickens*. 2 vols. London: Chapman and Hall, 1908.

Fulton, Joe B. *The Reconstruction of Mark Twain*. Baton Rouge: Louisiana State University Press, 2010.

Garfield, James A. *The Life and Letters of James Abram Garfield*. ed. Theodore Clarke Smith. 2 vols. New Haven: Yale University Press, 1925.

Glonek, James F. "Lincoln, Johnson, and the Baltimore Ticket." *Abraham Lincoln Quarterly*. March 1951: 255–71.

Gordon-Reed, Annette. *Andrew Johnson*. New York: Times Books, 2011.

Grant, Julia Dent. *The Personal Memoirs of Julia Dent Grant. Edited by* John Simon. Carbondale: Southern Illinois University Press, 1988.

Great Impeachment and Trial of Andrew Johnson. Philadelphia: T. B. Peterson & Bros., 1868.

Hahn, Steven. *A Nation Under Our Feet*. Cambridge: Harvard University Press, 2003.

Hamlin, Hannibal. *The Life and Times of Hannibal Hamlin*. Cambridge: Riverside Press, 1899.

Hancock, Almira Russell. *Reminiscences of Winfield Scott Hancock.* New York: Charles Webster & Co., 1887.

Hardison, Edwin T. *In the Toils of War: Andrew Johnson and the Federal Occupation of Tennessee, 1862–1865.* Knoxville: University of Tennessee, 1981. Unpublished dissertation.

Harris, Alexander, ed. *A Biographical History of Lancaster County, Pennsylvania.* Lancaster: Elias Baer & Co. 1872.

Harris, Alexander. *A Review of the Political Conflict in America.* New York: T. H. Pollack, 1876.

Hatch, Frederick. *John Surratt: Rebel, Lincoln Conspirator, Fugitive.* McFarland, 2016.

Hayes, Rutherford B. *The Diary and Letters of Rutherford Birchard Hayes.* ed. Charles Richard Williams. 5 vols. Columbus, Ohio: Ohio State Archeological and Historical Society, 1922.

Henderson, John B. "Emancipation and Impeachment." *The Century.* 1912: 196–209.

Hendrick, Burton J. *Lincoln's War Cabinet.* Boston: Little, Brown and Company, 1946.

Higginson, Thomas Wentworth. *Cheerful Yesterdays.* Cambridge: Riverside Press, 1898.

——. *Wendell Phillips.* Boston: Lee and Shepard, 1884.

Hill, Sherman Adams. "The Chicago Convention." *North American Review.* July 1868: 167–86.

Hinsdale, Mary L., ed. *Garfield-Hinsdale Letters.* Ann Arbor: University of Michigan Press, 1949.

Hoar, George F. *The Autobiography of Seventy Years.* 2 vols. New York: Scribner's, 1903.

Hodes, Martha. *Mourning Lincoln.* New Haven: Yale University Press, 2015.

Hoffert, Sylvia D. *Jane Grey Swisshelm: An Unconventional Life.* Chapel Hill: University of North Carolina Press, 2004.

Hofstadter, Richard. *The American Political Tradition.* New York: Vintage, 1957.

Hogue, Arthur Reed. *Charles Sumner, An Essay by Carl Schurz.* Urbana: The University of Illinois Press, 1951.

Hogue, James. *Uncivil War: Five New Orleans Street Battles and the Rise and Fall of Radical Reconstruction.* Baton Rouge: Louisiana State University Press, 2006.

Hollandsworth, James G. *An Absolute Massacre: The New Orleans Race Riot.* Baton Rouge: Louisiana State University Press, 2004.

Hollister, James Ovando. *Life of Schuyler Colfax.* New York: Funk and Wagnalls, 1886.

Holmes, Oliver Wendell. *Ralph Waldo Emerson.* Boston: Houghton Mifflin, 1886.

Hood, Alexander. "Thaddeus Stevens," in *A Biographical History of Lancaster County, Pennsylvania.* Lancaster: Elias Baer & Co. 1872.

Horowitz, Robert F. *The Great Impeacher: A Political Biography of James M. Ashley.* Brooklyn: Brooklyn College Press, 1979.

Howard, Oliver Otis. *The Autobiography of Oliver Otis Howard,* 2 vols. New York: Baker & Taylor, 1908.

Howe, Julia Ward. *Reminiscences 1819–1899.* Boston: Houghton Mifflin, 1899.

Howe, Mark deWolfe, ed. *Memories of a Hostess: a Chronicle of Eminent Friendships*. Boston: Atlantic Monthly Press, 1922.

Howe, Mark deWolfe. *Moorfield Storey: Portrait of an Independent*. Boston: Houghton Mifflin, 1932.

Howells, William Dean. "The Next President," *Atlantic Monthly*. May 1868: 628–32.

Hunt, Gaillard. "The President's Defense: His Side of the Case, as Told by His Correspondence," *Century Magazine*. January 1913: 422–34.

Hyman, Harold M. "Johnson, Stanton, and Grant: A Reconsideration of the Army's Role in the Events Leading to Impeachment," *American Historical Review*. October 1960: 85–100.

Jellison, Charles A. *Fessenden of Maine*. Syracuse: Syracuse University Press, 1962.

Jennings, L. J. "Mr. Raymond and Journalism." *Galaxy*. April 1870: 466–74.

Johnson, Albert E. H. "Reminiscences of the Hon. Edwin M. Stanton, Secretary of War." *Records of the Columbia Historical Society*. 1910: 69–97.

Johnson, Charles W. ed. *Proceedings of the First Three Republican National Conventions, 1856, 1860, and 1864*. Minneapolis: Harrison and Smith, 1893.

Johnson, Patricia, ed. "Sensitivity and Civil War: The Selected Diaries and Papers, 1858–1866, of Frances Adeline [Fanny] Seward." University of Rochester, 1964. Unpublished dissertation.

Jordan, David. *Winfield Scott Hancock: A Soldier's Life*. Bloomington: Indiana University Press, 1995.

Josephson, Matthew. *The Politicos*. New York: Harcourt Brace & Co., 1938.

Julian, George Washington. "George W. Julian's Journal." *Indiana Magazine of History*. 1915: 324–37.

———. *Political Recollections, 1840–1872*, Chicago: Jansen, McClurg and Company, 1884.

Kendrick, Benjamin B. *The Journal of the Joint Committee of Fifteen on Reconstruction*. New York: Columbia University, 1914.

Krug, Mark M. *Lyman Trumbull: Conservative Radical*. New York: A. S. Barnes, 1965.

Langston, John Mercer. *From the Virginia Plantation to the National Capitol*. Hartford, CT: American Publishing Co., 1894.

Larsen, Arthur, ed. *Crusader and Feminist: The Letters of Jane Swisshelm*. St. Paul: Minnesota Historical Society, 1934.

Latham, Henry. *Black and White: A Journal of a Three Months' Tour in the United States*. London: Macmillan, 1867.

Leach, Richard. "Benjamin R. Curtis: Judicial Misfit." *New England Quarterly*. 1952: 507–23.

Lee, Elizabeth Blair. *Wartime Washington*, ed. Virginia Jeans Laas. Urbana: University of Illinois Press, 1999.

Lichtenstein, Gaston. *Andrew Johnson as He Really Was*. Richmond: H. T. Ezekiel, 1911.

Lincoln, Abraham. *Lincoln: Speeches and Writings*, ed. Don E. Fehrenbacher. 2 vols. New York: Library of America, 1989.

———. *The Recollected Words of Abraham Lincoln*, ed. Don E. and Virginia Fehrenbacher. Palo Alto: Stanford University Press, 1996.

Litwack, Leon. *Been in the Storm So Long*. New York: Vintage, 1980.

———. *North of Slavery: The Negro in the Free States*. Chicago: University of Chicago Press, 1961.

Lowe, David W., ed. *Meade's Army, The Private Notebooks of Lt. Col. Theodore Lyman*. Kent, OH: Kent State University Press, 2007.

Lowell, James Russell. "The President on the Stump." *North American Review*. April 1866: 530–44.

———. "The Seward-Johnson Reaction." *North American Review*. Oct. 1866: 520–49.

Macrae, David. *The Americans at Home: Pen and Ink Sketches*. Edinburgh: Edmonston and Douglas, 1870.

Magliocca, Gerard N. *American Founding Son: John A. Bingham and the Making of the Fourteenth Amendment*. New York: New York University Press, 2013.

Mardock, Robert. *The Reformers and the American Indian*. Columbia: University of Missouri Press, 1971.

Marszalek, John. *Sherman: A Soldier's Passion for Order*. Carbondale: Southern Illinois University Press, 2007.

Marvel, William. *Lincoln's Autocrat: The Life of Edwin Stanton*. Chapel Hill: University of North Carolina Press, 2015.

Marx, Karl. *Capital: A Critique of Political Economy*. vol. 1, trans. Samuel Moore and Edward Aveling. London: Sonnenschein & Co., 1906 (originally published 1867).

Maverick, Augustus. *Henry J. Raymond and the New York Press*. Hartford, CT: A. S. Hale and Co., 1870.

McClure, Alexander K. *Abraham Lincoln and Men of War-Times*. Philadelphia: The Times Publishing Company, 1892.

McCulloch, Hugh. *Men and Measures of Half a Century*. London: Sampson Low, Marston, Searle and Rivington, 1888.

McFeely, William. *Grant*. New York: W. W. Norton, 1982.

———. *Yankee Stepfather: General O. O. Howard and the Freedmen*. New Haven: Yale University Press, 1968.

McJimsey, George T. *Genteel Partisan: Manton Marble*. Ames: Iowa State University Press, 1971.

McKitrick, Eric. *Andrew Johnson and Reconstruction*. Chicago: University of Chicago Press, 1960.

McPherson, James. "Grant or Greeley? The Abolitionist Dilemma in the Election of 1872." *American Historical Review*. October 1965: 43–61.

———. *The Struggle for Equality. Abolitionists and the Negro in the Civil War and Reconstruction*. Princeton: University of Princeton Press, 1964.

Melville, Herman. *Battle-Pieces and Aspects of War*. New York: Harper & Bros., 1866.

Memorial Addresses on the Life and Character of Thaddeus Stevens, Delivered in the House of Representatives, December 17, 1868. Washington: Government Printing, 1868.

Milton, George. *The Age of Hate: Andrew Johnson and the Radicals*. New York: McCann Howard, 1930.

Moore, Frank, ed. *Speeches of Andrew Johnson, President of the United States*. Boston: Little, Brown, 1865.

Moore, W. G. "Notes of Colonel W. G. Moore, Private Secretary to Andrew Johnson," ed. St. George L. Siousset. *American Historical Review*. October 1913: 98–131.

Motley, John Lothrop. *The Correspondence of John Lothrop Motley.* ed. George William Curtis. 3 vols. New York: Harper & Bros., 1900.

Napton, William Barclay. *The Union on Trial: The Political Journals.* eds. Christopher Phillips and Jason L. Pendleton. Columbia, MO: University of Missouri Press, 2005.

Nelson, Russell K. *Early Life of Elihu Washburne.* Grand Forks: University of North Dakota, 1853. Unpublished dissertation.

Nevins, Allan. *Hamilton Fish.* New York: Dodd, Mead, 1936.

Niven, John. *Samuel Chase: A Biography.* New York: Oxford University Press, 1995.

O'Connell, Robert L. *Fierce Patriot: The Tangled Lives of William Tecumseh Sherman.* New York: Random House, 2014.

Palmer, John M. *Personal Recollections.* Cincinnati: Robert Clarke Company, 1901.

Parton, James. "Log-Rolling at Washington." *Atlantic Monthly.* September 1869: 361–78.

———. "The 'Strikers' of the Washington Lobby." *Atlantic Monthly.* August 1869: 216–31.

———. *Topics of the Times.* Boston: James R. Osgood & Co., 1871.

Perman, Michael. *Reunion Without Compromise: The South and Reconstruction.* New York: Cambridge University Press, 1973.

Perdue, Kathleen. "Salmon P. Chase and the Impeachment Trial of Andrew Johnson." *The Historian.* 1964: 75–92.

Perry, Thomas Sergeant, ed. *The Life and Letters of Francis Lieber.* Boston: J. R. Osgood & Col., 1882.

Piatt, Donn. *Memories of Men Who Saved the Union.* New York: Bedford, Clarke and Company, 1887.

Pierce, Edward, ed. *Memoir and Letters of Charles Sumner.* London: Low, 1893.

Phillips, Ulrich, ed. "The Correspondence of Robert Toombs, Alexander Stephens, and Howell Cobb." *Annual Report of the American Historical Association Annual Report 1911.* Washington: Government Printing Office, 1913.

Plummer, Mark A. "Profile in Courage? Edmund G. Ross and the Impeachment Trial." *Midwest Quarterly.* Autumn 1985: 30–48.

Pomeroy, Marcus M. *Soliloquies of the Bondholder, the Poor Farmer, the Soldier's Widow.* New York: Van Evrie, Horton, & Co. 1866.

Poore, Benjamin Perley. *Perley's Reminiscences of Sixty Years in the National Metropolis.* 2 vols. Philadelphia: Hubbard Bros., 1886.

Porter, Horace. *Campaigning with Grant.* New York: Century, 1897.

Quaife, Milo M. ed. *Diary of James Polk During His Presidency.* 4 vols. Chicago: University of Chicago Press, 1910.

Quarles, Benjamin. *Frederick Douglass.* Washington: Associated Publishers, 1948.

Rable, George. *But There Was No Peace: The Role of Violence in the Politics of Reconstruction.* Athens: University of Georgia Press, 1984.

Raymond, Henry J. "Extracts from the Journal of Henry J. Raymond." *Scribner's Monthly.* June 1880: 275–80.

Reed, George, inter alia. ed. *The Bench and Bar of Ohio.* 2 vols. Chicago: Century Publishing, 1897.

Reid, Whitelaw. *After the War, a Southern Tour: May 1, 1865 to May 1, 1866.* New York: Moore, Wilstach & Baldwin, 1866.

Report of the Committee on Reconstruction. 4 vols. Washington, D.C.: Government Printing Office, 1866.

Report of the Joint Committee on Reconstruction, at the First Session, Thirty-ninth Congress. Washington: Government Printing Office, 1866.

Reports of the Committees of the House of Representatives, 1865–1866. 3 vols. Washington: Government Printing Office, 1866.

Reports of the Special Committee of the House of Representatives, 1871–1872. Washington: Government Printing Office, 1872.

Reynolds, David S. *John Brown: The Man Who Killed Slavery, Sparked the Civil War, and Seeded Civil Rights.* New York: Alfred A. Knopf, 2005.

——. *Walt Whitman: A Cultural Biography.* New York: Alfred A. Knopf, 1995.

Reynolds, Donald E. "The New Orleans Riot of 1866, Reconsidered." *Louisiana History: The Journal of the Louisiana Historical Association.* Winter 1964: 5–27.

Rhodes, James. *A History of the United States.* 8 vols. New York: Macmillan, 1920.

Richardson, Heather Cox. *The Death of Reconstruction: Race, Labor, and Politics in the Post–Civil War North.* Cambridge: Harvard University Press, 2004.

——. *West from Appomattox: The Reconstruction of America after the Civil War.* New Haven: Yale University Press, 2007.

Riddleberger, Patrick W. *1866: The Critical Year Revisited.* Carbondale: Southern Illinois University Press, 1979.

Robbins, Chandler. *A Memoir of Benjamin Robbins Curtis.* Boston: John Wilson, 1878.

Roberts, Clayton. "The Law of Impeachment in Stuart England: A Reply to Raoul Berger." *The Yale Law Journal.* June 1975: 1419–39.

Robinson, William S. "*Warrington*." *Pen-Portraits.* Boston: Mrs. W. S. Robinson, 1877.

Romero, Matías. "The Mexican Minister Describes Andrew Johnson's 'Swing Around the Circle,'" ed. Thomas Schoonover, *Civil War History.* June 1973: 149–61.

Ruchames, Louis. "Charles Sumner and American Historiography." *The Journal of Negro History.* April 1953: 139–60.

Ruddy, Richard A. *Edmund G. Ross: Soldier, Senator, Abolitionist.* Albuquerque: University of New Mexico Press, 2014.

Salter, William. *The Life of James W. Grimes.* New York: D. Appleton & Co., 1876.

Savage, John. *The Life and Public Services of Andrew Johnson, Seventeenth President.* New York: Derby and Miller, 1866.

Scally, Sister Anthony. "Two Nuns and Old Thad Stevens." *Biography.* Winter 1982: 66–73.

Schofield, John. *Forty-six Years in the Army.* New York: Century, 1897.

Schurz, Carl. *The Intimate Letters of Carl Schurz, 1841–1869.* Joseph Shafer, ed. and trans. Evansville, WI: Publications of the Wisconsin Historical Collections, 1928.

——. *The Reminiscences of Carl Schurz.* 3 vols. New York: The McClure Company, 1907.

——. *Report on the Condition of the South.* 39th Congress, 1st Session, Senate Ex. Doc. No. 2. Washington, 1865.

——. *The Speeches, Correspondence and Political Papers of Carl Schurz,* ed. Frederic Bancroft. 6 vols. New York: G. P. Putnam's Col, 1913.

———. *Charles Sumner, An Essay By Carl Schurz*. ed. Arthur Reed Hogue. Urbana: University of Illinois Press, 1951.

Sheridan, Philip H. *Personal Memoirs of P.H. Sheridan, General, United States Army*. 2 vols. New York: Charles L. Webster & Company. 1888.

Sherman, John. *Recollections of Forty Years in the House, Senate, and Cabinet*. 2 vols. Chicago: The Werner Co., 1895.

Sherman, John, and William Tecumseh Sherman. *The Sherman Letters: Correspondence between General and Senator Sherman*, ed. Rachel Thorndike Sherman. New York: Charles Scribner's Sons, 1894.

Sherman, William Tecumseh. *Memoirs of General W. T. Sherman*. New York: Library of America, 1990.

Sherwin, Oscar. *The Prophet of Liberty: The Life and Times of Wendell Phillips*. New York: Bookman Associates, 1958.

Simpson, Brooks D., ed. *Advice After Appomattox: Letters to Andrew Johnson, 1865–1866*. Knoxville: University of Tennessee Press, 1987.

———. *Let Us Have Peace: Ulysses S. Grant and the Politics of War and Reconstruction, 1861–1868*. Chapel Hill: University of North Carolina Press, 1991.

———. *The Reconstruction Presidents*. Lawrence: University Press of Kansas, 2009.

Small, Abraham, ed. *The American Speaker, A Selection of Popular, Parliamentary, and Forensic Eloquence*. Philadelphia: Abraham Small, 1816.

Smalley, George W. *Anglo-American Memories*. New York: G.P. Putnam's Sons, 1911.

Smallwood, James, inter alia. *Murder and Mayhem: The War of Reconstruction in Texas*. College Station: Texas A & M Press, 2003.

Stahr, Walter. *Seward: Lincoln's Indispensable Man*. New York: Simon & Schuster, 2013.

———. *Stanton: Lincoln's War Secretary*. New York: Simon & Schuster, 2017.

Stampp, Kenneth M. *The Era of Reconstruction*. New York: Knopf, 1965.

Stanbery, Henry. *Opinion of Attorney General Stanbery: June 12, 1867*. Washington: Government Printing Office, 1867.

Stanton, Elizabeth Cady. *Elizabeth Cady Stanton as Revealed in Her Letters, Diary and Reminiscences*. New York: Harper & Brothers, 1922.

Stearns, Frank Preston. *The Life and Public Services of George Luther Stearns*. Philadelphia: J.B. Lippincott Company, 1907.

Steiner, Bernard C. *The Life of Henry Winter Davis*. Baltimore: John Murphy Co., 1916.

Stevens, Thaddeus. *Reconstruction: Speech of the Honorable Thaddeus Stevens, September 7, 1865*. Lancaster, PA: Examiner & Herald, 1865.

———. *The Selected Papers of Thaddeus Stevens*, eds. Beverly Palmer and Holly Ochoa. 2 vols. Pittsburgh: University of Pittsburgh Press, 1998.

Stewart, Donald O. *Impeached: The Trial of Andrew Johnson and the Fight for Lincoln's Legacy*. New York: Simon and Schuster, 2009.

Strong, George Templeton. *The Diary of George Templeton Strong*. eds. Allan Nevins and Milton Thomas Halsey. 4 vols. New York: Macmillan, 1952.

Stryker, Lloyd. *Andrew Johnson: A Study in Courage*. New York: Macmillan, 1929.

Summers, Mark W. *A Dangerous Stir: Fear, Paranoia, and the Making of Reconstruction*. Chapel Hill: University of North Carolina Press, 2014.

———. *The Era of Good Stealings.* New York: Oxford University Press, 1993.

Sumner, Charles. "Clemency and Common Sense." *Atlantic Monthly.* December 1865: 745–60.

———. "Our Domestic Relations." *Atlantic Monthly.* October 1863: 507–29.

———. *The Selected Letters of Charles Sumner.* ed. Beverly Wilson Palmer. 2 vols. Boston: Northeastern University Press, 1990.

———. *The Works of Charles Sumner.* 20 vols. Boston: Lee and Shepard, 1875.

Sunstein, Cass R. *Impeachment: A Citizen's Guide.* Cambridge: Harvard University Press, 2017.

Tade, Reverend Ewing. "The Memphis Race Riot and Its Aftermath, Report by a Northern Missionary." ed. Joe M. Richardson. *Tennessee Historical Quarterly,* Spring 1965: 63–69.

Taylor, Joe Gray. "New Orleans and Reconstruction." *Louisiana History: The Journal of the Louisiana Historical Association,* Summer 1968: 189–208.

Taylor, Richard. *Destruction and Reconstruction: Personal Experiences of the Late War.* New York: D. Appleton and Company, 1879.

Temple, Oliver Perry. *East Tennessee and the Civil War.* Cincinnati: The Robert Clarke Company, 1899.

———. *Notable Men of Tennessee: From 1833 to 1875, Their Times and Their Contemporaries.* New York: Cosmopolitan Press, 1912.

Testimony Taken Before the House Judiciary Committee in the Charges Against Andrew Johnson. Washington: Government Printing Office, 1867.

Testimony Taken Before the Judiciary Committee of the House of Representatives, Thirty-ninth and Fortieth Congress. Washington: Government Printing Office, 1867.

Thayer, William Roscoe. *The Life and Letters of John Hay.* 2 vols. Boston: Houghton Mifflin, 1916.

Thomas, Benjamin P., and Harold Hyman. *Edwin Stanton: The Life and Times of Lincoln's Secretary of War.* New York: Knopf, 1962.

Thomas, Lately. *Sam Ward: King of the Lobby.* Boston: Houghton Mifflin, 1965.

Townsend, Edward D. *Anecdotes of Civil War in the United States.* New York: Appleton & Co., 1884.

Townsend, George A. *Washington Outside and In.* Hartford, CT: James Betts & Co., 1874.

Traubel, Horace. *With Walt Whitman in Camden.* 9 vols. ed. Horace Traubel, Gertrude Traubel, Sculley Bradley, inter alia. Boston-New York-California-Oregon, 1906–1996.

Trefousse, Hans L. *Andrew Johnson: A Biography.* New York: W. W. Norton, 1997.

———. *Ben Butler: The South Called Him Beast!* New York: Octagon Books, 1974.

———. *The Impeachment of a President: Andrew Johnson, the Blacks, and Reconstruction.* New York: Fordham University Press, 1999.

———. *The Radical Republicans: Lincoln's Vanguard for Racial Justice.* New York: Alfred A. Knopf, 1968.

Tribe, Lawrence. *To End a Presidency: The Power of Impeachment.* New York: Basic, 2018.

Trowbridge, John Townsend. *A Picture of the Desolated States and the Work of Restoration: 1865–1868.* Hartford, CT: L. Stebbins, 1868.

Truman, Benjamin. "Anecdotes of Andrew Johnson." *Century*, January 1913: 435–40.

Turner, Harriet S. "Recollections of Andrew Johnson. *Harper's*, January 1910: 168–76.

Turner, Justin G. and Linda Levitt. *Life and Letters of Mary Todd Lincoln*. New York: Alfred A. Knopf, 1972.

Twain, Mark. *Mark Twain's Letters*, eds. Victor Fischer and Michael B. Frank. 6 vols. Berkeley: University of California Press, 1992.

———. *Mark Twain Newspaper Correspondent: Newspaper Articles, 1862–1881*. Australia: Project Gutenberg, 2011.

Twain, Mark. ed. *Mark Twain's Notebooks & Journals*, ed. Frederick Anderson, inter alia. 3 vols. Berkeley: University of California Press, 1975.

Van der Zee, John. *Bound Over: Indentured Servitude and American Conscience*. New York: Simon and Schuster, 1985.

Van Deusen, Glyndon. *Thurlow Weed: Wizard of the Lobby*. Boston: Little, Brown, 1947.

———. *William Henry Seward*. New York: Oxford University Press, 1967.

Veenendaal, Jr., Augustus J. *The Diary of Claude August Crommelin, A Young Dutchman Views Post-Civil War America*. Bloomington, University of Indiana Press, 2011.

Wagstaff, Thomas. "The Arm-in-Arm Convention." *Civil War History*, June 1968: 101–19.

Warden, Robert. *An Account of the Private Life and Public Services of Salmon Portland Chase*. Cincinnati: Wilstach, Baldwin & Co., 1874.

Waugh, C. John. *Re-electing Lincoln: The Battle for the 1864 Presidency*. New York: DaCapo, 1997.

Weed, Thurlow. *The Autobiography of Thurlow Weed*, ed. Harriet Weed. Boston: Houghton Mifflin, 1883.

Weld, Theodore Dwight. *Memorial Services upon the Seventy-Fourth Birthday of Wendell Phillips, Held at the Residence of William Sumner Crosby. South Boston, Nov. 29th, 1885*. Boston: James Cooper, 1886.

Welles, Gideon. *The Diary of Gideon Welles*. 3 vols. ed. Howard K. Beale. Boston: Houghton Mifflin, 1911.

Whipple, Edwin P. "The President and Congress." *Atlantic Monthly*. April 1866: 500–507.

———. "The Johnson Party." *Atlantic Monthly*. September 1866: 374–80.

Whitaker, John. *Sketches of Life and Character in Louisiana: The Portraits Selected Principally from the Bench and Bar*. New Orleans: Ferguson & Crosby, 1847.

White, Ronald C. *American Ulysses*. New York: Random House, 2016.

Whitman, Walt. *Poetry and Prose*, ed. Justin Kaplan. New York: Library of America, 1983.

———. *The Correspondence*, ed. Edwin Havilland Miller. 2 vols. New York: New York University Press, 1961.

———. "Democracy." *Galaxy*, December 1867: 919–33.

———. *Memoranda during the War*. Camden, New Jersey: Privately published, 1875.

Whittier, John Greenleaf. *The Letters of John Greenleaf Whittier*, ed. John B. Pickard. 3 vols. Cambridge: Harvard University Press, 1975.

Wigfall Wright, Louise. *A Southern Girl in '61: The War-Time Memories of a Confederate Senator's Daughter*. New York: Doubleday, Page & Company, 1905.

Wilson, Henry. "Edwin M. Stanton." *Atlantic Monthly*. February 1870: 234–46.

——. "Jeremiah S. Black and Edwin M Stanton." *Atlantic Monthly*. October 1870: 463–75.

Wilson, James H. *The Life of Charles A. Dana*. New York: Harper & Bros., 1907.

Wineapple, Brenda. *Ecstatic Nation: Confidence, Crisis, and Compromise, 1848–1877*. New York: Harper, 2013.

Winston, Robert W. *Andrew Johnson, Plebeian and Patriot*. New York: Henry Holt, 1928.

Winthrop, Robert Jr. *A Memoir of Robert C. Winthrop*. Boston: Little, Brown, 1897.

Wolcott, Pamphila Stanton. *Edwin M. Stanton. A Biographical Sketch by his Sister, Pamphila Stanton Wolcott*. Columbus, Ohio: Ohio History Connection.

Wyman, Lillie Buffum Chace and Arthur Wyman. *Elizabeth Buffum Chace*. Boston: W. B. Clarke Company, 1914.

Young, John Russell. *Around the World with General Grant*. New York: The American News Company, 1879.

Illustration Credits

Index

Page numbers of illustrations appear in italics.

ABOUT THE AUTHOR

BRENDA WINEAPPLE is the author of several books, including *Ecstatic Nation: Confidence, Crisis, and Compromise, 1848–1877*, named a best book of the year by *The New York Times*, among other publications; *White Heat: The Friendship of Emily Dickinson and Thomas Wentworth Higginson*, a finalist for the National Book Critics Circle Award; *Hawthorne: A Life*, winner of the Ambassador Book Award for Best Biography of the Year; and *Sister Brother: Gertrude and Leo Stein*. Her numerous other honors include a Literature Award from the American Academy of Arts and Letters, a Pushcart Prize, a Guggenheim Fellowship, an American Council of Learned Societies Fellowship, two National Endowment Fellowships in the Humanities, and, most recently, a National Endowment Public Scholars Award. She is an elected member of the American Academy of Arts and Sciences and of the Society of American Historians and regularly contributes to major publications such as *The New York Times Book Review, The New York Review of Books, The Wall Street Journal,* and *The Nation*.

brendawineapple.com